In Search of Empire

The decades between 1670 and 1730 were the most formative in the history of the French colonies in the Americas. A sufficient number of migrants arrived from France and Africa to create settlements, establish economies of production, develop networks of exchange and trade, and adapt institutions of government and law to give substance and form to their resulting societies. *In Search of Empire* is the first full account of how French settlers came to the Americas during these years. It examines how they and thousands of African slaves, together with Amerindians, constructed settlements and produced and traded commodities for export. Bringing together much new evidence, the author explores how the newly constructed societies and new economies, without precedent in France, interacted with the growing international violence in the Atlantic world in order to present a fresh perspective of the multifarious French colonising experience in the Americas.

James Pritchard is Professor Emeritus in the Department of History at Queen's University. He is the author of *Louis XV's Navy, 1748–1762* (1987), and *Anatomy of a Naval Disaster* (1995), which was awarded the Keith Matthews Prize by the Canadian Nautical Research Society and received a John Lyman Book Award from the North American Society for Oceanic History.

In Search of Empire

The French in the Americas, 1670–1730

JAMES PRITCHARD
Queen's University

CAMBRIDGE
UNIVERSITY PRESS

PUBLISHED BY THE PRESS SYNDICATE OF THE UNIVERSITY OF CAMBRIDGE
The Pitt Building, Trumpington Street, Cambridge, United Kingdom

CAMBRIDGE UNIVERSITY PRESS
The Edinburgh Building, Cambridge CB2 2RU, UK
40 West 20th Street, New York, NY 10011-4211, USA
477 Williamstown Road, Port Melbourne, VIC 3207, Australia
Ruiz de Alarcón 13, 28014 Madrid, Spain
Dock House, The Waterfront, Cape Town 8001, South Africa

http://www.cambridge.org

© James Pritchard 2004

First published 2004

Printed in the United Kingdom at the University Press, Cambridge

Typeface Sabon 10/12pt.   *System* LATEX 2_ε [TB]

A catalog record for this book is available from the British Library.

Library of Congress Cataloging in Publication Data

Pritchard, James S., 1939–
In Search of Empire: the French in the Americas, 1670–1730 / James Pritchard.
p. cm.
Includes bibliographical references and index.
ISBN 0-521-82742-6 (hardback)
1. French–America–History–17th century. 2. French–America–History–18th century.
3. France–Colonies–America. 4. America–History–To 1810. 5. Frontier and pioneer
life–America. 6. America–Ethnic relations. I. Title.
E29.F8P75 2003
970'0971244–dc21   2003043592

ISBN 0 521 82742 6 hardback

Dedicated to my students,
who taught me that to teach is truly to learn

Contents

Illustrations

Maps and Graphs

Tables

Preface

The French occupied, founded, and settled at least fourteen colonies in the Americas during the late seventeenth and early eighteenth centuries. They were located in two broad climatic zones: tropical and temperate. The tropical colonies, founded only after Europeans had commercialised the idea of colonisation, were intended for settlement. All but one of the southern group were islands in the West Indies. The exception was Cayenne, or French Guiana, which along with similar English and Dutch possessions was located between the Amazon and Orinoco Rivers on the northeast coast of South America. The northern colonies were colonies of trade or industry. Four or five, depending on how one counts them, were located in the semitropical and temperate zones of North America. Only war appears to have given the colonies any kind of unity. Whether they achieved a more permanent unity is the subject of this book.

Eight of the island colonies were scattered along the sweeping thousand-kilometre arc of the Lesser Antilles, known as *les Isles du vent* or the Windward Islands: Grenada, Martinique, Marie Galante, Guadeloupe, Saint-Christophe, Saint-Barthélémy, Saint-Martin, and Sainte-Croix. The colony of Saint-Domingue, which occupied the western third of the island of Hispaniola, was in the Greater Antilles, called *les Isles sous le vent* or the Leeward Islands. Louisiana and Canada were located along the lower valleys of North America's greatest rivers, the Mississippi and the St. Lawrence, while Acadia, Placentia, and Île Royale were in the northeast maritime region.

The name by which France's South American colony is most commonly known, Cayenne, refers more accurately to a small island a pistol shot off the mainland. Guiana or, as the mainland was more commonly called in the seventeenth century, *la France équinoxiale*, is bounded by the Atlantic Ocean on the north, Brazil to the east and south, and Dutch Surinam to the west. Covering more than 90,000 square kilometres, its coastline runs about

320 kilometres. The colonial claim extended deep into the continent, but the low, swampy coastal region, 15 to 50 kilometres wide, discouraged penetration. Most of the colony was covered by equatorial rain forest, and the heavy rainfall from December to July with only a brief interruption in February or March made life extremely difficult.[1]

Grenada (350 km²), nearly 1,000 kilometres northeast of Guiana, is the southernmost of the Windward Islands. It includes the southern Grenadines, the largest of which is Carriacou. Seized by the French in 1650, Grenada is situated in the track of the major hurricanes that have visited destruction on the island over the centuries. Martinique, lying some 260 kilometres northwards, became France's major colonial possession before 1730. It encompasses 1,080 square kilometres and is largely mountainous. Its two highest peaks are active volcanoes. Guadeloupe, (1,530 km²) about 200 kilometres farther north, lies midway along the curving island chain. A narrow salt water channel actually divides it into two islands. Basseterre has a 1,467-metre-high active volcano, La Soufrière, while Grand Terre is low and encircled by coral reefs. Marie Galante (158 km²), 25 kilometres south of Grand Terre and equidistant from Basseterre to the west, is the largest of several nearby islands that are remarkable for their complex geology. The major part of Marie Galante, like Grand Terre, is formed from limestone and protected by coral reefs. La Désirade (20 km²), an eastern projection of Grand Terre, is similar. Îles des Saintes are volcanic islets off the south coast of Basseterre, and Îles de la Petite Terre are coral. All these islands may be treated as dependencies of the larger colony.

Four colonies lay in the northern arc of the Lesser Antilles. Saint-Christophe or St. Christopher (178 km²) lies about 150 kilometres northwest of Guadeloupe. The French occupied both ends of the island, sharing it with the English who held the middle portion. There was always friction and frequently conflict. Fifty kilometres further north along the northern rim of the island chain lie the much smaller islands of Saint-Barthélemy (St. Barts) and Saint-Martin, which the French still share with the Dutch. Sainte-Croix (215 km²), the largest of the Virgin Islands, lies at the western end of the Lesser Antilles about 100 kilometres from Puerto Rico.

Saint-Domingue's geography created three provinces that remained as separate from each other as the island colonies in the Lesser Antilles, and its great geographical area (27,989 km²) is deceptive. The land is very mountainous; more than two-thirds is unsuitable for cultivation. With highland and lowland zones, the western, northern, and southern districts of Saint-Domingue developed varied populations and economies, and one might best refer to three colonies rather than one because of the lack of land communication between them.

---

[1]   Pierre Pluchon, dir., *Histoire des Antilles et de la Guyane* (Toulouse: Privat, 1982), 26–31.

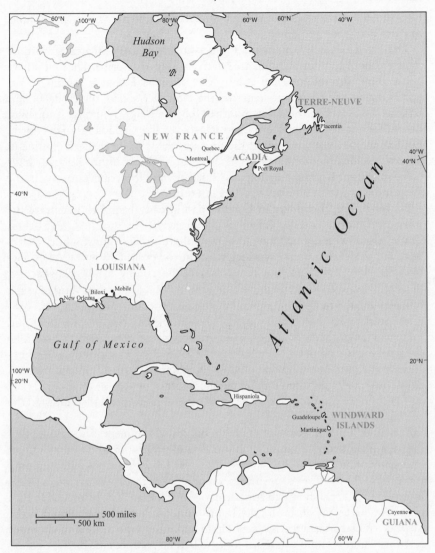

French colonies in America.

The southern French colonies were much farther apart from one another than is commonly believed. Le Cap François (today Cap-Haïtien) on the north coast of Saint-Domingue lies about 2,500 kilometres north and west of Cayenne, which, for its part, lies farther east than Placentia, Newfoundland. In the age of sail, some colonies lay many weeks apart from one another. If Fort Royal, Martinique (today Fort-de-France), was not too far from

Léogane, Saint-Domingue, the latter was as distant in time from Martinique, as Paris was from Moscow.

The French North American colonies covered vastly greater areas than their southern counterparts but are relatively easy to describe. The first salient point about the semitropical colony of Louisiana is that it lay far to the northwest of Saint-Domingue across the Gulf of Mexico, which itself is as large as the Caribbean Sea. The mouth of the Mississippi is almost 1,900 kilometres distant from Saint-Domingue. Moreover, like Canada far to the north, Louisiana was oriented toward the interior of the vast northern continent. Sometimes identified as part of what geographers and anthropologists have come to call the Circum-Caribbean, Louisiana had few connections with the West Indies and its colonists had less interest.

By 1670, French traders in Canada had already begun to penetrate the interior of North America via the St. Lawrence River and the Great Lakes. Trade, along with connections to metropolitan France, grew, while settlers were left to develop their own society in the lower St. Lawrence Valley. Geography shaped Acadia, but it was scarcely a colony at all. Plaisance or Placentia, Newfoundland, and its successor, Île Royale, were both French colonies related to the commercial development of the North Atlantic fisheries. Settlement scarcely mattered. The differences between the real and imagined geographies of imperialism are very great in the French case. The French North American colonies were separated by vast distances and extremely varied climates, geography, and economic activities. Only a common need for security connected them to one another or to France. Even if they had been more similar, commercial rivalries in France precluded unity in the colonies.

French colonial history suffers from historical fragmentation and lack of demographic, social, economic, cultural, and geographical contexts. There are plenty of political and economic histories of individual colonies, but only rarely have the histories of even a few colonies been incorporated into a single interpretation, be they North American or West Indian. The history of France in the Americas has oft been told, but too often it has been recounted in the absence of research into the lives of the colonists who settled in different territories and without reference to its maritime component.

This book aims to accomplish both. It is intended chiefly to be a synthesis, attractive to students and a broad readership as well as to scholars. It draws on classic works as well as on recent research, but it was not written simply to add another tome to the growing library of histories of *la France d'outre-mer*. It offers a reinterpretation of that history. It reexamines much original evidence and challenges accepted notions about early French imperialism during the Old Regime by suggesting that little worth the name existed before 1730.

Although a colony is a dependent territory within an empire, and to speak of colonies assumes an empire's existence, not too much should be drawn from this rather obvious semantic conclusion.[2] One of this book's themes is the French state's unsuccessful struggle to foster overseas colonial development. It argues that settlers and slaves rather than the metropolitan or even colonial governments largely made their own societies. It also claims that the six decades between 1670 and 1730 were the most critical in shaping those societies. Though most colonial histories focus on the six decades following 1730, perhaps because more evidence is available in archives than for the earlier period and the later decades lead directly to the great revolutions in France and Saint-Domingue, it is argued here that what came later was largely a continuation of what occurred before 1730. Between 1670 and 1730 a sufficient number of migrants arrived from Europe and Africa to create settlements, establish economies and trade, and shape social and governing institutions to their needs. These decades were also ones of almost unremitting warfare wherever the French found themselves in the Americas. This had great consequences for the future.

In order to make these arguments, I have divided the text into two parts. The first part, "Colonies Formed," examines five critically important topics: demography, social formation, production, exchange, and government in order to show how the newcomers, both white and black, made their own worlds. The second part, "Colonies Defended," moves from topical analysis to chronological narrative to tell a poorly known yet vitally important story and explore the impact of war on the colonies. Despite its best efforts, the French navy failed to defend the colonies effectively during the decades between 1670 and 1730. While the navy did not find a role in imperial defence, colonies became increasingly reliant upon fortifications, detachments of colonial infantry, and local forces. The wars of the period, the manner in which they were fought, and their outcome had an unexpected impact on the colonial societies. The French empire, indeed, became very elusive.

I am indebted to many scholars whose work, both old and new, has informed my own. My aim has been to show how their work fits into the larger picture rather than to debate their conclusions. I am also grateful to many people who shared their knowledge and enthusiasm with me and who offered advice and support at critical moments. Philip Boucher deserves special thanks in all respects. His criticism and knowledge of French Caribbean history proved essential. David Eltis helped me to clarify many ideas and generously shared his data with me, often reworking it to meet my requests. David Geggus generously sent me copies of Bertrand Ogeron's correspondence. Daniel Baugh read a version of Chapter 6 and provided advice at an early moment. Frederick Thorpe read versions of several chapters, happily sharing his deep knowledge of the history of Acadia and New France. I am also grateful to David Eltis, Frederick Quinn, Gerald Tulchinsky, and

[2] David B. Abernethy, *The Dynamics of Global Dominance: European Overseas Empires 1415–1980* (New York: Yale University Press, 2001), 21.

Cambridge University Press's readers who read the complete manuscript. Their comments were supportive, constructive, and often to the point. Finally, I thank my wife Suzanne, who carefully proofread the manuscript, saving me from committing many errors of grammar, syntax, and punctuation.

Earlier versions of parts of some chapters were presented at seminars held at Queen's University and the Université de Montréal at several annual meetings of the French Colonial Historical Society, the Canadian Nautical Research Society, and at the Naval History Symposium at Annapolis, Maryland, in 1997, the Iberville Tercentenary Symposium at Biloxi, Mississippi, in 1999, and the Canadian Military History Conference at Ottawa in 2000. An early version of Chapter 6 appeared as "The Franco-Dutch War in the West Indies, 1672–1678: An Early 'Lesson' in Imperial Defence" in *New Interpretations in Naval History, Selected Papers from the Thirteenth Naval History Symposium*, edited by William M. McBride. Annapolis: Naval Institute Press, 1998; parts of Chapter 7 appeared as "Le Profit et La Gloire": The French Navy's Alliance with Private Enterprise in the Defense of Newfoundland, 1691–1697" in *Newfoundland Studies*, 15, no. 2 (Fall, 1999) and as "The French West Indies During the Nine Years' War, 1688–1697: A Review and Reappraisal" in *French Colonial History*, Volume 2, edited by Robert Duplessis, East Lansing: Michigan State University Press, 2002; part of Chapter 8 appeared as "Canada and the Defence of Newfoundland During the War of the Spanish Succession, 1702–1713," in *Canadian Military History since the 17th Century* edited by Yves Tremblay, Ottawa: Department of National Defense, 2001. I thank the publishers of these volumes for permission to include revised versions of their texts in the present volume.

I also gratefully acknowledge the financial support of the Social Sciences and Humanities Research Council of Canada for a research grant in 1994 and for several annual extensions. I thank The Office of Research Service, Queen's University, for support and Ela Rusak who constructed the maps that so effectively enhance the text. Finally, I thank the libraries of my own university for their support of my interlibrary loan requests over many years and the W. D. Jordan Special Collections and Music Library, Queen's University at Kingston, Canada, for permission to reproduce several of the contemporary illustrations that appear here. The presence of works by Du Tertre, Labat, Froger, Lahontan, Charlevoix, Savary des Bruslons, and others in the university library collections considerably aided my research.

Dates, Weights, Measures, and Currency

Dates throughout the text conform with the present-day Gregorian calendar that the French, but not the English, employed during the seventeenth and early eighteenth century. Contemporary English and American dates, still based on the Julian calendar, fell ten and eleven days earlier in the seventeenth and eighteenth centuries, respectively, and each year commenced on 25 March. These dates have been indicated as Old Style [o.s.] in the Notes when reference is made to English documents.

The French livre weight of 489.5 grams was about 8 percent heavier than the English pound (lb) of 453.5 grams. The quintal of 100 livres [48.95 kilograms] was nearly 4 percent lighter than the English hundredweight (cwt) of 112 pounds [50.96 kilograms]. The Bordeaux quintal of 101 livres has been ignored. A much greater source of confusion is the French *tonneau* or ton of 2,000 livres weight, 979 kilograms, or 2,159 lb English. In order to allow for easier comparisons I have often converted figures in the text to freight or metric tonnes, abbreviated to "tonnes," of 1,000 kilograms, equivalent to 2,045 livres' weight or 2,205 lb English. In 1681, the volume of the old French freight ton, the *tonneau de mer*, was fixed at 42 cubic French feet or *pieds* (1.44 cubic metres). A ton weight of Bordeaux wine (913 litres), however, does not quite fill 28 French cubic feet of space. The difference seems to arise from a ship's load being two-thirds its capacity to carry the weight put into it. The old French freight ton was nearly 12 percent larger than the modern freight ton, equivalent to 1,000 kg (one tonne) or 40 English cubic feet (1.13 cubic metres). Any ships' capacities given in the text remain in *tonneaux de mer*.

Linear measurement varied within France, but the colonies generally followed Paris or royal measure. The French *pied du roi* of 12 *pouces* or inches was equivalent to 1.06575 English feet. Six *pieds* comprised 1 *toise* (1.949 metres); 3 *toises* equalled one *perche*, and 10 *perches* equalled one arpent (58.47 metres). There were 84 arpents in a common league (*lieue*). The linear arpent, equivalent to 192 English feet, was the common measure employed in land surveys other than in the West Indies. The superficial arpent was equivalent to about five-sixths of an acre. The two local systems of land measurement that prevailed in the French West Indies centered on the *carré* or *carreau*, the area bounded on each side by 100 surveyor's paces. Just to keep things interesting, the pace on Guadeloupe and Saint-Domingue measured three *pieds* (0.974 metre), while on Martinique it was equivalent to three and a half *pieds* (1.137 metres). The Guadeloupe and Saint-Domingue *carré* was equivalent to 0.9487 hectare while at Martinique *carré* was one-third larger, being equivalent to 1.2928 hectares. One hectare contains 2.47 acres, but for easy convenience 100 large or Martinique *carreaux* were equivalent to approximately 319 acres.

Ancient wet and dry measures are arcane topics, and I invite correction. Merchants employed two kinds of casks regardless of size, wet and dry, to ship goods to and from the colonies. Wet casks were tight, equipped with a bilge board and a bung hole. Dry casks, also called slack, were generally looser, had no bung holes, and were closed at the ends. Both kinds required great skill in manufacture. Wet measurement was based on the *pot* of 2.2648 litres (roughly half an English gallon). The *ancre, tierçon, barrique,* and *pipe* followed. The *ancre*, employed solely to carry brandy, was the smallest wet cask; it probably contained 32 *veltes* of 7.45 or 7.61 litres. The *baril* (wet measure) contained 55 *pots*. The *tierçon* was one-third of a *pipe*. Four *barriques*, each of 110 *pots*, made up a wine ton (*tonneau*) as did two *pipes*. The French do not seem to have employed the puncheon (*poinçon*), three of which made up a *tonneau*.

Dry measure included the *baril* and the *quart*. The size of *barils* varied according to the commodities they contained. In 1712, 3 *barils* of indigo weighed 436.5 livres net, (i.e., excluding the tare or weight of the empty cask), which gives the average net weight of indigo casks as 145.5 livres. In 1729, 30 casks of indigo weighing 11,209 livres at Léogane and sold at Bordeaux yielded only 9,358 livres, indicating the tare was 16.5 percent.[3] The *quart* was generally larger, holding about 180 livres weight net of the container, which might be either tight or slack depending on the commodity (e.g., pickled beef or flour). Allowing 10 percent for the tare, a *quart's* gross weight was about 200 livres, but this was only approximate.[4] Cereal grains were normally measured in *minots* equivalent to 37 litres or 1.05 bushels.

---

[3]   M. Morineau, "Quelques recherches à la balance du commerce exterieur français au xviiie siècle: ou cette fois un egal deux" dans *Aires et structures de commerce française aux xviiie siècle*. dir., Pierre Léon (Paris: Centre d'histoire économique et sociale de la région lyonnais, 1975), 31.

[4]   Col., C¹¹A 51, f. 203. In 1729, eight *quarts* of pure wheaten flour embarked at Quebec had a gross weight of 1,567 livres. After deducting an average tare of 20 livres per cask, the average net weight per cask equalled 176 livres.

The *boucault* appears to have been a freight ton for dry goods. Colonial tobacco was exported in *rolles* weighing 50 livres, and cotton was shipped in bales of 200 livres.

A marine league contained 2,853 *toises* or 3 nautical miles, the distance subtended by 3 minutes of latitude or 3 minutes of a great circle. One degree of latitude is equivalent to 20 leagues (approximately 112 kilometres or 69 statute miles).

France's money of account, the livre tournois (l.t.), was divided into 20 sols, and each sol into 12 deniers. French currency was found in the *petit* or silver *écu* (crown) worth three livres tournois and the gold *louis d'or* worth 24 livres. The *petit louis* was a silver coin. In the West Indies, however, the major currency was the Spanish silver peso or piece of eight, also called by the French *piastre*. It was equivalent to 42.29 grams of pure silver.

NOTE ON SUGAR CASKS

Sugar was normally packed in *barriques* and *barils*, but chiefly in the former. Their size varied widely and grew steadily. For the purposes of levying entry duties on their arrival in France, the net weight of sugar casks was set at 500 livres. However, planters sought to reduce duties by packing more sugar into larger casks. In 1719, 4 *barriques* or hogsheads of clayed sugar weighed 2,000 livres for payment of duty, but when sold, the same casks held 2,622 livres net, after the tare had been deducted. Merchants deducted 10 percent of the gross weight of muscovado (*sucre brut*) to represent the tare weight of the empty casks, but in this instance clayed sugar was involved and a tare of 17 percent was deducted. The gross weight of these four casks was likely 3,159 livres.[5] By the beginning of the eighteenth century, according to Father Labat, a sugar cask weighed an average of 550 livres.[6] But 5 hogsheads of white or clayed sugar sold at Bordeaux in 1708 weighed on average 495 livres net, while 2 casks of muscovado purchased by the same merchant had an average net weight of 486 livres.[7] By 1713, the net weight of some casks exceeded 700 livres, but variation remained very great. Individual net weights in one transaction involving 12 hogsheads of muscovado varied between 572 and 786 livres. In another, involving 17 hogsheads of clayed sugar, the average net weight per cask was 652 livres, but some casks contained

5 Jean-Baptiste Labat, *Nouveau voyage aux Isles de l'Amérique*. 2 vols. (La Haye: P. Husson, T. Johnson, etc., [1722] 1724), 1²: 319; and ADG., 7B/1857 Livre journal de Jean Pellet, entries for 8 July and 18 August 1719.

6 Labat, *Nouveaux voyage aux isles*, 1²: 317; also John J. McCusker, *Rum and the American Revolution: The Rum Trade and the Balance of Payments of the Thirteen Continental Colonies*, 2 vols. (New York & London: Garland Publishing Inc., 1989), 2: 860, n. 123.

7 ADG., 7B/1971 Livre journal de Jacques Pradie, entry for 8 June 1708.

more than 750 livres while one held just 464 livres.[8] A similar average net weight of 655 livres occurred in a sale recorded at Bordeaux six years later.[9] During 29 months, commencing in August of 1720, Jean-Baptiste Montuy purchased 420,718 livres (206 tonnes) of sugar, muscovado and clayed types, chiefly from planters on Marie Galante and Grenada, but also from some on Martinique and Guadeloupe. The fifty separate transactions involved 703 hogsheads. The average net weight per cask was 598 livres, but individual containers continued to vary from less than 500 to more than 700 livres. What is perhaps more important, neither the island of origin nor type of sugar was reflected in cask size. In most cases, transactions involving large purchases were generally packed in larger casks.[10] By 1730, another variant appeared. For purposes of determining the value of sugar imports at Bordeaux, all sugar casks from Saint-Domingue were assumed to contain 600 livres net while sugar casks from the Windward Islands were assumed to weigh 500 livres net of muscovado and 600 livres net of clayed sugars. As 97.9 percent of all sugar exported from Saint-Domingue was muscovado, it appears that sugar casks were beginning to vary by type and region.[11]

[8] Ibid., 7B/2813 Livre brouillard de J.-B. Montuy, 1713.
[9] Ibid., 7B/1857 Livre journal de Jean Pellet, entry for 18 August 1719.
[10] Ibid., 7B/3100 Livre brouillard de J.-B. Montuy, August 1720 to December 1722.
[11] Morineau, "Quelques recherches relatives à la balance du commerce", 33–4.

Abbreviations

ADCM	Archives departementales de Charente Maritime (La Rochelle)
ADG	Archives departementales de la Gironde (Bordeaux)
AN	Archives Nationales (Paris)
AN, SOM	Archives Nationales, Section Outre-mer (Aix-en-Provence)
BB	Bibliothèque de Bordeaux
BL	British Library (London)
BN	Bibliothèque nationale (Paris)
BSHM	Bibliothèque de la service historique de la marine (Vincennes)
Col.	Archives de Colonies (Paris, now at Aix-en-Provence)
Coll. de Mss.	*Collection de manuscrits contenant letters, mémoires et autre documents historiques relatifs à la nouvelle france*, 4 vols. (Québec: 1883–85)
CSP, CS	*Calendar of State Papers, Colonial Series*, edited by W. Noel Sainsbury, 10 vols. (London, HMSO 1860–1878)
DCB	*Dictionary of Canadian Biography*, 4 vols (Toronto: University of Toronto Press 1966–1979)
Marine	Archives de la Marine (Paris, A.N.)
n.a.f.	nouvelles acquisitions françaises
RAPQ	*Rapport de l'archiviste de la province de Quebec* [many volumes, 1921–1965]
RFHOM	*Revue française d'histoire d'outre-mer*
RHAF	*Revue d'histoire de l'amérique francaise*
RHC	*Revue d'histoire des colonies*

Part 1

Colonies Formed

1

Colonial Populations

Ambiguity characterised the French presence in the Americas. Whether in the vastness of North America or on the small islands in the Caribbean Sea, the magnitude of the disproportionate numbers of French men and women in the colonies and the geographical extent of the territories claimed by France became apparent between 1670 and 1730. In only one major colony did the French comprise more than half the total population in 1730. Although the number of French in the Americas tripled during the six decades after 1670, fewer than 74,000 lived there in 1730. Nearly as many Amerindians and more than twice as many Africans as Europeans inhabited these colonies. French colonial populations included three major components: Amerindian, European, and African, but each developed along very dissimilar lines. From Newfoundland to South America, Amerindian populations experienced massive declines that began long before 1670 and continued long after 1730. The French population, on the other hand, grew slowly after 1670 by natural increase, while African populations increased rapidly from forced migration. The relative distribution of these three populations in each colony was so different that it precluded the formation of any single model of French colonial development. In addition, each colonial population developed quite differently from the previous demographic histories of their constituent parts.

Appendix 1 shows the estimated population of the French Americas by ethnicity and region from 1670 to 1730. This is not the first attempt to gather all of the population data, but it is the most up-to-date and most heavily based on primary sources.[1] It is unique in its ambition to pull the data for

---

[1] See John McCusker, *Rum and the American Revolution: The Rum Trade and the Balance of Payments of the Thirteen Continental Colonies*, 2 vols. (New York and London: Garland Publishing, Inc. 1989), [548]–767; Appendix B, "Population Estimates for the

3

all the French American colonies together and to provide total population estimates for five separate years, each fifteen years apart, between 1670 and 1730. These estimates enable some general observations to be made about the populations of the French Americas during their formative years, and permit comparisons with other European colonies.

1.2 ABORIGINAL POPULATIONS

French migrants to the Americas encountered few Amerindians wherever they settled except in Guiana and Louisiana. Unlike the situation encountered by the Spanish, only a few thousand native people lived along the Atlantic coast of present-day Canada and even fewer French men and women settled there. Long before 1670, disease and war had virtually emptied the St. Lawrence Valley and Lower Great Lakes region as far west as the shores of Lake Huron of its aboriginal inhabitants. It was the activities of the French that encouraged some Amerindians to return to the region. The French encountered the largest native populations farther west in the Upper and Central Mississippi Valley stretching westwards from the ridge of the Appalachian Mountains to the Great Plains. However, there and even in the Lower Mississippi Valley the already devastated Amerindian populations continued to decline rapidly after 1670.

The French met few natives in the West Indies. Less than 50 years after first contact, Hispaniola's aboriginal population, once estimated to be several millions, had become more or less extinct.[2] In the Lesser Antilles, French and English pioneers had united earlier in the century to drive the Caribs out of their major settlements on St. Christopher, while the French alone fought for possession of Guadeloupe and Martinique. By 1670, few Caribs remained. The survivors either found temporary refuge on the mountainous islands of Dominica, St. Lucia, and St. Vincent, or fled to the South American mainland. In Guiana, along the coast of *Terre firme*, few Amerindians survived after

---

British Isles and the Western Hemisphere, 1680–1775" is based on secondary sources for non-British colonies. His population estimates for Canada, Nova Scotia, and Newfoundland for 1670, 1700, and 1730 are also for white populations only and mingle French and English populations together in the last two cases. They also precede the work of Hubert Charbonneau and the members of the Programme de recherches en démographie historique at the Universitéde Montréal. The estimates for the French West Indian colonies were all gathered from secondary sources. The recent study by Stanley L. Engerman and B. W. Higman, "The demographic structure of the Caribbean slave societies in the eighteenth and nineteenth centuries" in *General History of the Caribbean*, vol. 3, *The Slave Societies of the Caribbean*, ed., Franklin W. Knight (London: UNESCO, 1997), 45–104, ignores the seventeenth century and relies on McCusker for the early eighteenth century.

[2]   Shelburne F. Cook and Woodrow Borah, *Essays in Population History: Mexico and the Caribbean* (Berkeley: University of California Press, 1971), 401.

one and a half centuries of contact with Europeans. French settlers found few natives to contest their areas of settlement.

About 10,000 aboriginals lived in what is now Atlantic Canada before European contact. This included about 1,000 Beothucks who dwelt in New-foundland, but few if any lived along the south coast by 1670.[3] Epidemic diseases substantially reduced the number of Algonkian-speaking Mi'kmaq long before the early seventeenth century when the French established their first small trading posts in Acadia. As early as 1611, Father Pierre Biard, SJ recorded increasing mortality among the Mi'kmaq inhabitants of Nova Scotia.[4] Population densities may have been relatively high among these seminomadic hunters of the sea as well as of the eastern boreal forests, but by 1670 they probably numbered about 2,000 after more than a century and a half of contact with European fishermen and traders. The decline con-tinued into the second quarter of the eighteenth century. A 1705 estimate claimed there were two French for every Indian in Acadia, which is not far off the numbers in Appendix 1.[5]

By 1670, however, the native population in the Saint Lawrence Valley had more than recovered its earlier levels. Warfare and probably disease decimated the populations inhabiting this region during the sixteenth cen-tury. While the French encountered many seasonal migrants, they found few permanent inhabitants when they returned during the first decade of the seventeenth century. After an initial decline from 500 to 200 individuals in

---

[3] Hubert Charbonneau, "Trois siècles de dépopulation amérindienne" in *Les popula-tions amérindiennes et inuit du Canada, Aperçu démographique* (Montréal: Presses de l'université de Montréal, 1984), 32; and Olive Dickason, *The Myth of the Savage and the Beginnings of French Colonialism in the Americas* (Edmonton: University of Alberta Press, 1984), 100.

[4] Cited in Virginia P. Miller, "Aboriginal Micmac Population: A Review of the Evidence", *Ethnohistory*, 23, 2 (Spring, 1976), 117–27; also Dickason, *The Myth of the Savage*, 100–4.

[5] Mi'kmaq population estimates are in a very unsatisfactory state. Charbonneau, "Trois siècles", 32, indicates approximately 9,000 precontact Micmac and Abenaki, but Miller, op. cit., argues for a precontact population of 35,000 based on her acceptance of Biard's revised 1616 estimate of 3,500 as "the nadir population". She rejects earlier conserva-tive estimates of population densities for composite hunting bands and then halves the chief maximalist aboriginal/nadir population ratio, all of which amounts to selecting a number she feels comfortable with. Her own evidence, adduced from later seventeenth century sources, reduction of life expectancy, diminished family size, polygyny giving way to monogamy, and diminished birth rates all suggests that Biard's 1616 estimate cannot be accepted as a "nadir population" and that the Micmac continued to suffer serious population decline at least until the beginning of the eighteenth century. John G. Reid, "1686–1720: Imperial Intrusions" in *The Atlantic Region to Confederation: A History*, eds., Philip A. Buckner and John G. Reid (Fredericton: Acadiensis Press, 1994), 79, suggests this much smaller nadir population. See also Olive P. Dickason, *Canada's First Nations: A History of Founding Peoples from Earliest Times* (Toronto: McClelland and Stewart, 1992), 111.

the 1620s and 1630s due to the impact of European disease, the population began to recover during the 1650s as refugees from Huronia entered the area. Iroquois and Abenaki followed later and lived among the French.[6] By 1676, 20 to 30 percent of the Mohawk nation had moved to the Canadian mission of Kanawake; 300 were reported living there compared to between 900 and 1,500 in Iroquoia. By 1680 the mission held at least 400 Christian Mohawks.[7] In 1682 the French established the mission of St. François de Sales on the Chaudière River for Abenaki refugees from the Atlantic coastal region. Three years later the total population of domiciled natives had grown to about 2,100. More than three-quarters of them (1,598 in all) lived in four villages whose residents came to play a remarkable role in the history of New France. War and disease continued to exact their dreadful tolls, but new captives and additional refugees increased the domiciled Amerindian population slowly to about 2,600 by 1730.

The original population of the vast region known to the French as the *pays d'en haut* or Upper Country remains unknown. The Upper Country stretched westward from Montreal to the head waters of the Mississippi, including the Great Lakes' drainage basin north to James Bay and south to the mouth of the Ohio River. Minimum, moderate, and maximum population estimates provide fuel for countless learned debates among anthropologists, ethnohistorians, and historians, but only studies of discrete groups will add to the scant knowledge currently available.[8] Following the Iroquois wars against the Huron, Neutral, and Erie, and the pushing back of Algonkian-speaking peoples to the northern margins of the Great Lakes Basin, no one occupied the lands of present-day southern Ontario. A few dispersed peoples may have resumed hunting and fishing by 1670, but this region remained sparsely populated for a long time afterward.[9] Oral history claims that large-scale warfare between the Iroquois and Ojibwa during the final decades of the seventeenth century left the latter in possession of most of present-day Ontario, but when, where, and how many were involved remain a matter

6   J. A. Dickinson et J. Grabowski, "Les populations amérindiennes de la vallée laurentienne, 1608–1765", *Annales de démographie historique* (1993), 51–66; but also see Dickason, *The Myth of the Savage*, 107.

7   Francis Jennings, *Ambiguous Iroquois Empire: The covenant chain confederation of Indian tribes with English colonies* (New York: W.W. Norton, 1984), 176.

8   See John D. Daniels, "The Indian Populations of North America in 1492", *William and Mary Quarterly*, 3rd ser., 49, 2 (April, 1992), 298–320. John A. Dickinson, "The Pre-contact Huron Population: A reappraisal", *Ontario History*, 72, no. 1 (March, 1980): 173–4, revises figures for the Huron upwards to between 25,000 and 30,000 after Champlain. Bruce G. Trigger, *Natives and Newcomers: Canada's "Heroic Age" Reconsidered*, (Kingston and Montreal: McGill-Queen's University Press, 1985), 231–42, discusses the evidence and methodologies for determining both population estimates and declines.

9   Lucien Campeau, sj. *Catastrophe démographique sur les Grands Lacs; les premiers habitants du Quebec*, Cahiers d'histoire des Jésuites, No. 7 (Montréal: Editions Bellarmain, 1986), 95–7.

of conjecture.[10] The Iroquois nations living south of the lower Great Lakes lost more than half of their population to war, famine, and disease between 1689 and 1700.[11] Between 1670 and 1730, native populations in the vast region to the west experienced major transformations and shifts frequently characterised by large fluctuations, but always in steady decline.[12]

The once powerful if loose confederation of Illinois nations who numbered approximately 10,500 in 1670 quickly rose and fell during the next twenty years.[13] Even the most remote nations quickly experienced rapid declines. West of Lake Michigan, the Winnebago, Menominee, Sauk, and Fox each declined from many thousands in the early seventeenth century to a few hundred by 1709. They probably numbered no more than 1,800 by 1730.[14] The population of the Fox Indians faced genocide, dropping from an estimated 12,000 in 1665 to a mere 400 by 1736.[15] The total number in the region will never be known because hundreds of refugees and captives swirled in from eastern, western, and southern areas replacing thousands of dead and dying, the victims of pathogenic invasions and intertribal warfare which occurred on scales never before experienced. These continual migrations spread smallpox, influenza, measles, and scarlet fever throughout northeastern North America from the Atlantic to the Great Plains, north to Hudson Bay and south to the Gulf Coast.

The microbial invasion attacked people living south of the Ohio in the Mississippi Valley from both south and north. Diseases, epidemics, and slave raiding radically altered Amerindian societies of the Lower Mississippi long before the French arrived at the end of the seventeenth century. The estimated 70,000 natives in 1700 were far fewer than just two decades before, and the number was decreased by half again during the next quarter of a century. Around 1726, the Indian population was no more than 35,000.[16] A detailed estimate of a slightly larger area stretching north from the Gulf of Mexico to the mouth of the Ohio, as far west as East Texas and Arkansas, and in the east

[10] Leroy V. Eid, "The Ojibwa-Iroquois War: The War the Five Nations Didn't Win", *Ethnohistory*, 24, 4 (Fall, 1979), 197–234.

[11] Jennings, *Ambiguous Iroquois Empire*, 206–7.

[12] Conrad E. Heidenreich and J. V. Wright, "Population and Subsistence" in *Historical Atlas of Canada*, ed. R. C. Harris (Toronto: University of Toronto Press, 1987), Plate 18. Also, see Plates 35 and 37–40 by Heidenreich showing the great movements of population during the seventeenth and early eighteenth centuries.

[13] Ian K. Steele, *Warpaths, Invasions of North America* (New York and Oxford: Oxford University Press, 1994), 124; also George T. Hunt, *The Wars of the Iroquois* (Madison: University of Wisconsin Press 1940), 145–61.

[14] Jeanne Kay, "The Fur Trade and Native American Population Growth", *Ethnohistory*, 31 (1984), 276–8.

[15] Ibid., 275.

[16] Daniel H. Usner, Jr., *Indians, Settlers, and Slaves in a Frontier Exchange Economy: The Lower Mississippi Valley Before 1783* (Chapel Hill and London: University of North Carolina Press, 1992), 17, 44.

to below the ridge of the Appalachian chain, gives larger numbers but draws similar conclusions. Peter H. Wood indicates that the estimated aboriginal population of 160,500 in 1685 had declined by nearly two-thirds to 59,000 only forty-five years later. French Louisiana was a misnomer if ever there was one. In 1730, Amerindians still comprised more than 90 percent of the total population of the region, and while this does not disguise the massive decline in their numbers during the previous half century, the white, largely French population, had been recently surpassed by Africans who already made up more than 5.5 percent of the total.[17]

Conditions in the West Indies were different. On Saint-Domingue, the western, French-occupied portion of the island of Hispaniola, none of the precontact population survived. In 1685, Governor de Cussy claimed that the only Indians in the French settlements were female captives taken during pirate raids and brought back to the island.[18] The census of 1687 indicated some Indians in the colony, but two-thirds of them were indentured or enslaved and all lived on the island of Tortuga.[19] Most were probably Caribs captured in raids. According to Father Jean-Baptiste Margat, s.c. in 1729 not a single native remained in Saint-Domingue. Indeed, he added, not a trace of their passing could be found.[20]

The situation was equally tragic in the Lesser Antilles. By 1670, few native people survived. Historian Philip Boucher claims as "a reasonable guess" that 7,000 to 15,000 Caribs once inhabited many of the Lesser Antilles.[21] Shortly before the middle of the seventeenth century, after the French and English had expelled them from St. Christopher, Guadeloupe, and other islands, as many as 5,000, including refugees, may have lived on the island of Dominica. Coupled with emigration to the South American mainland, ongoing disease and war led to further catastrophic decline. African-derived, mosquito-employing pathogens such as falciparum malaria and yellow fever may also have played deadly roles among the Caribs who had lived for

[17] Peter H. Wood, "The Changing Population of the Colonial South: An Overview by Race and Region, 1685–1790", in *Powhatan's Mantle: Indians in the Colonial Southeast*, eds., P. H. Wood, G. A. Waselkov, and M. T. Hatley (Lincoln: University of Nebraska Press, 1989), 36–7 and Table 1, 38–9. I have incorporated data for subregions V to X as making up French Louisiana.

[18] Pierre de Vaissière, *Saint-Domingue: la société et la vie créole sous l'ancien régime, 1629–1789* (Paris: Perrin et Cie., 1909), 74–5.

[19] AN, SOM, G¹ 499, no. 18.

[20] Jean-Baptiste Margat de Tilly, S.C., *Lettres édifiantes et curieuses écrits des missions étrangères*, nlle. éd., Tome 7, *Mémoires d'Amérique* (Paris: J.G. Merigot, le jeune 1781), 153; from a letter dated 2 February 1729 concerning the history of the destruction of the island's original inhabitants.

[21] Philip P. Boucher, *Cannibal Encounters: Europeans and Island Caribs, 1492–1763* (Baltimore: The Johns Hopkins University Press, 1992), 35. Gérard Lafleur, *Les Caraïbes des Petites Antilles* (Paris: Karthala, 1992), 21, gives a much larger number, estimating that, as late as the 1620s, 20,000 to 30,000 Caribs inhabited the Lesser Antilles.

more than a century with Africans captured from the Spanish.[22] An English estimate of Indians on St. Vincent, St. Lucia, and Dominica in 1672 reported 1,500 bowmen but added, "w[h]ereof 600 are negroes".[23] Father Jean-Baptiste Labat visited Dominica in 1700 and estimated Carib numbers at less than 2,000, which appears far too high. Other estimates indicate Dominica's Carib population had declined to 600 by 1683 and to 400 in 1730.[24]

Other Caribs fled further down the island chain to St. Vincent, which reportedly had a population of 6,000 in 1683.[25] Two-thirds of this number were thought to be Black Caribs, the offspring of African female captives brought to the island by polygamous Island Carib males, or possibly the offspring of escaped slaves from Martinique and Barbados who seized the daughters and wives of native people. This estimate may be too high though, and the two groups may have lived apart. Thirteen years later, the two populations of St. Vincent were reported to be living on opposite sides of the island: 1,200 to 1,500 runaway slaves from neighbouring islands on one side, and two to 3,000 natives who had great commerce with those of the Orinoco River in South America on the other.[26] A 1704 estimate gave their number as nearly 5,000.[27] Whether these people emerged as an autonomous Afro-Carib community remains unknown. A French estimate that 4,000 to 5,000, including both Black and Island Caribs, inhabited the Lesser Antilles in 1713 may be low. The same year a report claimed between 7,000 and 8,000 Indians and former slaves (or maroons) lived on St. Vincent; another report dated 1719 placed St. Vincent's population at 7,000.[28] Well before the turn of the eighteenth century, the majority were probably Black Caribs, because Yellow or Island Caribs were as susceptible to African pathogens as they were to European ones.[29]

Many Caribs appear to have departed Martinique and Guadeloupe following the peace negotiated in 1660 betweenthemselves and the French. They

---

22 Jean-Pierre Moreau, *Les Petites Antilles de Christophe Colombe à Richelieu, 1493–1635* (Paris: Karthala, 1992), 69–74. For a contrary view see Kenneth F. Kiple and Kriemhild C. Ornelas, "After the Encounter: Disease and Demographics in the Lesser Antilles", in *The Lesser Antilles in the Age of European Expansion,* eds., Robert L. Paquette and Stanley L. Engerman (Gainsville: University of Florida Press, 1996), 50–67.

23 *CSP, CS,* vol. 8, no. 896, Enclosure in Governor Stapleton to the Council of Trade and Plantations, 17 July [o.s.] 1672.

24 Boucher, *Cannibal Encounters,* 96–7; he also gives a 1713 estimate of 400 to 500 Indians.

25 Ibid., citing Col., C⁸ᴬ 3, f. 268v Bégon and Blénac to Seignelay, 13 February 1683.

26 [François] Froger, *Relation d'un voyage fait en 1695, 1696, 1697 aux côtes de l'Afrique ... par Monsieur de Gennes* (Paris: Chez Nicolas Le Gras [1697], 1700), 195.

27 Col., C⁸ᴮ 2, no. 73, Du Parquet to Pontchartrain, 20 October, 1704.

28 Col., C⁸ᴮ 3, no. 42 extract, Phélypeaux to Pontchartrain, 8 March 1713; ADG-7B/1826 Pierre to Jean Pellet, Martinique, 20 August 1719, recounting a disastrous slave-raiding expedition.

29 Boucher, *Cannibal Encounters,* 97, citing Col., C⁸ᴬ 19, ff. 72–3.

virtually disappeared from Guadeloupe after 1671 when the 51 "sauvages, métis et tapouis" listed in the census represented less than 1 percent of the island's population. None were listed in 1686, although 16 appeared in the island's census a decade later.[30] Afterwards, Amerindians were usually listed together with other nonwhites as slave or free. The last census to record the presence of Caribs on Guadeloupe in 1730, enumerated 76, including 23 children.[31] The same general conclusion held true on the more populous islands of St. Christopher and Martinique. Caribs generally disappeared into the nonwhite population listed as either slave or free.[32] By 1686, the census recorded only 254 Caribs, both free and slave, in all the French Lesser Antilles and Cayenne.[33]

Disease and slave hunting devastated the Amerindians of Guiana on the South American mainland. Of the estimated 13,000 in the interior about 1670, perhaps only one-fifth remained in 1730.[34] By the time of French contact with the Galibis between the Maroni and the Oyapock Rivers at the beginning of the seventeenth century, the latter had become masters of the coast. They had arrived from the lower Amazon and Orinoco Rivers shortly before and pushed out the resident Arawak people. However, the coastal region proved to be fatal, and the Galibis population declined by 90 percent during the seventeenth and early eighteenth centuries.[35] Thought to number 9,500 in 1604, they totaled no more than 3,500 in 1666. A steady flow of refugees from the Amazon estuary fleeing Portuguese slavers disguised their continuing decline after 1685, but the French offered little protection. Pirates were notorious slave raiders, and after 1704, Governor Ferolles encouraged attacks on the natives and promoted their sale in the slave markets of the Antilles. Indeed, after 1687 only Indian slaves (about 100 annually) were counted in the few surviving censuses.

The most extraordinary feature of this dismal account of death and social destruction is that, despite the devastation visited upon the native peoples of the Americas, the survivors continued to play important roles in the history of the French colonies: as warriors fiercely resisting colonial incursions, as partners in trade, as agents of imperial conflict, and as independent actors pursuing their own tribal policies. They continually exercised their varied interests for as long as their reduced numbers and diminished resources allowed. Whether because of the nature of the colonial economies or the

[30] AN, SOM, G¹ 468, no. 56; 499, no. 18; and 469, f. 13.
[31] Guy Lasserre, *La Guadeloupe, étude géographique*, 2 vols. (Bordeaux: Union française d'impression, 1961), 1: 270.
[32] AN, SOM, G¹ 498, no. 56; and 499, nos. 13–14 and 78.
[33] Ibid., G¹ 498, no. 56.
[34] This paragraph is largely based on Jean Hurault, *Français et Indiens en Guyane, 1604–1972* (Paris: Union générale d'éditions, 1972), 23–4, 84–9, 92–3, 120–1, 353–5, 358, and 363.
[35] Bernard Chérubini, *Cayenne: ville créole et polyethnique, essai d'anthropologie urbain* (Paris: Karthala-Cennadom, 1988), 30.

small number of European immigrants, Amerindians influenced the shape of French colonial societies in ways that are only now beginning to be studied.[36]

1.3 AFRICAN IMMIGRANTS

The invading populations of Africans and Europeans grew by immigration and by natural increase, but their respective roles in the development of the French colonies are neither well-known nor clearly understood. Historians make far too much of government immigration policies, for example, without acknowledging that they largely failed. Historians also generally exclude Africans from any demographic consideration at all. The forced migration of Africans is normally studied from an economic rather than a demographic perspective. Studies of Africans in the Americas are in their infancy, but it seems clear that population increases in most parts of the Caribbean and Brazil came through continual forced migration.

The accurate number of slaves carried from Africa to French American colonies will never be known, especially for the period preceding 1715. Work on early African demography in the French West Indies is just now getting under way.[37] The evidence is scant and chiefly anecdotal. The picture is also complicated by the limited nature of the French slave trade during the seventeenth century.[38] Current historiography contends that most Africans were brought to the colonies by French slave traders, but little evidence exists to support the claim.[39] Fewer than 6,000 slaves were acknowledged in official correspondence to have reached the islands and Guiana during

[36] See Jan Grabowski, "French Criminial Justice and Indians in Montreal, 1670–1760", *Ethnohistory*, 43, 3 (Summer, 1996), 405–29 for a particularly important example.

[37] See David Eltis et al., *The Trans-Atlantic Slave Trade: A Database on CD-ROM* (Cambridge: Cambridge University Press, 1999); also, David Geggus, "The French Slave Trade: An Overview", *William and Mary Quarterly*, 58, 1 (January 2001) 34 paras. 2 april 2002: http//www.historycooperative.org/journals/wm/58.1/geggus.html

[38] Though his CD-ROM identifies 23 French slaving voyages and 6,300 imputed slaves embarked at Africa during the seventeenth century, Professor Eltis has kindly provided an update of his data. He has added 26 additional voyages between 1646 and 1700 and revised his imputed total of Africans embarked to 15,000. Eric Saugera, *Bordeaux port négrier, chronologie, économie, idéologie, XVIIe–XVIIIe siècles* (Paris: Karthala, 1995), claims 53 voyages occurred between 1643 and 1700, but an average of less than one slaving ship per year during the century does not make a slave trade.

[39] Robert L. Stein, *The French Slave Trade in the Eighteenth Century an Old Regime Business*, (Madison: University of Wisconsin Press, 1979), 11–12, leaves the mistaken impression that during the seventeenth century the French organised a regular slave trade, which though small, "displayed all the major characteristics of its eighteenth century successor". See also Herbert S. Klein, *African Slavery in Latin America and the Caribbean* (New York and Oxford: Oxford University Press, 1986), 52. Clarence Munford, *The Black Ordeal of Slavery and Slave Trading in the French West Indies, 1625–1715*, 3 vols. (Lewiston, NY: Edward Mellen Press, 1991), 1: 155–238, provides a disappointing, unconnected narrative that is anecdotal rather than analytical. The few numbers given (156, 160–1, and 174) are unreliable.

the three decades before 1700 when the estimated total slave population exceeded 33,000. One estimate is that about four times that number of Africans (124,500) were imported into the French Caribbean during the previous quarter century.[40] Not all slaves were delivered by interloping traders. Pirates were notorious suppliers of cheap slave labor. The French also raided other islands for slaves and purchased them from Carib raiders. The English claimed that during the 1667 war, the French carried off some 1,500 slaves from St. Christopher, Antigua, and Montserrat, and during the early 1680s Caribs sold captured slaves to French planters for rum and firearms despite a royal order prohibiting the practice.[41]

By 1670, Africans were already shaping French West Indian societies. While the source of these early forced migrants remains hidden in the unknown actions of interlopers and raiders, nearly 16,000 Africans resided in the French Lesser Antilles, where they comprised more than half the total population (see Appendix 1). Fifteen years later, the number of slaves in the colonies, including Guiana and Saint-Domingue, had risen to 25,000. The rate of increase declined considerably thereafter, but by 1700 slaves were nearly twice as numerous as whites, comprising nearly 65 percent of the French Circum-Caribbean population. Yet, the question remains: How did this occur? Moreover, half the period was occupied with the Nine Years' War, or the War of the League of Augsburg, when French slave ships were scarce on the Atlantic. The mystery deepens. Between 1701 and 1715, the number of Africans in the French West Indies grew more rapidly than at any time during the previous 30 years, even faster than during the subsequent fifteen years. By 1715 the slave population numbered nearly 77,000 – more than three times the white population in the French islands. In addition, between 1716 and 1730, more than 110,000 Africans were probably carried into the French colonies.

An estimated 390,000 slaves were imported into the French Circum-Caribbean during the years before 1730 (see Table 1.1). Whether surprisingly large or not, the figure is 2.4 times greater than the total number of Africans residing in the colonies in 1730. Owing to the striking similarity in the growth of slave populations in Jamaica and Saint-Domingue and the fact that the French islands were "sugar islands" with intensive land cultivation, high African-to-creole slave populations, and high male–female sex ratios among the slaves, Philip Curtin assumed a net annual rate of natural decrease of 5.4 percent, which largely accounts for the discrepancy between

---

[40] Philip D. Curtin, *The Atlantic Slave Trade: A Census* (Madison: University of Wisconsin Press, 1969), 26 and 119.

[41] *CSP, CS, 1669–1674*, no. 896; Richard S. Dunn, *Sugar and Slaves; The Rise of the Planter Class in the English West Indies, 1624–1713* (New York: W. W. Norton & Co., 1972), 124. See also *CSP, CS, 1681–1685*, no. 1126; and Col., B 10, f. 41 royal ordinance, 23 September 1683.

Table 1.1. *Estimated Slave Imports into French American Colonies to 1730*

Colony	Years	Slaves Imported	Annual Average	Percentage
Saint-Domingue	to 1680	4,000		
	1681–1730	176,560	3,530	
	Subtotal	180,560		46.1
Martinique	to 1670	15,830		
	1671–1730	91,260	1,690	
	Subtotal	107,090		27.3
Guadeloupe	to 1699	10,000		
	1700–1730	83,080	2,680	
	Subtotal	93,080		23.8
Louisiana	to 1730	7,000		1.8
Guiana	to 1730	4,000		1.0
Total		391,730		100

Source: Philip D. Curtin, *The Atlantic Slave Trade: A Census* (Madison: University of Wisconsin Press, 1969), 75–84; see especially Tables 20 and 21.

the high import and low population estimates.[42] This may be quite reasonable, even conservative. Gabriel Debien claimed slave mortality between 5 and 6 percent was a minimum.[43] During a fourteen-year period later in the eighteenth century, at least 129 new slaves were added to a Saint-Domingue plantation in order to keep the number around 150, which implies an annual depletion rate of 6.1 percent when the harshness of living conditions may have increased along with the supply of slaves.[44] Nevertheless, the number of imported Africans was at least 10 (perhaps as much as 20) times greater than all of the permanent European migrants to French America, including New France.

At least three-quarters of the Africans carried into the French colonies were transported in non-French ships.[45] Otherwise, the slave population

---

[42] Philip D. Curtin, *The Atlantic Slave Trade: A Census* (Madison: University of Wisconsin Press, 1969), 26.

[43] Gabriel Debien, *Les Esclaves aux antilles françaises (XVIIe – XVIIIe siècles)*, (Basse-Terre: Société d'Histoire de la Guadeloupe; Fort-de-France: Société d'histoire de la Martinique, 1974), 345.

[44] Gabriel Debien, *Plantations et esclaves à Saint-Domingue* (Dakar: Université de Dakar, 1962), 50–1, cited in K. G. Davies, *The North Atlantic World in the Seventeenth Century* (Minneapolis: University of Minnesota Press, 1974), 76, n28.

[45] Col., C9A 3, Du Casse to Pontchartrain, 15 December 1696, claimed the majority of slaves came from smuggling. The French, he declared, had never transported one-quarter of the number that arrived.

could not have reached the estimated levels in 1700. Dutch interlopers who did so much to develop sugar production in the French colonies might have carried Africans to the islands during the seventeenth century, but the most recent study of the Dutch slave trade found virtually no evidence. The Dutch, who landed nearly 13,000 slaves at Spanish American ports while they held the *asiento*, failed to deliver the contracted numbers.[46] They probably had no slaves for the French. This is not the place to recount the failure of French monopolists to establish a slave trade during the final quarter of the seventeenth century. It is sufficient to report that they came nowhere near supplying the 44,000 slaves called for in their contracts.

The first 15 years of the eighteenth century also remain an enigma. War returned to the West Indies, but it did not appear to affect slave migration. Between 1700 and 1715, slave populations increased faster than during any other time between 1670 and 1730, growing by 131 percent from 33,343 to 76,893. Yet, the slave population of the French Circum-Caribbean grew by 43,450 despite a negative rate of natural increase.[47] A recent estimate that French slave traders carried an average of 1,416 slaves annually from Africa to the West Indies between 1708 and 1713 may be quite accurate.[48] Others delivered the rest. The French took 3,200 captives from Nevis in 1706.[49] Although French raiders may have delivered several thousand captured slaves from other West Indian colonies, and planters undoubtedly sailed to Dutch and Danish colonies to acquire more, foreign interlopers probably delivered the largest portion of more than 50,000 Africans who arrived in the colonies from 1700 to 1715.

Between 1713 and 1730 the French slave trade grew by leaps and bounds as private entrepreneurs responded to easier access to credit and capital to supply a larger proportion of Africans to the West Indies than before. The largest change to the trade occurred in January of 1716, when letters patent opened Africa from the Sierra Leone River to the Cape of Good Hope to all French merchants on the condition that they pay a 20-livre head tax on each African landed in the Americas and fit out in one of five specified seaports.[50] Important new studies on the French slave trade have yielded an improved view of the number of slave imports for this period. Using shipping records rather than Curtin's assumptions and arithmetical calculations, Robert Stein estimated the French delivered 89,294 Africans

[46] Johannes M. Postma, *The Dutch in the Atlantic Slave Trade, 1600–1815* (Cambridge: Cambridge University Press, 1989), 34–5, 40.

[47] Curtin, *The Atlantic Slave Trade*, 170; also Paul Lachance, "The Demography of French Slave Colonies, Part 1 (1700–1760)", unpublished paper presented to the Social Science History Association, Chicago, November 1998, 14.

[48] David Eltis, *The Rise of African Slavery in the Americas* (Cambridge: Cambridge University Press, 2000), 166.

[49] Richard Pares, *War and Trade in the West Indies, 1739–1763*, reprint (London: Frank Cass, [1936] 1963), 181–2.

[50] Stein, *The French Slave Trade*, 13–16.

Table 1.2. *Slaves Arriving in French America, 1713–1730,*
by Quinquennial and by Colony

Years	Total Africans	Average Per Year
1713–1715	14,756.2	4,891.7
1716–1720	21,414.8	4,283.0
1721–1725	24,961.4	4,992.3
1726–1730	29,578.3	5,915.7
1713–1730	90,710.0	5,039.5

Colony	Number of Africans	Percent Slaves
Saint-Domingue	48,659.4	53.6
Martinique	33,439.7	36.9
Louisiana	4,660.0	5.1
Guiana	2,234.6	2.5
Guadeloupe Grenada	1,717.0	1.9
Total	90,710.7	100.0

Source: From David Eltis's calculations based chiefly on the Mettas-Daget, *Répertoire numerique.*

to the French colonies during the period.[51] Work by the late Jean Mettas, edited and published by Serge Daget, is more specific and involves real slaves carried in actual ships.[52] According to David Eltis who has rendered the records into computer readable form, 90,710 Africans reached French America in French ships during the 18 years from 1713 to 1730, inclusive (see Table 1.2).[53]

Eltis' number receives independent confirmation from a contemporary document reporting the French slave trade delivered a total of 54,057 Africans to the Americas between 1 July 1722 and 1730.[54] However, even

[51] Ibid., 211 Table A9.

[52] Jean Mettas, *Répertoire des expéditions négriers françaises au XVIIIe siècle*, édité par Serge Daget, 2 vols. (Paris: Société française d'histoire d'outre-mer et Librairie Orientaliste Paul Geuthner, 1978–1986).

[53] I gratefully acknowledge Professor Eltis's generous assistance and draw attention to his ongoing research on the Atlantic slave trade in association with members of the W. B. De Bois Institute at Harvard University. He generously reworked the data from the Mettas-Daget *Répertoire* for the eighteen-year period, adding imputed totals for eleven ships for which data on slave numbers were unavailable, and gave me the result, which appears in Table 1.2.

[54] Jean-Claude Nardin, "Encore des chiffres: La traite négrière française pendant la première moitiédu XVIIIe siècle", RFHOM 57 (1970), 425. Table 1.2 shows 54,539.7 slaves delivered for a slightly longer period, 1721–1730.

so, the number includes only slaves carried in French ships. Many Africans continued to be imported into the French colonies via British, Dutch, and Danish slave ships. Between 1715 and 1730, the black population increased by 83,385 (see Appendix 1), which is 15 percent greater than the number of arrivals via the French slave trade during the same period. If the average annual negative rate of increase was 5.4 percent, more than 126,000 new arrivals would have had to have landed since 1715 in order for the total black population to more than double to 164,278 during the next fifteen years. If true, the French slave trade may have supplied about 60 percent of the slaves landed in the French colonies between 1715 and 1730 compared to delivering less than one-fifth of the total during the seventeenth century.[55]

1.4 EUROPEAN IMMIGRANTS

Whether one looks at North America or at the West Indies and Guiana, the two streams of French immigration to the temperate and tropical colonies were very thin compared to the broad rivers of white migration that ran first from Spain and then England to the New World.[56] Between 1561 and 1650 Spanish migration to the Americas exceeded 350,000.[57] More than 400,000 English emigrated to the Americas during the seventeenth century. The British Caribbean alone received an estimated 222,000 migrants from the British Isles between 1630 and 1700, and during the last four decades of the century at least 100,000 emigrated from England to North America.[58] Tiny Portugal sent more than 1.1 million emigrants overseas between 1580 and 1760.[59] The numbers of other Europeans far exceeded the trickle of men

---

55 Assuming an annual negative rate of increase of 5.4 percent, the 76,793 slaves in the colonies in 1715 would number only 33,395 in 1730. Of the 160,278 slaves in the French West Indies and Cayenne in 1730, 83,385 (160,278–76,893) arrived between the beginning of 1716 and the end of 1730 and survived a similar negative rate of natural increase. Assuming continuous monthly arrivals during 180 months, 7,285.2 slaves arrived each year. During the 15-year period, 109,278 Africans, or 43.9 percent more than have been documented, entered the French West Indies. I gratefully acknowledge the assistance of Joan Geramita of the Department of Mathematics and Statistics, Queen's University, who worked out the solution to the problem.

56 See W. Borah, "The Mixing of Populations", and M. Mörner, "Spanish Migration to the New World prior to 1800", in *First Images: The Impact of the New World on the Old*, 2 vols., ed., F. Chiapelli (Berkeley: University of California Press, 1976), 2: 707–22 and 737–82.

57 Lyle N. McAlister, *Spain and Portugal in the New World, 1492–1700* (Minneapolis: University of Minnesota Press, 1984), 333.

58 Engerman and Higman, "Demographic Structure of Caribbean Slave Societies", 62; Anthony McFarlane, *The British in the Americas, 1480–1815* (London and New York: Longman, 1994), 60; and Robert Jütte, *Poverty and Deviance in Early Modern Europe* (New York: Cambridge University Press, 1994), 190.

59 Vitorino Magalhaes Godinho, "Portuguese Emigration from the Fifteenth to the Twentieth Century: Constants and Changes" in *European Expansion and Migration: Essays on*

and women who voyaged from France to the New World during the seventeenth and early eighteenth centuries, and who, for the most part, sought to return home again as quickly as possible.[60] It is highly unlikely that even 100,000 emigrants ever left the shores of "la douce France" for the harsh conditions of the New World, or that one-quarter of that number settled there.[61] Fewer than 3,000 French men and women actually settled in New France during the 60 years between 1670 and 1730, and though a few thousand more may have colonized the West Indies during the same period, the total for both regions may not have exceeded 10,000.

That the most populous country of Europe contributed only about 5 percent of the total European intercontinental migration between 1500 and 1800 deserves comment. While there may have been a cultural reluctance to depart from France, to sever ties of place and kinship forever, reliance on such an argument for the whole explanation is unconvincing. Recent research confirms earlier suggestions that French migration overseas was an extension of other perennial movements within France such as rural exodus or interurban labour migrations rather than a new phenomenon.[62] Yet, the question of why so few left France remains unanswered. Despite the dreadful impact of war, famine, and disease that led to the destruction of one-third of the peasantry of eastern France during the Thirty Years' War and to the devastation of the Paris basin during the Fronde, France's rural economy did not experience any significant restructuring such as occurred in England, nor was the political and religious oppression as grinding as in the Iberian peninsula. Above all, peasants owned nearly half the land in France and the security of peasant land tenure remained intact.[63] As long as the peasant hold on land remained firm, expanding French cities and the growing royal army absorbed most of the surplus population that appeared during the last quarter of the seventeenth century.

---

the *Intercontinental Migration from Africa, Asia, and Europe*, eds., P. C. Emmer and M. Möner (New York and Oxford: Berg, 1992), 18; and McAlister, *Spain and Portugal*, 340–2.

60 P. N. Moogk, "Reluctant Exiles: Emigrants from France in Canada before 1760", *William and Mary Quarterly*, 3rd series, 46 (July, 1989): [463]–505.

61 Pierre Pluchon, éd., *Histoire des Antilles et de la Guyane* (Toulouse: Privat, 1882) claims the estimate of 100,000 is too low because it excludes soldiers. He offers a revised estimate of the total number of pre-1789 overseas migrants of 300,000 but gives no compelling reason for accepting it. Jean Meyer, "Des Origines à 1763" dans *Histoire de la France coloniale des origines à 1914*, éds., J. Meyer *et al.* (Paris: Armand Colin, 1991), 14–16, is more discrete; he gives no number at all for total colonial migration.

62 See Leslie Choquette, *Frenchmen into Peasants, Modernity and Tradition in the Peopling of French Canada* (Cambridge: Harvard University Press, 1997).

63 See Pierre Goubert, "Le Paysan et la terre: seigneurie, tenure, exploitation" dans F. Braudel et E. Labrousse, éds., *Histoire économique et sociale de la France*, vol. 2, *Des derniers temps de l'âge seigneurial aux préludes de l'âge industriel, (1660–1789)*, (Paris: Presses universitaires de France, 1970), 130–9; also Ralph Davis, *The Rise of the Atlantic Economies* (London: Weidenfeld and Nicolson, [1973] 1975), 119–22.

Before 1663, recruitment of immigrants to all French colonies remained the preserve of colonial proprietors, seigneurs, and private entrepreneurs, including religious orders.[64] Afterward the Crown engaged in similar activity, but earlier recruiters only ceased to play their important roles a decade later. Thereafter, the government dominated in fostering emigration to the French colonies. The thin trickle of immigrants that flowed to the Americas during the next five and a half decades reveals the government's complete ineptitude as the major recruiting agency to settle the colonies.[65] Louisiana is a special case about which more will be said later.

Despite Jean-Baptiste Colbert's reputation as a promoter of French colonial settlement and rational economic development, his colonial immigration and settlement policies were confused, short-sighted, and frequently contradictory. They contributed little to establishing French colonies in the Americas.[66] Following his death in 1683, his successors' policies and efforts also proved ineffectual during the next half century. Close examination of colonial migration, population growth, and settlement reveals very clearly that the French government's policy was animated chiefly by economic conditions in France and environmental and market forces in the colonies. When the state played any role at all, it did so chiefly in reaction to forces beyond its control. Of policy, there was little that can be identified with either imperial ambition or rational development.

During the first decade of royal control of the American colonies, from 1663 to 1672, the Crown subsidized the transportation of 3,295 immigrants to New France, but few to the West Indies, where the emigration of indentured servants had peaked in 1663.[67] While emigration remained state-directed, little in the way of direct support appeared again until after Louis XIV's death. Never a strong proponent of immigration to the colonies,

---

64 Marcel Trudel, *The Beginnings of New France, 1524–1663*, trans. Patricia Caxton (Toronto: McClelland and Stewart, 1973), 184–90; and Lucien Campeau, *Les Cent-Associés et le peuplement de la Nouvelle-France, (1633–1663)*, Cahiers d'histoire des Jesuites 2 (Montréal: Bellarmain, 1974).

65 Leslie Choquette, "Recruitment of French Emigrants to Canada, 1600–1760" in *"To Make America", European Emigration in the Early Modern Period*, eds., Ida Altman and James Horn (Berkeley and Los Angeles: University of California Press, 1991), 133.

66 W. J. Eccles, *Canada Under Louis XIV, 1663–1701*, (Toronto: McClelland and Stewart, 1964), 6–13, contains the clearest statement in favour of the coherent rationality of Colbert's colonial policies, but similar views can be found in virtually every historical account. Contrary views exist chiefly in more specialised literature that has had little impact on texts intended for wider audiences; e.g., H. Charbonneau and Yves Landry, "La politique démographique en Nouvelle France", *Annales de démographie historique*, 1979, 29–57.

67 Marcel Trudel, *Histoire de la Nouvelle France*, [Tome] IV, *La seigneurie de la Compagnie des Indes Occidentales, 1663–1674* (Montréal: Fides, 1997), 251, 252–3; also Gabriel Debien, "Les Engagés pour les Antilles, 1634–1715", *RHC*, 37 (1951), 248–9, Tableau générale.

Colbert, like most French statesmen, had good reason to believe that France was underpopulated.[68] In his opinion neither men nor money was required to build colonies. Not surprisingly, the quality of the immigrants destined for New France rapidly declined.[69] As early as January of 1666, Colbert rejected a proposal to increase assistance to immigrants. The king regarded the proposal as impractical and believed it imprudent to depopulate his kingdom to settle Canada.[70] Four years later Colbert expressed similar sentiments to Governor-General de Baas in the Windward Islands, advising him that the king lacked the power to people the islands by force.[71] Sixteen years later, his son and successor at the Marine, the marquis de Seignelay advised the intendant of Martinique not to ask for workers or bondsmen from France. This did not prevent him, however, from sending nearly 2,000 forced Huguenot deportees to the West Indies to be sold into indentured servitude shortly afterwards.[72]

The quality of subsidized immigrants was also poor. Toward the end of 1667, the Canadian intendant complained that the 127 men who reached the colony were weak, excessively young, and unfit for service. Equally ominous, the number represented less than one-third of the 400 expected that year. The intendant requested that in future, idiots, cripples, the chronically ill, and wayward young men (*fils de familles*) not be sent.[73] In 1670, in a gesture sometimes thought to encourage immigration, Colbert reduced the length of service for indentured servants in the Antilles from 36 to 18 months, but planters, merchants, and ship captains quickly subverted the minister's intention by subsequently issuing contracts that specified forfeiture of the new shortened period of service and upheld the old term. This practice prevailed for nearly three decades until 1698, when the older three-year term was legally restored.[74] After 1673, the last year of assisted immigration to the colonies, Colbert did nothing at all during the remaining 10 years of his life. The Franco-Dutch War (1672–8) virtually halted emigration to the French colonies. Colbert and his successors continued to approve of indentured servants as immigrants because they increased the white population

[68] See M. W. Flinn, *The European Demographic System, 1500–1820* (Baltimore: The Johns Hopkins University Press, 1981), 77.

[69] Moogk, "Reluctant Exiles", 480–1.

[70] *RAPQ, 1930–31*, 41 Colbert to Talon, 5 January 1666; quoted in Moogk, "Reluctant Exiles", 466. See ibid., 36 Talon to Colbert, 4 October 1665 for the former's proposal to prepare homesteads for more than the year's quota of 300 assisted emigrants.

[71] L. P. May, *Histoire économique de la Martinique*, Réédité (Fort-de-France: Société de distribution et de culture, [1930] 1972), 36.

[72] Ibid.; also Debien, "Les Engagés pour les Antilles", 192–4.

[73] *RAPQ, 1930–31*, 81, 87 Talon to Colbert, 27 et 29 October 1667, quoted in Moogk, "Reluctant Exiles", 466, 480.

[74] Debien, "Les Engagés pour les Antilles", 64, 241; Christian Huetz de Lemps, "Indentured Servants Bound for the French Antilles in the Seventeenth and Eighteenth Centuries" in *"To Make America"*, eds., Altman and Horne, 182.

and could defend the colonies from external threat and internal slave revolt, but colonists and ship captains increasingly considered them an unnecessary burden on the cost of transportation, especially to the West Indies, where sugar and slaves were reducing the demand for white labour.[75]

After 1680, immigration to Canada slowed to a trickle, but it continued to flow to the West Indies. The reasons for the change reflected the altered circumstances which developed in France and in the colonies and changed the character of the two immigration streams. Canada was growing quite nicely by natural increase, but the islands still needed assistance to form families. During the next six years some 500 young white women, chiefly recruited from the general hospitals of Paris and Rouen, were shipped to the islands, but the convoys of immigrants were halted at the request of colonial authorities.[76] White female fertility appeared quite high, and after 1687 growth was chiefly through natural increase.[77]

The growing number of Africans proved a continual worry to colonial officials, for while slave resistance was real and fueled a concern to maintain white numbers, colonists were not prepared to pay for assisted immigration. As the pool of indentured servants dried up, the government turned to forced deportations. Intendant Michel Bégon did not interest himself much in indentured servants while in the Antilles, but following his appointment as intendant of the galley corps at Marseille in 1684, he discovered the benefit of ridding the arsenal of invalids and the elderly, and promoted the emigration of convicts to the New World, especially Guiana.[78] After a few trial voyages involving several hundred galley slaves in 1686 and 1687, the experiment came to an end.[79] Colonial authorities were appalled at the aged, decrepit, and crippled lifers who proved to be utterly worthless additions to the population. Some of the convict migration proved to be a cover for the continuing forced deportation of Huguenots. Between 1687 and 1688, more than 500 deportees were transported to Martinique alone.[80]

Every immigrant experience was a personal one. The decision to leave France and the factors leading to it were individual. These reasons shall always remain impenetrable, but the collective experience of immigration, as much as it remains open, can be explored a little further. Immigration to the colonies took place in currents, chiefly characterised by social type and sex. Some currents operated throughout the 60-year period and beyond, but

[75] See BN, n.a.f. 9,325, f. 307v Mémoire du Sr de Pouançay, 1682, for an extreme statement on the worth of indentured servants as immigrants.
[76] May, *Histoire économique de la Martinique*, 46; Jacques Petitjean-Roget, "Les femmes des colons à Martinique au XVIIe et XVIIIe siècle", *RHAF*, 9 (1955–56), 176–235.
[77] May, *Histoire économique de la Martinique*, 30, 38.
[78] Yvonne Bezard, *Fonctionnaires maritimes et coloniaux sous Louis XIV: les Bégon* (Paris: Editions Albin Michel, 1932), 73–4.
[79] Debien, "Les Engagés pour les Antilles", 178–9.
[80] Ibid., 43.

Table 1.3. *Known French Immigration to Canada, 1670–1729,*
By Decade and by Sex

Period	Men Number	Men Percent	Women Number	Women Percent	Total Number	Total Percent
1670–1679	429	54.4	369	46.2	798	27.4
1680–1689	483	89.6	56	10.4	539	18.5
1690–1699	490	93.9	32	6.1	522	17.9
1700–1709	283	92.2	24	7.8	307	10.5
1710–1719	293	94.2	18	5.8	311	10.7
1720–1729	420	96.8	14	3.2	434	14.9
Totals	2398	82.4	513	17.6	2911	100

Source: Hubert Charbonneau and Normand Robert, "The French Origins of the Canadian Population, 1608–1759" in *The Historical Atlas of Canada*, Vol. 1, *From the Beginning to 1800*, ed., R. C. Harris (Toronto: University of Toronto Press, 1987), Plate 45.

were heaviest at certain short intervals. Others appeared only later during the eighteenth century. In general, French immigrants to New France can be grouped into five general categories: indentured servants, soldiers, eligible young women, convicts, and freemen. The same categories may also be employed for the white migrants to the West Indies, Cayenne, and Louisiana. Any figures are very approximate – those for the West Indies are too sparse – but historians have also arranged them chronologically by decades in order to show the rhythm as well as the type of immigration to the colonies. Table 1.3 for New France immigration is as precise as can be reasonably demanded, but any observations and tentative conclusions need not depend on exact numbers.

The number of immigrants who settled in Canada during the six decades between 1670 and 1729 represent a little more than one-third (34.2 percent) of the total number of all migrants to New France.[81] Although more than four times as many men as women established themselves in the colony during this period, only the women traveled with the intention to stay. Almost all of them reached the colony during the early 1670s. They were the final part of the only significant wave of female immigration ever to reach Canada.[82]

---

[81] H. Charbonneau, Normand Robert, "The French Origins of the Canadian Population, 1608–1759" in *The Historical Atlas of Canada*, Volume 1, *From the Beginning to 1800*, ed., R. C. Harris (Toronto: University of Toronto Press, 1987), Plate 45.

[82] Yves Landry, *Orphelines en France, pionnières au Canada; les filles du roi au XVIIe siècle* (Montréal: Leméac, 1992) is the most thorough demographic study of these women to date.

Indeed, after 1672 less than three women immigrated annually to the colony during the next half century.

Immigrants who arrived in the West Indies and New France before 1680 comprised the pioneering generation. Whether in the Antilles or Canada, they included a large proportion of free men and women, merchants, soldiers hired as fighters who settled in the colony, and gentlemen settlers and their families who sailed at their own expense. Fewer than 500 freemen and women ever settled in Canada, and the same is probably true of the Antilles; almost none arrived in either region after 1670. Most who immigrated later voyaged alone.[83]

Between 1683 and 1727, some 4,577 soldiers were sent to New France of whom perhaps one-quarter died and one-fifth stayed.[84] Sick and wounded left every year; a few deserted or fled westward, but the remainder returned to France. Between 1683 and 1688, 2,100 soldiers were sent to Canada, but the impact of disease and war was such that only 1,418 remained to be organized into 28 companies during the autumn of 1689.[85] A further 861 recruits were sent to Canada between 1693 and 1697, but only 764 effectives could be mustered in the colony in 1699.[86] Between 1698 and the outbreak of hostilities in 1702, 337 men were sent out before the exhaustive manpower demands of the king's armies during the War of the Spanish Succession dried up the supply. None were sent in 1703, 1706, 1708, and 1709. Only 221 reached the colony during the war. In 1712, Governor-General Vaudreuil at Quebec declared the new recruits were children who needed three or four more years before becoming fit for duty.[87] Troops proved no easier to recruit after the war. Age and height minimums were lowered to assist the process, but between 1713 and 1727 naval authorities managed to send only 1,058 soldiers to New France.[88]

Military recruits had little impact on colonial demography.[89] They were poor prospects as settlers, and while some married in the colony, most

[83] Hubert Charbonneau, André Guillemette, *et al.*, *The First French Canadians: Pioneers in the St. Lawrence Valley* (Newark: University of Delaware Press, [1987] 1993) presents the latest research concerning the pre-1680 colonists of Canada. See also Jacques Petitjean-Roget, *La Société d'habitation à la Martinique: Un demi-siècle de formation, 1635–1685*, 2 vols. (Lille-Paris: Université de Lille III – Librairie Honoré Champion, 1980).

[84] J. Cassel, "Les Troupes de la marine in Canada, 1683–1760, Men and Material" (unpublished Ph.D. thesis, University of Toronto, 1987), 515–23.

[85] *Ibid.*, 515; J. Leclerc, *Le Marquis de Denonville, gouverneur de la nouvelle-france, 1685–1689* (Montréal: Fides, 1876), 86, gives 2,050.

[86] Cassel, "Les Troupes de la marine", 515; W. J. Eccles, *Frontenac, the Courtier Governor* (Toronto: McClelland and Stewart, 1959), 268, states that 615 reinforcements reached the colony from 1693 to the end of hostilities.

[87] *RAPQ, 1947–48*, 170 Vaudreuil to Pontchartrain, 6 November 1712.

[88] Cassel, "Les Troupes de la marine", 100, 102, and 516.

[89] Cf. J. Hamelin, *Economie et société en Nouvelle France* (Québec, Presses de l'Université Laval, 1960), 84, who claims soldiers and military recruits played a "fundamental role in the colonisation of New France, and the formation of the French Canadian population".

soldiers appeared quite content to remain in service. The desertion rate in Canada was only a tenth of the regular army; men who may have had few or no job skills were able to supplement their incomes by working for habitants and merchants.[90] Only a minority of soldiers ever faced the arduous conditions of the frontier. A surprising number obtained absolute discharges, buying their freedom from the service and leaving the colony. With half the ranks filled with urban dwellers, land and independence attracted only a few.[91] Only 20 percent of those who entered the colony before 1715 ever stayed on, and there is no reason to think the situation altered afterwards.[92]

Indentured servants known as *engagés* were the most important group of immigrants to settle in the French colonies. They represent about 39 percent of the total number of immigrants who settled in New France.[93] A still higher proportion of *engagés* probably colonized the West Indies. Five times as many indentures for those sailing to the West Indies than for Canada have survived in French archives.[94] Recent research on Canada stresses the high proportion of immigrants that returned to France from the colonies without settling there.[95] Returning bondsmen were noticed. From the days of the Crown's earliest involvement they were blamed for delays in the colonization of Canada.[96]

Though they came to New France on a slim but continuous basis, indentured servants were largely a feature of seventeenth-century immigration. Their geographic and social origins, social status, and eventual careers were extremely diverse, but the majority probably came from broken and dysfunctional families rather than the poorest groups in society. Some were farm labourers, carters, sawyers, textile workers, members of the landless, and rural labouring classes, but nearly half came from villages, towns, and cities.[97] Like soldiers, *engagés* were almost evenly divided between farm labourers and village artisans. Emigration from Angoumois, for example, was 51 percent peasant and 38 percent artisan.[98] Most migrants to New

---

90 *RAPQ, 1928–1929,* 288 Frontenac and Champigny to Pontchartrain, 10 November 1695, reported that soldiers earned about one-third less than the going wage. See also Cassel, "Les Troupes de la marine," 120.

91 Ibid., 95, 123, 127. Based on Table 10, which shows that for the period 1684 to 1725, 324 of 671 soldiers (48.3 percent) for whom data exists, had urban origins.

92 Louise Dechêne, *Habitants and Merchants in Seventeenth Century Montreal* (Montreal and Kingston: McGill-Queen's University Press, [1974] 1992), 41.

93 Hamelin, *Economie et Société en Nouvelle France,* 77.

94 Moogk, "Reluctant Exiles", 476–7; Debien, "Les Engagés pour les Antilles", 142.

95 Mario Boleda, "Trente mille Français à la conquête du Saint-Laurent", *Histoire sociale/Social History,* 23/45 (May 1990), 167, 172; Moogk, "Reluctant Exiles", 463–4; and Choquette, *Frenchmen into Peasants,* 279.

96 *RAPQ, 1926–27,* 8 King to Frontenac, 5 June 1672.

97 Charbonneau and Robert, "The French Origins of the Canadian Population", Plate 45.

98 M. Reible, "L'Emigration coloniale en Angoumois sous Louis XIV et la question protestant", *Mémoires de la société archéologique et historique de la Charente,* 1958 (Angoulême, 1959), 97-[178].

France were the offspring of the mobile, modern sector of a changing society rather than the rejects of a feudal one, hence, the large proportion of those with urban origins.[99]

The Crown's agents actively recruited *engagés* for Canada only during the 1660s when economic conditions in western France were so desperate that they simply signed up migrants coming into the seaports. By 1670, they had abandoned recruitment of bondsmen for Canada, leaving the onus on private enterprise. Authorities tried several times after the dissolution of the West India Company in 1674 to force ship captains to carry a fixed number of bondsmen based on ship tonnage. However, the regular appearance of similar ordinances throughout the entire subsequent period suggests that legislative regulations were neither observed nor enforced. Instead, ship captains and merchants undertook elaborate frauds to avoid their obligations or preferred to pay fines and carry extra cargo.[100]

Immigration figures are unavailable for the West Indies at the turn of the century. After 1680 population growth was chiefly through natural increase, and by 1700 the era of immigration had closed.[101] *Engagés* continued to arrive in the islands, but a general decline in their availability and a hardening attitude toward the "dangerous classes" following Louis XIV's death in 1715 gave rise to a new policy of transporting convicts to the colonies.[102] France's altered strategic position in North America, following the signing of the Treaty of Utrecht in 1713, also provided a new stimulus to settlement, and encouraged a more active promotion of colonial immigration. These changes gave rise to the largest single wave of immigration ever directed toward any French colony during the century before 1760, but the effort was not a success, nor did it point to any new role for the French government.

Three colonies needed government support if settlement was to be established after the war: Cayenne, Louisiana, and Cape Breton Island, recently renamed Île Royale. Antoine Crozat used the cession of Acadia and Placentia to the English and the consequent threat to the security of New France in a

---

99   Choquette, *Frenchmen into Peasants*, 279–305; unfortunately the author says nothing about migration to the French American tropical colonies.

100 Huetz de Lemps, "Indentured Servants Bound for the French Antilles", 170–203.

101 May, *Histoire économique de la Martinique*, 30, 38.

102 M. Gaucher, M. Delafosse, et G. Debien, "Les Engagés pour le Canada au XVIIIe siècle", *RHAF*, 13 (1959), 247–61, 402–21, 550–61, et 14 (1960), 87–108, 246–58, 430–40, and 583–602; also Charles Frostin, "Du peuplement pénal de l'Amérique française aux XVIIe et XVIIIe siècles: hésitations et contradictions du pouvoir royal en matière de déportation", *Annales de Bretagne*, 85 (1978), 67–94. Huetz de Lemps, "Indentured Servants)", 186, counted 8,500 indentures from 1698 to 1774, which led him to estimate that 13,000 *engagés* departed from Bordeaux for the Americas during the eighteenth century, but most of these voyaged after 1730. Few emigrated during the War of the Spanish Succession and most of those who sailed between 1715 and 1723 were forced emigrants (rounded-up vagabonds and salt smugglers without contracts) rather than voluntary *engagés*.

vain attempt to persuade Pontchartrain to assume the burden of immigration to Louisiana.[103] However, Pontchartrain proved incapable of providing a strong initiative. Nothing came of his modest proposal that the king support a small flow of immigrant families overseas from a deduction from lottery sales in France.[104] The plan had originated with Crozat, but Nicolas Desmaretz, Controller-General of Finances, rejected it. Desmaretz had ignored the navy's financial distress during the recent war, and during the peace, he shifted from indifference to outright hostility toward colonial immigration. According to Desmaretz, the security of French possessions in North America was better ensured by constructing fortifications rather than settling Île Royale, and he completely ignored Louisiana, which may have experienced a net decline in population between 1712 and 1715.[105] Immigration awaited the appearance of new initiators, the Regent of France and John Law.[106]

Only 215 French men and a very few women inhabited Louisiana at the time of Louis XIV's death in 1715.[107] About one-quarter of their number were settlers. War, absence of will, and a want of financial resources prevented the success of any immigration plan during the first 16 years of the colony's existence, but so too had the strategic reasons for its foundation. Established to prevent Spanish expansion from Florida and Texas into the Mississippi Valley and to block English access to the continental interior via the mouth of the Mississippi River, no economic reason ever existed for settling the region. Dreams of vast mineral wealth in the interior remained unfounded. The easy conquest of Spanish colonies also remained visionary, and, had a demand for furs existed, a settled, colonized Louisiana would only have undermined the Canadian fur trade by draining furs out of North America via the Mississippi rather than the St. Lawrence River. Between 1699 and 1715, whether under direct administration of the Crown or the private trade monopoly of Antoine Crozat, Louisiana survived largely thanks to Canadian *coureurs de bois* and canoemen who were able to defend and forage for themselves but who had no interest in becoming colonists.

As early as February of 1716, the new Navy Council, presided over by the comte de Toulouse, took the unreserved decision to transport criminals to the colonies. Salt smugglers, vagrants, and enclosed women (*femmes de mauvais vie*) were immediately targeted, and army deserters, tobacco smugglers, young rakes, prostitutes (*filles publiques*), and convicted

---

103 Marcel Giraud, *Histoire de la Louisiane*, 4 vols. (Paris: Presses universitaires de France, 1953–1974), 1:232.

104 Ibid., 240; Frostin, "Du peuplement pénal", 76.

105 Giraud, *Histoire de la Louisiane*, 1:240–5; also M. Allain, "L'Immigration française en Louisiane, 1718–1721", *RHAF*, 28, 4 (1975), 559.

106 Giraud, *Histoire de la Louisiane*, 2: 27–37.

107 Ibid., 1: 255.

criminals were quickly added. The first three transports with their cargoes arrived in Louisiana two years later.[108] Meanwhile, Antoine Crozat abandoned his trade monopoly and John Law's *Compagnie d'Occident*, or Western Company, was created by letters patent in August of 1717. By placing Louisiana in the very heart of his "system", Law gave an impetus to colonial immigration never before experienced. During the next four years, Law's ships and several naval vessels carried slightly more than 7,000 European immigrants to Louisiana.[109] These were reinforced by approximately 2,000 Africans brought to Louisiana during the same period.[110]

Fewer than 5 percent of the whites were free men. Given that 91.7 percent were indentured servants, transported prisoners, women, soldiers, and children, the remainder are best viewed as some form of coerced labour. Despite the impressive numbers though, the entire scheme failed. An estimated 2,000 white immigrants deserted or died of ill treatment during the crossing or returned to France. At least half of all the white migrants either died or abandoned the colony before 1726.[111] Few are numbered among Louisiana's founding families.[112]

Colonial and intercolonial migration also included non-French elements, perhaps more than is sometimes thought. Though European immigration usually occurred along national lines, intercolonial migration was more flexible. Only about 40 European migrants who settled in Canada were not of French origin, but at least 126 foreigners were granted letters of naturalisation between 1710 and 1714. They came primarily from New England and New York, captured during raids on the English colonies.[113] Only 53 foreigners were found among the approximately 6,200 engagés sent to the West Indies between 1634 and 1715, but Dutch, English, Scots, Irish, Flemish, and Portuguese were all present among the early settlers.[114] Some 1,200 Dutch including slaves settled in Martinique and Guadeloupe after fleeing Brazil following its reconquest by the Portuguese, and several hundred English remained on St. Christopher after it was captured by the French in 1666.[115] After the French captured Montserrat the next year, about 500

---

[108] Allain, "L'Immigration française", 560.

[109] Gwendolyn Midlo Hall, *Africans in Colonial Louisiana: The Development of Afro-Creole Culture in the Eighteenth Century* (Baton Rouge and London: Louisiana State University Press, 1992), 7, Table 1; also G. Conrad, trans. and ed., *Immigration and War, Louisiana: 1718–1721 from the Memoir of Charles Le Gac* (Lafayette: Center for Louisiana Studies of Southwestern Louisiana, 1970), 52–3.

[110] Usner, *Indians, Settlers, and Slaves*, 32–3.

[111] Ibid., 33.

[112] Allain, "L'Immigration française", 561.

[113] Charbonneau *et al.*, *The First French Canadians*, 66-7; and Moogk, "Reluctant Exiles", 499.

[114] Debien, "Les Engagés pour les Antilles", 90.

[115] Jean-Baptiste Du Tertre, *Histoire générale des Antilles habitées par les François*, 4 vols. (Paris: T. Jolly, 1667–71), 4: 460–5; and AN, SOM, G^1 471, Desnombrement générale 1671 gives 477 including slaves.

Irishmen swore allegiance to Louis XIV and more than 1,500 of their women and children remained on the island and later moved to the French islands nearby.[116] Though most did not survive to leave France, the Company of the Indies recruited about 1,300 Europeans from Alsace and parts of Germany for Louisiana.[117] Less well-known is the mingling of English at Placentia, and while the number of Scots who remained in Acadia after 1670 to increase the colony's small but vital population is unknown, historians insist on the importance of their contribution.[118] During the 1720s, more than one-tenth of the inhabitants of Louisbourg and a much larger proportion of the fishermen were Basques, and after 1722 at least one-fifth of the garrison included German-speaking Protestants from the Karrer Regiment of Swiss mercenaries that contracted for service in the French colonies.[119]

Growing religious intolerance in France during the 1680s led to expulsion of Jews and Protestants from the colonies. The former were Marranos among the Dutch settlers who reached Martinique and Guadeloupe during the 1650s and 60s; they numbered 226, including 132 slaves in 1683 when they were ordered from Martinique.[120] Jews disappeared by 1686, but returned during the eighteenth century, no longer as settlers but as merchants and factors.[121] Though legally excluded from the French colonies for many years, hundreds and perhaps thousands of Huguenots immigrated to the Antilles during the seventeenth century. Louis XIV's known attitude to orthodoxy prevented Colbert from endorsing and authorising Huguenot immigration, but he did nothing to prevent it. In 1685, the Revocation of the Edict of Nantes was accompanied by expulsion orders for Huguenots, who, unlike the Jews, numbered in the many hundreds including their slaves.[122] The few Protestants in Canada departed in 1686 and most in the West Indies soon followed. The hypocrisy and brutality of the expulsion is nowhere better revealed than in the fact that the children of French Calvinists were sometimes kidnapped from their parents, incarcerated, and deported to the islands as *engagés* during the decades after 1681. Between 1685 and 1711, one-fifth of the emigration from Angoumois was made up of these

---

[116] Donald Harman Akenson, *If the Irish Ruled the World: Monserrat, 1630–1730* (Montreal and Kingston: McGill-Queen's University Press, 1997), 85–6.

[117] Giraud, *Histoire de la Louisiane*, 4: 154–67; and Reinhart Kondert, "Les Allemands en Louisiane de 1721 à 1732", *RHAF*, 33 (1979–80), 51–65.

[118] See Naomi E.S. Griffiths, *The Context of Acadian History 1686–1784* (Montreal and Kingston: McGill-Queen's University Press, 1992), 30.

[119] A. J. B. Johnston, "The People of Eighteenth-Century Louisbourg", *Nova Scotia Historical Review*, 11, 2 (December, 1991), 79, 83.

[120] AN, SOM, G¹ 499, no. 44, "Dénombrement des Juifs demeurant en lisle de la Martinique", 3 February 1683; also Jacques Petitjean-Roget, "Les Juifs à la Martinique sous l'Ancien Régime", *RHC*, 43 (1956), 138–58.

[121] May, *Histoire économique de la Martinique*, 53.

[122] See Gérard Lafleur, *Les Protestants aux Antilles françaises du vent sous l'ancien régime* (Basseterre: La société d'histoire de la Guadeloupe, 1987) for detailed treatment.

children.[123] This desire for religious exclusiveness was chiefly the product of political conditions in France and, perhaps, the enthusiasm of the marquis de Seignelay who succeeded his father as minister of the marine until his death in 1690, but it did not last much beyond the end of the century. Religious authority was not strong in the colonies, even in Canada, and colonial officials were normally preoccupied with far more serious matters than exclusion.

If the Bourbon government's colonial immigration policy was incoherent, so too were its plans for social formation. Government ministers also failed to make up their minds about whether to transport convicted malefactors to increase colonial numbers and, in the end, resigned themselves to passing weak coercive measures forcing merchants and sea captains to carry emigrants in return for being permitted to depart for colonial destinations. The imbalance between the sexes and abnormal age structures that impeded family formation persisted in the colonies until well after the beginning of the eighteenth century. Whatever measures the government adopted, for however brief or long a period of time, they failed to affect the development of colonial populations.

The government could not prevent the return of immigrants to France. Fewer than one-third of all arriving migrants remained in Canada for sufficient time to establish a family. Numerous complaints about departing colonists from West Indies authorities suggest the same was true in the Antilles. French officials allowed few naturalizations of foreigners, were hostile to the presence of Jews and Protestants, and failed to assimilate any part of the native American population despite official support for such a policy. The high levels of natural growth of the French colonial populations in Canada and Acadia had nothing to do with any government policy whether under Louis XIV, the Regent, or Louis XV. Settlement and social formation occurred despite the government. The story of French colonial immigration is only one illustration of government ineptitude in virtually every sphere of activity it undertook in the colonies.

1.5 SIZE AND STRUCTURES

Demographers and historians first discover the size of total populations.[124] In spite of a great deal of recent work, little has been done to improve the knowledge of the total size of the population in the French colonies. Data for Canada stand apart from this generalization because demographers there have established new estimates of population size that are very impressive in their comprehensiveness, consistency, accuracy, and integrity of research

---

[123] Reible, "L'Emigration coloniale en Angoumois", 107, 112–14.
[124] John J. McCusker and Russell R. Menard, *The Economy of British America, 1607–1789* (Chapel Hill and London: University of North Carolina Press, 1985), 213.

methods.[125] For other French colonies, however, old estimates derived from contemporary censuses remain the chief basis for estimating the size and structure of both European and African colonial populations.

Seventeenth- and early eighteenth-century colonial censuses have to be used with caution even though they attempted to count total populations. Until civil administrators began asserting greater influence in the West Indies following the War of the Spanish Succession, military men normally collected data and few attached much importance to the task. In 1697, for example, the king's lieutenant on Saint-Domingue reported the work of militia officers was so inexact and drawn up "in such bad form" that he dared not send the general census of his district. He reported only a crude tabulation linking together white women and children and all adult slaves without distinction.[126] However, the same officer proved no more reliable himself. Four years later, he claimed there were more than 10,000 slaves at Léogane when that number did not inhabit the entire colony.[127] Authorities on Saint-Domingue assured officials at Versailles in 1715 that the census was made with "beaucoup d'exactitude," but the very next year acknowledged they were unable to ensure the "justesse" of the new census.[128] As colonies became more populated, accuracy was more difficult to achieve. Militia captains who collected and sent the data to the governor and intendant were generally so ignorant of the demands made of them that printed forms supplied by the ministry were of limited value.[129] After evaluating the censuses of Canada between 1685 and 1731, demographers recently concluded that women in the seventeenth century and young boys in the eighteenth century were underrecorded, and that the population in all censuses was under recorded by an average of just over 10 percent. They also noted that the increasing frequency of censuses between 1712 and 1724 led to an important decline in their quality.[130]

Though census returns invariably listed members of the first estate and their works at the head of any enumeration, the subsequent categories were more important. Populations were normally organized by militia companies;

[125] See Hubert Charbonneau, *Vie et mort de nos ancêtres: étude démographique* (Montréal: Les Presses de l'Universitéde Montréal, 1975) and Charbonneau, Guillemette, *et al.*, *The First French Canadians*.

[126] AN, SOM, G^1 509, no. 15 Gallifet to Pontchartrain, 8 January 1697.

[127] This error has been widely published. See Vaissière, *Saint Domingue*, 164, citing Col., C^{9A} 5, Gallifet to Pontchartrain 22 March 1701; also Gaston Martin, *Histoire de l'esclavage dans les colonies françaises* (Paris: Presses universitaires de France, 1948), 26; and Abdoulaye Ly, *La Compagnie du Sénégal* (Paris: Présence Africaine, 1958), 49. But see AN, SOM, G^1, 509, no. 8 "Recensement G[e]n[er]al du Cap, Port de Paix et Leoganne, Coste de St. Domingue en l'année 1700" for 9,082 slaves.

[128] Col., C^{9B} 2, extract, Blénac and Mithon to Navy Council, 24 November, 1715; and ibid., 3, extract, same to same, 15 July 1716.

[129] Col., C^{8A} 35, ff. 42-4v Feuquières and Blondel to Maurepas, 28 March 1726.

[130] R. Lalou and M. Boléda, "Une source en friche: les dénombrements sous le régime français", *RHAF*, 42, 1 (été, 1988), 67, 70.

the censuses indicated the number of men bearing arms and concluded with a list of muskets, pistols, swords, bayonets, and weight of powder, ball, and shot on hand. In 1682, the king's lieutenant at St. Christopher excluded 379 old or infirm men from the census as being unable to march for half an hour.[131] Viewing them as a useless burden on the colony, he consigned them to a separate entry at the end of the census. The 1715 Guadeloupe census excluded aged and infirm males, both white and black, which reduced the total by more than 7 percent.[132] Indentured servants and convicts were sometimes listed after slave labour. In that less colour-conscious society than our own, such people were conceived primarily as nonfighters or idle consumers; sometimes they were listed after horses and cattle.

The stress on men as fighters affected the number of white males counted as children. Between 1681 and 1700, the censuses for St. Christopher randomly designated as children those under 12, 14, and 15 years of age, which affected the number of youths bearing arms.[133] At St. Martin the census taker once distinguished between "boys bearing arms" and other boys "under 10 years"; he ignored the age of young white females, classifying them instead as "nubile", or "under puberty".[134] After reporting an increase in the number of young men bearing arms at Guadeloupe in 1699, Governor Auger sheepishly acknowledged one-third were between 12 and 16 years old.[135] In 1700, the governor of St. Christopher established three categories of young white males: "bearing arms", "under 15 to 6 years", and "under 6 years".[136] He designated young white girls similarly. While canon law decreed that girls 12 years and over were marriageable, the designation of children varied according to age, region, and probably to time and circumstances. The primacy given to boys bearing arms meant that the age of female nubility changed according to the male classification. The 1713 census of Saint-Domingue went so far as to omit the number of white girls under 12 years of age, thereby excluding about 13 percent of the white population.[137]

The age of slave and free coloured children is also unclear. The latter may have varied in line with whites, but as slave owners paid a head tax on all adult slaves, they may well have sought to preserve child status for Africans after they had reached 18 years of age. Some censuses refer to "working Negroes", but they do not distinguish between "negrillons" and "working boys". Agents of the Western Domain naturally sought to collect the head taxes, but military leaders in the colonies were invariably important planters who may have colluded with others to exaggerate the number of slave children in the colonies.

[131] Ibid., 472, f. 317.   [132] AN, SOM, G¹, 497, no. 8.   [133] Ibid., 472, ff. 306, 340, 348.
[134] Ibid., 498, no. 3a.
[135] Col., C⁷ᴬ 4 (non-foliated), Auger to Pontchartrain, 7 August 1699.
[136] AN, SOM, G¹472, f. 348.   [137] Ibid., 509, no. 12.

Despite the flaws and incompleteness in the old censuses, the data appear adequate to show how population size and structures shaped the new societies that emerged. What follows is tentative, but every effort has been made to ensure accuracy. The meaning of population size is obvious, but by structure, demographers and historians refer to age, sex, and race. The census data allow for some simple estimates of change in these categories over time and sometimes by regions and by urban–rural divisions.

1.6 NEW FRANCE

Between 1670 and 1730 New France contained seven separate colonies or regions: Placentia in Newfoundland, Acadia, Île Royale, Louisiana, Illinois, the *pays d'en haut* or Upper Country, and Canada. Canada, which stretched some 400 kilometres along the central valley of the St. Lawrence River from Vaudreuil to Les Eboulements along the north shore and from Chateauguay to Rimouski along the south shore, was its heart. A little more than 7,000 French men and women lived in all the vast regions of New France in 1670 compared to more than double that number who lived in the West Indies and Guiana, chiefly in the Windward Islands. Within six decades Canada had become the major centre of French population in the Americas. Nearly half of all the French in the Western Hemisphere, immigrants and colonial born, lived there. So central was Canada to the French presence in the Americas that its name was frequently, if incorrectly, used synonymously for all of New France. Yet, while the French North American population grew more than one and three-quarters times during the first 30 years of the eighteenth century, it actually declined from over 8 percent to just under 7 percent of the Anglo-American mainland population.[138]

The French settlements along the northeastern Atlantic seaboard had little to do with the rest of New France. Metropolitan fishing interests always remained more favoured over colonists so that French settlements on Newfoundland never counted more than 200 or 300 inhabitants. Fewer than 5,000 lived on Île Royale before 1730.[139] No settlements existed around the great northern peninsula of Newfoundland called *le petit nord* where fishermen from Saint-Malo were dominant. Settlement was chiefly confined along the south coast at Plaisance (Placentia), several locations on the Burin

---

[138] See Table 1.1 Row 10, and compare with J. Potter, "The Growth of Population in America, 1700–1860" in *Population in History: Essays in Historical Demography*, eds., D. V. Glass and D. E. C. Eversley, (London: Edward Arnold, 1965), 638–9.

[139] Fred. J. Thorpe, *Remparts Lointains: La politique française des travaux publics à Terre-Neuve et à l'île Royale, 1695–1758* (Ottawa: Editions de l'Universitéd' Ottawa, 1980), 22.

Peninsula to the west of Placentia Bay, and to the Island of St. Pierre where French Basques fished.

Well-known to French and Basque fishermen long before the state became involved in establishing a post there, Placentia possessed several natural advantages. It was above all a refuge for fishermen. It was ice-free early in the spring. It was a waystation en route to Canada and Acadia and for ships returning to France from the West Indies. Later, its garrison provided security to fishermen available nowhere else in Newfoundland. Only 73 residents were enumerated at Placentia in 1671 and 64 two years later.[140] Placentia in 1679 was described as fortified with a garrison of 20 men and 10 families, both English and French.[141] The population was very unstable. Only forty families were included among an overwintering population of perhaps one thousand in 1687. During the next quarter century, warfare and privateering probably reduced the number of permanent residents while swelling the ranks of soldiers and refugees. In 1698, Placentia had about the same number of resident families as 11 years before.[142] In 1709 an English report stated that 47 families, the greatest part boat keepers, lived on the Great Beach at Placentia. These people represented less than 15 percent of the total number of boat keepers there and at adjacent places. Those overwintering numbered 800, including 400 soldiers and 50 artificers employed as stone cutters, which revealed the French state's heavy involvement in fortifying the place.[143]

During the decade after the signing of the Treaty of Utrecht in 1713, French colonial development reverted to private companies with the very obvious exception of Île Royale. The designation Royal to the island formerly known as Cape Breton, and the attachment of new royal nomenclature to localities there, left no doubt of the French government's ambition to reestablish an American base for the North Atlantic fishery.[144] The state development of Île Royale was also a consequence of the structure of the international North Atlantic fishery, which could neither be controlled nor defended by a private

[140]   Canada, Dominion Bureau of Statistics, *Census of Canada, 1931*, vol. 1 (Ottawa, King's Printer 1936), 134; also Charles de La Morandière, *Histoire de la pêche française de la morue dans l'Amérique septentrionale*, 3 vols. (Paris: Maissoneuve & La Rose, 1962–1966), 2: 1009–10 for the complete enumeration of the 1671 census.

[141]   *CSP, CS*, 1677–1680, p. 418.

[142]   Canada, *Census of Canada, 1871*, vol. 4, *Censuses of Canada, 1665–1871* (Ottawa: 1876), 44; and corrections in *Census of Canada, 1931*, 1: 136; and John Mannion and Gordon Handcock, "The 17th Century Fishery" in *The Historical Atlas of Canada*, Vol. 1, ed., R. Cole Harris (Toronto: University of Toronto Press, 1987), Plate 23.

[143]   Cited in Jean-Pierre Proulx, *Military History of Placentia, a Study of French Fortifications, Placentia, 1713–1811* (Ottawa: National Historic Sites and Parks Branch, 1979), 61–2, 63–5.

[144]   In addition to changing the island's name to Île Royale, Havre à l'Anglois became Louisbourg, St. Pierre became Port Toulouse, and St. Anne was renamed Port Dauphin.

monopoly. As at Placentia, fishermen dominated the population of the new colony. During the years up to 1730 and beyond more than one-half of all the adults, including the soldiers of the garrison, worked in the fishery. Almost all were French migrants from Upper Normandy and western France and Basques from the southwest. Canadians and Acadians were notable by their relative scarcity in this new colonial population.[145] The state's primary investments to construct defensive fortifications, administrative buildings, and harbour installations were intended to support the fishery rather than colonial settlement. Both Placentia and Île Royale, resolutely facing eastward into the North Atlantic, were unique in America. Without hinterlands or agricultural support, nothing quite like them existed elsewhere in the New World, which has led to some woolly thinking about them. Historical geographer Andrew Hill Clark assumed that all colonies were created by farmers or slaves for the purpose of cultivating exportable crops. By their nature they are colonies of settlement and ought to have something to show for half a century of occupation. When that did not occur the colony must be underdeveloped.[146] This assumes that Île Royale had a problem, to wit, that the northern colonies of French America did not develop like middle American colonies of the British empire. Though the latter statement is correct, the French fishing colonies did not have a problem.

Though actually founded in 1713 when 116 men, 10 women, and 23 children relocated from Placentia, Île Royale's population had grown to nearly 1,500 three years later.[147] Louisbourg was only officially named the capital of the new colony in 1720 when the island's population stood at 1,740.[148] The colony also included the other islands in the Gulf of St. Lawrence as dependencies, and perhaps as many as 100 persons had settled on Île St. Jean, today known as Prince Edward Island. The Navy Council had granted the island to the comte de St. Pierre but his settlement came to naught. By 1725 his company was bankrupt and the island was virtually deserted.[149] The government moved to repossess the island in 1727 and encouraged Acadian migration. In 1730, its population consisted of 325 agricultural settlers and 140 fishermen located chiefly at Havre Saint-Pierre (today St. Peters)

[145] A. J. B. Johnston, "The Fishermen of Eighteenth-Century Cape Breton" in *Aspects of Louisbourg*, ed., E. Krause *et al.*, (Sydney: University College of Cape Breton, 1995), 198–208.

[146] Andrew Hill Clark, "New England's Role in the Underdevelopment of Cape Breton Island during the French Regime, 1713–1758", *The Canadian Geographer*, 9 (1965), 1–12. This paper illustrates the limits of historical geography or any other social science that employs counterfactuals and unspoken assumptions about human development in history.

[147] Canada, *Census of Canada, 1931*, 1: 137.

[148] Harold Adams Innis, "Cape Breton and the French Regime", *Transactions of the Royal Society of Canada*, 3rd ser., 29, sect. 2 (1935), 57, n27.

[149] Daniel Cobb Harvey, *The French Regime in Prince Edward Island* (New Haven: Yale University Press, 1926), 67–8.

on the north shore and Port La Joie (near present-day Charlottetown) on the south shore.[150]

The most accurate estimate of the total population of Île Royale and its dependencies appeared in 1726 when 3,131 inhabitants were enumerated[151] B. A. Balcom places the total at 3,950 after including the military garrison. Nearly 90 percent of the total (3,528, including 1,296 at Louisbourg) lived on Île Royale.[152] This was about equal to the total population of Louisiana and Illinois. The island's population alone had increased by 75 percent since 1719. If it were assumed that the same high annual rate of growth during the seven years prior to 1726 continued for the next four years, the estimated population of Île Royale and its dependencies in 1730 was 4,645. By then, however, Acadia was no longer a French colony.

Far more than any other French colony, the colonists themselves constructed Acadia. Restored to France by England in 1667, Acadia's effective reoccupation began three years later with the arrival of Captain Hector d'Andigné de Grandfontaine as the colony's new governor. At that time, Acadia may have numbered 500 persons.[153] Few colonists ever lived in the St. John River Valley or along the Maine coastline. Only 10 families lived in the region in 1695.[154] The bulk of the population resided at Port Royal, along the Annapolis River and elsewhere in peninsular Nova Scotia. Though few immigrants arrived after 1670, settlement expanded rapidly beyond Port Royal to Beaubassin in 1671 and to Minas in 1672. The location and role of the salt marshes scattered at the heads of bays and basins south and east of the Bay of Fundy, covering approximately 30,000 hectares, are the most critical factors to explain the establishment of Acadian settlements. Though not very extensive compared to the forest regions of Nova Scotia, the drained marshes, flat terrain, and natural wetness of soil yielded above average crops.[155]

During the next four decades of nominal French rule, the Acadian population tripled or quadrupled, but the population of Port Royal increased only by one-half. The push north and east was such that, by the end of the century, people in the Minas settlements outnumbered Port Royal, and

[150] Ibid., 103–8; also Andrew Hill Clark, *Three Centuries and the Island; a Historical Geography of Settlement and Agriculture in Prince Edward Island, Canada* (Toronto: University of Toronto Press, 1959), 29.

[151] Canada, *Census of Canada, 1931*, 1: 139; also A. J. B. Johnston, *Control and Order in French Colonial Louisbourg, 1713–1758* (East Lansing: Michigan State University Press, 2001), 37.

[152] B. A. Balcom, *The Cod Fishery of Ile Royale, 1713–58*, Studies in Archaeology, Architecture and History (Ottawa: Parks Canada, Environment Canada, 1984), 4.

[153] Clark, *Acadia*, 121.   [154] Canada, *Census of Canada, 1871*, 4: 39.

[155] Samuel P. Arsenault, "Geography and the Acadians", in *The Acadians of the Maritimes*, ed., Jean Daigle (Moncton: Centre d'études acadiennes, 1982), 96, 98.

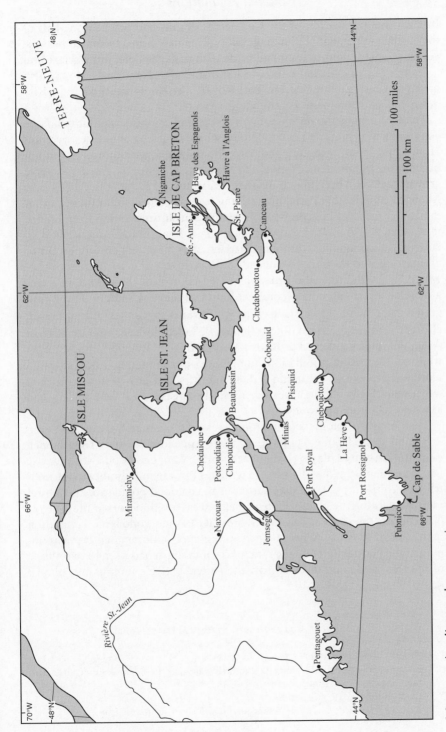

Map 1.1. Acadian settlements, *circa* 1700.

by 1710 the population of the Chignecto isthmus had reached one-half of the mother settlement.[156] These developments may have originated because young people sought to hunt and trade with native people, but warfare and a desire to escape official efforts to halt trade with New England may also have promoted migration from Port Royal, which was attacked and partly destroyed six times between 1690 and 1710.[157]

The astonishing population growth of Acadian colonists was due to unique conditions that prevailed in the colony, where sweeping epidemics were unknown and infant mortality was low. Population growth, however, did not occur in the isolation once thought to be characteristic of the Acadians. Some growth may have been due to Acadian absorption of Mi'kmaqs. Abbé Pierre Maillard claimed that racial intermixing had proceeded so far by 1753 that in fifty years it would be impossible to distinguish Amerindian from French in Acadia.[158] As for the growing number of English and Americans who entered the community through marriage after 1714, 25 to 30 percent of all marriages in the early eighteenth century involved a partner from elsewhere.[159] By the time the British assumed control of the colony in 1710, almost all Acadians were second- to fourth-generation settlers. A few emigrated to French-held Île St. Jean during the late 1720s, but official French efforts to encourage migration to Île Royale failed. Indeed, after 1726 most Acadian families returned to British Nova Scotia.[160] By 1730, the Acadians were an expanding population numbering approximately 5,000 souls.[161] During the previous six decades their numbers had grown in the order of ten times, chiefly through healthy natural increase, and their society had assumed its future contours.

The Canadian colonial population increased more than five times between 1670 and 1730: from 6,631 to 34,753 (see Appendix 1). After 1672 French immigration ceased playing a significant role in Canada's population increase for more than 60 years. The severe reduction of the immigrant stream contributed to the rapid Canadianisation of the colonial population as natural increase became the chief source of increase. Growth occurred most vigorously during the 1670s in the immediate wake of the second largest migration in the colony's history. Where French immigrants predominated at the beginning of the period, by 1681 the ratio of colonial-born had risen to two-thirds of the total and continued to grow thereafter.[162] Some immigrants, almost

---

[156]   Clark, *Acadia*, 124.
[157]   Griffiths, *The Context of Acadian History*, 17–18; and Haynes "Some Aspects", 6.
[158]   Dickason, *The Myth of the Savage*, 147.
[159]   Griffiths, *The Context of Acadian History*, 45–7.
[160]   Bernard Pothier, "Acadian Emigration to Île Royale after the Conquest of Acadia", *Histoire sociale/ Social History*, 6 (1970), 128, 131.
[161]   Clark, *Acadia*, 201.
[162]   Dechêne, *Habitants and Merchants in Seventeenth Century Montreal*, 47.

entirely male, continued to arrive in the colony, but they left less of a mark than their predecessors on what had become a rapidly growing population by the end of the century.

The geographical location of Canadians was not an important factor that affected the structure of the population, even though in 1670 and long afterward the colony consisted of three virtually separate settlements centered on Quebec, Trois-Rivières, and Montreal. The largest portion of the population continued to reside in the district of Quebec. Not quite two-thirds of the colonists lived there in 1667, and despite a slight decline during the last quarter of the seventeenth century, 65 percent of the population continued to live there in 1698. The number of settlers in the central district of Trois-Rivières grew slowly, but the proportion declined relative to the rest of the colony. Disease, war, and the vagaries of the fur trade caused Montreal's numbers to grow slowly during the last two decades of the seventeenth century. Its relative population fluctuated between 27.9 and 23.5 percent of the total.[163] During the first three decades of the eighteenth century, however, the colonial population shifted toward the western or Montreal-end of the colony, gradually occupying the empty space between the once isolated settlements. Though in-filling remained incomplete, by 1730 the colony had assumed the basic shape of an elongated village, stretching along both sides of the St. Lawrence River from Montreal to below Quebec that was to characterize it during the next century.[164]

Sex, age, and marital status are the true indicators of population structure. By 1681, the high male–female ratio of 163:100 of 15 years before had dropped to 133:100. In addition, male migration from France maintained the masculinity of the colony at artificially high levels for nearly 40 more years, but by 1720 the two sexes had achieved near balance.[165] During the 1720s, for the only time during the French regime, females became the majority in the colony.

Age structure evolved into a pyramid as youthful, single adult immigrants gave way to growing families and slowly aging parents. By 1700 most of the pre-1672 immigrants were 50 years of age or older. After analyzing the annual marriage, birth, and death data and decennial population figures, demographer-economist Jacques Henripen drew three important conclusions about Canada's French colonial population. First, the demographic character of the Canadian population remained constant throughout the

[163] Charbonneau, *Vie et mort de nos ancêtres*, Tableau 7, 40; also Trudel, *Histoire de la Nouvelle-France*, 4: 396–403.

[164] Dale Miquelon, *New France, 1701–1744: "A Supplement to Europe"* (Toronto: McClelland and Stewart, 1987), 191–4.

[165] Jacques Henripen, *La population canadienne au début du XVIIIe siècle: nuptialité-fécondité-mortalité infantile*, Institut national d'études démographiques, Travaux et Documents, Cahier No. 22 (Paris: Presses universitaires de France, 1954), 18; also Charbonneau, *Vie et mort de nos ancêtres*, 41.

years between 1660 and 1770. Second, family size also remained constant, and third, the slower growth of the total population was due to the death rate, which increased steadily in the colony during the entire period.[166] Prior to 1700, the colonial population contained very few elderly people; the increasing death rate during the eighteenth century indicated that the once youthful immigrant population was approaching maturity rather than facing some catastrophe or series of crises.

The age distribution of the island of Montreal's population between 1681 and 1732 confirms these conclusions. It clearly shows that the population structure changed little. The proportion of those who were 15 to 49 years of age (between 46.3 and 47.4 percent of the total) hardly varied at all during the 50-year period. The proportion of children 14 years of age and under varied a bit more (between 41.2 and 45.9 percent of the whole); not surprisingly, the small proportion of those who were 50 years and over varied more widely (between 7.7 and 11.3 percent). Like her predecessor, historian Louise Dechêne concluded that "the figures point to a broad-based [age] pyramid tapering off rapidly, reflecting a high rate of reproduction and a high rate of mortality", a conclusion that is valid for the entire colony.[167] In this respect, Canada's population was evolving similarly to the New England colonies to the south.

Canada's crude marriage rate varied between 185 and 210 per 10,000 inhabitants from the end of the seventeenth until the middle of the eighteenth century.[168] Fluctuations in the rates correspond to two waves of immigration; the first contained the only large number of females ever to reach Canada and occurred during the late 1660s and early 1670s, and the second arose as largely male immigration, chiefly soldiers, arrived after 1697. Since few single Canadian males were old enough or sufficiently well off to marry at the end of the century, these later migrants married the nubile colonial-born women and even the available widows. Celibacy remained high among colonial-born men until the 1720s, but even this impediment to marriage disappeared as the age pyramid broadened.

In the seventeenth century, women in Canada married young, about three years earlier than in France and a year and a half earlier than in colonial Massachusetts. Men, however, were more than three years older than in France and Massachusetts when they married. Women's mean age at marriage rose slightly in the early eighteenth century from 21.0 to 21.9 while men's mean age declined by nearly two years from 28.6 to 26.8.[169]

166 Henripen, *La population canadienne*, 14 and 119, graphique no. 1.

167 Dechêne, *Habitants and Merchants*, 48–9 and 344 n. 7. This contrasts markedly with France, where children made up only 30 to 35 percent of the population.

168 Ibid., 49, citing J. Henripen, *Tendances et facteurs de la fécondité au Canada* (Ottawa, 1968), 5.

169 Henripen, *La population canadienne*, 96; Dechêne, *Habitants and Merchants*, 51; Kenneth A. Lockridge, *A New England Town: The First Hundred Years, Dedham, Massachusetts, 1636–1736* (New York: W. W. Norton, 1970), 66–7.

Age differences between men and women may have been greater in the West Indies. Between 1686 and 1715, in three parishes in Martinique – admittedly a very small sample – slightly more than half of all white females in their first marriage were between 15 and 19 years old while half the white men were between 25 and 34.[170] The scarcity of women no doubt accounts for early matrimony among females in both colonies, while the arduous economic conditions forced men to delay marriage. Above all other considerations, early female matrimony had the greatest influence on the structure of the colonial population. It alone accounted for the high fertility levels of Canadian women, and though the rates were lower in the tropics, they remained higher than in France.[171]

The early mean age of marriage of women in the seventeenth century meant that families were larger before 1681 than afterward.[172] At Martinique, between 1686 and 1718 the average number of births per family was 4.9, lower than either France or Canada.[173] After 1700, the number of children per family in Canada declined to 5.6. Whether French- or colonial-born, married women in Canada and Martinique bore a child about every two years, displaying little difference at all from similar behaviour of their counterparts in northern and northwestern France whence most immigrants originated.[174]

Many years ago Pierre Goubert wrote that death was the first fact of life in seventeenth-century France, and it remained no less true in the colonies.[175] Though deaths were seriously underregistered and infant mortality was frequently ignored, demographer Richard Lalou established that Canadian infant mortality during the seventeenth century was 197.1 per thousand and increased to 241.6 between 1700 and 1729. At Martinique, on the other hand, the mortality rates as determined from the parish registers were so low as to confirm only that deaths were very much underregistered.[176] As the structure of the colonial population matured in Canada, infant mortality rates came to resemble those in France, where nearly one-quarter of all children died within their first year of life.[177] It is unlikely that the same evolution did not occur in the West Indies. During the first quarter of the eighteenth

---

[170]   Liliane Chauleau, *Case-Pilote, Le Prêcheur, Basse-Pointe: Étude démographique sur le Nord de la Martinique (XVIIe siècle)*, (Paris: Harmattan, 1990), 49.

[171]   Ibid., 71.

[172]   Charbonneau, *Vie et mort de nos ancêtres*, 221.

[173]   Ibid., 62.

[174]   Charbonneau et al., *The First French Canadians*, Table 66. 134; Chauleau, *Case-Pilote, Le Prêcheur, Basse-Pointe*, 75.

[175]   Pierre Goubert, *Louis XIV et vingt millions des français* (Paris: Fayard, 1966), 15.

[176]   Chauleau, *Case-Pilote, Le Prêcheur*, 83–4.

[177]   R. Lalou, "Des enfants pour le paradis: la mortalité des nouveaux-nés en Nouvelle-France" (unpublished Ph.D. thesis, démographie, Université de Montréal, 1990), 190, 238 cited in Y. Landry et R. Lessard, "Les causes de déces d'après les registres paroissiaux québécoise", *RHAF*, 48, no. 4 (printemps 1996), 525, n. 32.

century, prenuptial conceptions and illegitimate births also reached levels similar to those in France.[178]

Major mortality crises struck Canada. In 1687 and 1703, 1,400 and between 1,000 and 1,200 colonists, respectively, died. The number of deaths in both years more than cancelled the number of births, and in 1703 more than 8 percent of Montreal's population succumbed.[179] Disease, especially yellow fever, appeared to have the same effect in Martinique in 1690 and 1693.[180] Unlike Europe, though, periods of warfare are not reflected in the death rates of Canadians and most probably the West Indies. Whereas epidemics of measles (1687), smallpox (1699 and 1703), infant mortality, probably diarrhea (1714), and pertussis or whooping cough (1729–30) are reflected in the data, these diseases were not endemic in the colonies. They had little effect on rates of marriage or birth.[181] While they exacted their toll of misery and grief from the colonists, they were not preceded by great subsistence crises as occurred periodically in France. During the eighteenth century, Canada's white population grew vigorously at an average annual rate of 2.9 percent until, by 1730, it numbered nearly half of all the French in the Americas.[182]

French missionaries and fur traders began entering the Mississippi Valley during the 1670s, establishing themselves at Fort St. Louis (present-day Peoria, Illinois) on the Illinois River, at the Falls of St. Anthony, on the Mississippi (present-day Minneapolis, Minnesota), and at Cahokia and Kaskaskia also on the Mississippi below the mouth of the Missouri River during the final two decades of the seventeenth century. In 1717, over the objections of Governor-General Vaudreuil, these posts and small settlements in the Illinois country were transferred to Louisiana at the insistence of John Law, who believed reports of vast mineral wealth in the area. In 1719–21, Fort de Chartres was built to mark the new administrative arrangement, but the Illinois settlements grew slowly during the early eighteenth century because the Fox Indians fiercely resisted the French presence in the region until 1730.[183] In 1726, the French settlements in the Illinois country comprised nearly 500 people, including slaves.

178 Lyne Paquette and Réal Bates, "Les naissances illégitimes sur les rives du Saint Laurent avant 1730", *RHAF*, 40, 2 (autumne 1986), 242; and Réal Bates, "Les conceptions prénuptiales dans la vallée du Saint Laurent avant 1725", ibid., 258; also Chauleau, *Case-Pilote, Le Prêcheur*, 67.

179 Dechêne, *Habitants and Merchants*, 59–61 and 301, graph no. 5.

180 Chauleau, *Case-Pilote, Le Prêcheur*, 29, 81.

181 Henripen, *La population canadienne*, 15, 119.

182 At the same time, this number amounted to about 70 percent of the population of New York (see Robert V. Wells, *The Population of the British Colonies in America before 1776* (Princeton: Princeton University Press, 1975), 112.

183 See Giraud, *Histoire de la Louisiane*, 3: 371–80, and more recently, Carl J. Ekberg, *Colonial Ste. Geneviève: An Adventure on the Mississippi Frontier*, rev. ed. (Tucson: The Patrice Press, 1996), 4–8.

Although slavery became legal in Canada in 1709, it remained a product of circumstance rather than law. Only 48 Africans are known to have resided at one time or another in the colony and nine more resided at Louisbourg before 1730. These slaves appear to have been chiefly acquired as booty taken during raids on English colonies. A few may have been purchased by Quebec or Louisbourg merchants on rare trips to Boston or New York.[184] During the quarter century between 1706 and 1730, Amerindian rather than African slavery became a much more prominent feature of society. Marcel Trudel counted 482 such slaves during the period.[185] So many of them came from just one tribe, the Panis or Pawnee in the Missouri Valley, that *panis* became a synonym for *esclave* or slave. Slaves appeared to have had little economic value in New France and were held chiefly as symbols of elevated social status and social snobbery.[186]

The population in the Illinois country differed from other northern French colonies in the proportion of slaves. A recent claim that the region's economy remained connected to Canada rather than to the Lower Mississippi Valley may be true, but its social composition resembled Louisiana rather than Canada.[187] More than one-third of the total population were slaves. Moreover, Africans outnumbered Amerindians in the settlements by more than two to one. The 33 white indentured servants or *engagés* comprised only 15 percent of the coerced labour force. Concentration of slave ownership had also appeared; more than two-thirds of the Africans were owned by just nine families.[188]

Other fur traders and missionaries developed posts in the Upper Great Lakes region that remained more closely attached to the trade than those in the Illinois country. However, these suffered from the French withdrawal from the West in 1697; little remained to show for earlier efforts. Between 1701 and 1710, however, a small settlement began at Detroit some 1,000 kilometres west of Montreal. A census taken in 1710 showed 112 persons, including six families, who had established themselves near the fort, but this marked the high point of further settlement in the *pays d'en haut*. No more

---

[184] Marcel Trudel, *L'Esclavage au Canada français, histoire et conditions de l'esclavage* (Québec: Presses de l'universitéde Laval, 1960), 89–91 and [95]; also Robin W. Winks, *The Blacks in Canada: A History*, 2nd ed., (Kingston and Montreal: McGill-Queen's University Press, 1997), 21–3. See also Kenneth Donovan, "A Nominal List of Slaves and Their Owners in Ile Royale, 1713–1760", *Nova Scotia Historical Review*, 16, 1 (1996), 151–62 for evidence that 13 slaves including 9 blacks resided at Louisbourg.

[185] Ibid., 84–5; he counted only 64 native slaves between 1670 and 1705.

[186] J. R. Miller, *Skyscrapers Hide the Heavens: A History of Indian-White Relations in Canada*, rev. ed. (Toronto: University of Toronto Press, 1991), 45.

[187] Usner, *Indians, Settlers, and Slaves*, 7.

[188] Marthe Faribault-Beauregard, *La Population des forts français d'Amérique (XVIIIe siècle)*, 2 vols. (Montréal: Editions Bergson, 1982–1984), 2: 206–11. Charles R. Maduell Jr., *The Census Tables for the French Colony of Louisiana from 1699 through 1732* (Baltimore: Genealogical Publishing Co., 1972), 50, 57–60 gives slightly different numbers.

than 30 homesteaders resided at Detroit in 1727.[189] Except in the Illinois country, the French remained travelers and traders in the vast reaches of the North American interior. Most migrants remained part of the large floating population that garrisoned and serviced the interior posts, traded with Amerindians for furs, and manned the canoe brigades that regularly voyaged west of Montreal.

Louisiana's population in 1730 still remained largely subject to immigration rather than natural increase. Major European migration had occurred only nine to thirteen years before and continued to shape birth, marriage, and mortality rates.[190] Moreover, the sudden influx of approximately 7,000 Africans between 1718 and 1731 utterly transformed the structure of the colonial population.[191] Originally conceived as a strategic outpost to limit English westward expansion and as a base for trade with Spaniards and Indians around the Gulf of Mexico and in the Mississippi Valley, Louisiana was not considered an agricultural colony. It was viewed as a source of forest products for the West Indian colonies and a new Eldorado filled with mineral wealth awaiting discovery.[192] Canadians who played important roles as explorers, defenders, and traders during the colony's early years did not make good colonists. Their lack of discipline, inconstancy, and outlook did not support a settled life of backbreaking toil.[193] By 1708, only 77 colonists could be found, outnumbered by 80 Amerindian slaves and 122 soldiers and sailors.[194] A decade later, the populace numbered no more than 350 to 400 people, chiefly soldiers, officers, and officials in the king's service, scattered at posts along the Gulf Coast or deep in the interior at Fort Toulouse at the Forks of the Alabama River, at Natchitoches far to the west on the Red River, and at New Orleans just being built.[195] At least half of the approximately 7,000 Europeans and 2,000 slaves transported to Louisiana between 1718 and 1721 by the Company of the Indies either perished or abandoned the colony before 1726.[196] Europeans still outnumbered slaves in the colony, and the 233 indentured servants, like those in the Illinois country, formed

---

[189] See Lina Gouger, "Montréal et le peuplement de Détroit, 1701–1765", *Proceedings of the Eighteenth Meeting of the French Colonial Historical Society*, Montreal, 1992, ed., James Pritchard (Cleveland: French Colonial Historical Society, 1993), 46–9 for details.

[190] The best account of this European migration still remains Giraud, *Histoire de la Louisiane*, 3: 221–83.

[191] Usner, *Indians, Settlers and Slaves*, 34; Hall, *Africans in Colonial Louisiana*, 10.

[192] Jacob Price, *France and the Chesapeake: A History of the French Tobacco Monopoly, 1674–1791 and the Relationship to the British and American Tobacco Trades*, 2 vols. (Ann Arbor: University of Michigan Press, 1973), 1: 302.

[193] Giraud, *Histoire de la Louisiane*, 1: 84–5.

[194] Usner, *Indians, Settlers, and Slaves*, 25. See Giraud, *Histoire de la Louisiane*, 1: 255 for an enumeration of 1715 that gives a mere 215 persons.

[195] Usner, *Indians, Settlers, and Slaves*, 31–2.

[196] Ibid., 41.

less than 7 percent of the population compared to 46 percent represented by 1,616 habitants (men, women, and children). By that time, the population had shifted with two-thirds of the settlers living along the Lower Mississippi River below the mouth of the Red River and only one-fifth continuing to reside in the Gulf Coast settlements. The remainder inhabited the interior settlements and posts. Louisiana's transformation into a slave society occurred very rapidly. Still outnumbered in 1726, slaves were already the most geographically concentrated group in the colony. Nearly 70 percent of their total number toiled on lands along the Mississippi below Cannes Bruslées, and by 1731 they outnumbered whites by two to one.[197] Owing to the weakness of its economic base and high mortality, Louisiana remained insecure and unformed in 1730.

1.7 THE FRENCH CIRCUM-CARIBBEAN

Circum-Caribbean is an awkward term, but more accurately describes the wide range of French tropical colonies in the Americas than does the designation West Indies, which excludes South America. The Circum-Caribbean includes Louisiana, but this section concerns the colonies in the other three regions: South America, the Lesser Antilles, and the Greater Antilles. Each area contained colonial populations whose demographic history is not well-known. There exists no secondary literature comparable in quality to the work relating to Canada or even to Acadia and Louisiana. Except for a few recent studies of individual colonies, existing discussions are highly derivative and incomplete. They rely, like this one, upon the contemporary censuses of greater or lesser adequacy.

Guiana was the goal of four major French expeditions during the three decades before 1670, but none achieved success and no more occurred during the next 90 years.[198] Guiana haunted French overseas ambitions from the time of Cardinal Richelieu in the 1630s to the French Revolution 160 years later.[199] Its reputation as the entrance to El Dorado and a potential base from which to assault Spanish America proved dazzling. It continually distra cted government officials, including the supposedly hard-headed Colbert, from more solid colonizing accomplishments in the Lesser Antilles.[200]

---

[197] See ibid., 46–51, for a more complete discussion.

[198] For a brief contemporary history of these expeditions, see Du Tertre, *Histoire générale des Antilles*, 3: 9–35.

[199] M. Devèze, *Antilles, Guyanes, la mer des Caraïbes de 1492 à 1789* (Paris: SEDES, 1977), 122–30, 307–19 and David Lowenthal, "Colonial Experiments in French Guyane, 1760–1800", *Hispanic American Historical Review,* 32 (Feb., 1952), 22–43.

[200] For several excellent accounts of the early history of Guiana, see Philip P. Boucher, *Les Nouvelles Frances, France in America, 1500–1815, An Imperial Perspective* (Providence, RI: The John Carter Brown Library, 1989), 32–7 and 44–7; also his "A Colonial Company

Guiana illustrates the disproportion between metropolitan ambition, which claimed all the territory between the Amazon and the Maroni Rivers, and colonial reality where France occupied a small island separated from the continent by a channel about a pistol-shot wide. By 1670, the French population had also been substantially reduced from the 1,200 men including 800 soldiers, who had been sent out in 1664.[201] The Dutch who captured Cayenne in 1675 reported 16 great sugar mills and more than 100 plantations (i.e., fields) of indigo, cotton, and ginger with room for more than 100 sugar mills. In January of 1677, shortly after retaking the colony, French naval commissary Jean-Baptiste Patoulet counted 319 settlers (1,374 black, 48 native slaves, and 15 mulattos).[202] Eight years later the colony's total population had declined to 1,682, compared with nearly 30,000 people living in the Lesser Antilles.[203]

Isolation characterised Cayenne's demographic history. Few European immigrants arrived, and slave ships from Africa usually passed it by. In what must be unique in the annals of enumeration, the colony's 1687 census, which enumerated 321 whites, 1,700 slaves, and 100 natives, included 28 settlers who died that year.[204] The political neglect and economic subsistence may have been similar to Acadia, but unlike the North American colony, the positive Malthusian checks of famine and disease operated strongly in Guiana's tropical environment. Thirty-three years later, in 1722, Cayenne's population still had not doubled the 1687 number.[205]

The demographic and economic heart of French America remained the Lesser Antilles during the seventeenth century and during the first two and perhaps three decades of the next. Known to the French as *les isles du vent*, or Windward Islands, in 1671 they included eight island colonies with a combined population of just under 30,000 – more than four times the populations of Canada, Acadia, and Placentia (see Appendix 1). Two general censuses of the islands for 1682 and 1687 give total populations of 32,383 and 37,288, respectively (see Table 1.4). In 1683 the European population had actually

---

at the Time of the Fronde: The Compagnie de la Terre ferme de l'Amérique ou France équinoxiale" *Terrae Incognita*, 11, (1979), 43–58; and "Shadows of the Past: France and Guiana, 1655–57", *Proceedings of the French Colonial Historical Society*, 6 (1981), 13–26.

[201] Stewart L. Mims, *Colbert's West Indian Policy* (New Haven: Yale University Press, 1912), 66-7.

[202] *CSP, CS, 1675-76*, 391; and Col., C¹⁴ᴬ 1, f. 222 "Recensement général de l'ile de Cayenne et de Terreferme de l'Amérique" (undated); but on a partial census of one *côte* is written "avec la lettre du Sr. Patoulet du 23 jan[v]ier 1677" (f. 219). The numbers given in Devèze, *Antilles, Guyanes, la mer*, 311, exclude 18 free ex-convicts from the whites and 273 black and all the native slaves.

[203] Col., C¹⁴ᴬ 2, ff. 167–9 "Recensement du gouvernement de l'Isle de Cayenne faict par le sieur de Saint Marthe, gouverneur pour le Roy de la ditte Isle pendant l'année, 1685".

[204] Ibid., f. 184 "Recensement de l'Isle de Cayenne pour l'année, 1687".

[205] Ibid., 13, ff. 295–6 "Etat sommaire de la colonie", September-Octobre, 1722. The total includes 610 baptized Indians, a group that was not enumerated in 1685.

Table 1.4. *Distribution of Population in the French Windward Islands, 1682–1687, by Colour and Colony*

Colony	Blacks 1682	Blacks 1687	Whites 1682	Whites 1687	Coloured 1682	Coloured 1687	Total 1682	Total 1687
Martinique	9,364	10,801	4,505	5,019	251	433	14,120	16,253
St. Christopher	4,301	4,470	2,885	3,152	92	151	7,278	7,773
Guadeloupe	4,109	4,982	2,998	3,546		170	7,107	8,698
Sainte-Croix	533	546	791	589			1,324	1,135
Marie Galante	598	745	431	503		29	1,029	1,277
Saint Martin	134	278	456	720		21	590	1,019
Grenada	220	297	302	362	7	31	529	690
Saint-Barthélémy	87	81	319	355		7	406	443
Total	19,346	22,200	12,687	14,246	350	842	32,383	37,288
Increase %	14.8		12.3			140.6		15.1

Sources: Col., C⁸ᴮ 17, no. 9 Recensement des Isles de l'Amérique, 12 avril 1683, composed of individual enumerations made during the previous year (see AN, SOM, G¹ 469, f. 120 for Guadeloupe; ibid., 472, f. 317 for St. Christopher, St. Martin and St. Barthélémy, and ibid., 499 for Martinique); also AN, SOM, G¹ 498, no. 50 Recensement général des Isles françoises de l'Amérique du commencement de l'anné 1687.

declined slightly from a dozen years before, but during the mid-eighties it increased by nearly 3 percent annually. The proportion of slaves grew only slowly from 56.6 to 59.5 percent of the total population during the mid-1680s, and the equally slow change in the proportion of whites and blacks dramatically reveals the chief impediment to increased sugar production in the islands. Only on Martinique had the slave/settler ratio reached two to one.

Saint-Domingue was located in the third region of the Circum-Caribbean. Though its economic development had scarcely begun in 1685, its estimated population already numbered 7,544 people. Unlike the Lesser Antilles, its population had grown very rapidly, increasing by more than three and a half times during the previous 15 years.[206] Approximately 30,000 French men and women and their descendants lived in all the Americas. The total population of the French Circum-Caribbean was just over 44,000, of whom 18,000 were Europeans and 25,000 were Africans compared with less than 12,000 Europeans who occupied New France (see Appendix 1). Nearly four-fifths of all those living in the tropics resided in the Lesser Antilles. Almost three-quarters of the whites and more than four-fifths of all slaves lived chiefly on the islands of St. Christopher, Martinique, and Guadeloupe (see Map 1.2).

These three colonies had a combined population of 26,641, including 15,317 slaves in 1671. The few hundred free coloureds comprised less than 1 percent of the total.[207] By 1683, more than seven-eighths of the population of the Lesser Antilles, including nearly 92 percent of all slaves, lived on these three islands. During the late seventeenth century more than one-half of all French colonists in the Americas lived there.

In 1670 about 30 percent, and in 1686 nearly one-quarter, of the total population of the French West Indies inhabited the northern sector of the Lesser Antilles (see Map 1.3). The total population amounted to just over 10,000 living in whole or in part on four islands: St. Christopher, St. Martin, Saint-Barthélémy, and Sainte-Croix. War with the Dutch during the 1670s and with the English during the 1690s left them ravaged, vulnerable, and indefensible; by 1700, the total population had declined to less than 5 percent of the Lesser Antilles population and perhaps to less than 3 percent of the total in the French Circum-Caribbean. Shortly afterward they ceased to play any productive role in the French colonial economy. Sainte-Croix was evacuated in 1695. Seven years later, after changing hands for the seventh time,

---

[206] This crude estimate was obtained by a linear interpolation between the censuses of 1681 and 1687 (see Appendix 1).

[207] AN, SOM, G¹ 468, "Abrégégénéral du dénombrement des hommes, femmes, garcons, filles ... en l'Isle Guadeloupe", 1671; ibid., 471 "Desnombrement général des terres de l'Isle de St. Christophe, 1671"; and ibid., 499, no. 5 "Recapitulation du dénombrement général fait de l'Isle Martinique en l'année 1671 tant des personnes que bestiaux".

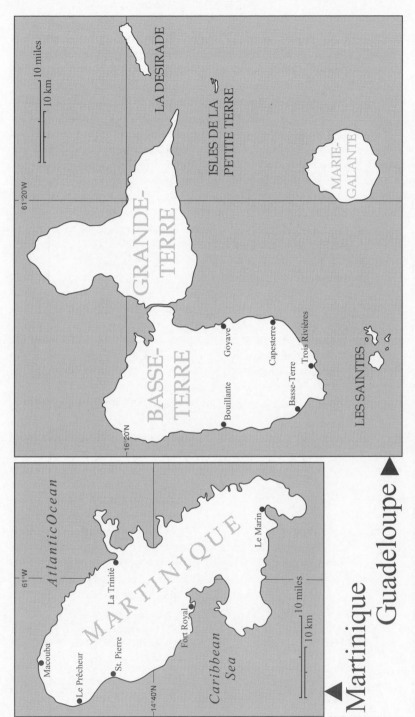

Map 1.2. Two maps of Guadeloupe and Martinique.

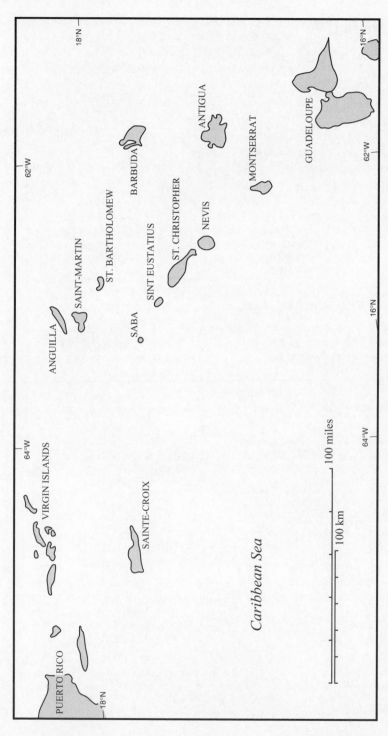

Map 1.3. Northern Lesser Antilles: St. Christopher, St. Bartholomew, Saint-Martin, and Sainte-Croix.

St. Christopher remained English. The continuing growth of populations in the Windward Islands and rapid growth of Saint-Domingue's population disguised these alterations, transforming what might have been a major social and economic setback into relatively insignificant changes in the French West Indies.

The French conquered the entire island of St. Christopher in 1666 and transported nearly 5,000 English colonists and their possessions elsewhere in the West Indies.[208] The terms of the Treaty of Breda, however, restored the *status quo ante* and the French handed back the English sector of the island in 1671 when the French-English proportions of the population had radically changed. Prior to the war, the English outnumbered the French by two to one, but during the 1670s the reverse held true. No basis for a direct comparison between the English and French sectors of the island exists, but in 1678 only 3,333 whites and slaves inhabited the English section of the island, less than half the total number in the French sections four years later, as shown in Table 1.5.

In 1670, St. Christopher contained the largest French population in the West Indies, but the continued division of the island between French and English severely impeded future French settlement. The French occupied both ends of the island, which left them with the best roadstead, but the English possessed more good farm land.[209] The French acknowledged this disadvantage as early as 1669 when the new governor-general of the islands, Jean-Charles de Baas, shifted his official residence to Martinique. But even though it was the most intensely cultivated French colony, instability due to continuing French-English rivalry confirmed the failure of sugar cane to become a significant crop on St. Christopher. Both the high proportion of European women and children during the 1680s and the low ratio of slaves to whites reveal the failure of the island to attract single white males. The total population and the number of sugar mills declined slowly between 1671 and 1689.

In August of 1689, the French captured the English garrison on St. Christopher, but their enemies reversed the situation the very next year and the French position on the island collapsed. The terms of the Treaty of Ryswick later restored the island to its prewar status, but the English only returned the French districts in 1699 after devoting nearly two years to destroying plantations, and as much other property as they could. One of five churches remained standing and when finally delivered into French hands, only 1,166 inhabitants remained to be enumerated. Six indigo works were operating, but no boiling houses or working plantations existed.[210] By 1701, the number

---

[208] Dunn, *Sugar and Slaves*, 124; Mims, *Colbert's West India Policy*, 126–7.
[209] Ibid., 32.
[210] AN, SOM, G¹ 472, ff. 341–6 "Etat des magasins, maisons et autres édifices de la Basseterre de St. Christophe detruit par les anglois depuis l'avis du traité du paix de Riswick", 20 February, 1699.

Table 1.5. *Distribution of Population on French St. Christopher,
1671–1701, by Age, Sex, and Colour*

Year	Population	Number	Men	Women	Children	Males	Females
					Percentages		
1671	Blacks	4,468	35.9	37.4	26.8		
	Whites	3,333	41.3	20.6	38.1	62.5	37.5
	Coloureds	112					
	Total (a)	7,913					
1682	Blacks	4,301	36.6	36.3	27	51.4	48.6
	Whites	2,885	35.1	19.1	45.8	57.5	42.5
	Coloureds	92				56.5	43.5
	Total	7,278					
1686	Blacks	4,348	37.6	35.1	27.3		
	Whites	2,383	34	31.7	34.3	49.8	50.2
	Coloureds	251					
	Total	6,982					
1689	Blacks	4,017	37	36.1	26.8		
	Whites	3,381	24.9	18.6	56.5	54.2	45.8
	Coloureds	200					
	Total	7,598					
1701	Blacks	934	45.5	35.1	19.4		
	Whites	901	42.3	29	28.7	59.2	40.8
	Coloured	19	47.4	31.6	21.1		
	Total	1,854	43.9	32	24.1		

[a] Includes 290 English settlers and their 187 slaves.
Coloureds include free and slave Caribs.
Sources: 1671, AN, SOM, G¹ 471; 1682, ibid., 498, no. 100 and 472, f. 317; 1686,
471, f. 329; 1689, ibid., ff.330–1; and 1701, ibid., 498, no. 63bis.

of slaves had nearly doubled from two years before, but efforts to rede-
velop St. Christopher were misguided. The very next year the English seized
the French sector once again, and, though the French sacked the island in
1706, the enemy retained possession at the war's end. The last 35 years of
French activity on St. Christopher from 1667 to 1702 had proved that joint
occupation was impossible.

The numbers on St. Martin and St. Bartholomew were never large.
These small island colonies were quite different from others moving toward
slave/sugar culture. Their purpose was to supply provisions to the more
populous French settlements on St. Christopher. Both colonies developed

important connections with the Dutch commercial empire, but with the loss of St. Christopher, their chief value waned. Absolute numbers peaked before the outbreak of war in 1689, and the inhabitants of these two islands probably comprised less than 2 percent of the total population for the French West Indies. In 1691 there were no plantations on St. Martin and the number of indigo works had fallen to 15 from 50 nine years before. In May of 1692, 1,100 souls, including 217 men under arms, were reported on the two islands, but they had no money to support themselves, about half of them being refugees transported from St. Christopher the previous summer.[211] Only 250 people resided on Saint Martin at the turn of the century alongside a Dutch population of about 300.[212] Little was produced there except for local consumption.[213]

The French only permanently occupied St. Bartholomew in 1658 following a fierce contest with Caribs.[214] Neither climate nor soil favoured sugar cultivation. Four-fifths of its residents were white.[215] That the indefensible island remained French during a quarter of a century of warfare was a reflection of its poverty.[216] By 1715 the French had abandoned the two islands in all but name. Forty families totaling 130 people lived peacefully with the Dutch on St. Martin, and during the war the commander of St. Bartholomew had accepted a commission from the English governor of St. Christopher to keep the peace.[217] Following an effort to assert royal authority in 1717, the French left the islands alone.[218] In 1730, the 445 French inhabitants on St. Martin were fewer than half a century before. Less than half that number probably resided on St. Bartholomew.[219]

French occupation of Sainte-Croix did not last to the end of the century. Originally taken from the Spanish in 1650 and settled a year later, the new colony was poorly governed during its early history, and by 1670 the island's establishments had been pretty well ruined.[220] The white population declined steadily between 1683 and 1695, and though the slave population

---

[211] Col., C^{8A}7, ff. 26-6v Blénac to Pontchartrain, 12 May 1692; and ibid., 6, f. 433 Du Maitz to Seignelay, 30 August 1691.

[212] Cornelius Ch. Goslinga, *The Dutch in the Caribbean and in the Guianas, 1680–1791* (Dover, NH: Van Goram, 1985), 131.

[213] AN, SOM, G^1 498, nos. 5 and 6a and b.

[214] Mims, *Colbert's West India Policy*, 43.

[215] Lasserre, *La Guadeloupe*, 2: 805.

[216] AN, SOM, G^1 472, f. 317; 498, nos. 89 and 101; also Lasserre, *La Guadeloupe*, 2: 804, 820.

[217] Col., C^{8A} 20, ff. 300-1v Duquesne to Pontchartrain, 20 October 1715.

[218] Col., C^{8B} 4, no. 49 Decision of the Navy Council, 18 June 1717; and Col., F^3 68, ff. 267–8 Navy Council to Feuquières, 15 March 1718.

[219] AN, SOM, G^1 498, no. 7 "Recensement de la partie françois de l'Isle de St. Martin de l'année 1730".

[220] Du Tertre, *Histoire générale des Antilles*, 3: 114–26; also Mims, *Colbert's West India Policy*, 44.

in 1695 was 30 percent higher than before the war, the total population remained below the level of twelve years earlier. The number of sugar works never exceeded the 14 recorded in 1682.[221] A retrospective report later claimed that there were 200 men bearing arms and 800 slaves working 11 plantations when the island was evacuated.[222] Sainte-Croix was renowned for its dye wood and timber, but the scarcity of springs, the brackish water of the island's only river, and supposedly bad air all contributed to its reputation for poor health and were used to justify its evacuation, carried out ostensibly to appease the tax-farmers of the Western Domain, who claimed that major revenues were being lost owing to virtual abandonment of the colony to the Danes from nearby St. Thomas.[223] The failure of French merchants to serve the colony had long thrown the colonists into Danish hands; the islanders received official permission to trade with the Danes as early as 1672.[224] Nothing changed during the next 23 years. The forced evacuation was chiefly carried out at the behest of the new governor of Saint-Domingue, Jean Du Casse.[225] Most of the 460 whites, 712 slaves, and 52 free coloureds enumerated in 1695 settled in the northern district of Saint Domingue.[226]

The net effect of these changes in the French "Leeward" Islands altered the balance of population in the French West Indies at the beginning of the eighteenth century. The French continued to occupy several small islands, especially Marie Galante and Grenada, but in future the bulk of the population resided in only three colonies: Guadeloupe, Martinique, and Saint Domingue, which, by 1700, held 90 percent of the population of the French Circum-Caribbean compared to less than 70 percent that resided there 30 years before. At the turn of the century, the French were producing about 12,000 tonnes of sugar annually, or slightly more than one-sixth of all the sugar in the Americas.[227] No one could have foreseen that during the next 30 years, the French colonies would grow so rapidly in contrast to their previous history, and that they would establish the conditions to become the greatest sugar producers in the world.

[221] AN, SOM, G¹ 493, no. 73; and 498, nos. 59 and 80.

[222] Col., C⁸ᴬ 19, ff. 337v-8 "Mémoire sur les Isles françaises … qui ont été degradées", May 1713.

[223] Pierre-François-Xavier Charlevoix, *Histoire de l'isle espagnol ou de S. Domingue* (Paris: Jacques Guerin, 1730–1731), 2: 287–8; also Jean-Baptiste Labat, *Nouveau Voyage aux Isles aux Isles de l'Amérique* (La Haye: P. Husson, T. Johnson, P. Gosse, Jvan Duren, R. Atberts, & C. Le Vier [1724]), 1 pt. 2: 73–4.

[224] Mims, *Colbert's West India Policy*, 323.

[225] Labat, *Nouveau voyage aux Isles*, 2: 242.

[226] AN, SOM, G¹ 498, no. 80 "Recensement générale de l'isle de Ste. Croix, 1695".

[227] David Eltis, "The slave economies of the Caribbean: Structure, performance, evolution and significance" in *General History of the Caribbean*, Vol. 3, *The Slave Societies of the Caribbean*, ed., Franklin W. Knight (London: UNESCO/Macmillan, 1997), 110; this upward revision is based on "muscovado equivalents" originally determined by McCusker, *The Rum Trade* (see Eltis, note 11). Cf. Dunn, *Sugar and Slaves*, 205 for the older, now outdated, estimates.

Stagnation marked Guadeloupe's late seventeenth-century demographic history. According to Father Raymond Breton, in 1656 Guadeloupe's population numbered 12,000 whites and slightly more than 3,000 blacks, but no compelling evidence confirms this estimate. If true, the island's white population fell by nearly three-quarters to about 3,000 during the next 15 years (which is highly unlikely), while the number of slaves increased to 4,267 (see Table 1.6).[228] Subsequent censuses reveal that during the next three decades, the number of whites remained steady, even declining slightly at times. The causes were contingent rather than structural. Immigration dried up during the Franco-Dutch War and never resumed in large numbers. Few slaves ever reached the island directly from Africa. Combined with the effect of tropical diseases, natural increase failed to maintain the population at existing levels.[229] The slave population grew slowly, but thereafter, Guadeloupe's population leapt forward.[230] Between 1699 and 1730, the island's total population increased four and a half times, the white population growing from 2,796 to 7,433. Slave numbers increased more than five and a half times from 6,185 to 26,801.[231] During the entire sixty-year period the proportion of whites on the island fell steadily from 39 to 21 percent of the total.[232]

The number of free blacks and coloureds remained small on Guadeloupe. The 1671 census recorded only 47 mulattos, and the free nonwhites, including natives, numbered only 349 or 3.3 percent of the colony's 10,453 inhabitants at the end of the century.[233] Despite the great increase of slaves on Guadeloupe during the next three decades, no real change occurred in the proportion of coloureds. They still comprised 3.6 percent of the colony's population in 1730. By then, however, they comprised 14.5 percent of the free population.[234]

The stagnation and recovery of Guadeloupe's white population during the late seventeenth century raises questions concerning the influence of war, disease, and famine on colonial populations. If war accounts for declines during the 1670s and 1690s, why did no corresponding decline occur between 1702 and 1713 during the War of the Spanish Succession? Indentured servants appeared to have had little interest in Guadeloupe after 1685; most

---

228 Lasserre, *La Guadeloupe*, 1: 275.
229 AN, SOM, G¹ 468 "Abrégé général du denombrement ... [1671]; and ibid., 469, f. 120 "Recensement général des habitants, nègres ... des Isles Guadeloupe, Grandterre et Saintes", 20 May 1682.
230 Charles Frostin, *Les Révoltes blanches à Saint-Domingue aux XVIIe et XVIIIe siècles (Haiti avant 1789)*, (Paris: L'École, 1975), 29.
231 Ibid., but see Anne Pérotin-Dumon, *La ville aux Iles, la ville dans l'île; Basse-Terre et Point-à-Pitre, 1650–1820* (Paris: Karthala, 2000), 292 for more data for the years 1700–1730.
232 Lasserre, *La Guadeloupe*, 1: 283 shows that the trend continued to 1848 when the proportion reached 8 percent.
233 Maurice Satineau, *Histoire de la Guadeloupe sous l'ancien régime, 1635–1789* (Paris: Payot, 1928), 380–1.
234 Ibid., 382–3.

Colonial Populations

Table 1.6. *Distribution of Populations on Martinique and Guadeloupe, 1671–1730, by Age, Sex, and Colour*

Colony	Colour	Number	Percentages					
			Men	Women	Children	Agd/Infrm	Male	Female
Martinique 1671	Black	6,582	36.6	34.2	29.2			
	White	4,326	54.6	15.2	30.2		71	29
	Coloured	—						
	Total	10,908						
Guadeloupe 1671	Black	4,267	39.3	35.5	25.2			
	White	3,331	50.6	16.4	33.1		69.3	30.6
	Coloured	98						
	Total	7,696						
Martinique 1682	Black	9,364	32.8	25.2	32.9	6.3		
	White	4,505	40.7	20.4	38.9			
	Coloured	251					75.7	24.3
	Total	14,120						
Guadeloupe 1682	Black	4,109	38	33.8	28.2		53.9	46.1
	White	2,998	32	20.1	47.9		59.1	40.9
	Coloured	70					54.4	45.6
	Total	7,186						
Martinique 1692	Black	12,857	37.4	31.5	31.2			
	White	6,413	26.4	20.2	53.5		54.6	45.4
	Coloured	344						
	Total	19,614						
Guadeloupe 1696	Black	6,431	31.6	33.5	34.9		48.5	51.5
	White	3,649	30.9	28.4	40.6		51.6	48.4
	Coloured	307					44.6	55.4
	Total	10,387						
Martinique 1702	Black	17,382	39	30.3	30.7			
	White	6,820	36.5	26.1	37.5		55.4	44.6
	Coloured	570			42.3			
	Total	24,772						
Guadeloupe 1710	Black	9,706	32.4	32.8	34.8			
	White	4,689	28.3	28.2	43.5			48.7
	Coloured	580	23.8	30.3	45.9			
	Total	14,975						
Martinique 1719	Black	35,475	31.7	24.8	30.2	13.3		
	White	9,106	42.1	28.4	29.5		57.3	42.7
	Coloured	993						
	Total	45,571						

Table 1.6. *(cont.)*

Colony	Colony	Number	Men	Women	Children	Agd/Infrm	Male	Female
					Percentages			
Guadeloupe	Black	17,184	31.5	25.5	30.7	12.4		
1720	White	6,238	34.4	28.2	37.4		53.6	46.4
	Coloured	895	23.5	27.5	49.1			
	Total	24,317						
Martinique	Black	40,403	33.9	25.5	25.7	14.9		
1726	White	10,959	36.9	28.1	35		55.9	44.1
	Coloured	1,304	18.5	32.4	49.2			
	Total	52,666						
Guadeloupe	Black	26,801	32	22	32	14		
1730	White	7,433	37	26.4	36.5		56.1	43.9
	Coloured	1,262	25.7	24.2	50.1			
	Total	35,496						

Sources: For Martinique, AN, SOM, G¹ 499, no. 5 (1671); no. 11 (1682); "néant" (1692); 470bis, no. 3 (1702); 499, no. 33 (1719); and Col., C^8A 37, ff. 14–36 (1726). For Guadeloupe, AN, SOM, G¹, 468 (1671); 469, f. 120 (1682); ibid., f. 13 (1696); ibid., f. 140 (1720); 497, no. 5 (1710); Satineau, *Histoire de la Guadeloupe*, 382–3.

headed to Saint-Domingue. In 1702, Intendant Blondel complained that no more than 50 engagés had reached Guadeloupe annually since 1686.[235] On the other hand, migration from St. Christopher rather than natural increase may have contributed to the increase in Guadeloupe's population after 1702. Nevertheless, natural increase cannot be ruled out. Table 1.6 reveals a near balance among white adults and that the percentages of white children under twelve years of age on Guadeloupe in 1682, 1696, 1710, and 1720 were similar to those in Canada.

The growth of Guadeloupe's slave population raises several questions, not the least of which is how it occurred. Slave numbers increased by less than half during the final three decades of the seventeenth century. However, during the next 30 years their numbers increased more than four times, doubling during the War of the Spanish Succession to reach 12,562 by 1714, nearly doubling again during the next decade, and finally reaching 26,801 in 1730.[236]

[235] Debien, "Les Engagés pour les Antilles", 242.
[236] AN, SOM, G¹ 497, no. 7 Desnombrements general de l'Ille Guadeloupe et dependences de l'année 1714"; and 469, ff. 140–9 "Recensement La Guadeloupe 1724". Satineau, *Histoire de la Guadeloupe*, 380–1.

The proportion of slave children born in the colonies is unknown, but the low percentage of children among the slave populations of Martinique and Guadeloupe, between 25.2 and 34.5 percent during the six decades in question, indicates that growth relied chiefly on continuous imports. The higher percentage of children among Guadeloupe's slave population in 1696 and 1710 may reflect the decline in new arrivals during the period and the temporary importance of natural increase. The curve of increasing numbers reflected the slave trade, both legal and illegal. Though some slaves may have been legally transshipped from Martinique to Guadeloupe, the legal slave trade provided the latter with few Africans. In 1687, Governor Hincelin claimed that more slaves died than were sold and fewer than 400 had arrived during the previous five years. Lack of slaves was the chief reason for the "better families" to depart for Martinique in 1694, and 25 years later in 1719, the situation remained unchanged. Governor de Moyencourt claimed, perhaps with some exaggeration, that during the previous quarter century only three small French ships had reached Guadeloupe with fewer than 500 slaves.[237] Some of the increase in slave numbers was due to the recently concluded war. In July of 1712, 500 to 600 slaves remained from 1,200 landed from Jacques Cassard's attack on Montserrat, but six months later he had been able to sell only about 300.[238] Nevertheless, in April of 1713, Governor Malmaison reported the arrival of more than 1,000 slaves during the past year.[239] A sharp increase in the slave population occurred in 1720, but the cause was local. Many of the reported 2,000 newcomers arrived with their owners from Martinique to take up new concessions, but Governor de Moyencourt's hope that Guadeloupe's population would surpass Martinique's in 10 years was not achieved.[240] Heavy mortality among slaves in 1726 led some colonists to depart, and in 1730, Guadeloupe's population of 35,496 remained less than two-thirds of Martinique's.[241]

Marie Galante, originally settled in 1648, quickly proved indefensible. Caribs from Dominica slaughtered the colonists in 1653 and the French began again. In 1675 the Dutch ravaged the island, burning everything they could not carry off, and the island remained abandoned until the end of the war. Planters began rebuilding after the Franco-Dutch War, and the population grew by more than 80 percent from 703 to 1,277 between 1680 and 1687. Slave numbers increased 136 percent. The number of sugar and indigo

---

[237] Lasserre, *La Guadeloupe*, 1: 292; Eltis's dataset confirms these three ships as arriving in 1714 and indicates that two more ships arrived in 1716; these were the only ones to do so before 1727.

[238] Col., C7A 6 Malmaison to Pontchartrain 5 and 20 August, 1712, and same to same 28 March 1713.

[239] Ibid., same to same 6 April, 1713.

[240] Col., C7A 8 ff. 127-7v Moyencourt to Navy Council 6 September 1720.

[241] Satineau, *Histoire de la Guadeloupe*, 382-3.

works grew to 16 and 51, respectively.[242] However, this promising recovery came to an end after the English devastated the island in 1691 and 1702. In 1700, the island's 492 settlers possessed a mere 191 slaves, and twelve years later, the total population numbered fewer than 1,000, including 550 slaves.[243] The inhabitants of Marie Galante paid a heavier price than any other French island for the colonial wars of the period. Significant development occurred only after 1713. Recovery was slow. There were far fewer slaves on the island in 1713 than in 1671, and only two of 24 sugar works were in working order.[244] Seven years later there were nine sugar works and six planters. The other whites, *petits blancs* who could afford only three or four slaves, produced indigo.[245] The increase in slaves paralleled the growth of sugar plantations. From 550 in 1713, slave numbers grew to 1,434 six years later and to 1,806 in 1726, by which time they comprised nearly three-quarters of the island's population. Between 1719 and 1727 the number of indigo works fell from 86 to 17, while sugar plantations increased from 12 to 20.[246]

Martinique remained the most populous French colony in the Americas until 1713. The black and white populations probably reached parity about 1659 or 1660, and thereafter blacks outnumbered whites.[247] The proportion of whites fell slowly as the French failed to meet the growing demand for slaves. Though the black–white ratio exceeded 2:1 by 1682, more than 30 years passed before the ratio increased to 3:1, indicating a very slow transition from tobacco and indigo to sugar monoculture.[248] The total population increased more than five and a half times between 1670 and 1731. European numbers grew three times, while the African population increased more than seven times. The number of whites did not double the 1670 figure, however, until 1706. Martinique's white population reached a peak in 1742.[249]

Gabriel Debien's anecdotal evidence from the second half of the eighteenth century suggests that half of all slaves reaching the French colonies died within eight years of their arrival, and this probably held true during

[242] AN, SOM, G¹ 498, nos. 17 and 59; also Christian Schnakenbourg, "Recherches sur l'histoire de l'industrie sucrière à Marie Galante", Extrait du *Bulletin de la société d'histoire de la Guadeloupe*, nos. 48–50, 2–4 trimestres (1981): 18–19.

[243] Ibid., and Col., C⁸ᴮ no. 42 extract, Phélypeaux to Pontchantrain, 16 January 1713.

[244] Col., C⁷ᴮ 1, no. 100 extract of Feuquières and Besnard to Navy Council, 6 May 1721.

[245] Col., C⁸ᴬ 6, no. 1 extract of a report by Sr. Desrucaux-Hardouin, 1720.

[246] Schnakenbourg, "Recherches sur ... Marie Galante", 19–20; and AN, SOM, G¹ 498, nos. 21 and 22.

[247] May, *Histoire économique de la Martinique*, 55.

[248] Richard S. Dunn, *Sugar and Slaves: The Rise of the Planter Class in the English West Indies, 1624–1713* (New York: W.W. Norton, 1972), 87 claims that when a plantation society such as Barbados was moving toward a 3:1 ratio of Africans to Europeans, it was in rapid transition to mature plantation monoculture.

[249] May, *Histoire économique de la Martinique*, 322.

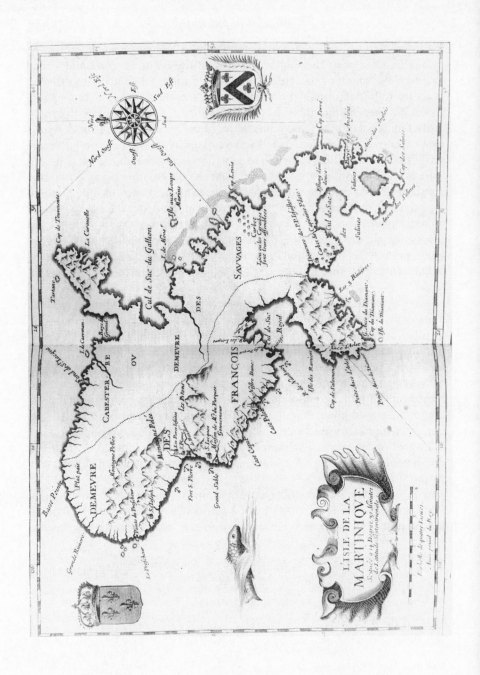

the earlier period.[250] Nevertheless, Martinique's slave population grew dramatically. Numbers doubled between 1671 and 1692 to 12,587 and doubled again before 1715, when the total reached 26,865. The War of the Spanish Succession did not seem to affect population growth, which increased 70 percent between 1700 and 1715. Between 1715 and 1730, the number of slaves increased by 60 percent, but the slave–white ratio remained fairly stable, varying slightly between 3.7 and 3.9, owing to the equally vigorous increase in white persons. In 1731, the island's total population stood at 58,548. The French appeared to have solved their labour supply problem, but it remains an open question whether the increase in the white population was due to a new stream of immigrants or to natural increase. According to L.-P. May, immigration to the colony ceased by the end of the seventeenth century, but the low percentage of white women and the proportion of children in the white population in 1719 and 1726 does not appear sufficient to account for the growth in numbers (see Table 1.6).[251]

Grenada, the most southerly of the Windward Islands, experienced little development during the seventeenth century, but by 1730 its population approached Île Royale's in numbers. Early colonizing attempts failed in the face of successful Carib attacks, internal divisions among the settlers, and the brutal tyranny of the island's owner.[252] In 1669, Colbert encouraged new efforts to settle the island with the vague idea of establishing a base for contraband trade with Spanish America.[253] However, with no real incentives, continuing conflict, and little capital, agriculture developed slowly. Between 1669 and 1696 the number of slaves more than doubled, but the island still contained fewer than 900 people at the end of the century.[254] Numbers continued to increase during the War of the Spanish Succession, and afterward, the French briefly considered Grenada as a replacement for St. Christopher. Some believed Grenada could be transformed into a base from which to attack the Dutch at Curaçao, but Governor-General Phélypeaux viewed it as fit only for indigo, claiming defence costs would be far too high and concluded the island was indefensible.[255] Grenada was left

---

[250] Debien, *Les Esclaves aux Antilles francaises*, 345.

[251] May, *Histoire économique de la Martinique*, 38 and 48.

[252] George Brizan, *Grenada, Island of Conflict from Amerindians to People's Revolution, 1498–1979* (London: Zed Books, 1984), 15–22.

[253] Clément, éd., *Lettres ... de Colbert*, 3, pt. 2: 460; also Mims, *Colbert's West India Policy*, 192.

[254] AN, SOM, G¹ 498, nos. 28 and 39; also Brizan, *Grenada*, 25.

[255] Col., C⁸ᴮ 2, no. 89 extract, Bouloc to Pontchartrain, 1 March 1708; ibid., 3, no. 42 extract, Phélypeaux to Pontchartrain, 8 March 1713.

Illustration 1.1. Map of Martinique, *circa* 1670.
From Jean-Baptiste Du Tertre, *Histoire générale des Antilles, habitées par les François*. 4 vols. (Paris: T. Jolly, 1667–1671), 1: inter pages 98–9.

to grow on its own. An influx of settlers from Martinique occurred in 1714, and four years later the island's population numbered nearly 3,500, including 2,779 slaves.[256] Grenada became a mature plantation society more rapidly than any other French colony. Though the island held a high concentration of slaves, it lay too close to the South American mainland to hold them. Slaves continually deserted, easily stealing small boats along the shore and making their way south. More than 10 percent of the adult slaves deserted in 1721 alone, which probably accounts for the 5 percent decline in population from just three years before.[257] Nevertheless, the population grew. In 1726 numbers reached nearly 4,500.[258] Though small in size, the colony contained a vigorous economy with approximately fifty plantations.

The French came relatively late to Saint-Domingue. Their starting point was the small island of Tortuga off the northern coastline of Hispaniola, which had become home to an international collection of masterless buccaneers, French, Dutch, and English. After gaining control of Tortuga in 1659, the French moved onto the main island during the next decade. In 1665 they began a 127-year reign over the western third of the island that brought untold profits to sugar planters, and death and destruction to unknown hundreds of thousands of African slaves. The Spanish Crown ceded the territory known as Saint-Domingue to the French in 1697 more than 40 years after their de facto occupation. This fact, along with the absence of sugar cane agriculture and its accompanying large scale slave labour force, meant that the population of Saint-Domingue evolved under rather singular conditions during the seventeenth century. Nevertheless, its final shape and structure, which became the epitome of the plantation sugar complex, appeared very rapidly during the first three decades of the eighteenth century. Though the black–white ratio was not yet 2:1 in 1700, it had climbed to the astonishing level of 4.6:1 15 years later. By 1730, when the African–European ratio had grown to 7.6:1, all was in place for what came later.

The first of the colony's three districts comprised the north coast and island of Tortuga; the second, or Western District, called Cul-de-Sac, incorporated settlements in the Gulf of Gonâve on the west coast; and the third was the south coast and Isle à Vache. During the seventeenth century, the latter remained virtually uninhabited. In 1669, Bertrand Ogeron claimed there were more than 1,600 fighters, hunters, settlers, and indentured servants on Tortuga and the coast of Saint-Domingue.[259] He also indicated that there were no slaves in the settlements. Two years later, navy captain Louis Gabaret

[256] Noell Deerr, *The History of Sugar*, 2 vols. (London: Chapman and Hall, 1949–50), 1: 177; and AN, SOM, G¹ 498, nos. 40 and 41.
[257] Col., C⁸ᴮ 7, no. 115 extract Pradines to Navy Council, 8 November 1721; and ibid., no. 34 "Recensement, année 1721".
[258] AN, SOM, G¹ 498, no. 45.
[259] Michel Camus, éd., "Correspondance de Bertrand Ogeron, gouverneur de l'île de la Tortue et coste de Saint-Domingue au xviie siècle", *Revue de la Société Haitienne d' Histoire et de Géographie*, 43, no. 146 (Mars, 1985), 94, 223.

Table 1.7. *Distribution of White Settlers on Saint-Domingue, May 1681,*
by Area, Age, Sex, and Occupation

Areas and Districts	Heads of Households	Women	Children	Servants Free	Servants Indentured	Total
Tortuga	75	33	72	19	69	268
Cap François	451	142	137	137	772	1,639
Port de Paix	88	42	57	93	160	440
Nrthrn. Distrct.	614	217	266	249	1,001	2,347
Léogane	356	91	77	68	381	973
Pt. et Gde Gôave	237	68	42	118	119	584
Nippe et Rochelois	122	33	29	26	24	234
Gde Anse et Gde. Riv.	71	22	24	16	30	163
Western Dist.	786	214	172	228	554	1,954
Isle à Vache	21	4			10	35
Total	1,421	435	438	477	1,565	4,336

Source: AN, Col., C⁹ᴬ 1 (nonfoliated), "Dénombrement général de l'Isle de la Tortue
et coste de St. Domingue, en mai 1681".

estimated that 1,000 to 1,200 habitants, 500 or 600 freebooters, and about
100 *boucaniers*, or hunters of feral cattle, lived in Cul-de-Sac.[260] These estimates for two separate regions suggest that by 1670 about 3,400 people
resided on Saint-Domingue, which seems to agree with two more estimates
made seven years later. Some growth may have occurred during the interim,
for though war with the United Provinces and Spain dominated the 1670s,
Saint-Domingue attracted single males with no capital fleeing the collapsed
tobacco economy of Martinique. A report of 1677, estimated the population,
both white and black, at between 4,000 and 5,000.[261] This may be about
right, for the same year an enumeration counted only 3,500 whites residing in a dozen settlements and estimated the number of freebooters at more
than 1,000.[262] Finally, a more detailed general enumeration made in 1681
reported a total population of 6,648 persons, of whom nearly two-thirds
were white (see Table 1.7).[263]

[260] Col., C⁹ᴬ 1 (nonfoliated) "Mémoire sur l'état de la colonie de St. Domingue", joined
      to Gabaret to [Colbert], June 1671. The distinction between *boucaniers* or buccaneers
      and *flibustiers* or freebooters long remained among the French after others had grown
      accustomed to using the terms synonymously.
[261] C. H. Haring, *The Buccaneers in the West Indies* (London: Methuen, 1910), 218 n2.
[262] Camus, éd., "Correspondance d'Ogeron" 17 n27 citing Col., 9B 1", "Mémoire sur les
      boucaniers".
[263] Col., C⁹ᴬ 1, "Denombrement général de l'isle de la Tortue et coste de St. Domingue, en
      mai 1681. An accurate copy is in the Margry Papers in BN, n.a.f., vol. 9,325, f. 305.

Saint-Domingue remained a collection of widely scattered settlements without connecting roads. More than four-fifths of the population lived in four areas (see Map 1.4). Cap François (also called Le Cap) on the north coast was the largest single settlement, but the population was small. In 1692, it numbered 257, including just 34 slaves.[264] The majority of the population lived in the Western District, chiefly at Léogane and Petit Goâve. The original settlement and pirate haven on Tortuga had declined to a shadow of its former self. The ethnic divisions in the colony indicate the minimal importance of commercial agriculture. Whites still generally outnumbered blacks by more than 2:1, and in the north by even more. The Northern District held only 36 percent of all slaves; 62 percent resided in the Western District where some cultivation, chiefly tobacco, had begun. The free coloureds (4.6 percent) comprised a larger proportion of the population than in the Windward Islands.

Tables 1.7 and 1.8 show the distribution of whites, slaves, and coloureds by district and settlement, by sex and age, and by occupation. They reveal that the Northern and Western districts had very different demographic profiles, which reflected the differences in their economies. More than half the whites lived in the Northern District, but only 25 percent were heads of households compared to 40 percent in the Western District. White servants, both indentured and free, made up nearly half the white population; indeed, they nearly equaled the total number of slaves. They may safely be assumed to have been males.[265] Like slaves, white servants were unevenly distributed in the two districts. In the north there were 165 white servants for every 100 African slaves, while in the west there were 166 slaves for each 100 servants. In the north, the 1,250 servants, four-fifths of whom were indentured bondsmen, far outnumbered the 632 adult slaves.

There was virtually no increase in the white population before the turn of the century, yet there may have been great movement to and from the island. Two thousand *petit blancs* and freebooters reportedly left during the 1680s, while the white population was virtually the same in 1687 as six years earlier.[266] Nevertheless, Saint-Domingue's population was utterly transformed during the half century after 1681, increasing 13.5 times. The white population grew by less than two and a half times, underperforming every other major French colony in the Americas, but slave numbers increased

---

[264]   David Geggus, "The Major Port Towns of Saint-Domingue in the later Eighteenth Century" in *Atlantic Port Cities: Economy, Culture, and Society in the Atlantic World, 1650–1850*, eds., Franklin W. Knight and Peggy Liss (Knoxville: University of Tennessee Press, 1991), Table 4.5, 105.

[265]   Arlette Gautier, *Les Soeurs de Solitude: la condition féminine dans l'esclavage aux Antilles du XVIIe au XIXe siècle* (Paris: Éditions Caribéennes, 1985), 72 assumes all domestics are male.

[266]   Charlevoix, *Histoire de l'isle espagnol ou de S. Domingue*, 2: 144, 236; AN, SOM, G¹ 498, no. 59 Recensement général des Isles françoise ... 1687.

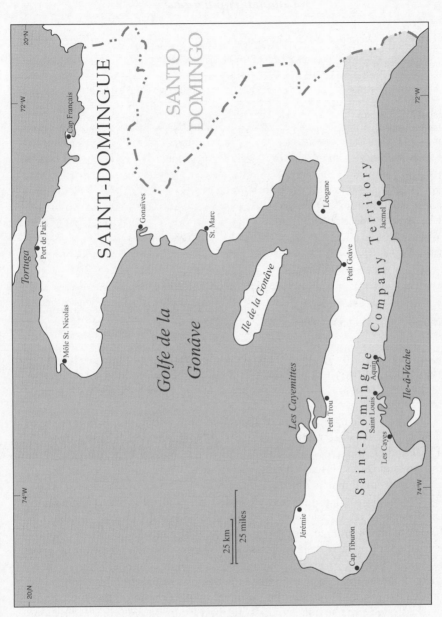

Map 1.4. Saint-Domingue showing lands of the Saint-Domingue Company, 1698–1720.

Table 1.8. *Distribution of Slaves and Coloureds in Saint-Domingue, 1681,*
by Area, Age, and Sex

Areas and Districts	Males	Females	Children	Slaves Total	Coloured
Island of Tortuga	58	22	9	89	17
Cap François	144	132	37	313	20
Port de Paix	159	117	81	357	11
Northern District	361	271	127	759	48
Léogane	350	173	68	591	34
Pte. et Gde Gôave	188	178	80	446	66
Nippe et Rochelois	98	53	13	164	23
Gde. Anse et Gde. Riv.	49	35	17	101	16
Western District	685	439	178	1,303	139
Isle à Vache	17	15	9	41	23
Total	1,063	725	314	2,102	210

Source: Col., C⁹ᴬ 1 (nonfoliated), "Dénombrement général de l'Isle de la Tortue et coste de St. Domingue, en mai 1681".

more than 34 times. This growth, emerging during the first quarter of the eighteenth century, negated the effect of all the losses in territory, population, and property that had occurred in the French "Leeward" Islands (see Table 1.9).

Despite the near stagnation of the white population, numbers more than doubled those of 20 years before in the Northern and Western districts. The number of slaves more than quadrupled. Most of the increase came during the 1690s, largely owing to between 1,600 and 2,000 slaves carried off from Jamaica during Governor Du Casse's great raid of 1694. By 1700, the total population exceeded the approximately eleven thousand persons on Guadeloupe and roughly equalled that of Canada. The Royal Saint-Domingue Company had only recently acquired the Southern District and was beginning its development. An enumeration in 1703 reported that 1,369 people, including 409 whites and 908 slaves, lived there.[267] More than seven-eighths of the colony's population lived in the two other districts.[268] However, the numbers in the Southern District contrast markedly with the sparse activities inspired by Le Moyne d'Iberville along the northern coast of the Gulf of Mexico during the same period.[269]

How the population grew during the War of the Spanish Succession remains a puzzle. Some increase in slave numbers came from war booty as when 700 to 800 slaves were carried into Petit Goâve in 1711, but these

[267] Ibid., G¹ 509, nos. 9 and 10. [268] Ibid., G¹ 509, no. 8
[269] Giraud, *Histoire de la Louisiane,* 1: 89–93.

Table 1.9. *Distribution of Population on Saint Domingue, 1681–1730,*
by Colour

Year	Blacks 1	Whites 2	Coloured 3	Total 4	Ratio 1/2	% 2/4	Ratio 3/2 + 3
1681	2,102	4,336	210	6,648	0.5	65	4.6
1687	3,358	4,411	224	7,993	0.8	55	4.8
1700 (a)	9,082	4,560	n/a	13,642	2	33	10.9
1713 (b)	24,156	4,970	1,117	30,243	4.9	16	16.4
1715 (a)	30,651	6,668	1,404	38,723	4.6	17	17.4
1720 (b)	47,077	7,956	1,573	56,606	5.9	14	16.6
1730 (b)	79,545	10,449	2,456	92,450	7.6	11	19.0

Notes: (a) Excludes the Southern District, which in 1703 held 908 blacks, 409 whites, and 52 coloureds, and in 1715 held 500 white families and 4,800 slaves. (b) Includes the Southern District.
Sources: AN, SOM, 498, no. 59; 509, nos. 2, 8, 9, 10, 12, 13, 17, 18; Col; C^{9B} 2; and Frostin, *Les Révoltes blanches à Saint-Domingue*, 144–5.

episodic events cannot account for the major increase in numbers.[270] During the 13 years after 1700, the total population more than doubled. Moreover, the crude slave–white ratio rose to 4.9, far surpassing the same ratio for Martinique.[271] By 1713 nearly four out of every five residents of Saint-Domingue were slaves. Whites made up less than one-sixth and free people of colour just under 4 percent of the total population.

White sex distribution showed little change (see Table 1.10). At 205 males to 100 females, the adult sex ratio remained very high. The low number of 52 children per 100 adult female slaves indicates clearly that the enormous increase in the slave population during wartime was due to imports from Africa and to interisland trade rather than from natural increase. Yet, all of this activity was but a precursor to further phenomenal growth.

From 1713 to 1730, Saint-Domingue's population more than doubled, reaching beyond 90,000.[272] By 1715, Saint-Domingue may have surpassed Martinique as the most populous French colony in the West Indies, indeed, in all French America. The separate administration of the southern district by a private company and the carelessness of militia officers in the other two

---

[270] E.g. Col. C^{9B} 2 extract from Charite to Pontchartrain, 23 June 1711.
[271] AN, SOM, 509, no. 12 "Recensement général de la Coste Saint-Domingue année 1713" does not include white girls under 12 years. This exclusion represents about 13 percent of the white population, which, if included, would bring the total population to about 31,500.
[272] Frostin, *Les révoltes blanches*, 144–5.

Table 1.10. *Distribution of Population on Saint-Domingue, 1681–1730,*
by Age, Sex, and Colour

Year	Number Slaves	Men	Women	Children	Aged/Infrm	Males	Females
				Percentages			
1681	2,102	50.6	34.5	14.9			
1687	3,358	41.7	44.6	13.7			
1700	9,083	41.6	32.8	25.6			
1713	24,156	43.1	29.6	27.3			
1715	30,651	40.8	24.4	25.5	7.7		
1720	47,077	42.2	26	23.8	7.9		
1730	79,545						

Year	Whites	Men	Women	Children		Males	Females
1681	4,336	79.9	10	10.1			
1687	4,411	60.4	13.3	26.3		77.6	22.4
1700	4,560	44.2	20.9	24.1		62.6	37.4
1713	4,970	54.9	21	24.1		73.6	26.4
1715	6,668	49.3	21.8	28.9		64.8	35.2
1720	7,956	51.2	20.9	28.7		66.3	33.7
1730	10,449						

Year	Coloured	Men	Women	Children		Males	Females
1681	210						
1687	224					63.4	36.6
1700(a)	500						
1713	1,117	19.5	28.3	52.2			
1716	1,213	23.4	30.5	46.1			
1720*	1,573					38.4	61.6
1730	2,456						

* The percentage of white males and females in 1720 is for 90 percent of the total population.
(a) Estimate; Coloureds were not enumerated in the 1700 census.
Sources: AN, SOM, G¹ 498, no. 59 (1687); ibid., 509, no. 2 (1681); no. 8 (1700); no. 12 (1713); no. 13 (1715); nos. 17 and 18 (1720); Col., C⁹ᴮ 3, extract from Blénac and Mithon to Navy Council, 15 July 1716; and Frostin, *Les Révoltes blanches à Saint-Domingue*, 28, 145 (1730).

districts yield confusing, unreliable data, but that year 500 white families and 4,800 slaves were reported in the south, then called St. Louis after its largest settlement, which brought the total number of slaves in the colony to more than 35,000. The presence of nearly 5,000 slaves in the south may be good evidence of an interisland slave trade because the company's ships had only carried 700 to 800 from Africa. Nor was the company's trade a matter of smuggling. In 1718, the Navy Council confirmed the directors' claim to trade legally with foreigners, and there is little doubt that they availed themselves of this privilege. At the same time, from 1714 to 1720, inclusive, 19,349 slaves arrived in the other parts of the colony, which compares nicely with the 18,551 in the Eltis data set.[273]

No two colonies contrasted more sharply than French Saint-Domingue and Spanish Hispaniola. In 1717, Saint-Domingue's population of 46,000 was 2.5 times larger than the population of the Spanish part of the island, and whereas Santo Domingo's population comprised 15,130 whites and 3,280 slaves, Saint-Domingue contained less than half the number of whites, 7,264, and more than 11 times the number of slaves, 37,474.[274]

Following the revocation of the Saint-Domingue Company's privileges in 1720, a detailed nominative census of most of St. Louis included nearly 800 whites and 4,367 slaves, which, when added to the enumeration of the northern and western districts, gives the colony's total population as 56,606, suggesting that seven-eighths of the population continued to reside in the Northern and Western districts.[275] Unfortunately, the official census of 1721 did not include St. Louis; Intendant Duclos reported only 49,669 in his enumeration of the other two districts.[276] No additional censuses from the 1720s have been found, but one for 1730 for all three districts indicates that the population grew to nearly 90,000, including 79,545 slaves and 10,449 whites.[277]

The growth of slave populations by natural increase was a rarity confined almost entirely to colonies with marginal economies or temperate climates. White populations in French tropical America performed better than slaves and sometimes as well as populations living in temperate colonies. Lack of data does not allow low reproductive performance to be attributed to low fertility, high mortality, age structure, sex ratios, or any other factors; birth rates are not available.[278] The proportion of children and the number of children per adult female in the black, white, and free coloured and other populations are crude, imperfect measures that allow us to say that birth rates among white populations in the French West Indies were sometimes surprisingly high. Table 1.6 indicates that the proportion of white children on St. Christopher was far higher than in rural France during the 1680s.

[273] Col., C9A 12 and 16 and C9B 2, 5, and 7 extracts from Blénac and Mithon to the Navy Council, 15 July 1716; also, Eltis *et al.*, *The Trans-AtlanticSlave Trade: A Database on CD-ROM*.

[274] AN, SOM, G1 509, no. 14; and Col., C9B 3 "Journal du voyage fait ... par le sieur Buttet", (ff. 62–6) who bribed a Spanish clerk at Santa Domingo to obtain the estimate.

[275] AN, SOM, G1 509, nos. 17 and 18.

[276] Col., C9B 7 Duclos to Navy Council, 25 June 1721; also AN, SOM, G1 509, no. 19.

[277] Frostin, *Les Révoltes blanches*, 144–5.

[278] Engerman and Higman, "Demographic Structure of the Caribbean Slave Societies in the Eighteenth and Nineteenth Centuries", 88–9.

The same could be said of Martinique during the last two decades of the seventeenth century and Guadeloupe for a longer period.[279] Not surprisingly, the proportion of children among the white populations in the Windward Islands never fell as low as levels experienced by the slave populations after 1670. The same may have been true on Saint-Domingue. Despite the small number of white women in 1681, there was 1.0 child for each adult female, whereas, in spite of the more equal sex ratio among adult slaves, fewer than one child existed for every two African adult females. Adult sex ratios also varied significantly by ethnicity and area. The average ratio among slaves in 1681 was 147 males per 100 females, but it varied greatly between 109 at Cap François to 202 at Léogane.

The proportion of children among slave populations varied between 25.2 and 34.9 percent in the Windward Islands (see Table 1.6). This compares with similar proportions among slaves in the English West Indies.[280] The exceptionally low proportion of slave children on St. Christopher in 1701 probably reflects the sudden influx of new slaves during the previous two or three years, while the generally higher proportions for Guadeloupe in 1696, 1710, and 1730 may reflect the slow rate of arrival of new slaves. The very low proportion of children among slaves on Saint-Domingue during the 1680s and after 1700 may also reflect their relatively recent arrival.

Free blacks and mulattos were normally enumerated together. Whether they were more likely than Europeans or Africans to live in nuclear families (nurture) or were more resistant to tropical diseases (nature), a far higher percentage of children were included in their totals than was the case for either whites or slaves. During the late seventeenth and early eighteenth century on Martinique and Guadeloupe, children comprised between 42 and 50 percent of the free coloured and free black population (Table 1.6), which matches or exceeds the percentages among Canadians at Montreal. The same was true at Saint-Domingue (Table 1.10) where the proportion of children was as high as 52.2 percent in 1713. The 1718 census of Saint-Domingue separately enumerated free coloured and free black adults. Children were undifferentiated, but despite the fact that the adult sex ratios contrasted sharply, they comprised 42.2 percent of the total. While there were 114 coloured females per

---

[279]   Chauleau, *Case-Pilote, Le Prêcheur, Basse-Pointe*, 71 contradicts this general observation based on Table 1.6; also see above, page 60.

[280]   Cf. Dunn, *Sugar and Slaves*, 316.

Illustration 1.2. Map of Saint-Domingue, 1731.

From Pierre-François-Xavier Charlevoix. *Histoire de l'Isle espagnole ou de Saint-Domingue écrit particulièrement sur les mémoires manuscrits du P. Jean-Baptiste Le Pers.* 2 vols. (Paris: Jacques Guerin, 1730–1731), 2: facing page 485.

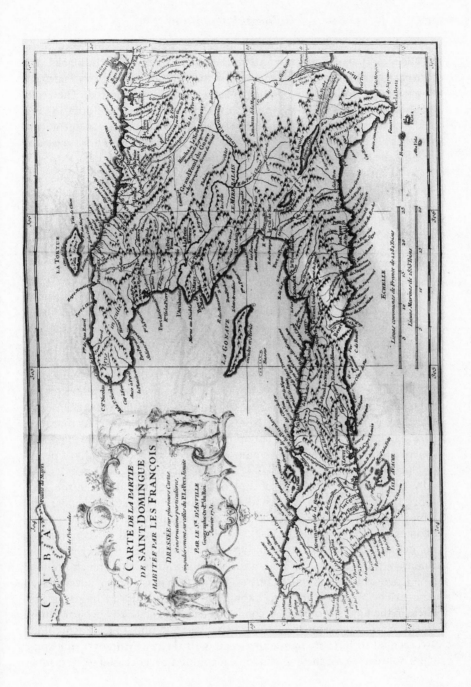

CARTE DE LA PARTIE
DE SAINT-DOMINGUE
HABITÉE PAR LES FRANÇOIS

DRESSÉE sur plusieurs Cartes
et instructions particulieres,
singulierement sur celle du Pr. et Pers. Jesuite

PAR LE Sr. D'ANVILLE
Geographe Ord.re du Roi
Janvier 1731.

ECHELLE
Lieuë commune de France de 2282 Toises
Lieuë Marine de 2853 Toises

100 males, there were 175 black females per 100 males.[281] A similar situation prevailed on Guadeloupe in 1730 among 1,262 free coloureds, blacks, and natives. The adult sex ratios among mulattos and métis was 109 males per 100 females, while at 134 among blacks it was less balanced. The really significant difference, however, lay in the proportion of children in each racial group: mulattos and métis 52.6 percent, blacks 34.1 percent, and natives 30.3 percent.[282] These may have been artificially raised, however, by the absence of white fathers from the populations being counted.

1.8 CONCLUSION

Colonial demography remains in its infancy, but it seems clear that no model of French colonial demographic behaviour existed. At the most general level whites were replacing native populations in North America while blacks replaced natives in the West Indies. French colonial populations displayed great diversity not simply owing to differences between their tropical and temperate locations, but because more profound differences between the colonies occurred in each zone owing to economic activity and the contingencies of warfare. Each colony's demography was also more complex than is often thought. To what degree size and structure were due to local processes and to kinds of economic activity remains to be explored in the following chapters.

Colonial populations were among the most free during the seventeenth and eighteenth centuries. European and African peasant societies came nowhere near the openness of the young frontier societies in the Americas that were growing amid the wreckage of collapsing aboriginal populations. These new societies had no demographic traditions; indeed, they did not have demographic histories.

By 1730, the development of indigo and sugar plantations in the West Indies had transformed what had been colonies of white settlement into colonies of exploitation based on African slave labour. From slave-owning colonies to slave societies, slavery was now fundamental to economic life and defined and shaped the social lives of all who lived there. Despite the similarity provided by the plantation-sugar complex, the French colonial experience was not similar to others. In the first place, sugar never played the overwhelming role in the economies of the French West Indies as elsewhere in the English colonies. Second, social change generally occurred more slowly over half a century or more between 1670 and 1730. Each colony also seemed to have its own experience with slavery. Moreover, the small white populations in the French tropical colonies never ceased to be frontier

---

[281] Col., C⁹ᴮ 5 extract from Mithon to Navy Council, 26 July 1719; also Marine Bᴵ 43, ff. 95-6v.

[282] Satineau, *Histoire de la Guadeloupe*, 382–3.

communities before 1730. In North America, Acadians, Canadians, and residents of Île Royale rapidly transformed their communities into different but equally unusual societies. Acadia grew virtually independent of any but local forces into a republic of subsistence farmers, while Canada rapidly evolved toward a replica of a western European peasant society. On Île Royale, neither sugar nor fur but fish and trade shaped the contours of a society without agriculture.

French expansion overseas was not embedded in a matrix of a rapidly increasing metropolitan population or expanding maritime commerce, nor was it an imperial endeavour. French governments were concerned with territorial acquisition, but the question of settlement remained ambiguous. French statesmen were populationists opposed to emigration. They hoped colonial acquisitions would increase French prestige, encourage trade, and contribute to the enrichment of the nation, but they did little to promote investment in shipping or encourage people to leave France and settle in the Americas. While French colonies were state directed – indeed, French authorities were obsessed with regulation and control – they were not really creations of absolute monarchy. Their development was profoundly shaped by the small number of Europeans who migrated to them and the small proportion of Africans carried there in French ships. Colonial institutions imported from France had little effect in shaping the contours of emerging colonial societies, which largely arose from the interplay of biology, economics, and contingency.

2

Settlements and Societies

2.1 INTRODUCTION

Colonial societies emerged spontaneously from individual seeds scattered over a wide variety of environmental conditions, mutating into something new rather than evolving from old French roots carefully transplanted into new environments. One thing was clear by 1670. People, both slave and free, were constructing the settlements and fashioning the societies emerging in the colonies. French colonial historiography has long been bedeviled by the opposite proposition. Whether concerning Canada or Saint-Domingue, historians have viewed the French state as the primary agent in the development of French colonies. Individual colonists and enterprises were essential to any colony's growth to be sure, but the French government, it is often claimed, was the key to that development.[1] The reason for the predominance of this view is interesting but need not concern us. Suffice it to assert that material factors, social institutions, and economies far more than metropolitan government erected French colonial structures and shaped their contours. Though social institutions can be traced to France, their colonial forms often became something else. The population and social makeup of each colony was like nothing found in France. All French colonial societies were multiethnic and multicultural, but each was unique. The product of economies of production and exchange, colonial social relations remained largely in a state of flux everywhere in the French Americas between 1670 and 1730.

---

[1]   Cf. W. J. Eccles, *Canada Under Louis XIV, 1663–1701* (Toronto: McClelland and Stewart, 1964), 251–2; and James E. McClellan III, *Colonialism and Science: Saint Domingue in the Old Regime* (Baltimore and London: The Johns Hopkins University Press, 1992), 9. Pierre Pluchon, *Histoire de la colonisation française*, Tome 1, *Le Premier Empire coloniale des origines à la Restauration* (Paris: Fayard, 1991) assumed there was a national interest obvious to all participants who were morally bound to follow it.

Though the linkages are not always clear, by the second quarter of the eighteenth century, the basic structures of these societies had emerged and were in place in the colonies.

Attitudes, values, and beliefs, what are sometimes collectively termed *mentalités*, of immigrants changed slowly in the face of the New World's shocking novelty. All the more so as the familiar institutions, customs, and routines that enclosed social life at home were incompletely transferred to the Americas and only partially recreated. Not all the institutions that emerged in the colonies owed their origins to France. Some were rooted in Africa and others in America itself. The new societies that appeared were not mirror images of the worlds left behind, nor were they the product of a single set of factors giving rise to a general type of French colonial society, one that was Catholic and authoritarian. Social relations in each colony evolved differently. Some emerged to be quite unique while others had more in common with non-French societies that engaged in similar forms of production. To understand this and grasp the nature of the multifaceted French colonial experience, one must consider material conditions; the legal framework of owning land and inheritance; the elusive characteristics of different social groups, including some never seen in France; and analysis of the institutions that enclosed and preyed upon social life: the family, the seigneury, the plantation, the parish, and the town. Above all, the social worlds of the French American colonies were made by the colonists, slaves and natives, themselves.

The Bourbon government's settlement policies and plans for social formation were as incoherent as its colonial immigration policy. While it encouraged indentured servants, bondsmen, former soldiers, and young women to settle in the Windward Islands and in Canada, it refused to allow its own Protestants access to the colonies. The case of Jews is instructive. After excluding them in the mid-1680s, the Crown ignored their reappearance in the colonies during the 1720s. Government leaders failed to make up their minds about whether to transport convicted malefactors to increase colonial numbers. Whatever measures were adopted, for however brief or long periods of time, they failed to affect the development of colonial populations in the Americas. Colonial societies remained chiefly the product of human interaction with geographical and environmental conditions, local modes of production, and circumstances largely beyond the government's ability to control.

Louis XIV's government facilitated marriages in the colonies and offered financial rewards to promote the growth of large families, but these measures were cast in unrealistic terms and did not significantly contribute to family formation.[2] The government even failed to prevent the return of

2   Louise Dechêne, *Habitants and Merchants in Seventeenth Century Montreal*, trans. Liana Vardi (Montreal and Kingston: McGill-Queen's University Press, [1974] 1992), 56.

migrants to France. In the West Indies, naval and merchant captains needing to replace crew members lost through death and desertion provided returning immigrants with an easy way home. More than 400 colonists reportedly left Martinique in 1693 alone.[3] In the case of Canada, fewer than one-third of all arriving emigrants remained in the colony for a sufficient length of time to establish a family. Some immigrants died during the transatlantic crossing or soon after arriving in the colony. Others deserted to the south. The vast majority went home as quickly as they could arrange their passage. The high levels of natural growth of the French colonial populations in Canada and Acadia had nothing to do with any government policy whether under Louis XIV, the Regent, or Louis XV. As with population growth, settlement and social formation occurred in response to changing material conditions in the colonies.

Any colony's social formation was a complex process. Countless factors influenced development so that no one society can be said to be typical of French colonies. French traditions, institutions, and government policies and actions affected social formation, but only along with environment, climate and typography, demography, war, forms of production, capital, and markets or the lack thereof. The history of land concessions in the seigneuries of La Prairie and Sault Saint-Louis on the south shore of the St. Lawrence River opposite Montreal best illustrates war's constraining effect on settlement. Eighty-five land concessions totaling 4,297 arpents were granted between 1672 and 1681, while only 67 (7,865 arpents) appeared during the next thirty years. Following these decades of warfare, 256 concessions totaling 18,232 arpents were granted between 1712 and 1731.[4] Some factors were more important than others at particular times, but which ones seem to depend on each historian's school of thought. The currently fashionable "genes, germs, and geography" school that denies the influence of human exceptionalism is a fad. History continues to be about people rather than things. The challenge is to think about how they interacted with each other and with the world in which they lived.

2.2 MATERIAL CONDITIONS

Local space and environments affected the historical development of individual colonies in ways that historians are just now beginning to explore. The physical settings of colonies fundamentally affected their social organisation. Geographical location, climate, topography, and soil type profoundly

3 E.g., Col., C⁸ᴬ 7, ff. 139–41v, 336–56, Dumaitz to Pontchartrain, 2 July 1692 and 16 June 1693.
4 Louis Lavallée, *La Prairie en Nouvelle France, 1647–1760, étude d'histoire sociale* (Montréal et Kingston: McGill-Queen's University Press, 1992), 70–1.

influenced the nature of production and exchange of each one. Fishing, for example, required little or no settlement at all because it had no need of agricultural support. The small societies at Placentia and its successor colony Île Royale were largely transient and never self-sufficient. Fishermen lived scattered along the shores of Newfoundland and Île Royale largely beyond government influence. The rich Bay of Fundy marshlands of peninsular Acadia (today Nova Scotia) shaped the subsequent agricultural society as clearly as any sculptor's knife.[5] The clay deposits in the glacial tills of the St. Lawrence Valley also exerted a strong influence over the rural settlements that arose there. The worthlessness of the sandy soils around Mobile Bay and on Dauphin Island on the north coast of the Gulf of Mexico rendered the first French settlements in the region useless and forced the survivors to move to the great alluvial basin of the Mississippi River. Though slavery was ultimately the greatest force in shaping West Indian societies, the fragile volcanic soils of the islands that enclose the Caribbean Sea and the nature of the island microclimates affected agricultural everywhere.[6] The topography of Saint-Domingue transformed that colony into at least three distinct societies.[7]

None of the local colonial geographies was contiguous to France. All were far away in both time and space. All the West Indian islands were closer to France than New France. Newfoundland was far from Breton fishing ports, but any ship on the Grand Banks was a brief two- or three-week sail away from France. Geographically and climatically the islands of the Lesser Antilles fall into two arcs, an inner and an outer one. The larger, inner arc composed of mountainous volcanic islands includes Martinique, Basse-Terre (Guadeloupe), Les Saintes, Saint-Christopher, and Sainte-Croix. The eastern half of Guadeloupe, called Grand Terre, Marie Galante, Desirade, Saint-Martin, and Saint-Barthélémy are the French islands of the outer arc. They are flat, primarily formed of limestone, and have drier climates than their volcanic neighbours. Indeed, the lack of water so reduced Grande Terre's fitness for settlement that it remained largely uninhabited before the eighteenth century, when planters acquired sufficient capital to build needed cisterns.[8] Saint-Domingue occupying the western portion of Hispaniola is the only French portion of the four islands known as the Greater Antilles that enclose the northern side of the Caribbean Sea. About two-thirds of the colony is mountainous terrain unsuitable for cultivation. In the west, the valley of the Artibonite River, which rises in Spanish Santo Domingo and empties

5 Clark, *Acadia*, 48–9, 53–4.
6 Lucien-René Abénon, *La Guadeloupe de 1670 à 1759: Etude politique, économique, et sociale*, 2 vols. (Paris: L'Harmattan, 1987), 1: 23–5.
7 McClellan, *Colonialism and Science*, 24–5.
8 Jean-Baptiste Labat, *Nouveau voyage aux Isles de l'Amérique*. 2 vols. (La Haye: P. Husson, T. Johnson, P. Gosse, Jvan Duren, R. Alberts, and C. Le Vier [1722] 1724), 1: 139–40.

into the Gulf of Gonâve, and the Plain of Cul-de-Sac are ideal for sugar. All these islands are south of the Tropic of Cancer and surrounded by warm waters throughout the year. The constant moisture-laden trade winds keep their climates moderate. Rainfall is heaviest on the north coasts. Indeed, the areas southeast of Mount Pelée, which rises over 1,400 metres on Martinique, northwest of La Souffrière, rising 1,467 metres on Guadaloupe and the west and southern parts of Saint-Domingue are semiarid. The Artibonite Plain receives an average annual rainfall of only 0.76 metres, whereas tropical rain forests dominate Saint-Domingue's northern coast.[9] Though lush, dense vegetation characterize the West Indies, their environments are fragile. Soil erodes easily and quickly, and volcanic soils are not very fertile.

Weather profoundly affected colonial life. The length of winter at Quebec reinforced its harshness. It constrained shipping to a brief six months of the year, from May to October, after which travel ceased until sufficient snow and frost permitted snowshoes and horse-drawn sleighs (*carrioles*) to alleviate some of the isolation. At Quebec, snow ordinarily accumulated six or seven feet high, leaving only very narrow passages between houses and ground floor windows.[10] After storms residents often found that they could not move at all.[11] Sudden thaws, on the other hand, sometimes left the colonists up to their ears in mud. At Montreal, located to the southwest, winter lasted only four months. The region also possessed some of the best soils in all of eastern Canada.[12] Though these two factors eventually drew settlers westward, weak economic forces retarded the phenomenon, leaving the Quebec district the most heavily settled during the French regime.

Unpredictable hurricanes frequently crossed the Lesser Antilles between July and October, causing extraordinary damage to lives and property. On 12 August 1680, the worst hurricane in Martinique's history left hardly a building, tree, or plant standing. It ruined even the stone citadel at Fort Royal and sank several ships laid up in the normally safe refuge of nearby Cul-de-Sac.[13] Fourteen years later high seas from a hurricane carried away the Dauphine Battery and adjacent buildings of the fort at St. Pierre, cast ships ashore, and swept vast amounts of soil out to sea. Forty-six houses and buildings worth an estimated one million livres were lost.[14] Hurricanes

---

9   See David Watts, *The West Indies: Patterns of Development Culture and Environmental Change since 1492* (Cambridge: Cambridge University Press, 1987), 1–40 for an excellent summary of the West Indian environment.

10 Quoted in Kathryn Young, *Kin, Commerce, and Community: Merchants in the Port of Quebec from 1717 to 1745* (New York: Peter Lang, 1995), 143, n23.

11 Ibid., 12.   12 Dechêne, *Habitants and Merchants*, 129–31.

13 Col., C[8A], 2, ff. 376–9 Patoulet to Colbert, 18 August 1680; and ibid., ff. 380–4 Procèsverbal des dégats provoqués par l'ouragan aux batiments de Fort Royal.

14 Ibid., 8, ff. 274–5 Gabaret to Pontchartrain, 10 November 1694; and ibid., ff. 276–7, "Estat des maisons et cazes qui ont estées emportées par le mauvais temps au quartier de fort St. Pierre", 10 November 1694.

ravaged Guadeloupe in 1713 and 1714. For five years during the mid-1720s, hurricanes, together with torrential rains, nearly wiped out the island's economy as they annually swept across the island, destroying not only sugar cane but slaves' provisions: manioc, potatoes, and yams. For the first time in their history, colonists kept themselves armed as starving slaves, who were dying at a rate of 20 a day in March of 1723, and ate anything they could find. Guadeloupe, always subordinate to its smaller neighbour, became merely an appendage of Martinique.[15] On 7 November 1727, Martinique suffered the most violent earthquake ever to strike the island. The shocks lasted three days and most strong buildings collapsed, though few lives were lost.[16] Total losses attributed to the earthquake and the subsequent loss of cacao trees exceeded 8 million livres.[17] Droughts such as the one that afflicted Cap François in 1726 were not uncommon. Fires were another hazard. One that broke out at Basse-Terre, Guadeloupe, between midnight and one o'clock on the night of 11–12 May 1681, destroyed more than 50 houses in less than three hours.[18] It also destroyed all hopes of a prosperous year despite an abundance of merchandise and good prices. A fire that devastated Quebec's lower town in 1682 led to a decline in population between 1681 and 1685.[19]

Disease was another material condition affecting colonial development, but how seriously remains an open question. Europeans and Africans found themselves in new pathogenic environments afflicted by diseases in both endemic and epidemic forms. Both also lived in unsanitary conditions. Acclimatization was especially difficult in the West Indies. The fact that Africans came from semitropical and tropical areas made no difference. New pathogens abounded, and Africans, like Europeans, were highly vulnerable owing to their unhealthy state and the brutality of their working conditions. Conversely, the absence of endemic diseases may have been one of the greatest forces shaping the small Acadian settlements by encouraging large families. In general, however, the migratory exchange of pathogens around the world following the quarter century between Columbus and Magellan meant that bacterial, viral, and parasitic infections struck the new forming societies in unpredictable ways. By 1670 syphilis was endemic in France and French colonies. Malaria and dysentery were endemic in the West Indies, and yellow fever, known as *le mal de Siam* after a ship from the East Indies introduced the disease into the French West Indies in 1690, quickly became so. Typhus,

---

[15] Col., C7A 6 (n.f.) La Malmaison to Pontchartrain, 23 September 1713; Abénon, *La Guadeloupe de 1670–1759*, 1: 161, 236–40.

[16] Col., C8A 38, f. 399 Blondel to Maurepas, 1 December 1727; Daney, *Histoire de la Martinique*, 2: 73.

[17] Ibid., 40, ff. 58–73 Extrait des procès verbaux (signed) Champigny and Blondel, 13 April 1728.

[18] Col., C7A 3, Hinselin to Colbert, 22 May 1681.

[19] Rémi Chénier, *Quebec: A French Colonial Town in America, 1660 to 1690* (Ottawa: Parks Services, Environment Canada, 1991), 185.

or the bloody flux, became so common during the eighteenth century that it was called ship fever. Shipborne fevers reached New France in 1710–11, 1718, 1720–21, and later.[20]

In New France, in 1687, an unknown contagious disease – perhaps a form of plague – killed 1,400 people. During the first half of 1703 smallpox claimed 400 victims, local Indians as well as French; 8 percent of the European population succumbed in Montreal.[21] Measles, in violent viral form, often struck adults in the West Indies with fatal consequences.[22] Nevertheless, the overall effect of contagion may have been less significant than expected. Smallpox, measles, influenza, whooping cough, and typhus all struck New France, yet careful examination of the available vital statistics indicates that birth and marriage rates generally remained unaffected. Mortality crises were temporary events that had no lasting effect on colonial social formation.[23] Malaria, yellow, fever, and other pestilential fevers struck the tropical colonies with devastating force. Disease and early death may have played a far greater role in shaping societies and attitudes there than in New France. However, if death was the first fact of life, vital forces always remained sufficiently strong to overcome it.[24]

2.3 LANDHOLDING

Though nature in all its forms appeared dominant, it quickly gave way before the African-European onslaught. By 1670, agriculture and settlement were becoming the first order of business everywhere. Even in Canada, where trade had always predominated, the appearance of women and the formation of families were laying the foundations of the largest ethnically French community in the Western Hemisphere. The French had been installed in Canada and the Lesser Antilles for more than a generation, but little existed to show for all the effort. Canada remained chiefly a fur-trading colony and a mission field to Amerindians. Settlement had been left largely in the hands of devout lay Catholics who aimed to erect a colonial society of Christian perfection in order to aid the conversion of the natives. The islands of St. Christopher, Martinique, and Guadeloupe, on the other hand, were intended as colonies of settlement from their initial establishment in the 1620s and 30s. Buccaneers on the island of Tortuga were beginning to settle the north coast of Saint-Domingue, where they hunted feral cattle and pigs and grew a little

---

[20] Dale Miquelon, *New France, 1701–1744, A Supplement to Europe* (Toronto: McClelland and Stewart, 1987), 225.

[21] Ibid., and Dechêne, *Habitants and Merchants*, 59–60.

[22] McClellan, *Colonialism and Science*, 29.

[23] Dechêne, *Habitants and Merchants*, 59–61.

[24] E. g. Liliane Chauleau, *Case-Pilote, Le Prêcheur, Basse-Pointe: Étude démographique sur le nord de la Martinique (XVII e siècle)*, (Paris: L'Harmattan, 1990), 26.

tobacco. In Acadia, long abandoned to the English, the few settlers were returning to French rule. Only following the royal government's suppression of the earlier monopoly companies in 1663 did settlement become an object of policy and direct assistance. Paradoxically, the government initially ignored already-established colonies and turned once again to Guiana to institute its first major effort at directly assisted settlement.

It is true that immigrants were assisted to Canada and the colony received its first intendant with a mandate to encourage rapid settlement, but Colbert's major effort dispatched an expedition of 650 settlers and four companies of infantry to Cayenne under the authority of Lieutenant General Alexandre de Prouville de Tracy. Colbert's decision to ignore the growing settlements in the Windward Islands reflected his lack of knowledge about the colonies.[25] His Guiana adventure, which failed, reveals how little he knew about the Americas and the debt he owed his political enemy, Nicolas Fouquet.[26] Tracy had a double mission: first, to capture Cayenne from the Dutch and leave the settlers there under the authority of Antoine-Joseph Le Febvre de la Barre, and second, to install royal governors in the French West Indies and in Canada.[27] He accomplished the first task during 1664 and early the following year sailed for Canada to take command of troops sent from France to carry war to the Iroquois and ensure the installation of new royal officials. Colbert also commissioned 30-year-old Jean Talon as intendant of New France, and sent him off the same spring to reorganize the colony's administration and supervise settlement of new immigrants who arrived during the next half dozen years. What remains memorable, however, is the ineffectiveness of most of the government's legislation concerning settlement. Conditions in the colonies even altered the normal system of French land tenure.

Land preceded colonisation. Uncleared, it was virtually worthless to the settlers, remaining so abundant relative to population, even in the Windward Islands, that during the seventeenth century they continued to receive free tracts until the century's end. The French system of land tenure also preceded settlement, and while the pattern of occupation tended to follow the contours of the land closely, the legal system which blurred the distinction between land ownership and land possession erected contours of its own that gave further shape and meaning to the emerging colonial societies.

There are two memorable features of the land owning system in the French colonies. The first is that very little land was bought or sold, nor was it granted for later sale to occupiers. It was granted freely. The consequence of

[25] Stewart L. Mims, *Colbert's West India Policy* (New Haven: Yale University Press, 1912), 62–7, summarizes the reasons but does not draw this conclusion.

[26] See Philip P. Boucher, "Comment se forme un ministre coloniale: l'initiation de Colbert, 1651–1664", *RHAF* 37, no. 3 (décembre 1983), 431–52; and his "A Colonial Company at the Time of the Fronde", 43–58.

[27] Léopold Lamontage, "Prouville de Tracy, Alexandre de", *DCB*, 1: 554–7.

this policy was that land was imperfectly integrated into the capitalist system of production in French colonies. The second remarkable feature of French colonial land owning was that the seigneurial system took root only in New France. Elsewhere land ownership reflected the new colonial environment in America. This occurred largely because new economic opportunities for agricultural exploitation quickly appeared in most tropical colonies but not in the northern ones. In Canada, a combination of abundant land, the inability of the fur trade to generate ancillary occupations (what economists call forward or backward linkages) or even to absorb the naturally increasing population, and lack of market opportunities led to the spontaneous generation of a unique colonial society of peasants whose possession of the land, though unshakeable, was blurred by the proprietory rights of their lords. In short, local conditions gave life to a land-tenure system that proved ineffective and never took hold elsewhere in the Americas.

Often thought to be no more than a collection of a few quaint customs, as in *The Marriage of Figaro* when his seigneur claims the right to bed his bride, feudalism survived into eighteenth-century France.[28] In August of 1789, Frenchmen even thought they were abolishing it.[29] In its land-owning guise, feudalism in Canada endured beyond the middle of the nineteenth century, more than ninety years after the colony ceased to be French. The seigneurial system was primarily designed to allocate income to members of the first two orders of Old Regime society: clergy and nobles.[30] It was only secondarily intended to accord land to immigrant settlers. It was based on the feudal notion that all land should be held from lords, both temporal and spiritual, who possessed proprietory rights over the fruits of peasant labour. This should not appear very startling. After examining the *cens et rentes*, today's cynic in a liberal democracy might claim the feudal burden was simply an early version of property taxes and a relatively light one at that.

Early proprietary companies in the Windward Islands, Acadia, and Canada were reluctant to give title or to acknowledge ownership of land to non-noble, indentured bondsmen who cleared and cultivated it. The resulting confusion between settlers who squatted on "their" land and lord-proprietors who claimed "ownership" produced an ever growing tangle of claims and counterclaims to properties, most of which had never been

[28] See J. Q. C. Mackrell, *The Attack on "Feudalism" in Eighteenth-Century France* (London and Toronto: Routledge & Kegan Paul and University of Toronto Press, 1973), 1–2. See also, Pierre Goubert, *The Ancien Régime, French Society, 1600–1750*, trans., Steve Cox (New York: Harper Torchbooks, [1969] 1973, 15–17, 96–7.

[29] John Markoff, *The Abolition of Feudalism: Peasants, Lords, and Legislators in the French Revolution* (University Park: Pennsylvania State University Press, 1996).

[30] Fernand Ouellet, "Seigneurial Property and Social Structure, 1663–1840" in *Economy, Class, and Nation in Quebec: Interpretative Essays,* ed. and trans., Jacques A. Bernier (Toronto: Copp Clark Pitman, 1991), 61.

surveyed, that could only end in chaos. It was no coincidence that by 1670 the first land registers, or *papiers terriers*, were being produced throughout the colonies. In 1666, the Sulpicians, the corporate seigneur of the island of Montreal, prepared their first land register.[31] Four years later Colbert ordered similar registers prepared for the entire islands of Martinique, Guadeloupe, and the French parts of Saint-Christopher in an attempt to sort out the growing confusion.[32] Land was allotted in a relatively orderly fashion, but disorder continued as homesteaders often proved unable to demonstrate clear title to their original concessions. Nevertheless, though the legal system of land holding supported seigneurs' policies of settlement, colonists often contested their ability to define boundaries and land use.[33]

Other factors confounded the issue. When Jean Talon proposed to settle new immigrants in villages which were more defensible against Indian attack, they proved to be a failure. Settlers preferred the more scattered result of occupying their own *rotures* along the river.[34] Plans for three radial villages north of Quebec were not renewed. Colonists may have seen them as official attempts to regulate their behaviour and control their movements, but just as likely they preferred to live on their own lands, which were sufficient to support a family.[35] In France, peasants often possessed a number of separate fields of insufficient size to support their families, which led them to live in villages. In 1674, Colbert was still advising Governor Frontenac that the king wished him to "crowd [settlers] together, and group them and settle them in towns and villages, and so give them the greater possibility of protecting themselves well", but to no avail.[36] Following the failure of the West India Company in 1674, the islands reverted to the king, and land was held in *franc-aleu* directly from the Crown. It quickly became marketable and was freely bought and sold. The sale of plantations for more than 1 million livres was not unknown in the 1720s.[37]

The great distinction between land in the West Indies and in New France was its changing relative availability and value. Economy and geography affected these distinctions, but the switch from tobacco to sugar production in the islands forced small landowners to sell. The techniques of sugar

---

[31] Dechêne, *Habitants and Merchants*, 134–6.

[32] AN, SOM, G¹ 468 Abrègé général du denombrement des hommes . . . en l'Isle Guadeloupe; ibid., 471 ditto re: St. Christopher; and ibid., 470, ff. 143–268 Estat du procès verbal des terres de l'isle de la Martinique.

[33] Colin M. Coates, *The Metamorphoses of Landscape and Community in Early Quebec* (Montreal and Kingston: McGill-Queen's University Press, 2000), 35.

[34] A *roture* was a piece of land held from a seigneur that could not be subinfeudated.

[35] R. C. Harris, *The Seigneurial System in Early Canada: A Geographical Study* (Kingston and Montreal: McGill-Queen's University Press, [1966] 1984), 177–9.

[36] Col., B 6, ff. 28–35 Colbert to Frontenac, 17 May 1674.

[37] E. g. Col., C⁸ᴬ 36, ff. 1–8v Blondel to Maurepas, 18 January 1726.

manufacture placed limits on plantation size. By 1720 the occupation of Martinique was complete and land had become very valuable.[38]

The absence of *retrait lignager* in the West Indies illustrates the modern, capitalist attitude toward land sales there. Though the Custom of Paris was registered in the islands and allowed *retraits* – the right of one whose inheritance was affected by a sale to assume the alienated property on payment of the purchase price within one year to the buyer – even when land was in *franc-aleu*, the custom had never been observed. Moreover, the Superior Council of Martinique blocked attempts to bring *retraits* against land sales, and the minister was independently advised to issue a declaration that lands would no longer be subject to the custom.[39] In New France, on the other hand, *retrait lignager* persisted. There, the absence of commercial agriculture and the extremely favourable man-to-land ratio constrained ownership and discouraged speculation. Land remained unaffected by feudal estate liabilities, for merchants would not take it and usually did not extend loans beyond the value of moveables (i.e., livestock and tools).[40]

The seigneurial system was more in name than real in Acadia. Having been under English control for 16 years between 1654 and 1670, Acadian settlers ignored those who claimed seigneurial rights over their lands. Though the French government largely ignored Acadia for the next 40 years, it was sensitive to those already occupying the land. New grants to seigneurial proprietors in Acadia usually acknowledged the rights of those already occupying the soil.[41] There were no seigneuries at Minas, which became Acadia's largest settlement and principal agricultural center at the end of the seventeenth century with one sawmill and seven or eight gristmills reported there.[42] In 1699, Governor Saint Ovide de Brouillan's attempt to have seigneuries granted along the southeast coast to himself and his cronies failed.[43]

The seigneurial system was not imposed by the Crown, indeed, Louis XIV did not like it, and even in Canada not all land was held *en seigneurie*. Both the Company of New France and the king granted lots *en roture* or nonnobly, and Jean Talon in the 1660s and Governor-General Frontenac and Intendant Champigny during the century's final decade did the same. Louis

38   Louis-Philippe May, *Histoire économique de la Martinique, (1635–1763)*, reédité (Fort-de-France: Société de distribution et de culture, [1930] 1972), 65–6.
39   Col., C⁸ᴬ 36, ff. 159–61 Memoir of Superior Council, 6 April 1726; ibid., f. 158 feuille au ministre 26 August 1726. See Harris, *The Seigneurial System in Early Canada*, 57, 230.
40   Dechêne, *Habitants and Merchants*, 137, 229.
41   Naomi E. S. Griffiths, *The Contexts of Acadian History, 1686–1784* (Kingston: McGill-Queen's University Press, 1992), 20; see also J.-R. Comeau, "Leneuf de la Vallière", *DCB*, 2: 409–10.
42   J. C. Webster, ed., *Acadia at the End of the Seventeenth Century* (St. John: The New Brunswick Museum, 1934), 132–33.
43   Col., C¹¹ᴰ 4, f. 81v Memoir of Brouillon attached to his letter to Pontchartrain, 6 October 1701.

XIV had been convinced since the beginning of his rule that seigneurs were ineffective colonizers. He blamed them for lagging settlement in Canada. In 1672, the Crown considerably tightened up the loose conditions that had originally governed seigneurial grants, reduced the size of seigneuries, and ordered that land be cleared or forfeited.[44] It renewed the threat seven years later. By the early eighteenth century the seigneurial system had fallen even further from favour. Secretary of State Pontchartrain, writing to intendants in both the Antilles and Canada, displayed strong opposition to granting large concessions to colonists at the expense of new settlers. In reiterating the monarch's own hostility, he attacked the system in New France and forbade its extension to Louisiana. Pontchartrain also rejected Antoine Laumet de Cadillac's earlier request to create a marquisate at Detroit, and he was especially opposed to subinfeudation, or the act of conceding land nobly *en fief* with seigneurial rights.[45] Far too many seigneuries had been granted in Canada, and he accused seigneurs of hindering settlement by withholding land and demanding exorbitant rents. In 1711, Louis XIV issued some reforming decrees which required seigneurs to grant land *en roture* freely on demand and forbade them to sell it.[46] Three years later, the king also proclaimed his intention to grant no more seigneuries in Canada. Almost none were granted during the next 18 years.[47] In keeping with the government's inconsistency, however, the Crown also made no grants *en roture* or *en franc-aleu*.

The seigneurial system was never implemented in the Windward Islands. After 1674 the king granted a few *fief-nobles* as counties and marquisates in return for fealty and homage, but appropriations and concessions soon led to private property. *Lods et ventes*, a seigneurial right to levy one-twelfth of the sale price of non-noble land (i.e., a roture) that passed out of the direct line of succession, quickly disappeared, perhaps, because there was a serious war going on. The desire to establish a fighting militia capable of defending the colony did not lead to the decline of the seigneurial system in New France, but it may have contributed to putting an end to it quickly in the islands. Seigneurial dues stood between the habitant-occupier of the land by allowing the seigneurial owner to claim rights, which may have discouraged habitants desperately wanted by governments fearful of slave revolts. The growing scarcity of white labour may also have been a factor, as was the lack of capital. However, above all the commercial, capitalist nature of sugar production put *finis* to seigneurialism in the West Indies.

44 Harris, *The Seigneurial System in Early Canada*, 26–7, 105, and 107–8.
45 Marcel Giraud, *Histoire de la Louisiane*, 4 vols. (Paris: Presses universitaires de France, 1953–1974), 1: 170 citing Col., B 28, f. 39v Pontchartrain to Vaucresson, 14 April 1706; and ibid., 30, f. 139 same to Raudot, 6 July 1709.
46 Harris, *The Seigneurial System*, 108, 198.
47 Miquelon, *New France, 1701–1744*, 195.

Concessions on Martinique followed arrangements first developed at St. Christopher where the original proprietors had granted small lots of 200 by 1,000 paces or 20 *carrés*. The island's land register of 1671 revealed the result. Little more than one-third of the entire area had been conceded, but concentration of ownership was already well-developed. More than 40 percent of all conceded land was in the hands of just 30 owners, including three who held 4,300 *carrés* (5,558.6 hectares). Less than one-sixth of the owners held two-thirds of the land, while 60 percent of all owners occupied only 15 percent of the land, chiefly on plots less than 10 *carrés*.[48] The original concessions had been halved for most habitants. By 1674 general regulations called for one-third of a concession to be cleared within three years of receipt, but even in the eighteenth century many uncleared lots remained.[49] Despite the simple conditions for acquiring land in the Windward Islands, Father Labat complained that an excessive amount of land lay in particular hands in 1700. Some colonists, possessing several grants on the same island, had cleared no more than 1.5 *carrés* to mark their possession.[50]

The shift to large land concessions on Guadeloupe, from between 10 and 20 *carreaux* to 50 to 60 *carreaux*, followed Colbert's placement of increased duties on tobacco, additional protection afforded the French sugar industry, and the improved technology in the islands for whitening sugar. By 1671, landholdings on Guadeloupe were already extremely concentrated. More than two-thirds of all conceded lands were gathered into less than 5 percent of the estates (i.e., those greater than 100 hectares). Nearly half of all properties, those of less than 10 hectares, comprised scarcely 4 percent of the lands.[51] Though covering less than 1,500 square kilometres, perceptible differences existed on the island. Small, cultivated holdings predominated south of a line between Capesterre and Bouillante, and large estates dominated in the north around Cul-de-Sac. Finally, by 1671 sugar had become Guadeloupe's only significant export crop. Indeed, the colony's sugar production roughly equaled Martinique's. Nearly 90 percent of all the land devoted to export crops, more than 3,000 hectares, was in sugar. Nearly as much land was devoted to producing provisions. Only 100 hectares was given over to cultivating tobacco, the island's first crop.[52]

---

48 Eugène Revert, *La Martinique, étude géographique et humaine* (Paris: Nouvelles Editions Latines, 1949), 255–6.

49 Guy Lasserre, *La Guadeloupe, étude géographique,* 2 vols. (Bordeaux: Union française d'impresion, 1961), 1: 333–7.

50 Jean-Baptiste Labat, *Nouveau voyage aux Isles de l'Amérique* (La Haye: P. Husson, T. Johnson, P. Gosse, Jvan Duren, R. Alberts, and C. Le Vier [1722] 1724), 1, pt. 2: 199; see Maurice Satineau, *Histoire de la Guadeloupe sous l'ancien régime, 1635–1789,* (Paris: Payot, 1928), 113–17.

51 Christian Schnakenbourg, "Le 'terrier' de 1671 et le partage de la terre en Guadeloupe au XVIIE siècle" *RFHOM,* 67 (1980), 42.

52 Ibid., 49–50.

In 1669, the colony had 113 plantations. The number declined to only 65 by 1697 chiefly owing to Colbert's policies of encouraging diversification, failing to deal with the labour supply problem, and deliberately undermining the island's economy by levying a punitive tax in 1682 on sugar refined in the islands in order to protect metropolitan refiners, forcing planters to deliver muscovado (*sucre brut*) at low prices.[53] Enemy hostilities during the Nine Years' War contributed to the decline, but government constraints were the chief cause of this failure of economic growth. Recovery during the War of the Spanish Succession, when the government's grip on the colonies slipped, supports this claim.

Claims to seigneurial rights seriously impeded settlement on Guadeloupe. As late as 1696, the heirs of the original proprietary lords who had been forced to sell the island to the West India Company in 1664 sought to exercise seigneurial rights over the district stretching from Gros Morne to Rivière Salée on Basse-Terre, but no settler would take up land other than from the king who gave it freely excluding even fealty and homage.[54] Seventeen years later, Governor-General Phélypeaux complained that "infinite breaches of trust, confusion, and disorderliness" were present without exception in all the concessions on Guadeloupe. He doubted whether any man living possessed sufficient rectitude, integrity, lack of bias, and understanding to sort out the mess. Abuses were common. M. Cloche, nephew of the island's governor, was a tyrant who ordered unauthorised slave corvées to build roads throughout his property, while M. Houel, descendant of the island's original owners, failed to develop his enormous holdings, which he had erected into a marquisate. Despite room for 60 plantations, there were none.[55]

Larger properties employing 30 to 40 slaves in 1669 were worked by 60 to 70 slaves by 1692.[56] Labat's description of an ideal plantation of 300 *carrés*, approximately 300 hectares, however, appears excessively large.[57] Grande Terre, Guadeloupe's other island, was settled during the early part of the eighteenth century. In 1732 it contained 651 properties. Only 119 of them were sugar plantations, generally between 100 and 200 hectares. Others were much smaller and a few were much larger, but the majority of homesteads were confined to the inhospitable margins along the south and southeast portion of the island where low rainfall rendered sugar cultivation unsuitable.[58]

Census data for 1687 reveal the continued mediocrity and extent of plantations in the Lesser Antilles. There were still fewer than two slaves for every

53 Lasserre, *La Guadeloupe*, 1: 352.
54 Labat, *Nouveau Voyage aux Isles*, 1, pt 2: 134.
55 Col., C^8A 19, ff. 40v–4, Phélypeaux to Pontchartrain, 16 January 1713.
56 Satineau, *Histoire de la Guadeloupe*, 121 n3.
57 Labat, *Nouveau voyage aux Isles*, 1, pt. 3: 323.
58 La Serre, *La Guadeloupe*, 1: 349–51.

white person. Among the latter, 8,000 to 9,000 seem to have been indentured whereas only 5,000 to 6,000 were heads of households. When added to
some 27,000 slaves, there were approximately 35,000 coerced agricultural
labourers or seven to eight workers per plantation. These low numbers
strongly underlie the still scattered, middling character of estates in the
French islands despite the presence of large land holdings.[59] Lack of capital and poor access to slave labour left the French islands in this condition
until the end of the century.

On Saint-Domingue the majority of colonists still lived by hunting during
the 1670s, though the number of feral cattle and pigs was rapidly declining. Those with plots took little care of them. In 1673, Governor-General
de Baas reported that little of the forest cover had been cleared.[60] Always
suspicious of the unruly population of buccaneers, Colbert did little to assist settlement on Saint-Domingue. Governor Pouançay later claimed settlers
had abandoned more than 100 properties at Cul-de-Sac alone because of the
poor prices for tobacco paid by monopolists.[61] Though Pouançay referred to
habitations, he did not mean plantations. The word still had a generic meaning referring to homesteads. Before the plantation complex reached Saint-
Domingue, early in the eighteenth century, properties were many and small.
Habitants devoted themselves to growing food, indigo, and tobacco.[62] No
plantation in Nippes Parish, Saint-Domingue, during the 1720s employed
more than 50 slaves.[63]

In Canada, the shift to larger farms was a function of need rather than
market forces. Initial land concessions on Montreal Island were too small.
Habitants quickly sought to consolidate their holdings by obtaining an aug-
mentation from their seigneur or purchasing an adjoining *roture*. Between
1698 and 1731, on Côte des Neiges, forty farms all between 40 and 60 arpents in size, had evolved into a smaller number of more diverse holdings.
Whereas none initially contained more than 60 arpents, 35 years later eleven
occupied between 80 to 160 arpents. The greatest change was to the smallest lots. Nearly three-quarters of all habitants held only 40 arpents in 1698,
but fewer than one-third did so in 1731.[64] The same increase occurred in
the seigneury of Sorel, where family need to achieve self-sufficiency rather
than market conditions governed the amount of arable land in *rotures*. By

59   Gaston Martin, *Histoire de l'esclavage dans les colonies françaises* (Paris: Presses univer-
      sitaires de France, 1948), 26–7.
60   Col., C8A 1, f. 232 De Baas to Colbert, 16 April 1673.
61   Col., C9B 1 (unfoliated) Pouançay to Colbert, 4 March 1677.
62   Gabriel Debien, *Une Plantation de Saint-Domingue: La Sucrerie Galbaud du Fort (1690–
      1802)*, (Cairo: Les Presses de l'Institute français d'archéologie orientale du Caire, 1941),
      22.
63   Arlette Gautier, *Les Soeurs de solitude: la condition féminine dans l'esclavage aux Antilles
      du XVIIe au XIXe siècle* (Paris: Editions Caribéennes, 1985), 83.
64   Dechêne, *Habitants and Merchants*, 150.

1724, the average arable holding had increased 75 percent per household from four decades earlier.[65] As Canadian seigneurialism grew, however, it increasingly enmeshed the population in its toils of appropriation and debt.

Elsewhere in continental French America, the same pattern of dispersed settlement in long lots perpendicular to major rivers appeared, but without the seigneurial system.[66] Settlers in the upper and lower Mississippi Valley usually cultivated a mixture of crops, especially corn and rice (both non-European cereals) on 200-arpent farms. During the 1720s these homesteads gradually spread along the banks of the Mississippi between New Orleans and Point Coupée as the India Company offered settlers free land, usually with 5 arpents of river frontage and a depth of 40 arpents.[67]

Though habitants in Canada had large families, their landholdings were not fragmented despite laws of inheritance that directed heirs of non-noble lands to receive equal shares of real estate. In the West Indies, too, plantations were not broken up in fulfillment of the laws of inheritance.[68] The evolution of colonial customs in spite of the existing legal code is yet another important illustration of how colonists interacting with their environment, rather than French institutions alone, shaped the new societies. With no complimentary resources or tradition of community sharing available and an abundance of land, Canadian settlers relied solely on their land to achieve self-sufficiency. Fragmentation was impossible.[69] Despite the law, which decreed equal inheritances to all children, and the egalitarian tendencies of Canadian agrarian individualism which existed beyond market forces, land was not divided equally. Instead, one heir gradually bought out the others. While Dechêne sees this as occurring during most of the eighteenth century, Greer views the pragmatic, egalitarian spirit and harmony prevailing in the lower Richelieu Valley only during the early decades. Afterward, as land became scarcer and markets for wheat emerged, procedures with less egalitarian effects appeared.[70] Both agree, however, that equality and social harmony among Canadian habitants were functions of their self-sufficient, traditional (i.e., nonmarket) agriculture, which prevailed throughout the colony before 1730.

---

[65] Alan Greer, *Peasant, Lord, and Merchant: Rural Society in Three Quebec Parishes, 1740–1840* (Toronto: University of Toronto Press, 1985), 17–18.

[66] For an excellent review see Carl J. Ekberg, *French Roots in the Illinois Country: The Mississippi Frontier in Colonial Times* (Urbana and Chicago: University of Illinois Press, 1998), 5–30.

[67] Daniel H. Usner, Jr., *Indians, Settlers, and Slaves in a Frontier Exchange Economy: The Lower Mississippi Valley before 1783* (Chapel Hill: University of North Carolina Press, 1992), 155.

[68] Lasserre, *La Guadeloupe*, 1: 347; and Eugène Revert, *La Martinique, étude géographique et humaine* (Paris: Nouvelles Éditions Latines, 1949), 265.

[69] Dechêne, *Habitants and Merchants*, 165–8, 214–15, and 244–9; see Coates, *The Metamorphoses of Landscape and Community*, 114–19 on the lack of community in the Canadian countryside.

[70] Greer, *Peasant, Lord, and Merchant*, 74.

The same characteristics probably applied to Acadia and early Louisiana, which before 1730 was still in too formative a stage to be certain of anything.

In the West Indies, where land became increasingly scarce and ever more valuable as sugar and slavery dominated agricultural production, social inequalities became even more pronounced. By 1671 landholding in the Windward Islands was already inequitable, and this development continued without any major check during the next six decades. The same process was merely delayed on Saint-Domingue. While tobacco and indigo attracted men with little land and few slaves, land reorganisation and consolidation quickly followed during the first three decades of the eighteenth century as sugar began to play a significant role in the colony's economy.

2.4 SOCIAL GROUPS

1. Slaves

Slaves formed the largest human groups in European areas of settlement in tropical French America. Though illegal in France, slavery was present in the French colonies for more than half a century before the government introduced the Black Code in 1685. No greater characteristic distinguished metropolitan from colonial life.[71] Slavery's scale and impact also divided the colonies into two broad social categories based nominally on geography, but really on economic activity. In 1670, African slaves barely outnumbered European free men and women in the West Indies and Guiana. Thirty years later, the number of slaves in the tropical colonies had more than doubled and was nearly twice that of Europeans. This was not yet true of Guadeloupe or Saint-Domingue, but the trend to more slaves was in full swing everywhere. By 1730, the number of slaves in the French tropical colonies had increased to almost five times the number at the turn of the century, while the number of Europeans barely doubled during the six decades after 1670. Though the ratio of slaves to whites became more extreme as the century progressed, the mechanism of change was in place early on. The coloured population (both mulatto and free black) made up, as yet, an insignificant portion of the population. Their numbers had increased more than 23 times between 1670 and 1730, but they still represented less than 1.5 percent of the total. It is not clear that race was the crucial distinguishing feature. The censuses before 1730 were generally concerned with whether persons were slave or free. Fine distinctions of colour that later prevailed in Saint-Domingue do not seem to be present, but the basic racial makeup of the tropical colonies was already in existence. By 1730, slaves comprised more

---

[71] For a recent review of changing French attitudes toward slavery in France, see Sue Peabody, *"There Are No Slaves in France": The Political Culture of Race and Slavery in the Ancien Régime* (New York: Oxford University Press, 1996), 11–22.

than four-fifths of the entire population of the French West Indies, including Guiana. Though they evolved slowly, French West Indian colonies already had more in common with their English counterparts than with the northern French mainland colonies.

Most slaves were born in Africa. Their many cultures contributed to colonial social development in ways that are now being explored. Some slaves were employed in households and in colonial towns, but most were employed as agricultural labourers of various degrees of skill.[72] Though men generally outnumbered them, more women laboured in the fields as most specialised work was reserved for men.[73] Slaves suffered generally from high mortality and low birth rates. The Black Code did nothing to encourage or preserve family formation among slaves. Early French settlers encouraged reproduction of slave families within the bonds of Christian marriage, but the development of sugarcane, increases in slave arrivals in the islands, and declining slave prices led to changing priorities before 1700.[74] Reproduction continued to be encouraged but was no longer based upon marriage or family formation. During the eighteenth century, female slaves were directly targeted but resisted marriage and having children whether by white masters or male slaves. Settlers resorted to harsh penal sanctions and physical torture to halt this female slave resistance but to little avail.[75]

Subsequent slave families fended for themselves and were liable to be broken up. Slaves lived in huts of their own construction on most plantations. They had few or no possessions. Many owners failed to provide slaves with the means to cover their nakedness or to grow their own food. Malnutrition and physical exhaustion were their common lot. Even if slaves had been allowed a day or two a week to cultivate their own gardens, they were too exhausted from their labours to fulfill these additional tasks.[76] Though slaves were considered chattels, constituting valuable capital stock, their owners found it cheaper to buy continually new imports from Africa than to maintain those they already owned in the colony.[77]

---

[72] The most authoritative study of French slavery continues to be Gabriel Debien, *Les Esclaves aux Antilles françaises* (Basse-Terre, Guadeloupe et Fort-de-France, Martinique: Sociétés d' Histoire de La Guadeloupe et de La Martinique, 1974).

[73] Bernard Moitt, *Women and Slavery in the French Antilles, 1635–1848* (Bloomington and Indianapolis: Indiana University Press, 2001), 43–7.

[74] Ibid., 351.

[75] The best account of the condition of female slaves in the French colonies remains Gautier, *Les Soeurs de Solitude*. Moitt's *Women and Slavery in the French Antilles* presents a topical approach. A more theoretical account may be found in Marietta Morrissey, *Slave Women in the New World: Gender Stratification in the Caribbean* (Lawrence: University Press of Kansas, 1991).

[76] M. Devèze, *Antilles, Guyanes, La Mer des Caraïbes de 1492 à 1789* (Paris: SEDES, 1977), 284; Debien, *Les Esclaves aux Antilles*, 179–82.

[77] François Girod, *La vie quotidienne de la société créole (Saint-Domingue au 18e siècle)*, (Paris: Hachette, 1972), 132–7.

The Black Code provided for slaves to be fed adequate nourishing meals, to be clothed, and to have Sundays and religious feast days without labouring, but this was a dead letter.[78] Though the code outlawed torture, it only limited the use of the branding iron and the lash. It forbade owners to abandon aged and infirm slaves, but did not provide for their care. The code denied slaves civil status though it allowed them a religious one. Slaves could be baptized and marry, but could not give evidence in court, nor could they own property or engage in trade. The law was more often honoured in the breach than in the observance, and slaves did sometimes testify against cruel masters.

Slaves lived debased lives in all colonies, but despite oppression, slave cultures developed wherever slavery predominated. African religious practices, music, dance, and language provided the chief nexus of social cohesion, promoting identity and resistance to white oppression.[79] French was the language of the masters, who forbade the use of African languages on the plantations. French became the basis of slave identity. Slaves developed a jargon of their own that gradually evolved into a creole tongue in each slave colony.[80] It is likely that all of those born in the islands spoke the language of slaves, which began to appear before 1670 in the Lesser Antilles and by 1730 in Louisiana.[81]

Violence was the chief characteristic of slave societies. Slaves constantly threatened European society, which employed enormous resources to suppress them.[82] Slave uprisings occurred early in the histories of the French island colonies and became endemic, breaking out wherever and whenever oppressors relaxed their guard for an instant. Slaves fought back both directly and indirectly. They ran away. They committed suicide. They poisoned working animals to disrupt labour routines and, in some cases, poisoned

---

[78]   For a brief discussion of the Black Code see Antoine Gisler, *L'Esclavage aux Antilles françaises (XVIIe-XIXe siècles): contribution au problème de l'esclavage* (Fribourg: Editions universitaires Fribourg Suisse, 1965), 19–34; a more complete analysis is in Louis Sala-Molins, *Le Code noir ou le calvaire de Canaan*, 3éd. (Paris: Presses universitaires de France, [1987] 1993), 90–203.

[79]   Girod, *La Vie quotidienne de la société créole*, 155–61 points out that African dancing is a religious rite rather than a social distraction.

[80]   Robert Chaudenson, *Creolization of Language and Culture*, revised in collaboration with Solikoko S. Mufwene, trans., Sheri Pargman, Solikoko S. Mufwene, Sabrina Billings, and Michelle AuCoin (London and New York: Routledge [1992] 2001), 144.

[81]   Albert Valdman, "Creole, the Language of Slavery" in *Slavery in the Caribbean Francophone World: Distant Voices, Forgotten Acts, Forged Identities*, ed., Doris Y. Kadish (Athens and London: University of Georgia Press, 2000), [143]–63; also Hall, *Africans in Colonial Louisiana*, 162–5, 191–200.

[82]   See Pierre Pluchon, *Nègres et juifs au xviiie siècle: le racisme au siècle des lumières* (Paris: Tallandier, 1984), 164–88 for an extended discussion of violence against slaves that stresses its sadistic dimensions; also Moitt, *Women and Slavery*, 101–4.

their masters and themselves.[83] Whites' fear of poison may have had greater disruptive effect than the poison itself.[84]

Slaves escaped and formed permanent and semipermanent marauding gangs that attacked plantations, which by their very nature were isolated. Escape was so endemic that planters more or less legitimised short-term escape as absence without leave, calling it *petit marronage* to distinguish it from the more permanent variety, *grand marronage*.[85] Planters expended enormous energy and resources, sometimes against their will, hunting down runaway slaves. They were assisted in their task by governing authorities who sometimes assembled large forces, including soldiers, in order to mount veritable military campaigns against slaves with greater or lesser degrees of success. In 1671, a judgment of the Superior Council of Guadeloupe tried to halt runaways by taxing slave owners on a graduated scale according to a slave's length of absence. This legislation allowed owners to cripple runaways by cutting their hamstrings in cases of recidivism and to inflict death in repeated cases.[86] Such punishments were confirmed in the Black Code (Article 38) in 1685, but remained ineffective. Pontchartrain instructed Intendant Robert and Governor-General d'Amblimont to consider the feasibility of seizing an estimated 1,200 runaway slaves on St. Vincent and neighbouring islands. If successful, he hoped the costs could be recovered by employing the maroons on Martinique's fortifications or by sales to advance their construction.[87] Of 24 slaves hunted down on Grenada in 1724, fourteen, including one woman, were killed.[88] An estimated 1,000 slaves inhabited the woods of Saint-Domingue in 1721, and reports of disquieting mobs being seen in the north, at Cul-de-Sac and at Maribeau, led to the creation of a special company of fifty men to pursue the fugitives on a regular basis.[89] In 1726, French officials on Martinique actually acknowledged the presence of 525 maroons in that year's census while officials on Guadeloupe reported more than 600 maroons in four bands were pillaging the colony daily.[90] Clearly,

---

[83] Col., C^{8A} 36, ff. 37–7v Mémoire sur les nègres empoisonneurs et sur les mesures à prendre pour réprimer les désordres qu'ils provoquent, 6 April 1726; also Moitt, *Women and Slavery*, 139–40.

[84] Satineau, *Histoire de la Guadeloupe*, 284–91; Girod, *La Vie quotidienne de la société creole*, 186–9 on poison; and McClellan, *Colonialism and Science*, 55; and Debien, *Les Esclaves aux Antilles*, 399–402.

[85] Ibid., 412.

[86] Satineau, *Histoire de la Guadeloupe*, 292 n. 2.

[87] Col., F^3 54, f. 372 Pontchartrain to Robert, 2 December 1699.

[88] Col., C^{8A} 35, ff. 197–7v Extrait de l'état dressé de 9 juillet 1726 ... par Sr. Rouve de Saint-Laurent.

[89] Girod, *La Vie quotidienne de la société créole*, 174.

[90] Col., C^{8A} 37, ff. 37–7v Recensement générale de l'isle Martinique fait à la fin de l'année mil sept cent vingt six; Debien, *Les Esclaves aux Antilles*, 414.

slave societies lived with enormous pressures, but they worked and successfully produced large quantities of agricultural products at marketable prices.

Slavery was also present in the French North American colonies. Though only introduced into Louisiana in 1719, Africans quickly transformed colonial society by transplanting rice cultivation from Senegambia, which gave the colony its first secure cereal grain for consumption by all. The Black Code was formally introduced *mutatis mutandi* in 1724.[91] Almost immediately after 1730, African slaves surpassed Louisiana's combined European population.[92] Slavery also played an important if little known role in the development of French Illinois. By 1720 slave labour was already transforming Cahokia (founded in 1699) and Kaskaskia (founded in 1703) into agricultural communities. At first Indian and then both Indian and African slaves, introduced in 1721, were employed.[93]

Slaves played negligible roles in the social development of Canada, Acadia, and Placentia/Île Royale.[94] The royal government encouraged the introduction of slaves to New France in 1689, 1701, 1716, 1719, and 1721, but no influx occurred, not even after Intendant Jacques Raudot's ordinance proclaimed the legality of slavery in 1709.[95] There was simply no economic reason for slavery to take hold in these colonies. Lack of wealth before the second quarter of the eighteenth century delayed employment of Africans as household servants by the rich and powerful.

2. Nobles and *Grands Blancs*

Whites formed a declining proportion of the total population of the Circum-Caribbean colonies. Between 1670 and 1730, their numbers declined from less than one-half to just under one-sixth of the total. Whites were becoming the minority of the settled population in Louisiana in 1730, but in Martinique they had declined from 40 percent in 1670 to just 20 percent six decades later. On Guadeloupe the decline was about the same. In 1718, whites of Grenada were only 13.5 percent of the population.[96] The greatest relative change occurred more rapidly on Saint-Domingue, where the proportion of

91 Sala-Molins, *Le Code noir*, 84 *passim* for a detailed comparison of the Louisiana version with the original.

92 Usner, *Indians, Settlers, and Slaves in a Frontier Exchange Economy*, 46–56; and Hall, *Africans in Colonial Louisiana*, 121–3.

93 Ekberg, *French Roots in the Illinois Country*, 33, 46–7.

94 See Robin W. Winks, *The Blacks in Canada: A History*, 2nd ed. (Kingston and Montreal: McGill-Queen's University Press, 1997), 1–23; Marcel Trudel, *Dictionnaire des esclaves et de leurs propriétaires au Canada française* (La Salle: Hurtubise HMH, 1990); and Kenneth Donovan, "Slaves and Their Owners in Ile Royale, 1713–1760", *Acadiensis*, 25, no. 1 (Autumn, 1995), 3–32.

95 Miquelon, *New France, 1701–1744*, 238–9.   96 AN, SOM, G¹ 498, no. 41.

whites remained as high as one-third of the total population as late as 1700, but fell to less than one-eighth by 1730 (Appendix 1). Whites eventually represented less than one-sixteenth of the population, but the trend clearly began during the century's first three decades.

If violence and sadism characterized slave societies, class and the economy also separated people according to traditional status and wealth. Although hierarchy was a crucial feature of all French colonial societies, it was challenged. In the West Indies, the richest and most powerful planters, the so-called *grands blancs*, stood at the top of the social pyramid, but traditional forms of social authority exemplified by other landowners, nobles, clergy, senior government officials, and military leaders challenged their power and ability to influence events. The six decades before 1730 were much more fluid than succeeding ones, and estimates of the number of *grands blancs* during the later period ought not to be read back into the earlier period. Few had noble antecedents.

Only 25 noble families lived in Martinique during the seventeenth century even though the right to engage in trade in the colonies was permitted without derogation of status.[97] Unlike Canada, where great wealth was unknown and status derived from one's official position or military reputation, wealth chiefly determined status in the West Indies.[98] It was much easier in the colonies than in France for talented, ambitious men to adopt the attitudes and values of the nobility, even become ennobled, and move up the social scale. Several factors account for this in Canada: the availability of free land, the economic opportunities provided by the fur trade, royal permission for members of the nobility resident in Canada to engage directly in trade and industry, and the presence, after 1683, of a large corps of regular troops.[99] The hierarchical nature of society was also more closely connected to imported social structures and values from France owing to the absence of capitalistic agriculture than in the West Indies. Their mutation in the presence of the fur trade and near constant warfare with the Amerindians gave rise to a closed caste of a seigneurial, land-owning elite holding military commissions in the standing infantry companies sent to serve in the colonies.[100] Throughout the colonies French males between the ages of 16 and 60 had to serve in the militia, but in the islands the wealthy monopolised the commissioned ranks and gained equivalent status to nobles by receiving exemptions

97 Liliane Chauleau, *Histoire Antillaise. La Martinique et la Guadeloupe du XVIIe siècle à la fin du XIXe siècle* (Paris, Fort de France et Pointe à Pitre: Desormeaux, 1973), 63.

98 W. J. Eccles, *France in America*, rev. ed. (Toronto: Fitzhenry & Whiteside, 1990 [1972]), 165.

99 Col., B 11, f. 108 arrêt du conseil, 10 March,1685; W. J. Eccles, *The Canadian Frontier, 1534–1760*, rev. ed. (Albuquerque: University of New Mexico Press, [1969] 1983), 100.

100 W. J. Eccles, "The Social, Economic, and Political Significance of the Military Establishment in New France", reprinted in *Essays on New France* (Toronto: Oxford University Press, 1987), 110–24.

from the poll tax on slaves according to their rank (e.g., captains 12 slaves, lieutenants 8, and ensigns 4). *Grands blancs* also monopolised seats on the Superior Councils, intermarried, and became castes. In Canada officers were becoming members of a closed caste by 1730, but in the West Indies the situation among the wealthiest inhabitants remained fluid for a few decades longer.

3. Habitants and Éngagés

Habitants, best translated as homesteaders, constituted the bulk of the white population in all the French colonies, but several elements fall within the general term, including small planters in the tropical islands (especially those not engaged in sugar production) and the farmers of the mainland colonies. In the West Indies, habitant included *petits blancs*, a disparaging term, while in Canada, the term habitant was a proud self-identifier distinguishing new colonial settlers from the despised peasant status left behind in France.

Éngagés or bondsmen could be found in all the colonies at any time between 1670 and 1730, but the number arriving there had already peaked before the beginning of the period. In the Windward Islands the total number of *engagés* declined from more than 2,000 in 1671 to less than 30 by 1698.[101] Some *engagés* may have resented working alongside African slaves but this was not the chief reason for their decline as claimed by Father Du Tertre.[102] The cause was economic. Slave labour was cheaper than coerced white labour in the West Indies, and in Europe, Spain proved to be a more attractive destination for French migrants as the century wore on.[103] During these years most bondsmen headed for Saint-Domingue where 1,565 of them, far outnumbering the 1,063 male slaves, comprised 45 percent of the white males in 1681.[104] Nevertheless, by 1700 their numbers, too, had fallen to just 463.[105] A similar decline occurred in Canada.

A slight revival occurred during the brief period of peace between 1698 and 1702, but thereafter the number of indentured servants declined rapidly. After Louis XIV's death the government briefly renewed efforts to stimulate colonial migration by forcing merchants and sea captains to transport *engagés* in return for being allowed to depart for the colonies. In the islands, however, enumerators mingled bondsmen with white domestics so that, while a few hundred were recorded in each colony, the designation *engagé* disappeared along with the indentured servants themselves. Only in Canada

---

101   AN, SOM, G¹ 468, 471, 499, no. 5; 498, no. 59; 499, no. 31; 469, f. 137; and 472, f. 340.

102   Jean-Baptiste Du Tertre, *Histoire général des Antilles, habitée par les françois,* 4 vols. (Paris: T. Jolly, 1667–1671), 2: 448.

103   Giraud, *Histoire de la Louisiane,* 1: 150.

104   AN, SOM, G¹ 509, no. 2.   105 Ibid., G¹ 498, no. 59 and 509, no. 8

did the term remain, identifying men hired annually to paddle the canoes
that voyaged west in pursuit of furs.

4. Merchants

Merchants who engaged in export and import trades, the men called *négociants* to distinguish them from petty shopkeepers, were normally connected to their counterparts in the French seaports rather than to colonists.
Metropolitan merchants preferred to employ men like themselves, temporarily residing in the colonies even if for several decades. Many were factors, that
is, employees in a merchant's service. Others were partners, often junior ones
connected by kinship and religion. It would be surprising if some, at least,
were not also joint venturers. In addition to assembling cargoes and distributing assortments of dry goods and provisions, these men acted as commission-
agents (*commissionnaires*), engaging in reciprocity of action with their con-
freres in France.[106] By 1700, or shortly thereafter, some of them at St. Pierre
were becoming independent, importing and exporting goods, collecting return cargoes, arranging for their prompt sale to ship captains, and assembling assortments of goods for distribution to planters. This centralisation of
commerce in the Windward Islands led to higher prices elsewhere, especially
at Guadeloupe, reducing the latter colony to dependence on Martinique.[107]

Many merchants were initially peddlers (*pacotilleurs*) who travelled sea-
sonally to the colonies with their goods. In Canada they were called
marchands forains. In the Windward Islands they were known as hucksters
(*regrattiers*). In both regions they were hated. These merchants sold directly
to settlers, competing directly with colonial factors and shopkeepers.[108] They
had no permanent connections to the colonies.

France may well have denied itself a transatlantic empire because it pursued a religious policy of intolerance and persecution.[109] Louis XIV drove
Protestant merchants who had been active in French overseas expansion
since the sixteenth century out of the colonies for a generation following

[106] See Jean Cavignac. *Jean Pellet, commerçant en gros, 1694–1772: contribution à l'étude
du négoce bordelais du XVIIIe siècle* (Paris: SEVPEN, 1967), 169–210 for the colonial
careers of two such commission-agents at St. Pierre in the 1720s.

[107] Anne Pérotin-Dumon, "Cabotage, Contraband, and Corsaires: The Port Cities of Guadeloupe and Their Inhabitants, 1650–1800" in *Atlantic Port Cities: Economy Culture and
Society in the Atlantic World, 1650–1850*, 59.

[108] May, *Histoire économique de la Martinique*, 243–44.; Peter N. Moogk, *La Nouvelle
France, The Making of French Canada – A Cultural History* (East Lansing: Michigan
State University Press, 2000), 192–3.

[109] Jacques Petitjean-Roget, "Les Protestants à la Martinique sous l'ancien régime", *RHC* 42
(1955), 220–65; J. F. Bosher, "The Imperial Environment of French Trade with Canada,
1660–1685", reprinted in *Business and Religion in the Age of New France, 1600–1760:
Twenty-Two Studies* (Toronto: Canadian Scholars' Press, 1994), 216–56.

the revocation of the Edict of Nantes. Though they and Jewish merchants, expelled in 1683, began returning during the 1720s, a critically important consequence was that France's integration into the new European international trade structure was seriously delayed and never completed.[110] Family and religious life governed the conduct of merchants trading to the colonies, and to ignore the cultural dimensions of trade gravely exaggerates the importance of purely economic considerations.

At Quebec, more permanent merchants who annually shipped furs and other colonial goods to France for metropolitan firms and imported textiles, metalware, wines, and other spirits were becoming a stable community by the second decade of the eighteenth century. The 1717 letters patent governing colonial trade granted colonial merchants the right to assemble freely and discuss their business. Whether, as a recent study claims, they were also becoming attached to Canada by marriages, their commerce, and their community involvement is more questionable.[111] Some of these merchants, like those in the Windward Islands, married colonial women and gained access to the governor and intendant's patronage, but these aspects of their lives most likely did not override the overwhelming influence of their transatlantic connections. In Quebec these men and women followed French fashion, and in the tropical colonies the commission-agents of St. Pierre and Cap François continued to have little in common with the societies in which they lived. Indeed, their fortunes made, they usually returned to France.[112]

Louise Dechêne's study of the Canadianized merchants of Montreal who assembled the goods, fitted out the fur trade, and shipped furs to Quebec is the most detailed collective portrait of colonial merchants anywhere in the French Americas.[113] Postmortem inventories of 29 of these merchant outfitters who dominated the Canadian fur trade between 1680 and 1718 reveal they played a primary role in town affairs. The average net value of their estates amounted to between 25,000 and 30,000 livres, but by the beginning of the eighteenth century the five wealthiest had assets in excess

---

110 For more on this see Eric S. Schubert, "Innovations, debts and bubbles: international integration of financial markets in western Europe, 1688–1720", *Journal of Economic History*, 48 (1988), 299–306; David Ormerod, "The Atlantic Economy and the 'Protestant Capitalist International', 1651–1775", *Historical Research*, 66 (1993), 197–208; also Larry Neal, *The Rise of Financial Capitalism: International Capital Markets in the Age of Reason* (New York: Cambridge University Press, 1991). J. F. Bosher, *The Canada Merchants, 1713–1763* (Oxford: Clarendon Press, 1987) recounts the story of how Protestant merchants reappeared in Canada during the 1730s. For the West Indies, see Gérard Lafleur, *Les Protestants aux Antilles françaises du vent sous l'ancien régime* (Basse-Terre: Société d'histoire de la Guadeloupe, 1988)

111 See Young, *Kin, Commerce, and Community*, xvii, 3, 5.

112 May, *Histoire économique de la Martinique*, 218–19; Moogk, *La Nouvelle France*, 194–5; Girod, *La vie quotidienne de la société créole*, 83.

113 See Dechêne, *Habitants and Merchants*, 220–22.

of five or six times the average. Their assets also differed markedly from their French counterparts. Nearly one-quarter owned no arable land, and farms amounted to no more than a fifth of the estates of the remainder. *Rentes* or annuities rarely accounted for more than 5 percent of their wealth, the greatest part of which was in stock and commercial claims (i.e., accounts receivables). Lifestyles also contrasted markedly from French merchants. Life in Montreal even for the well-off remained modest during the years of social formation. Merchants shared their fine cutstone houses with their shops and their goods. Modesty characterised their furnishings, which were often locally crafted. They did not ape the nobility in life. Neither idleness nor dissipation featured in their conduct. Wives often managed husbands' businesses in their absence. Accumulating wealth was both hard work and a serious matter. Orderly behaviour, responsibility in public affairs, and generous charity were the hallmarks of their conduct.[114]

5. Artisans

Little is known about the artisans in French colonial towns.[115] Suffice it to note that, in the extremely fluid conditions prevailing there, artisans often enjoyed freedom of opportunity encountered nowhere else in the colonies because they were never in sufficient supply. Governor-General Blénac complained that there were only eight wheelwrights in all of Martinique to build and service the carts (*cabrouets*) on 200 sugar plantations.[116] No distinctions were enforced between journeymen and masters. Lack of guilds or restraints on labour left colonial towns wide open to the ambitious and the fortunate. Jean Roy came to Martinique from Bordeaux as an indentured servant. He was a tailor by trade. Following the termination of his indenture, he began spinning tobacco and practising his former trade in the off season. Spinning was a skilled occupation whose practitioners were entitled to one-tenth the weight of their output.[117] Roy entered into a partnership with another spinner whose estate he inherited a few years later. He went privateering; soon after he acquired a plantation and several other establishments. By 1694 he owned six sugar works and a refinery, and worked more than 800 slaves. His eldest son became a militia captain. One of his daughters married a naval captain. When he died in 1707, Roy was dean of the Superior Council or High Court, first militia captain of the island, and the colony's oldest

---

[114] Miquelon, *New France, 1701–1744*, 242.
[115] What is known is chiefly the work of Peter Moogk, "The Craftsmen of New France" (unpublished Ph.D. thesis, University of Toronto, 1973); also his *La Nouvelle France*, 195–209. See, too, Dechêne *Habitants and Merchants*, 222–26, and Miquelon, *New France, 1701–1744*, 209–11.
[116] Col., C^{8A} 7, f. 20 Blénac to Pontchartrain, 12 May 1692.
[117] Price, *France and the Chesapeake*, 1: 77, 88.

inhabitant being over 90 years old. He left his wife and each of his 11 children 72 slaves and half a plantation.[118]

Commercial and business opportunities abounded in the colonies for ambitious, energetic young men. Seven years after his arrival in Canada in 1692 as an indentured cooper, Pierre Plassan was endorsing bills of exchange to a correspondent at Bordeaux. In 1702, he hired three employees to assist him with his enterprises at Quebec. A year later he formed a partnership with the clerk of the Treasurer-General of the Marine in the colony. During the next five years he sailed annually to France to purchase goods for the Canada trade and invested in shares of at least five ships. By 1708, when the partnership was dissolved, this one-time bondsman was in Rochefort negotiating with no less a person than the naval intendant himself.[119] Pierre Plassan was not alone. Colonial societies, especially those of the towns where artisans were to be found, were unstructured.[120] However, the stories of Roy and Plassan are also exceptions that prove the opposite. The important part of Jean Roy's story of accumulating wealth was that it was largely due to longevity, circumstances, and luck, whereas Plassan's good fortune was undoubtedly owed to his fortuitous connection to the clerk of the treasurer-general of the marine. The lack of artisans in the colonies may have had its greatest impact on slaves. From 1700 onward the decline in indentured servants and the growing demand for skilled artisans led to high prices for the latter. Cart building, wheel making, and cooperage on Saint-Domingue were all taken over by slaves, often after a very limited apprenticeship.[121]

6. Soldiers, Sailors, and Fishermen

Thousands of soldiers, sailors, and fishermen gave an air of permanent transience to all white colonial populations, especially after 1683 when the navy began recruiting regular infantrymen for service in the Americas. Ten companies of *troupes de la marine*, best viewed as colonial infantry rather than marines, were authorised for the first transport to the West Indies. Three companies were destined for Canada.[122] The 150 soldiers sent to Quebec grew to 1,514 five years later. Actual strength declined thereafter, and during the early eighteenth century numbers in the colony fluctuated between 600 and 1,000 annually.[123] Numbers in maritime New France remained

---

[118] Labat, *Nouveau voyage aux Isles,* 1: 76–7.

[119] J. F. Bosher, "Partners of the French Navy in Supplying Canada, 1701–1713" in *Business and Religion,* 292–5.

[120] Cf. Dechêne, *Habitants and Merchants,* 223.

[121] Debien, *Une Plantation de Saint-Domingue,* 88; also Debien, *Les Esclaves aux Antilles,* 95–104.

[122] Col., B 10, f. 38 order du roi, 23 September 1683.

[123] Jay Cassel, "The 'Troupes de la marine' in Canada, 1683–1760: men and materiel" (unpublished Ph.D. thesis, University of Toronto, 1987), 518–20.

modest, growing from about 80 in Acadia in 1690 to 350 at Placentia in 1709.[124] Later, at Louisbourg, soldiers comprised one–third of the entire population during the early 1720s.[125] Four understrength companies made up of 12 officers and 137 men were stationed in Louisiana in 1716, but a decade later their numbers had grown to 448 officers and men garrisoning 11 different posts.[126] In 1720, the India Company hired 183 Swiss soldier-workers to serve in the colony, and before the end of the decade similar foreign mercenary companies were sent to Quebec, Louisbourg, Martinique, and Saint-Domingue.[127]

Colonists comprised 30 percent of the officers in the colonial infantry by the early 1690s, but Canadianization occurred more gradually than previously believed. Nevertheless, colonists surpassed the number of French officers during the 1720s.[128] The rank and file remained French. Unlike infantry of the line (*troupes de terre*) who were often recruited by captains from specific areas of France, professional recruiters or crimps, pejoratively called *racoleurs*, recruited naval infantry. Frequently employing trickery and coercion, they gathered recruits from all over the kingdom. The minimum engagement period was six years, but many served at the king's pleasure (i.e., for life). Some were foreign, and like *engagés*, at least half of them had urban origins. Colonial soldiers had no regional identity or *esprit de corps*, and often arrived in the colonies as frightened young boys. Class as well as their heterogeneous origins separated them from their officers.

Few soldiers married and settled in the colonies though the government encouraged it. In Canada, soldiers were billeted with colonists. Only a few lived in garrison. Some obtained discharges and married, but their impact on colonial development has been exaggerated.[129] Many died in the colonies, and the remainder returned to France. They were minor consumers. Deductions for food, uniforms, and pensions left them with a mere pittance, about 24 sols per month, which they supplemented by working. Authorities were anxious that soldiers work for colonists, but frequently they had to surrender their army pay to their commanding officers to get permission to do so. Officers may have employed some, but by 1730 this practice had died out.[130]

---

[124] Col., C^{11D} 4, f. 12 Acadie fonds, 1696–1699.

[125] A. J. B. Johnston, "The People of Eighteenth-Century Louisbourg", *Nova Scotia Historical Review*, 11, 2 (December 1991), 151.

[126] Col., D^{2C} 51, Extrait de la revue des compagnies détachées de la marine à la Louisiane ..., 1716; and ibid., 50, ff. 9–10v Estat des officiers entretenus à la Louisiane. 1730.

[127] Col., C^{8A} 36, f. 58–8v Etat de la depense ... May 1727.

[128] Cassel, "The 'Troupes de la marine' in Canada", 77; see also W. J. Eccles, "The Social, Economic, and Political Significance of the Military Establishment in New France", *CHR* 52 (1971), 1–21.

[129] Cassel, "The 'Troupes de la marine' in Canada", 124–5. For an alternative view see Moogh, *La Nouvelle France*, 114–16.

[130] Cassel, "The 'Troupes de la marine' in Canada", 147, 152.

Few soldiers, drawn largely from the nonproductive, surplus population of France, provided much skilled labour in the colonies. Poorly trained, poorly supervised, and poorly paid, soldiers chiefly impacted the colonies as criminals. Though numbering fewer than 1,000 in a continually growing colony, soldiers in Canada were accused of 15 percent of all crimes and commonly found guilty of murder, theft, felony, and counterfeiting.[131]

French sailors were explicitly forbidden to become soldiers, so great was the need of their skills and so scarce were their numbers. Thousands arrived annually in the colonies, especially in the West Indies, where they formed large bodies of marginalised workers in the towns. During the quarter century before 1713, they drifted back and forth between royal and merchant service, privateering and buccaneering, continually upsetting authorities and blurring the distinctions that others sought to impose on them. In 1696, 700 to 800 freebooters and their families resided at Saint Pierre, where all Martinique's privateers were fitted out.[132] Ten years later an estimated 1,200 to 1,300 privateersmen, equivalent to about half the town's adult population, resided at Saint Pierre.[133] How many were family men is unknown.

The number of transient sailors reaching Martinique in a year could be greater than the number of adult males and adolescents bearing arms in the entire colony.[134] Between 1 July 1710 and 30 June 1711 (one of the few year-long periods for which data are available), 46 ships arrived at Martinique from France with 2,179 sailors on board. Seventy-five died and 479, more than one in five, deserted. Some of the deserters may have been among the 727 seamen who manned colonial vessels fitted out during the period.[135] Fishermen, too, were transients. At the end of each fishing season, most sailed back to France, but in the summer they often doubled or tripled the number of settlers at Placentia and Île Royale. In 1711, 406 fishermen were enumerated at Placentia and elsewhere together with only 235 colonists; two years earlier as many as 3,000 men manned the ships that called at

131   André Lachance, *Crimes et criminels en Nouvelle France* (Montréal: Boréal Express, 1984), 106–9.

132   Col., C[8A] 9, f. 271 "Memoire de L'Etat present de L'Isle de la Martinique," 21 April 1696, cited in May, *Histoire économique de la Martinique*, 215.

133   Col., C[8A] 16, ff. 109–16 Mithon de Senneville to Vaucresson, 10 May 1706; Labat, *Nouveau Voyage aux Isles*, 1: 26 gives the population of two parishes and three districts constituting St. Pierre as about 2,400 communicants and as many slaves and children.

134   AN, SOM, G[1] 470[bis], no. 11 The 1709 census of Martinique, shows 2,433 men and youths bearing arms living on Martinique. Data for half of each of 1715, 1716, and 1717 indicate that about 3,000 sailors reached Martinique annually, whereas the number of adult males and youths bearing arms in 1716 was 2,915. See Col., C[8A] 21, f. 261, 1716 census of Martinique, and ibid., 20, f. 443 and 22, ff. 273 and 274 "Etat des navires marchands partis de la Martinique ...".

135   Col., C[8A] 18, ff. 64, 149 "Estats des bâtimens ... 5", January and 3 July 1711.

Placentia.[136] At Louisbourg in 1720 and in 1724, fishermen and soldiers made up 72.5 and 64.9 percent, respectively, of the town's total population.[137] Over one-half of all adults on Île Royale worked in the fishery. The ubiquitous, concentrated presence of soldiers, sailors, and fishermen amidst an already rootless urban population gave colonial towns a particularly unstable aspect.

7. Free Blacks, Mulattos, and Métis

Free people of colour stood between whites and slaves. Their slowly growing numbers and economic activity appeared to have no counterpart in English and Dutch colonies.[138] Free blacks were predominantly female slaves who had been freed by masters and fathers of their children. Whites convicted of fathering a child with a slave were fined, and both slave and child were to be confiscated to the benefit of the work house in each colony, but this was easily avoided by having slaves declare the fathers to be sailors or soldiers unknown and no longer resident in the colony.[139] During the 1690s a free black, Louis Galère, operated the finest ferry service on Martinique between St. Pierre and Fort Royal, charging one *écu* to transport passengers daily on their 30-kilometre journey in three or four hours. In three years, Galère built a commercial operation of three or four boats and 20 of his own slaves, each vessel manned by a slave coxswain and four or five rowers.[140]

Mulattos treated legally free Africans with deep suspicion, and viewed them as inferiors. But they, in their turn, were similarly viewed by whites. Between 1704 and 1713, Intendant Mithon and Governor-General Phélypeaux severally and jointly denounced free coloured tavernkeepers – one of their few routes to economic success – as thieves, receivers of stolen goods, and protectors of runaway slaves. Above all they were insolent,[141] but views varied. Militia colonel Jean Dubuc attributed the growth of privateering at St. Pierre during the War of the Spanish Succession to the attractions of free black and mulatto women to freebooters; they were a stabilising

---

[136] Canada, *Censuses of Canada, 1665 to 1871*, 4: 48; and *Seventh Census of Canada, 1931*, 1: 137.

[137] Johnston, "The People of Eighteenth-Century Louisbourg", 75–83; also his "The Fishermen of Eighteenth-Century Cape Breton: Numbers and Origins", in *Aspects of Louisbourg*, ed., E. Krause *et al.*, (Sydney: University College of Cape Breton, 1995), 198–208.

[138] Richard S. Dunn, *Sugar and Slaves: The Rise of the Planter Class in the English West Indies, 1724–1713*, (New York: W. W. Norton, 1972), 255.

[139] Labat, *Nouveau voyage aux Isles*, 1, pt. 2: 32–7.

[140] Ibid., 1: 65–6.

[141] Léo Elisabeth, "The French Antilles" in *Neither Slave Nor Free: The Freedman of African Descent in the Slave Societies of the New World*, David W. Cohen and Jack P. Greene, eds. (Baltimore and London: The John Hopkins University, Press, 1974), 160.

influence on these men who possessed notoriously fickle loyalties.[142] Free coloured life became more difficult after 1713 when the first restrictions on movement appeared. Thirteen years later, in 1726, free coloured farmers' access to capital was blocked when deeds of gift between whites and blacks were denied.[143]

Yet, Father Labat sounds a cautionary note about racial stereotyping while illustrating the remarkable complexity of human relations in the colonies. A former galley slave called Dauphiné had been a slave driver (*commandeur*) for five or six years when he kidnapped a mulatto slave, married her, and took her to another part of Martinique where they lived for some time, perhaps several years. After the couple was found, the union was declared null, and Dauphiné was fined one *écu* for each day the slave had been absent from her master. Both were imprisoned. Dauphiné's ability to pay was not an issue, for he later bought his wife and her three children for 1,800 livres from her master. Labat published the banns and married them.[144]

Mulattos formed distinct groups in island societies. Between 1679 and 1729 at Fort Royal, 58 marriages involved mulatto and free black women. Twenty-four mulatto and 18 white men married mulatto females, and 16 black males married 15 free black and one mulatto females. The white males were artisans or soldiers, and their descendants generally sought their spouses among the newly arrived from France.[145] Mulattos were the only locally born group, and consequently, their numbers were more sexually balanced than others in society. As with free Africans however, they were too few in number to exert much influence before 1730.

Racial mixing occurred in the mainland colonies, and though Colbert encouraged it, little resulted until later. Not everyone was similarly inclined as Louis XIV's minister. Responding to Cadillac's plan to encourage racial intermarriage at Detroit, Governor-General Vaudreuil recommended that it be discouraged. Whether this was due to criticism of Cadillac or a genuine concern, his objection was couched in the prejudices of his class: "I am persuaded that one must never mix bad blood with good. The experience we have had in the country, that all the French who have married native women have been licentious, lazy, and insufferably independent, and that the children they have had have been as lazy as the natives themselves must prevent any such kinds of marriages".[146] Unions between French men and Indian women on the fringes of New France, both in the *pays d'en haut* and in the east, began long before 1670 and were more significant than those in the

---

[142] Émile Hayot, "Les gens de couleur libres du Fort Royal, 1679–1823", *RFHOM* 56 (1969), 8.

[143] Ibid., 136, 141, and 149.

[144] Labat, *Nouveau voyage aux Isles*, 1, pt. 2: 32–7.

[145] Hayot, "Les gens de couleur libres", 77, 83.

[146] *RAPQ*, 1942–43, 420 Vaudreuil and Raudot to Pontchartrain, 14 November 1709.

St. Lawrence settlements. Eventually they gave rise to an entirely new social group, the Métis, who peopled the Illinois and later the northwestern plains of Canada. The term, *métis*, was never employed in Acadia. The degree to which peaceful relations between Acadian settlers and Mi'kmaq people were consolidated by marriage and similar unions is unclear. La Have-Mirligueche on the southeast coast of Acadia contained a conspicuous Métis settlement of 75 or more at the turn of the century, and there were undoubtedly other similar settlements, for it seems doubtful that such peaceful relations as existed between French and Indian could have survived without mixed marriages.[147]

Nevertheless, the degree to which Amerindians impacted French colonial societies is moot. Though Acadia, the Illinois, and the *pays d'en haut* were all affected by daily contact with natives, the uniqueness of Saint-Domingue lay in the lack of any Amerindian presence at all. The Spanish had exterminated the original Arawak inhabitants during the first quarter of the sixteenth century. Though the French fought fierce battles for control of the Windward Islands, the number of remaining Caribs rapidly declined after 1670. In Canada, on the other hand, native Americans provided the entire *raison d'être* for the colony's existence. They were the object of the early and continuing apostolic missions; they harvested the furs the French sought so eagerly in trade; and they were valuable military allies without which the colony would not have survived. Yet, no middle ground was ever established between the two peoples.[148] Natives residing among French colonists in the St. Lawrence Valley governed themselves largely independent of French law, and the French sought continuously to conciliate them.[149]

8. Buccaneers and *Coureurs de bois*

Slaves constituted the largest group of marginalised people who gave unique contours to French colonial societies, but soldiers, convicts, and others added to this estate. Among the most original and picaresque were *coureurs de bois* and buccaneers. *Coureurs de bois*, to distinguish them from *voyageurs*, were outlaws who appeared in New France shortly before 1670 when the French began to penetrate the lower Great Lakes and the West. They were a product of sexual imbalance in the colony and chaos in the fur trade following the conclusion of the first two Iroquois wars. Without wives, unable to form

[147] Clark, *Acadia*, 128, 129 n27.
[148] This claim is unconvincingly argued by Richard White, *The Middle Ground: Indians, Empires, and Republics in the Region of the Great Lakes, 1650–1815* (New York: Cambridge University Press, 1991).
[149] For further discussion see the ground-breaking article by Jan Grabowski. "Searching for Common Ground: Natives and French in Montreal, 1700–1730", *Proceedings of the Eighteenth Meeting of the French Colonial Historical Society,* Montreal, May 1992 (Cleveland: French Colonial Historical Society, 1993), 59–73.

families or to clear land, hundreds of men soon ventured westward to trade directly with Indians for furs, the colony's sole source of income. By 1672, one estimate placed their number at 400. It was they who accompanied Cavalier de La Salle to the Illinois and Mississippi Valleys. By 1680 there were at least 800 *coureurs de bois* in the West.[150] During the 1680s they made Michilimackinac, at the junction of Lakes Michigan and Huron, their chief meeting place and pushed on to build new trading posts west, southwest and north of Lake Superior.[151]

Voyageurs were independent, licensed – therefore legal – fur traders who appeared after 1681. They were initially a small nucleus of independent men emerging from among the *coureurs de bois* who quickly disappeared under the influence of fur trade rationalization. The fur trade was the *voyageurs'* sole occupation. A larger group worked occasionally in the trade often as the employees of *voyageurs*.[152] The growing presence of indentured servants in the fur trade after 1700 reflected the increasing organization and consolidation of the trade, which led to the transformation of the mass of once independent canoemen into waged workers during the eighteenth century. Between 1716 and 1730, the nearly 1,800 surviving *engagements* represent only about 39 percent of the more than 4,600 mentioned in the licenses (*congés*) for the period.[153] Early in the eighteenth century, habitants who ventured westward once or twice in their youth before becoming immured on their small farms in the St. Lawrence Valley replaced the professional *voyageurs*. They were like their predecessors in name only. The few *voyageurs* who survived the economic forces of proletarianization moved upward in New France's social structure. Through partnerships and marriage they joined the class of fur trade merchants of Montreal, and by the 1720s these new *voyageur-marchands*, for so they were called, were consolidating their social and business positions in the colony by extending partnerships to military officers and post commandants who controlled access to trade at the western posts.[154]

Like the *coureurs de bois* of New France, pirates and buccaneers in the West Indies had disappeared by 1730, but their influence, like the product

---

[150]   Eccles, *The Canadian Frontier*, 109–10.

[151]   Jesuit missionaries originally established a mission at Sault Sainte Marie in 1668, but soon moved to St. Ignace on the Strait of Mackinac where most fur trading occurred. Soldiers were sent to protect the mission in 1683, but whether from the Indians or *coureurs de bois* is unclear.

[152]   See Dechêne, *Habitants and Merchants*, 117–25, for a detailed analysis of 668 *voyageurs* who journeyed west during the decade 1708–1717.

[153]   Gratien Allaire, "Fur Trade Engagés, 1701–1745" in *Rendezvous: Selected Papers of the Fourth North American Fur Trade Conference, 1981.* ed., Thomas C. Buckley, (n.p. n.d.), 15–26.

[154]   Gratien Allaire, "Officiers et marchands: les sociétés de commerce des fourrures, 1715–1760", *RHAF*, 40, 3 (hiver, 1987), 409–28. See also Dechêne, *Habitants and Merchants*, 89, 96.

of the first real French presence in the *pays d'en haut*, lived on in the Antilles. Pirates and privateers, even more than *coureurs de bois* and *voyageurs*, have fascinated the popular imagination since the seventeenth century. Their numerous published memories leave no doubt,[155] but the terms require some clarification.

The terms *pirate*, freebooter, and *buccaneer* tend to be employed synonymously to denote sea robbers of varying degrees of frightfulness. Freebooter, from the Dutch *vrijbuiter*, is a softer term than pirate, hearkening back to the Dutch military tradition of soldiering without pay for booty. The French translation is *flibustier*. Colonial privateersmen often went to sea under similar arrangements, thereby blurring the distinction between themselves and pirates. Not surprisingly, the French employed *flibustier* interchangeably with *corsair* or privateersman. The French sometimes privileged the term buccaneer (*boucanier*) to denote those bandits from western Hispaniola who, earlier in the seventeenth century, had hunted feral cattle and cured the meat by smoking it on a "boucan" or frame of green wood.[156] For many years after 1670 men continued to live on Saint-Domingue hunting and curing their meat because there were few other means of survival. The colony remained under very loose government authority for several decades after the first royal governor was appointed in 1665, and it continued to attract hundreds of *petit blancs* and *engagés* who fled Martinique and Guadeloupe unable to compete with slave labour.

Hunting wild cattle and piracy went together for masterless men of all nations. The buccaneers of Saint-Domingue initially attracted people of many nations and creeds, which calls attention to an important fact that not all buccaneers and freebooters were sailors.[157] Many were former soldiers. Exquemelin describes how pirates often attacked in good order, marching "with drums beating and banners flying".[158] Buccaneers were excellent marksmen, and the famous *fusil boucanier* was known throughout the West Indies. The problem for anyone seeking to harness their energies was that they were reluctant to go to sea as long as they had money for drink, and they were equally reluctant to attack disciplined military forces.

---

[155]   Two excellent accounts of French buccaneers available in English are A. O. Exquemelin, *The Buccaneers of America*, trans., Alexis Brown (Harmondsworth: Penguin Books, 1969) and Sieur Raveneau de Lussan, *Raveneau de Lussan: Buccaneer of the Spanish Main an early French Filibuster of the Pacific*, trans., Marguerite Eyer Wilbur (Cleveland: Arthur H. Clark Co., 1930), originally published as *Journal du voyage fait à la mer du Sud avec les flibustiers de l'Amérique en 1684 et années suivantes* (Paris: 1689).

[156]   *Boucan* is a Tupi Indian word denoting the smoking frame. Today *la boucane* is a French-Canadian word for smoke and the verb *boucaner* means to cure.

[157]   See Charlevoix, *Histoire de l'isle espagnole ou de S. Domingue*, 3, pt 2, 54–67; cited in John S. Bromley, *Corsaires and Navies, 1660–1760* (London and Ronceverte: The Hambleton Press, 1987), 2–3.

[158]   Exquemelin, *The Buccaneers of America*, 130.

In the West Indies, the pirates' heyday passed soon after 1670, and though the French continued to employ them during the wars of the next 45 years, they were scarcely worth the effort. The hundreds of indentured servants arriving at Saint-Domingue and *petit blancs* leaving the Windward Islands for the new settlements were also changing the composition of the white population. As Saint-Domingue gradually moved over to sugar culture, aided by slave raids on Jamaica and the proceeds from the raid on Cartagena during the 1690s, the buccaneer leaders became planters, and many of the remainder came ashore for good. After the War of the Spanish Succession, English naval forces drove the remaining pirates out of the Caribbean, but their legacy lived on in the French islands in the constant insubordination that, according to French authorities, characterised colonial societies.

2.5 INSTITUTIONS OF SOCIAL LIFE

1. Homestead and Plantation

In France, men and women lived their lives largely enclosed in three social institutions beyond the family that defined and preyed upon them. These were the seigneury, the village, and the parish. Like all parasites that survive from generation to generation, these institutions both supported and fed off their hosts. Relationships between individuals and institutions then were biological as much as social, for only within the parameters of seigneury, village, and parish was any kind of French existence viable.[159] In the French colonies, on the other hand, these vital institutions were imperfectly present. Except in Canada, the seigneury gave way to other forms of land owning, and the plantation or plantation complex – unheard of in France – became the major landed institution that incorporated most black labour. The village and parish, too, were very imperfectly planted in the colonies. Colonial towns held a large proportion of the white populations were poor substitutes, which left the family as the single most significant social institution to emerge in the colonies. Unlike France, where the family existed within and alongside the seigneury, village, and parish, it existed largely alone in the New World, and wherever it took hold, it became the dominant institution, particularly in North America. Tropical colonies, on the other hand, were notorious for their lack of family life as a result of ever-present pathogens, sexual imbalances, and the mode of production existing everywhere among both blacks and whites.

The *habitation*, or homestead, appeared with the first French settlements in the Americas. In Canada, Acadia, and Louisiana, where it was the basic economic institution of family support, it continued to develop long after

---

[159] Pierre Goubert, *The Ancien Régime: French Society, 1600–1750* (New York: Harper Torchbooks, [1969] 1973), 78–94.

1730. Prior to 1685, Martinique was evolving into a society of homesteads. During the previous half century, slaves impacted society slowly. They did not outnumber whites by even two to one.[160] Though plantations appeared before 1670, plantation society, the most important phase of colonial development in the tropics, came only slowly afterward. In two parishes on Martinique, in 1680, only 1 plantation out of 138 properties was worked by as many as 75 slaves. More than one-half were worked by fewer than five slaves, and more than one-quarter employed no slaves at all.[161] Homesteads continued to hold the bulk of the white population until long after 1730. In 1787, Martinique still had an average of only 15 slaves on its 1,320 homesteads.[162]

The plantation, however, enclosed the lives of most Africans. Many descriptions of life exist, and it is unnecessary to repeat what is already well-known. I wish only to make a few points that are sometimes overlooked or insufficiently emphasised. The plantation-complex refers to the socio-economic features of the plantation and acknowledges its differences from other forms of social organization. Philip Curtin identifies six of its features, setting it apart from other contemporary societies. They are not the only features of the system and perhaps not all deserve mention, but they are defining. First, almost all labour on plantations was coerced from slaves. Second, this labour was not self-sustaining. Third, agricultural production was capitalist rather than feudal or traditional. Fourth, it was conducted on a larger scale than could be found in Europe, including France. Fifth, though capitalist production prevailed, certain vestigial features of feudalism remained. The origins of the plantation complex lay several centuries in the past, and it was compatible with other (i.e., feudal) modes of production. Finally, plantation agriculture supplied a distant market with a highly processed commodity.[163] The critically important point was that capitalist production on the plantation meant that owners of the land also owned the labour and capital equipment, and controlled and managed all aspects of production. Seigneurial lords, in contrast, claimed to own their land, but never asserted control over their subordinate owners' production. Even if plantation owners did not control marketing the way they controlled production and processing, the entire plantation complex was capitalist in ownership.[164] The degree to which planters were innovators freely determining alternative

---

160 Jacques Petitjean-Roget, *La Société d'habitation à la Martinique, 1635–1685*, 2 vols. (Lille-Paris: Universitéde Lille III-Honoré Champion, 1980.)

161 Liliane Chauleau, *Case-Pilote, Le Prêcheur, Basse-Pointe: étude démographique du nord de la Martinique* (Paris: Harmattan, 1991), 24–5.

162 Chaudenson, *Creolization of Language and Culture*, 113.

163 Philip D. Curtin, *The Rise and Fall of the Plantation Complex: Essays in Atlantic History* (Cambridge: Cambridge University Press, 1990), 11–13, 46–8.

164 Michael Craton, "The Historical Roots of the Plantation Model", *Slavery and Abolition*, 5, no. 3 (December, 1984), 191.

possibilities may be questionable, but it needs saying that such a form of agricultural production scarcely existed in France.

In addition to the capitalist nature of its production, the sugar plantation later came to contain 100 to 300 people, most of whom were slaves organised on a basis of sadistic brutality and persistent aggression. The societies that emerged possessed no traditions, rules of behaviour, or values of honour and birth. Consequently, many whites lived lives unrestrained by culture or by law. Government was virtually nonexistent. Though little evidence for the years before the middle of the eighteenth century exists, there is no good reason not to think that the appalling conditions described during the latter half of the century emerged by or soon after 1670 and were firmly in place well before 1730. Daily life in the islands was reduced to its basic atavisms.[165]

Economies of scale influenced the size of plantations, but so did the technology employed to extract juice from sugar cane. The need to mill fresh-cut canes within 24 hours in order to halt rapid fermentation of the juice and ensure marketable quality of sugar limited plantation size to the amount of cane that could be accommodated in the boiling house twice in 12 hours in an age of slow, cumbersome haulage.[166] For these and other reasons plantations of 300 acres (121 hectares) employing 300 to 350 African slaves were optimum size. Most plantations during the late seventeenth and early eighteenth century were very much smaller and employed far smaller labour forces.[167] In 1710, the large plantation of Galbaud du Fort on Saint-Domingue employed 141 slaves, including 35 children.[168]

Whether plantations produced cotton, indigo, sugar, or coffee, the labour of field hands began before dawn and remained closely supervised until long after nightfall. Slaves ate their meals where they worked. According to Governor Galiffet, in 1702 most settlers on Saint-Domingue made their slaves work beyond what was humanly possible all day and during the greatest part of the night.[169]

2. Parish

The Roman Catholic Church was not strongly represented in the French colonies, and state support undermined its influence among the faithful. The King of France was never able to persuade the Pope to create an episcopal see

[165] Robert Forster, "Planters, Slaves, and Gens de Couleur on Saint-Domingue in the Eighteenth Century", *The Consortium on Revolutionary Europe, Proceedings, 1983* (Athens, GA: 1985), 6.
[166] Richard Sheridan, *The Development of Plantations to 1750* (Barbados: Caribbean Universities Press, 1970), 17–18. Ralph Davis, *The Rise of the Atlantic Economies* (London: Weidenfeld & Nicolson, 1973), 258–9.
[167] Abénon, *La Guadeloupe de 1671 à 1759*, 131.
[168] Debien, *Une plantation de Saint-Domingue*, 39.
[169] Girod, *La Vie quotidienne de la société créole*, 127.

in the West Indies. There, missionary priests who ministered to both slaves and colonists belonged to several competitive, plantation-owning religious orders that did not make for either cooperation or consolidation of influence.[170] In Canada, a few secular priests under the authority of the Bishop of Quebec aided missionaries to the Amerindians, but provision for their maintenance proved meager. In the early eighteenth century, four-fifths of the clergy in the colony continued to live in the towns, although only one-quarter of the population did so. One-fifth of the clergy served three-quarters of the Canadian population who lived in the countryside where they were poorly housed and received little from the tithe.[171]

From the beginning of French religious enterprise in the New World, ecclesiastical organization was affected by French domestic politics, foreign policy considerations, and the colonial environment. Religious energy was originally directed toward native Americans. It was also highly competitive. Ecclesiastical authorities viewed colonies as mission fields and considered them as extensions of metropolitan jurisdictions. The colonial church emerged only slowly and partially. The transfer of episcopal authority occurred only in New France and not at all in the West Indies. In Canada, the appointed bishop, François de Laval, was first named Bishop of Petrea *in partibus infidelum* and vicar apostolic in 1658 to ensure his dependence on Rome. Shortly afterward, in 1664, he erected the first parish church in the French colonies in the Americas. A year earlier, Laval founded the Quebec Seminary in keeping with the Tridentine injunction that each diocese train its own clergy. Monseigneur de Laval was named bishop of Quebec later in 1674.

In the West Indies a much more confused situation prevailed. After replacing the West India Company in 1674, the king took charge of everything affecting religion, requesting the provincials of several orders to fill the demand for clergymen in the islands, paying their passage, and providing them with royal pensions. The Pope refused to reduce the jurisdiction of the Spanish bishop of the West Indies at Santo Domingo. In 1692, one Dominican father who escorted 14 missionaries to the Windward Islands was appointed prefect apostolic and vicar general, but ecclesiastical order remained confused and disorderly. Missionaries had been paid originally by the company proprietors of the islands, and later the private owners of each colony who favoured different religious orders. After the Crown assumed control, ecclesiastical jurisdiction remained divided among Jacobins (Dominicans), Capuchins (Franciscans), Carmelites, and Jesuits whose conduct

---

[170] Capuchins were an exception in not owning plantations; see Sue Peabody, "A Dangerous Zeal": Catholic Missions to Slaves in the French Antilles, 1635–1800, *French Historical Studies*, 25, 1 (2002), 70.

[171] Miquelon, *New France, 1701–1744*, 233.

varied greatly.[172] As the number of parishes grew, so did the need for priests (*curés*) and for greater order. The king failed to introduce the tithe into the islands, and habitants refused to pay. They were supported by local authorities who pleaded their poverty. Governor-General Blénac and Intendant Bégon found an expedient solution in financial legerdemain, manipulating the price of sugar on payments made to the receiver of the Western Domain in order to find a means to support missionaries performing parochial duties.[173]

If parish creation and delimitation in the islands were the concern of the state, parish organisation was the product of the colonists. Customs quickly became established and laws were made, bringing greater stability than before to religious life. Elections of church wardens and the building of churches and manses went ahead, but at speeds and intensities established by the settlers. Churches were very humble. Most lacked any ornamentation. In 1696, the priest of Saint-François parish on Guadeloupe described his church as a slave hut (*une case des nègres*) decorated with painted cloth. Father Labat described the parish church at Cap François as being like an ordinary house, built of timbers stuck in the ground and covered with palm fronds; the altar was the least fitting he had ever seen. Church wardens administered parish properties, pew rents, and collections, and though they were elected annually, the office was a burden rather than a status symbol. Wardens were frequently negligent.[174]

Perhaps because the clergy lacked any authority over the colonists, they found the latter welcoming and appreciative of their efforts. Fathers Du Tertre and Labat, writing in the 1660s and around 1700, respectively, testified that regardless of a priest's origins and conduct, colonists welcomed the mass and the liturgy, familiar events in a harsh world. Not only did habitants build chapels and churches, they donated land and goods to the priests. After arriving at Macuba in northern Martinique, Father Labat received two demijohns of Madeira, one of Canary, and ten dozen chickens.[175]

Reliance upon state subsidies to build hospitals, hospices, and workhouses reduced the Church everywhere to loyal handmaiden of the state. In Louisiana and Île Royale the Church ran the risk of complete subservience.[176] As major landowners in every colony, the Church loyally promoted obedience to the Crown. In Canada, Bishop Laval's appointment marked the beginning of the reduction of the church's independence in New France.

---

[172] J. E. Rennaud, *Histoire religieuse des Antilles françaises des origines à 1914* (Paris: Librairie: Larose et Societéd'histoire des colonies françaises, 1954), 67–74; also Peabody, "A Dangerous Zeal: Catholic Missions to Slaves", 53–90.

[173] Rennaud, *Histoire religieuse des Antilles*, 86.

[174] Ibid., 104–7.   [175] Quoted in ibid., 64–6.

[176] Charles E. O. Neill, *Church and State in French Colonial Louisiana: Policy and Politics to 1732* (New Haven and London: Yale University Press, 1966), 286; A. J. B. Johnston, *Control and Order in French Colonial Louisbourg, 1713–1758* (East Lansing: Michigan State University Press, 2001) 21–3.

Episcopal absenteeism between 1704 and 1713 and again from 1727 to 1729 further weakened the Church in New France as did several unedifying disputes that arose from clashes between personalities. The second bishop of Quebec, Jean-Baptiste de La Croix de Chevrières de Saint-Vallier, consecrated in 1688, proved to be a disputatious priest whose quarrels with other clergy weakened the Church's authority during the next sixteen years. His decade-long absence was not followed by reconciliation and peace, and at his death in Quebec in 1727, the colonial church was rent by disputes between the clergy and colonial officials.[177] The third bishop never made an episcopal visit to Quebec, and his successor, Pierre-Herman Dosquet who arrived at Quebec in September, 1729, proved too quarrelsome to bring peace.[178]

Spiritual jurisdiction over the faithful in the colonies remained unclear. Though colonists from the earliest days viewed missionary chapels as parish churches where the sacraments of baptism, communion, and matrimony were administered by whichever missionary was available, they were not. Lack of human resources was also a major failing in the colonies. Without a bishop or an archdeacon, there could be no parishes, parish boundaries, or appointed priests. In Quebec, that occurred after 1664, and in the West Indies only after the king began to erect parishes 10 years later. This was not mere punctiliousness. Twenty years after Bishop Laval's first appointment, the Archbishop of Rouen continued to claim jurisdiction over New France.[179]

Provision for the maintenance of a colonial clergy fell on stony ground from the beginning. Bishop Laval introduced the tithe into Canada in 1663, but failed to impose the usual appropriation of one-thirteenth of the produce of the land. Habitants, supported by the Crown, agreed to pay only half the amount, which was levied on their cereal grains alone.[180] Laval had also wanted the tithe paid to the Seminary of Quebec in order to finance missions to the settlers, but in this he also failed. The tithe was paid only to priests residing in parishes. In 1722, long after Laval had died, most areas of rural Canada were finally organized into parishes.[181] Most parishes were established in the West Indies about a decade earlier.[182] In Acadia and Placentia, neither parishes nor the tithe appeared. There, a few missionaries ministered

177 Alfred Rambaud, "La Croix de Chevrières de Saint-Vallier, Jean-Baptiste", *DCB*, 2: 328–34. See also Cornelius Jaenen, *The Role of the Church in New France* (Toronto: McGraw-Hill Ryerson, 1976).

178 Jean-Guy Pelletier, "Dosquet, Pierre-Herman", *DCB*, 4: 220–2.

179 See Luca Codignola, "Roman Catholicism: French Colonies" in *Encyclopedia of the North American Colonies*, ed. in chief, Jacob Ernest Cook, 3 vols. (New York: Charles Scribner & Sons, 1993), 3: 546–7.

180 Eccles, *France in America*, 75; also Moogk, *La Nouvelle-France*, 210.

181 Miquelon, *New France, 1701–1744*, 234; Greer, *Peasant, Lord, and Merchant*, 18.

182 Peabody, "A Dangerous Zeal", 70–1.

to both Acadians and their Mi'kmaq neighbours. On Île Royale, the residents of Louisbourg outright refused to support the Recollet priests.[183]

From the beginning of French settlement on Saint-Domingue, religion held an insignificant place in society in contrast to the Windward Islands where Fathers Du Tertre and Labat praised the piety of settlers.[184] In 1701, Father Labat complained about the lack of devotion of the faithful at Cap François.[185] More than elsewhere the secular clergy in Saint-Domingue appeared to be few in number and lacking in zeal. Many were in some sort of trouble with their bishops in France, owing to some reprehensible behaviour, and had fled to the colonies. Members of religious orders did little to improve the tepid religiosity of the colony. Conditions did not improve during the next several decades. Indifference characterised the religion of the Saint-Domingue colonists. If the Catholic clergy reached out to slaves during the seventeenth century, the same cannot be said of the next. Indeed, plantation managers often viewed priests as a real danger to discipline and good order, and discouraged religious instruction and administration of the sacraments as the century wore on.[186]

3. Colonial Towns

Though they held small populations, colonial towns were important in the social and economic lives of all French colonists. Though most accounts give weight to Quebec, in 1726, Saint-Pierre, Martinique was the largest, most cosmopolitan, unruly town in all of French America. With nearly 8,000 inhabitants (5,248 slaves, 2,356 whites, and 343 free coloureds), it held 21.5 percent of Martinique's white population and 14.3 percent of the colony's total. It was more than two and a half times more populous than Quebec and Cap Français.[187] In 1730, Le Cap included 1,075 whites, 62 free people of colour, and 1,749 slaves.[188] When Charlevoix travelled the Mississippi in 1722, he found New Orleans unequal to the meanest French village; it was an encampment of tents housing about 300 men and some

[183] A. J. B. Johnston, *Religion in Life at Louisbourg, 1713–1758* (Kingston and Montreal: McGill-Queen's University Press, 1984), reprinted in 1996 as *Life and Religion at Louisbourg, 1713–1758*.

[184] Quoted in Debien, *Les Esclaves aux Antilles françaises*, 251, 255.

[185] Quoted in Girod, *La vie quotidienne de la société créole*, 162.

[186] Ibid., 164–8; also Peabody, "A Dangerous Zeal", 53–90.

[187] Kenneth Banks, "Commerce and Imperial Absolutism" (unpublished Ph. D thesis, Queen's University, 1994), 128, 140, 152–3; also Col., C^{8A} 37, ff. 14–37 recensement 16 February 1727.

[188] David Geggus, "The Port Towns of Saint Domingue in the later Eighteenth Century" in *Atlantic Port Cities: Economy, Culture, and Society in the Atlantic World, 1650–1850*, eds., Franklin W. Knight and Peggy Liss (Knoxville: University of Tennessee Press, 1991).

women.[189] It was probably little different from Basse-Terre, Guadeloupe, half a century before.[190] St. Pierre, on the other hand, was Martinique's center of commerce and government. Intendants resisted all attempts to move them to the colony's official capital, Fort Royal, and the courts were only shifted in 1692.

While many colonists lived in towns, they did not live in the most common form of collective domicile in France, the village. Colonial settlements in the West Indies were commonly called bourgs, but they were little more than collections of rude huts and sheds in the early days rather than market towns. According to Father Du Tertre, the so-called towns at Guadeloupe were "simply several rows of warehouses ... where foreign merchants sell what they bring and where several artisans have established themselves".[191] In 1694, Father Labat passed through Basse-Pointe, Martinique, which he described as "15 or 20 houses occupied by merchants, workers, and taverns".[192] Villages and village life were absent from the colonies. Attempts to create villages in Canada failed. None emerged naturally before 1730. The extreme youthfulness of the population during the seventeenth century, the scarcity of skilled tradesmen, and lack of local markets mitigated against their appearance. The availability of sufficient free land to support a family in the countryside was another factor. In brief, there were no demographic, economic, or political reasons for villages to appear in the colonies.

As administrative, judicial, military, religious, economic, and cultural centers, towns became crucial to defining the emerging colonial societies, but these towns were unique in a major respect. They lacked any community identity. French municipal traditions of local government did not develop. Colonial towns lacked mayors, town councils or consular jurisdictions, and bourses.[193] Any nascent corporate identity died with the abolition of syndics following Louis XIV's assumption of royal rule. Though French towns normally incorporated franchises and privileges, Colbert quickly suppressed attempts by misguided authorities like Governor-General Frontenac to introduce such concepts into the colonies. Such urban privileges ran completely counter to royal centralisation.[194] Though dominated by the state, colonial towns were also centers of colonial resistance.

[189]   Pierre-François-Xavier Charlevoix, *Histoire et description générale de la Nouvelle France avec le journal historique d'un voyage fait par ordre du roi dans l'Amérique septentrionale*, 6 vols. (Paris: P.-F. Giffart, 1744), 6: 192–3.
[190]   Pérotin-Dumon, "Cabotage, Contraband, and Corsairs", 76.
[191]   Du Tertre, *Histoire général des Antilles*, 2: 449–50; quoted in Pérotin-Dumon, "Cabotage, Contraband and Corsairs", 76.
[192]   Quoted in Chauleau, *Case-Pilote, Le Prêcheur, Basse-Pointe*, 14.
[193]   Cf. Goubert, *The Ancien Régime*, 203–17.
[194]   René Chénier, *Quebec: a French Colonial Town in America, 1660 to 1690* (Ottawa: Parks Services, Environment Canada, 1991), 26.

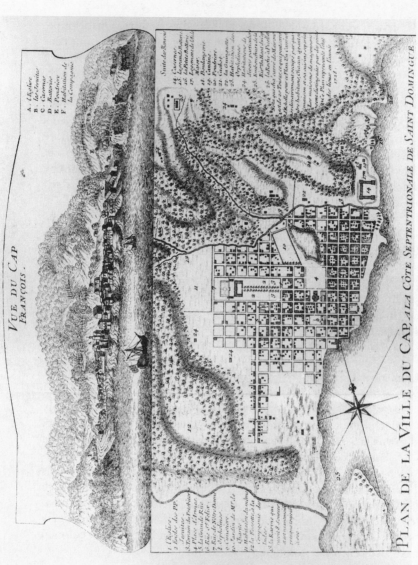

Illustration 2.1. The town of Le Cap François, 1728.
From Pierre François-Xavier Charlevoix. *Histoire de l'Isle espagnole ou de Saint-Domingue*
écrit particulièrement sur les mémoires manuscrits du P. Jean-Baptiste Le Pers. 2 vols.
(Paris: Jacques Guerin, 1730–1731), 1: facing page 101.

All colonial towns, except Montreal, were seaports, and though most were isolated from one another and from France for long periods of time, they remained connected to a wider world. Poor roads, lack of bridges over large rivers, and the absence of ferries left colonial towns poorly connected with the rural homesteads and plantations where the bulk of the colonists and their slaves resided, but the presence of gardens, cow sheds, and livestock reminded them that the countryside was close by. Effective land communications developed only slowly and were scarcely underway by 1730. West Indian colonies relied on coastal transport as did those on North America's Atlantic shores. Roads on Martinique and Guadeloupe were very primitive. In 1696, the road between Fort Royal and St. Pierre remained incomplete; the one between Fort Royal and La Trinité on the windward coast was impassable for two-thirds of the year. Travel was largely along the coast by pirogue.[195] The interior portions of West Indian islands remained very isolated. In New France and later in Illinois and Louisiana, *bateaux*, the ubiquitous canoe and, in winter, horse-drawn sleighs, connected people and places.

All towns in the French colonies were planned. Even the oldest, Quebec (1608) and St. Pierre (1635), displayed features that reflected seventeenth-century French urban planning.[196] Fort Royal, Cap François, and later New Orleans and Louisbourg were laid out in rectilinear grids by military engineers. In addition to the waterfront, colonial towns had a church and an adjacent *place d'armes*. Streets were laid out and markets located. French colonial town life was regulated early on but to little effect. Arrangements were made to halt burials within church walls, to set aside land for cemeteries, and to dispose of garbage. Attempts to clean up towns began in the 1670s with the promulgation of police regulations banning the discharge of night soil and animal entrails into the streets, but the battle for improved sanitation remained a never-ending struggle. Though contemporary France appeared to be the model for colonial towns, absent traditions and local conditions undermined apparent metropolitan influence.

French colonial towns also revealed and reflected the social role played by the Roman Catholic Church. In addition to convents and monasteries in many towns, poor houses (*hopitaux généraux*), hospitals (*hotêls dieus*) and schools run by members of religious orders could be found from Quebec to Fort Royal. At Quebec, Saint Pierre, and New Orleans, Ursuline nuns taught a few young girls. Royal hospitals known as *hopitaux de la charité*, run by

---

195 Col., C⁸ᴬ 9, ff. 276–6v "Mémoire de Robert", 21 April 1696; ibid., 10, ff. 149–50v Mareuil to Pontchartrain, 15 May 1697.

196 Josef W. Konvetz, *Cities and the Sea: Port City Planning in Early Modern Europe* (Baltimore and London: The Johns Hopkins University Press, 1978), Part 2, 73–147; also Chénier, *Quebec: A French Colonial Town in America*, and Johnston, *Control and Order in French Colonial Louisbourg*, 68–88.

Brothers of Charity, who contracted with the minister of marine to care for soldiers of colonial garrisons, also appeared.

Urban space was fragmented social space. Nothing in colonial life encouraged or fostered the development of social relations. Authorities frowned on assemblies as smacking of sedition and faction. The absence of municipal corporations and craft guilds and the presence of slaves, natives, transient soldiers, fishermen, and sailors reinforced the predominant role of family. In Canada, winter brought with it a virtual cessation of all outdoor work, rendering employment seasonal and making existence for the working poor precarious. Little public recreation occurred beyond official ceremonies marking the arrival of new governors-general or Te Deums ordered on news of the King's victories or the coming of peace in far off Europe. Secular and religious processions separated and segregated townsfolk as much as they may have united them. So, too, did religious worship. The clergy who belonged to the first estate lived in their own hierarchies. Nobles, military officers, senior colonial officials – actually civil officers of the navy – and judges occupied the top rungs on the colonial social ladder. Merchants, exporters and importers, and commission agents, not to be confused with shopkeepers, occupied the next highest social positions, but the majority of townspeople lived more modest lives. Skilled artisans were few and highly sought after.[197] Hierarchy also existed in the world of work; silversmiths and master builders stood at the top and hauliers and day labourers at the bottom.

In contrast with Canada and Acadia, the ports and bourgs of the tropical colonies contained a larger proportion of the white population of each colony. There artisans, innkeepers, dock workers, carters, fishermen, and clerks mingled with soldiers from local garrisons and sailors from ships newly arrived from France and elsewhere to comprise a motley crowd of rootless individuals. Little separated these *petit blancs* from mulattos, who also lived in the towns in growing numbers, in lifestyle or occupation. The racial mixing and cultural diversity in colonial towns, especially in the tropical colonies, made them cosmopolitan rather than provincial, but it did not reduce individual alienation. Though not yet numerous in 1730, mulattos already kept apart from *petits blancs* and increasingly competed with them. Not surprisingly, by 1730, whites began to set increasing store on colour differences, which added to the already heavy tensions in these insecure societies.

4. Family

Most students of the New World slave family claim that capitalist ownership and control of women prevented family formation by limiting marriage,

[197] Moogk, *La Nouvelle France*, 164–8.

disallowing paternity, and preventing extended kinship.[198] Though slave marriages were encouraged earlier during the seventeenth century, recognition of marriage and legitimate family formation quickly declined after 1700.[199] As the slave trade improved and sugar production increased, drawing the French West Indian colonies deeper into the nexus of commercial production and marketing, the earlier reasons to encourage slave families declined. At Nippes parish in Saint-Domingue during the 1720s, married slave couples could be found in only 10 of 38 plantations.[200] Childrearing was an unwanted expense to planters. Slave couples existed and were tolerated. They may have considered themselves married, but owners treated them as single if their mates lived on other plantations. They sold spouses and their children. Mother–child bonding undoubtedly existed, but as the average life span of slaves in the West Indies was about seven years and infant mortality was high, such bonds were rare and short lasting.

Louise Dechêne insisted that the importance of the Canadian family at Montreal was due to the initial isolation of the settlement and the weakness of public institutions, and despite the dearth of historical studies of families in the tropical colonies, the same might be said regarding all French colonies before 1730.[201] The family was the only social institution in the colonies that permitted individuals to escape the alienation and loneliness arising from their solitary condition. It is important, then, to ask whether colonial families developed fully in the West Indies. Commodity production based on slavery was essentially a white male enterprise. Wives were replaced by housekeepers and concubines in much of the West Indies. White women were rare in the tropical colonies, and those present appear to have been extremely marginalised. While white family formation occurred during the seventeenth century, the growth of the plantation complex worked against it in the next.

Households predated families. In the Windward Islands, colonial households gave rise to residences of unrelated men and the custom of *matelotage*, or mateship, wherein one man left his share to his comrade. French immigrants generally formed families only after arriving in the New World. Demographers point to an astonishing fact that between 1608 and 1759, a century and a half, only 250 couples married in France before leaving for New France.[202] Similar conditions prevailed in all of the colonies. Family formation, governed as it was by the imbalance between the sexes and the

---

198 Morrissey, *Slave Women in the New World*, 81.
199 Peabody, "A Dangerous Zeal: Catholic Missions", 68.
200 Gautier, *Les Soeurs de solitude*, 82.
201 Dechêne, *Habitants and Merchants*, 237.
202 Hubert Charbonneau and Normand Robert, "The French Origins of the Canadian Population, 1608–1759", *The Historical Atlas of Canada*, Vol. 1, *From the Beginning to 1800* (Toronto: University of Toronto Press, 1987), Plate 45.

extraordinary youthfulness of the populations, occurred only very slowly
after females in sufficient numbers arrived to stay in the colonies. The modern, nuclear, economically independent, two-generation family quickly predominated. In 1681, 76 percent of the 276 households on Montreal Island
contained single families with or without children. Extended and multiple
family households were uncommon. Young married couples rarely lived with
their parents.[203] Montreal families had on average 3.4 living children at
any one time in the seventeenth century, though later on, as the age pyramid assumed the shape of a more mature population, the number fell to
three.

Family formation proceeded even more slowly in the West Indies, where
white societies remained masculinised for a far longer period of time than in
New France. In Martinique, there were still two white men for each white
woman between 1678 and 1687, while in Saint-Domingue, the number of
men per white woman fell from eight to two in 1700. In Guadaloupe, sexual
balance among the adult whites was achieved only after 1733.[204]

Marriage customs quickly became unique in the colonies in response to
settlers' needs. While signing a marriage contract was normally confined to
the well-off in France, the practice became nearly universal in Canada and
elsewhere owing to the need for legal convention in absence of any real estate or kin at the time young couples decided to marry. Several assumptions
of the family law sections of the Custom of Paris did not fit colonial conditions.[205] Immigrants were usually so poor that they brought nothing of
their own to the marriage community, which amounted to little more than
an investment in the future. Most colonists were without kin in the colonies
and signed marriage contracts to avoid any later estate's being escheated (i.e.,
being appropriated by seigneurs or the Crown through the *droit d'aubaine*)
and to ensure the mutual gift of all property and moveables to the surviving
spouse, providing there were no children. While family law provisions of the
Custom of Paris provided for the lateral devolution of property brought into
a marriage to blood relatives of the deceased, colonial necessity demanded
marriage agreements be employed to protect the surviving spouse and children above all other considerations. While French jurisprudence aimed to
protect each spouse's patrimony, colonial custom recognised that few young
people had a patrimony to be protected and instead evolved to protect the
new family's patrimony.

Family needs also shaped inheritance practices in the colonies. The absence of wealth and crippling taxes in New France and the availability of
free land undermined the inheritance provisions of the Custom of Paris.

---

[203] Dechêne, *Habitants and Merchants*, 222–3.
[204] Gauthier, *Les Soeurs de solitude*, 33.
[205] Dechêne, *Habitants and Merchants*, 240–4.

About 25 percent of Canadians employed wills, but chiefly to express their last wishes concerning token gifts, advice to their loved ones, the settlement of old grievances, their own souls and burial place, masses to be said, and charitable bequests. Rarely was there mention of moveables and real estate. The law called for equal sharing of inheritances, but this did not happen. Parents favoured some heirs over others, but out of necessity rather than temperament. Parents wishing to favour one heir over another did so increasingly by deed of gift while still living (*intra vivos*) rather than by will. Gifts were usually made by elderly parents needing care and depending on the good will of their children for their continued well-being. They were made in favour of one heir with the assent of all heirs. Few such elderly couples existed in the seventeenth century, but by 1730 they were more numerous in the colonies, where immigrant populations had been replaced by colonial born.[206]

Remarriage of widows also shows the growing importance of family in the absence of other social institutions enclosing daily life in the colonies. While uncommon in France, remarriages of widows became the norm in the colonies. At Léogane, between 1666 and 1735, 10 percent of all marriages involved widows and widowers; 104 of 117 remarriages involved females.[207] Between 1686 and 1715, fully 50 or 15.5 percent of 323 recorded marriages in three Martinique parishes involved widows.[208] Procedures laid out in the Custom of Paris were generally ignored. The complicated legal procedures to inventory assets of the first marriage community before dissolving it in order to preserve the widow's claim to one-half and childrens' claims to the other half before they were put into the second marriage community were ignored. Colonists marrying widows with small children usually adopted them, thereby making them heirs of the second marriage community. This practice, like others growing in the colonies, was simple, efficient, and above all designed to reinforce the security of the living nuclear family. Patriarchy and authority were its watchwords, but the family was all that lay between the individual and the harsher world beyond.

Traditional forms of extra family relations scarcely existed in the colonies. The absence of craft guilds, religious associations, and village fêtes and the isolation of settlers from one another on individual farms lots left the family as the only institution where lasting social relations developed. Problems arising from ditching, road construction, church building, and bridge building in the Canadian countryside during the early eighteenth century provide compelling evidence of the absence of rural community in New

---

206 Ibid., 244–6.
207 Philippe Haudrère, "Les premiers colons de Léogane, 1666–1735, dans *Commerce et plantation dans la Caraïbe* (Bordeaux: Maison des Pays Ibériques, 1992), 72.
208 Chauleau, *Case-Pilote, Le Prêcheur, Basse-Pointe*, 52–3.

France. Poor settlers obtained few benefits from working for the common good usually defined by others, local notables, parish priests, or outside authorities.[209]

Unfortunately, little is known of affective ties between husbands and wives, parents and children, and between siblings.[210] Colonial conditions ensured that certain characteristics soon came to the fore. The views of the upper classes, however, need to be salted to one's own taste. Colonial authorities and the clergy who were from France constantly complained about disrespectful colonists. Was there ever a priest who did not moan about the behaviour of his flock? Colonists lived like Indians, they asserted; and horror of horrors, like them, they indulged their children, failing to discipline them or teach them respect for their betters. Such examples of individualism were merely evidence of the robustness of families and not to be taken as literally true. All boys 14 years and over learned to fire a musket. Who was going to chastise them?

Women had time to consider marriage. Not even the orphaned "daughters" of the king who arrived in the late 1660s and early 1670s could be stampeded into marriage. Some signed up to four different marriage agreements before settling on their mate.[211] Later on, a few young couples married themselves by the curious custom of "à la gaumine," indicating a certain independence from clerical and parental authority and willingness to commit themselves to one another.[212] Premarital conceptions in New France in the eighteenth century were not exceptional. About one in 10 brides was pregnant on her wedding day.[213]

Despite the high birthrate among women in the northern colonies, parents may not have invested much emotional capital in their children.[214] As noted in the previous chapter, half of them died before reaching adulthood. Children were put to work early on colonial farms. Girls followed their mothers

---

209 Coates, *The Metamorphoses of Landscape*, 114–19.

210 See, however, Denise Lemieux, "La famille en Nouvelle France: des cadres de la vie matérielle aux signes de l'affectivité" dans *De France en Nouvelle-France: société fondatrice et société nouvelle*, dir., Hubert Watelet (Ottawa: Les Presses de l'Université d'Ottawa, 1994), 45–70; and André Lachance, *Vivre, aimer et mourir en Nouvelle France: La vie quotidienne aux xviie at xviiie siècles* (Montréal: Libre Expression, 2000), 56–7, 88–93.

211 Yves Landry, *Orphelines en France: pionnières au Canada: les Filles du roi au XVIIe siècle* (Montéal: Leméac, 1992), 151.

212 Dechêne, *Habitants and Merchants*, 251; Jaenen, *The Role of the Church*, 138; also Coates, *The Metamorphoses of Landscape*, 66.

213 Henripen, *La Population canadienne*, 55, cited in Dechêne, *Habitants and Merchants*, 252.

214 See Linda Pollcock, *Forgotten Children; Parent-Child Relations from 1500 to 1900* (Cambridge: Cambridge University Press, 1983) for an introduction to the debate and extensive literature on whether European children were ignored and unwanted or loved and desired during the early modern period.

and boys their fathers, but work was not coercive as much as integrative, for, particularly on a farm, the family was also a production unit. The terrible fate of young children of widowed mothers dramatically illustrates how broken families failed to ensure any security for the young. Young widows often had no other recourse but to indenture their children as young as three and four years old to ensure the basics of life and a roof over their heads.[215] Family ties appeared to be based on explicit and implicit recognition that no better alternatives existed. The family provided employment, education, and welfare. It regulated conduct. Reciprocity prevailed. Parents aided their children to marry and children cared for their elderly, infirm parents. Orphans were cared for. Kinship ties developed rapidly in Canada as the eighteenth replaced the seventeenth century, and in this manner families spread across New France and Acadia.[216]

2.6 CONCLUSION

French colonial settlements were sometimes founded and constructed by the state; Louisiana and Île Royale are examples. But colonial societies were constructed by the colonists themselves. They transported a certain amount of cultural baggage with them to the New World, but they constructed their new societies during the course of earning their daily bread. New conditions such as the long winters in Canada and the tropical diseases in the Windward Islands and Saint-Domingue, to name only two, were sufficiently radical to challenge French men and women wherever they arrived in the New World. While patriarchy prevailed, the deference derived from rigid social hierarchy in France was missing as a result of the laxness of order.[217]

In Canada where the state had an observable role, the colony evolved from the fur trade into an agricultural colony with a strong military calling whose traditions quickly dissipated during the 1720s, leaving only the traditional agricultural economy to continue. The fur trade continued at Montreal and Quebec, but after 1700 the bulk of the population in the countryside scarcely noticed except when young men found employment as indentured canoemen for one or two seasons before returning to their farms. The state played a negligible role in social formation alongside the biological forces of reproduction and the moral imperatives that drove nonmarket agricultural production.

---

[215] Peter N. Moogk, "Les Petits Sauvages: The Children of Eighteenth-Century New France" in *Childhood and Family in Canadian History*, ed., Joy Parr (Toronto: McClelland and Stewart, 1982), 17–43.

[216] Dechêne, *Habitants and Merchants*, 259.

[217] Moogk, *La Nouvelle France,* presents a view of colonial society that is more highly structured and less free and open than what is argued here.

At the same time, French colonial societies bore little resemblance to one another. Indeed, slavery and capitalism shaped those given over to the plantation complex. In the West Indies and Guiana, colonial societies remained heavily masculine. Individuals were isolated and alone, perpetually brutalised by the mode of economic production. Societies contained few institutions or processes that permitted or encouraged social integration. Consequently, Martinique and other tropical colonies had difficulty developing and maintaining the social coherence and cultural integrity necessary to establish colonial identity.[218]

The uniqueness of Canadian society is all the more striking because it did not resemble other contemporary North American societies. This was not due to French culture. Language and religion disguised a much more basic difference, namely that the St. Lawrence Valley colony existed largely outside the nexus of capitalist production. By 1730, the great majority of Canadian colonists lived in the countryside, where they were creating a peasant society of the western European type based on a traditional nonmarket economy, the likes of which could not be found elsewhere in the New World. On the Atlantic littoral, fishing shaped the transient, masculine societies of Placentia and Île Royale. With their backs to America, firmly facing the sea, and their markets in France, Placentia and later Île Royale were unlike colonial societies in Canada and in the West Indies.

The differences between French colonial societies were far greater than any cultural features that might be thought to unite them. Combined with weak public institutions, only the French state and an unworkable colonial policy might be said to unite them, but the French government's involvement in overseas expansion is chiefly noticeable because there was so little else. It appeared dominant only in the absence of a dynamic commercial impetus.

[218] See Peter Hulme, *Colonial Encounters, Europe, and the Native Caribbean, 1492–1797* (London: Routledge, 1986), 139.

3

Production

3.1 INTRODUCTION

The Americas were more important as a source of commodities than as markets for manufactured goods. From a French or even a European perspective, American products can be divided into three categories. The first were those replacing or supplementing products already available. The second were Asian commodities successfully transferred to America, and the third comprised indigenous American products wholly unknown in the Old World.[1] Combined with demographics, commodity production for export (or in the case of Canada not for export) shaped colonial societies more forcefully than is often imagined.

Historians sometimes forget that early explorers made as much of the familiar and the commonplace (fish, furs, cereals, grapes, and nuts) found in the New World as of the exotic and strange, and that propagandists often stressed the easy acquisition of the former. After gold and silver, fish were the first goods sought in the New World. Indeed, fish may have preceded gold as the first New World commodity hunted by Europeans.[2] Though America was filled with as many trees as the North Atlantic was filled with fish, timber, potash, and other forest products proved too costly to transport. For a long time only dye woods from Central and South America could carry the freight charges from the New World to the Old. Furs became a more significant commodity. Not only did they supplement and replace the products of a dying European industry, their exchange later contoured and textured the French colonial society that emerged in the Saint Lawrence Valley.[3]

[1]   See K. G. Davies, *The North Atlantic World in the Seventeenth Century* (Minneapolis: University of Minnesota Press, 1974), 141–3.
[2]   David Harris Sachs, *The Widening Gate: Bristol and the Atlantic Economy, 1450–1700* (Berkeley: University of California Press, 1991), 35.
[3]   Harold Adams Innis, *The Fur Trade in Canada, An Introduction to Canadian Economic*

Other familiar products failed to appear for a variety of reasons. The demand for naval stores, masts, timber, pitch, tar, and hemp grew steadily, but despite heavy subsidies colonial supplies appeared, if at all, only during the second quarter of the eighteenth century.[4] Intendant Jean Talon enthusiastically established the first tar works in New France in 1671 and announced the manufacture of tar of excellent quality, but the high cost of production prevented it from becoming a colonial export. The best that could be done was to manufacture a sufficient quantity at a price that allowed colonial shipbuilders to cease importing supplies from metropolitan France after 1730.[5] The same could not be said of hemp. In 1720 Intendant Michel Bégon offered heavily subsidised prices, agreeing to take all that was presented and to pay two and a half to three times French prices. However, poor quality of colonial hemp led the minister to eliminate the subsidy by 1730, and exports quickly ceased. Local shipbuilders continued importing rope from France.[6] America was also capable of producing wool, cotton, and flax, but once again costs and sometimes ideology prevented success. In 1702, Intendant François de Beauharnois encouraged flax cultivation, but the secretary of state for the marine categorically refused to send weavers to Canada. "The colony", he asserted, "must not harm the industries in the mother country".[7]

Goods originating in Asia were much more successfully reproduced in America. Sugar, first manufactured in India many centuries before the modern era, became the greatest fashioner of French colonial societies in tropical America. Ginger was grown on Guadeloupe. When mixed with pepper, cloves, and cinnamon and sold in Europe as "mild spice", it proved popular. When crystallized into a *confit*, it benefited the digestion and was considered a strong antiscorbutic. Between 1698 and 1702 ginger on Guadeloupe fetched from 10 to 14 livres per quintal.[8] Indigo, cotton, and coffee, also from the East, became successful export commodities as well, but only indigo developed before 1700. Cotton grew naturally in Cayenne and the Lesser Antilles. It was introduced into St. Christopher and Martinique as early as 1636 in order to diversify colonial production. By the 1660s, growing profits from sugar discouraged production, and cotton became a crop for

---

History (Toronto: University of Toronto Press, 1930) is badly in need of replacement. See W. J. Eccles, *Essays on New France* (Toronto: Oxford Universty Press, 1987) and Dale Miquelon, *New France, 1701–1744; "A Supplement to Europe"* (Toronto: McClelland and Stewart, 1987).

4   See Paul W. Bamford, *Forests and French Sea Power, 1660–1789* (Toronto: University of Toronto Press, 1956), 117–28.

5   Joseph-Noël Fauteux, *Essai sur l'industrie au Canada sous le régime française,* 2 vols. (Québec: Ls.-A. Proulx, 1927), 2: 309–19; A.J.E. Lunn, "Economic Development in New France, 1713–1760" (unpublished Ph.D. thesis, McGill University, 1942), 236–7, 471.

6   Ibid., 75–9; also Colin Coates, *The Metamorphoses of Landscape and Community in Early Quebec* (Montreal and Kingston: McGill-Queens University Press, 2000), 434.

7   Jean-Claude Dubé, "Beauharnois de La Chaussaye, François de", *DCB*, 3: 52.

8   Jean-Baptiste Labat, *Nouveau voyage aux Isles de l'Amérique,* 2 vols. (La Haye: P. Husson, T. Johnson, P. Gosse, Ivan Duren, R. Atberts, and C. Le Vier [1722] 1724), 1: pt 2, 147–50.

the poor. Many *petit blancs* grew cotton on Guadeloupe in 1682 following the sacrifice of their interests to tobacco monopolists.[9] Colonists on Saint-Domingue turned to cotton about the same time for similar reasons.[10] During the early eighteenth century, cotton production increased substantially in response to growing European demand. In 1730, more than 10 million *pieds* of cotton – 1,500 *pieds* per hectare – worth about 2.5 million livres, were under cultivation on Guadeloupe. Only a very small amount of cotton was grown in Saint-Domingue, but the number of feet of cotton planted on Martinique reached 2.9 million in 1731, and more than 10,000 quintals were exported two years later.[11]

Cocoa refers to beans from the cacao tree, which is native to the West Indies. These beans were shipped to chocolate makers. The first plantation was established in Martinique around 1660, and Governor Ogeron encouraged similar developments on Saint-Domingue shortly afterward.[12] Fifteen or so slaves could maintain 100,000 trees, and with a yield of one livre weight of cocoa, worth 7 or 8 sols per tree, a colonist could count on an annual revenue of 40,000 livres. The government showed little interest in cocoa, giving priority to increasing revenues rather than developing markets. In September of 1697, insignificant consumption of cocoa in France was the stated reason for refusing to remove entry duties to encourage production.[13] Nevertheless, by the early eighteenth century, cocoa planters were achieving greater wealth than three-quarters of the sugar planters in the colonies. Martinique exported about 6,000 quintals of cocoa in 1710. However, between 1715 and 1720 insects destroyed nearly the entire Martinique cocoa crop.[14] The same occurred on Saint-Domingue. There, the climate was deemed unsuitable and planting was abandoned.[15] Planters on Martinique quickly recovered, exporting 14,000 quintals of cocoa in 1722. Cocoa became the major crop in Martinique's Gros-Morne district, reaching its greatest extent of 17,492,950 *pieds* (about 11,400 hectares) in 1726.[16] Several years of heavy rains, hurricanes, an earthquake in the winter of 1727, and disease attacked all the trees

9   AN, SOM, G¹ 469, f. 120.
10 Stewart L. Mims, *Colbert's West India Policy* (New Haven: Yale University, 1912), 30, 65, 242, 258, 261 and 269; also Labat, *Nouveau voyage aux Isles*, 1, pt. 2: 125–31.
11 Maurice Satineau, *Histoire de la Guadeloupe, 1635–1789* (Paris: Payot, 1928), 383; Louis-Philippe May, *Histoire économique de la Martinique, (1635–1763)*, Fort-de-France: Société de distribution et de culture, [1930] 1972), 86, Tableau II [307]; AN, SOM, G¹ 509, no. 19 Recensement générale de la coste de St. Domingue de l'année, 1721.
12 Ibid., 89–91 citing Labat, *Nouveau voyage aux Isles*, 2: 349; also Pierre-François-Xavier Charlevoix, *Histoire de l'isle espagnol ou de S. Domingue*, 2 vols. (Paris: Jacques Guerin, 1730–31), 2: 390.
13 Col., B 18, ff. 501v–2 Memoir of the King to Amblimont and Robert, 4 September 1697.
14 May, *Histoire économique de la Martinique*, 92.
15 Col., C⁹ᴮ Extrait from Chateaumorand and Mithon to Navy Council, 18 November 1717.
16 Col., C⁸ᴬ 37, ff. 37–7v Recensement generale de l'isle Martinique … [1726]. Eugène Revert, *La Martinique, étude géographique et humaine* (Paris: Nouvelles Editions Latines, 1949), 343 gives 14,462,620 *pieds* in 1727 as the greatest extent.

in the colony, and cocoa never recovered. It ceased to be an important crop in the island's economy. On Saint-Domingue cocoa survived only because of the careful cultivation of single trees in a few private gardens.

The loss of cocoa after 1715 led the government to send some coffee plants to the West Indies, which ultimately proved to be serendipitous. Coffee appeared to be the salvation of cocoa planters. Originally from Arabia and well-known in Dutch colonies, it was introduced into the French tropical colonies during the Regency, first to Cayenne and then to Martinique. Guadeloupe remained a minor producer. Only 20,000 feet of coffee trees yielding a mere 10,000 livres' weight were being cultivated there in 1730, but "coffee fever" seized Martinique. Between 1727 and 1737, the number of coffee trees on the island increased from 100,000 to 12.8 million, and exports attained 600 tonnes by 1733.[17]

The great spices from the East – pepper, cloves, nutmeg, and cinnamon – were all tried in Martinique, first in 1699 and again in 1719, but the results were inconsequential.[18] Lack of skill or perhaps just bad luck may have been the chief reason for failure because today, by a supreme irony, the tiny island of Grenada is one of the largest producers of nutmeg in the world.[19]

Attempts to produce silk on Martinique failed miserably despite a major effort. Production had been successfully transferred to France, and in 1673 Colbert suggested that silk might encourage greater diversification of crops among the island's planters. Whether he was really convinced, or only loyally serving his master, who took a personal interest in expanding silk production, is unclear. It was Seignelay who actually initiated the project, sending workers and seeds of the mulberry bush to the colony in 1682.[20] Intendant Michel Bégon took a lively interest in the project and personally carried the first silkworm cocoons to the island.[21] Within two years, thousands of seedings had been propagated and were ready for distribution, and by 1687 two skeins of silk were dispatched to the French court, where they were greatly admired. The crown obliged all landowners to plant mulberry bushes to feed the silkworms, but serious problems quickly occurred.[22] Governor-General Blénac ordered an inquiry to seek reasons for the death of the mulberry trees but prejudiced the case by demanding to know whether human negligence or unsuitable soil was to blame. Colonial authorities became discouraged,

17 Michel Devèze, *Antilles, Guyanes, la mer des Caraïbes de 1492 à 1789* (Paris: SEDES, 1977), 257; Satineau, *Histoire de la Guadeloupe*, 383.

18 May, *Histoire économique de la Martinique*, 101–2.

19 George Brizan, *Grenada, Island of Conflict, From Amerindians to People's Revolution, 1498–1979* (London: Zed Books, 1985), 298–9.

20 May, *Histoire économique de la Martinique*, 99–100.

21 Col., C^{8A} 3, ff. 243–4 Bégon to Colbert, 29 May 1683; Yvonne Bezard, *Fonctionnaires maritimes et coloniaux sous Louis XIV: Les Bégon* (Paris: Albin Michel, 1932), 40–1.

22 Pierre-Regis Dessalles, *Annales du conseil souverain de la Martinique*, 2 vols. in 4 (Paris: L'Harmattan, [1786] 1995), 1: 297.

and in 1694 Bégon's successor concluded the silk project was hopeless.[23] The high cost of land and continuing labour shortages removed any incentive to experiment with outlandish, specialised crops when cane sugar guaranteed a profit. Earlier evidence of a mass dying off of young mulberry trees suggests they failed to adapt to their new environment.

In Guiana colonists manufactured rocou, a red dye made from a cooked mash of seeds and surrounding pulp from *uruca*, a bush or tree native to South America. Rocou's great advantage to homesteaders was that it required almost no investment and could be produced by all family members, including children.[24] Its disadvantage lay in the free entry of foreign imports into France, which often destroyed prices, leaving colonists victims of over-production.[25] In 1715, rocou accounted for more than half of Cayenne's exports, but the growing number of settlers producing rocou led to ever-increasing supplies and falling prices. Attempts to cut production or to fix prices failed.[26] French prices fell by 50 percent as French merchants refused to accept any quantities at all, and the Navy Council refused to forbid production in the West Indies.[27] The solution appeared to lie in coffee. By 1722 some 16,270 young coffee trees and more than 30,000 seeds were under cultivation,[28] but the need for slave labour and work discipline soon revealed that only wealthy colonists could make a success of the new crop.

In the West Indies, especially Saint-Domingue, the French also produced indigo, which became the most important of all the subsidiary crops. Originally an Asian dye stuff, it was a source of blue, quite superior to European woad, and had been imported into Europe since ancient times. It was also very expensive. Spanish discovery of a wild species of American indigo, its subsequent cultivation in Guatemala and introduction into the French and English West Indies in the 1630s and 1640s, led to a rapidly reduced dependence on the Asian product and a growing market for American indigo.[29]

[23] May, *Histoire économique de la Martinique*, 196–7 for copy of Blénac's order, dated 5 January 1689; also Col. C⁸ᴬ 8, f. 15 Blénac and Dumaitz to Pontchartrain, 19 April 1694; and ibid., f. 154 Dumaittz to Pontchartrain, 1 March 1694.

[24] Labat, *Nouveau voyage aux Isles*, 1: 85–90; Satineau, *Histoire de la Guadeloupe*, 383.

[25] Col., C¹⁴ 2, f. 6 Saint-Marthe to Seignelay, 13 August 1686.

[26] Col., C¹⁴ᴬ X 8, ff. 16–26v Granval to Pontchartrain, 7 March 1714; ibid., ff. 99–104 Lefebvre d'Albon to Pontchartrain, 8 January 1715; and ibid., 105–12 same to same, 8 March 1715. Ibid., 8, ff. 99–104 Lefebvre d'Albon to Navy Council, 9 January 1717; ibid., f. 105–12 same to same, 5 March 1715; ibid., 9, ff. 198–200 same to same, 13 September 1716.

[27] Ibid., 11, ff. 37–9 Decisions of the Navy Council, 6 September 1718.

[28] Ibid., 13, ff. 91–2 La Mothe Aigron to Navy Council, 27 March 1722; ibid., ff. 161–2v Lefebvre d'Albon to Council, 22 January 1723; and ff. 295–6 Etat sommaire de la colonie, October 1722.

[29] Lyle N. McAlister, *Spain and Portugal in the New World, 1492–1700* (Minneapolis: University of Minnesota Press, 1984), 221, 365; Holden Furber, *Rival Empires of Trade in the Orient, 1600–1800* (Minneapolis: University of Minnesota Press, 1976), 259.

Governor-General de Baas exempted indigo plantations from taxes for two years in 1671 to encourage production but with little apparent effect.[30] By 1683 only 48 indigo works were operating, chiefly on Marie Galante and to a much lesser degree on Guadeloupe.[31] Four years later, however, 171 indigo works were reported on St. Christopher and the smaller islands; none were located on Guadeloupe or Saint-Domingue.[32]

Indigo was a transitional crop for colonists lacking sufficient capital to begin cultivating sugarcane. It was adopted increasingly after 1680 in the wake of collapsing tobacco prices. Successful indigo producers required more capital than had been initially believed, and during the 1690s, only richer planters continued. As sugar became profitable at the end of the Nine Years' War, indigo ceased to be an important crop in the Windward Islands. Little was ever produced on Martinique, and exports were no longer reported after 1726.[33] The number of Guadeloupe's indigo works never exceeded seven after 1715 and declined to zero by 1730.[34]

The history of indigo on Saint-Domingue, where the number of indigo works and sugar boiling houses grew in tandem, provides a strong contrast. In 1694, indigo was succeeding where tobacco and cotton had earlier failed.[35] Two years later, indigo appeared to be the colony's only profitable export.[36] By 1713 the colony could boast of 1,182 indigo works, including 829 in the southern district, and in 1730 there were 2,744.[37] The value of indigo exported from Saint-Domingue during these early years sometimes surpassed the value of sugar. Indigo accounted for 60 percent of the colony's total exports, two and a half times the value of sugar in 1709–10, and the proportion would have been greater had exports from the southern district been included.[38] Production increased, but in 1717 indigo accounted for just 38 percent of the colony's exports. Nevertheless, in 1720, the crop, worth 2.97 million livres, accounted for 53 percent of the colony's total exports.[39]

[30] May, *Histoire économique de la Martinique*, 86.
[31] Col., C^{8B} 17, no. 19 Recensements des isles de l'Amérique, 12 April 1683; Satineau, *Histoire de la Guadeloupe*, 126.
[32] AN., SOM., G¹, 498, no. 59 Recensement générale des Isles françaises de l'Amérique, [1686].
[33] May, *Histoire économique de la Martinique*, 86.
[34] AN, SOM, G¹, 469, ff. 140–9 Guadeloupe censuses 1720 to 1725; Satineau, *Histoire de la Guadeloupe*, 383.
[35] Charlevoix, *Histoire de l'isle espagnol ou de S.. Domingue*, 2: 253–4.
[36] Marine, B⁴ 17, f. 324; Col., C^{9B} 1, Ducasse to Pontchartrain, 15 December 1696; and ibid., 4, arrêt du conseil, 18 July 1696.
[37] Charles Frostin, *Les Révoltes blanches à Saint-Domingue aux XVIIe et XVIIIe siècle, (Haiti avant 1789)*, (Paris: L'École, 1975), 144–5.
[38] Col., C^{9B} 1 Estat des marchandises des Isles chargés pour France dans les vaisseaux marchants non compris le quartier de St. Louis depuis le premier may 1709 jusqu'au 1 may 1710.
[39] Ibid., 7, "Extrait de l'Etat des Vaisseaux pour 1720" in Duclos to Navy Council, 25 June 1721.

Strong foreign demand encouraged this production. Indigo was largely re-exported to Holland, Sweden, Denmark, Hamburg, and Poland.[40] Between 1717 and 1720, the value of Bordeaux's imports from the West Indies grew from nearly 600,000 to more than 2 million livres.[41] The value of indigo imported into La Rochelle – about 240 tonnes – roughly matched that of sugar until the middle of the eighteenth century; for the port's merchants, it was the primary re-export to northern Europe.[42] In 1729, 490,500 livres' weight of indigo entered Bordeaux from the West Indies; about 86 percent of it originated at Saint-Domingue.[43] The indigo grown in Saint-Domingue's southern quarter entered European markets illegally owing to strong demand and the exceptional ease of transport to Jamaica. Unlike sugar and sirop, which were very heavy and required time to load, indigo produced in this distant area of the colony, where habitant leaders ignored the king's authority and actively collaborated with smugglers, was easy to carry away.[44] So much contraband trade was carried on in the south by 1732 that the minister of the marine approved the governor-general's suggestion to either fill in the main harbour on Île à Vaches opposite Les Cayes, or divert its freshwater source into the sea in order to discourage smugglers based there.[45] During the early eighteenth century, indigo, cotton, cocoa, and coffee, like sugar itself, seemed primarily affected by international price increases due to heightened demand rather than government encouragement of production.

The biological exchange between the Old and New Worlds was pro-found, but the actual process of transfer was very slow. Though study of the transoceanic exchange of flora and fauna and of pathogenic bacteria and viruses has only begun, it is clear that America's greatest treasure was not gold and silver, but food crops: cassava, maize, potatoes, tomatoes, paprika, peppers, pineapples, cocoa, tobacco, Jerusalem artichokes, squashes, and

---

[40] Michel Morineau, "Quelques recherches relatives à la balance du commerce exterieur français au XVIIIe ou cette fois un egale deux", *Aires et structures de commerce français au XVIIIe siècles*, Pierre Léon dir. (Paris: Centre d'histoire économique et sociale de la région lyonnais, 1975), 34.

[41] ADG., C 4268, ff. 73v–4, 89v–90, 113v–14, and 134–4v. Charlevoix, *Histoire de l'isle espagnole ou de S. Domingue*, 2: 489 claimed the colony's indigo was worth three million in 1724.

[42] John C. Clark, *La Rochelle and the Atlantic Economy during the Eighteenth Century* (Baltimore and London: The Johns Hopkins University Press, 1981), 163–4; and Henri Robert, "Les trafics coloniaux du port de la Rochelle au xviiie siècle", *Mémoires de la société des antiquaires de l'ouest*, 4ème série (1960), 5.

[43] Morineau, "Quelquel recherches relative à la balance du commerce exterieur français au XVIIIe siècle, 32–4.

[44] Col., C⁹ᴮ 5 "Mémoire sur le commerce étrangère, 1719". See also Richard Pares, *War and Trade in the West Indies, 1739–1761*, reprint (London: Frank Cass, [1936] 1963), 101, 182–3, 330, 357 and 417–19.

[45] John Garrigus, "Blue and Brown: Contraband Indigo and the Rise of a Free Coloured Planter Class in French Saint-Domingue", *The Americas*, 50 (1993), 240–44.

beans.[46] Without them the industrialisation of northern Europe might not have occurred, and the present human population of the world could not be sustained. Today two-thirds of the world's potatoes and maize are grown in Europe, Africa, and Asia, and 80 percent of the world's sweet potatoes are harvested in China.[47] However, of the rich store of indigenous crops, only tobacco found a ready market in Europe before 1700. Cocoa appeared during the final quarter of the century, but the demand remained small. Other crops were sometimes another two centuries before finding markets overseas.

The conditions of trade lay at the heart of the erratic adoption and transfer of American crops. While the policies of metropolitan governments cannot be ignored, it was the factors of production, capital, land, labour, and conditions of transportation that created the economic problems of the colonial period. Except for indigenous tobacco and cocoa, the commodities exported from the colonies were all available elsewhere. Fish, fur, sugar, indigo, ginger, and cotton had to compete, as did tobacco. For this as well as for another important reason, by 1670 tobacco was rapidly ceasing to be a French colonial export.

3.2 TOBACCO

A European market for tobacco existed well before the second quarter of the seventeenth century. The first generation of colonists found tobacco easy to plant alongside their provisions of manioc and beans needed to support life. According to one early account a single man could grow 1,000 pounds of tobacco in addition to his own food. Father Du Tertre claimed that a plot or "jardin" 100 paces square, containing 10,000 plants, each spaced 3 feet from the other, ideally yielded between 1,500 and 2,000 pounds of tobacco.[48] Few men worked alone, however, and Father Labat estimated that two or three men working on a standard concession of 10,000 to 15,000 square paces might harvest annually between 3,000 and 4,000 pounds of leaf from which they could earn sufficient to pay off their creditors and to purchase white indentured bondsmen and even African slaves to increase production.[49] Tobacco was ideally suited to first generation settlers. It grew in varied soils under different climatic conditions, required little land and capital, and yielded

[46]   See Alfred W. Crosby, *Ecological Imperialism: The Biological Expansion of Europe, 900–1900* (New York: Cambridge University Press, 1986), and Herman J. Viola and Carolyn Margolis, eds., *Seeds of Change, A Quincentennial commemoration* (Washington and London: Smithsonian Institution, 1991).

[47]   William H. McNeill, "American Food Crops in the Old World", in *Seeds of Change*, eds., Viola and Margolis, 43–59.

[48]   May, *Histoire de la Martinique*, 84; and Jean-Baptiste Du Tertre, *Histoire générale des Antilles habitées par les Françoise*, 4 vols. (Paris: T. Jolly, 1667–1671), 2: 100.

[49]   Labat, *Nouveau Voyage aux Isles*, 1: pt. 2, 179; also cited in Satineau, *Histoire de la Guadeloupe*, 113.

a quick return. A crop could be grown in nine months. By 1640, tobacco had become the only export crop from the French West Indies.[50]

However, the same qualities that made tobacco a pioneer crop undermined its continuing success. Tobacco could be grown almost anywhere in the world, including France, but it also quickly exhausted the soil. Its success was the precondition of glut, and the secular downward trend in prices had already set in before French settlers began to cultivate the crop. All planter strategies to respond to lower prices failed. Finally, a much better quality leaf was grown in more temperate climates than in the tropics, and the West Indian islands lost any comparative advantage they might have previously enjoyed. By the 1660s French planters in the Windward Islands were rapidly abandoning tobacco cultivation, and in 1674 Colbert completed its demise as a colonial export crop. The subsequent history of tobacco in the French colonies, however, provides a revealing insight into just how little, if any, policy planning lay behind the colonial activities of Colbert and his successors.

Duties had been levied on tobacco entering France as early as 1621; a proposal in 1629 to exempt colonial tobacco came to naught. By 1662, West Indian tobacco paid duty of at least 11 livres per quintal, which in some areas amounted to more than 100 percent of its market value. The size of the tariff was less significant, however, than the absence of legislative, administrative, and judicial unity in France, without which no means to achieve an equitable national customs duty existed. A tax-farmed monopoly may have been the only means available to raise an equitable revenue for the Crown from colonial products.

Colbert is commonly credited with encouraging tobacco cultivation in the islands, not only by restricting its cultivation in France and Canada, but by favourable tariff treatment.[51] At first, he sought to levy an import duty of 4 and 13 livres per quintal, respectively, on colonial and foreign tobacco. These duties were quite light in contrast to the existing ones and were clearly intended to encourage increased production at home and overseas, but colonial preference was negligible. The same year, the West India Company was granted exemption from all duties on colonial imports destined for re-export, and this, it may be argued, did promote colonial cultivation. From 1666 to 1673, however, Colbert also reduced duties on foreign imports and repeatedly confirmed his action, thereby negating colonial tobacco's privileged position.[52] Moreover, until its dissolution in 1674, the West India Company also collected an additional 5 percent *ad valorem* duty (reduced

[50] Mims, *Colbert's West India Policy*, 250.
[51] E.g., Charles W. Cole, *Colbert and a Century of French Mercantilism*, 2 vols. (New York: Columbia University Press, 1939), 2: 22, 45–9.
[52] Jacob Price, *France and the Chesapeake: A History of the French Tobacco Monopoly, 1674–1791 and Its Relationship to the British and American Tobacco Trades*, 2 vols., (Ann Arbor: University of Michigan Press, 1973), 15–16.

to 3 percent in July of 1671) from private importers of colonial tobacco.[53] In brief, Colbert did nothing to promote tobacco production in the colonies.

The quality of French tobacco was inferior to most American leaf. A prices-current list from Rouen from 1669 lists St. Christopher tobacco at well below Virginia prices.[54] Production had also declined below earlier levels. By 1670, the amount of Guadeloupe's 80,000 to 100,000 livres' weight annually was matched by the island's cotton and ginger; it was no contest compared to the millions of pounds of sugar being produced.[55] A similar development was occurring on Martinique, where only 364 *carreaux* of arable were given over to tobacco compared to 1,070 *carreaux* for provisions and 767 *carreaux* for sugarcane.[56] In 1671, only four fields of tobacco existed on St. Christopher compared to sixty of ginger.[57] Tobacco was among the least of the Windward Islands' exports. At La Rochelle, between 1670 and 1675, tobacco was in fifth place behind indigo, ginger, cotton, and sugar, which accounted for 90 percent by weight of colonial imports entering the seaport.[58] Only on Saint-Domingue, where it continued to be a pioneer crop, did tobacco production increase after 1670. Production, which reached 1,200,000 pounds by 1669, doubled five years later. By 1674 total French colonial production probably came to no more than 3 million pounds.[59] In 1668–9, London alone received 9 million pounds mostly from Virginia and Maryland.[60] French colonial production was modest, declining, and of poor quality. Why, then, was so much effort expended on it during the next half century?

Before the outbreak of the Dutch War in 1672, Colbert sought to improve the quality of colonial tobacco imported into France rather than encourage colonists to produce more. Thus, in 1669, Governor Ogeron issued an ordinance abolishing the settlement of debts on Saint-Domingue and Tortuga in tobacco in order to reduce fraud and improve quality. The ordinance proved ineffective and old practices continued, but because the use of tobacco currency encouraged overproduction and poor quality, Colbert's intention seems clear. In 1671 Governor-General de Baas attempted to limit production on Martinique by setting standards for cultivating, harvesting, drying, and spinning tobacco, but to no avail.[61] Finally, in 1672, Colbert forbad tobacco cultivation in New France in order, he wrote, to reduce competition

---

53   Mims, *Colbert's West India Policy*, p. 251; and Price, *France and the Chesapeake*, 82.

54   Price, *France and the Chesapeake*, 173, 174.

55   Satineau, *Histoire de la Guadeloupe*, 206.

56   May, *Histoire économique de la Martinique*, 85.

57   AN, SOM, G^1, 471 Denombrement générale des terres de l'île de St. Christophe, 1671.

58   Marcel Delafosse, "La Rochelle et les Îles au XVIIe siècle", *RHC*, 36 (1949), 257.

59   Mims, *Colbert's West India Policy*, 251; Price, *France and the Chesapeake*, 83, points out that the second figure appeared only retrospectively in 1692 and may be for all colonies rather than just St. Domingue as Mims suggested.

60   Davies, *North Atlantic World*, 145–6.

61   Col., A 24, f. 145 ordonnance de Baas, 5 February, 1671; Dessalles, *Annales du conseil souverain de la Martinique*, 1: 128–9, 139.

for the Caribbean product,[62] but the order had no effect. West Indian tobacco failed to find a market in New France, and Canadian settlers grew white tobacco for their own use while merchants imported Brazilian (black) tobacco for the fur trade.[63]

Colbert had no alternative. By removing Dutch competitors and increasing freights, his tariff policy had raised production costs and lowered tobacco prices in the colonies. Improving quality was the only way to overcome the new economic obstacles. Whatever Colbert and his successors may have thought about colonial development, their ideas were discrete notions that did not add up to empire building.[64] The fisc alone was central to Colbert's thought.[65] His ideas about colonies were not sufficiently well-thought-out nor consistent enough to be called policy. Even before the Franco-Dutch War they were always part of a much larger, though not necessarily coherent, context of state building that included such intangibles as the king's prestige and his *gloire*, on the one hand, and the harsh reality of short-term fiscal demands of the state on the other.

During the course of liquidating the West India Company, Colbert leased its rights to collect taxes and duties in the colonies. The tax-farm became known as the *Domaine d'occident*. The press of wartime finances called for more revenue-enhancing measures, however, and in 1674, Colbert established a new tax-farm on tobacco out of the ruins of the old company, creating a single buyer in France for domestic, colonial, and foreign tobacco, and fixing wholesale prices at 20 and 40 sols per livre for French and foreign tobacco, respectively.[66] Private importers intending to re-export could do so, but only if they held their stocks in the buyer's warehouse. In short, all duties on tobacco were removed and replaced by a monopsony – a single buyer rather than a monopoly, which is a single seller – in order to provide a new revenue for the Crown during wartime. The tax-farm lease was a brilliant introduction of a consumption tax of the type that no modern state can do without.

The idea for the new tax-farm did not originate from any concern for the colonies, their development, or a desire to improve tobacco production. It may not even have originated with Colbert; it may owe its origins to a number of ambitious financiers who were deeply involved in court politics at the very highest level.[67] However, the financiers did not obtain a cash cow.

---

62 *RAPQ, 1930–31*, 168 Colbert to Talon, 4 June 1672.
63 Louise Dechêne, *Habitants and Merchants in Seventeenth Century Montreal*, trans., Liana Vardi (Montreal and Kingston: McGill-Queen's University Press, [1974] 1992), 83.
64 Price, *France and the Chesapeake*, 78–80, 81.
65 Daniel Dessert, *Argent, pouvoir et société au Grand siècle* (Paris: Fayard, 1985), 325–38.
66 Mims, *Colbert's West India Policy*, 252–3 has been superseded by Price, *France and the Chesapeake*, 17–25.
67 Price, *France and the Chesapeake*, 17–51; and Dessert, *Argent, pouvoir et société*, 389, 511–12.

MENAGERIE

1. Coffe à Petun.
2. Negre qui étambe le petun.
3. Negre qui le torque à 33.
4. Negre qui le monte.
5. Il qui ratiffent le Manioc.
6. Moulin a greger le Manioc.
7. Ancienne maniere de greger le Manioc 11a.

Y. La Preffe.
9. Negreffe paffant la farine.
10. Negreffe qui cuit la caffaue.
11. La Poye de manitre.

12. La Cuifine.
13. Caffaue qui feiche.
14. Coraffole à 111.

Acquiring the tax-farm was a risky business, and in time, it proved unsuccessful. Tobacco was initially expected to raise only three-fifths of the 3.4 million livres to be paid to the Crown during the six-year lease beginning on 1 December 1674. The remainder was to come from a second, wholly unrelated monopoly on hallmarking and stamping pewter. Concern for revenue and administrative convenience drove this arrangement, not ideas about colonial expansion or development. Gross receipts during the first few years exceeded the lease price, but they did not cover the costs of setting up, collecting, and regulating tobacco purchases and sales in France. Receipts declined annually after 1676. Total income paid to the government amounted to approximately 85 percent of the leased price, and the tax-farmers asked to be relieved of their burden.

Colbert clearly understood the primacy of the state's short-term fiscal demands over economic development, especially during wartime. He was not the dupe of financiers. As controller-general of finances, in effect the state's chief auditor, he was their closest associate. In order to assist them, the government began restricting domestic cultivation of tobacco starting in 1676. Colbert initially claimed this was a means to protect colonial production, but he refused every anguished appeal not to destroy the work of small settlers who lacked sufficient labour and capital to diversify into some other commodity. Colbert was not unaware of the growing misery in the colonies. In the years after peace was achieved in 1678, Governor Pouançay wrote him repeatedly with the same message of desperate men becoming pirates or emigrating from Saint-Domingue to Dutch Curaçao or to English Jamaica, men to whom he held out false hopes that the tobacco monopoly would be cancelled at the termination of the lease.[68] In 1680 Intendant Jean-Baptiste Patoulet claimed that four to 5,000 men in the islands had withdrawn from tobacco cultivation.[69] The decline of tobacco production is a major reason why freebooting and piracy increased again during the 1680s. Small planters were left with no alternative. Many migrated from the Windward Islands to Saint-Domingue, where hunting could supplement buccaneering. The poorest colonists, unable to make indigo and reduced to extreme poverty, were forced into piracy.[70] Thousands of settlers who were

[68]   Price, *France and the Chesapeake*, 1: 85–6.
[69]   Col., C[8B] 1, Patoulet to Colbert, cited in May, *Histoire de la Martinique*, 85 and others.
[70]   Charlevoix, *Histoire de l'isle espagnole ou de S. Domingue*, 1: 210.

Illustration 3.1. Tobacco curing, spinning, and twisting, *circa* 1670. These operations are shown on the right. At the left and in the center slaves are preparing cassava flour from manioc roots.

From Jean-Baptiste Du Tertre. *Histoire générale des Antilles, habités par les François.* 4 vols. (Paris: T. Jolly, 1617–1671), 2: inter pages 418–19.

land poor and lacking capital were victims of the fiscal needs of the French state.[71]

At the same time as colonial production ceased in the Windward Islands and declined at Saint-Domingue, the tobacco monopoly was transferred to the United General Farms and increased its imports of English, chiefly Virginia, leaf. At a time when the monopoly paid the equivalent of 41/2-5d (pence sterling) per pound for French tobacco, it could buy a similar quantity at Bristol FOB for half that price.[72] Responding to low prices, Colbert hoped that these measures, a larger, more sophisticated administration, and tighter policing offered by the United General Farms would increase the Crown's revenue. During the 1680s the tax-farmers purchased only about one-third of Saint-Domingue's crop in order to force French prices down.[73] By 1688–9, Saint-Domingue production had shrunk to between twelve and fifteen thousand rolls (600,000–750,000 livres weight), and Governor de Cussy warned of a revolt among small planters.[74] The war temporarily relieved the problem of unrest by providing poor settlers with the occasion for their last great hurrah of organised violence.

By strange irony, the final collapse of colonial tobacco production was chiefly due to the great success of French privateers off the coasts of France. They brought so much English tobacco into the seaports that the tax-farmers were supplied with more leaf of superior quality than France could consume, at prices well below those paid for colonial imports. Saint-Domingue tobacco virtually ceased to enter France between 1690 and 1696. When privateers captured a large quantity of very high quality Verinas tobacco at Cartagena in 1697, their leader had it shipped directly to Amsterdam to avoid the low prices in France.[75]

The idea of tobacco's ability to contribute to colonial development recurred repeatedly for as long as colonies existed, but no one, except historians, mistook rhetoric for policy. Louis Phélypeaux, comte de Pontchartrain, was no different than his predecessors. While the government was fully aware of the need to support the white settlers on Saint-Domingue, it refused to take any action prejudicial to the tobacco monopoly that held down prices and

---

[71]   Frostin, *Les Révoltes blanches*, 52–3, offers a fourfold contradictory explanation for the decline, pointing to overproduction in the West Indies, competition from Virginia, tax-farmer ruthlessness, and planter fraud. Jean Meyer, *Histoire de la France coloniale*. vol. 1. *des origines à 1914* (Paris: Armand Colin, 1991), 1: 47–8 ignores the role of the tax-farm, attributing the production decline entirely to natural causes: too much rain, tropical climate, lack of fertilizer, and overproduction.

[72]   Price, *France and the Chesapeake*, 1: 178.

[73]   Ibid., 1: 44–5, 90, 176. Not surprisingly, in 1688 Intendant Dumaitz de Goimpy reported that tobacco had disappeared from the lesser islands; see Col., F³ 163, ff. 255–6. Cited in Price, *France and the Chesapeake*, 2: 877 n27.

[74]   Ibid., 1: 89, 92–3.   [75]   Ibid., 1: 182.

maximized revenues to the Crown.[76] By the end of the war, the monopoly was actually achieving Colbert's modest goal of 1680, increasing revenues paid to the Crown by about one and a half times. Henceforth, the tobacco monopolists were able to argue convincingly that importing foreign tobacco contributed more to Crown revenues than any encouragement of cultivating domestic or colonial tobacco.[77]

In 1697 and for 33 years afterward, the tobacco farm was legally separated from the United General Farms and erected into an independent lease. While the entire French tax-farming system collapsed during the last years of the reign of Louis XIV, the tobacco farm's revenues grew by leaps and bounds. By the 1720s, the revenues that it paid to the Crown exceeded Colbert's modest aspirations by at least a factor of twenty.[78]

Tobacco became a valuable revenue source that was made to yield even more by very wealthy lessees possessing international financial and mercantile connections. Between 1697 and 1701, Louis de Pontchartrain left the offices of controller-general of finances and secretary of state for the marine. He was succeeded at finances by Michel de Chamillart who was also the secretary of state for war. This decline of colonial and naval influence in the government was partially offset by new arrangements that ensued between Louis's son, Jérôme Phélypeaux de Pontchartrain, who became secretary of state for the marine in 1699, and a small coterie of associates, not more than a dozen, who acquired the tobacco farm in 1697. Led by Pontchartrain's closest associate, Samuel Bernard, these men belonged to the world of finance rather than commerce, and under Jérôme de Pontchartrain's aegis they created new companies, revived old ones, and refinanced French colonial expansion overseas. As in Colbert's day, the government's short-term financial demands prevailed. By the century's end, colonial tobacco production was dormant; its quality was poor owing to the continuation of such traditional shoddy practices as mixing second and third growth leaves with first growth, and its reputation was ruined.[79] By 1717 only free blacks cultivated tobacco for local consumption on Saint-Domingue.[80]

Tobacco ought to have disappeared from any concern about colonial development after 1700 and likely would have, but for the strange sequence of events following the establishment of Louisiana. During the War of the Spanish Succession and afterwards, tobacco did not serve even as a pioneer crop that men without labour and capital could grow along with their

---

[76] Col. B 18, ff. 275–6 Pontchartrain to Ducasse, 28 May 1696, cited in Price, *France and the Chesapeake*, 1: 96.

[77] Ibid., 1: 93–5, 178–81.   [78] Ibid., 1: 288.

[79] Labat, *Nouveau voyage aux Isles*, 2: 177, quoted in Price, *France and the Chesapeake*, 1: 86.

[80] AN, SOM, G¹ 509, no. 14 Recensement générale [dated] 15 November [1717].

provisions. The need for food was too great.[81] Only in 1717 when the government of the Duc d' Orléans, the Regent of France, became obsessed with the economic virtues of self-sufficiency and the notion that Louisiana could replace English sources for France's tobacco did anything change.[82] Thereafter, tobacco cultivation became a fiscal and financial matter. Louisiana's agricultural potential attracted members of the government only after they recognised a need to provide investors in John Law's India Company with some staple to yield a return.[83] His *Compagnie d'Occident* had had mixed success in attracting investment. In August of 1718, the Regent decided to give it a sounder financial foundation than its current limited overseas trading base could provide by allowing it to take over the tobacco tax-farm.[84] In short, without the tobacco farm no intelligent investor would put a sou into Louisiana. With it, anything was possible.[85] The directors of Law's Occidental Company and later his India Company poured millions of livres into Louisiana. Between 1670 and 1730, no other French colony was the recipient of so much investment.

During the decade after 1719 tobacco cultivation became more heavily promoted than at any other time in French colonial history. The directors sent seed and tobacco workers from France, and located major tobacco-growing concessions on excellent land located on high bluffs above the Mississippi River near the villages of Natchez Indians some 270 kilometres above New Orleans. They paid artificially high prices for tobacco, offered long-term credit and bounties to concessionaires who planted the crop, and subsidized slave prices and transportation from Africa. Promotion was primarily the function of influential people who received concessions. Much that passed for policy was simply rhetoric intended to dupe the greedy and mislead the gullible. By 1 October 1721, when France's colonies were supposed to be able to supply all of the kingdom's tobacco needs – between 4 and 6 million

---

[81]   Marcel Giraud, *Histoire de la Louisiane*, 4 vols. (Paris: Presses universitaires de France, 1953–1874), 1: 133–5.

[82]   Price, *France and the Chesapeake*, 1: 196–220 and 306.

[83]   Daniel H. Usner, Jr., *Indians, Settlers, and Slaves in a Frontier Exchange Economy: The Lower Mississippi before 1783* (Chapel Hill: University of North Carolina Press, 1991), 32.

[84]   Col., A 22, f. 58 déclaration...à propos de l'adjudication qui lui a été fait le 1er aout [1718] de la ferme générale de la vente exclusive des tabacs pour la somme de 4,020,000 l. par an; and George T. Matthews, *Royal General Farms in Eighteenth-Century France* (New York: Columbia University Press, 1958), 118.

[85]   J. H. Shennan, *Philippe, Duke of Orléans, Regent of France, 1715–1723* (London: Thames and Hudson, 1979), 111; Price, *France and the Chesapeake*, 1: 220. For a fuller account of John Law and his "System" see Paul Harsin, "La finance et l'État jusqu'au système de Law" dans *Histoire économique et sociale de la France*, Vol. 2, *Des derniers temps de l'âge seigneurial aux préludes de l'âge industriel, (1660–1789)*, (Paris: Presses universitaires de France, 1970), 267–99. For a brief synopsis see John Kenneth Galbraith, *Money, Whence it came, Where it went* (New York: Bantam Books, [1975] 1976), 27–34.

pounds annually – a mere 500 pounds was shipped from Louisiana.[86] Five years later, Louisiana produced only 20,000 livres weight of tobacco, equivalent to the annual production of one medium-sized Virginia plantation.[87] The concession of two large land grants for tobacco cultivation at Natchez in 1726 led directly to the massacre three years later that ended tobacco cultivation for export in Louisiana for more than a decade. On the morning of 28 November 1729, Natchez warriors killed 237 French men, women, and children, and captured nearly 300 slaves and 50 white women and children.[88]

That year the Company's directors declined to pay the previous heavy subsidies for Louisiana tobacco, and in July of 1730, they leased the monopoly to the United General Farms. They wrapped up the Louisiana adventure, writing off all their bad investments. In September, the Council of State confirmed the terms; the new lessees agreed to buy all of Louisiana's tobacco, but only at Virginia prices, effectively ending any market for French colonial tobacco and the bizarre dream of autarky. On 22 January 1731, the company directors offered to retrocede Louisiana to the King and to compensate him for surrendering their obligations. A gracious monarch accepted the next day after first reducing the offer of compensation by more than one-half.[89]

3.3 FISH

Though the Newfoundland fishery was the vital centre of New World economic activity in the Northern Hemisphere, the question of including fish among colonial staples is debatable. In several respects the new fish from the abundant seas of the northwestern Atlantic were not colonial commodities at all. They did not originate in the Americas and, for nearly one and a half centuries, they were neither harvested by colonists from the New World, nor were they sold there. Moreover, fishing was not a new activity. The northwestern Atlantic cod and whale fisheries developed from earlier activities off European shores. Fishing may also be viewed as a form of aquatic hunting, part of Europeans' search for new sources of protein in response to demographic growth.[90] Fishing was a high-risk activity and an early form of

---

[86] Price, *France and the Chesapeake*, 1: 308.

[87] Ibid., 1: 319.

[88] Marcel Giraud, *History of French Louisiana*, Vol. 5, *The Company of the Indies, 1723–1731* (Baton Rouge: Louisiana State University Press, 1974), 398; Usner, *Indians, Settlers, and Slaves*, 72.

[89] Price, *France and the Chesapeake*, 1: 328.

[90] Jean-François Brière, *La Pêche français en Amérique du Nord au XVIIIe siècle* (Montréal: Fides, 1990), 28; A.R. Michell, "The European Fisheries in Early Modern History", *The Cambridge Economic History of Europe*, vol. 5, eds., E.E. Rich and C.H. Wilson (London: Cambridge University Press, 1977), 132.

capitalist activity, where the division of labour was already well-developed.[91] The new sources of fish contributed significantly to expand and integrate European markets, but the discovery of new grounds only fostered further development of already existing commercial organisation and employment practices. Long-distance fishing hastened the shift from shares to wages to pay crew members. Fishing continued to be both capital and labour intensive.

Large numbers of French fishermen sailed to the Grand Banks, where they fished as far as 320 kilometres off Newfoundland, salted their catch, and returned to France never having sighted land (see Map 3.1). Their ships were called "bankers". This practice appeared during the second half of the sixteenth century in response to a growing Catholic taste for salted fish at Lenten season. In 1670, it still occupied about one-third of the French fleet. It was known as the "green" fishery after the name, *morue verte*, given to the cod caught and preserved in this manner. The older, more common practice of the majority of fishermen was to carry fish ashore in the Americas, split them, spread them out to dry, and, after being air-cured and lightly salted, load them back on board for transport to Europe. This was called the sedentary (*pêche sedentaire*) or dry fishery in contrast to the wandering fishery (*pêche errante*), another apt name for the banks fishery. As some ships landed fish caught on the nearer banks about 80 kilometres off shore, the dry fishery also became known as the inshore fishery. It was chiefly conducted in small craft called shallops that normally operated within a dozen or so miles of land.[92]

While economists claim that relative access to supplies of sea salt accounted for the different techniques, the need to match product to markets was also an important consideration. The green fishery was conducted for the rapidly growing urban markets of northern France, including Paris, whose wealthy inhabitants would pay a premium for delivery early in the year, while the air-cured, lightly salted product of the sedentary fishery kept well in the warm climates of Italy, Portugal, and Spain where it was mainly sold.[93] Regardless of the practice followed, the French fishery had the largest domestic market of any European fishing fleet and, together with its large export market, primarily shaped its structure. It was almost entirely a migratory fishery. Techniques and markets imposed rhythms wherein some

---

[91] See John T. Gilchrist, "Enterprise and Exploration – the Newfoundland Fishery, c. 1497–1677", in *Canadian Business History, Selected Papers, 1497–1971*, ed. David S. Macmillan (Toronto: McClelland and Stewart, 1972), 7–26; and Laurier Turgeon, "Le temps des pêches lointains, permanences et transformation vers 1500-vers 1850", dans *Histoire des pêches maritimes en France*, éd., Michel Mollat (Toulouse: Privat, 1987), 134.

[92] Nicolas Denys, *Description and Natural History of the Coasts of North America (Acadia)*, 2 vols., trans., Wm. F. Ganong, (Toronto: The Champlain Society, [1672] 1908); vol. 2 is almost exclusively devoted to a detailed description of the North Atlantic cod fishery.

[93] Charles de la Morandière, *Histoire de la pêche française de la morue dans l'Amérique septentrionale*, 3 vols. (Paris: Maissoneuve & La Rose, 1962–6), 1: 345.

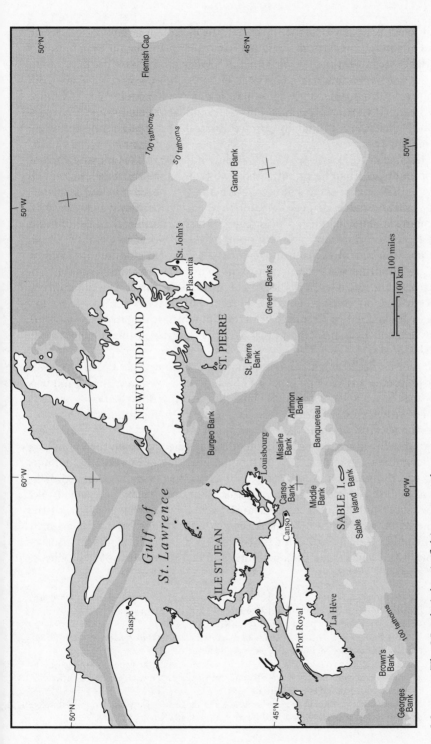

Map 3.1. The North Atlantic fishing grounds.

ships sailed as early as January and others returned as late as December, but French fishermen normally sailed anew each year to the fishing grounds. With the great wealth that the fisheries generated, we may still ask why a French colonial or residential fishery failed to develop before the eighteenth century. Did colonists try to profit from the "gold" of the sea? We also need to account for the eventual appearance of a colonial fishery during the eighteenth century, and finally, can we assess the fishery's overall impact on colonial development?

The characteristics of the French fishing industry and New England competition, rather than monopoly, were two reasons that a residential French colonial fishery failed to emerge before 1713.[94] Fishing techniques, markets, and the widely dispersed locations of the dry fishery, which left small numbers of ships scattered almost everywhere, discouraged a colonial fishery. Fierce competition from metropolitan fishermen and well-organised fish merchants with strong urban and regional ties in France also militated against the growth of colonial fishing industries. In brief, no demand or commercial encouragement existed, and the large, well-organised metropolitan industry discouraged its development. The French cod fishery began to decline before 1650 and did not improve before 1730, which stimulated metropolitan merchants to fight fiercely to preserve their position in the North Atlantic world.[95]

In the mid-seventeenth century, the French fishing fleet comprised over 400 ships and almost 10,000 men.[96] It originated from more ports and was dispersed over a far wider area than ships of any other nation.[97] French fishing vessels came from 17 ports and could be found along the shores of Newfoundland, the Gulf of St. Lawrence, and Nova Scotia.[98] Expanded, more integrated markets had forced many smaller ports out of the fishing business earlier in the century. Fishing had become more specialised. Ships had become larger, and with larger crews they were more costly to operate and required greater capital investment than before. By 1664, the banks fishery was based chiefly at Le Havre and Honfleur in the mouth of the Seine River, and at Nantes and Sables d'Olonne on the Atlantic coast near the mouth of the Loire. Ships that produced chiefly dry cod had also become more concentrated at Saint-Malo and the Biscay ports of La Rochelle,

---

94 Cf. Harold Adams Innis, *The Cod Fisheries; The History of an International Economy*, rev. ed. (Toronto: University of Toronto Press, [1940] 1954), 119–38 .

95 Turgeon, "Colbert et la pêche française", 261.

96 R. Cole Harris, ed., *Historical Atlas of Canada*, Vol. 1, *From the Beginning to 1800* (Toronto: University of Toronto Press, n.d.), Plate 23.

97 Turgeon, "Le temps des pêches lointains", 137–8, notes that the fishery was larger at the end of the sixteenth century when 500 ships and 12,000 men were employed. Brière, *La Pêche français*, 125, gives 372 ships in 1683.

98 La Morandière, *Histoire de la pêche française*, 1: 232; Laurier Turgeon, "Pour une histoire de la pêche", *Histoire Sociale/Social History*, 14, no. 28 (Nov. 1981), 295.

Bordeaux, and St. Jean de Luz.[99] No one port emerged and consolidated itself as the sole source of fishing capital and skilled labour. The French fishery remained decentralised and, together with declining yields, decreased domestic consumption and increased foreign competition, reinforcing already existing rivalries among seaports and continuing to prevent a colonial fishery from starting up. With high overheads, fluctuating markets, and low profits, the strong demand for capital in the highly competitive French fishery meant that virtually none was available for colonists.

Colbert attempted to foster a colonial fishery in New France, but it failed despite permission granted to colonists in 1669 to export cod to France on payment of the same duties as residents of Le Havre and granting concessions and privileges to establish fisheries along the lower St. Lawrence River and Gaspé peninsula during the 1670s.[100] The presence of migratory fishermen in most favourable locations ensured that colonists faced strong opposition wherever they fished. In 1686, Intendant Jacques De Meulles reported that the fierce competition between fishermen from Bayonne, La Rochelle, and Honfleur for drying space at Île Percée in the Gaspé had moved to open warfare.[101]

Even without the presence of French competitors, geography doomed a Canadian colonial fishery, and Intendant Demeulles admitted as much.[102] The St. Lawrence River was impassable for half the year and too far away from even the Gulf fishery during the other half to be exploited from New France. Lack of salt and the high cost of fishing gear also persisted, but the attraction of the fur trade ensured that fishing in New France would always want for local capital and labour. Only during the early decades of the eighteenth century did some colonial fishing become possible. War between 1702 and 1713 seriously disrupted overseas fishing; increased colonial population encouraged local markets to appear at Quebec and at Louisbourg, and special conditions arising from climatic changes beyond the colony's ability to influence gave rise temporarily to favourable conditions.

During those decades intendants of New France, first Raudot and then Bégon, awarded a monopoly to develop a white whale fishery in the St. Lawrence River off the Rivière Ouelle. Their aim was to prime the pump of economic development and encourage diversification rather than to award an exclusive privilege. Although the settlers won and fishing became free, the colonists did not gain access to capital or international markets for train oil.

---

99 Michell, "The European fisheries", 159, notes that in 1664 Le Havre, Honfleur, Saint-Malo, Nantes, and Sables d'Olonne provided 71 percent of the ships involved.

100 Cole, *Colbert and a Century of French Mercantilism*, 2: 79; W. J. Eccles, *Canada Under Louis XIV, 1663–1701* (Toronto: McClelland and Stewart, 1964), 211–14; and La Morandière, *Histoire de la pêche française*, 1: 374–8.

101 Innis, *The Cod Fisheries*, 124; and La Morandière, *Histoire de la pêche françaises*, 1: 367.

102 *Coll. de Mss.* 1; 300

While colonial merchants managed to send some dried cod and a little seal and train oil to French markets, and small markets appeared in France for such expensive delicacies as smoked salmon and jellied eels, fish never joined fur as a second great colonial staple exported from New France. Instead, where it was pursued at all, fishing became an adjunct of local agricultural activity.[103]

Attempts to establish residential colonial fisheries at Placentia and Acadia during the seventeenth century illustrate more clearly the obstructive effect of the metropolitan fishery and the mixed aims of the state. Both attempts ignored a significant feature of the fishing industry: its freedom. They arose from the state's misapprehended interests rather than the needs of the industry. Disputes over occupation of bays and coves, insecurity of boats and fishing gear left over the winter, and attacks from thieves and pirates had always been adjuncts of the overseas fishery. For a century and a half European fishermen had roughly regulated their own activities through negotiation rather than war. Their ability to act in their own interests, developing a strong body of custom without state interference, is one of the most fascinating aspects of their early history. However, changes in fishing practices and the constant growth and ever more visible evidence of riches could not be hidden forever from ambitious statesmen always on the lookout for new sources of wealth to fill their coffers. State appropriation of fishing revenue could only be delayed, not denied.

A few Frenchmen may have wintered along the south coast of Newfoundland in earlier times, but it was the growing practice of English fishermen to winter in the bays of the Avalon peninsula during the second quarter of the seventeenth century that challenged the French. The practice appeared to supply the French state with a pretext to interfere and claim a role for itself in the fishery. Prior to this time the French decentralised fishery had been entirely unregulated. Beginning in the mid-1650s, however, Nicolas Fouquet and later Colbert sought to constrain the fishery's freedom by offering protection from pirates and foreign fishermen. In the early 1660s in the absence of an effective, operational navy, they sought to establish a garrisoned settlement at Placentia on Newfoundland's south coast in the bay of the same name.[104] Placentia harbour was sheltered from the winds, ice-free early in the year, easy to defend, able to hold a vast fleet seeking refuge from ocean storms, and close to abundant supplies of cod. The immediate pretext for the settlement was the fear that resident Englishmen in growing numbers would deny the French access to drying room ashore. The settlement never amounted to much. Lack of arable land and local capital left resident

---

[103]   Alain Laberge, "Etat, entrepreneurs, habitants et monopole: le privilège de la pêche du marsouin dans le Bas Saint-Laurent, 1700–1730", *RHAF*, 37, 4 (mars, 1984), 543–56.

[104]   La Morandière, *Histoire de la pêche française*, 1: 403–507, provides a detailed narrative history of the residential fishery at Placentia.

fishermen and their families wholly dependent on offshore suppliers for their provisions, salt, fishing gear, and transportation of fish to market. The need to import these goods and services from France made them costly and uncompetitive. One garrison commander possessed so little leadership that his men murdered him soon after his arrival.[105] Others seemed bent on extorting fish from local fishermen rather than protecting them from foreigners.[106] In 1670, the new commandant, Sieur de La Poipe, agreed *not* to extort one-third of the fishing catch from resident fishermen.[107] Little wonder that Placentia grew slowly and that the majority of French residents lived elsewhere along Newfoundland's south coast. In 1687, only 256 or 40 percent of the 640 French inhabitants residing on the south coast lived at Placentia.[108]

The outbreak of war in 1689 set back the colonial fishery during the next eight years. Though Placentia continued to be provisioned and resupplied from France, its survival was ensured only after the comte de Pontchartrain contracted for services from private merchants chiefly from Nantes.[109] After the war, residents of Placentia quickly renewed their summer, autumn, and spring fisheries, and in 1698 sent more than 80,000 quintals (3,916 tonnes) of cod to France.[110] The fishery continued to develop during the next five years and even after the renewal of hostilities. In 1703 and 1704, 71,200 and 123,000 quintals of dried cod, respectively, reached France,[111] but the government's rigorous application of the system of naval recruitment threatened the continuation of the fishery, as did its efforts to control the movement of fishing ships by imposing convoys to and from France. Forcing fishing vessels to carry cannon to defend themselves also added to costs. The government tried to shift major costs of fortifying Placentia onto the fishing industry by requiring ships to transport salt, provisions for colonists and workmen, livestock, and even materials for the fortifications.[112] In an industry characterised by high overheads and low profits, investors fiercely resisted such exactions. Crews ate the animals intended for the settlers, and fishing captains refused the governor's attempts to tax them to pay for a hospital that he wanted.[113]

[105] Ibid., 1: 417–18.   [106] Ibid., 1: 422.
[107] BN, Mélanges de Colbert, 176, f. 127v Colbert de Terron to the King, 1 May 1670.
[108] La Morandière, *Histoire de la pêche française*, 1: 432.
[109] See James Pritchard, "'Le Profit et la Gloire': The French Navy's Alliance with Private Enterprise in the Defense of Newfoundland, 1691–1697", *Newfoundland Studies*, 15, 2 (Fall, 1999), 161–75.
[110] La Morandière, *Histoire de la pêche française*, 1: 475.
[111] Ibid., 1: 496–7. By comparison, in 1704 the English fishing fleet carried home 68,000 quintals, see B.L., Egerton Mss, 921, p. 4v.
[112] Frederick J. Thorpe, *Remparts lointains: La politique française des travaux publics à Terre-Neuve et à l'Île Royale, 1695–1758* (Ottawa: Université d'Ottawa, 1980), 136–40.
[113] La Morandière, *Histoire de la pêche française*, 1: 496–504.

The original reason for establishing Placentia was as much political as economic. During the half century after 1664 the French government failed to develop a role for the navy, either to protect the residents along Newfoundland's south coast from the growing presence of the English or to increase the security of the fishery. With no clear idea of what to do with the navy, French authorities sought to fortify Placentia largely at the expense of the fishing industry. At the end of the War of the Spanish Succession, when the French had not lost any territory in Newfoundland, had successfully defended Placentia from two English naval assaults, and launched three successful, destructive raids against enemy settlers, France surrendered its sovereignty over Newfoundland. French fishing interests made no protest. Indeed, two years before, one of Pontchartrain's advisors, Jean Bochart de Champigny, former intendant of New France, had insisted that as long as French rights to dry fish along the coast were preserved no irremediable damage would be done.[114] Metropolitan fishing interests had no interest in continuing a residential fishery that had increasingly become a burdensome liability.

It comes as no surprise that political considerations predominated when Colbert attempted to establish a colonial fishery in Acadia. Though long the state's main instrument of colonial development, monopoly had never been the way of the free fishery. It says little for Colbert's grasp of fishing that in February of 1682, the Council of State granted the newly formed *Compagnie de la pêche sédentaire de l'Acadie* a monopoly to dry its catch on the southeastern coast of Nova Scotia and in the Bay of Fundy to the mouth of the St. John River. The origins of the Sedentary Fishing Company of Acadia represented a more aggressive stance by the French government than before in attempting to put an end to an increasingly intolerable situation. While political control of Acadia was ostensibly returned to France in 1670, economic control remained in the hands of several New England merchants who continued trading with Acadian settlers and increasingly with Huguenot merchants.[115] The new company was intended to rid Acadia of the New England and possible Huguenot influence over fishing and trading in the region, but it appears that its merchant backers had aims other than fishing in mind.[116]

The company was formed under the authority of Charles Duret, marquis de Chevry, and several of Colbert's closest associates, including François Bellinzanni, financiers and Parisian merchants. Clerbaud Bergier, a Huguenot

---

[114] Ibid., 1: 505.
[115] See L.-A. Vigneras, ed., "Letters of an Acadian Trader, 1674–1676", in *New England Quarterly*, 13 (1940): 98–110; also J.F. Bosher, "Huguenot Merchants and the Protestant International in the Seventeenth Century", *William and Mary Quarterly*, 3rd Series, 52, 1 (January 1995): 77–102.
[116] La Morandière, *Histoire de la pêche française de la morue*, 1: 356–67 contains a brief history of the Company.

merchant of La Rochelle who had once traded at Quebec and resided in the West Indies whence he traded with New England, was an investor and the new company's man in Acadia.[117] The interested parties in the fishing company were granted exemption from salt duties and a bounty of 1,000 livres annually for each ship sent to the fishery.[118] Despite competition from French migratory fishermen, a growing demand for slave provisions in the West Indies ought to have aided the company. The Antilles constituted a valuable market for poorer quality dried cod called "rebut" that was unfit for European markets, but once again a colonial fishery failed to emerge.

The true aim of the Acadian Company may have been fur trading. It collected the duty on beaver from Acadian colonists for nearly eight years before they refused to pay any longer. The Company's letters patent included a 20-year privilege to send all beaver to France without paying any export duties to the Western Domain. Acadia was neither mentioned in the original tax-farm, nor in 1684, when the agent-general petitioned the king concerning beaver from Hudson Bay. The Royal Council declared that all beaver in New France "except in Acadia" had to be carried to Quebec to pay the duty. Finally, the son of the Company's director in Acadia, Bergier Desormeaux, was arrested and his pelts seized in May of 1685.

With sufficient capital to operate a single establishment at Chedabouctou (near present-day Guysborough, N.S.), the Acadian Company fulfilled no need and caught few fish. Indeed, it scarcely got off the ground. Possession of a monopoly only encouraged the holders to deny drying room to others, extort fish from migratory fishermen, trade for furs with the Amerindians, and license New Englanders to do the fishing. Bergier initially protested the Acadian practice of licensing New England fishermen, seized several English ships, and carried them off to a French admiralty court to be judged good prizes, but in 1687, Governor Meneval, with the Company's acquiescence, continued the practice. The Company does not seem to have done much cod fishing. It received a concession of the Magdelen Islands in the Gulf of St. Lawrence in 1686, but they had never been a site for drying fish. New England freebooters sacked the Company's establishment at Chedabouctou in 1688, and two years later an expeditionary force seized the company's warehouse at Port Royal.

The Acadian Sedentary Fishing Company does not seem to have existed through the war, though some claim that its monopoly was only canceled in

---

117 C. Bruce Ferguson, "Bergier", *DCB*, 1: 89–90. J.F. Bosher, *Men and Ships in the Canada Trade, 1660–1760: A Biographical Dictionary* (Ottawa: Environment Canada, Parks Service, 1992), 38; Frédéric Deloffre, "Chronique de Chedabouctou: La Colonie Rocheloise de Chedabouctou racontée par un Témoin" in *France and the New World: Proceedings of the 22nd Annual Meeting of the French Colonial Historical Society*, ed., David Buisseret (East Lansing: Michigan State University Press, 1998), 91–106.

118 *Coll de Mss*, 1: 290.

the middle of the next war.[119] Granting a monopoly to a group of metropolitan investors who may or may not have attempted to establish a colonial fishery shows just how little the French authorities understood the French fishery.[120] Though monopoly did not provide support for a colonial fishery, competition from New England's colonial fishery was the chief reason why a colonial fishery did not appear until after 1713.[121]

New Englanders murdered and ransacked wherever they could get away with it. The French navy did little to defend either colonial or migratory fishermen. More importantly New Englanders developed a vigorous, cost-effective, residential fishery of their own. With local capital and manpower and able to provision themselves with cheap colonial foodstuffs, New England fishermen quickly carved a place in the international fishery, seriously threatening the southern markets of the French metropolitan fishing industry. By 1700, more than 100 fishing vessels worked the Acadian coast, pushing the French out of the way and competing successfully in traditional French markets of Portugal and Spain where they annually sold 50,000 quintals of dried cod.[122] During the War of the Spanish Succession Acadia fell to English forces, but the colonial fishery had disappeared long before, unlamented by both Acadian farmers and French metropolitan fishermen alike.

The terms of the Treaty of Utrecht, the loss of Acadia, and the demise of Placentia's residential fishery testify to the continuing power of the metropolitan migratory fishing interests and to the importance of overseas fish in the French economy. The loss of so much territory in northeastern North America gave rise to a more strategic view of the fishery at Versailles and a sharp awareness of the need to replace the former possessions in order to strengthen France's maritime position and assure the continued possession of New France.

The comte de Pontchartrain had been seeking a location for storm-damaged ships of the migratory fishery and a new centre for the colonial fishery before the treaty negotiations commenced. After canvassing Cape Breton and Labrador, he settled on Havre à l'Anglais on the east coast of Cape Breton Island, and, early in 1713, he ordered the transfer of the remaining resident fishermen and their families from Placentia and elsewhere along the south coast of Newfoundland. The French government was intent on founding a new settlement based on fishing and trade. In order that no one doubt the king's intentions, Louis XIV approved naming the new settlement Louisbourg and renamed Sainte Anne, Saint Pierre, and Cape Breton

---

119 But see also Robert Guitard, "Le déclin de la Compagnie de la pêche sédentaire en Acadie de 1697–1702", *Cahiers de la société d'histoire acadienne.* 9, no. 1 (mars, 1978), 5–21; La Morandière, *Histoire de la pêche française*, 1: 360–2.
120 See Brière, *La Pêche français*, 248.
121 Innis, *The Cod Fisheries*, 126–7, claims that the failure of a French residential fishery was another example of monopoly's failure to withstand free competition.
122 Turgeon, "Le temps des pêches lointains", 154; La Morandière, *Histoire de la pêche française*, 1: 359.

itself, Port Dauphin, Port Toulouse, and Île Royale, respectively.[123] The new colony's nomenclature could not have been more closely associated with the royal family.

From the beginning, the new colony was envisioned as something other than Placentia. Settlement, trade, and security were all included among its objectives. The fishery got off to a poor start after the government attempted to tax merchants for support of the garrison. This led to a decline in the number of ships in 1716, but after assuming all direct costs of fortifying Île Royale and interpreting its obligation broadly to include the construction of port facilities as well, the government provided a valuable subsidy to the residential fishery.[124] The arrival at Île Royale of large numbers of migratory fishermen each year from France was an important factor in future growth. From 1713 to 1724, French sedentary fishermen abandoned the Newfoundland coast for Île Royale, Labrador, and, beginning in 1720, Gaspé. An abnormal drop in yields noted in the English Newfoundland fishery during these years probably triggered the exodus, and new exemptions from export duties for ships fitting out for New France added further incentives.[125] Despite competition from New Englanders in Chedabouctou Bay, in 1718 Île Royale achieved the highest annual volume of dried cod exports prior to 1730. That year and next, more than 150,000 quintals of dried cod were produced.[126] English forces attacked French fishermen on Canso Island that year and stole their property, and though the latter was never restored, the government effectively asserted its position that British Nova Scotia consisted only of the mainland. By then, because their share of the catch rose to half the total, residential fishermen dominated Île Royale's fishery.[127]

The adoption of new technology in the form of the New England schooner, which one historian believes led to the appearance of a new kind of fishery at Île Royale, may well provide another reason for the new fishery's success. During the fishing season, cod migrated from the shore out to the banks off Nova Scotia. This required a larger vessel than was normally employed in the French inshore fishery and a swifter, more maneuverable craft than the square-riggers normally used in the green fishery.[128]

Three other significant developments also aided the growth of the colonial fishery. First, a major change in the conduct of the metropolitan migratory fishery saw a virtual abandonment of the northern peninsula of Newfoundland and a major shift to Labrador, the Gaspé, and, as just noted, Île Royale,

[123] A. J. B. Johnston, *Control and Order in French Colonial Louisbourg, 1713–1758* (East Lansing: Michigan State University Press, 2001), 81. Today Port Dauphin is known as Englishtown and Port Toulouse is called St. Peters.

[124] Thorpe, *Remparts lointains*, 22, 164.

[125] Brière, *La Pêche française*, 170.

[126] B.A. Balcom, *The Cod Fishery of Isle Royale, 1713–58* (Ottawa: Parks Canada, Environment Canada, 1984), 15–16.

[127] Miquelon, *New France, 1701–1744*, 114; also Turgeon, "Pour une histoire", 312–13.

[128] La Morandière, *Histoire de la pêche française*, 2: 666–7.

with greater emphasis than before on the dry fishery. This may have been caused by the altered dynamics of fish stocks.[129] By 1720, the green fishery employed less than half the French ships and only a quarter of all the men in the industry.[130] Second, the climatic changes during the 1720s forced serious contractions in the metropolitan fishery. Any increase in metropolitan yields reflected attempts to maintain profits in the face of declining prices.[131] Though production at Île Royale also declined, the milder impact of these changes may have eased the situation for colonial fishermen.[132] Finally, the rapid transformation of Louisbourg into a trade entrepôt overcame the two greatest obstacles to the development of a colonial fishery during the previous half century: its reliance on costly French provisions and fishing supplies, and its inability to encourage local economic diversification. As an entrepôt, Louisbourg did not need to depend upon French sources or a nonexistent agricultural hinterland for its survival. Instead, goods and provisions flowed into the new colony from Canada and New England in return for dried cod. There was also a tremendous surge in demand for dried cod in the French West Indies.

Though France remained the new colony's largest export market, the West Indies came second. Dried cod came to account for between 70 and 80 percent of Île Royale's exports to the West Indies. By the mid-1720s, the total value of fish exports from Île Royale exceeded the value of all exports, including furs, from Canada.[133] By then, the colonial fishery may have been contributing about one-fifth of the entire French northwestern Atlantic fishing catch.[134] Over the first half of the eighteenth century, Île Royale probably produced more than 10 percent of the entire North Atlantic cod catch and one-third of the total French share.[135]

3.4 FUR

Furs, particularly beaver skins, were the primary export of New France, and remained so for nearly two centuries. Yet, if fur provided the economic vitality, the *vis viva*, of New France, it was of minor significance to the French economy. Just as fish, or the lack of it, profoundly affected the emerging colonial societies on the northeastern coast of North America and sugar

---

129 Turgeon, "Pour une histoire", 310.
130 La Morandière, *Histoire de la pêche française*, 2: 635.
131 Turgeon, "Pour une histoire", 313–16.
132 Balcom, *The Cod Fishery*, 16; also Brière, *La pêche français*, 100, Tableau 1.
133 Balcom, *The Cod Fishery*, 8–9 and 18.
134 Thorpe cited in ibid.
135 Christopher Moore, "Cape Breton and the North Atlantic World in the Eighteenth Century" in *The Island: New Perspectives on Cape Breton History, 1713–1990*, ed., Kenneth Donovan (Fredericton, NB: Acadiensis Press, 1990), 34.

shaped social developments in the West Indies, so fur or its absence, fashioned Canadian colonial society. Its greatest influence, however, was more indirect than is often acknowledged.

Three frequently unconsidered features of the fur trade profoundly affected colonial society. First, fur was the only American colonial staple produced by a free labour force. The fur trade's reliance upon free hunters is the exception to Mintz's claim that "the saga of post-conquest production in the Americas meant work, workers, and worker control".[136] Fur could only be harvested by free people hunting over hundreds of thousands of square kilometres of North America. The fact that the hunters were the continent's indigenous inhabitants may have made the exchange remarkable or picaresque depending on one's point of view, but it is less important than the freedom of the Amerindians who traded furs with equally free Frenchmen. Despite all that has been written about Amerindian dependency, the natives of North America remained "partners in furs" long after the French ceased to participate in the trade.[137] Fur's second important feature is that it was obtained through exchange and trade rather than conquest or settlement. The symbiotic relationship between native hunters and French traders gave rise to a set of socioeconomic and politicomilitary relations during the late seventeenth and early eighteenth centuries that became unique in the Western Hemisphere. These two characteristics ought to have ensured the special nature of the French colonial society that emerged in the St. Lawrence Valley, but a third, less obvious feature, also shaped the contours of colonial society. This was that progressively fewer colonists became involved in the trade as time passed.

The lack of connection between the trade and the colony's agricultural economy reinforced the significance of this third characteristic. The fur trade provided no inducement to invest elsewhere in colonial production for export or to add value to the export commodity itself, and only very limited inducements to invest in local ancillary activities. The trade also reinforced the effect of the colony's poor location vis-à-vis New England and the West Indies, which retarded development of commercial agriculture, lumbering, the carrying trade, and shipbuilding until the second quarter of the eighteenth century. In the absence of backward, forward, and demand linkages, the commercial fur trade long remained a quasifeudal venture based on limited exports of high value and low bulk. Like the long-distance trades of earlier times it was small, sturdy, and resilient; it adapted quickly to change and responded well to repeated challenges. However, it had very few

---

[136] Sidney Mintz, "Pleasure, Profit, and Satiation" in *Seeds of Change*, 114.

[137] See Arthur J. Ray, *Indians in the Fur Trade: Their Roles as Hunters, Trappers, and Middlemen in the Lands Southwest of Hudson Bay* (Toronto: University of Toronto Press, 1974); and Daniel Francis and Toby Morantz, *Partners in Furs: A history of the fur trade in eastern James Bay, 1600–1870* (Kingston and Montreal: McGill-Queen's University Press, 1983).

Illustration 3.2. The beaver as revealed to French audiences in 1706.
From [Louis-Armand de Lom d'Arce], baron de la Hontan. *Voyages du baron de la Hontan dans l'Amérique septentrionale*. La Haye: 1706, facing page 174.

connections to the remainder of the colonial economy that embraced the lives of the majority of colonists.[138]

Labour demand continually declined relative to demographic growth. During the decade 1708–17, the 668 men known to have travelled to the upper country represented no more than 2 percent of the adult males in the colony.[139] In the decade prior to this, the first colonial-born habitants surged upon the land; the proportion of the population in the towns declined from previous decades.[140] More important was the lack of connection between the commercial, urban fur trade and the noncapitalist, rural agricultural economy occupied by a growing proportion of colonists.[141] Consequently, New France's rural colonial society developed largely outside the market economy apart from capitalist productive forces.

---

[138] Dechêne, *Habitants and Merchants*, 124–5; see also M. H. Watkins, "A Staple Theory of Economic Growth" in *Approaches to Canadian Economic History*, W. T. Easterbrook and M. H. Watkins (Toronto: McClelland and Stewart, 1967), 55 and 67 .

[139] Dechêne, *Habitants and Merchants*, 117–18.

[140] Jacques Mathieu, "Province de France, (1663–1700)"; "Un pays à statu colonial 1701–1755)", dans in *Histoire du Quebec*, dir., Jean Hamelin (Montréal: France-Amérique, 1976), 194.

[141] Dechêne, *Habitant and Merchants*, 146.

During the six decades between 1670 and 1730, market forces drove the Canadian fur trade toward an oligopoly of merchant traders. Despite the government's obsessive concern for law, regulation, and revenue, it proved unable to halt the process or to influence its outcome. Fur trade legislation indicates the government's concern for order and the influence of short-term revenue demands on its decisions, but as in the case of tobacco, it reveals little coherent policy. The fur trade, then, is best viewed as a business.

The long fall in beaver prices after 1664 pushed small participants out of the fur trade.[142] Chaos characterised the trade between 1668 and 1682, but so did territorial expansion, illicit trade, bankruptcy and rapid turnover, wealth accumulation, and professionalisation.[143] In 1670, the fur trade continued to be conducted within the confines of the colony at Montreal where Indians carried down the bulk of the furs to be traded. Twelve years later the fur fairs had all but been abandoned, and French colonists roamed the interior of North America in search of furs. All of this occurred despite Colbert's repeated injunctions that the fur trade cease.[144]

Colbert's attempts to regulate the trade through admonitions, prohibitions, and injunctions failed in part because his attitude toward expansion was ambiguous. The minister opposed expanding settlement, but encouraged exploration and searches for new resources and mission fields. After the outbreak of the Franco-Dutch War in 1672, demands for revenue dominated his concern for colonies. The nature of the fur trade itself also encouraged expansion. The exhaustion of the resource and the need to cultivate new native hunters kept traders on the move. Failure to find and develop an alternate staple and the misunderstandings and misdeeds of men also contributed to expansion. Above all, Colbert's obsessive concern with increasing the Crown's revenue probably contributed as much to foster expansion as all the other factors combined.

In 1681, Intendant Jacques de Meulles recommended the minister regulate access to the west by issuing licenses to meritorious individuals and sending out perhaps a score of canoes laden with trade goods. To everyone's surprise, Colbert granted amnesty to all *coureurs de bois* who returned to the settlements and authorised the governor-general and intendant to issue 25 licenses, called *congés*, to deserving persons.[145] These quickly gained a monetary value and a brisk trade became associated with the system. Deserving officers "bleached" in the king's service, impoverished widows of noblemen, and religious institutions all received licenses. Some recipients participated in the trade while others sold their licenses. Licenses were too valuable to

---

[142] Ibid., 74. [143] Ibid., 91–3.
[144] See Eccles, *Canada Under Louis XIV*, 61–2 on the fur fairs; and his *The Canadian Frontier, 1534–1760*, rev. ed. (Albuquerque: University of New Mexico Press, [1969] 1983), 111–12 on their demise.
[145] Eccles, *Canada Under Louis XIV*, 109–10.

remain for long in the hands of the deserving. They greatly enhanced the patronage opportunities of senior colonial officials. The number of *congés* increased along with the number of canoes covered by each license. Gradually, they came into the hands of larger merchants at Montreal who outfitted entire ventures, hiring the canoes, employing crews, and provisioning them with victuals and trade goods.

Though a certain looseness prevailed, the growing contrast between illicit and lawful trade more than offset any defects of the new system. In a virtually cashless society, debt recovery was both vitally important and difficult to achieve. The increased stability that came from dealing with men who had a stake in the community, the greater security of debt and credit, the improved cooperation between licensees and colonial officials and the tax-farmer's agent, and the slow return of many renegades to the colony all aided to concentrate the trade in fewer hands. Before the end of the century, Montreal merchants, who fitted out the canoes for virtually all licensees each year, numbered less than 20, and the annual number of participants, canoemen, and voyageurs fell below 200.[146] Left alone the fur trade was becoming increasingly rationalized, better organised, and more efficient. Had market forces alone prevailed, all might have been well, but Colbert did not leave the trade alone.

In 1666, the West India Company obtained the right to collect preexisting duties of 10 and 25 percent, respectively, on the value of moose hides and beaver pelts exported from Quebec.[147] In return for payment of the duties at Quebec, the Company allowed colonists the right to sell their furs freely in France. Peace with the Iroquois after 1667 permitted western Indians to deliver more furs to Montreal, and beaver prices plummeted. As the number of beaver pelts increased, revenues seriously declined to less than three-quarters of the expected sum.[148] An orderly response to the sudden influx of fur was occurring with improved results on the revenue side. In 1672, a wealthy Quebec merchant paid the Company 47,000 livres – 500 livres more than he paid nine years earlier – to renew his lease to these rights.[149] By 1672, however, the West India Company was effectively defunct, and during the next two years, growing demands for enhanced revenues brought on by the Dutch War led Colbert to create the new tax-farm out of the Company's privileges known as the *domain d'occident* or the Western Domain. It was leased to Jean Oudiette and associates for 350,000 livres annually for 10 years.[150] Oudiette sublet the Canadian portions of the lease for 119,000

146 Dechêne, *Habitants and Merchants*, 93–5.
147 [Canada, Legislative Assembly], *Edits, ordonnances, déclarations et arrêts du conseil du roi concernant le Canada*, 3 vols. (Quebec: E.R. Frechette, 1854–1856), 1: 60.
148 Innis, *The Fur Trade*, 63–4.
149 Yves Zoltvany, "Aubert de La Chesnaye, Charles" *DCB*, 2: 27–9.
150 Mims, *Colbert's West India Policy*, 178.

livres in order to turn his full attention to more lucrative revenues in the West Indies and the slave trade.[151]

In Canada, a tax-farmer received a monopoly on all furs traded at Tadoussac at the mouth of the Saguenay River and another on all the trade of the huge territory on the north shore of the St. Lawrence River drained by the Saguenay-Lake St. Jean basin, which came to be called the King's Domain. He also received the right to collect 10 percent *ad valorem* duties on all wine, spirits, and tobacco entering the colony. The tax-farmer chiefly received the right to levy the duties on moose hides and beaver skins formerly collected by the West India Company. In return for becoming the sole seller of beaver pelts in France, the tax-farmer was obliged to accept all beaver offered for sale at Quebec at a fixed price of 4 livres 10 sols regardless of quality and to sell them in France for no more than 10 livres.[152]

Knowing that beaver fur was manufactured into felt hats and the distinctions between coat (*castor gras*) and parchment (*castor sec*) beaver are fundamental to understanding the colonial fur trade that was based on the pelts of this monogamous rodent. Coat beaver was sewn into robes and then worn for about 18 months by Amerindians living north of the St. Lawrence River and the Great Lakes. Their natural body oils conditioned the pelts and allowed the long, deep-rooted guard hairs to fall out, leaving only the soft underfur, called *duvet* or wool, for the felt maker. Parchment beaver had been sun-dried after being skinned from the carcass; it still carried its guard hairs. Good quality parchment was sent to Russia where a secret industrial process allowed the underfur to be combed out for return to the felt maker, leaving a fine pelt of lustrous guard hairs for the fine or fancy fur industry. These furs were called *castor de muscovie*. Northern beavers were smaller than those from the south, but their pelts carried a heavier load of underfur. Southern beaver also were not worn by Amerindians and were often poorly prepared, being hunted only for the trade. They were the most easily obtained, and in 1676, the price was adjusted in an effort to counter the flood of poor quality furs coming down from the upper country.[153] While continuing to pay 90 sols for some categories of beaver, the tax-farmer agreed to pay 110 sols for coat beaver, but only 70 sols for parchment.[154] These prices remained in effect until the end of the century. Despite the adjustment, Colbert's tax-farm had driven a sharpened stake through the heart of the colonial fur trade and seriously distorted the colony's future economic development.

Colbert and his successors could advise, reject, encourage, or recommend this and that, but fur became the only game in town. Colbert continually

[151] Ibid., 290–1; and Abdoulaye Ly, *La Compangie du Sénégal* (Paris: Présence Africaine, 1958), 127–9.

[152] Innis, *Fur Trade*, 64; and Eccles, *Canada under Louis XIV*, 101.

[153] Innis, *The Fur Trade*, 64; and E.E. Rich, *The Fur Trade and the Northwest to 1857* (Toronto: McClelland and Stewart, 1967), 45–6.

[154] [Canada, Legislative Assembly], *Édits, ordonnances*, 1: 86–9; Innis, *The Fur Trade*, 66.

encouraged colonists to diversify their economic pursuits to produce alternative exports, but the tax-farm offered such opportunities for gain that the little capital in evidence went directly into the fur trade. Some historians argue that the fixed price for beaver pelts in 1674 was a necessary mechanism to provide for an orderly market in the wake of overcompetition that had resulted from dumping Canadian beaver on the French market at less than cost price,[155] but these claims are not convincing. The previous decade had been characterised by a downward trend in prices; colonists themselves had paid the duties on beaver and sold their peltry freely on the open metropolitan market. The notion that they were dumping fur at below cost is inappropriate for the seventeenth century and inapplicable in any case. The decline in beaver prices indicated the market was responding in an orderly manner to the sudden influx of furs. The claim that the monopoly was intended to halt the glut and control local fur traders is also not persuasive, for monopoly promoted the ensuing glut and the chaos that characterised the subsequent decade. The tax-farm was created to increase the Crown's revenues, not to create an orderly market for beaver. Another reason for the tax-farm lay in the minister's desire to keep the fixed costs of administration off the government's back and on the colonists' shoulders. The duty of 25 percent collected on all beaver exported from Quebec was a form of colonial taxation.

Balancing the ratio between coat and parchment skins became an impossible task. The hat makers wanted 40,000 livres weight of coat and 20,000 of parchment beaver in 1676, but the tax-farmer had a surfeit of poor quality parchment and only 3,000 to 4,000 livres weight of coat. The next year 92,000 livres' weight of pelts were shipped from Quebec, of which only 4,000 were coat.[156] During the decade, 1675–85, the average annual amount of beaver exported from New France was 89,588 livres weight, and between 1685 and 1687, it rose wildly to 140,000 livres weight.[157] Illicit trade with Albany grew by leaps and bounds. Not only did colonists receive nearly three times the price paid at Quebec for their beaver pelts and valuable English trade goods, in return, they were paid in cash rather than in heavily discounted bills of exchange payable several months in the future.[158] The ever-accumulating supply of beaver contributed nothing to the wealth of the colony, but it did concentrate the trade in the hands of major traders.[159]

In 1681, during his attempts to reorganise several revenue farms into a monolithic company, Colbert joined the Western Domain to the new lease

[155] Miquelon, *New France, 1701–1744*, 58; and Michael Bliss, *Northern Enterprise; Five Centuries of Canadian Business* (Toronto: McClelland and Stewart, 1987), 44.

[156] Innis, *The Fur Trade*, 65–6; and Rich, *The Fur Trade and the Northwest*, 45.

[157] Innis, *The Fur Trade*, 70.

[158] Eccles, *Canada Under Louis XIV*, 110; and Thomas E. Norton, *The Fur Trade in Colonial New York, 1686–1776* (Madison: The University of Wisconsin Press, 1974), 121 *passim*.

[159] *RAPQ*, 1927–28, 21 Frontenac to Seignelay, 15 November 1689.

of the United General Farms, known as the Jean Fauconnet lease, to run for six years.[160] In 1687, the Western Domain lease was renewed for 500,000 livres and was to run another 10 years.[161] At the end of the second term, however, the fur trade was on the verge of ruin. Production fluctuated violently during the 1690s, and large numbers of poorly prepared, low quality beaver pelts continued to flow in from south of the Great Lakes.[162] In 1697, after more than twenty years of paying fixed prices at Quebec, the tax-farmer's warehouse at La Rochelle bulged with 850,185 livres weight (416 tonnes) of unsold beaver pelts. Yet, scarcely 620,669 livres weight had been sold during the previous dozen years.[163] Current consumption may have been less than during the 1670s. The contraband trade with Albany had combined with furs from the English Hudson's Bay Company to glut the Dutch market at Amsterdam, thereby closing off any hope that re-exports would help to reduce the glut in France.[164]

The approaching renewal of the Western Domain lease in 1696 forced Pontchartrain to respond to the growing problem. Financial questions dominated his daily concern; nothing could be more serious than a threat to the Crown's revenues. The lessees of the United General Farms refused to include the Western Domain in their offer of renewal. The minister ordered that no more beaver be accepted at Quebec, the license system be abolished, all traders be withdrawn from the west, and all but one interior post be closed; he set out to find a new group of investors to take up the Western Domain.[165] Pontchartrain's abrupt reaction was ill-considered. More than an air of unreality surrounded his orders. They reflected a complete lack of knowledge of France's position in North America and the primacy of fiscal considerations in his daily thinking.

As controller-general of finances, the comte de Pontchartrain's concerns may not be too surprising, but his orders provide still another illustration of the lack of colonial policy and the prevalence of short-term fiscal demands. So too does his next move, for in order to enhance the new farm's attractiveness, Pontchartrain added a small but potentially lucrative new revenue farm, *la marque des chapeaux*, the right to tax and hallmark fur hats. The lease was signed by a new group under the name of Louis Guigues on 18 March 1697, and was to run for 12 years from the following 1 October.[166] Pontchartrain could not have been very pleased. While the total value of the new lease

---

[160]   Guy Frégault, "La Compagnie de la colonie" in *Le XVIIIe siècle canadien: études*, (Montréal: HMH, 1968), 244.

[161]   Eccles, *Canada Under Louis XIV*, 102.   [162]   Innis, *The Fur Trade*, 70–1.

[163]   Hamelin, *Economie et société*, 50, citing C^{11A}, 17: 159, 304.

[164]   See Frégault, "La Compagnie de la colonie", 244; see also Innis, *The Fur Trade*, 65–6; E.E. Rich, "Russia and the Colonial Fur Trade," *Economic Historical Review*, 2nd Series, 7 (1954–55), 307–28.

[165]   Eccles, *Canada Under Louis XIV*, 102–4.

[166]   Miquelon, *New France*, 1701–1744, 58.

came to nearly 5 million livres, the same value as the previous one, it was to run for two more years, making the annual payments of 415,000 livres, or 17 percent less, even with the *marque des chapeaux* thrown in.

The group of investors behind the lease may have been closely connected to the hatmaking industry. Though only a *prêt-nom* or surrogate, Louis Guigues was a Paris hat maker.[167] The new associates may have seen the farm as an opportunity to obtain a cheap, long-term supply of beaver skins because they had demanded a halt to beaver shipments from Quebec. With the coming of peace they may also have been sufficiently sanguine to think they could dispose of surpluses by re-export to the rest of Europe. They also recognised the hallmarking privilege as more than a device to control the quality of manufacturing. It could be a splendid means to exercise a monopoly over the sale of hats through the entire kingdom by refusing to mark the products of other manufacturers.[168] The Guigues syndicate sublet the Western Domain; the lessee in turn separated the Canadian taxes from the rest of the Domain and sublet them to a third party.[169] All of these financial maneuvres were designed to put as much distance as possible between serious money and the collapsing fur trade.

Canadian merchants refused the request to halt beaver shipments from Quebec. Instead, their sense of righteous anger fueled by a generation of fixed prices for beaver led them in 1699 to propose taking over the Canadian obligations of the Western Domain. With the aid of some Paris bankers and the collusion of the governor-general and intendant, the chief among them created a colonial company called *La Compagnie de la Colonie*. It assumed the obligations of the tax-farmer and continued to trade.[170] The effect was disastrous. In 1699 alone, 296,000 livres' weight of beaver pelts, well over five times the annual amount consumed, reached France.[171]

The Colony Company was formed with the blessing of Jérôme Phélypeaux de Pontchartrain. It was not a partnership such as might be found among solid merchants but a joint-stock company established by royal letters patent. This was a suspicious device for such a small endeavour as the Canadian fur trade. While ostensibly designed to raise a capital stock, the joint-stock company may have been intended to place the company's assets, chiefly unsalable beaver skins, in the hands of its directors beyond the influence of other colonial shareholders. The former purchased scarcely any shares. The sale of some beaver in 1702 at Amsterdam, and in 1705 at Hamburg, provided temporary optimism to the naive. The very next year however, Pontchartrain acknowledged his error by sending a new intendant

167 Frégault, "La Compagnie de la colonie", 244.
168 Miquelon, *New France, 1701–1744*, 58.
169 Frégault, "La Compagnie de la colonie", 244–8.
170 Ibid.; and Miquelon, *New France, 1701–1744*, 61–5.
171 Innis, *The Fur Trade*, 72.

to New France to shut down the Company. The Colony Company was a dirty trick played by a desperate, financially crippled monarchy on ignorant, irresponsible, greedy colonial fur traders.

If greed, ignorance, and corruption account for some of the difficulties – they certainly did in the eyes of condescending, mistrustful authorities – the Colony Company could not dissolve the great block of unsalable fur. Moreover, the French government so overburdened the Company with obligations that the abolition of the tax on beaver did not help. Compensation to the tax-farmer for suppression of the *marque des chapeaux* was one weight. Annual fixed charges of colonial administration was another. The heavy interest rates paid to the Company's backers, the annual requirement to reprovision and supply posts at Cataraqui and at Detroit, and the 1.5 million livres owed for the stock of unsalable beaver at La Rochelle also contributed to the company's ruin. In brief, the government divested itself of its Canadian liabilities, kept them firmly on the backs of colonial fur traders, and then abandoned Canada during the ensuing War of the Spanish Succession.

Colonists were on their own. Imports dried up. The Colony Company died, and its financial affairs passed into the hands of several groups of French financiers for more than a decade. During the next two decades, 1706–26, the fur trade was marked by smuggling, slow recovery, reorganisation, and consolidation, during which the oligarchy of the 1680s was reestablished with new players on a sounder basis than before.

Beaver prices collapsed during the remainder of the war. Any trade that survived was illegal, carried on largely at Albany via the Mission Iroquois of Montreal.[172] This trade provided a valuable outlet for coat beaver whose export to France was banned between 1705 and 1717. It also supplied Canadian traders with a steady stream of quality merchandise that aided in repositioning themselves among the interior tribes. Its negative impact on the colony has been exaggerated. From a business perspective, Montreal's illegal fur trade could not have had a more positive effect. Its chief role may have been to keep the colony's entire commercial structure afloat.[173]

In 1714, the great backlog of beaver skins in France finally succumbed to rodents, damp, and moths. Together with the commercial history of the previous quarter of a century, they left a valuable legacy. The reduced profit margins that fur traders appeared willing to accept in future were probably the result of the hard lessons learned. This also may have led to greater willingness among colonists to enter into other commercial ventures, and hence, to increased diversification of the local economy so long sought by Colbert and his successors.

[172] Frégault, "La Compagnie de la colonie", 275–80; J. E. Lunn, "Illegal Fur Trade Out of New France", *Canadian Historical Association Report*, 1939, 61–76; and Norton, *The Fur Trade in Colonial New York*, 129–39.
[173] Dechêne, *Habitants and Merchants*, 95.

Financial and technical changes also led toward revival and concentration in the trade. First, the 25 percent duty on beaver pelts, suspended in 1702, was never revived.[174] Duties continued to be collected on goods entering and leaving New France, but furs never again had to bear any of the fixed costs of the colonial administration. Second, in 1717 the Navy Council abrogated the distinction between colonial and metropolitan money. The distinction whereby an *écu* of 3 livres tournois was worth four livres in the colonies had been a device to keep the burden of taxation on the colonial fur trade, but since the suppression of the *quart*, it had been pointless.[175] While import prices did not fall as a result of the Council's reform, the profits on French and colonial goods, formerly hidden in the devaluation of the colonial money of account, stood out for all to see. This change, which increased the transparency of commercial transactions after 1717, aided in putting the colony's primary commercial activity on more secure foundations than in the past.

Following the slow revival of the beaver trade under the aegis of the continuing ban on coat beaver and very low prices, monopoly came to play a more positive role in this age of imperfect markets. No sudden upsurge in supply occurred after the backlog's disappearance. The value of furs imported into La Rochelle increased more than two and a half times between 1718 and 1730. Nonbeaver fur exports grew in importance, up to 75 percent of the total value between 1706 and 1720 when beaver demand remained low, and fell to nearly half the annual value of all skins exported from Quebec afterward.[176] While beaver pelts were processed in the highly concentrated hat making industry and subject to contingent crises, other furs, chiefly marten, raccoon, and bear, but also otter, fisher, and fox, found much wider distribution in the more scattered fancy fur industry and re-export markets throughout Europe, where prices tended to remain more stable over long periods of time.[177]

In 1718, the reconstituted French East India Company, *La Compagnie des Indes*, inherited the privileges of John Law's short-lived Occidental Company, including the beaver export monopoly, and in an attempt to save on freight, insurance, demurrage, storage, and commissions, beaver pelts left Quebec freely for nearly two years. In May of 1720, Law instructed the India Company to renounce its privilege, but it reverted to enforcing the beaver

174 Miquelon, *New France, 1701–1744*, 63.

175 See Innis, *The Fur Trade*, 62 quoting [Louis-Armand de Lom d'Arce], baron d'Lahontan, *New Voyages to North America*. 2 vols., ed., Reuben Gold Thwaites, (Chicago: A.C. McClung & Co., [1703] 1905), 1: 101 who is quite clear on the point.

176 Lunn, "Economic Development of New France", 464; Dechêne, *Habitants and Merchants*, 76. In 1736, nonbeaver pelts accounted for 56.3 percent of the total value of furs exported from Quebec, see Frégault, "Les Finances", 291.

177 Thomas Wien, "Castor peaux et pelleteries dans le commerce canadien des fourrures, 1720–1790", in *Le Castor Fait Tout: Selected Papers of the Fifth North American Fur Trade Conference*, eds., B. Trigger, T. Morantz, and Louise Dechêne (Montreal: [n.p.] 1987), 72–92.

monopoly early in 1722, which encouraged more illicit trade to Albany.[178] During the 1720s, annual beaver shipments to France varied between 90,000 and 125,000 livres' weight. Whether this indicates that the French hat industry had grown considerably from 30 years before or if the increase was in re-exports arising from generally increasing prosperity on the continent requires study.[179]

In Canada, the monopoly combined with smuggling to act like a flywheel on the colony's small but rugged commercial engine, smoothing out fluctuations, reinforcing stability, and adding to the security of trade.[180] By providing an assured market for beaver and regularly cashing bills of exchange drawn on itself at Paris, the India Company's beaver monopoly provided New France with the surest means to sell its primary export and ready access to credit in France. Continuing contraband trade with Albany reinforced these positive features by preventing the Company from dictating too strongly to the colonial traders or from easily escaping international competition. The combination of English competition and English collusion, along with the increasing proportion of nonbeaver furs and skins being exported from New France, may also have prevented the fur trade from experiencing its nemesis from the previous century, overproduction. Finally, the monopoly that was not a monopoly may also have curbed the fierce internecine competition among colonial traders that one historian recently identified as the most damaging feature of the French colonial fur trade.[181]

Changes of a technical nature and to the labour force were symptomatic of the reorganised fur trade, but they were no less important indicators of consolidation and growing efficiency. Where formerly, in the 1680s, canoes were 4 or 5 metres long and carried three men and 40 packs of beaver, less than 1,000 livres' weight of goods, by 1715 they had increased to between 9 and 12 metres in length, were propelled by five men, and carried more than three times the load of a quarter century before.[182] Though La Salle's construction of barks on Lake Ontario in 1677 and *Le Griffon* on Lake Erie in 1679 marked the beginning of Great Lakes navigation, regular transportation of trade goods on Lake Ontario by sailing vessels only began after 1725.[183] The appearance of a schooner and a bateau that year was one more bit of evidence of the growing rationalisation of the trade as well as a response to English competition. The changing nature of labour also reflected the

---

[178] Marine, B³ 267, ff. 58–9 Law to duc d'Orléans, 5 May 1720. Innis, *The Fur Trade*, 103; Miquelon, *New France, 1701–1744*, 81.

[179] Thomas Wien, "Selling Beaver Skins in North America and Europe, 1720–1760; The Uses of Fur Trade Imperialism", *Journal of the Canadian Historical Association*, New Series, 1 (1990), 293–317.

[180] Extrapolated from ibid., Fig. 4, 309.   [181] Ibid., 297.

[182] Lahontan, *New Voyages*, 1: 100–1; Dechêne, *Habitants and Merchants*, 67.

[183] Col. CᴵᴵA. 47, ff. 231–8v Bégon to Maurepas, 10 June 1725; also Innis, *The Fur Trade*, 46.

trade's growing sophistication. The colony's labour supply far exceeded the demands of the trade and brought its own docility. The proletarianisation of the labour force and concentration of traders indicated the fur trade's transformation to a more capitalistic form of enterprise.[184]

During the early 1720s the Canadian fur trade assumed the form it possessed until its demise a century later. The merchant-outfitters of Montreal remained subordinate to their creditors and suppliers in the metropolis like those who came afterward, but nothing hindered their domination of the great commerce of North America's interior. Nevertheless, it must be acknowledged that in 1730 the total value of New France's exports was equivalent to less than 7 percent of the total value of West Indian exports to France.[185]

3.5 SUGAR

Nothing could be further removed from the fur trade than sugar manufacture. The factors of production could not be more clearly reversed. Fur was native to North America, requiring an entire continent to be successful, whereas sugar, imported into the New World, needed only a few small, indeed, minuscule, islands to be profitable and became the major colonial export of the eighteenth century. Where the occasional labour needed to gather furs had to be free, the intensive labour to make sugar had to be coerced. Fur trading relied on stone-age hunter-gatherers while sugar came as close to industrial production as could be found in the late seventeenth and early eighteenth centuries. The fur trade demanded very little capital, while sugar manufacture called for major investments in slaves, machinery, and equipment. While the fur trade marked the triumph of free individuals bringing order out of chaos, sugar, embedded in its own odious commerce, created chaos in the form of the most hellish society on earth before which all humane values perished.

The reasons for sugar manufacture's slow penetration of the French Caribbean have been attributed to lack of security in the French islands prior to 1660, excessive government regulation after that date, heavy taxation, inappropriate land-granting policies, lack of venture capital, problems with the slave trade, and the ravages of warfare. Though all six factors influenced the outcome, they were not crucial. What must be explained is not retarded growth, but vigorous growth. During the six decades from 1670 to 1730, the total amount of sugar produced in the West Indies more than

---

[184] See Dechêne, *Habitants and Merchants*, 94–6, and 117–24; and Gratien Allaire, "Fur Trade Engagés, 1701–1745" in *Rendezvous: Selected Papers of the Fourth North American Fur Trade Conference*, 1981, ed., Thos. C. Buckley, 15–26.

[185] Cf. Lunn, "Economic Development of New France", 477; and Col., C⁸ᴬ 42, f. 338 Commerce général des Isles françoise tant de sortie que d'entée en 1730 et 1731 [n.d.].

quadrupled, but French production grew much more rapidly.[186] By 1730 it equaled and may have surpassed the output of its better known competitor, the British West Indies.[187] The French West Indies were on their way to becoming the world's largest producers of cane sugar. Yet, this occurred while France fought three major wars in the Americas, each longer, more exhausting, and more damaging than the last: the Dutch War (1672–1678), the War of the League of Augsburg (1688–1697), and the War of the Spanish Succession (1702–1713). Most scholarly attention has focused on the subsequent sixty years, but these witnessed little or no significant change. The earlier decades were the most important in the entire history of sugar in the New World, for it was then that all the structures of production, distribution, and oppression were put in place. The chief aim of this section is to account for the growth of the French portion of what one historian calls "the plantation complex".[188]

Neither the French nor the English started anything new when they began to cultivate sugarcane. The wild cane that Father Bouton saw soon after arriving on Martinique had probably been planted much earlier by Carib Indians. They had carried the plants throughout the Lesser Antilles from Hispaniola, where very early in the sixteenth century Spaniards had experimented with cane cultivation and sugar making.[189] Interest in sugar appeared nearly simultaneously during the 1630s on Saint Christopher, Martinique, and Guadeloupe. Production, requiring heavy investments in machinery and labour, got under way only during the next two or three decades. By 1664, sugar had become the major export crop on all three islands, where cultivation remained largely confined to the colonial leaders and wealthier settlers.[190] The transformation of the French Caribbean

---

[186] Jean Meyer, *Histoire du sucre* (Paris: Éditions Desjonquères, 1989), 124.

[187] Ralph Davis, *The Rise of the Atlantic Economies* (London: Weidenfeld and Nicolson, 1975), 257, Table 4 shows total French and British production of 24,000 tons [i.e., 21,768 tonnes] each in 1720, compared to 20,000 tons from Brazil. Noel Deerr, *History of Sugar*, 2 vols. (London: Chapman and Hall, 1949–50), 1: 193–4, on the other hand, shows total British production in 1720 over 34,000 tons, which increased by about 50 percent to 51,000 tons during the subsequent decade. Pierre Pluchon, *Histoire des Antilles et de la Guyenne*, 114 reported sugar production in 1720 for Saint-Domingue as exceeding ten thousand metric tonnes. Total French production is much harder to arrive at, but an estimate is presented later in this chapter.

[188] See Philip Curtin, *The Rise and Fall of the Plantation Complex; Essays in Atlantic History* (New York: Cambridge University Press, 1990).

[189] Labat, *Nouveau voyage aux Isles*, 1: 225–6 claimed that sugarcane grew naturally in the West Indies, but see May, *Histoire économique de la Martinique*, 87, and J. H. Galloway, *The Sugar Cane Industry: An historical geography from its origins to 1914* (Cambridge: Cambridge University Press, 1989), 62–3.

[190] Mims, *Colbert's West India Policy*, 260 gives 1664; Satineau, *Histoire de la Guadeloupe*, 128 dates sugar predominance from 1656. See also Cole, *Colbert and a Century of French Mercantilism*, 1: 189–90.

islands from small plantations employing white bondsmen on small properties raising several export crops to large estates devoted to sugar monoculture
employing large gangs of African slave labour began quite early, developed
only very slowly, continued until well into the eighteenth century, and was
never complete. While sugar production may have stimulated an influx of
private traders venturing from France during the late 1660s, most plantations continued to employ only a few field hands each for several more
decades.[191]

Raw sugar (*sucre brut*), called muscovado in English, was manufactured
on plantations in sugar works; the process of refining sugar began with removing impurities from raw sugar and involved additional industrial treatment.[192] A desire to create a domestic sugar refining industry in order to halt
the export of specie to the United Provinces rather than a sudden interest
in colonial development drove the French policy toward colonial sugar production during the reign of Louis XIV. Enhancement of the state's revenues
was, as always, a vitally important consideration. The government sought
chiefly to encourage a domestic sugar refining industry. In this way its ambition differed only slightly from its tobacco policies, which were entirely
revenue driven.

Until the mid-1660s most French colonial sugar was shipped directly to
Holland by Dutch merchants in Dutch ships. Anxious to halt the practice,
indeed, to drive the Dutch out of the West Indies by all available means,
Colbert subsidized merchants willing to build sugar refineries in France.
Through tariff reform he sought to create a domestic refining industry. His
first tariff, in 1664, imposed a high duty of 15 livres per quintal on foreign
refined sugar and a lower entry duty of 4 livres on all other sugars, including
those from the French colonies.[193] The next year, following requests that
colonial sugars receive a preference, Colbert left the 4 livres' duty on colonial
sugar and increased the duties on all foreign sugar entering France, raising
the tariff on refined sugar to 22 livres 10 sols.[194] The new tariff may have
stimulated private trade with the islands as French ships began to arrive in
never before seen numbers.

However, all was not well. Inequities became apparent. First, the West
India Company had paid a duty of only 2 livres per quintal since 1668,
while private merchants paid the full tariff, double the rate paid by the
Company. Second, though muscovado (*sucre brut*) that was warehoused for

---

[191] Mims, *Colbert's West India Policy*, 34–6, 236–7; May, *Histoire économique de la
Martinique*, 89–90; and Cole, *Colbert and a Century of French Mercantilism*, 1: 243.

[192] John J. McCusker, *Rum and the American Revolution: The Rum Trade and the Balance of
Payments of the Thirteen Continental Colonies*, 2 Vols. (New York and London: Garland
Publishing, 1989), 2: 1194.

[193] Ibid., 1: 39–40; Mims, *Colbert's West India Policy*, 266.

[194] Ibid., 262–3; Cole, *Colbert and a Century of French Mercantilism*, 1: 432 and 2: 50–1
and 359.

re-export paid no import duty, Colbert's tariff schedules contained no provision for re-exporting raw sugar that had been refined in France.[195] Finally, sugar prices had fallen so low that planters complained that they could not make a profit.[196] Both company agents and private traders demanded a rebate of all import duties paid on muscovado that was refined and re-exported from France. They also claimed that the rebate should be prorated as 1 livre of refined sugar required 2.5 livres of raw sugar. Not surprisingly, the tax-farmers strenuously objected, and after due consideration, the Royal Council ordered duties restored on imported raw sugar and all refined reexports at the rate of 6 livres per quintal. In keeping with his encouragement of new domestic refining, Colbert forced colonial planters deeper into the refiners' control because the decree also forbade any rebate of import duties paid on raw sugar re-exports.[197]

As usual with colonial commodities, demand frequently fell behind supply, and sugar prices, which had been slowly falling since before sugar cultivation began in the Lesser Antilles, declined more rapidly. In London, they fell by 70 percent between 1645 and 1670.[198] In France, the price decline lent an urgency to planter complaints. In December of 1670, the Council reduced by one-half the duty on French West Indian sugar paid by private traders to 2 livres per quintal.[199] A month later, the duties on sugars previously applicable only to the jurisdiction of the Cinq Grosses Fermes were extended to include almost all of France, and less than a fortnight later, responding to the previous month's reduction in duties for private traders, the rebate on reexports of refined sugar were also adjusted downward.[200]

Later, Colbert viewed the adjustments as too great a deviation from his original tariff and too much of a concession to colonial planters. In May of 1675, in what amounted to a search for additional revenue during wartime, Colbert returned the import duty on colonial sugar to its former level of four livres, where it remained until the close of his ministry. None of these adjustments aided colonial planters. Increased sugar production after 1670 led European demand to level off, and markets were oversupplied. European sugar prices plunged sharply, bottoming out in the mid-1680s, and did not recover until a decade later.[201] Between 1677 and 1687, the Amsterdam price of muscovado fell by more than one-third; in England the price fell in 1686

---

[195] Muscovado or *sucre brut*, literally raw sugar, is made from evaporating sugarcane juice and draining off the molasses.
[196] Mims, *Colbert's West India Policy*, 267.
[197] Ibid., 264–5; Cole, *Colbert and a Century of French Mercantilism*, 2: 51.
[198] Davies, *The North Atlantic World*, 188.
[199] Mims, *Colbert's West India Policy*, 266; Cole, *Colbert and a Century of French Mercantilism*, 1: 433.
[200] Ibid., 2: 359.
[201] Deerr, *History of Sugar*, 2: 528–30. William Doyle, *The Old European Order, 1660–1800* (Oxford: Oxford University Press, 1978), 53.

to a level lower than at any time during the next two centuries; French prices may have fallen earlier.[202]

At the end of the Dutch War in 1678 the price of sugar in the islands fell to between 2.5 and 3 livres per quintal. Planters accused metropolitan refiners of price fixing and complained the import duties were more onerous than ever, but Colbert would not reduce them.[203] Destroying Dutch trade was Colbert's guiding aim, and he refused to relieve planters' distress by permitting colonial raw sugar exports to foreign destinations. Colbert always maintained an ambiguous attitude toward colonial sugar producers. Earlier, he had sought to limit sugar production, advising local officials to encourage cultivation of a variety of export crops, while acknowledging sugar-making to be the way to further colonial development.

In the face of collapsing sugar prices and also colonial tobacco cultivation, Colbert promoted two options. In 1679, he advised the new intendant to the Windward Islands, Jean-Baptiste Patoulet, to support planters who invested in local sugar refineries, and he attempted to open a market for colonial sugar in Spanish America. While experiments in sugar refining in the Antilles had gone on for more than a score of years, lack of both capital and technical knowledge inhibited colonial planters. Refining refers to recrystallizing sugar from the raw stage. Planters' early attempts may have been crude given that their creditors insisted on accepting any refined sugar on the same basis as muscovado.[204] Colbert intermittently encouraged planters, but he seemed chiefly interested in promoting sales of a cleaner, more attractive product in France. By 1679, five small refineries with a combined annual capacity of about 1,000,000 livres' weight had been built: three on Martinique and two on Guadeloupe.[205] Always the pragmatist, Colbert saw no contradiction between encouraging a metropolitan refining industry and promoting similar activity in the colonies. Patoulet enthusiastically accepted Colbert's advice and quickly reported that two large refineries with a capacity of nearly 1 million livres weight were to be built by the largest planter on Martinique.[206]

Authorities had long sought access for French manufacturers to Spanish America's rich and varied markets, and in 1680 Seignelay seized on the sugar glut as an opportunity to enter Spanish America by permitting the marquis' de Maintenon to annually export 500,000 livres weight of sugar (about

---

[202] Richard S. Dunn, *Sugar and Slaves; The Rise of the Planter Class in the English West Indies, 1624–1713* (New York: W.W. Norton, 1972), 205. Deerr, *History of Sugar*, 2: 529; also Henri Hauser, *Recherches et documents sur l'histoire des prix en France de 1500–1800* (Paris: Les Presses modernes, 1936), 497; and McCusker, *Rum and the American Revolution*, 2: 1144–5, Table E-45.

[203] Col., C⁸ᴬ 3, f. 188 Mémoire de Patoulet pour M. Bégon, 20 December 1682, cited in Mims, *Colbert's West India Policy*, 267.

[204] Ibid., 272.   [206] Deerr, *History of Sugar*, 1: 232.

[206] Cole, *Colbert and a Century of French Mercantilism*, 2: 54; and Deerr, *History of Sugar*, 1: 230–33.

245 tonnes) for four years to Spanish America.[207] Trade with Spanish American colonies was illegal and the venture was to be kept secret, but whether this or the previous encouragement of colonial refining should be taken as evidence of government policy is moot. Colbert or his son may not have encouraged a colonial sugar refining industry so much as fulfilled a patron's obligation toward a client. Expediency, not policy, may be the operative word.

The beneficiary of all this encouragement was Charles-François d'Angennes, marquis de Maintenon, former buccaneer leader, current governor of Marie Galante, and the largest sugarcane planter on Martinique. In 1675, he had sold his chateau and estate near Chartres to Louis XIV.[208] D'Angennes arrived in the West Indies, where he put himself at the head of some freebooters and ravaged the Dutch possessions of Sainte Marguerite Island and the Trinity Islands. The declaration of peace in August of 1678 put a halt to his buccaneering. He purchased the large estate on Martinique once owned by Esnambuc and got himself appointed governor of Marie Galante.[209] In 1680, he was clearly a man of wealth and influence. In addition to receiving a monopoly on all trade between the French West Indies and Spanish America in 1682, he was building the largest sugar refinery in the colonies.[210] By 1685, Michel Bégon reported d'Angennes' property had 200 slaves and annually produced 400,000 livres weight of sugar. Thirty years later, in 1714, d'Angennes' heirs sold the plantation, including 129 *carreaux* in cane, for 318,067 livres.[211] The marquis de Maintenon appears to have been the chief if not the sole benefactor of Colbert's patronage in the 1680s.

All this activity had some short-term effect. Local sugar prices on Martinique rose to 5 and later 6.5 livres per quintal,[212] but the impact on metropolitan refiners was even greater. The new colonial competition broke the monopoly over the market for raw sugar and, in April of 1682, quickly persuaded Colbert to increase the import duty on colonial refined sugar to 8 livres per quintal.[213] Such expediency from the same man who only two years earlier had advised Patoulet "to increase by every means the number of colonial refineries" reinforces the interpretation that colonial policy was no more than patronage. Colbert had always viewed colonial sugar production as ancillary to establishing a domestic refining industry.

---

[207] Cole, *Colbert and a Century of French Mercantilism*, 1: 409.

[208] The king purchased it for Françoise d'Aubigné, Mme. Scarron, governess of his natural children. Henceforth, she assumed the title of marquise de Maintenon and later became Louis's morganatic wife.

[209] Charlevoix, *Histoire de l'Isle espagnole ou S. Domingue*, 2: 122; and Col., B 9, f. 37v provisions de gouverneur pour M. d'Angennes de Maintenon, 24 April 1679.

[210] Ibid., f. 138 King to Blénac, 2 November 1680; and ibid., f. 254 passport 4 November 1682; also Deerr, *History of Sugar*, 1: 230.

[211] Mims, *Colbert's West India Policy*, 275; and Deerr, *History of Sugar*, 1: 230.

[212] Col., C^{8A} 3, ff. 188 Mémoire de Patoulet pour M. Bégon, 20 December 1682, cited in Mims, *Colbert's West India Policy*, 275.

[213] Ibid., 278.

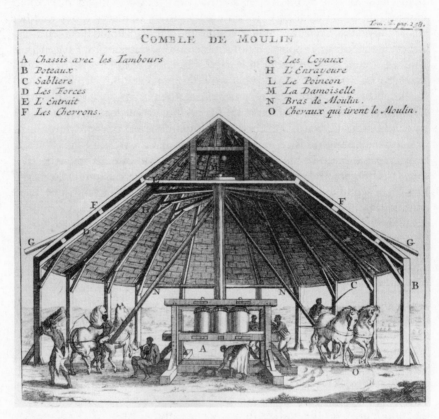

Illustration 3.3. Crushing sugar cane in the seventeenth century. Although published in 1724, this illustration harkens back to about 1670 or earlier. From Jean-Baptiste Labat. *Nouveau voyage aux Isles de l'Amérique.* 2 vols. La Haye: P. Husson, T. Johnson, P. Gosse, Jvan Duren, R. Alberts, and C. Le Vier [1722] 1724, 1, part 2: facing page 258.

Colbert died in September of 1683, and his son and successor at the ministry of the marine, the marquis de Seignelay, assumed his father's role as protector of the refining industry. On 21 January 1684, a new royal decree forbade construction of any additional refineries in the colonies on pain of 3,000 livres fine.[214] The prohibition did not appear to adversely affect sugar production in the Windward Islands. Eight refineries remained on Martinique and Guadeloupe during the five years after 1682, while the number of sugar works or boiling houses grew by 35 percent from 203 to 274.

[214] Ibid., 279.

Data concerning French colonial sugar production in the late seventeenth century are insubstantial, and historians' estimates of production frequently fail to provide any indication of the fragility of the evidence.[215] Censuses during the period enumerate the number of sugar works (*sucreries*) on each island, and some production figures are based on estimated averages of annual sugar production of these works. Thus, in 1669, 113 sugar works on Guadeloupe produced an estimated 43,750 quintals or 2,142 tonnes of sugar.[216] However, two years later, on Martinique, roughly the same number of sugar works, 111, produced 77,080 quintals or 3,773 tonnes.[217] The mean annual production on each island varies so considerably as to cast doubt on these results.

Shortly before 1674, Jacques Savary estimated French West Indian sugar production at a little over 14 million livres (6,877 tonnes): St. Christopher 55,500 quintals, Martinique 45,000 quintals, Guadeloupe 35,000 quintals, and Marie Galante 5,000 quintals.[218] St. Christopher accounted for 40 percent of the total. Savary's estimate that Martinique produced between 40,000 and 50,000 quintals annually throws doubt on the volume reported in 1671. The estimate of 12 million livres' weight (5,874 tonnes) of sugar reportedly produced in 1674 appeared in a retrospective account written 17 years later by Intendant Gabriel du Maitz de Goimpy. The report of 18 million livres weight (8,811 tonnes) of sugar is taken from a report written in 1682.[219] A fourth total estimate, dated 1683, gives the amount of muscovado consumed by French domestic and colonial refineries. Twenty-nine metropolitan refineries consumed 17,700,000 livres weight and five colonial refineries used 3 million more, making in all 20,700,000 livres weight (10,133 tonnes) of raw sugar.[220] During the last eight years of Colbert's ministry, French West Indian sugar production may have grown by 50 percent to reach just over half the production of the English colonies. Though it surpassed total Dutch production by several times, it probably remained less

[215] According to Herbert S. Klein, *African Slavery in Latin America and the Caribbean* (New York: Oxford University Press, 1986), 51–2, by 1670 the French Windward Islands had some 300 sugar works producing close to 12,000 tonnes of sugar annually, is as much as twice as high as it should have been.

[216] Col., C7A 1, ff. 163–4 discussed in Christian Schnakenbourg, "Statistiques pour l'histoire de l'économie de plantation en Guadeloupe et Martinique (1635–1835)", *Bulletin de la Société d'Histoire de la Guadeloupe*, no. 31 (1977), 98.

[217] Ibid., based on AN, SOM, G1 470, ff. 143–267.

[218] Jacques Savary, *Le Parfait négociant ou instruction générale pour ce qui regarde le commerce des marchandises de France & des Pays Etangères*, 7eme éd., édité par Jacques Savary des Bruslons, 2 vols. (Paris: Michel Gignard et Claude Robustel, [1675] 1713), 1: 538.

[219] Col., C8B 2, Mémoire touchant le commerce des Isles, 1691; and Col., C8A 3, ff. 188–97 Mémoire de Patoulet to Bégon, 20 December 1682; see also Cole, *Colbert and a Century of French Mercantilism*, 2: 54.

[220] Col., F3 142 Estat des rafineries de France, 1683; reproduced in Mims, *Colbert's West India Policy*, 263, n.11 albeit with an arithmetical error.

than half the annual exports from Brazil.[221] The key point is that the French colonies contributed to the sugar glut that held prices down in Europe.

Table 3.1 allows a glimpse of French West Indian production facilities in 1687, the only year for which a general enumeration was made. Sugar production during the century probably peaked that year. Growth had occurred on Martinique, but it may have been recent. In 1671 there were 233 sugar works on Martinique, Guadeloupe, and Marie Galante, but in 1682 there were only 224.[222] The number of sugar works had declined on Guadeloupe, and a similar decrease may have occurred on St. Christopher. A limited census made for Basseterre or Pointe de Sable in 1681, reported 60 sugar works and another made eight years later noted only 43 for the same area.[223]

Events in 1689 and estimates for 1701 confirm the lack of sufficient stability on Saint Christopher to ensure steady development. Only 86 sugar works were enumerated in the two French sectors in 1689 a few months before hostilities resumed. According to one report, cultivation declined, and the numbers of plantations diminished owing to a lack of slaves. No reliable data for St. Domingue exist, but in 1701 the colony was in the midst of a very recent boom. The number of sugar works on Martinique grew to 207 in 1692, but declined quickly thereafter. Nevertheless, between January 1696 and June 1697, about 5,000 tonnes of raw and white sugar were exported from Martinique's 166 plantations.[224] Though the number of sugar works in the Windward Islands declined from 407 to 233 between 1687 and 1696, Table 3.2 suggests that a vigorous recovery was underway by 1701. That year's total number of sugar works remained nearly 30 percent lower than the prewar figure. Professor Dunn's estimate of total French production as 10,000 tons (9,070 tonnes) *circa* 1700 is perhaps too high and does not mark an increase over prewar production.[225]

[221] Based on Dunn, *Sugar and Slaves*, Table 21, 203, which gives 18,202 [short] tons, converted to 16,509 tonnes. Richard B. Sheridan, *Sugar and Slavery; An Economic History of the British West Indies, 1623–1775*, (Baltimore: Johns Hopkins University Press, 1974), 398 gives 372,000 cwts, which is equivalent to $372,000 \times 112 \times 0.4535 \times 10^{-3} = 18,895$ tonnes, but he made a serious error trying to convert French production into hundredweights (cwts), failing to acknowledge that the French livre is 8 percent heavier than the pound. McAlister, *Spain and Portugal*, 382 indicates that the Portuguese industry was depressed in the 1680s but recovered to about 21,000 short tons (*c.* 19,000 tonnes) annually at the end of the century. Niels Steensgaard, "The growth and composition of the long-distance trade of England and the Dutch Republic before 1750" in *The Rise of Merchant Empires; Long-Distance Trade in the Early Modern World, 1350–1750*, ed., James D. Tracy (New York: Cambridge University Press, 1990), Table 3.18, 140 for Dutch production of 2,516 tonnes *c.* 1688. His erroneous figure of 9,315 tonnes for French production is derived by compounding the errors in Sheridan, *Sugar and Slavery*, 397–8.
[222] Schnakenbourg, "Statistiques", 85.
[223] See AN, SOM, G¹ 472, ff. 306–16 and 330–1.
[224] AN, SOM, G¹ 499, no. 28 Denombrement générale de l'isle de la Martinique de l'année 1696; and Col., C⁸ᴬ 10, f. 105v Robert to Pontchartrain 17 July 1697 reported 18,072 *barriques* and 4,668 *barils* estimated as 20,406 *barriques*; assuming a weight of 500 livres each gives a total of 4,994 tonnes.
[225] Dunn, *Sugar and Slaves*, 205.

Table 3.1. *Sugar Works and Refineries in the French West Indies,*
1687–1701

Colony	Sugar Works 1687	Sugar Works 1701	Refineries 1687	Refineries 1701
Martinique	184	186	4	
Grenada*	4	c.3		
Guadeloupe	86	81	3	1
Marie Galante	16			
St. Christopher	101	16	1	
St. Martin				
St. Bartholomew				
Sainte-Croix	12			
Saint-Domingue		35		
Cayenne**	24	17		
Total	427	338	8	1

* 1701 based on data for 1696 and 1704
**1701 " " " " 1698 " 1704
Sources: AN, SOM, G¹, 498, no. 59 Recensement général des Isles
françoises de l'Amérique du commencement de l'année 1687; Col., C¹⁴ 2,
f. 185 Denombrement général de l'isle de Cayenne et Terreferme, année
1687; AN, SOM, G¹ 498, no. 63ᵇⁱˢ Denombrement général des isles de la
Martinique, la Guadeloupe et St. Christophe de l'année 1701, ibid., nos.
39 et 40 Recensement général de la Grenade de l' année 1696 [et de 1704];
Col., C¹⁴ 3, f. 227 Recensement de Cayenne année 1698; and ibid., 4,
f. 253 Recensement de Cayenne, année 1704.

It is a significant reflection of the industrial rather than the agricultural
side of sugar making that the French, like the Portuguese, counted boiling
houses (*sucreries*) rather than plantations (*habitations*) as the fundamental
units of sugar production. Planting, cultivation, and harvesting sugar cane
were but preliminary steps to crushing the cane in mills, boiling the expressed
juice until it crystallized, curing the sugar in moulds, and further purifying
it before packing it in casks for shipment to France. In view of the labour,
discipline, and organisation of work, the interchangeability of labour units,
time-consciousness owing to the crop's rapid perishability, the separation of
production from consumption and the slaves from their tools, sugar manufacture was the most industrialised form of human enterprise of the late
seventeenth and early eighteenth century.[226]

---

[226] These processes have been written about very extensively and may be profitably studied in
Sidney W. Mintz, *Sweetness and Power; The Place of Sugar in Modern History* (New York:
Viking, 1985), 48–52. See also J. H. Galloway, *The Sugar Cane Industry; An Historical*

Table 3.2. *Number of Sugar Works in the French Windward Islands, 1696–1701.*

Year	Martinique	Guadeloupe	St. Christopher	Total
1696	165	67		233*
1697	166	65		231
1698	166	62		228
1699	169	71		240
1700	183	73	1	257
1701	186	81	16	283

* Includes one reported on Grenada
Sources: C. Schnakenbourg, "Statistiques pour l' historie de
l'économie de plantation en Guadeloupe et Martinique, 1635–
1835", 85; also AN, SOM, G¹ 498, no. 63ᵇⁱˢ Denombrement général
des Isles de la Martinique, la Guadeloupe et St. Christophe de
l'année 1701; G¹ 472, f. 340 Denombrement général de l'Isle de
St. Christophe de l'anné 1699; ibid., f. 348 Recensement général des
deux quartiers françoises de St. Xphe, 1700.

Some idea of per unit production, annual yields, and earnings of French
West Indian sugar works allows consideration of the causes of growth and
some informed comparison with the much better known English sugar industry during this most formative period in the history of sugar manufacture.
While a study of sugar workings, including plantations, reveals an exotic variety of agroindustry, it also shows that, despite a reputation for indolence
and sloth, planters were hardworking capitalist entrepreneurs. Planters were
slave owners who consciously or not were inseparable from the slave cultures emerging throughout the West Indies, but they were also businessmen
labouring in a harsh commercial environment. Knowledge of sugar making
technology aids understanding, but must be considered alongside the social-
psychological dimensions of the modern history of sugar. It seems appropriate, then, to turn to Father Jean-Baptiste Labat, a missionary, a preaching
friar, a Jacobin as members of the Dominican order were called in France.
For though Labat had pastoral duties, he was also a planter. During the final years of the seventeenth century, he managed and operated his order's
plantation of Fond Saint-Jacques at Grand Rivière on Martinique, leaving a
valuable record of the production and yield of a large contemporary sugar
works.[227]

Geography from its Origin to 1914 (Cambridge: Cambridge University Press, 1898); also
Meyer, *Histoire du sucre*.

[227] Labat, *Nouveau voyage aux isles*, 1, pt. 2: 316–17. It would be useful to read the note on
sugar casks (pp. xxv–xxvi).

As described by Father Labat, his order's sugar works were much larger and better equipped than average. It possessed all the necessary cane and employed 120 slaves and six rather than the usual four copper boilers or cauldrons (*chaudières*) in the boiling house. The sugar works also possessed a water-driven mill that crushed the cane much more rapidly than one powered by animals. Often a plantation required more than one mill to crush sufficient cane to keep the boiling house in continuous operation, especially in such an ideal case as described by Labat, where the works remained in continual production for nearly 8 months or 30 weeks from December to July. If a sugar works made only muscovado sugar, Labat estimated production to be 23 to 24 hogsheads (*barriques*) weekly. Each cask weighed 550 livres, which gives a weekly production of 13,200 livres weight.

The Jacobin plantation made clayed sugar, which involved more sophisticated techniques. Clayed sugar was one of the features of the French colonial sugar industry that, except for Barbados, distinguished it from its English counterpart. Clayed sugar had been known for a long time; all Brazilian sugar was clayed.[228] The English referred to it as "plantation white", and some historians have mistakenly assumed it to be an inferior product to muscovado. Clayed sugar was made by placing a layer of wet clay over the upper surface of a magma of crystalline sugar and impurities in an inverted earthenware cone-shaped mould, and allowing the water therein to flush out additional molasses draining through a hole in the apex. The resultant clayed sugar was whiter than the raw variety and, in 1696, sold for 22 livres 10 sols per quintal. Though the process was costly, it was also profitable. In 30 weeks, the sugar works produced 6,000 sugar moulds each weighing 25 livres or 150,000 livres weight in total. The year's total value of clayed sugar amounted to 33,750 livres, but to this sum Father Labat added 1,890 livres earned from the sale of 8,400 livres weight of *sucre de sirop fin*.[229] He earned another 6,000 livres from 1,000 moulds of sugar made from *gros sirop* and 400 moulds made from *sirop d'ecumes*.[230] Produced from drainings from clayed sugar and foam skimmed off boiling cane juice, they yielded low-grade sugar worth only 7 livres 10 sols.[231] No less than 50,000 livres weight of this heavy moist sugar was produced during the season and when re-passed through the boiling house with additional sugarcane it yielded 80,000 livres

228 Deerr, *History of Sugar*, 1: 96 and 109.
229 Much lighter than cane syrup, *sirop fin*, drained from moulds of clayed sugar in the curing house, was itself moulded and set aside to produce a very light sugar; each mould weighed only eighteen livres. Labat estimated 6,000 ordinary moulds yielded 10 percent more sugar from this syrup. Thus, 600 moulds $\times$ 18 livres $\times$ -10^2 quintals $\times$ 22.5 livres = 1,890 livres tournois.
230 *Gros sirop*, literally "heavy syrup", drained from sugar moulds before claying; some was even collected from the hogsheads themselves. "Foam syrup" was skimmed from the first three cauldrons and taken to the *vinaigerie* or still to be manufactured into spirits, but much was set aside. After a few weeks it was passed through the boiling stage with fresh cane juice added and yielded more than half again the original amount of production.
231 Deerr, *History of Sugar*, 1: 109–10.

weight of raw sugar or muscovado to add to the original 150,000 livres of clayed sugar. In all, Labat's sugar works annually produced about 238,400 livres weight (116.7 tonnes) of sugar worth approximately 41,640 livres. About one-third of the establishment's total yield was raw sugar. Finally, the distillates from each stage of production yielded another 3,000 livres, leading Labat to inflate the total value of one year's production to 46,000 livres.

Labat claimed his picture of earnings was quite realistic; "moderate" was the word he chose. He reported that between 1699 and 1702 clayed sugar sold from 36 to 44 livres per quintal, but just as important as the high price of sugar is the demonstration that sugar byproducts significantly increased plantation returns. Estimates of returns on investment are very rare, but Labat claimed that during these same years the plantation of Houel de Varennes, son of Guadeloupe's first proprietor-governor, estimated to be worth 350,000 to 400,000 livres annually, earned 30,000 *écus*. Compared to Europe, where land might return at best 5 or 6 percent, estates in the islands might yield at least 15 percent and could go as high as 25 percent.[232] More than a quarter of a century later, Father Pierre Charlevoix, estimating plantation yields on the Plaine du Cap in the northern district of St. Domingue, claimed that each of more than 200 sugar works annually made 200,000 livres net weight of sugar. With an average price of sugar in the colony of 13 livres per quintal, each mill earned 30,000 livres without including the returns from syrups and spirits, which he set at 1,000 écus or an additional 10 percent.[233] Thus, while estimating the annual value of sugar earnings on the Plaine to be six million, the industry returned at least another 600,000 from sugar byproducts.

Whether Charlevoix's estimate ought to be accepted is debatable. His annual production estimate for only one area near Le Cap François as 40 million livres, or a staggering 19,580 tonnes, is nearly twice the amount of other figures. Each mill is credited with annually producing 98 tonnes of sugar. Christian Schnakenbourg determined the mean yield per sugar works on Guadeloupe in 1730 to be 450 quintals or 22 tonnes.[234]

Labat also attempted to determine the yield of 100 *carrées* of land. After several experiments, he concluded that this area, equivalent to about 250 acres, if well cared for, should yield about 150 moulds, more or less, and that the same cane, if made into muscovado, ought to yield 12 to 16 hogsheads of sugar. Labat argued that the difference between Guadeloupe and Martinique *carrées* was unimportant as other variables that affected yields, soil, climate, rainfall, and the relative location of fields to the trade winds so influence yields that it could be ignored.[235]

[232] Labat, *Nouveau voyage aux Isles*, 1, pt. 2: 317.
[233] Charlevoix, *Histoire de l'isle espagnole ou de S. Domingue*, 2: 489.
[234] Schnakenbourg, "Statistiques pour l'histoire de l'économie", 98–9.
[235] Cf. Jamaican production in N. Zahedieh, "Trade, plunder, and economic development in early Jamaica, 1655–89", *Economic History Review*, 39 (1986), 209–10.

Colonists did not strictly observe Seignelay's prohibition of colonial sugar refineries in later years as prices generally remained low during the 1690s. Privateers carried so much captured English sugar into French ports during the decade that prices remained low for refiners. Planters could only get 40 to 50 sols per quintal in 1694, and in 1695 perhaps slightly more if they accepted sugar notes (*billets du sucre*).[236] With freight rates of about 8 deniers and duty over 9 deniers per livre weight, sugar worth no more than six deniers could not carry the cost.[237] Little wonder that some discouraged planters switched to indigo. The per quintal price rose to 90 sols in 1696 in response to hopes for peace and to growing demand from refiners at Nantes. However, the fact that four or five refiners in Martinique suddenly proved willing to pay as much as 7 livres per quintal for muscovado was even more important.[238]

These developments led metropolitan refiners to seek a halt to further competition from the colonies and to secure a low price for raw sugar. Having enjoyed special protection for a generation, it is no surprise that they successfully petitioned Jérôme Phélypeaux, who had become his father's chief adviser on all matters concerning France overseas.[239] On 16 January 1698, less than 18 months after French diplomats signed the peace treaty with the Maritime Powers and Spain, the Royal Council increased import duties on all refined and semirefined colonial sugars. All sugars, whether refined or clayed, were hit with a levy of 7 livres per quintal, and the same sugar in loaf was to pay duty of 22 livres 10 sols. To encourage colonists to produce for metropolitan refiners, the duty on muscovado was diminished by 20 sols to 3 livres.[240] In 1697 and 1698, the Martinique censuses enumerated 13 and 18 refineries, respectively, but the new tariffs effectively destroyed them and further colonial exports of refined sugar.

The new tariff did not appear to help metropolitan refiners. It may be that so much superior English muscovado entering France during the war altered consumers' preference. Cultural factors ought not be ignored. It is common knowledge that the French taste for sweetness, as in all wine-olive oil cultures, developed only slowly and never to the extent found in northern Europe.[241] Despite the increase, higher overall tariffs seemed to give a strong impulse to producing whiter clayed sugar in the islands. Whiter sugar was

---

[236] Labat, *Nouveau voyage aux Isles*, 1, pt. 2: 293–4.; and Sidney Daney, *Histoire de la Martinique depuis la colonisation jusqu'en 1815*, 3 vols., facsimile (Fort-de-France: Société d'histoire de la Martinique, [1846] 1963), 1: 380.

[237] Pierre Margry, éd., *Relations et mémoires inédits pour servir à l'histoire de la France dans les pays d'outre-mer* (Paris: Challamel, 1867), 263. The original is in Col., C^{8A} 9, ff. 266–312.

[238] Margry, éd., *Relations et mémoires*, 263–8.

[239] E.g., Col., C^{8B} 2, no. 33 Response of the judge and consuls of Nantes merchants, 8 September 1696.

[240] Satineau, *Histoire de la Guadeloupe*, 158–9.

[241] Mintz, *Sweetness and Power*, 135–6.

far more attractive to consumers, and French planters seemed to awaken to the fact that clayed sugar gave them a means to bypass metropolitan refiners, but other reasons also account for the French switch to clayed sugars.

According to Intendant François-Roger Robert, the claying method had been learned five or six years earlier on Guadeloupe, and despite the extra costs and duties planters took up its manufacture for sound economic reasons. The low price of raw sugar was one. "The manufacture of *sucre brut* does not provide them with the wherewithall to exist", Robert wrote.[242] Nor could planters escape their debt loads. Their credit was ruined. The chief reason for changing to the new process, however, was to avoid the great wastage during the transport of raw sugar to France and to obtain the far higher price paid for clayed sugar. Most of the molasses from raw sugar manufacture was a pure loss. So much remained in the sugar after packing that as much as 25 percent of the total volume was lost during the voyage to France. Sugar casks were the object of reciprocal fraud by merchants and planters. Merchants supplied poorly made hogsheds, poorly joined and banded, so that syrup leaked from casks that therefore arrived lighter than when they left the islands. Together, waste and losses may have amounted to as much as one-third of the product, which also meant a loss of one-third of planters' investments in land, slaves, animals, machinery, and equipment. Planters remedied this by lining the casks with potter's clay to preserve the weight of the sugar for sale.[243]

Though more expensive to manufacture owing to the number of moulds, pots, and copper boilers required, the larger curing sheds and warehouses to be erected and the greater care in manufacture, increased work, and additional fuel for more boiling, Robert explained that planters adopted the claying process for three important reasons. First, little waste occurred during manufacture. Losses during the voyage to France were virtually eliminated. Moreover, clayed sugar cost less to transport. One hundred livres weight of muscovado gave only two-thirds that amount of clayed sugar, but none of the latter was lost. Moreover, as clayed sugar occupied one-third less cargo space than muscovado, shipping costs were reduced. Clayed sugar also yielded more molasses than muscovado, which may have benefited the planter's illicit trade with English and Dutch interlopers. Finally, the price of clayed sugar was far higher than for muscovado. While raw sugar at Martinique in 1696 fetched 4 livres 10 sols per quintal, a similar amount of clayed sugar brought 22 livres 10 sols. After deducting one-third for the reduction in the quantity of clayed sugar, the planter still earned 15 livres for two-thirds of clayed sugar that remained. By 1699, Guadeloupe plantations were producing half muscovado and half white sugar.[244]

[242] Margry, éd., *Relations et mémoires*, 263–8; also Col., C^{8A} 10, ff. 376v–8 Robert to Pontchartrain, 11 July 1698.

[243] Josa, *Les industries de sucre et du rhum*, 52; Revert, *La Martinique*, 369;

[244] Col., C^{7A}, 4 (n.f.) Auger to Pontchartrain, 7 August 1699; also McCusker, *Rum and the American Revolution*, 1: 309.

The new duties on clayed sugars did not block potential earnings. Indeed, the legislation was interpreted as authorising production of the whiter sugar, and metropolitan merchants quickly shipped pots and clay to the West Indies in the wake of peace. Marseilles merchants began to develop markets for sugar in the Mediterranean, and other French merchants were expanding the domestic market.[245] The new attractive product could be sold directly to the French consumer, thus breaking the metropolitan refiners' hold over colonial production. Whatever the causes, clayed sugar became associated with stability and prosperity in the French Windward Islands.

Prices remained strong, rising from 36 to 44 livres per quintal between 1699 and 1702, nearly double the price of only a few years earlier. The price of muscovado rose to 12 and 14 livres.[246] Between 1698 to 1702, the number of sugar works on Martinique and Guadeloupe grew by about one quarter. Even the wartime devastation on St. Christopher was rapidly overcome.[247] No sugar mill was left standing in 1699, but two years later, the number of sugar works had increased to 16.[248]

Events during the war and interwar period also stimulated developments on Saint-Domingue. The slaves, settlers, and gold injected into the western and northern sectors of the colony following the assault on eastern Jamaica in 1694, the evacuation of Sainte-Croix in 1695, and the sacking and pillaging of Cartagena in 1697 made significant contributions. At the very end of the century, Saint-Domingue experienced a boom fueled by these capital inputs. In 1699, an ordinary sugar works reportedly yielded 10,000 *écus* annually. Property values increased so rapidly that in October of 1700, 2,000 *écus* were refused for an unimproved plantation purchased only 18 months before for 70. A year later, 35 sugar works were reported operating, 20 more were about to commence production, and the construction of 90 more was reported underway.[249] Acting Governor Gallifet's enthusiasm may have been exaggerated, but clearly local conditions for growth had greatly improved, leaving settlers able to respond to rising sugar prices.

Why the War of the Spanish Succession had little impact on the continuing growth of the French sugar industry is not clear. Perhaps the answer lies in the continuing high prices paid in France.[250] Neither the permanent loss of St. Christopher to the English in July of 1702 nor the pillaging of Marie Galante in 1703 and 1708 had much overall impact. Planters on the latter had not invested in sugar production since 1696, and their plantations

[245]   Charles Carrière, *Négociants marseillais au XVIIIe siècle: contribution à l'étude des économies maritimes*, 2 vols. (Marseille: Institut historique de Provence, 1973), 1: 331–2.
[246]   Labat, *Nouveau voyage aux Isles*, 1, pt. 2: 317; Daney, *Histoire de la Martinique*, 1: 382.
[247]   AN, SOM, G¹ 472, ff. 341–6.   [248]   Ibid., f. 340 and ibid., 498, no. 63bis.
[249]   Col., C⁹ᴬ 4, Gallifet to Pontchartrain, 27 December 1699; ibid., 5 same to same, 10 October 1701; ibid., same to same, 24 September 1701, all quoted in Pierre de Vaissière, *Saint-Domingue: la société et la vie créole sous l'ancien régime (1629–1789)* (Paris: Perrin et Cie., 1909), 61–2.
[250]   See ADG 7B, 2,631–2 waste books of Paul Hugon for anecodal evidence from 1708.

remained abandoned for the next sixteen years.[251] The English assault on Guadeloupe in 1703 also had little effect. The number of sugar works there grew by 52 percent between 1701 and 1711.[252] The French do not appear to have suffered setbacks in the Lesser Antilles similar to those experienced by their English enemies. Sugar imports into England and Wales from Barbados declined 46 percent during the war years, and shipping losses dealt a "dreadful blow" to planters and merchants.[253] Following the French attacks on St. Christopher and Nevis in 1706, sugar production in the Leewards fell to a lowly annual average of just one-fifth of mean production between 1699 and 1704.[254] The slaves carried away to Saint-Domingue and Martinique may well have contributed to continuing growth on the French Islands.

The most important conclusion to draw from Table 3.3 is that the loss of St. Christopher did not matter. Between 1701 and 1704, the number of sugar works on Martinique grew by three times the number lost at St. Christopher, leveling off at about 240 during the middle years of the war. Growth resumed during the war's final years.

Growth on Saint-Domingue more than compensated for losses encountered elsewhere. In 1713, the approximately 138 sugar works nearly quadrupled the prewar number. Saint-Domingue's population grew by 127 percent, from 13,156 to 29,855, but the number of slaves grew more than two and half times from 9,082 to 24,146.[255] The 138 sugar works at Saint-Domingue compare with 280 at Martinique in 1713. Why Saint-Domingue's slave population of 24,146 almost equaled Martinique's estimated slave population when the number of sugar plantations was less than half the number on Martinique is a matter for conjecture.[256] A large number of slaves worked on Saint-Domingue's indigo plantations; individual sugar plantations may also have been larger, employing more slaves per plantation than at Martinique. Taking the entire French West Indies into consideration, the number of sugar works may have increased during the war by 168 percent. All of these factors suggest that the growth of the French West Indies commenced before the end of the previous war around 1696.

The problem remains as to how to explain it. Where did all of the slaves come from? How much growth can be attributed to illicit trade with Spanish, Dutch, and English colonies? How much of the increased production did French markets absorb? The tentative answer is that rising sugar prices

---

[251] Christian Schnakenbourg, "Recherches sur l'histoire de l'industrie sucrière à Marie Galante", *Bulletin de la Société d'histoire de la Guadeloupe*, nos. 48–50 (1981), 19–20.

[252] Lasserre, *La Guadeloupe, étude géographique*, 1: 284.

[253] Sheridan, *Sugar and Slavery*, 409–10, Table 17.2.

[254] Dunn, *Sugar and Slaves*, 136–8; and Deerr, *History of Sugar*, 194.

[255] Charles Frostin, *Les Révoltes blanches à St. Domingue aux XVIIe et XVIIIe siècles. (Haiti avant 1789)* (Paris: L'École, 1975), 32, 138–9.

[256] See Appendix 2. Martinique's 1713 estimated slave population of 25,371 is a linear progression from 1709 to 1715.

Table 3.3. *Number of Sugar Works in the French West Indies,*
1701–1730

Year	Martinique	Guadeloupe	St. Domingue	Others	Total
1701	186	81	35	36[a]	c. 338
1702	203		50		
1703	221				
1704	234		120	22[b]	
1705	236				
1706	236				
1707		105		14	
1708	246				
1709	242			14	
1710	264	111			
1711		123	130	12	
1712					
1713	280*	129*	138	12	c. 553
1714		133		11	
1715		127	158		
1716		140		12	
1717		144	185	12	
1718		149	196	9[c]	
1719	338	157	199*	28[d]	c. 722
1720		168	202		
1721		172	167?		
1722		180		17[e]	
1723		187		17[c]	
1724		190			
1725		200		18[c]	
1726				40[f]	
1727	413				
1728					
1729		246			
1730	437	252	339	85[g]	c. 1,113

* Estimates based on linear progressions: between 242 in 1709 and 338 in 1719 for Martinique, between 123 in 1711 and 133 in 1714 for Guadeloupe, and between 1718 and 1720 for Saint-Domingue. Except where indicated in the "Others" column, numbers refer to Cayenne, where indigo was also produced on some sugar plantations.
[a] Includes 16 sugar works on St. Christopher and estimates of 3 and 17 for Grenada and Cayenne, respectively (see Table 3.1).
[b] Includes 6 on Grenada.
[c] Grenada only.
[d] Includes 12 on Marie Galant, 9 on Grenada, and 7 at Cayenne.

(*continued*)

appear to have been more influential than any other factor, but the question is by no means closed.

Sugar production continued growing rapidly after the Treaty of Utrecht. Planters increased their lands under cultivation so rapidly that the supply of African slaves could not keep pace. Conservative colonial officals, fearing a sugar glut, issued an ordinance in 1717 forbidding erection of new plantations, but colonists strongly objected. The number of sugar works on Saint-Domingue increased by 146 percent between 1713 and 1739; 95 percent of them continued to produce muscovado.[257] Growing demand in Europe stimulated yet additional demand, for colonial production exceeded French consumption. Sugar was shipped abroad directly from the islands on payment of a 3 percent *ad valorem* duty and a duty of 40 sols per quintal to the receiver of the Western Domain.

How prices affected the postwar expansion of sugar production requires more research, especially as monetary manipulations in the wake of the government's financial collapse characterised the 13 years after 1713. Relative sugar prices declined from their wartime highs, but the downward trend was slight – in the neighbourhood of 10 percent between 1715 and 1725. Lower prices stimulated French and European consumption, which appeared to match the growing supply from the West Indies. Supply only began to exceed demand in the 1720s when weakening prices after 1722 portended a precipitous plunge four years later. Real sugar prices were extremely unstable during the 1720s. Raw and clayed sugars reached highs of 20 and 57 livres per quintal respectively in 1722, but fell suddenly to 11 and 40 livres three years later before partially recovering between 1727 and

---

[257]   Frostin, *Les Révoltes blanches*, 32.

Table 3.3 (*cont.*)

[e] Cayenne and Grenada.
[f] Marie Galante and Grenada.
[g] This is an estimate based on a linear progression from 20 to 57 sugar works on Grenada between 1726 and 1731, yielding 50, and a similar progression from 20 to 60 on Marie Galante from 1726 to 1738, which yields 35.
Sources: Schnakenbourg, "Statistiques", 85–6 and "Recherches sur l'histoire de l'industrie sucrière à Marie Galante"; Deerr, *History of Sugar*, 1: 233; Vaissière, *Saint-Domingue*, 61; Frostin, "Les Pontchartrain et la pénétration commerciale", 309 n. 5 and *Les Révoltes blanches*, 144–5; AN, SOM, G¹ 509, nos. 12, 13, 14, 17, 18 and 19 Censuses of Saint-Domingue for 1713, 1715, 1717, 1720 and 1721; ibid., 498, no. 40 Recensement générale de la Grenade de l'année 1704. For Cayenne, see censuses at Col., C¹⁴ 4, f. 253; 5, ff. 263–71; 6, ff. 183–9; 7, ff. 229–41, 242–50 and 255–9; 9, ff. 281–81v; 10, ff. 232–4.

1730 as the money situation stabilized.[258] During the ten years after 1726, the relative price of sugar fell to its lowest level in a century.[259] By then the French West Indies were becoming the world's largest suppliers of cane sugar and would remain so until the revolution on Saint-Domingue in 1791 destroyed the house of sugar.

During these years of growth, quarrelsome metropolitan sugar refiners engaged in fierce internecine rivalry that had little effect on the current transformations going on around them. Their competition was privilege-based rather than market-based. Representatives from Bordeaux, Marseilles, La Rochelle, Nantes, Saint-Malo, and Rouen struggled to defend their "liberties" by preventing them from being extended to others. They sought to undermine those enjoyed by their rivals, but changes wrought in marketing sugar marginalised the refiners, who never again enjoyed the privileged position of the previous century.[260]

Peace unleashed a flood of French shipping to the West Indies, and refiners soon proved unable to handle the greatly increased quantity of sugar and sugar byproducts reaching the ports. Brandy manufacuring interests successfully arranged to have the manufacture of rum in France banned in 1713, but that did not halt imports of syrup and molasses.[261] These products simply encouraged re-export, opening up new economic opportunities that others were quick to seize and that transformed the port cities. Nowhere was this more pronounced than at Bordeaux, where the colonial re-export trade very quickly transformed a sleepy, commercial relic of the Middle Ages into one of the strongest engines of commercial growth in the entire kingdom.[262]

In May of 1715, the directors of Bordeaux's Chamber of Commerce claimed French refiners could not handle the 80,000 quintals (3,916 tonnes) of muscovado in the kingdom's ports and proposed removing all duties on raw and refined sugar destined for foreign markets as a solution. They also blamed local refiners for the flood of bankruptcies that struck the city in 1714 and 1715. The intendant of Guienne, Lamoignon de Curson, concurred, supporting the Chamber's proposal to free French sugar of import duties to allow the French to undersell English and Dutch sugar abroad.[263]

---

[258] Cavignac, *Jean Pellet, commercant en gros*, 201; see also Robert Louis Stein, *The French Sugar Business in the Eighteenth Century* (Baton Rouge and London: Louisiana State University Press, 1988).

[259] McCusker, *Rum and the American Revolution*, 2: 1144–5, Table E-45. The century in question is from 1680 and 1780.

[260] Paul Bondois, "L'Industrie sucrière française au XVIIIe siècle: la fabrication et les rivalités entre les raffineries", *Revue d'histoire économique et sociale*, 19, 3 (1931), 316–46.

[261] Ibid., 332 n. 79; and McCusker, *Rum and the American Revolution*, 1: 58.

[262] Christian Huetz de Lemps, *Géographie du commerce de Bordeaux à la fin du règne de Louis XIV.* (Paris-La Haye: Mouton, 1975); and Paul Butel, *Les Négociants bordelais l'Europe et les Isles au XVIIIe siècle* (Paris: Aubier-Montagne, 1974).

[263] BB, Ms. no. 734, ff. 27v–8 Curson's report; also Huetz de Lemps, *Géographie du commerce*, 473.

In the wake of the crisis, the controller-general of finances replaced the import duties with a 3 percent *ad valorem* tax payable to the Western Domain. It was subsequently extended until April of 1717, when it became part of the new letters patent that governed colonial trade until the Revolution.[264] The letters patent also reordered the duties on colonial sugar entering France, reducing those on muscovado but leaving those on clayed sugars unchanged. This had an immediate effect. Between 1713 and 1723, English exports to the continent declined by nearly two-thirds to about 2,900 tonnes under the onslaught of French competition, and shortly thereafter French sugar drove the English and Dutch entirely out of European markets.[265]

New groups of merchants, ship outfitters, slave traders, and commercial re-exporters also appeared in the Atlantic ports. Their interests allowed planters greater freedom from refiners' control than in the past. The presence of these new groups encouraged refiners to quarrel over their privileges, preventing them from combining in the face of competition.[266] Colonial trade grew by leaps and bounds; commercial re-exports grew significantly.[267] At Bordeaux, sugar imports doubled from 5.5 to 11 million livres weight (2,700 to 5,400 tonnes) between 1717 and 1719. By 1720, nearly 30 percent of the value of all Bordeaux's colonial imports, including indigo and cacao, were re-exported. In just four years, re-exports increased two and a half times to account for one-sixth of the total value of Bordeaux's exports.[268] In 1729, 98 percent of all clayed sugar (*sucre blanc*) imports to Bordeaux and 58 percent of muscovado, 26,146 hogsheads in all, were re-exported to Hamburg, Holland, Bremen, Middleburg, Lubeck, Geneva, Flanders, and Spain. Despite low profit margins, Amsterdam alone received 3,634.9 tonnes of sugar worth 2,282,230 livres.[269]

The postwar sugar boom occurred largely on three islands, Martinique, Guadeloupe, and Saint-Domingue. The smaller islands prospered, although their output declined in overall importance. Marie Galante recovered rapidly after 1713. The number of operating sugar works increased from two at the war's end to 20 in 1726. The 550 slaves on the island in 1713, less than three-quarters of the number on the island a quarter of a century before, increased to 1,806 in 1726. The new plantations were much larger than their seventeenth-century predecessors, and the island was fast approaching

[264] Ibid., 474.
[265] Frank Wesley Pitman, *The Development of the British West Indies, 1700–1763* (New Haven: Yale University Press, 1917). Reprinted [London: Cass, 1967], 168. Competition accounts for only some of the retreat from the continent for British domestic consumption grew very rapidly during these postwar years.
[266] Bondois, "L'Industrie sucrière", 338.
[267] Butel, *Les Négociant bordelais*, 393.
[268] Huetz de Lemps, *Géographie du commerce*, 474, 482–3.
[269] Morineau, "Quelques recherches relatives à la balance du commerce", 33–4.

a condition of sugar monoculture.[270] On Grenada, sugar played a significant role only after the mid-1720s, when the number of mills rose from 15 in 1722 to 20 in 1726.[271] By 1730, however, production had grown so rapidly that Grenada and Marie Galante accounted for 11 percent of all the sugar works in the French Windward Islands (see Figure 3.1).

Cayenne never took part in the sugar boom. Its isolated location on the South American mainland, the rigidly controlled, private, even military, nature of the settlements, and limited production left metropolitan merchants and slave traders reluctant to trade. During the entire six decades and beyond, Cayenne remained a virtual fief of the Lefebvre family's descendants. The colony got off to a good start, and the number of sugar mills increased from 10 to 16 between 1667 and 1675,[272] but the colony's promise was never fulfilled though the number of sugar works grew to 24 in 1687.[273] Thereafter numbers declined to 12 in 1713.[274] By then, annual sugar production had fallen to a quarter of the 600,000 livres reported in 1695.[275] During 13 months in 1719 and 1720, the total value of Cayenne's sugar exports accounted for just under one-half the total value of the colony's exports, and by 1722 only two sugar works remained in the colony.[276]

The larger islands still had plenty of undeveloped land in the 1720s. The interior of Martinique remained largely unexplored and impenetrable. Much undeveloped land belonged to planters with five or six concessions and insufficient means to bring them into cultivation. Seeking to encourage development, the king threatened to reunite uncleared land to the royal domain in 1722.[277] Grande Terre, the larger of the two islands that make up Guadeloupe, remained virtually unsettled and undeveloped until after 1713.[278] On Saint-Domingue low rainfall in the Western District was a serious

---

[270] Schnakenbourg, "Recherches . . . à Marie Galante", 21, n. 41.

[271] Ibid., nos. 42 to 45 censuses for 1722, 1723, 1725, and 1726.

[272] *CSP, CS*, 1661–68, no. 1540.

[273] Col., C^{14A} 1, f. 220 "Recensement générale de l'île de Cayenne et Terreferme de l'Amérique", undated, [c. 1677]; ibid., 2, f. 185 Denombrement générale de l'Isle de Cayenne et Terreferme, année 1687; and AN, SOM, G^{I} 498, no. 59 Recensement générale des isles françaises de l'Amérique du commencement de l'année 1687.

[274] Ibid., 2, ff. 201–1v Recensement de l'isle de Cayenne, 1691; ibid., 3, ff. 213–13v Recensement de l'île de Cayenne au mois de may 1692; ibid., f. 215 Recensement de Cayenne en 1695; ibid., f. 227 Recensement de Cayenne année 1698; ibid., 4, f. 253 Recensement de Cayenne [1704]; ibid., 5, ff. 263–7 Recensement générale, 1707; ibid., 6, ff. 183–9 Recensement des habitants . . . juillet 1709; ibid. 7, ff. 229–41 Recensement . . . décembre 1711; and ibid., ff. 242–50 Recensement générale . . . pour l'année 1713.

[275] Ibid., 7. ff. 248–59 Recensement générale de Cayenne pour l'année 1713; and C^{8A} 9, f. 11v Extrait des despeches, 11 September 1695.

[276] Ibid., 12, f. 353 Etat des vaisseaux marchands qui ont fait le commerce à Cayenne pendant l'année 1719; and ibid., 13, ff. 295–6 Etat sommaire de la colonies, [1722].

[277] Ibid., 2: 52.

[278] Satineau, *Histoire de la Guadeloupe*, 380–1.

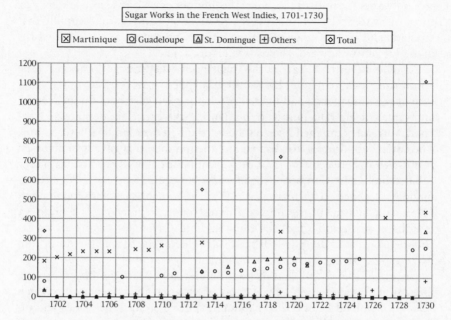

Figure 3.1. Number of sugar works in the French West Indies, 1701–31.

constraint on extensive areas of level land suitable for sugar plantations such as the Artibonite Plain and Cul-de-Sac. Irrigation was not attempted before 1730.[279]

Between 1713 and 1730, the number of sugar works on Saint-Domingue grew nearly two and a half times from 138 to 339, and the number of slaves by 3.3 times from 24,100 to 79,500 (see Figure 3.1).[280] Production probably surpassed Guadeloupe before the war's end, and during the next 17 years exceeded it by a considerable amount. Nevertheless, the number of sugar works on Guadeloupe increased steadily from 133 in 1714 to 252 in 1730, but the slave numbers tell the story.[281] Saint-Domingue already had twice as many slaves as Guadeloupe in 1713 and almost three times as many in 1730.

The situation on Martinique can only be estimated. A linear progression between 1709 and 1719 suggests approximately 280 sugar works existed on the island in 1713.[282] Because Martinique already possessed the most mature

[279]   Galloway, *The Sugar Cane Industry*, 102–3.
[280]   Devèze, *Antilles, Guyanes, la mer des Caraïbes*, 256.
[281]   AN, SOM, G¹ 497, no. 7 Desnombrement générale de l'isle de Guadeloupe et dependencies de l'année 1714.
[282]   Schnakenbourg, "Statistiques", 85–6.

sugar economy in the French islands with more sugar works than existed on Guadeloupe and Saint-Domingue, it was no surprise that during the next 17 years the rate of increase was slower than elsewhere. Even so, by 1730 the number of sugar works on Martinique increased 1.6 times to 437, nearly 100 more than on Saint-Domingue. The slower increase in the number of slaves than in the other two colonies indicated that Martinique was approaching a limit.[283]

Estimates of sugar production are much more difficult to obtain. Christian Schnakenbourg, estimating the mean annual production of Guadeloupe sugar works in 1730, concluded that the theoretical mean number of adult slaves per sugar works on Martinique and Guadeloupe was roughly the same.[284] Adding an estimate of 85 for the number of sugar works on Marie Galante and Grenada in 1730 to the known totals for Guadeloupe and Martinique gives the estimated number of sugar works in the French Windward Islands as 774 in 1730.[285] Multiplying by the mean annual production of 21.6 tonnes suggests that sugar production in the French Windward Islands may have exceeded 16,000 tonnes.[286]

Sugar export figures may not be reliable, but checks and balances between planters reporting false data seeking to avoid tax and tax-farmers' agents demanding access to volumes of sugar in order to levy duties may give some veracity to the figures. Export figures must not be mistaken for production estimates. Table 3.4 shows that between 1717 and 1732, sugar exports to France increased two and a half times. Those from Martinique more than tripled, while Guadeloupe's exports grew only marginally and declined quite seriously after 1722. The proportion of clayed sugar exports was already high in the Windward Islands by 1717 (66.3 percent at Martinique), and rose even higher by 1732, when they accounted for over 90 percent of all

---

[283] The number of slaves on Martinique is unknown. Supposing a linear progression between the number of slaves on Martinique in 1709 and 1719, 22,384 and 35,472, respectively, suggests that in 1713 the slave population amounted to approximately 27,620. This estimate may not be far off, for taking the lower Martinique–Guadeloupe slave ratio of 2.3 and 2.2 in 1707–8 and 1719, respectively, and multiplying by the number of slaves known for Guadeloupe in 1714, the estimated slave population that year would be 27,636.

[284] Schnakenbourg, "Statistiques", 98–9 based on four consecutive estimates of annual sugar production from 1729 to 1732 in order to smooth out any anomalies arising from using only one year. Had only the numbers for 1730 been used, for example, the annual mean would be 25.3 tonnes; see Satineau, *Histoire de la Guadeloupe*, 383–4. The respective mean number of adult slaves per sugar works on Martinique and Guadeloupe was 55 and 57.

[285] The estimate was derived from linear projections and progressions, respectively, between known numbers of sugar works on Marie Galante in 1719 and 1726, 12 and 20, and on Grenada in 1726 and 1731, 20 and 57. See AN, SOM, G^1 498, nos. 21, 22, 45, and 47.

[286] The actual product from the multiplication is 16,170.

Table 3.4. *Sugar Exports to France from the*
French West Indies, 1713–1732

Colonies	Sugar (1,000 kg)		
	Muscovado	Clayed	Total
Martinique			
1717	1,120	3,508	4,628
1722	2,937	5,830	8,767
1725	5,638	7,716	13,354
1732	1,200	13,489	14,689
Guadeloupe			
1718	640	901	1,541
1722	498	1,124	1,622
1725	215	870	1,085
1732	216	709	925
St. Domingue			
1714	6,800		6,800
1720	10,093	185	10,278
1721			10,784
1722			9,984
1724			19,576
1730			

Sources: Schnakenbourg, "Statistiques", 115, 119;
Deerr, *History of Sugar*, 1: 239.

sugar exported from Martinique and Guadeloupe.[287] Exports from Saint-
Domingue tell a similar tale to Martinique except that almost all its sugar
was shipped to France in raw form. From approximately 6,800 tonnes in
1714, exports to France increased to an astonishing 19,576 tonnes by 1724,
a nearly threefold increase for the decade.[288] In 1729, 123 ships carried
10,260 tonnes of sugar into Bordeaux alone; nearly two-thirds (63.9%) was
muscovado and the remainder clayed sugar.[289]

[287] May, *Histoire économique de la Martinique*, Tableau II, [307]; and Alain-Philippe Blérald,
Histoire économique de la Guadeloupe et de la Martinique: du XVIIe siècle à nos jours
(Paris: Karthala, 1986), 23.

[288] McCusker, *Rum and the American Revolution*, 1: 316 Table V-I and 365 n. 34 for sources,
chiefly Deerr, *History of Sugar*, 1: 240, with the latter's errors of omission and commission
corrected. I converted McCusker's hundred weights to tonnes as follows: no. cwt $\times$ 112 $\times$
0.4535 $\times -10^3$ = no. tonnes.

[289] Morineau, "Quelques recherches relatives à la balance du commerce", 32–4.

3.6 CONCLUSION

From 1672 to 1731, short-term fiscal requirements dominated the French government's concern for its colonies. The history of colonial tobacco provides a cautionary note when discussing other commodities such as fish, fur, and sugar. In each case, colonial development, an inherently long-term concept, was sacrificed to the short-term demands of the French state for tax revenue. Only by ignoring the evidence does any idea of policy emerge at all. Indeed, policy as a course of action adopted by government, separate and distinct from politics, thought of as sagacious, prudent, or expedient actions, is not apparent from the evidence. Perhaps this should not be surprising, for the French do not distinguish between policy and politics. *La politique* includes notions of both, and in the late seventeenth and early eighteenth centuries colonial policy was never anything more than domestic politics.

After half a century of effort, a residential colonial fishery appeared in North America, and though it met with a large measure of success, its earlier failure was of greater significance. The failure of a colonial fishery to emerge during the seventeenth century contributed to the isolation of French colonial markets from one another and from France. It was precisely at this time that the expanding New England colonial fishery performed its integrative function, drawing the French as well as the English West Indies into the English imperial economic system. While Colbert and his successors understood the value of intercolonial trade to integrate the small, distant colonial markets of the time, they stressed the need to exchange colonial commodities only to satisfy the interests of the metropolis. They did not grasp the role to be played by low cost, colonial-caught dried cod in joining these markets together. Only dried cod could be traded in sufficient quantities to provide the stability to develop other trades and to complete links. They did not or could not see that the French metropolitan fishery was a great obstacle to creating an integrated French overseas colonial economy. In the next chapter we will see that the failure of a large French slave trade to appear in the seventeenth century reinforced the effect of the metropolitan fishery to obstruct colonial trade.

The fur trade's history during the sixty years after 1670 brings out yet another often overlooked feature of the Old Regime. Private merchants competed fiercely among themselves, but they made a success of the trade. Government interference provided little assistance. Legislation and regulation hindered traders by appealing to their greed and inexperience. Local officials, ministers, and secretaries of state frequently viewed traders as enemies of the public good. While sometimes seeing fur traders as military agents, guerrilla warriors to be launched in penny packets against the state's enemies whether Amerindian or English, and viewing merchants as cash cows, rarely, if ever, did they consider merchants, planters, and fur traders to be creators of the very wealth they so anxiously sought in order to justify French expansion overseas.[290]

Except for its introduction, all major developments concerning the French colonial sugar industry occurred during the 60 years between 1670 and 1730. No sugar revolution ever occurred in the French West Indies. No sudden change in export crops or rapid displacement of one labour force by another ever occurred. Sugar replaced tobacco rather than displacing it. The number of slaves only slowly outnumbered whites long after sugar had been introduced. On some islands like Martinique, Grenada, and Marie Galante a form of sugar monoculture occurred, but not on others, including the largest, Saint-Domingue. Even after becoming the world's largest producer of cane sugar shortly after 1730, French West Indian exports remained more diversified than on British islands. As with other colonial commodities, government policies did little to encourage sugar production, but they also did little to retard it. Colbert's policies were chiefly intended to develop a domestic refining industry, but he only endowed France with an uncompetitive, high-cost industry. His successors at the ministry of marine were no better. Lower duties and the easing of restrictions on re-exports after 1715 did not harm the colonial industry, and may have encouraged it through restructuring the economies of the French ports, but by then the growth of sugar production had been underway for nearly a score of years.

Warfare may have temporarily damaged colonial sugar production, but then again, there were occasions when war may have aided it. Growth occurred nearly everywhere during the War of the Spanish Succession, reinforcing the notion that war was not a critical factor. The Franco-Spanish alliance in 1700 and the creation of the Royal Asiento Company the following year may have influenced the growth of Saint-Domingue, and captured slaves delivered to Martinique by privateers and French raiders may have aided colonial trade, but closer analysis presented in Chapter 8 suggests otherwise. The key factor accounting for the growth of French colonial sugar production seems to have been the real and relative price of sugar, what it cost in France, and what it cost relative to English and Dutch products. The number of sugar works built in the colonies seemed to be directly related to this one factor above all others, which, if true, reinforces the view that government intervention and regulation had little or no significance in the development of the West Indies or elsewhere in French America.

[290] See Wien, "Selling Beaver Skins", who argues this most persuasively.

4

Trade and Exchange

4.1 INTRODUCTION

Well before 1670, European merchants had assimilated once separate networks of exchange and nearly autonomous economies into a loose world
trading system. Shortly before 1670, the international trading system ceased
its century-and-a-half-long expansion and began evolving anew, deepening
existing trade links and creating new trade opportunities. Three features im-
parted a new dynamism to trade: the intervention of merchants attuning production to markets, the replacement of bilateral by multilateral exchanges,
and the reduction of transactions costs.[1] French merchants had played an insignificant role during the preceding period of European international trade
and did not play an important role in the new financial and commodity trading system which arose under the United Provinces of the Netherlands and
England.[2] Religious persecution that drove French Protestants to flee France
just before William III introduced the Dutch financial system to England
helped unite London and Amsterdam, and international warfare on an
unheard-of scale between 1688 and 1713 fostered the creation of international capital markets as states spent far beyond their means. Persecuted religious minorities, both Jews and French Huguenots, circulated in northeastern Europe spreading new financial capitalism from which France remained

---

[1] Jan De Vries, *The Economy of Europe in an Age of Crisis, 1660–1750* (London and New
    York: Cambridge University Press, 1976), 113–16; also David Hackett Fischer, *The Great
    Wave, Price Revolutions, and the Rhythm of History* (New York: Oxford University Press,
    1996).
[2] Eric S. Schubert, "Innovations, debts, and bubbles: International integration of financial
    markets in western Europe, 1688–1720", *Journal of Economic History*, 48 (1988), 299–
    306; David Ormerod, "The Atlantic Economy and the 'Protestant Capitalist International',
    1651–1775", *Historical Research*, 66 (1993), 197–208; and J. F. Bosher, "Huguenot Mer-
    chants and the Protestant International in the Seventeenth Century", *William and Mary
    Quarterly*, 3rd Series, 52, 1 (January 1995), 77–102.

largely excluded.[3] The questions to be answered then are How were French overseas possessions and their colonial trades merged into the new system, and How did the slow integration affect the elusiveness of empire?

The total capacity of French shipping in 1670 was about 80,000 tons, less than 6 percent of Europe's combined tonnage. This compared with Dutch capacity of about 600,000 tons.[4] While the French economy was the largest in Europe, it was predominantly local, regional, and poorly connected. Its lack of shipping indicates the challenge facing French merchants to recapture and integrate French colonial trade into France's recovery between 1670 and 1730. Colbert's claim that 150 Dutch ships annually carried away the production of the French West Indies in exchange for foodstuffs from Germany and manufactures from Holland may be too high, but the Dutch long dominated colonial trade.[5] Well before the end of the period, however, French merchants had driven the Dutch from the colonial trades and were resisting competition from the English, who dominated the new trade system, while integrating most colonial production into the expanding French and European economy. This chapter describes and accounts for these developments by looking at the roles of government, commercial trade, transportation, the development of markets, the slave trade, and problems of money and payments.[6]

4.2 INEFFECTUAL POLICIES, LEGISLATIVE FUTILITY

From the beginning, French colonial trade developed under severe legislative constraints that restricted its conduct to French vessels. The resources of French maritime commerce proved inadequate to meet the needs of colonists, who were never considered important in any case. This became even more clear during the six decades after 1670 when the government strove unsuccessfully to restrict trade exclusively to French shipping. Moreover, French overseas trade policy was often incoherent and contradictory. The acquisition of transmaritime bases, the establishment of long-distance trading

---

3 Larry Neal, *The Rise of Financial Capitalism: International Capital Markets in the Age of Reason* (New York: Cambridge University Press, 1990), Chapter 1, 1–19.

4 Richard W. Unger, "The Tonnage of Europe's Merchant Fleets, 1300–1800", *The American Neptune*, 52, 4 (Fall, 1992): 258, 261.

5 Pierre Clément, éd., *Lettres, instructions et mémoires de Colbert*, 7 vols. bound as 9, (Paris: Imprimerie impériale, 1859–82), 2 pt. 1: cclxxi, "Mémoire sur le commerce", quoted in Stewart L. Mims, *Colbert's West India Policy* (New York: Yale University Press, 1912), 2–3.

6 Evidence of colonial trade under Louis XIV is scarce and fragmentary. A single carton containing commercial data (AN, SOM, Série F²ᴮ, Commerce des colonies, vol. 1) is all that exists in the colonial archives. The rest is scattered through hundreds of cartons and registers of general correspondence of colonial governors-general, intendants, and their subordinates; its accuracy and usefulness remain moot.

companies, and the pursuit of colonisation were not always compatible objectives. The futility of trade policy stands revealed after studying the development of commerce with the colonies. Government legislation and regulation make clear that well-being and prosperity were products of changing circumstances and material conditions rather than state intervention.

Not surprisingly, Jean-Baptiste Colbert was anti-Dutch. In 1664, he introduced high tariffs against Dutch goods. Three years later he raised the tariff wall even higher. This had little positive effect. If anything, it increased the costs of French trade. Dutch merchants continued to dominate French West Indian trade because their chief port, Amsterdam, remained Europe's largest entrepôt for colonial goods. The greatest obstacle to developing French commerce was the limited nature of French demand for colonial products. Moreover, the system of monopoly and state legislation designed to keep foreigners out of the French colonies actually encouraged them to intrude. Charter companies like the West India Company (1664), Senegal Company (1674), Guinea Company (1685), and Saint-Domingue Company (1698) were primarily established to provide services to the French state rather than to be commercial enterprises. Also, monopoly and the right to conduct trade under monopolistic conditions dominated merchant thinking.

Legislation advanced the interests of the state and occasionally those of metropolitan merchants. Sometimes legislation had to contradict the government's intention to restrict colonial trade to French goods because its objectives were unobtainable. In 1668, for example, a judgment forbade all foreign trade to the colonies and granted all exchange to the West India Company.[7] In June 1670, a royal ordinance prevented foreign ships from anchoring in the colonies, denying colonists any right to trade with them; less than two years later a second royal ordinance disallowed all trade in foreign goods.[8] Yet, in 1673, the government acknowledged the unreality of its restrictive policies and permitted French merchants to sell the very product, Irish salt beef, forbidden for sale in the colonies less than two years before.[9] For the next half century and long afterward, legal fiction, ambiguity, and contradiction characterised the French government's policies and legislation governing trade with the colonies. The so-called *exclusif* or *pacte coloniale* existed chiefly in the minds of later economists and historians. Louis XIV's ministers and their successors were pragmatists chiefly driven by short-term demands of fiscal expediency. They were unable to devise anything we would recognise today as coherent policy.

Following judgements of 1670 and 1671, which granted the rights of entrepôt and transit to the West India Company, and the latter's suppression in 1674, colonial trade lay exposed to the demands and exactions of

---

[7] Col., A 24, f. 206 arrêt, 10 September 1668.
[8] Ibid., f. 191 no. 2.
[9] Col., A 24, f. 93v ordonnance du roi, 10 May 1673.

tax-farmers of the Western Domain and their employees. Until the end of Louis XIV's reign, several edicts exempted goods leaving France for the colonies from exit duties, and colonists struggled with some success against the retarding policies and behaviour of tax-farmers and customs clerks who were private contractors rather than government officials.

Under Louis XIV, measures to control trade were piecemeal, half-heartedly enforced, or not enforced at all. The first real attempt to regulate colonial trade occurred when the government of the Regent issued two letters patent, dated 1716 and 1717. The first dealt with the slave trade and the second with colonial commerce in general. The letters patent were the definitive statement of early post-war colonial trade policy. The preamble of the 1717 letters patent reflected continuity with the past, clarifying older regulations and introducing freer trade to the colonies by opening commerce to merchants in 13 seaports stretching from Calais in the north to Sète in the south provided they met certain obligations and paid exit duties.[10] It had the effect of doubling the number of ports permitted to trade with the colonies. The addition of a 14 and 15 port in 1719 and 1721 freed trade even more. Though it preserved the principle of restricted ports of entry and exit to and from the colonies, the new law virtually opened colonial trade to all and may have contributed to the growth of colonial trade during the next decade.

In 1727, soon after Louis XV began to rule as well as to reign, the new minister of marine, the comte de Maurepas, sponsored new letters patent governing colonial commerce. Maurepas ignored developments that were integrating the colonies into the broader, international, commercial, Atlantic world. He intended to establish a closed commercial system once and for all. These letters patent were regressive and ineffective. They made trade with Spanish America illegal where it had never been forbidden in the past.[11] Trade with Spanish America was quickly restored, but the incident clearly revealed the minister's attitude. While the letters patent merely reiterated the previous legislation against foreign trade, the new penalties were so severe that the law could not be enforced. Until 1727, confiscation and fines had been decreed to punish offenders, but under the new enactment, ships' captains found guilty of importing slaves from foreign sources or goods from anywhere but France were threatened with banishment to the galleys, a form of living death from which few escaped. All foreign ships discovered within one league of a French island were liable to seizure. Captains of French ships suspected of carrying foreign goods could be judged summarily by the intendant. The minister left no doubt about his enthusiasm for the new law.

---

[10]   Col., A 25, f. 51v Lettres patentes du roi portant reglement du commerce dans les colonies françaises..., April 1717.

[11]   See Col., C^{8B} 9, no. 55 [anonymous], "Commerce aux colonies", 20 October 1727, for Maurepas' "bon" written in the margin where this is mentioned.

He credited it with encouraging French merchants to send 64 heavily laden ships to Martinique in the first five months after the letters patent were issued. He demanded Governor-General de Champigny and Intendant d'Orgeville enforce the regulations and recommended extending the full rigour of the law to punish those who broke it.[12] Colonists were less than enthusiastic. The law was duly registered at Martinique and Quebec before September of 1728. However, at Louisbourg officials registered it only two years later.[13] Registration did not ensure compliance. Local officials continued to permit foreign vessels to call and trade, and in 1733, after reluctantly acknowledging the reality of French inability to supply Ile Royale, Maurepas approved a local decision to permit trade with New England.[14] Colonists refused to denounce offenders, and colonial authorities acknowledged the injustice of turning colonists into prisoners of metropolitan merchants who complained to the minister as they failed to meet colonists' needs. The law's chief thrust was to preserve the illusion that absolutism was in control.

4.3 COMMERCIAL TRADE

1. France

Almost all maritime traffic to the colonies in 1670 was in French hands, but this was a very new, relatively fragile and partially illusory arrangement. To this point, colonial commerce in the Antilles had been in Dutch hands; Dutch ships had also sailed to Canada.[15] Under the French, goods became scarce, expensive, and poor in quality and assortment. Trade in the islands commonly took several months to complete, which may be why the governor of Guadeloupe congratulated himself in 1671 after a La Rochelle merchant completed his transactions in 28 days.[16] Ships at Cayenne late in the seventeenth century sometimes waited a year for a cargo.[17]

---

[12]   Col., C8A 39, ff. 1–8v Mémoire du roi pour servir d'instructions à MM Champigny et d'Orgeville, 27 April 1728.

[13]   [Assembée Legislative du Canada], *Edits, ordonnances, royaux, declarations et arrêts du conseil d'état du roi concernant le Canada*, 3 vols. (Québec: E.-R. Fréchette, 1854–56), 1: 464–76; Col., B 54, 498–9 Maurepas to Admiralty officers, 30 June 1730; also Miquelon, *New France, 1701–1744*, 117.

[14]   A. J. B. Johnston, *Control and Order in French Colonial Louisbourg, 1713–1758* (East Lansing: Michigan State University Press, 2001), 141.

[15]   James S. Pritchard, "Ships, Men, and Commerce: A Study of Maritime Activity in New France" (unpublished Ph.D. thesis, University of Toronto, 1971), 85.

[16]   Louis-Philippe May, *Histoire économique de la Martinique, (1635–1763)*, (Fort-de-France: Société de distribution et de culture, [1930] 1972), 130–1; Lucien-René Abénon, *La Guadeloupe de 1671 à 1759: Etude politique, économique et sociale*, 2 vols. (Paris: L'Harmattan, 1987), 1: 157.

[17]   [François] Froger, *Relation d'un voyage fait en 1695, 1696 et 1697 aux côtes d'Afrique, Detroit de Magellan, Brézil, Cayenne, & Isles Antilles, par un escadre des vaisseaux du roi, commandé pas M de Gennes*. (Paris: Chez Nicolas Le Gras, 1700), 158.

Surprisingly, lack of shipping did not hinder this early trade, though it
is unlikely that French ships trading to the West Indies during the 1660s
amounted to even 10 percent of the Dutch. The number of French ships of
more than 100 tons capacity doubled between 1664 and 1704.[18] However,
this slow expansion did not appear to benefit the colonies. Colbert did not
establish the West India Company to diminish trade with the colonies, but
such was the Company's impact that it had that effect. Colonists were initially excluded from trade with France. Only after the Company's bankrupt
condition became obvious and Colbert opened the colonies to private traders
in 1669 did merchants begin to send ships on their own accounts to New
France and the West Indies.[19] Governor-General de Baas continued to favour
Company clerks who obstructed private merchants, hindered them from obtaining return cargoes, and tied up planter's crops.[20]

The number of French ships sailing to the West Indies increased from 59
to 134 between 1670 and 1674,[21] and as the Company fell into bankruptcy
these private merchants quickly imposed a stranglehold, charging high prices,
combining to fix prices, and failing to meet demand.[22] War with the United
Provinces severely constrained trade thereafter as many merchants withdrew
for the duration. The wealthiest merchant in Canada, for example, sat out
the war in La Rochelle.[23] The nature of the colony's exports also led to the
stagnation of Canada's trade. While it possessed great value compared to
its volume, the annual fur harvest from Canada could be carried to France
on a single ship. Canada's major export could not stimulate shipping, and
falling beaver prices discouraged metropolitan merchants from fitting out
ships to New France. Merchants also had little chance of finding return
cargoes to send to France. Moreover, the reoccupation of Acadia attracted
some La Rochelle merchants there in order to explore opportunities or to
connect with New England and sources of cargoes for the West Indies.[24]
Fifty-nine ships, more than two-thirds from La Rochelle, sailed from France

[18]   F. Braudel et E. Labrousse, dirs. *Histoire économique et sociale de la France*, Tome II. *Des
       derniers temps de l'âge seigneurial aux préludes de l'âge industriel (1660–1789)*, (Paris:
       Presses Universitaires de France, 1970), 189.
[19]   Col., C^{11A}, 3, f. 61 Patoulet to Colbert, 11 November 1669, also May, *Histoire
       économique de la Martinique*, 109–10; and Mims, *Colbert's West India Policy*, 225–6;
[20]   Clément, éd. *Lettres ... de Colbert*, 3: 459 Louis XIV to de Baas, 4 August 1669.
[21]   Col., B 2, ff. 148–9 Etat des passeports délivrés aux navires française pendant l'année
       1670; ibid., 6, ff. 60–6 Etat des passeports delivrés aux marchands française et étrangers
       pour les Isles de l'Amerique pendant 1674.
[22]   E.g. *RAPQ*, 1926–27, 10, 48 Frontenac to Colbert, 2 November 1672 and 13 September
       1673.
[23]   Yves F. Zoltvany, "Aubert de la Chesnaye, Charles", *DCB*, 2: 28.
[24]   See L. A. Vigneras, "Letters of an Acadian Trader, 1674–1676", *The New England Quar-
       terly*, 13, (1940), 98–110; and J. F. Bosher, "The Lyon and Bordeaux Connections of
       Émmanuel Le Borgne, c. 1605–1681." *Acadiensis*, 23 (1993), 128–45.

to Canada between 1673 and 1682.[25] Most of the remainder sailed from Bordeaux, where merchant bankers, several of whom were foreign, willingly provided capital.[26] The Dutch War and harmful policy also led trade to the West Indies to stagnate. The French navy effectively cleared Dutch ships from the waters around the French islands, but could not bring the vessels required to replace them. Colbert's suppression of tobacco production in favour of the tax-farmers also removed the stimulative effect of a valuable, bulky commodity from the list of colonial products.

The relatively peaceful 1680s saw growth in colonial maritime traffic, though sometimes it was deceptive. The annual volume of shipping to arrive at Quebec from France in 1684 was not reached again for more than half a century, but this development reflected the transport of troops to the colony rather than growth in colonial trade. In the West Indies, the situation was more complicated. More than 100 ships reached Martinique in 1684 in response to peace and increased production.[27] Slightly more than one-quarter of all the shipping clearing Saint-Malo for the Caribbean during the final two decades of the century arrived between 1686 and 1688, and more than one-third of all the returning traffic occurred during the same brief period.[28] Limited domestic demand for colonial products led metropolitan merchants to send out small cargoes, which pushed colonists into the willing embrace of English and New England traders. According to intendant Michel Bégon, French merchants deliberately sent small cargoes to the colonies to keep prices high and the colonists under their domination, but lack of demand in France was the deeper cause.[29] Little changed before the end of the War of the Spanish Succesion.

French West Indian trade grew remarkably after 1713, but still not rapidly enough to force out foreigners. Colonial production grew faster. The total value of France's colonial trade, excluding the African trade increased 4.5 times between 1716 and 1730.[30] The Atlantic ports of Bordeaux and Nantes grew in conjunction with the sugar and slave trades. Saint-Domingue sugar exports grew twice as fast as Jamaica's, and during the 1720s, they surpassed

[25] Pritchard, "Ships, Men, and Commerce", 95–6; Marcel Delafosse, "La Rochelle et le Canada au XVIIe siècle", *RHAF*, 4 (1950–51), 500–4.

[26] J.F. Bosher, "The Canadian Trade at Bordeaux, 1671–1684" in *Business and Religion in the Age of New France, 1600–1760* (Toronto: Canadian Scholars Press, 1994), 164–72.

[27] May, *Histoire économique de la Martinique*, 134.

[28] Jean Delumeau, *Le Mouvement du port de Saint-Malo, 1681–1720: bilan statistique* (Paris: Librarie C. Klincksieck, 1966), 297.

[29] Col., C⁸ᴮ 1, Mémoire pour Monsieur Metz [Dumaitz] par Bégon, 12 April 1685.

[30] Paul Butel, *Les Negociants bordelais, l'Europe et les Iles au XVIIIe siècle,* (Paris: Aubier 1974), 20–1; also François Crouzet, "Économie et société (1715–1789)", dans *Bordeaux au XVIIIe siècle.* dir. F.-G. Parizet (Bordeaux: Fédération historique du Sud-Ouest, 1968), 199.

Illustration 4.1. *The Complete Merchant, circa* 1675, standing in front of his shop near the quay among his colleagues, clients, and goods, some of which are still being unloaded from a ship. Behind him a porter opens a bale. At the shop entrance customers examine cloth. Nearby his clerk presents a cargo manifest or list of goods to the tax-farmer's agent who is recording items in a register.

From Jacques Savary des Bruslons, *Le Parfait négociant ou instruction générale pour ce qui regarde le commerce des marchandises de France et des pays estrangers.* 7ème éd. (Paris: M. Guignard & C. Robustel [1675] 1713), frontispiece.

the exports of the English colony. Martinique's sugar production kept pace. In 1729, more than 7.5 million livres worth of sugar, indigo, hides, and cotton entered Bordeaux alone from the West Indies. Martinique and Guadeloupe accounted for 47.5 and 4.1 percent, respectively. The rest came from Saint-Domingue. Sugar comprised about 80 percent of the total value.[31] Secondary staples such as coffee, indigo, and cacao, however, remained important French colonial exports.

French foreign trade grew annually at a rate of 4.1 percent between 1716 and 1748, but New World markets for French manufactures did not grow at the same rate and old practices continued. At the end of 1726, Governor-General de Feuquières and Intendant Blondel issued an ordinance to prevent ship captains from colluding to refuse credit, artificially fixing prices, and refusing to sell goods brought to the colonies.[32] As a consequence of this imperfect integration of colonial products into the French economy, the Atlantic trades that so enriched the seaports never developed beyond a series of intense but temporary booms in commodity imports.[33]

2. Intercolonial Trade

The last thirty years of the seventeenth century saw the rise and fall of official attempts to create a maritime commercial link between Canada and the West Indies. It ended with official disapproval of any but metropolitan ships being employed in intercolonial trade and the exclusion, albeit temporary, of colonial ships from trade between the two regions. A second period, marked off from the first by colonial initiatives, arose from the circumstances of the War of the Spanish Succession rather than structural alterations in the economy or changes in government policy. The period was notable for attempts to free the trade between the colonies from metropolitan control. It continued during the Regency period, which was marked by the government's effort to introduce freer, if not free, trade to the colonies. Finally, in the wake of the 1727 letters patent, the government moved from excluding to encouraging colonists to participate in intercolonial trade.[34] Despite legislative prohibitions against foreign trade and administrative support for colonial merchants, self-sufficiency within the French colonial system was never achieved nor was foreign trade excluded or even significantly reduced.

---

[31] Michel Morineau, "Quelques recherches relatives à la balance du commerce exterieur français au XVIIIe siècle: ou cette fois un egale deux," dans *Aires et structures de commerce française au XVIIIe siècle*. dir. Pierre Leon (Paris: Centre d'histoire économique et sociale de la région lyonnaise 1975), 33–4.

[32] Col., C[8A] 35, ff. 202–4v ordinance, 24 December 1726.

[33] De Vries, *The Economy of Europe in an Age of Crisis*, 144.

[34] See Jacques Mathieu, *Le commerce entre la Nouvelle-France et les Antilles au XVIIIe siècle* (Montréal: Fidès, 1981).

Fewer than 75 cargoes moved between Quebec and the West Indies during the last three decades of the seventeenth century. The largest number of ships to be involved were owned by the same La Rochelle merchants that dominated maritime traffic between France and Canada. Their decision to direct their ships to the Antilles, chiefly Martinique, after leaving Quebec marked recognition that few profitable return cargoes could be found in Canada where the expanding fur trade increasingly focused and absorbed the colony's limited economic resources.[35]

A small number of ships, some of which initiated the commercial connection, belonged to colonists. In 1670, two Canadian ships sailed for Cayenne and Tortuga, but apparently ended up at Martinique.[36] Encouragement originally took the form of shipbuilding subsidies and intendant Jean Talon's personal encouragement and involvement, but changing circumstances and the contradictions between Colbert's policy and colonists' abilities soon brought the modest venture to a close. Changes in the fur trade, the outbreak of war with the Netherlands, which increased costs, the comparative advantage enjoyed by New England traders, and the character of the French New World fishery all overrode Colbert's attempts to encourage intercolonial trade. Colbert demanded large ships in pursuit of his anti-Dutch policy, while market realities and colonists' means required small vessels.[37] Both the closure of the St. Lawrence River to navigation for six months each year and the expense of transporting low-cost foodstuffs cut into profitability. Merchants lacked sufficient capital to build a trade connection, and many failed to make their expenses.[38] Finally, the rapid expansion of the Canadian population in the 1670s and the introduction of thousands of soldiers during the next decade created local markets for foodstuffs where none had previously existed. Intercolonial trade between Canada and the West Indies declined.

Efforts to encourage trade from Martinique to New France had even less consequence. Increasingly aware that the English islands owed some of their new prosperity to sales of molasses and rum to New England, yet, forbidden to export this byproduct of sugar manufacture to France in order to protect the domestic brandy industry, the owners of two refineries in Martinique and Guadeloupe sent a small ship to New France with a cargo of rum, sugar, and tobacco in 1681. Misfortune intervened at Quebec, where fire consumed

35 Pritchard, "Ships, Men, and Commerce", 99–100.
36 *RAPQ, 1930–31*, 120, 136 Mémoire of Talon, 10 October 1670 and Talon to Colbert, 1 November 1670; also May, *Histoire économique de la Martinique*, 142.
37 Pritchard, "Ships, Men, and Commerce", 105–17; see also Col., C^{11A}, 8, f. 259, Mémoire de Riverin et Chalons, 7 February 1686 for claim that success in trade to Martinique depended upon small ships.
38 Col., C^{11A} 6, f. 81v Demeulles to Colbert, 12 November 1682; also C^{8A} 4, f. 197v Dumaitz to Seignelay, 18 December 1686; ibid., f. 246 Dumaitz and Blénac to Seignelay, 6 March, 1687; and ibid., 6, 337–7v Dumaitz to Pontchartrain, 16 February 1691; also Clarence P. Gould, "Trade Between the Windward Islands and the Continental Colonies of the French Empire, 1683–1763", *The Mississippi Valley Historical Review*, 25 (1939), 476.

both ship and cargo.[39] The owners of the colonial refineries had petitioned for a 10-year monopoly on trade between the islands and North American mainland colonies, both French and English.[40] West Indian merchants were not interested in trade with the French North American colonies unless exit duties were waived.[41] They recognised that the Canadian population could consume only small amounts of West Indian goods. Their real aim was to trade with New England. Lack of suitable returns from Canada was also a major problem. Canadian softwood lumber, chiefly pine, was less durable in the tropics than other timber, and oak used in casks was cheaper from New England. Under pressure from the tax-farmer of the Western Domain, Colbert would not hear of waiving Canadian duties on colonial imports.[42] It was cheaper to export rum and tafia to New England than to Canada and Acadia.[43]

A mutuality of interest between French colonial planters and New England merchants grew during the 1680s despite official attempts to halt any contacts. Both parties satisfied commercial demands that could not be met elsewhere. The English islands did not produce sufficient syrup, nor could they absorb the growing quantities of New England products of salt fish, flour, and staves. French planters fit the bill in both respects and also wiggled out from under the dominating thumb of metropolitan merchants. For the next decade and a half, Canada was irrelevant to the West Indian economy.

Trade between Canada and the West Indies grew during the War of the Spanish Succession, when French merchants virtually abandoned the northern colony. Necessity became the mother of invention as Quebec merchants bought or built ships and sent them off with local cargoes of foodstuffs and lumber to Martinique,[44] but more regular traffic had to await the coming of peace and the establishment of Île Royale. Trade quickly sprang up between Quebec and the new colony partly owing to strong government stimulus, but also because settlers on Île Royale created a demand for provisions shortly after the Canadian populace had begun moving onto the land at an increased rate and was producing more food than ever before.[45] Shipments of Canadian peas, flour, other cereals, and lumber found a ready market.

---

39   May, *Histoire économique de la Martinique*, 151,

40   Col., C^{8A}, 3, ff. 66–70 and C^{11A}, 5, ff. 324–6v "Advis de M. Patoulet sur la proposition fait par les intéressez . . . , 28 February 1681; also ibid., C^{8A}, 3, ff. 71–1v Patoulet to Colbert, 8 March 1681.

41   Ibid., 3, f.76 extrait of Patoulet's letter, 15 November 1682.

42   Charles W. Cole, *French Mercantilism, 1683–1700* (New York, Columbia University Press, 1943), 64; May, *Histoire économique de la Martinique*, 151.

43   Col., C^{8A}, 4, f. 59 Blénac and Dumaitz to Seignelay, 1 October 1685; Gould, "Trade Between the Windward Islands and the Continental Colonies", 476.

44   Pritchard, "Ships, Men, and Commerce", 285–8.

45   *RAPQ*, 1947–48, 210 King's Memoir to Vaudreuil and Bégon, 25 June 1713; ibid., 245–6 same to same 19 March 1714.

Late in 1714, Intendant Bégon recommended forbidding flour exports to the West Indies while allowing those to Île Royale.[46] Canadian merchants might well profit from sending surplus flour to Saint-Domingue, but their small cargoes did not replace supplies from France. The 440 barrels that arrived from Quebec in 1714 represented less than 4 percent of the flour landed in Saint-Domingue that year.

Louisbourg quickly flourished in a way that Placentia never had. In 1715, a New England trader reported 40 vessels loading and six men-of-war in the port, which he claimed could accommodate 500 ships.[47] Three years later, eight colonial vessels from Quebec carried provisions to Île Royale.[48] In 1719, Intendant Bégon shipped 1,000 quintals of flour from Quebec and reported private trade was developing well.[49] A total of 88 ships, the vast majority of them fishing vessels, arrived at Île Royale that year. Included in their number were colonial ships from the West Indies.[50]

Fraud increased traffic from France to Louisbourg after 1724, as ships clearing for the colony were able to avoid the charges for *engagés* levied on all ships bound for the West Indies and Canada. However, the growing number of vessels sailing between Quebec and Louisbourg–about 30 annually during the final years of the decade–were a product of vigorous market forces. Louisbourg became a vital point linking the merchants of the West Indies, Canada, and Île Royale to each other and to those in New England.[51] By 1727, 32 Quebec merchants were sharing in the profits of Île Royale trade.[52] The next year the government ordered 2,000 quintals of flour (double the amount of 10 years before) and 340 *quarts* of peas shipped to Louisbourg.[53]

Louisbourg's own merchants played a larger role as the port's shipping expanded rapidly during the middle twenties. From 55 fishing shallops and 12 larger bateaux and schooners in 1724, the local fleet grew to 276 shallops and 57 larger vessels just two years later. In 1726, more than half of the latter were designated for trade rather than fishing.[54] Louisbourg

---

46 Ibid., f. 306 Bégon to Pontchartrain, 12 November 1714.
47 Quoted in J. S. McClennan, *Louisbourg from its Foundation to its Fall* (Toronto: Macmillan, 1918), 21.
48 Col., C^{IIA}, 39, f. 180 "Estat des pois, biscuits, et farine ... chargée en 1718", 14 October 1718.
49 Ibid., 40, f. 85v Vaudreuil and Bégon to Navy Council, 14 November 1719.
50 AN, SOM, G^I 466, no. 59 "Ressensement du vaisseaux qui sont venus de france et autre lieux à l'isle royale en l'année 1719".
51 McLennan, *Louisbourg from its Foundation to its Fall*, Appendix V, 382; also Col., C^{IIA}, 50, ff. 25–6 Beauharnois and d'Aigrmont to Maurepas, 1 October 1728.
52 Ibid., 49, memoir, 1727 cited in Allana G. Reid, "Intercolonial Trade During the French Regime", *Canadian Historical Review*, 32 (1951), 240; Gould, "Trade Between the Windward Islands and the Continental Colonies", 484.
53 Ibid., f. 556 (copy) Maurepas to Dupuy, 24 May 1728.
54 AN, SOM, G^I 466, nos. 67 & 68 Ship censuses, Île Royale, 1724 and 1726. For a good

fish merchants were beginning to ship several thousand quintals of cod to the West Indies each year. During 1728, 21 ships entered Martinique and Guadeloupe from Canada and Île Royale, and 16 departed in the opposite direction.[55]

By the end of the 1720s the integrative function of expanding markets was loosely tying together Canada, Île Royale, and Martinique and linking them more closely than before to New England. Fifty-six ships arrived at Martinique and Guadeloupe from Canada and Île Royale during 1730 and 1731, and 45 ships departed from the West Indies for the same destinations.[56] Only a few ships, chiefly from France, sailed directly from Quebec to the islands, but Louisbourg offered a counter to metropolitan domination of trade. Its relative proximity permitted colonists at both Saint-Pierre and Quebec to make two voyages annually and gave them easy access to the larger Atlantic trading world of the American mainland colonies. The scarcity of wheat and livestock in Canada, which interrupted traffic to Île Royale in 1729, sounded a cautionary note that signaled new difficulties in the future.[57] In truth, Île Royale, like the French West Indies, fell increasingly under the domination of the American mainland colonies.

3. Foreign Trade, Illicit Trade

Trade between the French colonies and the possessions of other European powers shows clearly that French colonial commerce was never a closed system. Recently, a few scholars have been presenting a valuable corrective in pointing to market forces rather than government policy as having shaped French colonial commerce.[58] Though Colbert sought to reserve trade to the colonies for French merchants and French ships, he had a certain ambivalence toward trade between the colonies and the possessions of other European powers. Between 1662 and 1698, Louis XIV permitted Denmark to trade with the French colonies.[59] Spanish America, which paid for imports with silver, naturally occupied a very important place in French overseas trade

history of the development of the fishery, see B.A. Balcom, *The Cod Fishery of Isle Royale, 1713–1758*, (Ottawa: Parks Canada, Environment Canada, 1984).

55 BN, n.a.f., 2,550, f. 102 "Commerce des Isles du vent, 1728".

56 Col., C⁸ᴬ 42, ff. 344–4v "Recapitulation du commerce des Isles du vent de 1730 et 1731".

57 Col., C¹¹ᴬ 53, ff. 120–1 Hocquart to Maurepas, 17 October 1730.

58 Christopher Moore, "The Other Louisbourg: Trade and Merchant Enterprise in Île Royale, 1713–1758", *Histoire sociale-Social History*, 12, no. 23 (1979), 79–96; also see his "Cape Breton and the North Atlantic World in the Eighteenth Century" in *The Island: New Perspectives on Cape Breton History, 1713–1790*, ed. Kenneth Donovan (Fredericton: Acadiensis Press, 1990), 31–48. Daniel H. Usner Jr. *Indians, Settlers, and Slaves in a Frontier Exchange Economy: The Lower Mississippi Valley Before 1783*, (Chapel Hill and London: North Carolina University Press, 1992), 244–56.

59 May, *Histoire économique de la Martinique*, also Col., C⁸ᴬ 7, ff. 304–19 Dumaitz to Pontchartrain, 27 February 1693.

202   *Trade and Exchange*

and in French thinking about trade with its own colonies. In 1670, French merchants at Cadiz owned more than 15 percent of the 8.5 million pesos on board the Mexican treasure fleet that reached Spain.[60] Colbert naturally sought to enhance that trade, suggesting that French colonies could become bases from which to trade with Spanish America.[61] Some exchanges did occur during the next several years, but results were slim. During the early 1680s, a trade in horses and hides sprang up between the French and Spanish on Saint-Domingue. It appeared to replace the recently ruined tobacco trade on the island.[62] In the 1680s, Louis XIV granted a four-year monopoly on trade to the Spanish Main to the marquis de Maintenon, a rich Martinique planter, but nothing came of that venture.[63] Indeed, by 1682, Colbert had so struggled with the issue of foreign trade in the colonies that he decided to forbid even trade with the Spanish Main.[64] After 1698, Pontchartrain hoped the unsettled southern coast of Saint-Domingue would develop as an entrepôt for smuggling goods into Spanish America, but the plan failed as English merchants from Jamaica bought the indigo, cacao, and tobacco produced by the region's settlers.[65]

Despite a growing French overseas merchant fleet, shipping proved insufficient to meet the demand for slaves, provisions, and manufactures. In his effort to create a closed trading system in 1670, Colbert had gone too far, excluding all foreign goods even if transported in French bottoms. In August of 1671, the Royal Council annulled the West India Company's right of entrepôt for Irish salt beef and forbade imports of foreign meats and wine into the colonies.[66] Even government subsidies failed to draw much dearer French beef to the colonies, so almost immediately foreign beef imports had to be allowed to re-enter. Many ships arrived from English colonies, some from as far away as Boston, as French merchants proved incapable of supplying the colonies during wartime in spite of government bounties.[67] In 1680, after nine years of misspent effort, Colbert finally acknowledged his policy of excluding Irish beef and Madeira wine was a failure. While insisting that Governor-General Blénac prevent direct trade with the colonies by seizing and selling any foreign ships found in colonial harbours, he allowed

[60] Lyle N. McAlister, *Spain and Portugal in the New World, 1492–1700* (Minneapolis: University of Minnesota Press, 1984), 375.
[61] Jean Meyer, *Colbert*, (Paris: Hachette, 1981), 130.
[62] BN, n.a.f. 9,325, ff. 303–4v Mémoire du Sr. de Pouançay … à M. de Colbert, 30 January 1681.
[63] See May, *Histoire économique de la Martinique*, 148–52 for a brief notice about the chequered career of Charles-François d'Angennes, marquis de Maintenon (1648–1692).
[64] Mims, *Colbert's West India Policy*, 192–3.
[65] Charles Frostin, "Les Pontchartrain et la pénétration commerciale française en Amérique espagnole", *Revue historique*, no. 245 (1971), 307–36.
[66] Mims, *Colbert's West India Policy*, 173–5, 209.
[67] Ibid., 209–11, 215.

foreign merchandise to enter provided it passed through France and paid the required duties.[68]

For the next half century, especially during wartime, colonial authorities normally turned a blind eye or granted special permission to foreign ships to enter colonial harbours and trade openly in return for payment of required duties and sometimes bribes. Governors and intendants often resorted to reporting the arrival of foreign ships needing wood and water whenever shortages threatened. Although the minister complained, his more customary silence acknowledged the failure of French merchants to supply the colonies. In 1717 and again in 1726, colonial authorities made identical complaints that French merchants failed to send adequate supplies of beef, and much that did arrive was of poor quality and short weight. Unless the situation improved, they added, foreign trade could not be prevented.[69]

French merchants lived in a world of privileges, subsidies, and monopolies. Market culture as we have come to know it did not really exist in Old Regime France, nor, for that matter, did entrepreneurship as an abstract factor of production as implied by the idea of a market system. Bourgeois liberties enjoyed by urban merchants were essentially privileges exacted from the king. Merchants viewed the colonies as theirs to treat as they saw fit. Ministers generally agreed, justifying their own interference on the grounds that merchants selfishly pursuing their own interests had no idea of the public good. French merchants lived in a noncapitalist world where most wealth was in offices, land, and annuities.[70]

Illicit trade differed from foreign trade, though not by much. Contraband was the next step beyond foreign trade with special permission. As the Dutch experience revealed, it was a major activity early on – well-developed – and, after 1670, largely carried out in secret.[71] The most common form in the Windward Islands was to sail from Guadeloupe and Martinique to St. Eustatius and Antigua, exchange colonial products for desired merchandise, including slaves, and return without being caught. Most traffic occurred at night from small coves around the islands and involved modest cargoes. Distances between the English and Dutch islands and Guadeloupe were short; exchanges were mutually beneficial. No demand existed in France for syrup or rum, which were in constant demand in the foreign colonies. French

---

68 Col., A 24, f.33 /no. 2704 (Extrait) King to Blénac, 30 April 1681; F³, 248, f. 243 quoted in Abénon, *La Guadeloupe de 1671 à 1759*, 143–4.

69 Col., C⁸ᴬ 22, 39–46 La Varenne to Navy Council, 24 February 1717; ibid., 35, ff. 190–3 Feuquières et Blondel to Maurepas, 12 December 1726.

70 See William Reedy, *The Rise of Market Culture: The Textile Trade and French Society, 1750–1900* (Cambridge: Cambridge University Press, 1984), 19–21. Also Fernand Braudel, *Civilization and Capitalism, 15th-18th Century*, Vol. 3. *The Perspective of the World*, trans., Siân Reynolds (London: Collins, 1982), 325–52.

71 See Wim Klooster, *Illicit Riches: The Dutch Trade in the Caribbean, 1648–1795* (Leiden: KITLV Press, 1995).

colonists found everything they needed in the way of salt beef, salt cod, flour, slaves, and manufactures from the interlopers.

By 1683, illicit trade involved major planters on the islands. Producers like the marquis de Maintenon, Nicolas de Gabaret, and other shareholders in the sugar refinery at Mouillage on Martinique are mentioned in complaints. Midnight sailings in small vessels on gentle island breezes gave way to major, well-organized frauds. One involved ship captains commonly loading 800 hogsheads of sugar at Martinique and, after making their declarations to the clerk of the Western Domain, sailing to St. Christopher, where they sold half the cargo to the English, replaced it with a similar amount purchased from French planters on the island, and sailed to France. Two benefits accrued to shippers and colonists. First, they avoided paying duties on 400 hogsheads of sugar, and second, selling more sugar might increase its price thereby allowing planters to purchase more slaves.[72] Five years later, even the king admitted to knowing the system of illegal trade in some detail. His Majesty acknowledged the complicity of the clerks of the tax-farmer of the Western Domain, claimed that trade between Guadeloupe and Montserrat occurred almost nightly, that the king's officers knew about it, and that other trades existed between St. Christopher and Nevis and St. Eustatius and between Martinique and Dominica. As usual, the king demanded vigilance in suppressing illegal trade, but to no avail.[73] Illicit trade was, and always had been, vital to the health of the island economies. Repeated injunctions to enforce the laws against foreign trade were useless.[74]

Just as there are few data concerning legitimate trade, almost no evidence exists on which to base conclusions about contraband trade. Few mentions occur in official correspondence in the late seventeenth century in contrast to constant complaints about it found during the next. Official silence appeared to mark tacit acceptance of the benefits of, and perhaps complicity in, illegal trade that could not be halted. It is not outlandish to suggest that official figures of French sugar exports must understate considerably, perhaps by as much as one-third or more, total French production. If so, the figures for English sugar exports are probably overstated owing to the continual passing off of French sugar as English. Lack of human and material resources constrained authorities trying to halt smuggling. Even after authorizing merchant ship captains to keep one-third of the goods seized from the foreign vessels they arrested, Intendant Robert had no results. One of his servants who tried to arrest slaves being landed clandestinely one night received no help from other royal authorities because all were planters.

[72] Col., C⁸ᴮ, 1, no. 69 "Mémoire sur le commerce des isles, 1683".
[73] Col., B 14, ff. 38–8v King to Blénac and Dumaitz, 1 September 1688.
[74] Ibid., 18, ff. 160–3 King to Robert, 12 October 1695; also C.A. Banbuck, *Histoire politique, économique et sociale de la Martinique sous l'ancien régime, 1635–1789*, reprinted (Fort-de-France: Sociétéde Distribution de culture, [1935] 1972), 259.

Tom.J.Part.J.P.78.

Illustration 4.2. Colonial vessels employed in the French colonies. From Jean-Baptiste Labat. *Nouveau voyage aux Isles de l'Amérique.* 2 vols. La Haye: P. Husson, T. Johnson, P. Gosse, Jvan Duren, R. Alberts, and C. Le Vier [1722] 1724. 1, part 2: facing page 78.

Robert was powerless to halt foreign trade, which "is being carried out with impunity".[75]

In 1696, Pierre Le Bègue, former town major at Martinique and king's lieutenant at Sainte-Croix, became the first royal officer to be arrested for illicit trade practices. The receiver of the Western Domain alleged that Le Bègue had extorted 200 *écus* from him and also obtained one *écu* from the agent of the Brandenburg Company for every hogshead of French sugar delivered to him at St. Thomas. Set up under the protection of Brandenburg-Prussia, the Brandenburg Company was a front for Dutch merchants

[75] Col., C^{8A}, 10, ff. 332–42v Robert to Pontchartrain, 31 May 1698.

excluded from membership in the East India and West India monopolies.[76] Le Bègue denied the allegations as did any witnesses who were interrogated. The case collapsed because former residents of Sainte-Croix evacuated to Saint-Domingue claimed they were beyond the intendant's jurisdiction. Intendant Robert at Martinique did not contest the assertion and displayed no further interest in pursuing the case.[77] Indeed, *de facto* free trade existed in the French islands. Warships were rarely available to enforce trade regulations. Naval officers were much more eager to engage in illegal trade than to suppress it. Officials of the Western Domain only purchased their first patrol vessel at the end of the century.

During the War of the Spanish Succession, better prices in Spanish America drew French merchants away from the Antilles while low commodity prices for colonial products proved attractive to foreign, ostensibly enemy, traders.[78] This did not prevent merchants at Bordeaux from strenuously opposing attempts by nonnaturalized residents of the port to bring in Dutch ships with the king's passport, flag them as French, and load them with cargoes for the West Indies.[79] Despite the absence of flour in France in 1709, Bordeaux's Chamber of Commerce successfully protested a government decision to allow Irish and Dutch shippers to send provisions directly to the colonies.[80] French merchants squeezed virtually any profit out of the colonial trade in French goods during the war, partly because of the high cost of insurance, freight, duties, and warehousing, all of which were passed on to the colonists, but also owing to low demand for colonial produce which kept prices low.[81]

Necessity drove colonists to find their own solutions. With the support of the governor-general, foreign ships frequently called at French islands. If data were available, according to Frank Wesley Pitman, illegal trade between the British mainland colonies and the French West Indies would show a marked ascent during the war.[82] Like their predecessors during the 1690s, Governor-General Machault and Intendant Vaucresson authorised local merchants to trade sugar for provisions, especially syrup and tafia for beef and other

[76] Eberhard Schmitt, "The Brandenburg Overseas Trading Companies in the 17th Century" in *Companies and Trade: Essays on Overseas Trading Companies during the Ancien Regime* (Leiden: University Press, 1981), 168.

[77] Col., C⁸ᴬ, 9, ff. 365–7v Robert to Pontchartrain, 24 May 1696; Col., B 18, f. 512v Pontchartrain to Le Bègue, 4 September 1697.

[78] Col., C⁸ᴬ, 17, ff. 298–300v Vaucresson to Pontchartrain, 1 April 1710.

[79] ADG, Série C/4251 f. 109 deliberations of the Chamber of Commerce, 28 June 1708.

[80] Ibid., ff. 169–70, 176 deliberations of 10 October and 28 November 1709.

[81] Col., C⁸ᴬ, 17, ff. 298–300v Vaucresson to Pontchartrain, 1 April 1710.

[82] Frank Wesley Pitman, *The Development of the British West Indies, 1700–1763*, reprinted. (London: Cass, [1917] 1967, 190; John J. McCusker, *Rum and the American Revolution: The Rum Trade and the Balance of Payments of the Thirteen Continental Colonies.* 2 vols. (New York and London: Garland Publishing, 1989), 1: 303–5 plays down the connection.

provisions at St. Thomas, Barbados, and St. Lucia. Foreigners introduced mules and slaves in such sufficient numbers into Martinique that the total number of plantations increased from 183 in 1700 to 264 in 1710, while the number of slaves rose from nearly 17,000 in 1702 to more than 22,000 in 1709.[83] On Guadeloupe, where scarcely any ships arrived from Africa or France during the war, the number of slaves increased by nearly 50 percent between 1701 and 1712 (see Appendix 1).

After 1715, when the French navy more or less withdrew from the Caribbean, pirates became the greatest threat to illegal trade. Yet, shipping from the British mainland colonies flooded into the French West Indies. In 1717, La Rochelle merchants virtually abandoned Martinique: "They do not have 10,000 livres worth of goods in the island", claimed the intendant.[84] Sieur Desrucaux Hardouin, a Nantes merchant, claimed in 1720 that one-third of all French sugar and cacao went to the English. He estimated that annual losses to the farmers-general in unpaid duties amounted to 400,000 livres and to French merchants 2 million livres in lost freight.[85] There was such a quantity of foreign provisions in the islands, complained one captain, that he sold his salt beef for less than it had cost him in France.[86] Yet, a short-age of salt beef and flour at Martinique in the autumn of 1720 led authorities to authorise several voyages to St. Thomas in search of provisions, to permit an English merchant to land 500 barrels of flour to sell, and to send local merchants off to Barbados and elsewhere on the pretext of recovering debts, in order to import ships and cargoes of salt meat, flour, and butter.[87] The same year, Governor de Moyencourt advised the Navy Council that foreign trade on Guadeloupe, especially in slaves, was uncontrollable. No colonist would denounce another. If blank *lettres de cachet* allowing the governor to send the guilty parties to France might deter some, they could also lead to mass desertion of the colony by others.[88] To this the conscientious comte de Toulouse could only add in the margin of the dispatch that there were grounds for hoping that recent laws would have a good effect.[89] Moyencourt took no action against foreign traders. In 1725, he allowed 24 foreign ships chiefly laden with livestock, lumber, and provisions to land at Guadeloupe.[90]

83 AN, SOM, G¹ 470bis Denombrement general de l'Isle de la Martinique de l'année 1700; ibid., no. 2 Estat general du recensement de l'Isle Martinique pour l'année 1701; no. 11 Recensement generale de la Martinique pour 1709.

84 Col., C^{8A} 22, f. 216v Ricouart to Navy Council, 11 April 1717.

85 Col., C^{8B} 6, no. 1 "Extrait du mémoire envoyé au conseil par le Sr. Desrucaux Hardouin. [1720].

86 Col., F^{2C}, 2, f. 143.

87 Col., C^{8A}, 27, ff. 93–8 ordinances of Feuquières and Bénard, 27 and 29 November and passeport 1 December 1720; and ibid., ff. 130–7 Feuquières and Bénard to Council, 30 November 1720.

88 Col., C^{7A}, 8, ff. 121–1v Moyencourt to Navy Council, 4 June 1720.

89 Col., C^{8B}, 6, no. 38 Extrait de Moyencourt to Council, 4 June 1720.

90 Maurice Satineau, *Histoire de la Guadeloupe, (1635–1789)*, (Paris: Payot, 1928), 48–9.

Consequently, even though the minister moved in 1726 to destroy foreign trade in the colonies altogether, French policy remained ineffective, or at best ambiguous and wasteful. The new letters patent did not repeal a recent edict that permitted exports of clayed sugars directly to Spain.[91] After ordering Governor de Moyencourt of Guadeloupe to prevent all foreign trade, comte de Maurepas concluded that foreign ships carrying horses, mules, lumber, staves, slaves, and provisions not carried from France would be allowed and even encouraged at Basse Terre.[92] While denying that insufficient French goods reached the islands, the directors of Bordeaux's Chamber of Commerce vigorously accused royal governors of regularly accepting bribes and openly maintaining warehouses where beef, flour, and other goods were available in return for goods and cash, and claimed that no more than half of all French colonial produce reached France.[93] Colonial officials replied that it was impossible to suppress foreign trade in slaves and provisions because planters and foreign merchants acted in perfect conjunction with each other. Governor-General de Champigny claimed that the purchase of New England-built vessels at Martinique in exchange for tafia and syrup was so advantageous and profitable that they should be taxed and the revenues applied to building the island's fortifications.[94] Nothing had really changed during the previous 60 years except that during the final half of the period, foreign and illicit trade had become vital to the colonies' economic health.

The struggle against foreign and illicit trade wasted resources and hindered the economic development of the colonies. Yet, it must be said, the colonies continued to develop. Colonial authorities refused to cooperate with metropolitan injunctions because increasingly they saw French merchants' complaints as unjustified in the light of their failure to supply sufficient goods at competitive prices. Efficient or otherwise, metropolitan merchants were purveyors of privilege, seeking to keep trade in their own hands at colonists' expense. French officials remained unable to see that integration of the colonial economies into the growing Atlantic world was a prerequisite rather than a hindrance to establishing a French empire. Far from tying France and its colonies together, government policies weakened colonial economies, thereby delaying and obstructing what they were trying to achieve.

4.4 SHIPPING

The establishment of the French colonies during the second quarter of the seventeenth century potentially gave French merchants a new position in

---

91   May, *Histoire économique de la Martinique*, 128–9.
92   Abénon, *La Guadeloupe de 1671 à 1759*, 1: 154–5.
93   ADG, C/4269, f. 90–1v Mémoire contre le commerce prohibité". 24 October 1726; Col., C^{8A} 35, ff. 171–4v Feuquières and Blondel to Maurepas, 27 October 1726.
94   Col., C^{8A} 40, ff. 158–9v Champigny to Maurepas, 4 June 1729.

international commerce, but shipping to the colonies grew painfully slowly after 1670. This was in part because of the regional nature of the French economy and the foreign domination of much of France's overseas commerce. As late as 1686, two-thirds of the French overseas fleet remained employed in the North Atlantic fishery.[95] That year, a little more than 10,000 tons cleared French ports for the West Indies compared with more than 30,000 tons from English ports.[96] However, shipping's slow growth was also owing to the limited number of French sailors. These totaled far less than the 60,000 Colbert believed were present in France in the 1660s. Seignelay, his son, continued the delusion two decades later when he believed the kingdom contained 80,000 sailors. His support of the Revocation of the Edict of Nantes, which may have reduced the French seafaring population by one-fifth to one-quarter, increased the problem of scarce manpower.[97]

Several economies existed in France, and only the Western or Atlantic one became connected to the colonies before the eighteenth century. Dutch merchants and foreign commission agents were the agents of this new development in the French Atlantic ports. They dominated the north–south trade links built on wine, salt, and textiles that integrated Bordeaux, La Rochelle, and Nantes into the commercial, maritime world stretching between the Iberian peninsula and the Baltic Sea. As demands for colonial products grew in Europe, new re-export trades supplied from the colonies appeared in the seaports.[98] The old commercial network became the basis for establishing the new colonial re-export trades. In spite of continuing Dutch competition, French colonial trade grew slowly and began to transform the western ports themselves.

During the 1670s, 273 ships departed from La Rochelle for Africa and the French colonies in America. In 1672, 15 ships were fitted out for the West Indies at Bordeaux whence only one had set out a decade earlier.[99] The same year, a total of 131 ships departed for the West Indies from all

---

95 Turgeon, "Colbert et la pêche française", 267.
96 Cf. Ralph Davis, *The Rise of the English Shipping Industry in the 17th and 18th Centuries*, National Maritime Museum Reprint (Greenwich: London: HMSO, [1962] n.d.), 268.
97 Meyer, *Colbert*, 218–20; T. J. A. Le Goff, "The Labour Market for Sailors in France" in *"Those Emblems of Hell"? European Sailors and the Maritime Labour Market, 1570–1870*, eds., Paul C. van Royen, Jaap Bruijn, and Jan Lucassen (St. John's: International Maritime Economic History Association, 1997), 300 estimates that France had 43,000 skilled sailors (i.e., excluding boys (*mousses*) and inexperienced young men (*novices*)) at the end of the seventeenth century.
98 See Paul Butel, "France, the Antilles, and Europe in the Seventeenth and Eighteenth Centuries: Renewals of Foreign Trade" in *The Rise of Merchant Empires: Long Distance Trade in the Early Modern World, 1350–1750*, ed., James D. Tracy (New York: Cambridge University Press, 1990), 153–60.
99 Jonathan Howes Webster, "The Merchants of Bordeaux in Trade to the French West Indies, 1664–1717" (unpublished Ph.D. thesis, University of Minnesota, 1972), 437.

French ports.[100] In 1674, the number of French ships departing for the West Indies was 134 whereas only 16 ships had sailed in 1664.[101] These numbers compare very favourably with shipping to the four English Leeward Island colonies, which were visited by about 100 ships annually during the late 1670s.[102] By 1683, the number of sailings of Bordeaux ships had risen to twenty-nine. Sixty-four ships left Nantes for the Antilles in 1674 and 1675, and the number doubled to 128 in 1687 and 1688. Four hundred and eleven ships departed La Rochelle for the colonies between 1680 and 1689.[103] At the time of Colbert's death in 1683, 205 French ships sailed for the West Indies and carried away some 4 million livres weight (2,000 *tonneaux*) of sugar formerly freighted by the Dutch.[104]

In 1685, 152 ships totaling 17,702 tons sailed from 14 different French ports for the West Indies. More than half departed from just two, La Rochelle and Nantes. Growth in trade with the West Indies provided the impetus for tripling La Rochelle's ship tonnage between 1664 and 1682.[105] In brief, French colonial shipping increased by more than eight times during the previous score of years though most of this occurred after the Dutch War.[106] Though the 1685 tonnage represented only half the volume that cleared English ports for the West Indies, it was more than sufficient to carry away the colonial products destined for France.[107] Less than 10,000 tons was required for sugar, and the available tobacco, indigo, cotton, and other products did not fill the remaining capacity. Ships bound for Saint-Domingue were particularly vulnerable to not finding a cargo, and the same can be said about ships sailing to Canada. Nevertheless, the number of ships reaching the colonies each year was directly connected to colonial well-being. Governor Hinselin of Guadeloupe had no doubt of it:

[Commerce] is carried on at present with more advantage for the colonists because having a quantity of ships and merchandise here they are cheap as is the freight on sugars being sent to France, which returns to the profit of the colonists other than the increased price of sugars and cotton here and in France.[108]

---

[100] Mims, *Colbert's West India Policy*, 236.
[101] Col., B 2, 6, ff. 60–6 Etat des passeports delivrées aux navires française et étrangers pour les Isles de l'Amérique pendant 1674; and Webster, "The Merchants of Bordeaux", 437.
[102] Ian K. Steele, *The English Atlantic, 1675–1740: An Exploration of Communication and Community* (New York: Oxford University Press, 1986), 29.
[103] Butel, "France, Antilles, and Europe", 161.
[104] Charles W. Cole, *Colbert and a Century of French Mercantilism*, 2 vols. (New York: Columbia University Press, 1939), 2: 34.
[105] John G. Clark, *La Rochelle and the Atlantic Economy during the Eighteenth Century* (Baltimore and London: The Johns Hopkins University Press, 1981), 26.
[106] Michel Morineau, "La Vraie nature des choses et leur enchainement entre la France et l'Europe, (XVIIe–XIXe siècle)", *RFHOM*, 84 (1997), 7.
[107] Davis, *The Rise of the English Shipping Industry*, 298.
[108] Col., C7A 3 (nonfoliated), Hinselin to Colbert, 16 July 1681.

But were the vessels really French? The traditional view of the sudden expansion of French colonial shipping during the quarter of a century after 1664 as positive proof that Colbert's policies to promote colonial shipping were farsighted and bore fruit has always been weak. There is no evidence of significant market growth for colonial goods in France during the 1670s or later.[109] Weak demand for colonial products in France quickly revealed itself with the sudden influx of ships whose captains sought only sugar to the detriment of small producers of tobacco, indigo, and ginger and the rapid fall in sugar prices as supply exceeded demand.[110] The growth in shipping may have merely reflected the maturing market for colonial products, but this, too, is weak. The failure of domestic markets for colonial products to develop in France was a key factor behind the shipping problem for decades to come. Only about one-tenth of colonial sugar was consumed in France as against nine-tenths of English-grown sugar in England.[111] Nevertheless, the growth of shipping illustrates how local French capital found an outlet to enter the new maritime trades when traditional ones were dominated by foreigners, Dutch, English, and Germans.[112] Private merchant initiative rather than government dirigisme may be appealing, but little evidence exists that French capital was significantly involved. The French Atlantic ports were still medieval cities where local merchants remained tied to their traditional trades.

The sudden expansion of French shipping probably owes its origin chiefly to the same Dutchmen that Colbert struggled to exclude from the French colonies rather than to any spontaneous appearance of French risk capital. The French navy forcibly excluded Dutch ships from the islands after 1670. The Dutch simply returned to the colonies via the French seaports whose maritime trades they already dominated.[113] Little French capital was available for risky seaborne commerce, but Dutch commission agents at Nantes, La Rochelle, and Bordeaux cheerfully supplied capital to French merchants willing to enter the transocean colonial trade.[114] Foreign ships that received passports for the West Indies in 1674 came from Bergen, London, Limerick, Galoway, Jersey, and Hamburg.[115] Dutch investment in French colonial shipping allowed foreign merchants to continue their profitable trade with new

---

[109] Mims, *Colbert's West India Policy*, 223–4; also Butel, "France, the Antilles, and Europe", 159.

[110] May, *Histoire économique de la Martinique*, 120.

[111] Fernand Braudel, *Civilization and Capitalism, 15th–18th Century*, Vol. 2 *The Wheels of Commerce*: trans., Siân Reynolds (London: Collins, [1979] 1982), 193.

[112] Butel, "France, the Antilles, and Europe," 159–60.

[113] May, *Histoire économique de la Martinique*, 110 citing, Clément, éd., *Lettres, ... de Colbert*, 3²: 637. See also Morineau, "La Vraie nature des choses et leur enchaînement entre la France et l'Europe", 8–9.

[114] Braudel, *Civilization and Capitalism*, 3: 256–60; also J. F. Bosher, "The Lyon and Bordeaux Connections of Émmanuel Le Borgne, c. 1605–1681". *Acadiensis*, 23 (1993), 128–45.

[115] Col., B 6, ff. 60–6 Etat des passeports ... pendant 1674".

French partners. Colbert's policies had little to do with it. Colbert only envisioned the expansion of French merchant shipping arising from a reduction of the Dutch fleet. He had no idea that expanding trade creates new markets and integrates formerly separate ones, and because he could do nothing else, he left the development of French overseas trade to the initiatives of individual merchants: "It pleases the king that the merchants having the whole of it, do what they desire".[116]

The decline of Norman ports in colonial trade after the 1660s reflected the inability of French markets for colonial products to develop. In 1672 and 1674, only 15 (16.9 percent) and 30 (22.4 percent) ships, respectively, came from Norman ports. Bordeaux, La Rochelle, and Nantes accounted for 67 (75.3 percent) and 81 (60.4 percent) ships, respectively.[117] Though the tonnage from Norman ports increased 2.8 times between 1672 and 1674, this appeared to represent a maximum effort. The absence of large markets for colonial products in France owing to the local nature of most of the economy is a frequently overlooked factor in the development of French colonial trade. The quarter century of warfare between 1688 and 1713 probably retarded market development.

A precipitous decline in shipping to the colonies marked the first half of the years between 1688 and 1713. The recovery and subsequent rise during the second half of the period points to improved general economic conditions. Though no document permits knowledge of total maritime traffic, shipping to Saint-Domingue declined severely from 33 to just eight ships between 1692 and 1695.[118] Between 1691 and 1700, the number and capacity of ships departing Saint-Malo for the West Indies declined by nearly half of that of the previous decade.[119] La Rochelle's commercial fleet suffered grievous losses at this time, and did not recover its previous numbers until long after 1730. The same fate befell Bordeaux merchants as well.[120] A recovery during the years from 1699 to 1701 occurred at Bordeaux where an average of 60 ships (6,244 tons) annually departed from and arrived at Bordeaux from the West Indies, Newfoundland, and Canada.[121] An ancient estimate that the number of French ships employed in the colonial trade in 1701 was probably only about two-thirds of the number employed 16 years earlier may not be inaccurate.[122]

---

[116] Clément, éd., *Lettres, ... de Colbert*, 32: 583 Colbert to de Baas, 8 November 1674.
[117] Col., B 4, 107–17 "Estat des passports delivrez ... 1672"; and ibid., 6, ff. 60–6 "Etat des passports ... 1674".
[118] Philippe Hrodej, *L'Amiral du Casse; L'Élévation d'un Gascon sous Louis XIV*, 2 vols. (Paris: Librairie de l'Inde, 1999), 1: 141.
[119] Based on Delumeau, *Le Mouvement du port de Saint-Malo*, 277.
[120] Webster, "The Merchants of Bordeaux", 437–8.
[121] Christian Huetz de Lemps, *Géographie du commerce de Bordeaux à la fin du règne de Louis XIV* (Paris-La Haye: Mouton, 1975), 525.
[122] Thomas Southey, *Chronological History of the West Indies*, 3 vols., reprinted (London: Frank Cass and Co., [1827] 1968), 2: 190.

The War of the Spanish Succession (1702–13) did not have the same effect on French colonial shipping. Fewer than five ships, less than 900 tons, departed the Breton port of Saint-Malo annually for the French Caribbean between 1701 and 1710.[123] However, this was exceptional, as merchants turned away from the colonies to mount a remarkably successful commercial invasion of Spanish America via the Great South Sea. Bordeaux, once thought to have suffered severely from a decline in departures for the West Indies, experienced strong growth in the number of local ships fitted out for the Caribbean during the war. This may have been due to the decline in the number of French ships from other ports that no longer arrived to load wine for the colonies. The number of local ships fitted out for the islands recovered to their prewar average by 1704–5 and grew steadily thereafter except for two brief dips during the war. The average number of Bordeaux ships bound for the West Indies during the first five years of the war, 1702–7, exceeded the same average for the preceding quinquennial period.[124] The largest volumes of colonial-bound traffic ever to depart La Rochelle left in 1705 and 1708 though few ships at all sailed to Canada.[125] Marseilles merchants who had not previously sent ships to the West Indies dispatched a "minimum" of 101 between 1700 and 1715.[126]

The anecdotal evidence for the West Indies shows continued growth. During the twelve months following 1 May 1709, 18 ships arrived at Saint-Domingue from France while 37 ships departed.[127] Thirty-seven ships left Martinique during the last six months of 1710.[128] This shipping growth during wartime was most probably because of a general improvement in economic conditions in Europe. The growth illustrates the integration of the French seaports into the international maritime economy rather than improvements in the local economies.

During the remainder of the eighteenth century, French colonial trade was constructed almost entirely of re-exports to the rest of Europe. Rising demand outside France ultimately caught up with excess supply but only about 1730. Until then the colonies remained in thrall to metropolitan merchants and commission agents who continually failed to meet colonial demand for provisions. Monetary devaluations and deflationary policies forced many

---

[123] Delumeau, *Le Mouvement du port de Saint-Malo*, 278–80.

[124] Huetz de Lemps, *Géographie du commerce de Bordeaux*, 552–5; also Paul Butel, *L'Économie française au XVIIIe siècle* (Paris: SEDES, 1993), 31.

[125] John S. Bromley, "La commerce de la France de l'ouest et la guerre maritime (1702–1713)", in *Corsaires and Navies, 1660–1760* (London and Ronceverte: The Hambleton Press, 1987), 404.

[126] Charles Carrière, *Négociants marseillais au XVIIIe siècle: contribution à l'étude des économies maritimes*, 2 vols. (Marseille: Institut historique de Provence, 1973), 1: 68, 80.

[127] Col., C^{9B}, 1 (nonfoliated) Etat des marchandises venues d'Europe …; ibid., Etat des Indigos, sucre brut et blanc et cuirs chargés pour france … [n.d.].

[128] Col., C^{8A}, 18, f. 64 Etat des batiments marchands …, 5 January 1711.

merchants to the wall, precipitating bankruptcies in 1715 and adding to insecurity and instability, but colonial trade quickly picked up thereafter. The French Atlantic ports regained their places in the north–south trade flows that dominated their seaborne commerce with the American colonies stimulating much of the new commercial growth.

At first, the intendant of Guienne accused Bordeaux's merchants of being no more than commission agents for foreigners. The few risk takers were young, inexperienced, and generally unsuccessful, while those who met with success left trade to acquire offices to pass on to their children. He feared the colonial trades would fall to others by default,[129] but his fears proved groundless. The number of ships departing Bordeaux for the colonies grew rapidly, from 45 in 1713 to 137 in 1722.[130] By 1729, Nantes and Bordeaux controlled nearly two-thirds (43 and 23 percent, respectively) of all French colonial trade.[131] Although La Rochelle fell behind Bordeaux and Nantes before 1713, colonial trade continued to dominate the activities of its merchants. Ninety percent of all ships clearing for the high seas during the 1720s departed for Africa, the West Indies, Canada, and other colonies. More than half sailed to Saint-Domingue.[132] At Marseilles, the new West India trades provided strong stimuli to broaden old connections in Italy and the Levant and a new market for products from its own hinterland.[133] By 1725, 33,000 tons of shipping (about the same amount as in the North Atlantic fishery) departed France annually for Canada, the West Indies, and Africa. Together, they represented about 90 percent of the high seas fleet,[134] but colonial shipping was expanding rapidly. Only five years later the colonial trades employed 51,000 tons of shipping whereas the tonnage in the deep-sea fishery had fallen to under 30,000.[135]

Martinique remained the major port in the colonies. In 1717, 132 ships departed Martinique compared with the 136 that left Saint-Domingue.[136] But thirteen years later in 1730, 268 ships carried away cargoes worth 11.6 million livres from Martinique while Saint-Domingue exports, worth

---

129 BB. ms. no. 734, ff. 29–30 Extrait du mémoire de M. de Curson sur la généralité de Guienne, [n.d.] *c.* 1714.

130 Crouzet, "Economie et société (1715–1789)", 306.

131 Ibid., 202.

132 Clark, *La Rochelle and the Atlantic Economy*, 29.

133 Carrière, *Négociants marsellais*, 1: 68, cited in Butel, *L'Economie française au XVIIIe siècle*, 32.

134 BN, n.a.f., 2,550, f. 30 cited in Turgeon, "Colbert et la pêche française", 267.

135 [NAC transcript, MG/7I. A2] BN, 11,332, ff. 663–700, "Situation du Commerce Extérieur du Roïaume exposée à Sa Majesté . . . le 30 octobre 1730".

136 Col., C8A 22, f. 273 Etat des navires marchands partis de la Martinique pour les ports de France pendant les derniers six mois de 1717, 30 January 1718; ibid., 25, f. 6 Etat des navires arrivés à la Martinique pendant les six derniers mois de 1717, 30 January 1718; ibid., C8B 4, no. 81 Extrait from Mesnier to Navy Council, 23 November 1717; Col., C9B 5 Extrait from Mithon to Navy Council, 20 August 1718.

8.5 million, left in 173 ships.[137] Few ships sailed to Guadeloupe in any given year. In 1730, Guadeloupe received only one-tenth of the vessels arriving in the Windward Islands and only 7 percent of the cargoes by value.[138]

Shipping between France and Canada increased nearly 60 percent between 1715 and 1730, but the average annual number of ships was less than ten. The volume reaching the port between 1726 and 1730 averaged about 1,250 tons annually.[139] The value of Canada's imports in 1730 was about 10 percent of the value of cargoes that arrived at Martinique alone.[140] Growth in local traffic in the Saint Lawrence River and intercolonial trade was more significant. By 1724 and 1725, nearly half the tonnage entering Quebec each year was either local or from Île Royale and Martinique.[141]

Demand for provisions in the colonies continually exceeded metropolitan demand for sugar, which left the colonies continually short of supply and planters always prepared to trade with others. Table 4.1 shows data collected by the Navy Council during an attempt to validate colonists' complaints, but such research had no effect on supply. Only as French merchants increased their ability to meet European demand through re-exports of sugar after 1730 did some balance begin to appear. Why Martinique received more than six times the amount of salt beef sent to Saint-Domingue, while the latter received 27 percent more flour than was sent to the former colony, is a matter for conjecture. Were slaves fed more poorly on Saint-Domingue than at Martinique? Was another commodity, such as salt cod, being supplied to Saint-Domingue from elsewhere, such as Louisbourg or the New England colonies? Was beef raised in sufficient quantity in the colony or imported from Spanish Santo Domingo to obviate imports? Clearly, further research is needed.

4.5 THE SLAVE TRADE

To grasp the nonimperial, noncapitalist nature of the transoceanic connections between France and its colonies, it is necessary to examine the slave trade. Only 53 French slaving voyages are known to have occurred during the seventeenth century.[142] The slave trade played the major role in transforming the Atlantic world into a complex of interdependent economies

---

[137] Col., C⁸ᴬ 42, f. 388 Commerce général des Isles françoise … [n.d.].

[138] Col., C⁸ᴬ 42, f. 344 Recapitulation du commerce des Isles du vent de 1730 et 1731 [n.d.].

[139] Based on Pritchard, "Ships, Men, and Commerce," Tables II–IX. The annual average is imputed.

[140] Lunn, "Economic Development in New France", 477.

[141] Col., Cᴵᴵᴬ 46, f. 300 Recensement des navires venus devant la ville de Quebec [1724]; ibid., 47, f. 308 Recensement des navires qui sont venus à … 1725.

[142] Eric Saugera, *Bordeaux, port négrier: chronique, économie, idéologie, XVIIe–XVIIIe siècles*, (Paris: Karthala, 1995), 201 gives the latest number that is likely to be revised.

Table 4.1. *Ships and Commodities Sent from France to the Colonies,*
1 October 1720 to 28 February 1722 (17 months)

Seaports	Marti-nique	Guadeloupe Cayenne	Saint-Domingue	Quebec	Unknown	Total Nos.	Total %
Bordeaux	84	1	42		12	139	88.4
Nantes	40	3	15			58	24.4
La Rochelle	7		30	4		41	17.2
Total	131	4	87	4	12	238	
Total (%)	55		36.6	1.7		100	100

Commodities							
Flour casks	11,925	60	15,166	—	—	27,151	
Salt Beef casks	26,137	70	4,124	—	—	30,331	
Wine tonneaux	8,602	40	6,394	—	—	15,036	
Brandy casks	4,914		2,642	—	—	7,556	

Source: Col., F²ᶜ 2 ff. 73-3v, 74v, 125-5v, 161, 171, 172, 176-6v, 192-2v, 199-9v, 218-18v, 224v-5, 301-1v, 355, 362v, 395v-6, 411v, 436v-7, 438v, 455, 476-6v, 481-1v; ibid., vol. 3, 25-5v, 91, 104v, 108-8v, 125, 128.
Note: 27,151 casks of flour @ 180 livres net each = 2,443.6 tonneaux
30,331 casks of salt beef @ 180 livres net each = 2,729.8 tonneaux
15,036 tonneaux of wine = 15,036 tonneaux
15,036 casks of brandy @ 8/tonneaux = 944.5 tonneaux
Total of the four major commodities = 21,153.9 tonneaux.

linking Europe, Africa, and the Americas.[143] The absence of a significant French slave trade in the seventeenth century slowed the integration of the French colonies into the Atlantic world for many decades, indeed, until after 1730. The inability of French slave traders to supply the colonies, however, stemmed less from the government's desire to prevent foreign access than from metropolitan monopolists' fighting to prevent competition from private merchants on the African coast. The monopolists had no incentive to meet colonial demands for labour.[144] The 1679 reorganization of the Senegal Company, for example, may have occurred to create a front for

[143] David Eltis, *The Rise of African Slavery in the Americas* (Cambridge: Cambridge University Press, 2000), 24, 114–15. Barbara Solow, ed., *Slavery and the Rise of the Atlantic System* (New York: Cambridge University Press, 1991) explores this theme in twelve essays.

[144] This was clearly acknowledged by Père Labat, *Nouveau voyage aux Isles*, quoted in Frostin, *Les Révoltes blanches*, 123.

certain royal officials to pocket the 13–livre gratuity paid to the Western Domain for each slave imported into the West Indies.[145] High profits were easily achieved in the absence of competition by maintaining a shortage of slaves. Slave traders usually refused credit to colonists who often lacked capital and cash. Traders also disliked leaving colonial product on the beach, demanding only sufficient goods to fill their ships' holds for the return voyage. These attitudes were in keeping with the lack of domestic demand for colonial produce.

The Dutch, on the other hand had long supplied African slaves to the French in exchange for tobacco, cotton, indigo, ginger, sugar, and other commodities. The huge gap between the number of slaves, 22,566, that reached Dutch Curaçao between 1668 and 1674 and the 12,766 shipped to official asiento ports on the Spanish Main suggests the French and others may have received the difference.[146] The French government displayed little interest in the slave trade until 1669 when the Council of State authorized the West India Company to trade for slaves on the African coast to the exclusion of all others. The following year the Council lifted the 5 percent tax on slaves landed in the islands to encourage the trade.[147] During the next six decades, seven monopoly slave trading companies rose and fell. These were the West India Company, 1664–74; the Senegal Company, 1675–84; the Guinea Company, 1685–96; the New Senegal Company, 1685–1700; the Royal Saint-Domingue Company, 1698–1720; the Royal Guinea or Asiento Company, 1701–15; and John Law's India Company.[148] Shortly after 1700, these monopolies became quiescent or focused elsewhere than on the French colonies and private merchants began to explore opportunities in the trade. After absorbing the Senegal, Guinea, and Saint-Domingue Companies, the India Company finally abandoned the trade to private merchants in 1725 in return for payment of 10 livres per head on all slaves landed in the colonies.[149]

---

[145] Pierre Boulle, "French Mercantilism, Commercial Companies, and Colonial Profitability", in *Compagnies and Trade: Essays on Overseas Trading Companies during the Ancien Règime*, eds., L. Blussé and F. Gaastra (Leiden: University of Leiden Press, 1981), 108 n28.

[146] Klooster, *Illicit Riches*, 109 n. 14. Johannes Postma, *The Dutch in the Atlantic Slave Trade, 1600–1815* (Cambridge: Cambridge University Press, 1989), 34–5 says little about this.

[147] Col., C^{8B} 9, no. 10 arrêt, 26 August 1670.

[148] I have not included the privilege of the tax-farmer of the Western Domain to sell slaves in the West Indies as a monopoly because between 1675 and 1679 he had no privilege to buy them in Africa.

[149] The history of these failures can be followed in Mims, *Colbert's West India Policy*; Abdoulye Ly, *La Compagnie du Sénégal* (Paris: Présence Africaine, 1958); Gaston Martin, *Histoire de l'esclavage dans les colonies françaises*, (Paris: Presses Universitaires de France, 1948). Charles Munford, *The Black Ordeal of Slavery and Slave Trading in the French West Indies, 1625–1715*, 3 vols. (Lewiston, NY: Edwin Mellen Press, 1991) is disappointing, being chiefly anecdotal.

As many as 5,000 slaves may have been delivered annually to French colonies during the last quarter of the seventeenth century, but French ships probably carried fewer than one-fifth of them.[150] In 1675 the tax-farmers of the Western Domain contracted to deliver 800 slaves annually for the next four years but failed miserably.[151] The Senegal Company imported no more than 600 or 700 slaves into the French Caribbean, including Saint-Domingue, between June 1679 and July 1680.[152] In 1683, 959 slaves were sold at Martinique.[153]

The monopoly companies all suffered from similar difficulties: insufficient capital and resources, lack of skilled agents in Africa, Dutch – and, later, English – competition, and lack of leadership leading to internal quarrels. In 1680, only a year after obtaining its monopoly, the Senegal Company obtained a two-year moratorium on paying its debts after losing seven vessels. After a reorganisation the following year, the Company's monopoly was revoked in September of 1684.[154] Officials at Martinique and Guadeloupe asked for access to foreign slave traders, but the king refused, creating instead the Guinea Company charged with the same burden as its predecessor of furnishing 2,000 slaves annually to the colonies. In 1688, the government reduced the duties on West Indian products entering France bought with the proceeds from slave sales by half, but this did little to assist colonial planters.[155]

With very little capital on hand and the more populous, wealthier island of Martinique close by, few slaves ever reached Guadeloupe directly in French ships. Colonists acquired slaves from the neighbouring colony when and if they were available, but almost all slaves on Guadeloupe were bought from foreign sources. Planters here and on Marie Galante and Grenada developed vigorous, interisland trades that became the backbone of illegal trade to which local authorities turned a blind eye for decades to come. In one effort to overcome irregularity of commercial traffic, Guadeloupean planters contracted in 1713 with the captain of a slaver for a supply of slaves. Governor de La Malmaison sent a copy to Pontchartrain because he feared French merchants would try to have it annulled. Captain Mosnier agreed to accept half cash then and half one year later. Had Mosnier allowed everyone who

---

[150] Philip D. Curtin, *The Atlantic Slave Trade: A Census* (Madison: University of Wisconsin Press, 1969), 121 argues that projections of Table 34 suggest French imports in excess of 4,980 slaves annually, but that French shipping carried fewer than 2,000. See Martin, *L'Histoire de l'esclavage*, 21 for the estimate of 1,000.

[151] Col., F²ᴬ 10 Traitez fait entre les directeurs du Domaine d'Occident et Jean Oudiette . . . . 16 October 1675.

[152] Mims, *Colbert's West Indian Policy*, 300, citing Col., C⁸ᴬ, 2 Blénac to Colbert, 13 July 1680.

[153] Col., C⁸ᴬ, 3, ff. 310–19 Blénac and Bégon to Seignelay, 18 June 1684; Ly, *La Compagnie du Sénégal*, 170 mistakenly transcribed 159 slaves.

[154] Ibid., 165–7, 182.

[155] Pierre Pluchon, *Histoire de la colonisation française*, Tome 1. *Le Premier Empire coloniale des origines à la Restauration* (Paris: Fayard, 1991), 1: 412.

wanted to sign the contract, he would have had a thousand signatures. In December of 1714, Mosnier and another slave trader reached Guadeloupe and sold their 367 slaves in a week,[156] but the experiment was not repeated.[157] Interlopers were probably able to beat the French competition. In 1719, Governor de Moyencourt claimed with only slight exaggeration that during the previous quarter of a century, only 500 slaves had reached Guadeloupe in French ships.[158]

During the Nine Years' War, between June 1691 and March 1694, the Guinea Company delivered fewer than 900 slaves to the Windward Islands.[159] The slave trade had virtually dried up. Irreparable losses from shipwreck and captures of the Senegal Company's forts in 1693 led the government to authorise its sale to one of its eight shareholders who became the sole owner acting for a syndicate of financial investors.[160] Slaves supplied by the Senegal Company were reputed to be poor workers and insufficiently numerous. At the end of the Nine Years' War, colonists asked that private merchants be allowed to trade in Africa and even to employ the Dutch to obtain slaves.[161]

French planters bought slaves from the Dutch at St. Eustatius and sailed to St. Thomas in the Virgin Islands to exchange goods for slaves under the neutral flags of Denmark and Brandenburg.[162] A unique slave trade sprang up temporarily on Grenada between the French and Carib Indians, who brought slaves from South America. Spaniards brought slaves to Martinique from Venezuela.[163] Pontchartrain allowed the colonists on Saint-Domingue to draw slaves from wherever they could be found. He even asked whether invalid convicts, no longer useful in the galleys, could be employed instead of Africans.[164] Governor Du Casse found Saint-Domingue's best source of slaves in Jamaica. Following his great raid of 1694, he claimed the colony's trade was flourishing.[165]

Though slave prices doubled between 1686 and 1696 and colonial officials called for free trade in slaves, the old Senegal Company's monopoly

[156] Abénon, *Guadeloupe de 1671 à 1759*, 1: 161.

[157] Ibid., 1: 162; also Jean Mettas, *Répertoire des expéditions négriers françaises au xviiie siècle*, edité par Serge Daget, 2 vols. (Paris: Société française d'histoire d'outre-mer et librairie orientaliste Paul Geuthner, 1978–1984) [hereafter Mettas-Daget, *Répertoire*], 2: 235.

[158] Col., C⁸ᴬ, 8, ff. 34–6 Moyencourt to Navy Council, 19 August 1719.

[159] Ibid., 6, 367–92 Dumaitz to Pontchartrain 5 June 1691; ibid., 7, ff. 268–94 same to same, 18 January 1693; and 8, ff. 132–65 same to same 1 March 1694 reports arrivals of 150, 489, and 250 slaves, respectively.

[160] Ly, *La Compagnie du Sénégal*, 207–14; Martin, *Histoire de l'esclavage*, 23; also K. G. Davies, *The Royal Africa Company* (London: Longmans Green & Co., 1957), 272.

[161] Col., C⁸ᴬ 10, ff. 150v–2 Mareuil, King's Lieutenant at Capesterre, to Pontchartrain, 15 May 1697.

[162] Klooster, *Illicit Riches*, 119.

[163] Col., C⁸ᴬ, 6, 324–42 Dumaitz to Pontchartrain, 16 February 1691.

[164] Col., B 14, ff. 402–2v Pontchartrain to Du Casse, 27 August 1692.

[165] Col., C⁸ᴬ, f. 12v Extrait des depêches, 11 September 1695.

was reconstituted once again. The new company was no more effective than its predecessors. Only a few hundred slaves were delivered to the colonies: 339 to Cayenne in 1697 and 235 to Martinique, of which 50 were sold at Guadeloupe in 1698 and 170 to Cayenne in 1699.[166] The acquisition of considerable capital during the Nine Years' War in the Channel and Atlantic ports may have led to increased calls to open the slave trade without restrictions; Pontchartrain began allowing private traders to fit out for Africa soon afterward.[167] In 1698, he acknowledged the Company's failure when he permitted a Sieur Boitard to import 2,000 slaves from the Danes and interlopers.[168] Colonists continually complained about the lack of slaves.[169] Despite the arrival of 1,000 slaves at Martinique in 1700, demand continued to outstrip supply, and foreign suppliers appeared unable to make up the difference.[170]

The War of the Spanish Succession changed all of that. The French colonies became virtually open to all. In 1701, the Guinea Company was reorganized under the direction of a dozen or so influential financiers close to the minister of the marine. It was given the appellation "royal" and the *asiento*, the contract to supply slaves to the Spanish colonies in America, and became the Royal Asiento Company.[171] Although an asiento ship carried 500 slaves into St. Louis, Saint-Domingue, early in 1703, the Company generally concentrated on supplying Spanish America.[172] French planters obtained slaves wherever they found them in greater numbers than before. On the eve of war, with the charter companies uninterested in supplying sufficient slaves to the French colonies, deputies of commerce from the French seaports succeeded in obtaining a government order forcing the Guinea Company to allow private merchants access to the African coast south of the Sierra Leone River.[173]

During the next 12 years these same deputies ensured that the Company obeyed the new rule to issue permits free of charge, but French merchants began exploring opportunities in the trade only midway through the war. During the last four months of 1702, 591 slaves entered Martinique

---

[166] Col., C^{14}, 3, ff. 114–16v Férolles to Pontchartrain, 15 January 1697; Col., C^{8A}, 10, ff. 301v–2 Robert to Pontchartrain, 6 March 1698; and Col., C^{14}, 4, ff. 14–15v Férolles to Pontchartrain, 8 April, 1699.

[167] Lionel Rothkrug, *Opposition to Louis XIV: Political and Social Origins of the French Enlightenment* (Princeton: Princeton University Press, 1965), 409–11.

[168] Col., B 21, ff. 117–17v King to d'Amblimont and Robert, 20 August 1698.

[169] E.g. Col., C^{8A}, 13, ff. 198–201v Robert to Pontchartrain, 4 November 1701.

[170] Col., C^{8A}, 12, ff. 58–81, 107, 149 Robert to Pontchartrain, 8 January, 6 March, and 26 May 1700. Also see Postma, *The Dutch in the Atlantic Slave Trade*, 49.

[171] Col., F^{2A}, 7, Acte de société, 15 November 1701.

[172] Col., C^{8A} 15, ff. 110–18 (extract) Galiffet to Pontchartrain, 24 January [1703]; also ibid., ff. 419–24 Mithon to Pontchartrain, 23 June 1705.

[173] Thomas Schaepper, "Colonial Trade Policies Late in the Reign of Louis XIV", *RFHOM*, 62, nos. 248–9 (1980), 207.

from English prizes.[174] The absence of slave deliveries at Martinique for two years prior to June of 1705, indicates they began slowly and intermittently.[175] In July of 1707, a ship belonging to a private trader from Nantes reached Martinique with 291 African men, women, and children on board; between October of 1708 and April of 1709, two ships arrived at Martinique with 530 slaves from Africa.[176] Local privateers introduced 480 slaves from successful raids on the Dutch colony of Essequibo, and six private slavers arrived from Africa during 1709 and 1710.[177] During the same period, 450 slaves arrived at Saint-Domingue.[178] In 1713, several hundred slaves entered Martinique from Barbados with the acquiescence of French authorities and payment of 1,000 livres per ship.[179]

With the signing of the Treaty of Utrecht, the French slave trade blossomed. The charter companies faded away. In November of 1713, the deputies of commerce succeeded in getting the Guinea trade opened to anyone willing to engage in it. Letters patent of January 1716 opened the slave trade to merchants from five seaports on payment of a head tax of 20 livres to the tax-farmer of the Western Domain. This attempt to control the trade by restricting it to merchants from Rouen, Nantes, La Rochelle, and Bordeaux failed. Saint-Malo, Honfleur, Le Havre, and others were soon added to the list of authorized ports.[180] To all intents and purposes, the trade was free to all.

Merchants from Nantes quickly emerged as major sources of capital and shipping to dominate the trade. One incomplete list shows 113 Nantais ships arriving in the West Indies from Africa between 1711 and 1722 with a total of 26,000 slaves on board.[181] Sixty-five percent of all French slavers were fitted out at Nantes during this period. The proportion rose to 70 percent during the decade, 1726–36.[182] From 1714 to 1720, 10,200 slaves carried from Africa in 68 ships reached Martinique. Nearly twice that number, 19,349,

---

[174] Col., C8A 14, ff. 247–51, 285–9 and 290–5 Robert to Pontchartrain, 25 September, 3 December, and 25 December 1702.

[175] Col., C8A 15, f. 426 Mithon to Pontchartrain, 23 June 1705.

[176] Col., C8A, 16, f. 246 Vaucresson to Pontchartrain, 24 July 1707.

[177] Ibid., 17, f. 90 Vaucresson to Pontchartrain, 18 April 1709; Ibid., 18, ff. 56–6v Etat des vaisseaux négriers; Mettas-Gaget, *Répertoire*, 1: 5–7.

[178] Col., C9B 1 Mémoire des prix ausquels les marchandises et denrées d' Europe ont été vendues à St. Domingue . . . [1 mai 1709–1 mai 1710], [n.d.].

[179] Col., C8A 19, ff. 408–15 Vaucresson to Pontchartrain, 25 July 1713; also David Eltis, "The British Transatlantic Slave Trade before 1714: Annual Estimate of Volume and Direction" in *The Lesser Antilles in the Age of European Expansion*, eds. Robert Paquette and Stanley L. Engerman (Gainsville: University of Florida Press, 1996), 195.

[180] See Robert Louis Stein, *The French Slave Trade in the Eighteenth Century: An Old Regime Business* (Madison: University of Wisconsin Press, 1978), 13–15.

[181] Quoted in Herbert S. Klein, *The Middle Passage: Comparative Studies in the Atlantic Slave Trade* (Princeton: Princeton University Press, 1978), 188.

[182] Mettas-Daget, *Répertoire*, 1: 3. Earlier studies exaggerated the domination of Nantes.

reached Saint-Domingue during the same period.[183] Between 1713 and 1730, 383 slave voyages occurred between Africa and the French colonies.[184] Some 5,850 Africans were traded annually during the period, of which 4,961 were delivered to the colonies,[185] but these numbers failed to meet demand.

Between 1719 and 1727, inclusive, approximately 11,000 slaves were carried into St. Eustatius. The majority were disposed of chiefly among neighbouring French colonies. Then, just as mysteriously as it began, this illicit trade disappeared.[186] High prices and increased demand at Saint-Domingue led French slavers to bypass the Windward Islands, leading to a severe, temporary shortage which the Dutch had filled. In September of 1719, Intendant Bénard claimed no slaves had reached Martinique during the previous two years.[187] The following year, Governor-General de Feuquières and Bénard complained bitterly of slavers sailing directly to Saint-Domingue where colonists were paying up to 900 livres for African males in order to resell them to the Spanish in Santo Domingo for 2,500 livres. Martiniquois were offering only 700 livres.[188] The 3,667 slaves, an increase of 36 percent over the previous four-year average, officially landed at Saint-Domingue in 1720 appear to bear this out.[189] In addition to the circumstances on Saint-Domingue, the India Company, which had absorbed all the defunct charter companies, attempted to exploit the slave trade in its own ships. Forty-six Company ships carried 16,000 slaves to the West Indies between 1723 and 1725, forcing private merchants to withdraw temporarily from the trade.[190] Possibly owing to pressure from the controller-general of finances, the Company abandoned the slave trade to private merchants in 1725 in return for payment of a head-tax of 20 livres per slave transported to the

---

[183] Col., C9A 12, Etat general des nègres, 22 February 1717; ibid., 16, Mithon to Council, 10 March 1719; Col., C9B 2 Etat des marchandises seiches et autre denrées qui ont été portées de France ... 1714; ibid., Extrait de la lettre de 16 June 1716; ibid., 5, Extrait de la lettre de Mithon to Council 20 August 1718 and 10 March 1719; and ibid., 7, Extrait des etat des vaisseaux pour 1719. L. Guet, *Origines de la Martinique–Le colonel François de Collart et la Martinique de son temps–colonisation, sièges, révoltes et combats de 1625 à 1720* (Vannes: Lafolye, 1893), 383.

[184] David Eltis, based on Mettas-Daget, *Répertoire*; this number includes 16 more voyages than claimed by Stein, *The French Slave Trade*, Table A1, 207.

[185] Ibid., 211.

[186] Postma, *The Dutch in the Atlantic Slave Trade*, 197–200; also Klooster, *Illicit Riches*, 119.

[187] Col., C8A, 26, f. 318v Bénard to Navy Council, 15 September 1719.

[188] Col., C8A, 27, ff. 132v–3 Feuquières and Bénard to Navy Council, 30 November 1720; ibid., f. 395v Bénard to Council, 29 November 1730. Liliane Crété, *La traite des nègres sous l'ancien régime: le nègre, le sucre, et la toile* (Paris: Perrin, 1989), 226. See also Col., C8B, 6, f. 38 Extrait de Moyencourt to Navy Council, 7 July 1720 for the same complaint concerning Guadeloupe.

[189] Col., C9B, 7 Extrait de l'etat general des negres ..., 1720.

[190] Klein, *The Middle Passage*, 179; Jean-Michel Deveau, *La Traite rochelais* (Paris: Karthala, 1990), 17–18

colonies.[191] Reduced by half in 1726, this levy remained in place for the next 40 years.[192]

Also in 1726, English traders using St. Lucia began to rival the Dutch traders at St. Eustatius, perhaps forcing them out of the contraband business.[193] English interlopers already played a major role in the French slave trade. Despite the growth in the number of French slavers, the increased demand in the colonies since the beginning of the century provided plenty of opportunity for interlopers to supply additional slaves. One English report of 1714 claimed that 3,800 of an estimated 6,100 Africans carried to the French colonies arrived in English and Dutch ships. The author, a Reverend Mr. Gordon, explained that owing to their inexperience and lack of influence in Africa, the French paid about 60 percent more for slaves than their competitors who delivered them at much cheaper prices.[194] A decade later, an English agent for Barbados estimated that more than half of an estimated 2,300 slaves re-exported annually from the colony were shipped to the French Windward Islands: 800 to Martinique, 150 each to Guadeloupe and Grenada, and 100 to Marie Galante.[195] If true, the number from Barbados was equal to nearly 30 percent of the official arrivals at Martinique. Both English reports claimed the entire slave trade to Guadeloupe, Marie Galante, and Grenada was in English and Dutch hands, which is roughly borne out by data in Table 1.2.

The slave trade was the last element of the plantation complex to appear in French America. The trade had been a hollow shell during the seventeenth century as financiers holding the slave monopoly manipulated the trade for their own gain. The charter companies were possibly the greatest retardant factor in the growth of the French colonies in the Americas. The trade grew slowly during the first quarter of the eighteenth century because of the companies' repeated failures. The needs of planters had little influence given their lack of capital and metropolitan merchants' reluctance to grant them credit. Despite three decades of failure at the end of the seventeenth century, the government and metropolitan merchants continued to support calls for monopoly and regulation. Even after the mid-1720s, when colonial

---

[191] See Col., F²ᴬ, 11 "Memoire sur la quantité des nègres qu'il est necessaire d'introduire chaque année aux isles d'Amerique," 5 September 1724; and ibid., "Commerce de Guinée, Mémoire" 10 November 1724.

[192] Clark, *La Rochelle and the Atlantic Economy*, 126.

[193] Col., C⁸ᴬ 36, f. 39v Blondel to Maurepas, 8 April 1726; ibid., 35, f. 77 Feuquières and Blondel to Maurepas, 16 June 1716; and Pitman, *The Development of the British West Indies*, 85–6.

[194] Huntington Library, San Marino, California, Stowe Ms. ST9, ff. 48–50 "Observations on the Trade of Africa and Angola by the Reverend Mr. Gordon (1714)". I thank David Eltis who provided the references for this and the following footnote.

[195] Huntington Library, San Marino, California, Stowe Ms. 9, ff. 43–5 "Some remarks on the trade from Africa to Barbadoes by Mr. John Ashley one of the Agts of the said Island [1725]".

trade began to contribute in a major way to the growth of the economies of France's largest seaports, the government continued to subsidise the trade. Only then did the French slave trade begin to develop quickly on a major scale, and sugar production began to rival and later surpass production in the English colonies.[196]

4.6 MONEY, CAPITAL, AND CREDIT

Lack of money, capital, and credit in the French colonies combined with legislative constraints and lack of domestic demand to limit trade during the years prior to 1730. Lack of coin in Guadeloupe explains why virtually no direct trade with France existed. When metropolitan ships did arrive, as happened in 1711, it was because a temporary shortage of coin in Martinique encouraged traders to seek cheaper colonial products through direct barter with the colonists. Moreover, in this case, agents at Martinique supplied ship captains with the names of good and bad payers.[197] Three kinds of exchange occurred in the colonies: barter, the exchange of goods as money equivalents, and real coin. In the Windward Islands prices were fixed in livres weight of tobacco, while beaver pelts and occasionally moose hides and wheat were used in Canada. Sugar and indigo began to replace tobacco during the 1660s and became paramount a decade or so later.[198] The little coin present in the Antilles was chiefly Spanish or Dutch, and on Saint-Domingue, pieces of eight remained a money of account without being expressed in livres tournois – at least until 1702.[199]

Before 1727, French coin circulated in the colonies at a premium of one-quarter greater than its nominal value in an attempt to keep it there as a circulating medium. The par of exchange was 133 1/3 livres colonial currency or *monnaie du pays* per 100 livres tournois (*monnaie de France*). In other words, the colonial livre was depreciated by one-third in comparison with the French livre. This system effectively prevented planters from making large profits because metropolitan merchants calculated trade balances in local prices, which increased the value of French goods sold in the colonies and decreased the value of colonial exports sold in France, where transportation costs and commissions were also determined. Most profits accrued to metropolitan merchants.

196 Meyer, *Histoire de la France coloniale*, 1: 49; Stein, *The French Slave Trade*, 15.

197 Abénon, *La Guadeloupe de 1671 à 1759*, 1: 161, 163.

198 Alain Buffon, *Monnaie et crédit en économie coloniale: Contribution à l'histoire économique de la Guadeloupe (1635–1919)*, (Basse Terre: Société d'Histoire de Guadaloupe 1979), 17; Adam Shortt, ed. *Documents Relating to Canadian Currency, Exchange and Finance during the French Period*, 2 vols. (Ottawa: King's Printer, 1925), 1: xxxiii–xxxix, 39 and 53.

199 Robert Richard, "A Propos de Saint-Domingue: La monnaie dans l'économie coloniale (1674–1803), *RHC*, 41 (1954), 28–9.

Initially applied to Canada in 1654, the depreciated colonial money of account became standard in all colonies in 1672.[200] In the West Indies, underweight coin circulated at full value (by tale or count) in a futile attempt to draw money into the colonies. A royal edict abolishing this colonial currency in July of 1717 applied only to Canada. Change did not occur in the Caribbean until a decade later when a new edict issued in 1726 increased the premium on French money in the colonies to one-third its value. Colonial currency was further depreciated by being set at a new level of 150 livres colonial per 100 livres tournois in response to the continual outflow of coin. These official rates of exchange ruled out any commercial rates until much later, reflecting the weakness of colonial economies before 1730.

A variety of financial and commercial paper circulated in the colonies in addition to pieces of eight (*piastres*), guilders, and any real coin of the realm. Private promissory notes, pay orders, acquitted receipts, drafts on the treasurers-general of the marine, and private bills of exchange also circulated, but merchants generally avoided both colonial money and personal notes. Colonists were reputed to be bad payers. Drafts on the treasurers-general were only reluctantly accepted because they required three different official documents to effect payment and loss of any one of them led to total loss.[201] Bills of exchange were promises to pay the bearer a specified sum on certain dates in the future, usually after three, six, and nine months. Before their "due" dates such bills traded at a discount – a practice that yielded good profits. Initially a form of compensation, bills of exchange became, wherever interest on loans was forbidden by the Church, the most frequent form of credit.[202] All these forms of exchange depreciated colonial currency and financial paper possessed different values because they were discounted at different rates. Not surprisingly, merchants preferred coin, though little was ever present in the colonies. The conduct of commerce was difficult and costly. Following the collapse of John Law's system, Pierre Pellet at St. Pierre congratulated his brother Jean at Bordeaux that their firm had not been crushed like so many others because they had eschewed money and bills and stuck to commodities in their trading.[203]

In Canada, where coin remained impossible to keep in circulation, the government resorted to many expedients. In the mid-1680s, the shortage of circulating currency was as desperate as it had ever been. Though regular

[200] Shortt, ed., *Documents*, 1: 3; Richard, "A Propos de Saint-Domingue", 28; Buffon, *Monnaie et crédit*, 48–9; and John J. McCusker, *Money and Exchange in Europe and America, 1600–1775: A Handbook* (Chapel Hill: University of North Carolina Press, 1978), 281.

[201] Jacques Mathieu, *Le Commerce entre la Nouvelle France et les Antilles* (Montréal: Fides 1981), 146.

[202] Braudel, *Civilization and Capitalism*, 2: 142.

[203] Jean Cavignac, *Jean Pellet, commercant en gros, 1694–1772: contribution à l'étude du négoce bordelais du XVIIIe siècle* (Paris: SEVPEN, 1967), 152 cited in Braudel *Civilization and Capitalism*, 2: 149.

soldiers had been introduced into the colonies in 1683 and had to be paid in cash, the minister of marine proved increasingly reluctant to send specie overseas. In June of 1685, after accusing naval authorities at Rochefort of failing to send sufficient coin to pay the troops or to meet immediate expenses, forbidding fur traders to take coin or bills of exchange into the interior, and after ten companies of soldiers had hired themselves out to colonists in the absence of their pay, intendant Jacques Demeulles issued his own currency to pay the soldiers. Issued in three denominations, the currency was made from individual playing cards bearing the intendant's arms and signature. Backed by Demeulles' personal, private promise to redeem them, the cards met with ready acceptance. Counterfeit cards appeared during the summer so that three months after their first issue, following the arrival of the king's ship carrying in specie, the cards were redeemed and withdrawn from circulation. Nevertheless, commerce had received a boost from the ease with which the cards circulated in the colony.

Cards were employed as currency in Canada off and on for the remainder of the French régime, but forgery was an ever-present danger, and French officials strongly disapproved of the practice. The constant excess of colonial government expenditures over allotted funds, losses of specie at sea, and the French government's growing financial difficulties all led intendants in Canada to continue to release card money into circulation. As long as trade expanded, the practice encouraged and facilitated commerce in the colony. During the War of the Spanish Succession, however, in the wake of the collapsing fur trade and contracting government expenditures, the cards led to uncontrolled inflation. As early as 1704, the treasurers-general of the marine protested bills of exchange drawn from Canada. Colonial merchants refused to accept cards. By the end of the war, cards with a nominal value of more than 2,000,000 livres were circulating in the colony. Later, in 1717, the government agreed to redeem the cards at half their nominal value but completed the job only in 1719 – an action that crushed several colonial merchants.

The government of the Regent imposed new discipline and financial orthodoxy in the colonies by disallowing intendants from issuing bills of exchange against future allocations of colonial expenses. In 1717, the new Navy Council ordered all money to circulate in the colonies at the same value as in France. Card money was abolished in Canada three years later. The move paralyzed commerce as the little remaining coin quickly flowed to France or into tiny hordes carefully hidden away by habitants. Coin remained impossible to keep in the local economy, and the government finally agreed in 1729 to recreate Canadian card money, issuing cards up to a nominal value of 400,000 livres. Deeply suspicious of paper, yet acknowledging a need, the government hoped to control the amount in circulation by redeeming 250,000 livres annually and releasing it back into the economy the next year.[204] The system worked well as trade expanded, at least until the next war.

The absence of sufficient currency in circulation was also a feature of the West Indies colonies and punished colonial merchants who quickly fell under the domination of commission-agents residing in the colonies. Commission-agents were neither factors, employees in a merchant's service, nor partners sharing risks and profits. They were independent merchants. All merchants worked on commission for other merchants, taking a small percentage on deals negotiated for third parties and expecting a similar percentage for a similar arrangement. The commission system was more flexible, less costly, and more time saving than other arrangements, and by the late seventeenth century it was in widespread general use.[205] The most famous or notorious commission-agents lived in Saint Pierre, but others lived in Quebec, Louisbourg, Léogane, and Cap Français, where their influence and numbers grew.

Risk capital, the kind required for seaborne commerce, was always in scarce supply in France. No central bank emerged during the *ancien régime*, nor were there large accumulations of capital on which merchants could draw. Credit resources shrank generally in Europe after 1630 and did not expand again until Spanish silver production improved during the last third of the century and new imports of gold from Brazil began to appear at the beginning of the next.[206] The French practice of purchasing venal offices and low-interest-bearing annuities called *rentes* absorbed much available capital. French annuities, usually tied up in inheritances, were quite useless as instruments of credit.[207] Little venture capital existed beyond the urban merchant communities, and many merchants removed themselves from trade through purchase of offices, *rentes*, and land. Those in search of capital to exploit colonial trade were confined chiefly to the seaports and competed fiercely amongst themselves for scarce resources. Slaves traders, whose needs were greater, relied heavily on Paris for capital.[208]

Few credit resources existed in the seventeenth century. Well into the eighteenth century, the capital needed to finance overseas ventures was obtained chiefly through bottomry loans (*à la grosse avanture*) at rates of between 25 and 30 percent in peace time. These loans covered both principal and insurance for loss of a ship (such as a bottom); cargo financed by such a loan led to cancellation of the borrower's obligation to repay should it be lost at

[204] Shortt, ed., *Documents*, 2: 591–5, 611.
[205] Braudel, *Civilization and Capitalism*, 2: 150.
[206] Pierre Goubert, "Le 'tragique' XVIIe siècle" dans Braudel et Labrousse, dirs. *Histoire économique et sociale de la France*, 2: 363–4; and Ernest Labrousse, "Les 'bons prix' agricoles du xviiie sièclle", ibid., 393; also Fischer, *The Great Wave*, 109.
[207] Braudel, *Civilization and Capitalism*, 2: 113.
[208] Stein, *The French Slave Trade*, 148–50.

sea. Under such conditions, the lender rather than the borrower accepted the risk. Money obtained through bottomry resembled direct equity investment rather than contemporary bond or debenture credit. Commerce carried on under such conditions was not an example of surplus capital seeking an outlet, but the reverse with entrepreneurs seeking scarce resources in an age of very little credit.

Much of the power of French merchants also lay in the traditional way in which they conducted business. For example, they customarily levied interest annually on advances made over the life of an association with a colonial merchant, while simultaneously taking commissions up to 5 percent on sales of any merchandise. Lenders also normally demanded interest on credits from the date of the request for a loan rather than from the date of issue. This may have been insignificant in face-to-face transactions of an earlier era, but when applied overseas in an age of slow communication it put colonists in a permanent subservient state because their requests often preceded by many months the granting of a loan.[209] Under such conditions small traders in the colonies quickly fell under the domination of metropolitan merchants.

4.7 CONCLUSION

The popular image of triangular trade between France, Africa, and the West Indies characterising French colonial trade before 1730 is misleading. First, only a minority of French ships sailed to the West Indies via Africa, and second, France's colonial trade grew strongly only after colonial products were re-exported from France to northern Europe. The centrality of overseas commerce to French colonial history outside the Caribbean also deserves questioning. In Canada, Acadia, Cayenne, and Louisiana commerce does not appear to have been central to people's lives. There, fewer and fewer people participated in export trades or even produced for such trades. Local markets emerged slowly and remained quite small. Few colonists initiated commercial activities since they possessed virtually no capital. Regardless of any hopes and expectations that they might improve their condition, almost all immigrants were single, poor bondsmen and women who brought no savings with them. Most nobles were poor. They sought to rebuild their fortunes rather than opportunities to invest current ones. Land, which was granted, not sold by the king and lords-proprietor, was virtually worthless until improved by the labour of slaves or homesteaders. Depreciated colonial currency hampered the few colonists who may have had capital of their own. Most had to borrow from France, but they encountered great reluctance among potential creditors to lend to them.

---

[209] Col., F²ᴬ, 7f. 62; discussed in Mathieu, *Le commerce entre la Nouvelle France et les Antilles*, 147.

The absence of savings in the colonies suggests that other means of accumulating capital (theft or privateering) may have played a more significant role in developing the colonies than might otherwise have been the case. Little evidence exists to suggest this occurred during the Franco-Dutch War in the 1670s, but slaves carried into the colonies by French privateers during the next two struggles between France and the Allies represented significant infusions of capital. This activity permitted introduction of the plantation complex to Saint-Domingue during the 1690s greatly increasing the growth of sugar production there. During the next war, the same occurred in the Windward Islands, where the plantation system was strongly reinforced.[210] Nevertheless, the absence of local capital remained long afterward the major barrier to developing colonial commerce.[211]

With little currency, capital, or credit, French colonists remained prisoners of their metropolitan creditors, who held them in a remorseless grip. The noncapitalist outlook of government ministers and lesser officials chiefly concerned with regulation and supervision of markets rather than yields and circuits of exchange provided little assistance.[212] Above all, the failure of French domestic markets for colonial products to develop before 1730 locked French colonists into a trap from which only foreign demand released them. While the re-export of colonial commodities to the rest of Europe created great prosperity in the French Atlantic seaports in the eighteenth century, it did little to link the colonies to France. It is little wonder that colonists welcomed, indeed, actively sought out, any and every opportunity to trade with others. Foreign and illicit trade remain the great unknowns of French colonial history. The evidence that exists is chiefly anecdotal. By 1730, the economic life of New England, New York, and Pennsylvania was more vitally connected to the slave economies of Saint-Domingue, Guadeloupe, and Martinique than to any English colony.[213] Thus, the answers to the two questions posed at the beginning of this chapter are more clearly revealed. French colonial economies, including trade, merged with the new international Atlantic world slowly and imperfectly before 1730, and this slow development reinforced the elusiveness of the French empire for long afterward. Trade with others was pervasive, persistent, and in sufficient quantity not only to shape the societies themselves, but to delay the formation of a French imperial economy.

---

[210] See the suggestive article by N. Zahedieh, "Trade, plunder, and economic development in early English Jamaica, 1655–89", *Economic History Review*, 39 (1986), 205–22.

[211] Col., C^{11A}, 76, 323v Mémoire sur le commerce, 1741 quoted in Mathieu, *Le commerce entre la Nouvelle-France et les Antilles*, 149.

[212] Braudel, *Civilization and Capitalism*, 2: 282.

[213] Pitman, *The Development of the British West Indies*, 190–1.

5

Government and Politics

France's first overseas colonies appeared to depend on the state more than other European settlements, yet, owing to their demographic weakness, they were never successfully united into a centrally run, economically integrated empire. Colonial policy, metropolitan direction, and colonial government had much less formative impact on the development of French colonies than historians normally assert. The overseas authority of the early French state of Louis XIV and his successors was not well-developed, elaborate, or effective. The physical settings in which colonists found themselves, their settlements, forms of production and exchange, and the wars they fought to defend their possessions had greater effect on the evolution of French colonies in the Americas than the metropolitan government ever did. The question of government cannot be ignored, but neither does it deserve the attention it is traditionally accorded.

In September of 1663, Louis XIV revoked the charter of the Company of New France, reunited Canada to the French Crown, and the colony became a royal French province. The following year the King created a new charter company, and New France and the proprietary colonies in the West Indies were conceded to the West India Company. This move manifested the newly invigorated French state's search for a means to control and regulate the exploitation of its colonies rather than any reluctance to participate directly in the development of France overseas as did earlier grants to private companies. While company agents sought to play directing roles, the state interfered, naming governors and confirming appointments to newly erected sovereign councils. The first attempt to centralize metropolitan authority in the islands occurred in 1667 with the appointment of the first governor-general of the islands of America. By 1670, the Company was in decline and royal government was in the ascendant throughout the colonies.

During the brief period of West India Company jurisdiction, the basic elements of French colonial government began to be put into place. Long after 1730, however, changes continued to occur in colonial government. The Crown never abandoned monopoly companies as a means to promote colonial economic development and settlement. Whether in Saint-Domingue in 1698, Louisiana in 1712 and 1717, or Île St. Jean in 1718, the state continued to employ private companies to achieve its ends overseas. This practice and continual tinkering with colonial administration illustrates absolutism's pragmatic nature and lack of any theoretical model of development. Further investigation also reveals colonial government's weak, often confused organisation, overlapping jurisdictions and near absence of policy, its capacity for pragmatic responses to short-term demands, and, above all, the relative insignificance of the colonies to French state building and foreign policy.

Though the nature of the connection between the Crown and its overseas colonies at this time was chiefly owed to events in France rather than in the Americas, the growing wealth of the tropical colonies, the increasing colonial reliance upon non-French sources for slaves, and the use of foreign shipping to carry goods to Europe attracted the metropolitan government's attention. The same could not be said of New France, where the colony had sunk to the nadir of its fortunes and appeared headed for the same fate as Acadia, which was abandoned during the previous decade. Events between 1659 and 1662 were crucial to the change; during these years, France finally achieved peace with Spain, France's prime minister Cardinal Mazarin died, and the young king began to rule in his own name. With the arrival of Louis XIV there appeared another, often overlooked, motive for reuniting the colonies to the Crown – *la gloire*.

Mazarin played a crucial if ambivalent role as a precursor to the reunification of France's American colonies to the Crown. On the one hand, he was an avowed anticolonialist, a European statesman deeply involved in international politics who had little understanding of, or interest in, commerce and industry. On the other hand, he was chiefly responsible for the state of peace and military preponderance that Louis XIV inherited upon his minister's death in March of 1661. Without peace with Spain it is doubtful whether Louis XIV would have displayed any interest in New France or the other American colonies.[1] The royal government was ripe for an appeal from Canada and elsewhere in the Americas, and the king and his new ministers were willing and able to respond.

5.2 ABSOLUTISM

Previous assertions that French colonial governments were centralised, authoritarian, and paternalistic fail to stand up to analysis. The French

---

[1]   Pierre Goubert, *Mazarin* (Paris: Fayard, 1990), 491.

government was absolutist to be sure, and so too were colonial governments, but explaining what that means has given rise to a complex, multifaceted debate. Historians interested in European state formation have revised earlier models that stress the early centralising trends and coercive powers of modern states. Some features commonly attributed to absolutism such as authoritarianism and paternalism are found in many other governments. Rather than link absolutism to evidence of the emerging modern state, some historians suggest it arose from the co-opting of centralisers by strong regional groups and local interests who represented resistance to modernizing tendencies. Far from a victory of centralising royal authority over local elites and a manifestation of the rise of modern bureaucracy, historians have recently argued that the concentration of power in the hands of Louis XIV was the culmination of a process that can be traced back to the Middle Ages.[2] Others deny that any evidence of the complex articulations of modern bureaucracy can be found in the absolute state prior to the French Revolution. Public authority was also not differentiated from private interests, and the system of government was far more personal and idiosyncratic than a rule-based bureaucracy.[3]

French absolutism, it appears, was the monarch's successful achievement of collaboration with provincial elites rather than their coercion. Thus, rather than a concentration of power into the hands of the monarch, it was a tendency to co-opt local, traditional, representative institutions, and corporate bodies to the military, economic, political and ideological requirements of the central government arising from the near chaos threatening the monarch's existence during the century before 1660.[4] This idea is not as contentious as it may first appear. It is not radically different from earlier views of absolutism except that it points to the continuing strength of regional interests,

[2] Among the strongest proponents of the former view is J. C. Rule; see "Le Roi-Bureaucrate" in *Louis XIV and the Craft of Kingship*, J. C. Rule, ed. (Columbus: Ohio State University Press, 1969), 3–101; and "Colbert de Torcy, an emergent bureaucracy and the formulation of French foreign policy, 1698–1715" in Ragnild Hatton, ed., *Louis XIV and Europe* (London: Macmillan, 1976), 261–88.

[3] See J. F. Bosher, *French Finances, 1770–1795: From Business to Bureaucracy* (Cambridge: Cambridge University Press, 1970); Robert R. Harding, *Anatomy of a Power Elite: The Provincial Governors of Early Modern France* (New Haven and London: Yale University Press, 1978); C. H. Church, *Revolution and Red Tape: The French Ministerial Bureaucracy, 1770–1850* (Oxford: Clarendon Press, 1981); and James Pritchard, *Louis XV's Navy, 1748–1762: A Study of Organization and Administration* (Kingston and Montreal: McGill-Queen's University Press, 1987).

[4] William Beik, *Absolutism and Society in Seventeenth-Century France: State Power and Provincial Aristocracy in Languedoc* (Cambridge: Cambridge University Press, 1985); Sharon Kettering, *Patrons, Brokers, and Clients in 17th Century France* (Oxford: Oxford University Press, 1986); and A. N. Hamscher, The Conseil Privé and the Parlements in the Age of Louis XIV: A Study in French Absolutism, *Transactions of the American Philosophical Society*, 72, 2 (1987), i–v, 1–162.

corporate rivalries, local privileges, religious nonconformity, and resistance to financial exactions amidst the growing expansion of the monarchy into new jurisdictions and new activities permitted by its access to new sources of wealth.[5] Such an interpretation can be usefully applied to France's overseas colonies, where the early state lacked administrative, financial, judicial, and military institutions and the human resources to overcome the effect of distance to impose its will upon the colonists. This does not mean, however, that colonial government under the absolute monarchy was a democracy in practice.[6] The view of an eminent American colonial historian writing about the English example (that early modern states were built on continuous negotiations and reciprocal bargaining between authority and people) may be equally applied to the French experience.[7]

Colonial government organisation remained vague for many decades after 1670. Although only one ministry, the Marine, dealt with the colonies, no central administration existed for 40 years after Louis XIV created the navy secretariat in 1669. François Bellinzanni was entrusted with the business of commerce and manufactures, including colonies, but they were managed from three different bureaux: Ponant, Levant, and *fonds*.[8] Government at the center remained intensely personal. In 1710, Jérôme de Pontchartrain created a colonial office, but chiefly to find an honourable retirement, a sinecure close to the court, for his cousin.[9] This characteristic of government enabled vigorous secretaries of state to profit from weak departmental structures and confused jurisdictions to extend their personal authority over large protoministries.[10] This feature of absolutism was briefly overthrown after the death of Louis XIV. Under the government of the Regency (1715–23), administrative councils of nobles replaced the secretaries of state. This did represent a revolution in government, but the innovation could not last. The legacy of the royal seizure of power at the center returned. Personal rule that

---

[5] David Parker, *The Making of French Absolutism* (London: Edward Arnold, 1983).

[6] The claim was made for Canada in Hubert Deschamps, *Les Méthodes et les doctrines coloniales de la France du XVIe siècle à nos jours*, (Paris: Armand Colin, 1953), 59 and quoted approvingly by Raymond F. Betts, *Europe Overseas, Phases of Imperialism* (New York: Basic Books, 1968), 39.

[7] Jack P. Greene, "Negotiated Authorities: The Problem of Governance in the Extended Politics of the Early Modern Atlantic World" in *Negotiated Authorities: Essays in Colonial Political and Constitutional History* (Charlottesville and London: University Press of Virginia, 1994), 1–24.

[8] The two major administrative offices, Ponant and Levant, refer respectively to the Ocean Sea, (that is, Atlantic affairs) and the Mediterranean Sea including the African coast; *fonds* or the funds office dealt with accounting.

[9] For a brief history of the central bureaux of the Marine, see Pritchard, *Louis XV's Navy*, 19–36.

[10] Charles Frostin, "L'organisation ministérielle sous Louis XIV: cumul d'attributions et situations conflictuelles (1690–1715)", *Revue historique de droit français et étranger*, 4ème série, (1980), 201–26.

accompanied absolutism was back in place by the mid-1720s and remained a feature of French government until some 70 years later.[11]

Although the French colonies did not pay for themselves and ministers continually complained about excess expenses, they were not a great drain on the French government. Expenses in excess of colonial revenues were met out of naval funds, which absorbed from 13 to 23 percent of France's total military expenses between 1690 and 1700; the proportion fell to between 11 and 14 percent during the first decade of the eighteenth century. Navy funds continued to decline both absolutely and relatively during the post-war period. By the late 1720s, when they comprised only about 4 or 5 percent of the government's general expenses, the colonies accounted for only about 10 percent of the department's expenditures.[12]

Despite the lack of any real burden, colonies had a contribution to make to further Louis XIV's greatness or *gloire*. Glory does not do justice to the word. *La gloire* included the nation's interest, defined dynastically to be sure, but also the king's own personal ambition and obsession with his reputation. In Voltaire's words, "every king who loves glory loves the public weal".[13] *La gloire* was the mainstay of power, but it also extended beyond amassing military victories. It was the concomitant of a fragile reputation.[14] We should never forget that French colonies were chiefly seen as a means to demonstrate Louis XIV's, and thereby France's, greatness rather than as sources of economic riches. This profoundly affected the ways governments thought about colonies. It reminds us, too, that colonies were considered as very small parts of a much greater whole, pawns to be used in France's pursuit of international affairs.

5.3 COLBERT AND HIS SUCCESSORS

If the nature of absolutism is contentious, so too is the career of Louis XIV's most famous minister, Jean-Baptiste Colbert (1619–83) and the work of his

---

[11]   See Michel Antoine, *Le Conseil du roi sous le règne de Louis XV* (Genève: Droz, 1970), 43–117.

[12]   Henri Legohérel, *Les Trésoriers généraux de la marine (1517–1788)*, (Paris, Éditions Cujas, 1965), 179–80. Also Catherine M. Desbarats, "France in North America: The Net Burden of Empire during the First Half of the Eighteenth Century", *French History*, 11, 1 (1997), 1–28.

[13]   [Jean-François-Marie Arouet de] Voltaire, *The Age of Louis XIV*, trans., M. P. Pollack (London: Dent [1926] 1966), 333.

[14]   See Andrew Lossky, "The Nature of Political Power According to Louis XIV" in L. Krieger and F. Stern, eds., *The Responsibility of Power: Historical Essays in Honor of Hajo Holborn* (Garden City, NY: Doubleday Anchor Books, [1968] 1969), 122; on *la gloire* see also Ragnild Hatton, "Louis XIV and His Fellow Monarchs" in J. C. Rule, ed., *Louis XIV and the Craft of Kingship*, 155–95; and Peter Burke, *The Fabrication of Louis XIV* (New York and London: Yale University Press, 1992), 5.

successors. Historians usually credit Colbert with pursuing a coherent vision of empire for a score of years until his death. This is partly because his life defies biographical treatment despite the recent appearance of studies based on new research.[15] Some of the problem also stems from a tradition of viewing this hard-working minister outside his own times, but historians are putting Colbert back into the social-political context of his own period.[16] Colbert still has his admirers, but today historians are generally more critical of his conduct and ideas than a generation ago. They no longer see Colbert as a key figure in European economic history nor as a founder of France's commercial and industrial economy.[17] They are much more conscious than before that France was not anyone's to change. Colbert is now more frequently seen as a loyal servant of the king who continued and extended policies best attributed to his predecessors.[18] Any view of Colbert as a reformer is anachronistic. Though a devoted royal servant and patriot, he was less a progressive thinker and moderniser than previously believed, and while he embodied the bourgeois values of hard work, self-discipline, and upward mobility, he also strove to succeed in a largely paternalistic, aristocratic, clan-based, precapitalist society.

Colbert was a pragmatist rather than an ideologue who hid his multiple responses to short-term crises behind a thin veneer of ideological justifications that were of little interest to him. His policies, especially financial ones, were driven chiefly by short-term expediency and were frequently contradictory and self-defeating. His attempts to unify and standardise the law had little immediate success, and his efforts to control tax-farmers have been misunderstood. Although Colbert increased Crown revenues, he did so by ruthless application of the existing system rather than reform. The financial attraction of colonies lay in the possibility of finding alternative sources of revenue to an already overburdened agriculture in which direct taxes had quadrupled in a generation. Colbert saw in the development of maritime, including colonial trade, the key to rapidly increasing indirect taxes.[19] Colbert never escaped the clutches of the powerful corps of financiers and judicial office holders who controlled so much of the power and business of France. Far from

[15] E. g. Andrew Trout, *Jean-Baptiste Colbert* (Boston: Twdyne Publishers, 1978); Ines Murat, *Colbert* (Charlottesville: University of Virginia Press, [1980] 1984); and Jean Meyer, *Colbert* (Paris: Hachette, 1981); Roland Mousnier, dir., *Un Nouveau Colbert Actes du colloque pour le tricentenaire de la mort de Colbert* (Paris: SEDES, 1985).

[16] See especially Daniel Dessert and J. L. Journet, "Le Lobby Colbert: un royaume ou une affaire de famille", *Annales E.S.C.*, 30 (1975), 1306–36.

[17] Jan De Vries, *The Economy of Europe in an Age of Crisis, 1600–1750* (London and New York: Cambridge University Press, 1976), 90.

[18] Pierre Goubert, *Louis XIV and Twenty Million Frenchmen*, trans., Anne Carter (New York: Vintage Books, [1966] 1970), 114–27; also Meyer, *Colbert*, 102, 124.

[19] Jean Meyer, *Histoire de la france coloniale*, Vol. 1. *des origines à 1914* (Paris: Armand Colin, 1991), 32.

being the enemy of financiers, he was their close collaborator. Nor could it have been otherwise, for they alone were capable of creating the military-industrial complex that Louis XIV needed to build his new powerful army and navy.[20]

Colbert's colonial policies fared no better. His efforts to promote immigration were haphazard and came to nought owing to his strong support for the war against the Dutch. His creation of a tobacco monopoly to meet the exigency of wartime finances destroyed the export crop of many West Indian settlers, and his lease of the tax on beaver pelts to the tax-farmer of the Western Domain removed the Canadian fur trade from the discipline of market forces with harmful consequences later in the century.

Colbert rose rapidly in Louis XIV's favour, organising the prosecution of Nicolas Fouquet during the early 1660s, turning his attention to French overseas commerce, introducing the first high tariff against Dutch shipping and manufactures, and founding the West India Company to close off Dutch access to the French colonies. He became controller-general of finances in 1665 and secretary of state for the marine in 1669. He united in his hands, albeit under the authority of the king, everything to do with economic administration.

Colbert was no economic theorist, though his name is still often associated with "mercantilism".[21] He was not as dogmatic as this suggests. Though many continue to discuss mercantilism, the effort confuses rather than enlightens. Historian Jan De Vries has argued convincingly that, while the term cannot be ignored, it is best avoided as an organising concept.[22] Colbert may very well have possessed a dream of colonial development intended to enhance Louis XIV's reputation or *gloire* by establishing overseas colonies to produce and export natural products to increase France's wealth and the king's revenue, but this vision remained a dream. Though well-intentioned, Colbert's policies and directives were frequently incoherent, contradictory, and ambiguous. He was never able to escape his master's demands – constrained his actions.[23] Colbert was a man of his time. He was the pragmatic servant of a pragmatic king whose state-building measures have been

---

20   See Daniel Dessert, *Argent, pouvoir et société au Grand Siècle*; also his *La Royale, vaisseaux et marins du Roi Soleil* (Paris: Fayard, 1996).

21   Eli F. Hecksher, *Mercantilism*, 2 vols., 2nd ed. (London: E. F. Sonderland, 1965) remains the classical study of mercantilism. Charles W. Cole, *Colbert and a Century of French Mercantilism*, 2 vols. (New York: Columbia University Press, 1939) and *French Mercantilism, 1683–1700* (New York: Columbia University Press, 1943) are the standard works on the subject.

22   De Vries, *The Economy of Europe*, 29 and 236. D.C. Coleman, ed., *Revisions in Mercantilism: Debates in Economic History* (London: Methuen, 1969) contains several articles that seek to redefine mercantilism, which illustrates De Vries' point.

23   Dessert, *Argent, pouvoir et société au grand siècle*, 384–91; Meyer, *Colbert*, 121–4.

overemphasised at the expense of seeing the state more accurately as providing economic stability and unity and whose policies focused perforce on the state's short-term fiscal demands. Colbert struggled continually to impose order on chaos by seeking to control and regulate the lives and activities of colonists. It was under Colbert that royal governors were appointed, the first intendants were established, royal justice was imposed, a comprehensive body of law was introduced, and security was reinforced by the dispatch of regular infantry to the colonies. Missionaries had been in the colonies long before Colbert and the reign of Louis XIV, but it was during the 1670s that parishes appeared in New France and the West Indies and a bishop was named to Quebec to provide a familiar Roman Catholic milieu for the settlers.

However, all of this remained in a continual state of evolution. No model of colonial government incorporating French absolutism ever existed nor can such a thing even be attributed to Colbert or his successors. Nor could one exist as long as idiosyncrasy remained the hallmark of the *ancien régime*. Whether authority was executive, legislative, judicial, military, or religious, in the French colonies it was intensely personal and remained in a continual state of becoming during the 60 years after 1670 and long after that.

The marquis de Seignelay, who succeeded his father as secretary of state and minister for the marine, was subjected to a pitiless regimen of training in preparation for the job from the time he reached 17 years of age.[24] After 1672, Seignelay became so closely involved in naval and colonial administration that it is not always easy to determine whether he or his father signed the colonial dispatches.[25] The death of his father in September of 1683 ushered in a new stage in Seignelay's career, and during the next seven years the construction of the navy and its logistical support system held a higher priority than colonial development. Possessing an iron will and enormous energy, Seignelay sought to make the French navy the primary instrument of French state power. Against staggering odds he succeeded in a few short years in fitting out fleets that approached in power the combined strength of the Anglo-Dutch naval forces arrayed against France. His ceaseless activity was combined with an epicurean lifestyle that led him to burn the candle at both ends. Sick unto death, he died in November of 1690, having seen the

---

[24] See Dessert, *La Royale*, 30–2.
[25] W. J. Eccles, *Frontenac, the Courtier Governor* (Toronto: McClelland and Stewart, 1959), 203n uses Colbert's brutal assessments of his son unfairly to characterise him as lazy and possessing limited ability. See Cole, *Colbert and a Century of French Mercantilism*, 1: 321–2 for a more balanced evaluation. A fuller treatment of Seignelay's career may be found in Laurent Dingli, *Colbert, marquis de Seignelay: le fils flamboyant* (Paris: Librairie Académique Perrin, 1997).

king's fleet win the greatest naval victory in its history rendered ineffective by the failure the previous year of Louis XIV's Irish campaign to restore James II to the English throne.[26]

The appointment of Louis Phélypeaux, comte de Pontchartrain, to become secretary of state of the royal household and to succeed Seignelay at the naval ministry may have surprised the Court, including the new appointee himself, but a certain logic was present. He had become the controller-general of finances in 1689, and like Colbert before him, was entrusted with the economy, finances, and the colonies during wartime. Pontchartrain belonged to one of the most powerful robe families in the kingdom, but the subordination of the war effort to finance drove him into the arms of the great entrepreneurs of privateering and the slave trade, some of whom married into his family.[27] Devout and possessing all the talents, training, and character of a member of his caste, Louis Phélypeaux was hard-working, pragmatic, and able to devise expedients with speed and decision. His career illustrates the strength of the Old Regime. Traditionally condemned as the gravedigger of the French navy, including the colonies, he further resembled Colbert in being forced to subordinate the war to finance.[28] In 1699, his job was done. The king appointed his faithful servant to the senior but largely honorific posts of chancellor and keeper of the seals. His son Jérôme succeeded to the navy department until 1715, and his grandson, the comte de Maurepas, followed in the same office in 1723.

Jérôme Phélypeaux became marquis de Pontchartrain in 1699. Heavy-jowled, thick-lipped, hunchbacked, one-eyed thanks to smallpox, and wearing a glass eye in an ill-fitting, weeping socket, he has never escaped his reputation as a loathsome beast with which the duc de Saint-Simon endowed him. Trained by his father in the details of naval and colonial administration and granted the succession to his father's two ministries, Jérôme Phélypeaux possessed a sharp analytical mind and a passion for work.[29] He was not a good judge of character though, and this failing clouded an otherwise sound judgment and hid a strong measure of humanitarian concern for sailors, dockyard workers, and the poor.[30] The harshness of the times

26   Geoffrey Symcox, *The Crisis of French Sea Power: From the guerre d'escadre to the guerre de course* (The Hague: Martinius Nijhoff, 1973), 102.

27   Lionel Rothkrug, *Opposition to Louis XIV; The Political and Social Origins of the French Enlightenment* (Princeton: Princeton University Press, 1965), 431–2.

28   Charles de La Roncière, *Histoire de la marine française*, 6 vols. (Paris: Plon, 1909–1932), 6: 81–4.

29   John C. Rule, "Jérôme Phélypeaux, comte de Pontchartrain and the Establishment of Louisiana, 1696–1715" in *Frenchmen and French Ways in the Mississippi Valley*, ed., John F. McDermott, (Urbana: University of Illinois Press, 1969), 179–97.

30   Dale Miquelon, *New France, 1701–1744, "A Supplement to Europe"* (Toronto: McClelland and Stewart, 1987), 9–13; and Marcel Giraud, "Crise de conscience et d'autorité à la fin du règne de Louis XIV", *Annales, E.S.C.* (Apr.–Sept. 1952), 172–90, 293–302.

during the War of the Spanish Succession pushed him to privilege the economy and finance over the military. He defended colonial interests when he could, but he was not a minister of state; he did not enter the Royal Council. Nor was he controller-general of finances, which further reduced his influence. Moreover, the controller-general of finances from 1701 to 1715 was Nicolas Desmaretz, Colbert's nephew, whose possession of office reflected the marginalisation of the navy and colonies in the government's planning and priorities during the war. Wartime exigencies overwhelmed Pontchartrain, leaving him unable to prevent either the controller-general of finances or the minister of foreign affairs from encroaching on his ministry, including colonies.[31]

The thirty years following Colbert's death were characterised by war and insecurity. The Franco-Dutch War of 1672–78 was only a precursor to much harsher struggles during the quarter century between 1688 and 1713. The American colonies became increasingly more involved in European wars and, toward the end of the period, were virtually abandoned as France poured out its human, material, and financial treasure on the battlefields of Europe. The island of Sainte-Croix reverted to its original proprietors, the Knights of Malta, and any French dream of empire in the interior of North America lay in ruins in the shambles that was Louisiana. By 1713, France and her colonies faced bankruptcy. The aging king was driven to cede Acadia, Newfoundland, and Hudson Bay in the north and St. Christopher in the south in order to achieve peace. If the Treaty of Utrecht checked Louis XIV's ambition of universal monarchy, he and his successors moved swiftly to compensate for the territorial losses.

Even before the war was concluded, French officials were considering a new strategic placement on Cape Breton Island. Louis XIV's death on 1 September 1715 signaled a change in colonial administration. The heir and successor, the late king's great-grandson, was a five-year-old orphan, and the governance of France fell to his great-uncle, Philippe, duc d'Orléans. The Regent of France, as he became known, suppressed the system of government established by Louis XIV, replacing the great secretaries of state by six administrative councils known collectively to history as the *polysynodie*. The comte de Pontchartrain surrendered his office, and responsibility for colonies was transferred to one of them, the *Conseil de Marine* or Navy Council, headed by Louis XIV's natural son, the comte de Toulouse, assisted by his brother-in-law, Vice-Admiral and Marshal of France Victor-Marie, comte d'Estrées. The council supervised French colonial affairs until 1723.

The Navy Council introduced several changes that can only be classified as attempts to make the colonial administration more efficient, but Louis XIV's administrative legacy was too strong for any real change to occur.

[31] Meyer, *Colbert*, 185–6; Dessert, *La Royale*, 33–4.

Nevertheless, much was done that bore fruit later. Though colonies were low on the Regent's list of priorities to revive the country, the Navy Council drafted and passed much useful colonial legislation affecting trade in general and the slave trade in particular. The Regent was persuaded to put Louisiana at the heart of John Law's system of financial renewal, and while this was not one of his successes, the establishment of a new base for the French fishery on Île Royale was. The failure of John Law's "system" led French policy away from the Americas to focus on relations with the Levant, Spain, and the rest of Europe.[32] The economic development of the West Indies moved forward largely on its own, maintaining the momentum generated during the recently concluded war and profiting from the Navy Council's new legislation. Metropolitan authorities under the Regency also displayed both wisdom and restraint in dealing with the most serious colonial revolts in French history at Martinique and Saint-Domingue.

The Regency Council disappeared on 25 February 1723, when Louis XV declared his majority. On 10 May, Cardinal Dubois informed the Navy Council of its suppression and that henceforth the comte de Morville would fulfill the functions of secretary of state for the marine.[33] Three months later, following Dubois' own death, the king confided the ministry of foreign affairs to Morville, and 22-year-old Jean-Frédéric Phélypeaux, comte de Maurepas, assumed the marine vacated by his father a decade before.[34] For the next two years Maurepas held the office under the tutelage of his mentor and father-in-law, Louis Phélypeaux, marquis de La Vrillière, and thereafter on his own until 1749.[35]

Maurepas' arrival at the ministry of marine marked no new departure. Like his father, he did not immediately become a member of the Royal Council, and many years passed before he did. Colonies continued to occupy a low place among the government's concerns. Maurepas consolidated much that had been initiated during the Regency and before. His most important act occurred in October of 1727 when he sponsored new letters patent intended to halt foreign trade with the colonies. Its chief thrust freed up trade with France in order to preserve the important illusion that absolutism was in

[32] Jeremy Black, *Natural and Necessary Enemies; Anglo-French Relations in the Eighteenth Century* (London: Duckworth, 1986), 42; Armin Reese, *Europäische Hegemonie und France d'outre mer. Kolonial Fragen in der franzosischen Aussenpolitik, 1700–1763*, (Stuttgart, 1988), 160.

[33] Antoine, *Le Conseil du roi*, 118–19, n. 4; and Sydney Daney, *Histoire de la Martinique depuis la colonisation jusqu'en 1815*, 3 vols. (Fort-de-France: Société d'histoire de la Martinique, [1846] 1963), 2: 52.

[34] Marine, B² 267, ff. 208v-9 Morville to Beauharnois, 14 August 1723; ibid., f. 683-3v Maurepas to same, 5 December 1723.

[35] For an evaluation of Maurepas see James Pritchard, *Anatomy of a Naval Disaster: The 1746 French Expedition to North America* (Montreal and Kingston: McGill-Queen's University Press, 1995), 21–2.

control.[36] Maurepas' view of the *pacte coloniale* was more rigid than Colbert's. The letters patent were far more than a reiteration of all that had gone before in prohibiting foreigners from trading in French America. It was the most savage piece of colonial economic legislation ever promulgated. The severity of the penalties made the letters unenforceable.[37] Nevertheless, the letters patent of 1727 remained the basic document regulating French colonial trade until the end of the Seven Years' War. The government's ability to control remained as ineffective in 1730 as it had been 60 years before. Examining the interaction of governors, intendants, and the courts with the colonists and their worlds makes clear what little influence the government really wielded.

5.4 COLONIAL GOVERNMENT

Colonial governments emerged as pragmatic responses to local needs. They owed their form chiefly to demographic increase, social development, political exigency, economic activity, and territorial expansion rather than to the distant, metropolitan authority that imposed them.[38] While the basic building blocks of government were put into place during the twenty years following the return of the colonies to the crown, they continued to grow in response to local requirements. Though the king announced his intention to establish admiralty courts in 1672, for example, 45 years passed before the first court of this kind was established at Martinique.[39] French absolutism did not impose a clearcut chain of command between the king and the lowest colonial official in his service – far from it. Colonial administration continually evolved for more than half a century after 1670. Its chief characteristics were patriarchal, patronage- and clientage-based, and noncapitalist.

After extinguishing the seigneurial rights of the various proprietors of the colonies in New France and the Windward Islands, Louis XIV replaced the governing structures with one more closely resembling a royal province with a governor, intendant, and sovereign council, but the similarity was only proximate. French provincial administrations were not headed by governors-general, nor did all colonies possess intendants or sovereign courts. For

---

[36] Colonies, Série A, 25, ff. 83v-90 Lettres patentes du roy, October 1727.

[37] Cf. Miquelon, *New France, 1701–1744*, 91; Pierre-Regis Dessaulles, fils, *Annales de la conseil souverain de la Martinique, ou Tableau Historique du Gouvernement de cette colonie depuis son premier établissement jusqu'a nos jours*, 2 vols. Reprinted (Fort-de-France and Paris: Société des Amis des Archives/L'Harmattan, 1995), 2: 3; and Daney, *Histoire de la Martinique*, 2: 72–3.

[38] For a detailed discussion from this point of view see André Vachon, "Administration", *DCB*, 2: xv–xxv.

[39] Dessalles, *Annales du conseil souverain de la Martinique*, 1: 467–8.

many years governors remained the only legally constituted authority in several colonies. The decision to endow colonial governments with intendants emerged slowly in response to local needs. Governors held all military and civil powers until the sovereign courts assumed civil and judicial powers. Thus, while colonial governors were assisted by king's lieutenants, town majors, and deputy town majors as might be found in France, New France and the West Indies were each headed by governors-general who resided at Quebec and at Fort Royal. Two governors resided at Montreal and Trois Rivières in New France, and others appeared later on at Port Royal, New Orleans, and Louisbourg. In the West Indies, governors initially existed on each of the islands and at Cayenne and Saint-Domingue.

A third governor-general was appointed in 1714 when the incumbent governor of Saint-Domingue became governor-general of the Leeward Islands (*Isles sous le vent*). Following the recall of Governor Choiseul-Beaupré from Saint-Domingue in 1710, the governor of Martinique, Nicolas de Gabaret, was named interim governor to replace him. However, this wealthy planter in the Lesser Antilles refused to take the position, and the commandant of Saint-Domingue's north coast, formerly the governor of Sainte-Croix, assumed the position. Two years later Louis de Courbon, comte de Blénac, son of the former governor-general of the Windward Islands, arrived bearing the unheard of title of governor of Saint-Domingue and lieutenant general of the islands, but his official appointment, making him the third governor-general in the Americas, occurred only in 1714.[40] The isolation of the colony's three districts from one another led to three governors being appointed under him, at St. Louis, Léogane, and Cap Français. All of these appointments simply acknowledged Saint-Domingue's growing population and economic development. They did not mirror Blénac's influence, the metropolitan government's imperial ambition, or a desire to rationalise colonial administration.

The first two governors-general of the West Indies, Jean-Charles de Baas and Charles de Courbon, comte de Blénac, with one brief exception, governed for 27 years (1669–96).[41] Louis de Buade, comte de Frontenac, governed New France for 20 years (1672–82 and 1689–98).[42] All three, iron men of the "iron" century, possessed strong personalities. Their naval officer successors in the West Indies, many of whom were carried off by yellow fever, were not as impressive. Regrettably, only a few modern studies

40 Pierre-François-Xavier Charlevoix, *Histoire de l'Isle espagnol de S. Domingue, ecrit particulièrement sur les mémoires manuscrits du P. Jean-Baptiste Le Pers*, 2 vols. (Paris: Jacques Guerin, 1730–31), 2: 388.

41 See André Baudrit, "Charles de Courbon, comte de Blénac (1622–1694)", *Mémoires de la Société d' Histoire de la Martinique*, 2 (1967), 1–205.

42 William J. Eccles, *Frontenac, The Courtier Governor* (Toronto: McClelland and Stewart, 1959) is a demolition of the myth created by Francis Parkman, *Count Frontenanc and New France under Louis XIV* (Boston: [many editions] 1877).

of French colonial governors exist.[43] The dilemmas and challenges that a governor-general faced are well-illustrated, however, by the career of Philippe de Rigaud de Vaudreuil who governed New France for nearly a quarter of a century from 1703 to 1725, guiding the colony through the greatest military and economic threats to its existence.[44] In contending with the Crown, the Indians, English colonists, and the ambitions of men at Detroit and in Louisiana, he had to be all things to all people, loyal servant of the king, but also protector and promoter of colonial interests. His many roles as arbitrator, negotiator, soldier, diplomat, politician, economist, and tactician as well as *bon père de famille*, illustrate the nature of the constantly negotiated and constructed authority and power in the colonies.

Intendants appeared in the colonies only gradually. The creation of the West India Company and the arrival of its agents in the colonies hindered their appearance in the West Indies for 15 years. The first one named to New France in 1663 never sailed to the colony. Instead, civil administration was placed in the hands of a Sovereign Council created the same year. The council was comprised of the governor-general, the vicar apostolic, or in his absence the senior cleric in the colony, five councillors, an attorney general, a recorder (*greffier*), and a bailiff (*huissier*).[45] At that time, the legislative, executive, and judicial powers in the colony were divided between the new governor-general and the council under the direct authority of the king. Two sovereign councils were created at Martinique and Guadeloupe the next year. Nothing appeared to be simpler, but the very next year, the creation of the West India Company, granting it full ownership of all the colonies in America, thereby returning them to seigneurial rule, albeit in mitigated form, introduced complications. Until 1674, colonial governments remained poorly formed and ineffective as company agents interfered with the setting up of royal governments.

The king had not extinguished all the rights of the former proprietors before creating the new company, leaving the latter to deal with the difficult task of accommodating their demands. Indecision over the appointment of intendants dragged on. The king appointed the second intendant of New France in 1665, but the decision to make intendants a permanent part of colonial administration remained in the future.[46] Governor-General Frontenac and the sovereign council shared the colony's civil administration between

43 Philippe Hrodej, *L'Amiral Du Casse: l'Élévation d'un Gascon sous Louis XIV*, 2 vols. (Paris: Librairie de l'Inde, 1999) is welcome although it deals chiefly with his maritime and naval career rather than his administration of Saint-Domingue.

44 Yves F. Zoltvany, *Philippe de Rigaud de Vaudreuil, Governor of New France, 1703–1725* (Toronto: McClelland and Stewart, 1974).

45 Raymond Du Bois Cahall, *The Sovereign Council of New France: A Study in Canadian Constitutional History* (New York: Columbia University Press, 1915), 22.

46 On Talon see André Vachon, "Talon", *DCB*, 1: 614–32.

1672 and 1675, which was quite in keeping with conditions in the West Indies, where Governor-General de Baas governed the colonies in conjunction with three Sovereign Councils.[47] Colbert never trusted the masterless men of Saint-Domingue, who continued to be ruled by a governor alone until after his death. The marquis de Seignelay established the colony's first sovereign council at Petit Goâve in 1685. In Cayenne, governors acted alone until 1703, and in Louisiana, they did so until 1714.

Jacques Duchesneau's appointment to New France in 1675 was a direct response to growing chaos in the colonial government owing to Governor-General Frontenac's quarrel with the councillors of the Sovereign Council. He continually interfered in their efforts to investigate his allegations against two critics of his behaviour.[48] As a consequence, Duchesneau arrived bearing a royal judgement which reorganised the Sovereign Council, increasing the number of councillors to seven and making their appointments independent of the governor. Intended to resolve difficulties and smooth the way for a more efficient conduct of business, the intendant's appointment did no such thing. For the next seven years, the governor-general and intendant quarrelled to such an extent that Colbert finally recalled both men in 1682.[49] In the islands, the comte de Blénac quarrelled continually with intendants Jean-Baptiste Patoulet and Gabriel Dumaitz de Goimpy. Only his absence during most of Michel Bégon's term prevented similar bad relations from developing with the island's second intendant.[50] The first colonial intendants were connected to Colbert and the worlds of law and finance, but increasingly royal administrators were to be connected to the ministry of the marine.

Local needs led to Jean-Baptiste Patoulet's appointment as the first intendant of the Antilles in 1679. Patoulet's career illustrates both the growing importance of local experience in making colonial appointments and the rapidly expanding connection between the colonial and naval administrations. He initially arrived in the colonies in 1665 as Jean Talon's private secretary. He sailed to France two years later but returned the next season with Claude de Boutroue, who greatly appreciated his talents. He sailed again to France in 1670 and was promoted to navy commissary (*commissaire de la marine*) before immediately sailing to Acadia, and then on to New France to serve again under Talon at Quebec. Though Talon recommended him as his replacement, Patoulet returned to France in 1672.[51] Afterwards, he served as senior navy commissary in Vice-Admiral d'Estées' two expeditions to the

---

47   Col., F³, 53, ff. 47–8 Lettres patentes pour l'établissement du conseil souveraine de l'isle de St. Christophe du 17 décembre 1670.

48   Eccles, *Canada under Louis XIV*, 89–98.

49   Eccles, *Frontenac*, 127–56 for a full account of those years.

50   Baudrit, "Charles de Courbon, comte de Blénac", 52–9.

51   J. Eccles, "Patoulet, Jean-Baptiste" and " Boutroue, Claude de", *DCB*, 1, 119–20, 534.

West Indies. The important reports that he prepared on problems related to these naval operations largely account for his appointment to the West Indies in 1679.[52] Recalled to France in 1682, where he became intendant of Dunkirk, he died there in 1695. Writing a year before Patoulet's death, the comte de Pontchartrain praised his honesty, agreeable manner, and conscientious attention to duty.

Patoulet provides an excellent example of the high calibre of royal servants Colbert brought into the navy. Their service in the colonies set a precedent, gradually becoming a prerequisite during the next century for further advancement in the hierarchy of naval administration. This, however, was no modern bureaucracy in the making. Venality of office was excluded from the navy, but it was not very far away in the tax-farmers of the Western Domain and treasurers-general of the marine. Family, patronage, and clientage prevailed over talent or administrative norms. Michel Bégon, son of an intendant of the West Indies and himself intendant of New France for 14 years, was brother-in-law to a former intendant and a future governor-general of the same colony.[53] Through his marriage to Elisabeth de Beauharnois he was related to Pontchartrain, who was notorious for making rash colonial appointments. In 1709, in the midst of war, he arranged for Louis XIV to appoint his cousin, Raymond-Balthzar, marquis de Phélypeaux, as governor-general of the Windward Islands despite his reputation for sloth and idleness. The chief reason for the appointment was to keep this courtier away from court, where his presence had become unacceptable, yet provide him with a comfortable income.[54] Abraham Duquesne-Guitton was appointed governor-general of the Windward Islands as a reward for abjuring his Protestant faith. Pontchartrain created the colonial bureau as a sinecure for his cousin, Antoine-Denis Raudot, former intendant of Canada, rather than from a desire to rationalise the central administration of the colonies.[55] Though deserving promotion in the administration, Raudot owed his rapid advancement to his family connection rather than to his intelligence and ability. Absolutism continued to be characterised by the rule of men rather than law.

Between 1680 and 1718, two intendants headed the civil administrations of New France and the West Indies. As time passed they were aided by a small but growing number of naval commissaries, storekeepers, writers, and clerks who were chiefly occupied with recordkeeping, issuing pay orders and stores,

52 See Chapter 6.
53 Yvonne Bezard *Fonctionnaires maritimes et coloniaux sous Louis XIV, les Bégon* (Paris: Éditions Albin Michel, 1932).
54 Jacques Petitjean-Roget, *La Gaoulé, la révolte de la Martinique en 1717* (Fort-de-France: Société d'histoire de la Martinique, 1966), 114–16.
55 Col., B 36, f. 87 Pontchartrain to Duquesne-Guitton, 28 February, 1714; Donald Horton, "Raudot, Antoine-Denis", *DCB*, 2: 549–54.

and accounting for their disbursements. A naval commissary ordinarily resided at Montreal as the intendant's subdelegate, and later *commissaires-ordonnateurs* served at Louisiana and Île Royale and at Cap Français in the West Indies, but some governors continued to exercise their powers alone. Acadia was one such jurisdiction; no Sovereign Council ever appeared there.

Financial commissaries, called *ordonnateurs*, were like junior intendants, possessing many of the latter's powers without the accompanying prestige. They were normally commissioned naval commissaries – officers of the pen – who had been given the all-important authority to issue orders to treasurers to make payments on behalf of colonial governments. French colonial governments did not have revenues, nor did they spend funds in the way modern readers might assume. Intendants and *ordonnateurs* were solely authorised to order payments to be made on behalf of the government. They never saw a sou of the funds assigned to meet a colony's expenses, nor did they control those who received, held, managed, and paid those funds. Governors continued to possess all civil, judicial, as well as military authority in the northern district of St. Domingue until 1704, when André Deslandes, a former director of the French East India and Asiento Companies, arrived to be the colony's first *ordonnateur* and to establish a Superior Council at Cap Français, which he did the following year. Only then did the governor of Saint-Domingue have to share his powers. Deslandes died in 1706, and the old arrangements continued until a new financial commissary arrived in 1708.[56]

A third colonial intendant appeared in 1718. Commissary Jean-Jacques Mithon de Senneville had been in the West Indies since 1697 serving under Intendant Robert at Martinique. He was named a councillor to the colony's Superior Council in 1703, and five years later became *ordonnateur* of Saint-Domingue. Ten years passed, however, before he was named the first intendant of the Leeward Islands on 9 August 1718.[57] Once again, local needs account for the delay and explain the appointment.

Following Maurepas' assumption of sole direction of the Ministry of Marine, he may have tried to reassert metropolitan control over the administration of the two largest colonies in America, Saint-Domingue and New France, especially as the first intendant he appointed, Claude-Thomas Dupuy, had such a disruptive influence. In 1725, Jean-Baptiste Dubois-Duclos, and in 1728, Gilles Hocquart were appointed *ordonnateurs* of their respective colonies of Saint-Domingue and Canada. Though Saint-Domingue had had an intendant for eight years and Duclos had served as financial commissary at Le Cap, he was only promoted after four years. Despite Canada having had an intendant for half a century, Gilles Hocquart remained at

---

56   Charlevoix, *Histoire de l'Isle espagnol de S. Domingue*, 2: 384-5.
57   Etienne Taillemite, *Inventaire analytique de la correspondence générale avec les colonies, Départ, série B*, vol. I (Paris: Ministère de la France d'Outre-mer, 1959), 301.

Table 5.1. *Colonial Sovereign Courts by Date of Establishment*

Location	Date
Quebec	April 1663
Martinique	11 October 1664
Guadeloupe	"
Saint Christopher	17 December 1670
Petit Goâve	August 1686
Léogane	?
Cap Français	June 1702
Cayenne	1703
New Orleans	18 December 1714
Louisbourg	September 1717

Sources: Col., A 21, f. 54; A 22, f. 19; Col., B 2, f. 143; B 3, f. 114. B 9, ff. 24 and 26; B 11, f. 188v; B 24, f. 299; C^{8A} 14, f. 14.

Quebec on probation until 1731, when he was finally named intendant. Whatever the secretary of state's motives, these measures could have affected only their personal behavior. By the late 1720s, the structure of colonial administration was firmly in place.

During this long period following Colbert's death the most important changes in French colonial government affected the Sovereign Councils, called Superior Councils after 1703 (see Table 5.1). By then the number of councillors had increased to 12. As governors vigorously defended their own prerogatives – indeed, sought to expand them – and intendants aggressively asserted their own extended powers of justice, police, and finances in the face of all contenders, the councils gradually lost their legislative and executive powers and evolved into the senior colonial appellate courts.[58] Indeed, the term *Conseil Superieur* might better be translated as High Court. The struggle was long and had not ended by 1730, but during the process the councils became the major institution for articulating, if not establishing, colonial identities and developing local politics. Although only three governors-general and three intendants held colonial appointments at any one time, by the 1720s the number of colonial high courts had grown to nine, each with 12 councillors chosen from among influential persons, and although appointed by the king, they could not help but be representatives of the major economic and social interests in each colony. In New France, for example,

[58] Cahall, *The Sovereign Council of New France*, 200–1.

31 councillors were appointed to the Council during the six decades after 1669, and virtually all were important men in the colony.[59]

If the judicial system was a strength introduced into the colonies, the administration of finances was not. French absolutism was built on the wreckage of a medieval system of finance. Particularly debilitating was the government's need to rely on tax-farmers, private tax gatherers, and treasurers organised into powerful corps of *officiers* who made it impossible to establish a system of salaried employees to collect and disburse the state's revenues or to establish a national debt on a sound basis.

The colonies were not subject to the most hated taxes in France, the head and salt taxes (*taille* and *gabelle*). In the West Indies, neither the tithe (*dîme*) nor feudal dues were collected. Following the demise of the West India Company, Colbert assigned the obligation to meet colonial expenses to the tax-farmer of the Western Domain and the treasurers-general of the marine, who installed their agents in the colonies at Quebec, St. Pierre, and later at Petit Goâve, Cap Français, New Orleans, and Louisbourg. These men collected the capitation duty, payable in sugar, levied on all males, free, indentured, and slave, between the ages of 14 and 60, a few other special levies, and all fines and confiscations in the West Indies. In New France, they collected a tax of one-quarter of the value of all beaver furs exported from the colony to 1702 and other special levies, fines, and confiscations. Clearly understanding the relation between political representation and direct taxation, Pontchartrain refused to introduce the latter into the colonies.[60] Agents of the treasurers-general and the tax-farmers were not royal officials. They were employees of private financiers who mingled the king's funds with their own, accepting the kings revenues with one hand and paying the king's expenses with the other. In the absence of a central banking system, tax-farmers provided the treasury with short-term credit to cover the difference between current expenditures and often delayed tax receipts. Their power lay in providing short-term credit to cover the gaps between slow, uneven flows in and rapid, uneven flows out. This indispensable service and the sums collected through the sale of offices forced the state into their hands.[61] Here lay the heart of absolutism's ambiguity, revealing the disproportion between the splendour of the French monarchy and its institutions and its crippled underpinnings. For all of Louis XIV's and his ministers' desires to give France a unitary government, they lacked sufficient power to ignore the privileges of the provinces,

59   J. Delalande, *Le Conseil souverain de la Nouvelle France* (Québec: Imprimeur de roi, 1927), 117–24 gives a list of appointees.
60   Y. F. Zoltvany, ed., *The Government of New France: Royal, Clerical, or Class Rule?* (Scarborough: Prentice-Hall of Canada, 1971), 15–16.
61   De Vries, *The Economy of Europe*, 201; see also J. F. Bosher, "Government and Private Interests in New France", *Canadian Public Administration*, 11 (June 1967), 244–57.

the legal particularism of local and regional parlements and estates, and the special interests of corps of *officiers,* tax gatherers, and other financiers.

The careers of two colonial treasurers illustrate the blurring of distinctions between public and private and the influence of financial officers. Jean Petit, who succeeded his uncle as treasurer in New France in 1701, married the daughter of a seigneur soon after arriving in Canada and later obtained half a seigneury. He was admitted to the Superior Council shortly before his death in 1720.[62] The case of his successor, Nicolas Lanouillier de Boisclerc, appointed treasurer in 1720, is more interesting. During the next decade, Lanouillier loaned merchandise to colonial officials at local retail prices as advances on their salaries, which he sent back to Paris as bills of exchange drawn on the treasurers-general of the marine. In Paris, Lanouillier's father used the sums realised from the bills to purchase merchandise to ship to Quebec. This was entirely legal, but Lanouillier's practice began to unravel as he overextended credit to men who were poor businessmen and bad risks. He was caught short of funds to meet pay orders issued by intendants, who ironically were among his greatest debtors. When arrested in 1730, Lanouillier's books revealed a deficit to the Crown of 300,000 livres. What he owed to private merchants in the colony is unclear,[63] but the affairs of treasurers and tax-gatherers in the colonies clearly reveal the government's underlying weakness.

5.5 COLONIAL JUSTICE

Justice was the primary responsibility of the kings of France. The same was true in the colonies. It was through the judicial and legal systems imposed on the colonies that the Crown directly delivered the popular experience of justice. The king did not tolerate governors' attempts to subrogate any judicial powers to themselves. The leading law officers in each colony, the intendant and attorney-general (*procureur général*), were appointed in France and were servants of the Crown, and despite claims of colonial sovereign councils, French laws did not have to be registered for them to be effective in the colonies.[64] Such was the appalling reputation of lawyers (*avocats*) that they were forbidden to practise in the colonies; few legal officials possessed any legal training, and there was no colonial bar. Until the Crown repossessed all the colonies during the 1660s, only seigneurial justice existed overseas. The

[62] W. S. Reid and B. Weilbrenner, "Petit, Jean", *DCB,* 2: 521.
[63] S. Dale Standen, "Lanouillier de Boisclerc, Nicolas", *DCB,* 3: 352–3.
[64] The following section on colonial law is heavily indebted to John A. Dickinson, *Justice et justiciables, la procédure civile à la Prévôté de Québec, 1667–1759* (Québec: Les Presses de l'université Laval, 1982) and his succinct summary, *Law in New France,* Canadian History Project, Working Paper Series (Winnipeg: University of Manitoba, 1992).

king easily and swiftly imposed a new juridical order throughout America. A single body of customary law called the Custom of Paris, a system of weights and measures, and a common civil procedure were adopted. A common criminal law was also introduced following the edict of 1673. Existing seigneurial courts in New France continued to operate and new ones appeared, for they chiefly settled disputes over money and enforced social hierarchy,[65] but throughout French America the king imposed a whole new system of royal justice. Like the administration, the judicial system evolved in response to local needs. Montreal's seigneurial court was replaced by a royal court, but only in 1693. Provisions for an admiralty court at Quebec were issued in France in 1699, but nearly a score of years passed before one was set one up, and then, chiefly to meet Intendant Bégon's needs for an additional source of patronage.[66] Royal courts were quickly established in the Windward Islands but did not appear in Saint-Domingue until 1685 at Petit Goâve, Cap Français, Port de Paix, and Léogane at the same time as the colony's first Sovereign Council.[67] The first royal judge only appeared at Cayenne in 1696.[68] In Louisiana, the Superior Council, provisionally established in 1714, served as the colony's only court, judging cases in first and second instances. It became permanent two years later.[69] The Bishop of Quebec created an ecclesiastical court in 1660 to deal with civil and criminal cases involving the clergy, but it was not officially recognized for nearly a quarter of a century.[70]

The presence of the West India Company instigated a struggle between its agents and royal officials over the administration of justice in the West Indies, but by 1670 the latter were clearly dominant and assumed complete control four years later. Both justice and law evolved in the colonies. In New France and the West Indies, the intendant was the first judicial officer in the colony. The governors-general were presidents of the Sovereign Councils, but from 1680 they were forbidden the title. Intendants acquired the greatest importance, presiding over sessions, taking opinions, collecting votes, and pronouncing judgement. They possessed enormous judicial authority, being able to hear cases in their own right and to pull cases out of other courts, including the Sovereign Council if they deemed it necessary.

The comte de Blénac resented this, and soon after Patoulet was appointed, he attempted to establish a militia council to judge settlers on the grounds that they were in military service. Colbert took strong exception to the

---

65 Colin M. Coates, *The Metamorphosis of Landscape and Community in Early Quebec* (Montreal and Kingston: McGill-Queen's University Press, 2000), 104–14.

66 Col., B 20, ff. 255v provisions de juge à l'amirauté, 30 May 1699.

67 Col., B 11, f. 192 provisions de juge, 6 August 1685.

68 Ibid., 18, f. 390v provisions de juge à Cayenne, 15 October 1696.

69 Marcel Giraud, *Histoire de la Louisiane française*, 4 vols. (Paris: Presses universitaires de France, 1953–1974), 1: 279–80.

70 Vachon, "The Administration of New France", *DCB*, 2: xxiv.

maneuver and ordered him never to do such a thing again.[71] Half a century later, Maurepas reprimanded Governor Saint Ovide of Île Royale for refusing to participate in sessions of the Superior Council.[72] Intendants also supervised the other courts, judges, and law officers to ensure obedience to all decrees, judgements, ordinances, and regulations. Naturally such great powers weighted the courts in favour of the Crown, but when the intendant was absent the weight shifted in favour of influential colonists. The Sovereign Council of New France was at its most important during the 1670s. When Intendant Robert left Martinique for France in 1704, leaving behind Jean-Jacques Mithon de Senneville as his subdelegate, he weakened the Crown's role in the administration of justice. As a navy commissary, Mithon had no connection with justice, nor could he preside over the Council. In Robert's absence, the senior councillor or "dean" of the Council was entrusted with powers normally exercised by the intendant.

The Sovereign Council acted as a court of first instance at Quebec until 1677. Royal courts called *prévôtés* or *sénéchausées* with both civil and criminal jurisdiction were established in Trois Rivières in 1667, Quebec in 1677, and Montreal in 1693. Similar courts appeared in each French colony in response to local needs. In 1721, for example, two were created in the southern district of Saint-Domingue at Saint-Louis and Jacmel.[73] Each was presided over by a judge (*lieutenant-général*) sometimes assisted by a deputy-judge (*lieutenant-particulier*), a king's attorney, a recorder, and several bailiffs. The latter were minor judicial officials who maintained order in the courts and enforced police regulations concerning fire prevention, town markets, public sanitation, respect in church, and road building. They were frequent targets of verbal abuse because their duties made them unpopular, and resistance to their authority was considered seditious. Invested with the king's authority, they also tended to be overbearing and self-important.[74]

The civil law in the French colonies was based on a comprehensive body of centuries-old property and family law called the Custom of Paris that was codified in 1579. It had little to say about commercial law and relations between masters and servants. The former was covered in the Code Marchand of 1673 and the latter by local edicts, police regulations, and ordinances issued by governors and Sovereign Councils or intendants. Specific colonial law was codified in 1685 and known as the Slave Code or Code Noir.[75] The

71 Dessalles, *Annales de la conseil souverain*, 1: 197 quoting from Colbert to Blénac, 11 June 1680; also Baudrit, "Charles de Courbon de Blénac", 88.
72 A. J. B. Johnston, *Control and Order in French Colonial Louisbourg, 1713–1758* (East Lansing: Michigan State University Press, 2001), 26.
73 Col., A 27, no. 6 Edit qui creée deux sénéchausées, 10 November 1721.
74 Peter Moogk, 'Thieving Buggers' and 'Stupid Sluts': Insults and Popular Culture in New France", *William and Mary Quarterly*, 3rd series, 36 (1979): 531.
75 An English translation may be found in *War, Diplomacy, and Imperialism*, ed. and trans., Geoffry Symcox (New York: Harper Torch Books, 1973), but for complete treatment

Slave Code did not break new ground. It codified the existing local order that had been developing during the previous half century, leaving to owners the right to order work and enforce discipline, excepting the use of mutilation and death. These were placed under judicial authority.

The most important point concerning French civil law in the colonies is that it identified the family as the fundamental unit in society rather than the individual. Individual rights were defined only by one's place in the family. The law sought to safeguard male authority within the family and the integrity of family property or patrimony. This was, of course, contrary to the new commercial reality of the times since it confined commerce in an essentially noncapitalist system deeply influenced by the canonical censure of usury. The absence of *retrait linager* in the islands, however, reveals how strongly the economics of the plantation complex reshaped notions of patrimony in the colonies.[76] Yet, a judgement of the Royal Council forbidding the seizure of slaves, boiling coppers, and/or livestock from working plantations for nonpayment of capitation duties or slave head taxes seriously limited freedom of action by denying absolute rights of property and the free distribution of one's goods.[77] The Custom of Paris limited the rights of individuals, including their right to alienate or dispose of property as they saw fit by sale or testament. Not surprisingly, there was little or no need for wills in French law.[78]

Civil procedure set down in the Civil Ordinance of 1667 was scrupulously observed in New France, where the courts became essentially debt collection agencies. Only 3.5 percent of the cases before the *prévôté* of Quebec involved criminal cases. Between 1685 and 1689 and again between 1715 and 1720, about three-quarters of all criminal cases concerned quarrels between neighbours that occasionally led to defamatory insults and malicious slander.[79] Personal reputation and honour mattered in French colonial culture. On the other hand, over one-half of all cases brought before the court during these same periods concerned commercial transactions or money owed for wages.[80] Very little of the court's attention was concerned with property

---

see Louis Sala-Molins, *Le Code Noir ou le calvaire de Canaan*, 3 éd., (Paris: Presses universitaires de France, [1987] 1993) for text and commentaries.

[76]   Col., C⁸ᴬ 36, ff. 158 internal memorandum for the minister 24 August 1726.

[77]   Col. B 9, f. 55v arrêt du conseil, 2 May 1679.

[78]   Yves F. Zoltvany, "Esquisse de la Coutume de Paris," *RHAF*, 25, 3 (décembre 1971), 367. Louise Dechêne, *Habitants and Merchants in Seventeenth Century Montreal*, trans. Liana Vardi (Kingston and Montreal: McGill-Queen's University Press [1974] 1992), 244–9 present a more flexible view of the inheritance provisions of the Custom of Paris.

[79]   Dickinson, *Justice et justiciables*, 117–18: also Peter N. Moogk, *La Nouvelle France: The Making of French Canada – A Cultural History* (East Lansing: Michigan State University Press, 2000), 136, 140, 216, 230, and 260 for several examples.

[80]   Dickinson, *Justice et justiciables*, 123.

cases, which indicates that notaries worked as effectively in the colonies as they did in France.

Royal notaries played a key role in French law. They were public officials recognised by the courts who drew up binding agreements that courts could not alter or break except in the very unlikely event that the notary had not drawn up a document as specified by the law.[81] Their chief occupation was with property, concessions, sales, leases, and exchanges. Secondarily, notaries dealt with families, dowries, marriage contracts, estate inventories, and deeds of gift. French colonial society could not have functioned without notaries.

French criminal law exercises a perennial if prurient fascination in English minds because it appears so alien, but all things considered it was fairer and more balanced than the operation of English criminal law at the time. Judges conducted trials in the colonies under the inquisitorial system of justice following procedure laid down in the Criminal Ordinance of 1673. Few colonial judges had training, as only the attorney-general of the Sovereign Council had to be a member of the Paris bar. Lack of legal training in the colonies does not appear to have been detrimental. Judges read the law carefully, and few people questioned their competence.[82] Criminal law with its secrecy and torture was probably as fair as the more open, brutal English adversarial system. Both systems sought to ensure social control and uphold the values of the state; unlike the English system, however, the French judicial system did not allow private criminal prosecutions and was remarkably free from scandal.

Theft was the most common crime punished in New France. Criminal justice dealt very severely with thefts, especially those committed at night. Sexual misdemeanors, rape, abortion, incest, bestiality, and adultery, followed by counterfeiting, were the next most common crimes committed in the seventeenth century.[83] Caning, branding, banishment, the galleys, and public shaming were the usual punishments,[84] but the extent of criminal activity in New France remains unknown because most reported cases occurred in the towns where only a minority of the population resided.

The law in the French colonies, John Dickinson concludes, mirrored the social structure favoured by the absolute monarchy. It was authoritarian and paternalistic. It also gave rise, at least in New France, to a profoundly

[81] Andre Vachon, *Histoire du notariat canadien, 1621–1960* (Quebec: Les Presses de l'université Laval, 1962), 16–35.

[82] See André Lachance, *La Justice Criminelle du roi au Canada au XVIIIe siècle* (Québec: Les Presses de l'université Laval, 1978).

[83] André Lachance, *Le Bourreau au Canada sous le régime française* (Québec: La sociétée historique du Québec, 1966), 47; Dickinson, "Crime and Law Enforcement", 409–11.

[84] Lachance, *Le Bourreau*, 36–44.

conservative outlook, for it transmitted religious moral values impregnated with tradition. It reinforced paternal authority, the sanctity of marriage, patrimony, and lineage. Fear of the power of female sexuality underlay much of the law, which also stressed hierarchy and the obligation to manage property carefully and to transmit it to the next generation. The law was insensitive to capitalist business practices as evidenced by secret mortgages, exemption of chattels from seizure for debt, insistence upon the integrity of patrimony within lineages, seigneurial monopolies, and protection afforded widows and orphans. Yet, it was not inflexible. The law continued to evolve in the colonies. As shown in the absence of *retrait linager* in the West Indies, jurisprudence and royal legislation modified it. The law did not prevent capitalism from flourishing in the French colonies of the ancien régime.

5.6 COLONIAL RESISTANCE

While royal justice prevailed in the colonies, the Crown's weak authority was nowhere more clearly revealed than in its mild response to colonial resistance between 1670 and 1730. Colbert's decision to halt contact between Dutch traders and colonists and the inability of the West India Company to supply the colonies led to serious trouble in Martinique in 1666 and provoked a major rebellion in the western district of Saint-Domingue four years later. The troubles of 1670–2, according to Charles Frostin, "gave birth to a true insurrectional tradition which continued to influence heavily the behaviour of the population".[85] Contrary to Louis XIV's practice in France, where disorders were ruthlessly suppressed, the government treated political disturbances in the colonies with relative mildness. No repression followed these first revolts in the West Indies. Still seeking to attract settlers, Colbert persuaded the king to grant a general amnesty to all the colonists on Saint-Domingue.[86] Such pragmatism speaks volumes against the existence of even a vision of empire.

Troubles broke out again in 1680 at Cap Français following the collapse of the French market for colonial tobacco and the enforcement of the Senegal Company's slave trade monopoly. With only 80 soldiers and the militia of doubtful loyalty in the face of 300 armed settlers, Governor Pouançay ended the disturbance by misleading them. He told the settlers that the Company

---

[85]   Charles Frostin, *Les Révoltes blanches à Saint-Domingue aux XVIIe et XVIIIe siècles (Haiti avant 1789)*, (Paris: L'École, 1975), 110. See Jean-Baptiste du Tertre, *Histoire générale des Antilles, habitées par les François*, 4 vols. (Paris: T. Jolly, 1667–1671), 3: 148–53 for a contemporary account of the initial attempt to establish the king's writ on Saint-Domingue.

[86]   Ibid., 94.

agents would henceforth trade only as private merchants. Fortunately the Senegal Company's bankruptcy the next year saved him from embarrassment, but there was no question of suppressing the populace.[87] The failure of the colonists to defend Saint-Domingue in 1691 and 1695 was partly the result of the deep divisions between rich and poor and also of the weak authority of the Crown.

As pawns in the growing rivalry between England and France, Acadian resistance took a unique form. Excluded from political authority, colonists isolated themselves from their rulers, who accused them of being seditious republicans. Acadians learned to coexist with both English and French so well that they referred to their New England neighbours as "our friends, the enemy".[88]

The situation differed somewhat in New France, where taxes never became an issue and commercial agriculture was negligible. Governor-General Vaudreuil dealt with two instances of habitant unrest with the mildest of measures. After some habitants had appeared under arms at Montreal to demand an end to engrossing of salt by local merchants in December of 1704, Vaudreuil gave one of the ringleaders a severe reprimand but, much to the disgust of the local governor, punished no one.[89] Thirteen years later, habitants on a seigneury stood to their arms over a matter of their forced labour on Montreal's fortifications. Hotheads among them insulted the governor-general, who could not let the insolence go unpunished, but his response could not have been milder. Following the pleas of other habitants that the rebels be pardoned, Vaudreuil agreed, saving the king's pleasure, on condition that the men be delivered to him. The ten contrite colonists voluntarily surrendered themselves and were confined in Montreal, but Vaudreuil released them at the onset of winter as their jail was so awful he feared that they would die if forced to remain; he pleaded with Versailles that they be pardoned. The Navy Council granted the request.[90] These were not serious examples of resistance. In neither case was sedition an issue. Governor-General Vaudreuil's response may well have reflected his paternalistic attitude toward the lower orders and his compassionate recognition of the harshness of their lives on the Canadian frontier, but it also illustrates the fragility of royal absolutism in the colonies. In 1730, Vaudreuil's less phlegmatic successor, the marquis de Beauharnois, requested that three companies of Swiss guards,

[87] Ibid., 122–3.
[88] Col., C^{11D} 4, ff. 55, 76v "Mémoire de ce qui regarde les Interets du roy ... " joined to Brouillon to Pontchartrain, 6 October 1701; ibid., Brouillon to Pontchartrain, 6 October 1702.; and ibid., ff. 278v-81 same to same, 25 November 1703. See also Jean Daigle, "Nos amis, les ennemis; relations commerciales de l'Acadie avec le Massachusetts, 1670–1711" (unpublished Ph.D. thesis, University of Maine, 1975).
[89] Zoltvany, *Philippe de Rigaud de Vaudreuil*, 57–8.
[90] Ibid., 156–7.

including German-speaking Protestants, be sent to Canada "to enforce the King's authority" as they were already doing elsewhere in the colonies.[91]

The weakness of metropolitan authority persisted because, while the government insisted on preserving a closed system of trade between France and the colonies, it could neither suppress smuggling nor ensure that an adequate amount of commercial shipping kept colonists supplied with goods or carried away their products. Royal authorities perforce had to collude. Smuggling was crucial to the economic development and growing prosperity of the colonies. A quarter century of warfare between 1688 and 1713 also moderated the tensions between colonists and their governments by uniting them in resistance against common enemies, but attempts to end the complicity of colonial officials, reassert crown rights, and force colonists to accept new taxes after the war quickly provoked resistance, including renewed insurrections in the West Indies.

Early in 1715, the new financial commissary at Louisbourg, Pierre de Soubras, attempted to collect a tax on alcohol sales to be used to build a hospital. This aroused widespread opposition from fishing interests, which forced him to drop the tax, and the hospital was built by the Crown.[92] In 1713, the metropolitan government introduced a tax called an *octroi* on slave holders and required that all merchants desiring to trade with foreign colonies purchase a passport from royal officials. The head tax was intended to force colonists to assume the costs of their defence, while the passports acknowledged that, as the government could not halt contraband, it might as well try to control and profit from it. The first protest came from Guadeloupe, where in June of 1715, 400 or 500 armed colonists called for the abolition of the *octroi* as being too onerous for a colony recovering from the devastation of a recent hurricane. They presented their appeal to king's lieutenant Coulet, who endorsed it to head off a revolt, or so he claimed. Governor La Malmaison believed Coulet was in league with the rebels but was powerless to do anything about it. In subsequent negotiations, the head tax was replaced by a tax on the island's trade, thereby forcing merchants to assume at least some of the burden initially placed entirely on planters.[93]

At Martinique, a general assembly of deputies agreed to the new tax under protest, but two years later conflict broke out again.[94] The protest in 1717

91 Robert Lionel Séguin, *La Civilisation traditionnelle de l'habitant aux XVIIe et XVIIIe siècles* (Montréal: Fides, 1967), 74; also Johnston, *Order and Control in French Colonial Louisbourg*, 47.

92 [Anonymous], "Soubras, Pierre-Auguste de", *DCB*, 2: 611.

93 Col., C^{8A} 20, ff. 349–53 Vaucresson to Pontchartrain, 21 June 1715; ibid., 268v-9, Duquesne to Pontchartrain, 5 July 1715. See also Robin Blackburn, *The Making of New World Slavery from the Baroque to the Modern, 1492–1800* (London and New York: Verso, 1997), 296.

94 Col., C^{8A}, 20, f. 276v Duquesne to Pontchartrain, 22 July 1715; Dessaulles, *Annales de la conseil souverain de la Martinique*, 1: 393–400.

was serious. Led by Latouche de Longpré whose extended family connections reinforced his influence, the revolt quickly forced the colonial authorities to abandon the levy on slaves. Colonial militia led by Colonel Jean Dubuc sided with the protesters, and after the authorities seized a Spanish ship which Latouche had chartered, Latouche and Dubuc arrested Governor-General La Varenne and Intendant Ricouart, accused them of arbitrary abuse of power, and deported them on the next ship sailing to France. The Superior Council then stepped in, confirmed the expulsion of its metropolitan leaders, and declared Martinique open to the trade of all nations.[95] The revolt became known as *La Gaoulé*, a creole word for rising.[96] French authorities greeted this astonishing activity, which included calls for independence and a republic, with the mildest of responses. Influential colonists quickly suppressed the aspirations of poor whites, and Colonel Dubuc surrendered his powers to king's lieutenant Pierre Lebègue, the island's veteran governor. A new governor-general and intendant were rushed to the colony with orders to adopt a conciliatory policy. Five infantry companies accompanied them to increase royal authority, and a general amnesty was declared in favour of all but four of Latouche's nephews, who left the island. Colonel Dubuc was briefly held, but lived to become the colony's most respected inhabitant and founder of a creole dynasty.[97]

However, the conflict between the Crown and Martinique's Superior Council continued amidst waning royal influence. In 1725, the latter refused to register the provisions naming a navy commissary as a councillor, but rather than strike down the council's refusal the king asked the council to amend its ruling. When this was refused, the commissary was appointed by royal letters patent.[98] A year later the king's lieutenant at St. Pierre complained to Maurepas about the Council's "independence" and "republican and tyrannical spirit", which was harassing him over two judgements he had recently disallowed.[99]

Colonial protest became more serious on Saint-Domingue where members of the Superior Councils imitated the colonial assembly of nearby Jamaica attempting to transform themselves into representative political bodies.[100]

95 Charles A. Julien, *Les Français en Amérique de 1713 à 1789*, 2 vols. (Paris: Centre de documentation universitaire, 1955), 1: 42.
96 Petitjean-Roget, *La Gaoulé, la révolte de la Martinique en 1717*, contains a fascinating if excessively detailed account, long on biography and narrative, but with extensive quotations from sources.
97 Michel Devèze, *Antilles, Guyane, la Mer des Caraïbesde 1492 à 1789* (Paris: SEDES, 1977), 229–31.
98 Daney, *Histoire de la Martinique*, 2: 68; Col., C^{8A} 35, ff. 99–103 Feuquières and Blondel to Maurepas, 3 August 1726.
99 Col., C^{8B} 9, no. 36 Du Rieux to Maurepas 15 April 1726 quoted in Kenneth Banks, "Communication and Imperial Absolutism", 167.
100 Paragraph based on Frostin, *Les Révoltes blanches*, 159–65.

As at Guadeloupe, the introduction of a head tax on slaves sparked the initial resistance, but on Saint-Domingue, where colonists had previously avoided paying any taxes at all, resistance was stronger. The government's weakness at the end of the war initially led it to try to co-opt the councils by having them set the amount of tax, the distribution of revenues, and the appointment of collectors. Councillors readily acquiesced, but two years later they suppressed the head tax and replaced it with duties on ships entering the colony and on indigo and sugar exports. They also imposed taxes payable by tavern and innkeepers on French wines, much to the fury of metropolitan merchants. The Councils did not stop there. They usurped the power of the governor and intendant by nominating agents, "commissaries", they called them, chosen from amongst themselves, to negotiate contracts for the repair and construction of fortifications and to inspect the regular troops in the colony. The entire system of government appeared overthrown.

A combination of metropolitan confusion arising from Louis XIV's death and changes in government administration, *la Gaoulé* at Martinique, and the weakness of the Regent in the face of parliamentary opposition in Paris led to inaction for nearly three years. Versailles did not respond until August of 1718, when the Navy Council disallowed the colonial legislation, suppressed the tax on shipping, reestablished the head tax on slave owners, and increased the duties on sugar exports. In order to put an end to "the infinite negligence" of the collectors of these revenues, the government ordered their receipts be remitted bimonthly to the clerk of the treasurers-general of the marine. Though the Crown reasserted authority, its response can only be considered mild. And well it might have been. Following a general tour of Martinique in 1720, Governor-General de Feuquières reported the colonists' loyalty was "very unsteady". He received no cooperation during his inspection; many militia officers failed to present themselves for review, and few local officials could be trusted. Colonists attributed the king's amnesty to their own power rather than to His Majesty's grace. "The interests of religion will not hold them for a moment", he concluded.[101]

On Saint-Domingue, in 1720, councillors claimed they must consent to new taxes in the name of the colonists, who held the ultimate right of consent because their fathers had conquered the island by force of arms.[102] The creation of the new India Company in the wake of the collapse of John Law's "system" was the chief cause of a year-long revolt that began late in 1722. The Company had acquired the rights to the slave trade previously possessed by the Saint-Domingue Company. The immediate cause was a new royal ordinance fixing the rate of exchange on foreign currency (i.e., Spanish pesos) at their real weight of silver, which meant a loss of about 20 percent

---

[101]   Col., C⁸ᴮ 6, no. 24 Extract from Feuquières to Navy Council, 17 April 1720.
[102]   Frostin, *Les Révoltes blanches*, 65.

to colonists.[103] The revolt first broke out among lower-class white women at Cap Français, who attacked the offices of the India Company. They were supported by men, bondsmen, small artisans, former buccaneers, and the like. The revolt reflected the persistence of deep class divisions that had existed in the colony since the 1690s and persisted throughout the eighteenth century. Some wealthy merchants and rich shippers from the French ports also became involved. In mid-1722, the India Company began to enforce its slave trade monopoly by refusing to issue trade licenses to independent traders.[104] French merchants spread rumours that the Company would seize all the colony's commerce, increase prices, and reduce the amount of goods available. The principal colonists seized the occasion to strike at their metropolitan creditors, who held large debts formerly worth one-quarter more and held in notes from Law's defunct bank.

Colonial authorities were powerless to resist demands that they abandon the India Company, send its local agents home, and accept regular sessions of the Superior Councils attended by deputies sent from the various districts in the colony to deliberate its general affairs. This transformed Saint-Domingue into a *pays d'etat*, where the king consulted provincial assemblies whose members voted and collected the *taille* or principal French property tax. On 1 March 1723, the Superior Council at Léogane renamed itself the Sovereign Council, directly challenging the king. Governor-General de Sorel and Intendant Mithon, fearing the Martiniquan "rising" was repeating itself, fled to the fort at Petit Goâve and requested military intervention from France. Reassertion of metropolitan authority only occurred in December with the arrival of a naval squadron commanded by the comte Denos de Champmeslin, appointed commandant of all French America, and carrying a new governor-general, Gaspard-Charles de Goussé, chevalier de la Rochalar to the colony.[105]

Cap Français's conciliatory Council, which had kept aloof from the attempted coup in the Western District, facilitated his task. Once again, the government ordered clemency in dealing with a colonial revolt. Champmeslin carried out an elaborate charade by accepting the "loyalty" of all. He annulled the agreement of 29 December 1722, but issued a general amnesty. The measures fixing the rate of exchange of foreign coin were not reestablished. Finally, the India Company lost its opportunity to trade for anything other than slaves at Saint-Domingue, and this concession lasted less than two years. In 1725, the Company reversed its monopolistic policy and began to sell licenses to private traders, reopening the slave trade until the Revolution.

---

103 See Joannès Tramond, "Les troubles de Saint-Domingue en 1722–1724", *RHC*, 22 (1929), 50; Frostin owes much of his third and fourth chapters to this lengthy article.

104 Robert Louis Stein, *The French Slave Trade in the Eighteenth Century: An Old Regime Business* (Madison: University of Wisconsin Press, 1979), 19.

105 See Frostin, *Les Revoltes blanches*, 219–65 for a full discussion.

The contraband trade was left intact and continued to contribute to Saint Domingue's growing economic development for the next 45 years. For all their obsession with control and fear that colonists would develop corporate identities, the kings of France and their secretaries of state for the marine were unable to control them. In effect, the colonists had won the struggle against the king's men and continued, as they had done all along, to make their own society.

5.7 CONCLUSION

While the French state appeared to rest on firm foundations of central administration, army, courts, and laws, features of colonial government continued to disturb the king and his minister of marine. Central institutions no more functioned in a sociopolitical vacuum in the colonies than they did at home. From the beginning of royal rule colonial subjects normally questioned, evaded, or modified laws. Only as a last resort did they obey them. Colonial governments operated a long way from France in societies that co-opted officials rather than confronted them. The comte de Blénac once complained that he was "the most forgotten gentleman of France".[106]

The politics of governing were just as important as the processes of administration. Officials had to negotiate obedience, not simply command it. Even secretaries of state were not free to give orders. Writing to a naval official at Placentia in 1700, Pontchartrain advised him to conciliate Malouin fish merchants, whom he wanted to contribute to the cost of fortifications. "Assure them", he wrote, "that I have no intention of punishing them. On the contrary, I seek only to please them and to establish secure bases during wartime".[107] Political maneuver was not alien to their own experience within the ministry of marine, and local officials did not always agree with the substance of laws and advice sent from France. Although they were the most important officers in the colonies, governors-general and intendants were part of a tripartite structure of power and agency that arose from a balance of interest groups that included other governing officials, the Church, and local elites. Colonial administration possessed little overt power. Opportunities for patronage in the colonies were limited. Government derived its authority and legitimacy from the king and the imperatives of administration. Its chief duty was to provide peace and order and to make the colonies pay or at least ensure that they did not cost too much.

The administration was not professionalised and displayed none of the complex articulations found in a nascent bureaucracy. Not even the

---

[106] Col. C⁸ᴬ 8, f. 64v Blénac to Pontchartrain, 20 March 1694.
[107] Thorpe, "Fish, Forts, and Finance: The Politics of French Construction at Placentia, 1699–1710", *Canadian Historical Association Historical Papers*, 1971, 59.

government viewed its administrators as faceless cogs in a machine. Colonial administration exhibited all of the signs of patronage and client networks that have been identified in French metropolitan administration. Jacques de Meulles and Michel Bégon de la Picardière, intendants of New France and the West Indies, respectively, during the 1680s, were brothers-in-law and related by marriage to Colbert. Bégon's son, also named Michel, later served as intendant of New France, and his younger brother, also Michel, was one of the comte de Pontchartrain's three private secretaries.[108] Almost all officials supplemented their stipends through participation in the colonial economies even though some, like the governor-general and intendant, were expressly forbidden to do so. Tarin de Cussy, to use just one example, arrived at Saint-Domingue in 1684 resembling a merchant rather than a governor. His critics accused him of landing 45 tons of wine, brandy, salt pork, flour, and dry goods. Two former members of Seignelay's entourage were his alleged partners.[109] The Crown continually sought to isolate colonial officials from local ties and pressures, but largely failed. Jacques-Charles de Bochart de Noray de Champigny, governor of Martinique since 1720 and governor-general of the Windward Islands from 1728 to 1748, was descended from the last proprietor of Guadeloupe and owned several plantations.[110] Philippe de Rigaud de Vaudreuil, governor-general of New France for nearly a quarter of a century, married a Canadian, Louise-Elisabeth de Joybert, who devoted her later years at Versailles to advancing the interests of her husband and creating careers for her sons, two of whom became governors-general of Saint-Domingue and New France, respectively, during the Seven Years' War. After winning the protection of Jérôme de Pontchartrain she became under-governess to the duc de Berry in 1712. She surrounded her husband with a large network of colonial clients recommending colonists for advancement and promotion.[111]

Despite its best efforts, the Crown could not even present a unified image of itself to colonists. Wherever the power of the French Crown appeared in the New World, it reached its subjects in fragmented form. In 1686, Intendant Jean Bochart de Champigny paid for and installed a bronze bust of Louis XIV in the center of the marketplace at Quebec, which was renamed Place Royale in honour of the occasion. Though clearly a vehicle for the glorification of the monarch and aggrandizement of his authority, merchants and tradespeople soon found the bust and its enclosure a nuisance. Someone proposed moving

[108] See Yvonne Bezard, *Fonctionnnaires maritimes et coloniaux sous Louis XIV: les Bégon* (Paris: Éditions Albin Michel, 1932).
[109] BN, Clairambault, 888, ff. 208–21 Mémoir [sur] la mauvais conduit du sieur de Cussi (n.d., post-1688).
[110] Michel Vergé-Franceschi, "Fortune et plantations des administrateurs coloniaux aux Iles d'Amérique aux XVIIe et XVIIIe siècles" dans *Commerce et plantations dans la Caraïbe XVIIe et XVIIIe siècles* (Bordeaux: Maison des Payes Ibériques, 1992), 115–42.
[111] Yves F. Zoltvany, "Joybert de Soulanges, Louise-Élisabeth", *DCB*, 3: 301–2.

it to the front of a house on the side of the square and subsequently into a recess above the door. Soon not even this would serve, and around 1700 the bust was removed to the intendant's palace, where it is believed to have been lost in a fire in 1713.[112] At Martinique, colonists resisted all efforts to move the intendant and sovereign council from the colony's commercial center of St. Pierre to Fort Royal, site of the governor-general's seat and location of the island's main fortifications. Merchants preferred St. Pierre, which straggled along the shore under Mount Pelée before an open roadstead which allowed ships to slip in and out of port at will to the Cul-de-Sac beside Fort Royal, though it was much better protected under the fort's cannons and was a snug refuge during the hurricane season. Half a century after Colbert had designated Fort Royal as the capital of the colony, the comte de Maurepas surrendered to reality when he authorised the new intendant, Charles-François Blondel de Jouvancourt, to live at St. Pierre, which was always the island's principal town.[113]

The Roman Catholic Church reinforced secular sovereignty. Its religious missions, both apostolic and pastoral, were backed by moral and material power as well as by law. Though a compliant handmaiden to the state, its economic, social, and ecclesiastical interests often linked to particular secular groups in society sometimes caused divisions in its own ranks, ensuring that it did not identify completely with the state. The Church added to faction rather than appeasing it. The greatest economic power lay with the local elites, property owners, and merchants, comprising an uneasy mixture of metropolitan French and colonial-born creoles. Despite the absence of representative institutions, their stakes in local economies and social structures created colonial politics, forcing officials into reciprocal bargains and compromises.[114] The growth and development of French America inevitably created interest groups, all of whom competed for resources and labour. Thus, the administration was drawn into networks of interests linking officials and colonists, metropolitans, and creoles and creating local oligarchies throughout French America. Colonial administrators were under continual pressure to modify laws in favour of one local interest group or another.

Colonial government was neither as uniform nor as strong as it appeared or its generic name suggests. Ministers and secretaries of state lived on one side of the Atlantic and colonial officials lived, not always in harmony, on the other among the people they governed. The Crown needed revenue and sought glory. Needs and desires are the weaknesses which gave the colonists

---

112   Robert Cole *et al.*, *Portraits du site et de l'habitat du Place-royale sous le régime français* (Québec: MAC, 1992), 1: 50. Also Jeffrey Merrick, "Politics on Pedestals: Royal Monuments in Eighteenth-Century France", *French History*, 5 (1991), 234–64.

113   Col., B 47, ff. 777–9 Maurepas to Feuquières and Blondel, 8 August 1724.

114   See Guy Frégault, "Politiques et politiciens ", *Le XVIIIe siècle canadien: études* (Montréal: HMH, 1968), 159–241.

essential leverage to deal with the metropolitan government instead of merely obeying it. The result was that government in the French colonies did not proceed by absolute command and unqualified obedience, but by negotiation and accommodation. This framework allowed for, indeed, was constructed of, collaborating colonial elites and conniving metropolitan officials. Cooperation was often grudgingly given. Several months after learning that he had been promoted to intendant of the galley corps and would be leaving Martinique, Blondel de Jouvancourt vented all his anger and frustration in the following outburst to the comte de Maurepas:

[I]t is no longer possible for me to remain on good terms with people in this land who for the most part are filled with vanity, uncivil, ungrateful, unfair, quarrelsome, jealous, and violent, refusing to pay the most legitimate and preferred debts and disobedient to all the king's ordinances and to those whom His Majesty has confided the administration of government and justice.[115]

The colonial environment undermined absolutism. It proved to be a very inadequate form of government for colonial conditions. It was unable to respond to the variety of demands made upon it. Widely differing local conditions, whether geographic, demographic, social, or economic, proved too much for the rigidity and control it sought but could not achieve. Absolutism contributed in a major way to the failure of the French colonies to evolve beyond a scattered collection of isolated towns and territories. The six decades between 1670 and 1730 revealed a degree of political, social, and economic vitality never before seen in French American colonies, which laid the foundations for all the ensuing developments that came during the remainder of the eighteenth century. The vigour and variety that appeared did not give rise to anything sufficiently unified to be called a French American empire. Indeed, absolutism could not make up for the lack of demographic weight and the disproportion between the economies of the colonies, which lacked a focus for its energies. What came to be called the first French or Bourbon empire proved to be little more than the remnants of dreams, the fragmentary pieces of statesmen's ambitions, and the lonely pleas of colonial authorities for succor against their foreign and domestic enemies. Only war provided any unity at all, and it was of the negative kind.

[115] Col., C[8A] 36, ff. 323–32 Blondel to Maurepas, 30 November 1726; ibid., ff. 72–3 same to same, 22 June 1726.

Part 2

Colonies Defended

The New World was well-known to French sailors. In the wake of Christopher Columbus, French privateers had led the way to Caribbean waters to plunder the wealth of the Indies. The French long understood the importance of attacking Spanish lines of communication between Spain and America and built a navy during the second half of the sixteenth century. By the seventeenth century, the French royal navy had shrunk; it had become a thing of the past. Its re-creation began during the 1620s and, following a brief decline at mid–century, increased in intensity during the 1660s. Warship construction increased to a new level of intensity under Louis XIV. The French fleet quickly grew to a magnificent force of 200 or more warships. The investment in warships and sweeping organisational changes were part of a major effort to foster maritime trade, to acquire colonies, and to make France a commercial trading society of first rank.[1] Yet, the main thrust of this naval development was part of a policy of prestige – *la gloire* – and remained focused on the traditional Hapsburg threat to the Bourbons rather than on the growing menace from the new maritime powers emerging to the north, England, and the United Provinces of the Netherlands.

During the six decades after 1670, indeed, beginning during the brief war between France and England in 1666 and 1667, French colonies in the Windward Islands became caught up in war with the Maritime Powers. France was allied to the United Provinces at the time and drawn in to support the latter in its war with England. In April of 1666, the English governor of Saint Christopher contemplated driving the French off the island, but the French attacked first. They seized control of the colony, appropriated 400 slaves, and deported nearly 5,000 English settlers. Afterwards, they attacked the English on Antigua and Montserrat, capturing 1,000 additional slaves.

[1] Jan Glete, *Navies and Nations, Warships, Navies and State Building in Europe and America, 1500–1860*. 2 vols. (Stockholm: Almquist & Wiksell International, 1993), 1: 125–9, 187–9.

The following year, in 1667, the navy became involved in the West Indies, and before the Treaty of Breda was signed French warships prevented the English from retaking Saint Christopher.[2] This brief war established the reputation of the colonial militia, and though the navy's defence of Martinique was less redoubtable, it was clear that the navy had a place in the defence of France's overseas possessions. Yet, no role as imperial defender ever emerged. Just as demographic, social, economic, and political developments in the colonies did not integrate the colonies, war also failed to draw the French colonies together, leaving them as isolated as before. This had major implications later in the middle of the eighteenth century. Despite a great deal of significant activity in American waters during the crucial decades between 1670 and 1730, the French navy did not find a role in imperial defence. Why this was the case is the subject of the four chapters in Part 2.

---

[2] Richard S. Dunn, *Sugar and Slaves: The Rise of the Planter Class in the English West Indies, 1624–1713* (New York: W. W. Norton, 1972), 124.

6

The Franco-Dutch War, 1672–1678

6.1 INTRODUCTION

Though England first declared war on the States General of the United Provinces on 27 March 1672, the ensuing hostilities were largely French inspired.[1] Louis XIV had been waging economic and political warfare against the Dutch with extraordinary tenacity during the previous four years. Employing high tariffs and secret diplomacy, the King of France had sought to reduce Dutch power and influence everywhere it appeared, including in the Americas.[2] No monocausal explanation such as the king's desire for revenge or Colbert's dream to crush the Dutch economy accounts for the war. Detailed analysis of the war's diplomacy stresses the importance of contingent factors: the personalities of the French leaders, short-term considerations, ministerial ambitions, and political expediency as important causes of the war.[3]

The war eventually resulted in a French victory, albeit an equivocal one, but Louis XIV failed to achieve his aims largely owing to his own inability to articulate a policy and his ministers' and generals' failure to execute the neatly planned strategy of 1672.[4] Colonial historians have virtually ignored

---

[1] An earlier version of this chapter appeared as "The Franco-Dutch War in the West Indies, 1672–1678: An Early "Lesson" in Imperial Defence" in *New Interpretations in Naval History*, ed., William M. McBride (Annapolis: Naval Institute Press, 1998), 5–22.

[2] See Herbert H. Rowen, *The Ambassador Prepares for War: The Dutch Embassy of Arnauld de Pomponne, 1669–1671* (The Hague: Martinus Nijhoff, 1957).

[3] Paul Sonnino, *Louis XIV and the Origins of the Dutch War* (Cambridge: Cambridge University Press, 1988).

[4] See Carl J. Ekberg, *The Failure of Louis XIV's Dutch War* (Chapel Hill: University of North Carolina Press, 1979) for a damning indictment of the king's personal ambition to pursue victory at the expense of the state's interest. John B. Wolf, *Louis XIV* (New York:

the war. English historians tend to confuse it with the Third Anglo-Dutch War that was a brief two-year struggle fought entirely at sea; its origins were wholly political and lay in the secret Anglo-French Treaty of Dover signed by Charles II in June of 1670.[5] It was, according to the latest historian to write on the subject, "a bogus affair from its aggressive start to its whimpering end".[6] It was also a side show.

The main conflict between the French and Dutch, which endured for six years between 1672 and 1678, was a very different affair. It occurred chiefly in the Low Countries and involved the largest armies seen in Europe since the days of the Roman Empire.[7] Its naval dimensions, including the campaigns in the North Sea as well as those in the Mediterranean and Caribbean Seas, were seconary. The French naval historian La Roncière divided his account of the naval war into two parts: dealing with the war in the North Sea and with the war against the continent, which included the West Indies.[8] Little wonder that the American dimensions of the Franco-Dutch war are usually conflated with the Third Anglo-Dutch War or virtually ignored.[9]

The importance of the maritime dimensions of the Franco-Dutch War lie in the fact that the new, inexperienced navy of Louis XIV achieved its first successes, and the "lessons" learned had lasting effects.[10] New research has shed much light on the American aspects of the conflict.[11] The war's colonial

W. W. Norton, 1968), 213–65 devoted three chapters to this war in his biography of the king, but nowhere mentioned its American aspects.

[5] See Sir Keith Feiling, *British Foreign Policy, 1660–1672* (London: Macmillan and Co., 1930), 267–309 for the negotiations leading to the Anglo-French alliance.

[6] J. R. Jones, *The Anglo-Dutch Wars of the Seventeenth Century* (London and New York: Longman, 1996), 216.

[7] John Lynn, "The Growth of the French Army during the Seventeenth Century", *Armed Forces and Society*, 6, (1980), 576. For the latest word on the growth of the French army see Lynn's *Giant of the Grand Siècle: The French Army, 1610–1715* (Cambridge: Cambridge University Press, 1997), 32–64.

[8] Charles de La Roncière, *Histoire de la marine française*, 6 vols. (Paris: Plon, Nourrit et Cie., 1899–1932), 5: 526–77 and 578–705.

[9] Mims, *Colbert's West India Policy*, 195–224 ignores the naval features of the conflict in favour of its commercial dimensions. Nellis M. Crouse, *The French Struggle for the West Indies, 1665–1713* (New York: Octagon Books, 1966 [1943], is both superficial and incomplete. A. P. Newton, *The European Nations in the West Indies, 1493–1688*, (London: A.&C. Black, 1933), 296–307 and J. H. Parry, P. Sherlock, and A. Maingot, *A Short History of the West Indies*, 4th edition (London and Basingstoke: Macmillan Caribbean, 1987), 79 conflate the two wars, and the latter account is so erroneous as to mislead.

[10] Meyer, *Colbert*, 131–2.

[11] For some of this new historical work see Cornelis Ch. Goslinga, *The Dutch in the Caribbean and the Wild Coast, 1580–1680*, (Gainesville: University of Florida Press, 1971); Donald G. Shomette and Robert D. Haslach, *Raid on America, The Dutch Naval Campaign of 1672–1674* (Columbia: University of South Carolina Press, 1988); Jaap Bruijn, *The Dutch Navy of the Seventeenth and Eighteenth Centuries*, (Columbus: University of South Carolina Press, 1993) devotes only a few pages to the American portion

dimensions possess much greater significance than some earlier historians believed.[12] The French dispatched a surprising amount of naval support to the West Indies, and the navy suffered its greatest losses of the war in American waters. Yet, despite disappointments and tragedies, it also contributed significantly to the war's outcome in the Americas. It was through naval action rather than commercial competition that the French excluded the Dutch from their colonies in the West Indies. The war also permanently altered the nature and direction of international colonial rivalry. The reduction of Dutch influence was a vital precondition to further French colonial expansion and economic exploitation of the West Indies. The war set the stage for the subsequent struggle between the English and French in the Americas. By excluding the Dutch from major political and military roles in the New World, the French also brought to the fore the irreconcilability of their own and England's colonial ambitions, a consequence they had not envisioned.[13] Finally, the war's outcome deeply affected the future limited role of the French navy in colonial defence. Owing to the "lessons" learned from the war, the navy was not accorded any significant role in the future defence of the French American colonies.

6.2 OPENING HOSTILITIES

Behind the animus of Louis XIV's attacks on the Dutch republic lay his desire to exploit continuing Spanish weakness in both the Netherlands and America. This twofold aim, however, led to a poorly focused, even ambivalent French policy in the West Indies. Frigates sent to the West Indies were intended to threaten Spanish treasure fleets as well as to drive Dutch merchant ships from French colonies. Vice-Admiral comte d'Estrées' instructions in 1668 included orders to reconnoiter all seas and routes, including the Spanish Main and the Gulf of Mexico, the exits and entries for the treasure fleets.[14] In 1670, six weeks after French diplomats signed the secret Treaty of Dover, Colbert directed d'Estrées to anticipate a rupture with the United Provinces and advised him to look to the defences of the colonies and plan to attack

---

of the war; Christian Buchet, *La Luttle pour l'espace caraïbe et la façade atlantique de l'Amérique centrale et du sud (1672–1763)*, 2 vols. (Paris: Librairie d'Inde Editeur, 1991) provides the best analysis of the war's impact on future imperial conflict in America. See also Philip P. Boucher, *Cannibal Encounters: Europeans and Island Caribs, 1492–1763* (Baltimore and London: The Johns Hopkins University Press, 1992) and Daniel Dessert, *La Royale: vaisseaux et marins du Roi-Soleil* (Paris: Fayard, 1996).

[12] E.g., Alfred T. Mahan, *The Influence of Sea Power upon History 1660–1783* (Boston: Little, Brown & Co., 1892), 158 dismissed the naval war in America as simply "one or two half-privateering expeditions to the West Indies".

[13] Arthur Percival Newton, *The European Nations in the West Indies, 1493–1688* (London: A.&C. Black, 1933), 286.

[14] Col., Série F³ 26, ff. 76–84 Mémoire du Roy au Sr. comte d'Estrées, 5 September 1668.

the Dutch there.[15] Previous attempts to exclude foreign shipping from trade with the French islands had proved ineffective. Cruises in 1667, 1668, and 1669 failed to obtain results.[16] Only after the king dispatched three warships in 1670 under the command of *chef d'escadre* Louis Gabaret with new instructions to sink or seize all foreign vessels in French waters, to continue "constantly cruising", and to maintain secrecy about his operations, did the Dutch begin to relinquish their grip on French colonial commerce.

Gabaret was an anachronism in Louis XIV's new expanding navy. He was a tarpaulin officer and one-time corsair. His skills as a navigator and seaman were freely acknowledged, but the new navy was being officered by nobles and few of the old school remained. The old sea dog may have been under the protection of Vice-Admiral d'Estrées, who admired his strength of character and acknowledged the lessons he could teach new inexperienced officers.[17] Colbert kept in continual touch with Gabaret, encouraged his brutality toward Dutch and English traders, and supported his refusal to accept orders from Governor-General de Baas.[18] However, if the Dutch fled French waters under Gabaret's harsh regime, his conduct failed to conjure up sufficient French sailors and shipping to replace the foreigners, which led to a full blown revolt in Saint-Domingue that Gabaret helped to put down.[19]

Despite these unstable conditions, Colbert did not consider the defence of the colonies a problem. The Dutch were in no position to mount an attack, and the French minister left no doubt about his own aggressive intention to replace them in the interloping trade with Spanish America. Colbert aimed to drive the Dutch from the West Indies and from the slave trade. He especially wanted to expel them from Curaçao where they refreshed their slaves after completing the Middle Passage before selling them in the Spanish colonies. He asked Vice-Admiral d'Estrées for a plan to drive the Dutch out of Africa as well as from St. Eustatius and Curaçao.[20] Colbert also

---

[15] Pierre Clément, éd., *Lettres, instructions et mémoires de Colbert,* 7 vols in 9 + one (Paris: Imprimerie imperiale 1859–1882), 3, pt. 1: 251–3 Colbert to d'Estrées, 15 July 1670.

[16] Col., F³ 26, ff. 72–5 and 84–4v d'Estrées to Colbert, 5 and 23 March and 16 April 1669.

[17] BN, *Mélanges de Colbert,* 176, f. 104 Mémoire de Colbert de Terron au Roi, 21 April 1670 calling for Gabaret's dismissal; also *ibid.,* f. 309 d'Estrées to Colbert, 11 September 1670.

[18] Col., B 2, ff. 47, 97v and 120 Louis XIV to Gabaret, 9 April, 3 July, and 12 October 1670; also Stewart L. Mims, *Colbert's West India Policy* (New Haven: Yale University Press, 1912), 195–201.

[19] Col., C⁹ᴬ 1 (nonfoliated) "Mémoire sur l'état de la colonies de St. Domingue" joined to Gabaret's letter of June 1671. For details of the revolt and its suppression see Charles Frostin, *Les Révoltes blanches à Saint-Domingue aux XVIIe et XVIIIe siècles (Haiti avant 1789),* (Paris: L'École, 1975), 101–5; also Jean Meyer, *Colbert* (Paris: Hachette, 1981), 264–6.

[20] Abdoulaye Ly, *La Compagnie du Sénégal* (Paris: Présence Africaine, 1958), 103–9 treats the African dimensions of the plan.

instructed Governor-General de Baas to drive the Dutch out of Tobago, "if possible without directly violating any of His Majesty's treaties with them". He secretly advised de Baas to aid the Carib Indians to make war by supplying them with arms and munitions, "always taking care", he added, "to prevent the Dutch from obtaining proof".[21] De Baas was already pursuing a silent war against the Dutch on the island, having refused to reply to the Dutch governor's requests for assistance against the Caribs and advising his major, M. de Laubière, to do nothing to intimidate the Indians.[22]

When hostilities finally broke out in April of 1672, however, Colbert's combination of contempt and animosity disguised the hollowness of his offensive aims against the Dutch and the lack of resources to support the islands (see Map 6.1). Colbert thought French colonists under their military leaders ought to be able to look after themselves, and he advised Governor-General de Baas to rely on his own resources. The navy's role remained modest, unchanged from the previous four years. A division of three frigates was sent to Martinique at the beginning of 1672, but the senior officer commanding died in the islands and *Le Bon* was wrecked on the coast of Saint-Domingue.[23] A second division, including *Le Belliqueux*, a 66-gun second-rate, and *La Marquis*, 46 guns, was significantly more powerful than previous forces, but it only arrived in December. A third division comprising *L'Alcion*, 44 guns, *Les Jeux*, 36, and *La Friponne*, 16 guns, commanded by Captain marquis d'Amblimont which reached the islands in 1673 represented a return to former strength.[24] The king's instructions to naval commanders remained defensive, and by the time the third division reached the islands only *La Marquis* remained from the earlier ships. The others had long since worn out and departed for France. A year after the opening of hostilities, the French position in the West Indies had actually weakened from two years earlier.

Half a dozen factors in the West Indies contributed to the new weakness in addition to the continuing emphasis on the naval war in the North Sea during 1672 and 1673. The first was the West India Company. Colbert initially placed the burden of the islands' defence on the Company, sending it cannon, powder, ball, match, and even six companies of infantry.[25] Undercapitalised from its beginnings and suffering severe losses earlier, by 1672, the Company was foundering amidst shoals of debt, maladministration, and continual inroads by Dutch competitors. During the next two years, its assets were liquidated, but the Company's continuing existence, interposed

---

[21]   Clément, *Lettres … de Colbert*, 3, pt. 1, 487 Colbert to de Baas, 3 July 1670.
[22]   Col., C⁸ᴬ 1, ff. 29v–30 de Baas to Colbert, 15 January 1670.
[23]   Col., B 4, ff. 29–9v King to de Baas, 14 March 1672; and ibid., C⁸ᴬ 1, f. 204 de Baas to Colbert, 28 December 1672.
[24]   Mims, *Colbert's West India Policy*, 195–201, 208.
[25]   Col., B 4, ff. 6–7v King to Colbert de Terron, 23 January 1672.

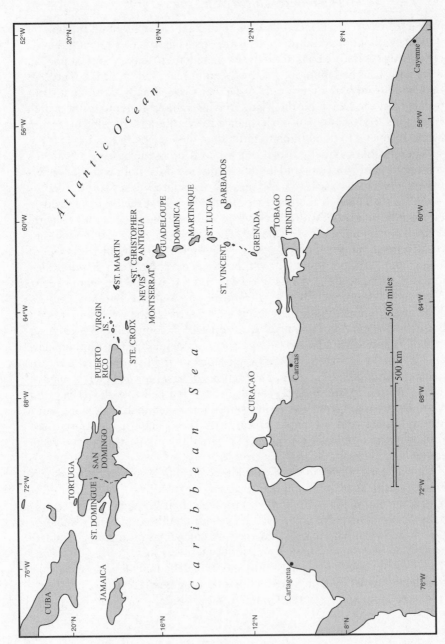

Map 6.1. The Southeastern Caribbean.

between royal authority and colonists, obscured lines of authority.[26] Second, the governors of the island colonies frequently undermined Colbert's efforts to control them from Paris and Versailles. Local, group, and class interests along with individual personalities continually contended for power and influence. Governor-General de Baas was an extremely prickly person. In the words of one recent historian, he was "temperamental, obstreperous, and independent".[27] His relations with Colbert were as difficult as those of his better known counterpart, the Governor-General of New France, Louis de Buade, comte de Frontenac. Both men were soldiers whose combination of disobedience and heedlessness was the price Colbert paid for their strong leadership and other military virtues. Their insouciant behaviour often exasperated Colbert. Early in 1672, after three years attempting to drive the Dutch from the waters around the French islands, de Baas cheerfully acknowledged his own profitable trading arrangements with a merchant residing at Curaçao without the slightest hint that anything was amiss.[28] Island governors also complained frequently about each other and about Governor-General de Baas. They proved reluctant to cooperate, often choosing to challenge his authority. Colbert once became so annoyed with Charles-François du Lion, governor of Guadeloupe, a notorious complainer, that he sharply informed him that his letters were "too long, too tedious, and too petty" to spend his time reading them.[29]

The increasing numbers of naval officers arriving in the West Indies during the war undermined attempts to achieve central command and control. The presence of the king's ships in the colonies was still relatively new, and relations between army and naval officers were only being established in France. Good relations proved to be especially difficult to achieve in the colonies; official correspondence is replete with complaints, disputes over precedence, and refusals of cooperation. The death in the islands of the senior naval captain in February of 1672 and his replacement immediately led to deteriorating relations owing to the latter's temperamental character. De Baas bitterly complained about Captain Montortier's pretentious claim that the naval officer corps was incomparably more noble and more highly regarded by the king than the corps of army officers and his refusal to accept de Baas' authority to detach warships and send them on missions of his own choosing.[30] In June, Captain Montortier's insolence left de Baas no alternative but to arrest him. Many captains in Louis XIV's new navy were former soldiers,

---

26 Mims, *Colbert's West India Policy*, 176–9.

27 Philip P. Boucher, *The Shaping of the French Colonial Empire, A Bio-bibliography of the Careers of Richelieu, Fouquet, and Colbert* (New York: Garland Press, 1985), 156.

28 Quoted in Mims, *Colbert's West India Policy*, 211–12.

29 Clément, *Lettres ... de Colbert*, 3, pt. 2: 572–3 Colbert to Lion, 6 September 1673; also see Mims, *Colbert's West India Policy*, 212–13.

30 Col., C[8A] 1, ff. 167–75 and 182–2v de Baas to Colbert, 28 February and 20 May 1672.

touchy about their dignity, yet uncertain of their place in France's military hierarchy, where birth so often outweighed rank. They were anxious to test their prerogatives ashore as well as afloat. De Baas released Montortier only after receiving Colbert's order to do so.[31]

The navy won a brief but temporary victory in 1674, when Colbert's son, the marquis de Seignelay, denied the governor-general authority to issue orders to the commanding officer of the Windward islands squadron,[32] but struggle continued. About 18 months later, Seignelay changed his mind in the face of the continuing independent actions of naval officers. In April of 1676, Colbert rejected *chef d'escadre* the marquis de Grancey's claim to exercise the rights of the Admiral of France in the West Indies, denying him the power to command or inspect troops ashore including those drawn from his own ships, and the authority to issue privateering commissions. These powers belonged solely to the lieutenant-general of the islands, (i.e., to the governor-general).[33] Naval officers' conduct continually forced Colbert to attempt reconciliation but with little success. Relations between *la terre et la mer* during the war remained idiosyncratic and unreliable, and undermined defence efforts.

The Carib Indians at Grenada posed another serious threat to French security. They proved to be deeply hostile to the settlement Colbert had been encouraging there since 1669.[34] Perhaps unknowingly, Colbert had placed the French athwart the Caribs' main route to the South American mainland, threatening their freedom of movement. Whether deliberate or not, this challenge to Carib independence weakened French security in the most sensitive area of the Lesser Antilles to windward of all other French island colonies and close to the Spanish Main.[35]

The French position on Saint-Domingue was not simply weak – it was precarious. Governor Bertrand Ogeron, aided by Captain Gabaret, had checked the settlers' revolt incited by Dutch merchants in 1670, but two years later sedition remained possible and he greatly feared for the colony's security at both Tortuga and Petit Goâve. Ogeron thought the habitants would rise again in the absence of a French warship, armed troops, and additional munitions. The distance from Martinique and the difficulty of communications also led him to expect no aid from Governor-General de Baas. In his opinion, one or two enemy corsairs cruising off the Caicos islands would be sufficient to seize all of the colony's merchant shipping.[36]

[31]   Ibid., ff. 184–6 and 205 de Baas to Colbert, 8 June and 28 December 1672.
[32]   Col., C[8B] 19, no. 20 memorandum dated 4 November 1674, signed Louis, but marginalia in Seignelay's hand.
[33]   Marine, B[4] 7, ff. 181–1v Monseigneur to Grancey, 9 April 1676.
[34]   Clément, *Lettres ... de Colbert,* 3, pt. 2, 460 Colbert to de Baas, 15 September 1669.
[35]   Boucher, *Cannibal Encounters,* 64–5, 86.
[36]   Michel Camus, éd., "Correspondance de Bertrand Ogeron, gouverneur de l'île de la Tortue et coste de Saint-Domingue au XVIIe siècle", *Revue de la société Haitienne d'histoire et de géographie,* 43, no. 146 (mars 1985), 158–9.

Finally, Louis XIV's own indifference to his colonies, especially after becoming caught up in the details of the great campaign in the Low Countries, left colonial governors very largely on their own to pursue individual policies. In New France, Intendant Jean Talon departed for France in November of 1672 and was not replaced for nearly three years, while in the West Indies, Governor-General de Baas continued to govern alone with only the assistance of a financial commissary sent out in 1675. As the European war progressed and quick victory failed to appear, the king's obsession grew. France lost its English ally, alienated neutrals, and allowed the war to be transformed into a major military struggle into which America was drawn.

6.3 COLONIAL INITIATIVES

French colonists in the West Indies initially remained passive. Martinique's Sovereign Council registered the declaration of war in June of 1672, placed the island on alert, raised two companies of horsed militia, and levied a tax on slaves to fortify the Cul-de-Sac, the island's superb harbour at Fort Royal.[37] Colbert early on sought assurances that English governors would take common measures for joint security. By the end of 1672, local English colonial forces had quickly seized Saint Eustatius, Saba, and Tobago from the Dutch, while the French remained on the defensive.[38] English attempts to seize Dominica, lying between Martinique and Guadeloupe, were more disturbing, but fortunately came to nought.[39] The French naval presence was ineffective. Not only did the naval commander spend the last half of the year under arrest, but by the end of November many crew members were dead or dying and provisions were short. De Baas wondered whether sufficient manpower remained to permit the ships to sail to France. After ordering three warships to cruise between Martinique and Barbados to support merchantmen expected from France, he had to reinforce their crews with local settlers.[40] It was not before mid-February of 1673 that de Baas could launch his expedition to seize Dutch Curaçao.

Conceived by de Baas and equipped and manned from the colonies, the expedition owed its origin to false reports that the Dutch colony was weakly protected.[41] De Baas seemed ignorant of the English failure to capture the

---

37 Pierre-Regis Dessalles, fils, *Annales du Conseil Souverain de la Martinique, Tableau historique du gouvernement de cette colonie depuis son premier établissement jusqu'à nos jours*, 2 vols. (Bergerac: Chez J. B. Puynesge, 1786), 1: 134–8

38 Clément, *Lettres ... de Colbert*, 3[1]: 431–2 Colbert to Colbert de Croissy, 11 May 1672. See BL, Stowe Mss., 201, f. 145 Lord Willoughby, Governor of Barbados, to Earl of Essex 6/16 August 1672 for an account of his capture of Tobago.

39 Col., C[8A] 1, ff. 187–9 de Baas to Colbert, 22 July 1672.

40 Ibid., ff. 192v–3 and 200–2 de Baas to Colbert 25 October, 20 November and "Addendum" dated 28 November 1672.

41 Ibid., ff. 221–2 de Baas to Colbert 16 February 1673.

colony the previous year.[42] Collecting a small force of 3 men-of-war and 3 merchantmen newly arrived from France, 14 local craft, and some 1,200 soldiers, de Baas headed north from Martinique to recruit additional men from Guadeloupe and St. Christopher. Governor Ogeron and 400 buccaneers were expected from Saint-Domingue but failed to arrive at the appointed rendezvous. However, others appeared and de Baas and his motley crew of soldiers, colonists, and freebooters sailed to Curaçao, where they landed in early March only to meet with ignominious failure for which de Baas accepted full responsibility.

After eight days on the island, the French withdrew.[43] An English report that the French simply "ran away and lost the design shamefully" reveals the animus between ostensible allies rather than an accurate assessment of what occurred.[44] The discovery that Fort Amsterdam at Willemstad was strongly fortified, well-garrisoned, and supported by armed ships in the harbour, together with the absence of an artillery train to besiege the fort and de Baas' keen awareness that he had stripped the French West Indies of their meager defences to mount the expedition left him no option but to return quickly to Martinique.[45] Nevertheless, he first sailed to Tortuga in search of Ogeron. Not finding him, he left an interim commander in charge before departing for Martinique. Later, Colbert refused to indulge in recriminations over the abortive attack. His greatest concern was for the disappearance of Ogeron and his men. The loss of 400 buccaneers left Saint-Domingue virtually unprotected and vulnerable to Spanish attack.[46]

Ogeron and his men had shipwrecked on the north shore of Puerto Rico. The Spanish were holding him and nearly 200 buccaneers prisoners at San Juan despite the existence of peace between France and Spain. The Spanish government had been pro-Dutch and anti-French from the war's outset, and long-suffering Spanish colonists killed many of the shipwrecked buccaneers after they came ashore, treating them as pirates. This should not be surprising. Privateering in the West Indies during these years was never anything more than piracy with a clear conscience, and there was no peace ever between Spaniards and buccaneers.

Ogeron escaped during the summer and made his way back to Tortuga. In October, he set out with a second force of 500 buccaneers in eight or ten craft to rescue the prisoners, but his attempt failed. A hurricane forced a return to Tortuga. Contrary winds prevented an early return to Puerto Rico, and when

[42] *CSP, CS*, 1669–1674, no. 954.

[43] Col., C⁸ᴬ 1, ff. 224–33 De Baas to Colbert 16 April 1673; also Crouse, *The French Struggle for the West Indies, 1665–1713*, 103.

[44] *CSP, CS*, 1669–74, no. 1082, p. 486. Lt.–Gov. Thos. Lynch to Council of Trade and Plantations, Jamaica, 28 April [O.S.] 1673.

[45] See Goslinga, *The Dutch in the Caribbean*, 471–2 for an account of the abortive attack. De Baas' own account is in Colonies C⁸ᴬ 1, ff. 224–33 de Baas to Colbert, 16 April 1673.

[46] Clément, *Lettres … de Colbert*, 3, pt. 2: 564–9 Colbert to de Baas, 5 September 1673.

the French finally reached their destination, a well-laid ambush led to more captures and additional atrocities.[47] In the summer of 1674, France declared war on Spain, sealing the fate of the French prisoners. By September, no more than 130 Frenchmen were still alive on Puerto Rico.[48] Starvation killed many. Others were worked to death on fortifications at Havana and Cartagena and in the silver mines of Peru.[49] A few reached Spain as replacement sailors on board the galleons, and after many representations, the last prisoners were exchanged in 1677. Some made their way back to Tortuga, where they never forgot their sufferings. Alexandre Exquemelin reported that they later joined the marquis de Maintenon's expedition to Trinidad armed with special knives and pincers to flay alive any Spaniard who fell into their hands.[50] Ogeron's story clearly reveals the lack of central command amongst the French in the West Indies, and that from 1673 onward the struggle with the Spaniards appeared to be a private war.

De Baas' return to Martinique toward the end of May was fortuitous. Unknown to him or even to each other, two Dutch squadrons were about to meet off the entry to the Cul-de-Sac. The first, composed of six ships from Zealand under the command of Cornelis Evertsen, was originally destined to seize the annual returning English East India Company fleet somewhere off St. Helena in the South Atlantic, but the English had delivered such a serious check in the Cape Verde islands that Evertsen made for the Americas.[51] He reached South America in mid-March and spent nearly two months there without attacking the French at Cayenne before sailing to Barbados. After failing to find any prizes there Evertsen made for Martinique, where on 22 May, he met up with six more Dutch ships outside the Cul-de-Sac.[52] These vessels belonged to an Amsterdam squadron commanded by Captain Jacob Binckes, sent out in December with orders to escort Spanish treasure ships from the Azores to Cadiz and afterward to sail to the West Indies to prey on English and French colonies and their trade. Neither Dutch commander knew of the other's existence. Binckes had arrived a few days earlier and taken two prizes. He had news that a large French warship wearing a commodore's pendant, an English frigate, and seven or eight merchantmen were cleared for action lying close by shore batteries at Fort Royal. These were *Le Belliqueux*, 66-guns, Captain marquis d'Amblimont, and HMS *Garland*, fifth-rate of 30 guns, Captain John Wyborne. The English frigate had left Carlisle Roads, Barbados, to investigate reports of strange ships nearby and, while patrolling

47   Camus, éd., "Correspondance d'Ogeron", 167–8, 169, 171.
48   Col., C9A 1 (n.f.) de Baas to Gov. of Puerto Rico, 12 September 1674.
49   Col., C9A 1 de Baas to Gov. of Puerto Rico, 26 November 1674; and C8A 1, ff. 318–20v Duclerc to Seignelay, 20 January 1675.
50   A. O. Exquemelin, *The Buccaneers of America*, trans., by Alexis Brown (Harmondsworth: Penguin Books, 1969), 127–33.
51   Shomette and Haslach, *Raid on America*, 41, 44–7, 65–8, and 73–5.
52   Ibid., 81–2, 91–4; and Goslinga, *The Dutch in the Caribbean*, 446.

between St. Lucia and Martinique sighted the Dutch vessels and fled into the Cul-de-Sac with the news.[53] There the French and English awaited an attack that never materialised.

Why the Dutch did not attack is unclear. *Le Belliqueux* was far larger than any of the Dutch warships and contrary winds may have prevented the Dutch from sailing into the bay. The French ships were also moored so close to shore as to present too formidable a challenge for a cutting out expedition by ships' boats.[54] This was just as well, for Governor-General de Baas had stripped Martinique for his Curaçao expedition, and according to Captain Wyborne, "the Island had not above 12 guns mounted nor 150 men".[55] In any case, the Dutch abandoned their attempt and sailed to Guadeloupe. The two leaders joined their squadrons, agreeing to alternate command weekly and to attack both English and French colonies.[56] After seizing three prizes at Guadeloupe, they continued northward through the Lesser Antilles. English colonists vigorously repulsed their attacks from Montserrat and Nevis, and both French and English did the same at St. Christopher. The Dutch managed to cut out one French prize, but the blood price was high.[57] In early June, they retook St. Eustatius but soon left it to be reoccupied by their enemies.

The Dutch sailed northward during the summer months. They burnt some ships in the James River, Virginia, and in August, they accepted the surrender of the colony of New York. Later, four ships attacked Ferryland on Newfoundland's Avalon Peninsula where the Dutch killed cattle, destroyed other property valued at 2,400 pounds sterling, burnt 70 fishing boats, and seized four great guns and as much fish as their holds could carry before sailing away to Fayal in the Azores.[58] As in the West Indies, the Dutch aimed to plunder and destroy property rather than conquer territory, and though the raid did not accomplish a great deal, it revealed French weakness in the Americas.

The French had been extremely fortunate that the Dutch commanders had not pressed home their attack on Martinique in May. Captain d'Amblimont's ship was of little practical use beyond serving as a shore battery. Amblimont himself was more cooperative than his predecessor, but his ships were in poor condition. *Le Belliqueux, La Fée,* and *La Sybille* had accompanied de Baas to Curaçao, but after six months in the islands, the ships had run out of victuals and were unfit for further service. Moreover, replenishing the warships' victuals in June from provisions purchased from merchantmen

53 *CSP, CS,* 1669–74, no. 1097 Minutes of the Council of Barbados, 27 May [o.s.] 1673; COL., C^{8A} 1, F. 242 de Baas to Colbert, 1 June 1673.
54 Col., C^{8A} 1 ff. 240 de Baas to Colbert, 1 June 1673.
55 See note 52.
56 Shomette and Haslach, *Raid on America,* 94–9.
57 Ibid., 109–10; also Col., C^{8A} 1, ff. 246–7v de Baas to Colbert, 5 July 1673.
58 Shomette and Haslach, *Raid on America,* 203–5; *CSP, CS,* 1675–76, no. 495 account by Dudley Lovelace, 29 March [o.s.] 1675.

consumed food intended for colonists. Louis XIV ordered all three ships home in July. After reaching Rochefort, naval authorities condemned the two small frigates to be broken up. Colbert decreed that warships were to serve for only one year in the West Indies, but as warships continued to be poorly fitted out, this proved too long for service in tropical waters.[59]

The Dutch launched a concerted effort to conquer the French West Indies the very next year. The seriousness of the threat is beyond a doubt. On 30 August 1673, Spain concluded an anti-French coalition with the Dutch, Austria, and the Duke of Lorraine out of fear that, once in control of the United Provinces, France would annex the Southern Netherlands.[60] Early in 1674, France lost her English ally and became isolated in Europe. Anti-French feeling reached a particularly high level during the last half of 1673 in England and combined with increasing anti-Popery fear to force Charles II out of the war.[61] In mid-February of 1674, after parliament denied him funds to continue the war, Charles II betrayed France by signing a separate peace with the Dutch called the Treaty of Westminster.[62] These developments set the stage for a brilliant strategic gamble by the Dutch. The object was to draw French forces away from the Netherlands by attacking the French Atlantic coast and colonial possessions overseas.

In the spring of 1674, the greatest admiral of his age, Michiel Adriaanzoon de Ruyter, anticipated British eighteenth-century naval strategy by nearly three-quarters of a century when he and Admiral Cornelis Tromp sailed down the English Channel with an enormous fleet of nearly 150 warships, troop transports, and victualers. Once into the Atlantic, the Dutch forces divided. Tromp sailed to attack the west coast of France, where he hoped to find support among French Protestant co-religionists, while de Ruyter led the remainder to conquer the French West Indies.[63] Only the previous September an overbearing, arrogant Colbert had assured Governor-General de Baas that no such attack need be expected because Louis XIV kept his enemies so well-occupied in Europe that there remained "neither enough time, nor enough

---

[59] Col., B 5, f. 31 King to de Baas, 1 July 1673; ibid., f. 47 Colbert to de Baas, 5 September 1673.

[60] Derek Mckay and Hamish Scott, *The Rise of the Great Powers, 1648–1815* (London: Longman, 1983), 30.

[61] C. R. Boxer, "Some Second Thoughts on the Third Dutch War, 1672–1674", *Transactions of the Royal Historical Society*, 5th Ser., 19 (1969): 89; and J. D. Davies, "The Navy, Parliament, and Political Crisis in the Reign of Charles II", *The Historical Journal*, 36, (1993), 272, 274.

[62] K. H. D. Haley, *William of Orange and the English Opposition, 1672–1674* (Oxford: Oxford University Press, 1953), 133–84 closely traces the disintegration of Charles II's ministry and the growth of English public and parliamentary hostility to the king and the war at this time. See also Sir Herbert Richmond, *The Navy as an Instrument of Policy, 1588–1727* (Cambridge: Cambridge University Press, 1953), 187–8; and Jones, *The Anglo–Dutch Wars*, 211–16.

[63] Goslinga, *The Dutch in the Caribbean*, 473–4; Bruijn, *The Dutch Navy*, 91.

money, nor enough troops to think of any enterprise against the islands".[64]
Like his royal master, Colbert continually underestimated his enemies.

De Ruyter steered directly for Martinique hoping to surprise the French defences. By mid-July, he lay off the Cul-de-Sac with 17 ships of the line, nine smaller warships, and 18 transports and provision ships, some 7,500 sailors and soldiers and 1,100 cannons.[65] French spies had learned his destination and news of his arrival preceded him.[66] Opposing him was a single worn-out fourth rate, *Les Jeux*, 36 guns, under the command of Captain marquis d'Amblimont and 161 men on shore commanded by Governor Antoine de Sainte-Marthe, manning 20 guns behind a double wooden palisade.[67] Governor-General de Baas was in bed at St. Pierre, too sick to reach the scene in time.

The engagement was fought the next day, 20 July 1674.[68] Governor Sainte-Marthe was an able military man and had sufficient warning to sink one or two French merchantmen in order to block the harbour entrance. He also posted his men well and placed his few guns effectively in cooperation with Captain d'Amblimont, who landed many of his ship's guns ashore, but the outcome of the subsequent battle remains difficult to explain.

Following a heavy bombardment, the Dutch landed a force of 1,000 men, who quickly became caught in a deadly crossfire as they frontally assaulted the fortified position. De Ruyter was unable to move his ships inshore to help the troops and a debacle unfolded during the day. Casualties rapidly mounted, especially among senior Dutch army officers. Counts Horne and Styrun and de Ruyter's son were killed during the attacks. Soldiers broke into warehouses along the shore and were soon drunk. In the evening, de Ruyter ordered a withdrawal to the ships, and panicking soldiers abandoned their

---

[64] Clément, éd., *Lettres ... de Colbert*, 3, pt. 2: 564 Colbert to de Baas, Paris, 5 September 1673.

[65] There is some variation concerning the numbers involved. A contemporary French account gives 26 vessels from 50 to 80 guns, 14 flutes, and 6 brigantines carrying 6,000 soldiers and 4,000 sailors; see BN, Clairambault, 888, f. 165 for an engraved record of the battle entitled, "Assaut des Hollondoise Repoussés du Fort Royal de la Martinique par M\u02b3 Le Chevalier de Sainte-Marthe, Gouverneur pour le Roy dans lisle". They are very close to the above figures, which are taken from Goslinga, *The Dutch in the Caribbean*, 475.

[66] BN, Clairambault, 888, ff. 167–8 A. de Saint–Marthe to Colbert, Martinique, 10 July 1674, acknowledging receipt on the 6th of the king's letter, dated 24 March, containing news of the expected attack.

[67] Col., F³ 26, ff. 97–8 "Mémoire de tout de ceux qui ont deffendu le Fort Roïal contre l'attaque de l'armée hollondoise conduit par Michel de Ruyter à la Martinique" has a list of all the officers and men present in the defense works.

[68] Col., F³ 26, ff. 99–106 "Relation de Sr de la Calle sur ce qui s'est passé à l'attack du fort Roïal de la Martinique par la flotte de Ruyter"; BN, Clairambault, 888, ff. 177–7v for copies of certificates and affidavits dated 20 July and 27 September 1674, respectively, concerning the sinking of *L'Hirondelle* of Honfleur in the entry to Le Carenage. For details see Crouse, *The French Struggle*, 104–10; and Goslinga, *The Dutch in the Caribbean*, 475–7.

dead and wounded, even their arms, as they stampeded into the boats sent to draw them off. Continuous French musketry increased the confusion, which lasted far into the night. Dutch casualties were later put at 461 dead and wounded while the French lost fewer than 20 men. That night de Ruyter abandoned the attempt and withdrew, first to Guadeloupe and then from the islands.[69] The French repulse of the Dutch attack was one of the most one-sided victories in French colonial history.

Ruyter's failure to make another attempt remains a puzzle. It is unlikely that the admiral had suddenly become timid or lost confidence. The deaths of the assault commanders may have prevented a second attempt. Though he might have captured another French island, perhaps Ruyter understood the meaninglessness of such a gesture. The retaking of St. Eustatius the year before had provided no benefit to the Dutch who had no ability to defend it. Nothing less than the conquest of the French West Indies where strong pro-Dutch sentiment existed among the populace would serve the admiral's strategy. Only Martinique, the most populous of the French Antilles, would do, but its defences had proved too formidable, and with his senior military officers dead, no one remained to lead another deadly frontal assault.[70]

The repulse of Dutch forces was indeed fortuitous. Since the spring of the year, the French had also been coping with a sudden, sharp deterioration in relations with the Carib Indians of St. Vincent who, with their arrows and wooden clubs, were wreaking more havoc than the Dutch. Quarrels among local military leaders at Grenada exacerbated the problem. Neither Governor de Canchy nor the marquis d'Amblimont, who had been entrusted with the colony's defence, could agree to be subordinate to the other.[71] Later in the year de Baas recalled Canchy and sent him home after replacing him with one of Governor de Sainte-Marthe's sons. While this contretemps had been developing, some Caribs murdered the crew of a vessel sent to evacuate Jesuit missionaries who were withdrawing from St. Vincent. While en route to the South American mainland, the killers passed through Grenada and murdered more French colonists. Dominican Caribs tried but failed to resolve the crisis and Colbert, pleading insufficient resources, denied de Baas' request to launch reprisals. This left the Carib problem unresolved and French settlers insecure.[72] The next year, the Amerindians struck Grenada again, forcing de Baas to send three companies of scarce troops and a warship to support the now terrified settlers.[73]

---

69 Col., F³ 26, ff. 108–9v "Extrait de la lettre de M. de Baas au ministre", 28 August 1674.

70 Buchet, *La Lutte pour l'espace Caraïbe*, 1: 97–102 for further speculation on Ruyter's withdrawal.

71 Col., C⁸ᴬ 1, ff. 260–98 three letters from de Baas to Colbert, 8 February, 3 June, and June 1674.

72 Ibid., ff. 281–4 de Baas to Seignelay, 8 June 1674; ibid., ff. 294–6 same to same, 25 June 1674.

73 See Boucher, *Cannibal Encounters*, 86.

Dutch privateers, who had carried more than 25 prizes into Curaçao during the previous year, were also a problem.[74] Shortly after Ruyter returned to the Netherlands, a Dutch privateer captain, Jurriaen Aernouts sailed from Curaçao to attack English and French possessions in North America. On reaching New York, he was told by English colonists of the Treaty of Westminster, and they persuaded him to attack the French in Acadia. On 10 August, Aernouts captured Fort Pentagouet on the Penobscot River and seized Governor Jacques de Chambly, who was wounded in the fray. After destroying the fort, Aernouts sailed along the coast pillaging French posts. At Fort Jemseg on the St. John River, he captured Chambly's lieutenant. Claiming Acadia for the States General, Aernouts deposited his French prisoners at Boston, sold his booty, including several captured French cannon, to New England merchants and returned to Curaçao.[75]

In December, another Dutch privateer pillaged and carried off slaves from four plantations on Grenada.[76] This was Jan Erasmus Reining, known to the French as Ramus. French authorities lost no time accusing the captain of the frigate La Friponne of disobeying orders to remain at Grenada and leaving the island unprotected in order to pursue his own commercial interests at Martinique.[77] Early in 1675 Aernouts joined Ramus to seize the weakly defended colony, but fortunately a French frigate sent post haste by de Baas slipped into the harbour behind the privateers and an infantry landing party quickly rounded up about 80 freebooters.[78] Sometime later, after being carried to Martinique, Ramus and Aernouts managed to escape.[79] The French probably allowed the Dutch to escape in return for surrendering on Grenada a few months earlier, a reasonable quid pro quo.

The Franco-Dutch War of 1672–8 occurred during the "golden age" of buccaneering, yet, it is remarkable for the absence of English and French corsairs. The loss of nearly 400 buccaneers from Saint-Domingue explains part of the absence, but very little privateering occurred out of Martinique or elsewhere in the French Windward Islands, probably due to Dutch naval operations during 1673 and 1674, the aggressiveness of Dutch privateers, and the decline in commercial traffic from France. Late in 1674 and early 1675, Governor Ogeron took to issuing privateering commissions to English buccaneers from Jamaica, even corresponding with Lieutenant-Governor Sir

74   Goslinga, The Dutch in the Caribbean, 478.
75   See "Aernoutsz" DCB., 1: 39–40.; also G. A. Rawlyk, Nova Scotia's Massachusetts: A Study of Massachusetts-Nova Scotia Relations, 1630 to 1784 (Montreal and London: McGill-Queen's University Press, 1973), 37–8.
76   Col., C⁸ᴬ 1, ff. 322–2 La Lande to [de Baas], Grenada, 26 December 1674.
77   Ibid., ff. 318v–19 Duclerc to Seignelay, 20 January 1675.
78   The account of this episode can be followed in a number of documents in Col., C⁸ᴬ 1, ff. 324–45 dated 28 to 31 March 1675.
79   Ibid., ff. 342–6 De Baas to Colbert 26 June 1675.

Henry Morgan's brother-in-law about recovering his share of their prize money in the English colony's prize courts![80]

6.4 METROPOLITAN RESPONSES

French merchantmen failed to carry sufficient stores and provisions for the king's ships during the war. Naval vessels became unfit for service so quickly after reaching the West Indies that it may have been due to poor careening and fitting out in France. Reunion of the French colonies to the royal domain following revocation of the West India Company's letters patent did not improve security. The month before, Colbert acknowledged his inability to supply the colonies, and advised Governor-General de Baas to avoid all disputes with either the English or the Caribs: "resolve to carry out whatever you may undertake with the sole forces that you can draw from the islands", and he stressed the importance of strengthening land fortifications and sent special funds to be expended on Fort Royal.[81]

Continuing French weakness in the West Indies can be traced to the failure of the French army to conquer the United Provinces, to a shift in military strategy owing to Louis XIV's decision that French interests required a major military thrust into western Germany, and to a decision in mid-1674 to support the revolt of the Sicilian city of Messina against Spain. Louis XIV and his generals had planned a single overwhelming campaign against the Netherlands in 1672, but found themselves bereft of allies and bogged down in a frightful slugging match incapable of resolution. As early as 1674, the colonies were feeling the effects of a sharp curtailment of naval and colonial expenditures. The French decision to support Messina in Sicily also drew the navy into the Mediterranean, provoking large, unforeseen expenses leading to virtual abandonment of the Atlantic except for a few small guard ships to protect coastal shipping. Naval activity in the West Indies was also curtailed despite the previous presence of Dutch squadrons there.

Though France and Spain were officially at war, Colbert denied any special assistance to Governor Ogeron, who continued his plans to rescue the French prisoners at Puerto Rico. Instead, Colbert requested that the defunct West India Company send Ogeron some arms and munitions to help the

---

[80]   See Camus, éd., "Correspondance d'Ogeron", 185–6 Commission for Captain John Bennett dated 21 November 1674 and another dated 3 April 1675; also *CSP., CS.*, 1675–76, no. 638 Ogeron's power of attorney issued to Colonel Robert Byndloss, Morgan's brother-in-law; and ibid., no. 1129 also referring to commissions issued by Ogeron and to Morgan's connivance; E. A. Cruikshank, *The Life of Sir Henry Morgan* (Toronto: Macmillan and Co., 1935), 228.

[81]   Clément, éd *Lettres … de Colbert*, 3, pt. 2: 584 Colbert to de Baas, 8 November 1674; ibid., 592 Colbert to de Baas, 17 May 1675.

colonists defend themselves, but made it clear that his chief concern was that the governor assist the company to recover its debts.[82] In August, he advised Rochefort's naval intendant that "the King's intention is to halt all naval expenses, and to allow only those which are indispensably necessary". In the face of the greatest land war in the history of the French monarchy, he added, all available funds, "sans aucune réserve," were being applied to the European war. Only six or seven warships were to be fitted out during the coming year for both coast guard duties and convoy escorts to the Americas.[83]

The important Newfoundland fishery received only grudging attention. Saint-Malo merchants who requested warships for protection were commanded to fit out two of their own strongest vessels for the task. Then, adding insult to injury, Colbert directed they be commanded and officered by the king's nominees allegedly to ensure they remain on patrol and not go off fishing while on the Grand Banks.[84] The minister relented a month later, ordering the dispatch of two warships to the fishery,[85] but he also levied a tax of three livres tournois per ton on all Newfoundland-bound fishing vessels to pay some of the costs. This arrangement became permanent later in the year, and in 1676, two more warships patrolled the Grand Banks, the harbours of Newfoundland's south coast, and the waters off the northern peninsula, for six months.[86] The example of fishery protection illustrates how, despite its great size, the navy reacted to external threats and pleas in the absence of any commitment to a naval policy. While Louis XIV and his minister built an enormous and very costly navy, they had no organized set of ideas about its function.

After three years of war, the French position in the West Indies remained embarrassingly static. Though the defence of Martinique had improved, the colony's security remained in doubt. The militia was as good as any in the islands, and the added presence of eight companies of trained soldiers (400 men) in the king's livery provided colonists with valuable stiffening. The one locally mounted offensive expedition had been a humiliating failure; the famed buccaneers of Saint-Domingue proved unable to look after themselves, and French-Carib relations were in a shambles. The one bright light was the growth in the number of passports issued to French merchantmen between

[82] Camus, éd., "Correspondance d'Ogeron", 172 Colbert to Ogeron, 20 January 1674.
[83] Clément, éd., *Lettres ... de Colbert*, 3, pt. 2: 523–4 Colbert to Demuyn, 13 August 1674.
[84] Ibid., 539–40 Colbert to Sacchi, 28 December 1674; also ibid., 2: 684 Colbert to Marillac, 24 November 1673, for a similar sarcastic response to fishermen's requests for protection.
[85] Marine, B² 30, ff. 32v King to Demuyn, 30 January 1675.
[86] Ibid., ff. 36–7 passport 6 February 1675; ibid., f. 314–15 judgement of the Council of State, 27 November 1675; and ibid., 33 f. 170 Colbert to Sacchi, 13 May 1676; also Marine, B⁴ 7, ff. 204–6v "Journal du voyage de Terreneuve par les navires du roy *Le Duc* et *L'Estoille*, commandés par le sieur de Sourdis", 12 November 1676.

1672 and 1674 as the West India Company went into liquidation,[87] but this proved temporary; no merchant vessels reached Martinique during the second half of 1674. Warships scheduled to remain in the islands for a year could not be maintained, and senior naval officers, like Captain Bitaut de Bléor, busied themselves loading sugar, indigo, cotton, rocou, and 80,000 livres weight of ginger into their worm-eaten ships' holds and storerooms in anticipation of their return voyages to France.[88] Scarcity of provisions and munitions was sufficiently widespread by the beginning of January 1675, that de Baas authorised four English merchantmen to trade at Martinique.[89]

Under these pressures the military situation in the West Indies became abysmal. Naval preparations in France fell to a new low. Indeed, 1675 marked the lowest level of naval expenditure during the quarter century before 1690.[90] In January, authorities assigned only two ships, a third-rate and a fifth-rate, and three *barques longues* or pinnaces to the Caribbean. These small vessels equipped with both oars and sails, to be manned by soldiers, were intended to reduce the St. Vincent Island Caribs to French authority.[91] *Chef d'escadre* marquis de Grancey was appointed to command the reduced division, whose departure was advanced to mid-April. The three third- and fourth-rates in the islands were in such poor condition by June of 1675 that they provided no security at all. Local settlers replaced dead crew members but dysentery continued to reduce numbers. *Le Galant*, 44 guns, lacked 40 men, while the hulls of *Le Marquis*, 44 guns, and *L'Emerillon*, 34 guns, were so fouled and full of worms because of long stays in harbour as to be ineffectual. Lack of careening facilities in the colonies obstructed all attempts to correct the situation. There was also a desperate need to care for sick sailors and to build a hangar to protect masts, yards, and spars from the rains and tropical sun.[92] While naval commissary Jolinet conferred on the best location for a storehouse at Fort Royal, Seignelay had yet to order one to be built. Seignelay's letter to de Baas about the coming campaign is a fascinating combination of flattery and doubletalk, largely designed to let the dying governor know that once again he was being abandoned to his own resources. Henceforth, de Baas was to send his letters directly to His Majesty and, as Colbert's son was now directing naval and colonial affairs, he was no longer to address his letters to "My Lord"; a simple "Monsieur" would suffice. Seignelay kindly admonished de Baas to look after himself

---

[87] Cf. Col., B 4, ff. 107–17 and ibid., vol. 6, ff. 60–6 Etat des passeports, for 1672 and 1674, respectively.

[88] Ibid.

[89] Col., C⁸ᴬ 1, ff. 316–17 Duclerc to Seignelay, 20 January 1675.

[90] Henri Legohérel, *Les Trésoriers généraux de la marine, 1517–1788* (Paris: Éditions Cujas, 1965), 164–5 and 170 tableau no. 5.

[91] Marine, B² 30, f. 126 King's instructions to Grancey, 26 April 1675.

[92] Col., C⁸ᴬ 1, ff. 347–52, Jolinet to Seignelay, 3 June 1675.

and not to fall ill! Finally, reporting that yet another Dutch squadron was expected to arrive in the islands, he sent another 20,000 livres to improve the Cul-de-Sac's fortifications. Both Seignelay and the king called upon the dying governor-general to exhibit the same sterling conduct as before in the face of the enemy.[93]

The marquis de Grancey's instructions also reveal the new policy of constraint. In view of the lack of funds, he was to extend his stay in the West Indies to 18 months, which directly contradicted the decision made in September of 1673 that ships stay only one year. Authorities made no provision for careening the warships, nor did they arrange to send storeships to re-victual and re-provision his ships for the longer stay. They only hoped that Grancey might find sufficient foodstuffs in the colonies. Grancey's primary mission was to defend the islands from attack and secure their trade. He was explicitly advised to accept de Baas' orders during the mission and instructed to avoid all disputes. His orders were anything but clearcut. In the case of de Baas' poor health or death, the king empowered Grancey to issue orders to island governors, but forbad him to go ashore.

Naval authorities in France had counted on the two fourth-rates and the light frigate already in the islands remaining operational and placed them under Grancey's orders. Thus, they hoped to have a strong squadron of five warships operating in the Windward islands before the hurricane season. Seignelay intended to maintain these numbers by fitting out three more naval vessels in August to reach the islands after the hurricane season, and to replace the original three ships, which were to return to France in September.[94] However, Colbert's son did not know that the three warships in the islands had already been laid up, nor had he counted on Grancey's own willful behaviour. In June, Grancey had not yet taken up his command at Rochefort though he had been ordered there two months earlier. Indeed, the *chef d'escadre* was still arguing with Seignelay about the size of his table allowance.[95] On 3 July, an exasperated Louis XIV relieved Grancey of his command, but with exquisite timing, the marquis had sailed two days earlier in *Le Fort*, 56 guns, and *Le Hardy*, 36 guns.[96]

François-Benédict Rouxel de Médary, marquis de Grancey (1635–79), was one of several courtiers whom Colbert drew into the navy along with the comte d'Estrées. Like the latter, Grancey was the son of a marshal of France, and there were other marshals in his immediate family. Though he entered

93 Clément, éd., *Lettres … de Colbert*,3, pt. 2, 590–4 Colbert to de Baas, Sceaux, 17 May 1675.
94 Marine, B² 30, ff. 123v–4 Liste des vaisseaux …, 26 April 1675; also ibid., ff. 149, 150 King to Demuyn, 29 April 1675.
95 Ibid., 31, ff. 127–7v, 163v–4, 199–9v, and 207v–8 four letters from the king and Colbert to Grancey from 3 May to 22 June expressing their growing surprise at the latter's conduct; also see ibid., 29, f. 62 Colbert to Demuyn, May 1675.
96 Ibid., 30, f. 182v Louis XIV to Demuyn, 3 July 1675.

the navy in 1665, he was promoted to general grade rank, *chef d'escadre*, just seven years later, apparently thanks to his privileged connection to Colbert.[97] Grancey reached the islands in August of 1675.

That month, the king's wrath fell on the unsuspecting Captain Bitaut de Bléor just returned from the Antilles. In order to make an example, Louis XIV had his name stricken from the captain's list for having freighted colonial cargoes in his ship.[98] The following spring, the king also ordered the seizure and sale of all the sugar, indigo, and other colonial products freighted to La Rochelle merchants on board three more returning warships and the funds delivered to the naval treasurer.[99] Naval officers were not contributing much to the defence of the islands, and by the end of 1675, after additional reinforcements, *L'Alcion*, 40 guns, *Le Hazardeux*, 40 guns, and *Les Jeux*, 36 guns, had arrived from France, the situation had not improved.[100] By the year's end, the three ships laid up in June had fallen into such a state of disrepair and their crews were so ravaged by sickness that they had to return to France as quickly as possible.[101] Grancey's flagship was seriously hogged and leaking badly, although she had been in the West Indies for less than six months.[102]

Much of the navy's ineffectiveness stemmed from its newness and inexperience. This gave rise to slackness at home and inadequate means to enforce discipline overseas. Not only did Colbert accuse naval captains of freighting so much merchandise for sale in the islands that ships' holds held no more than three months' provisions, but crews found their rations were short and poor in quality.[103] The daily issue of 40 ounces of salt pork for seven men, for example, ordinarily yielded 28 ounces after cooking, but Commissary Jolinet advised Seignelay that it yielded only 16 to 22 ounces after preparation. He also reported that all the pickled meat on hand was 18 to 24 months old and unreliable. The manner in which sailors received their rations also proved troublesome. Clerks of the purveyor-general on board the warships tended to issue a week's brandy ration to each seven-man mess at one time to avoid the tedium of issuing it daily. The result was easily predictable: drunkenness, colic, dysentery, and other sickness increased.[104]

97 Michel Vergé-Franceschi, "Dictionnaire des personnages et des batailles" dans *Mes Campagnes de Mer sous Louis XIV,* par Philippe de Villette-Mursay (Paris: Tallandier, 1991), 334–5.
98 Marine, B² 30, f. 207 King to Vauvré, 2 August 1675.
99 Ibid., 33, ff. 142v–3 Louis XIV to Patoulet, 24 April 1676.
100 BN, *Mélanges de Colbert,* 173, "Mémoire sur la solde des vaisseaux des isles de l'Amérique", 22 March 1676.
101 Col., C⁸ᴬ 1, ff. 361–72 Jolinet to Seignelay, 10 December 1675.
102 Col., C⁸ᴬ 1, f. 355 Jolinet to Seignelay, 6 December 1675.
103 Marine, B², 33, f. 194v Colbert to Demuyn, 29 May 1676, admonishing him to pay greater attention to fitting out the king's ships.
104 Ibid., ff. 354–4v Jolinet to Seignelay, 6 December 1675.

Naval defence of the West Indies continued to be as ineffective as before. Despite Grancey's explicit instructions to cooperate with de Baas, the two men quarrelled, and after the new naval commander angered the governor-general with his pretensions, the latter placed him under virtual house arrest, then sent him home.[105] In June of 1676, the government again dispatched only two ships, *Le Galant*, 46 guns, and *L'Emerillon*, 34 guns, under command of Captain de Montortier to replace *Le Fort* and *Le Hardy*, which were so badly worm-eaten they had to return to France before the hurricane season.[106] The French colonies continued to rely chiefly on the colonists for their defence, but all this was to change during the final two years of the war when events took a much more serious turn.

6.5 NAVAL ASSAULTS

Captain Jacob Binckes had been well-received on his return to Amsterdam in 1673. In the spring of 1676, he was promoted to vice-admiral, given command of seven men of war, a fire ship, and five lesser vessels, and sent back to the West Indies. He was to seize Cayenne from the French and settle the island of Tobago, which had been returned to the Dutch after the Treaty of Westminster. The new Dutch plan is a bit of a puzzle because the Dutch West India Company declared bankruptcy in 1674 after a combination of commercial losses and military expenditures overwhelmed its fragile finances.[107] Binckes reached Cayenne on 4 May 1676. The next day he landed 900 troops near Fort St. Louis, and Governor Cyprien Lefebvre de Lézy quickly surrendered. After placing a small garrison in command, Binckes departed for Marie Galante.[108] He quickly captured the small island and pillaged it.[109] Many colonists, including at least eight planters who were unhappy with Colbert's restrictive regulations, accepted Binckes' offer to settle them at Tobago. The Dutch also carried off 700 slaves and 80 to 100 horses, destroyed sugar boilers, and burnt everything they could not seize.[110] Marie Galante's plantations were still unoccupied at the war's end.[111]

[105]   Col., F³ 26, ff. 117–19 de Baas to Grancy, 10 April 1676; and Col., C⁸ᴬ 1, ff. 383–6 de Baas to Seignelay, 27 July 1676; also Crouse, *The French Struggle*, 111.

[106]   BN, *Mélanges de Colbert*, 173, ff. 231–1v Mémoire sur l'escadre des isles de l'Amérique, 22 March 1676.

[107]   Jan de Vries and Ad van der Woude, *The First Modern Economy, Success, Failure, and Perserverance of the Dutch Economy, 1500–1815* (Cambridge: Cambridge University Press, 1997), 466.

[108]   Goslinga, *The Dutch in the Caribbean*, 478; Shomette and Haslach, *Raid on America*, 319; and Buchet, *La Lutte pour l'espace Caraïbe*, 102–4.

[109]   Col., C⁷ᴬ 3 (nonfoliated), Copy of statement by de Vaeuluisant, notary, 19 June 1676 for account of the attack and pillage of Marie Galante; also Marine, B⁴ 7, f. 179 Copy of Binckes' call on the island's inhabitants to surrender, 31 May 1676.

[110]   Col., C⁷ᴬ 3, Témericourt to de Baas, 20 June 1676.

[111]   Christian Schnakenbourg, "Recherches sur l'histoire de l'industrie sucrière à Marie Galante", 18.

At Guadeloupe, Binckes encountered some of the marquis de Grancey's wornout ships that had taken shelter under the shore batteries at Basseterre, and though they may have aided in driving off the Dutch attackers, they did not seriously hinder them. At Saint Martin, the Dutch, half of which had been seized at the beginning of the war, Admiral Binckes made a more energetic effort, landing 500 men who carried the French defences and killed Governor de Maigne.[112] As at Marie Galante, they were more interested in plunder, and after carrying off about 100 slaves and a large number of cattle they left the French to reoccupy the island.[113] Afterward the Dutch fleet divided. One part, with the Dutch and newly recruited French colonists on board, headed south to Tobago, while Binckes with the larger part sailed for Saint-Domingue. Passing Guadeloupe en route to Tobago, some of the Dutch ships again encountered Grancey's squadron, and though the French kept them under fire for some time, they failed to halt or otherwise interrupt the progress of the Dutch ships laden with booty and passengers.[114] Meanwhile, at Saint-Domingue, Binckes called on the French populace to revolt against their masters, but his appeal failed.[115] At Petit Goâve, the Dutch attacked a fleet of 12 heavily laden merchantmen about to depart for France and seized nearly one million livres weight of tobacco, which they dispatched to Amsterdam.[116] Binckes then sailed to Tobago. Luckily for the French, the Dutch campaign was not aimed at conquest. It was a very profitable search for plunder intended to support another equally serious decision, namely the establishment of a new Dutch colony to windward of all the French settlements in the West Indies.[117]

The 1676 Dutch campaign provides yet another illustration of how the French reacted to, rather than initiated, events during the war. News of the Dutch depredations reached France in August, and Louis XIV responded with immediate orders. Scarcity of naval funds remained a problem, but Colbert found a solution in the private initiative of the comte d'Estrées, who had been virtually unemployed since the English withdrawal from the war in February of 1674. In addition to being under a cloud following the navy's disappointing performance in the North Sea during the first two years of the war, Vice-Admiral d'Estrées had no place in naval operations in the Mediterranean, where he was eclipsed by the duc de Vivonne. The latter was not only Captain-General of the Galley Corps, but the elder brother of Louis XIV's current influential mistress, Madame de Montespan, and since 1675, a marshal of France.

[112] Col., C^{8A} 1, ff. 383–8 de Baas to Colbert, 27 July and 12 September 1676.

[113] Goslinga, *The Dutch in the Caribbean*, 479.

[114] Col., C^{8A} 1, ff. 378–82, and 383–7 de Baas to Colbert, n.d. and 27 July 1676.

[115] See Mims, *Colbert's West India Policy*, 246 n72 for translation of Binckes' written appeal to the French colonists.

[116] Ibid., 247.

[117] Buchet, *La Lutte pour l'espace Caraïbe*, 103.

In November of 1675, d'Estrées, whose other options appeared to be to follow the king on campaign, to live in Paris, or to retire to his estates in the country, proposed to Colbert that, with very little expense, he could carry the maritime war to the Spanish and the Dutch. He initially conceived of an operation with seven or eight warships in the English Channel but quickly expanded the proposal to an attack on the Spanish treasure fleet. He offered to pay to fit out a number of warships and recruit 700 troops on his own account in return for a share of the booty.[118] By April, d'Estrées and his backers had revised the proposal to attack Curaçao instead. Four warships and two pinnaces would join the king's ships being fitted out for the Antilles, bringing the total number of French warships available for the attack to nine. Secrecy was essential to success, d'Estrées advised, but chiefly to keep Governor-General de Baas rather than the Dutch from finding out about the expedition![119] Louis XIV approved the plan, awarding d'Estrées one-third of the value of any booty taken during the campaign, and Colbert assured the admiral of his willingness to assist in any way possible in fitting out the vessels.[120] In August, following receipt of news that the Dutch had captured Cayenne, plundered Marie Galante, killed the governor of St. Martin, destroyed Petit Goâve, seized Saint-Domingue's tobacco harvest, and were settling Tobago, Colbert's son revised d'Estrées' proposal. Having no extra funds for colonial defence, he regarded the admiral's idea as more attractive than ever,[121] but the minister ordered that the expedition first recover Cayenne and drive the Dutch from Tobago before attacking Curaçao.

On 17 December 1676, Vice-Admiral d'Estrées in command of four ships of the line and eight smaller vessels reached Cayenne, and the following day, after overcoming a spirited but brief resistance, retook the fort from the Dutch.[122] Leaving the former French governor in command of a small garrison, he sailed for Martinique. Once there, he learned that Governor-General de Baas had died on 15 January. D'Estrées lost no time appealing for troops to support his enterprise and after collecting 300 or 400 volunteers and soldiers he quickly departed, arriving at Tobago on 15 February.[123] The

118   Marine, B⁴ 7, ff. 437–9 "Relation de la prise de l'isle".

119   Ibid., ff. 191–2v [Anonymous], "Mémoire pour Monsieur le marquis de Seignelay du mois d'avril d[erni]er".

120   Marine, B² 33, ff. 1565v–7, 199v Colbert to d'Estrées, 1 and 29 May 1676.

121   BN, Clairambault, 879, ff. 132–40 [anomymous], "Relation de la prise de l'isle et forts de Cayenne et de l'ataque de celle de Tobago contre less Hollondais en 1677 par les vaisseaux du Roy" [n.d.]; also Buchet, *La Lutte pour l'espace Caraïbe*, 2: 1018–19.

122   Marine, B⁴ 7, ff. 199–201 "Relation de la prise de Cayenne à l'Amérique par les françois sur les hollondois", 18 December 1676; Ibid., ff. 354–61v "Relation de la navigation de l'escadre des vaisseaux de Sa Majesté depuis Brest jusqu'à Cayenne, Cte d'Estrées, 21 January 1677; and ibid., ff. 363–8v d'Estrées to Seignelay, 9 February 1677. See Buchet, *La Lutte de l'espace caraïbe*, 1: 105–16 for an analysis of the campaign and 2: 588, 620 for details concerning the ships.

123   Colonies, C⁸ᴬ 2, ff. 11–12 Sainte-Marthe to Colbert 24 January 1676.

ensuing engagement, involving 15 French and 14 Dutch ships, was the largest naval action yet fought in the West Indies.

The French enjoyed undoubted superiority. Their fleet mounted 494 guns and carried more than 2,600 men against the Dutch force of 313 guns and 1,700 men.[124] D'Estrées' flagship, *Le Glorieux*, 60 guns, *L'Intrepide*, 56 guns, commanded by Louis Gabaret, his second-in-command, and *Le Fendant*, 54 guns, Captain comte de Blénac, were all larger than the Dutch flagship,[125] but the Dutch had been busy during the previous five or six months and were positioned behind strong fortifications. Unable to draw Binckes out of his strong defensive position inside the island's reef-strewn harbour, d'Estrées attempted to force the entrance, a tactic which failed badly. In a new effort, the French landed a large party of soldiers to seize the fort and turn its guns on the Dutch squadron anchored close inshore. With heavy losses though, the landing force failed to achieve its objective. On 3 March, d'Estrées attempted a second attack from the sea. The Dutch fleet was destroyed in the ensuing conflagration, but the French were still unable to take the fort. Moreover, d'Estrées' own losses were too severe to attempt another attack.[126] Four of the king's ships (the largest) were lost and several captains, including Louis Gabaret, and hundreds of sailors were killed or wounded.[127] A week later Vice-Admiral d'Estrées withdrew to Grenada, whence he dispatched two ships back to Tobago in order to contain half a dozen privateers operating out of the island. Afterwards, he sailed to France.[128]

The government went to great lengths to make it appear that d'Estrées had won a great naval victory even striking two medals, the first marking the recovery of Cayenne and the second the battle for Tobago.[129] However, the fact remained that the Dutch continued to possess Tobago, which strategically threatened Martinique and the French Windward islands while providing a forward defence for Curaçao and a windward refuge for privateers.[130] Despite the celebratory bonfires in Paris, the comte d'Estrées, Louis XIV, and Colbert understood that Tobago had to be taken.[131] Only six months after the failed attempt, a new fleet of seven of the line and four smaller warships,

---

[124]   Buchet, *La Lutte pour l'espace Caraïbe*, 1: 108 gives about 4,000 French to 1,700 Dutch.
[125]   Crouse, *The French Struggle*, 113–18; Goslinga, *The Dutch in the Caribbean*, 448–53; also Buchet, *La Lutte pour l'espace caraïbe*, 1: 107–16; and 2: 598, 620.
[126]   Marine, B⁴ 7, ff. 373–80v "Relation de ce qui s'est passé à la défaite de l'escadre des vaisseaux Hollondois à Tobago ... ", 26 May 1677 [printed account].
[127]   See Marine B⁴ 7, ff. 83 *passim* procès verbaux de la perte des vaisseaux, March 1677.
[128]   BN, *Mélanges de Colbert*, 174bis f.393 summary of d'Estrées to Seignelay, 25 June 1677.
[129]   Hotêl de la Monnaie, *La Médaille au temps de Louis XIV* (Paris: Imprimeris Nationale, 1970), nos. 393 and 394.
[130]   See Buchet, *La lutte pour l'espace caraïbe*, 1: 130–1.
[131]   Marine, B⁴ 7, ff. 370–2v d'Estrées to Colbert, 1 April 1677; ibid., ff. 410–11 "Mémoire touchant les dispositions nécesaires aux entrprises qu'on pourroit former à Brest, 28 June 1677 (signed) d'Estrées.

all fitted out at the king's expense, were lying in readiness for Vice-Admiral d'Estrées to once again assume command. Much stronger than the previous force, it contained three second-rates. Before there had been none. The large second-rates mounted 18 pounders in their main batteries compared to 12 pounders carried in third-rates.[132]

Vice-Admiral Jean d'Estrées (1624–1707) was an experienced sailor and a brave man. He was the nephew of Gabrielle d'Estrées, Henri IV's mistress, and son of a marshal of France. He had also been a high-ranking army officer, a lieutenant-general since 1655, and wounded in action. Though usually characterised as incompetent, an "*intru*" whose haughtiness ensured that he would never be accepted in the navy, this view has been recently challenged and denied.[133] D'Estrées entered the navy in 1668 after quarreling with the war minister, the marquis de Louvois. He received command of the naval squadron sent to the West Indies in 1669 and the very next year was appointed *vice-amiral du Ponant*. The extreme rapidity and clearly political nature of his advance to the senior command of the navy left him open to calumny, which was not long in coming. His reputation was of incompetence though the evidentiary basis is slim and highly politicized. Moreover, there is a case to be made in his favour. Throughout 1670, the year he was promoted to vice-admiral, d'Estrées showed himself to be a hard-working commander-in-chief afloat. Early in the year he took a squadron to Lisbon and cruised off Salé, Morocco. Almost immediately following his return, he departed again with a squadron of new ships to cruise between Grand Canary Island and Cape Verde, Africa. Far from being merely the courtier admiral that so many historians have depicted, the comte d'Estrées appeared anxious to master ship handling and naval practice.

Unlike the navies of other maritime powers, the French navy was brand new. During the eleven years after 1661, the number of warships in the fleet grew from 9 to 120 rated vessels.[134] D'Estrées' letters to Colbert are filled with observations about ships' performances, the constraints on long voyages imposed by insufficient space for provisions, and the lack of blue-water sailing experience of many captains. The vice-admiral's open and frank acknowledgement of his own need and desire to gain knowledge and skill is also worth noting.[135] D'Estrées served as commander-in-chief of the French navy during the opening years of the Franco-Dutch War when France and England were allies. The lack of any success during the two campaign seasons, the infighting within the English naval command, and d'Estrées' own

---

132 Buchet, *La Lutte pour l'espace caraïbe*, 2: 598, 620.
133 Ibid., 1: 119 is the latest to present the traditional view, but see Dessert, *La Royale*, 187–90, 225 for the revision.
134 Patrick Villiers, *Marine royale, corsaires et trafic dans l'Atlantique de Louis XIV a Louis XVI*, 2 vols. (Dunkerque: Société dunkerquois d'histoire et d'archéologie, 1991), 1: 64–5.
135 See BN, *Mélanges de Colbert*, no. 176, 410–12v and ibid., 176bis, ff. 480–1v.

tactical inexperience during the battles of Solebay, Schooneveldt, and Texel brought harsh accusations of cowardice and betrayal from his English allies. In truth, he may have been betrayed by some of his own officers.[136] Vice-Admiral d'Estrées obtained command of the West Indies squadron in 1676 in part, as we have seen, because he paid to fit out part of it, but also because he had always been advanced by Colbert, who was dazzled by the idea of allying a member of such an illustrious family to the navy.[137]

By 1677, the New World had begun to impinge on international relations in a wholly unexpected way, and d'Estrées' continuation in command had significant and lasting consequences. Flying his flag in *Le Terrible*, 68 guns, d'Estrées departed Brest for the West Indies on 3 October. His squadron comprised seven ships of the line from 50 to 68 guns, four fourth- and fifth-rates from 34 to 44 guns, five flûtes, and four fireships. It was the strongest French naval force ever sent to the Americas.[138] The marquis de Grancey, in *Le Tonnant*, 64 guns, replaced Gabaret as second-in-command and the comte de Blénac, commanding *Le Belliqueux*, 60 guns, carried the king's commission as the new governor-general of the French West Indies. Blénac also held instructions that, as soon as he reached Martinique, he was to recruit soldiers and colonists to reinforce the naval crews and to act in concert with Vice-Admiral d'Estrées.[139]

The squadron first sailed to the Cape Verde islands and on 31 October seized the island of Gorée, off present-day Dakar, from the Dutch. Afterward, d'Estrées quickly made for the Caribbean.[140] Learning from the previous year's experience to leave no time for a warning to reach the Dutch, he stopped only briefly at Barbados in search of intelligence about Dutch strength before anchoring off Tobago on 6 December.[141]

The French military plan proceeded smoothly. The Dutch had been only lightly reinforced, and Admiral Binckes had few resources. D'Estrées possessed overwhelming force at sea, and the comte de Blénac commanded a landing force of 950 troops and an all-important artillery train to lay siege to the fort that had so strongly resisted the previous spring. Hauling mortars

[136]　For discussion of these battles, see Mahan, *Influence of Sea Power*, 146–8; Richmond, *The Navy as an Instrument of Power*, 175–87, and Villiers, *Marine royale, corsaires*, 1:71–3. But see also J. D. Davies, *Gentlemen and Tarpaulins: The Officiers and Men of the Restoration Navy*, (Oxford: Clarendon Press, 1991), 159–63 and 172–3; Dessert, *La Royale*, 241, and Jones, *The Anglo-Dutch Wars*, 189–91, 203–5, 208–11.

[137]　Etienne Taillemite, *L'Histoire ignorée de la marine française* (Paris: Librairie Academique Perrin, 1988), 113–16.

[138]　Marine, B⁴ 7, f. 353 "Escadre des Isles de l''Amérique commandé par M. le Cte d'Estrées en 1677".

[139]　Col., F³ 26, f. 137 King to Blénac, 11 August 1677.

[140]　Marine, B⁴ 7, ff. 420–5v "Relation de la prise de l'Isle de Gorée et de ses forts possedez par les hollondois au Cap Vert", 13 November 1677.

[141]　Ibid., ff. 429–34v "Relation de la prise de l'Isle et fort de Tobago et des vaisseaux qui sont trouvez dans le port, 25 December 1677".

and cannons about four miles to a hilltop overlooking the fort was exhausting work, but after spending three days dragging them into position, the French engineer opened fire and dropped his third shell into the powder magazine, blowing up the fort, killing Admiral Binckes, 16 officers, and 250 men. French forces attacked immediately to forestall any rally and seized four sinking ships as well as the shattered fort in less than an hour.[142] They took 600 prisoners.[143] What had been inconceivable only four years before became a reality. With the capture of Tobago the French permanently expunged the Dutch military presence from the Lesser Antilles. After sending the most severely injured and sick prisoners to the Dutch, Admiral d'Estrées sailed to Martinique to prepare his attack on Curaçao. The French were finally on the verge of accomplishing Colbert's long-held aim of permanently destroying Dutch power in the New World.

Unaccountably, d'Estrées cruised through the Windward islands for the next four months from January to April seeking support for the attack on Curaçao. The long interval was probably due to the lack of resources in the islands to replenish the warships and refresh their crews. The king had ordered Governor Pouançay at Saint-Domingue to recruit 200 buccaneers and send them to Martinique in December, and to raise 1,000 to 1,200 more the following month.[144] It was not until early in May that d'Estrées met up with Pouançay and the buccaneers in 15 of their own ships at St. Christopher.[145] Relations between English and French on the island had grown very strained, and the previous year Governor Saint Laurent had offered a treaty of neutrality and continuing friendship in order to forestall an English declaration of war.[146] With such overwhelming French force on hand, it was just as well that the decidedly nervous English governor had earlier accepted the French offer.[147]

D'Estrées broadcast his intention to attack the Spanish at Puerto Rico, and on 7 May departed for Curaçao. Four days later, believing himself to be farther west than he actually was, the French fleet ran onto coral reefs surrounding the low-lying Aves islands some 60 miles east of its destination. Seven ships of the line, including the flagship, were lost along with a flute,

[142] Ibid., ff. 431–4v; also ff. 461–74 Patoulet to Seignelay, 23 January 1677.

[143] Crouse, *The French Struggle*, 118–20; Goslinga, *The Dutch in the Caribbean*, 454–6; and *CSP, CS*, 1677–80, no. 498 Gov. Atkins of Barbados to Council of Trade and Plantations, 2 January [o.s.], 1678.

[144] Marine, B⁴ 7 f. 412 copy of Louis XIV to Pouançay, 12 August 1677.

[145] BN, n.a.f., 9325, Pouançay to Colbert, 28 February 1678.

[146] Clément, éd., *Lettres ... Colbert*, 3, pt. 2: 626–8 Colbert to d'Estrées, 11 March 1678; Marine, B⁴ 8, ff. 250–3v "Mémoire du cinquieme may ..., 1678". (signed) le Cte d'Estrées; see Frances G. Davenport, *European Treaties bearing on the History of the Unites States and its Dependencies*, 4 vols., (Washington: Carnegie Institution, 1917–1937), 2: 256–60 for the terms of the treaty.

[147] *CSP, CS*, 1677–80, nos. 665 and 690 dated 18 and 26 April [o.s.] 1678.

three transports, and three privateers. How many French sailors drowned is unknown; estimates range from 80 to 500.[148] D'Estrées returned to France on the only ship of the line to survive. Though the disaster is tradition-ally explained as owing to the admiral's ignorance and arrogance, historian Daniel Dessert has recently subjected the entire incident to critical scrutiny and concluded that the most damaging testimony, written by d'Estrées' flag captain, de Méricourt, was little more than a fabrication.[149] The marquis de Seignelay, who thoroughly investigated the incident, appeared to agree. Vice-Admiral d'Estrées sailed twice more to the Americas in command of naval squadrons, and in 1684 Louis XIV named him a marshal of France.

While the disaster did have consequences, it did not affect the terms of the peace that France negotiated with the United Provinces, for it was not known in time. Two treaties, both dated 10 August 1678, were signed. The first dealt chiefly with Europe, but Article Seven, which left the parties in possession of territories currently held, gave the French Tobago, Cayenne, and the is-land of Gorée. The second was a commercial treaty which guaranteed the Dutch freedom of trade and navigation and represented a significant French concession, but the articles applied to Europe only.[150] The French had safe-guarded their overseas possessions. In the Franco-Spanish treaty signed on 17 September, Louis XIV failed to secure Spanish recognition of his pos-session of the western part of the island of Hispaniola, and, a point fre-quently overlooked, hostilities between the two parties continued "beyond the line".[151] France signed a fourth treaty with the Holy Roman Emperor in February of 1679. Together, these treaties are known as the Peace of Nijmegen.

6.6 CONCLUSION

The results of the Franco-Dutch War and the treaties that ended it influenced later developments in the Americas in three significant ways. First, they drove the Dutch militarily from the Lesser Antilles and substantially reduced Dutch commercial influence on the French colonies. Though their new English allies returned St. Eustatius to the Dutch, the island was waterless and useless as a naval base. Stewart L. Mims' argument that Colbert's West India policy and its vehicle the West India Company were primarily responsible for excluding

[148] Newton, *The European Nations*, 307; Buchet, *La Lutte pour l'espace Caraïbe*, 119; Vergé-Franceschi, "Dictionnaire" 246–7; and Dessert, *La Royale*, 190.

[149] Ibid., 187–91, and 250–2, who also reprints in full Méricourt's account of the disaster (ibid., 334–42).

[150] Davenport, *European Treaties*, 2: 262.

[151] McKay and Scott, *Rise of the Great Powers*, 34 incorrectly claims that Spain surrendered the western portion of Hispaniola to France. Spain acknowledged French sovereignty over the western one-third of the island only in 1697.

the Dutch from the French islands is untenable. So, too, is the success of French commercial shipping, which he claimed replaced the Dutch at this time. Dutch privateers remained active in the Windward islands until as late as June of 1677, when some reportedly burnt all the French vessels on the coast of Saint-Domingue.[152] Dutch access to the French colonies was denied through naval action. The French naval expeditions to the Caribbean brought a process begun by the English in 1666 to a successful conclusion in 1678. Curaçao remained an entrepôt, but it was too far leeward to threaten the French Antilles.

The comte d'Estrées' earlier successes in his West Indian campaigns weighed heavily in France's favour during the peace negotiations. The recapture of Cayenne in December of 1676, his destruction of the last Dutch squadron in the West Indies in March of 1677, and the capture of Gorée and Tobago in October and December, respectively, were major accomplishments that secured French colonial possessions from France's chief enemy. They also contributed significantly to France's future development of the slave trade. These successes not only outweighed the effects of the tragedy at the Aves islands, but in the long run had greater political significance than Abraham Duquesne's famous "victories" in the Mediterranean during the same period.[153]

The second, unforeseen consequence of d'Estrées' campaigns was that the Nijmegen treaties left France and England as the only remaining first-rank contenders in the West Indies. The very act of removing the Dutch from political and military contention clarified the stakes in any future contest. However, the most overlooked significance of the Franco-Dutch War is that for the first time it involved Louis XIV's large but young, untried navy in distant campaigns, and though the war taught many lessons, few were learned. The ships of the line and frigates sent to the West Indies greatly aided in driving foreign shipping from the French islands, but the navy's effectiveness was reduced by weak institutional boundaries and constant quarrels between navy and army officers, insufficient provisions, sickly crews, and the very rapid deterioration of warships in the warm tropical waters. Naval support proved difficult to maintain for any length of time in the islands. Ships and men quickly succumbed to the effects of the tropical climate.

Nevertheless, the comte d'Estrées' failure to take Curaçao cannot be dismissed. Although it failed to influence the peace negotiations, it significantly affected French domestic politics.[154] Not even the striking of yet a third medal commemorating the capture of Tobago could disguise the injury to

---

152   BN, *Mélanges de Colbert*, 174bis f. 393 summary of d'Estrées to Seignelay, 25 June 1677; and *CSP, CS*, 1677–80, no. 313 Governor Lord Vaughan to Secretary Coventry, 26 June [o.s.] 1677.

153   Dessert, *La Royal*, 251.

154   Hotel de la Monnaie, *La Médaille au temps de Louis XIV*, 170 planche no. 251.

the king's prestige of the Aves islands disaster. The loss of 11 ships of the line and hundreds if not thousands of sailors' lives in the West Indies during the war undermined the king's confidence in his navy. The navy may even be said to have created an embarrassment. *L'Intrépide*, sunk by the Dutch during the first attack on Tobago, was refloated and sailed to Amsterdam, where she remained a visible reminder of successful Dutch resistance to French aggression. At the end of the war, Louis XIV's agents quietly repurchased the vessel and returned it to France, thereby removing this visible stain on the king's *gloire*.[155] The failure to take Curaçao also meant that despite the ambitions of Colbert and his successors, France would never succeed in overcoming Dutch and later English competition in order to play the long-sought major role in the illicit trade with Spanish America. Finally, losses in the Americas and the ineffectual campaigns in the North Sea moderated the effect of any naval successes in the Mediterranean, and left Colbert and his son much diminished in their rivalry with the war minister.

While d'Estrées' two expeditions contained many lessons for the new navy, they also revealed its lack of overseas experience. Early in July of 1677, immediately after it returned to France, the first expedition's commissary, Jean-Baptiste Patoulet, reported a number of important observations and made several recommendations concerning future naval operations in the Caribbean.[156] Chiefly, he advised the navy to build a careening wharf and a small naval base at Fort Royal. Patoulet stressed that warships in the tropics had to be frequently careened in order to kill the ship worm, *teredo navalis*, that ate away submerged hulls, leaving flimsy, honeycombed shells. Careening and sheathing could not be accomplished without a wharf, which is why he ruled out stationing a hulk in the colony. Patoulet recommended that the naval base ought to contain at least a warehouse with special handling facilities for navy pitch, fish oil, and tallow, and a well-equipped forge, charcoal, and a skilled armorer. A storehouse would permit the navy to avoid the clutches of merchants and their exorbitant rates, and a navy forge at Martinique would allow tradesmen among ships' crews to work iron. D'Estrées had landed troops to assault shore positions and had found that many small arms proved to be useless or were damaged during the landings. Maintaining a well-supported armorer at Martinique was a sound recommendation, especially after the West Indies became part of the royal domain and the king sent increasing numbers of infantry and large quantities of arms to the colonies. There was also an unexpected need for extra spars and topmasts in the West Indies where warships beat continually to windward to regain their stations after chasing suspicious vessels. Patoulet blamed many deaths among d'Estrées' sailors on the absence of a hospital ship. He was probably

[155] Dessert, *La Royale*, 325.
[156] Colonies, C^{8B} 1, no. 45 mémoire et observations de Patoulet, Versailles, 6 July 1677; printed in Buchet, *La Lutte pour l'espace caraïbe*, 1: 134–6.

correct to state that the navy's chief enemy was dysentery rather than the Dutch. He recommended that any flûte employed as a hospital could carry sufficient extra spars for the entire expedition during the outbound voyage.

The most striking evidence of the navy's inexperience with long distance operations lay in flaws in food preparation, packing, and distribution. Patoulet recommended that in the future, rations be organised and distributed among groups of seven men, and consist only of biscuit, three and a half livres weight of salt pork, and a pint of brandy. Sailors should be issued with small kettles to facilitate preparation. Greater attention should also be paid to packing naval provisions in tight, well-made casks to reduce leakage and waste during long voyages. Finally, Patoulet recommended that naval commissaries, attached to future expeditions, be supplied with funds. Only by good fortune, in 1677 and 1678, had Commissary Jolinet arranged to meet Patoulet's pay orders for repairs to ships, purchases of goods, medicines, and linen and rent to house the sick and wounded.

Following the second expedition, Patoulet continued to identify serious problems concerning crews' victuals, insubordination of junior officers, and piloting. He strongly criticised many captains' practices.[157] Ships' holds were too much given over to the rations of captains' servants who traded them in the islands. He accused captains of taking a "sordid interest" (*un vilain petit interet*) or a portion of the rations issued to seamen. The result was that the crews' victuals were appalling. He proposed that sailors' rations be issued jointly by captains and commissaries. He also recommended that captains submit reports on the conduct of all ships' officers in order to improve discipline. According to the commissary, pilots were never employed on the king's ships because the art of pilotage was not a respected profession in France. Sailors who can read and write and who surpass their peers in knowledge, he wrote, quickly leave their low condition to become masters. They then find employment in merchantmen. The only solution, he added, was to advance pilots in the king's service and raise their pay. It is not surprising that a little more than six months after filing this second report, Jean-Baptiste Patoulet was appointed the first intendant of the French islands of America.[158]

Patoulet's recommendations, designed to improve sailors' living conditions at sea and in the West Indies, had a strong humanitarian aspect to them. Included in his instructions on the second expedition was the minister's admonition to establish a hospital for sick soldiers and sailors.[159] Except for the hospital which was soon erected, chiefly to care for soldiers of the colonial garrisons, the minister of marine did not adopt these sensible

[157] Col., C^{8B} 1, no. 48 "Mémoire des observations faites par le S. Patoulet dans son voyage à la suitte des escadres des Isles," September 1678.

[158] Col., B 9, ff. 8–9 pouvoir de l'intendant de justice, police et finances aux Isles d'Amérique, 1 April 1679.

[159] Col., B 7, ff. 133v–34v Colbert to Patoulet, 11 September 1677.

recommendations, and it is useful to ask why. The partial answer is that any administrator's views were always rather jaundiced. Patoulet, for example, saw only merchant greed. Like Colbert, he considered merchants incapable of acting in the public good or able to aid the navy. More importantly, lack of funds and uncertainty about the navy's contribution to the defence of the West Indies were also factors.

The French learned valuable lessons from the two naval expeditions overseas. The dreadful effects of ship worm, scurvy, and tropical fevers on warships and crews became well-known. So too were the effects of the rainy season and of hurricanes. Christian Buchet recently contrasted the failure of French campaigns in March with successful campaigning in December, but whether the highest officials in the naval ministry understood the limitations that tropical sailing conditions and weather imposed on warships and crews or if they acted upon these and similar recommendations remains unclear. No naval establishments, not a dockyard nor a careening wharf, nor a naval station, were ever constructed in the French colonies.

The primary reason for the inactivity on the sensible recommendations of naval commissaries in the colonies may well have related to the naval liabilities that arose during the war. The ostensible reason was undoubtedly logistical. First, warships were not well-fitted out in France. No other conclusion is possible in the face of the rapid deterioration of hulls soon after their arrival in tropical waters. Second, logistical problems were not easily solved. Seventeenth-century warships were not built to carry six months' worth of provisions for distant campaigns. The organisation and regulation of naval provisioning only occurred during the war itself; arrangements to re-victual warships were inadequate and lacked any sense of urgency. Transports and victualing ships arrived late or not at all.[160] Finally, and very importantly, the French West Indies were incapable of supplying provisions to re-victual the naval squadrons. Possessing only small populations and with a growing commitment to commercial agriculture based on slavery, the colonists had neither the land, labour, nor inclination to grow provisions for the navy. Unlike the English and Spanish, the French had no colonies in the Americas that produced agricultural surpluses; like their Dutch enemies, they had to carry all their provisions and stores from Europe.

Though the navy obtained its first experience attempting to project power overseas, Louis XIV gained no appreciation of the navy's function and his prestige suffered a serious blow. None of the ambiguities of administration, finances, and function that had been incorporated into Louis XIV's young navy were resolved during the Franco-Dutch War. The French may not have built naval facilities in the New World because government authorities never understood the possible role that naval defence of the colonies might play.

---

[160] See Buchet, *La Lutte pour l'espace Caraïbe*, 2: 1021–4, 1027–31.

They continued to rely, as in the past, on fortifications and local military forces. Louis XIV and Colbert failed to grasp that the navy had made major contributions to the defence of French possessions in the West Indies.

The final consequence of the naval campaigns to defend the West Indies during the Dutch War is that their results had mixed long-term effects that limited future naval activity in overseas defence. In warfare, as in economic development, short-term financial exigencies continually undermined the naval defence of the colonies. The fitting out of three naval vessels by the comte d'Estrées in August of 1676 provides an early example. The use of private capital to support or sustain France's war efforts overseas subverted naval defence. By giving priority to a quick return on investment at the same time as naval expenses assigned to the marine department were withdrawn during wartime or declined during the later years of Louis XIV's reign, not surprisingly, denied the navy an active role in the defence of the empire.

The war made clear that colonies of settlement were a precondition to continuing the struggle in the Americas. Despite the undeniable courage of the French defenders of the Cul-de-Sac at Martinique in 1674 and the military ability of Admiral Binckes and his Dutch sailors and soldiers in 1673 and 1677, success required support from the colonies themselves. Despite the failure of Governor-General de Baas to capture Curaçao in 1673 and Vice-Admiral d'Estrées' failure to take the same colony five years later, the French experience at Tobago in 1677 clearly demonstrated the need for naval expeditions to be supported and reinforced from the colonies. Without such support, naval expeditions in the West Indies were little more than raids for plunder and property. Even though the French and English possessed island bases from which to launch their hostilities, the Franco-Dutch War in the West Indies established a pernicious tradition from which the navy never escaped.

7

The Nine Years' War in America,
1688–1697

7.1 INTRODUCTION

Louis XIV's attack across the Rhine in September of 1688 was intended to be a short, sharp intervention into German politics. No one, least of all the king, anticipated that his action would usher in a quarter century of almost continual warfare during which both French power and France's territorial integrity became central issues in European international relations. France survived the wars of the next quarter century with its territory intact and a French Bourbon seated on the throne of Spain, but its hegemonic ambitions in Europe were beaten back for nearly 80 years. The overseas dimensions of the international conflict were small compared to the struggle in Europe, but they were not without significance. What was called the War of the League of Augsburg caught the French colonists and the minister of marine who was responsible for their security unexpectedly. Both were unprepared. The first so-called French overseas empire that emerged during this and the subsequent conflict was born of war rather than of peace. While settlers and their slaves remained the primary shapers of the new societies and empire remained elusive, they could not escape the impact of military imperialism.

During the decade after 1678, French colonies experienced a respite from European enemies and enjoyed a modest development, but Louis XIV's continuing aggression against neighbouring states had its counterparts in the Americas. Hostilities against the Spanish Low Countries were matched in the Gulf of Mexico by the sacking of Vera Cruz in 1683 and La Salle's projects in the Spanish borderlands, while schemes for the acquisition of New York and English fur trading posts in Hudson Bay were pursued farther north. In 1683, the minister of marine introduced regular infantry called *troupes de la marine* into the colonies for their defence. While imperial factors began to appear, French aggression in the American colonies was chiefly carried out by surrogates of the state, buccaneers and explorers in the West Indies and *coureurs de bois* and merchants in the northern interior. Moreover, during the 1680s Amerindians rather than European rivals administered the severest checks to New France's social and economic development.

The empire that emerged during the first great period of French-English conflict was characterised by uncertainty, disproportion, and incoherence. Demographically, *la France d'outre-mer* contained fewer than 60,000 people, both white and black in 1685, and not much more than double that number a generation later in 1715 (see Appendix 1). About 30,000 French faced hundreds of thousands of Spanish, English, and later Portuguese. Yet, territorially, it was among the largest empires, sprawling across a vast area of North America and islands in the West Indies, and extending to the northeast shoulder of South America. This was also true economically. During these war years, French colonial sugar production surpassed Brazil's, and France would soon overcome Great Britain as the greatest sugar-producing nation in the world. These disproportionate characteristics were so strong that it is difficult to delineate the shape of these territories. It lacked coherence. It had no centre. In the words of historian Jean Meyer, "nothing acted to concentrate human effort or physical resources".[1]

It is commonplace to state that naval operations played little part in the defence of French America and exerted little influence on the course of the great European wars during the period between 1689 and 1713, but this is to view events through the wrong end of the telescope. Of course early naval operations had little immediate impact, but they were not without effect or significance. Far more than the Franco-Dutch conflict in the West Indies during the 1670s, the quarter century after 1688 marked the beginning of colonial struggles that had profound influence upon European international relations during the eighteenth century. The French struggle in the colonies included Dutch, Spanish, as well as English opponents. Indeed, during the Nine Years' War, France's chief enemy in the Americas shifted from England to Spain as the conflict progressed. Considering that France also faced the Iroquois in New York, it is not surprising that the French relied heavily on local manpower and resources for self-defence. It was the appearance of the metropolitan factors, the navy and its colonial infantry, that often made the difference between success and failure. During the Nine Years' War, Colbert's big navy policy was first undermined, then rejected as changing circumstances forced adoption of privateering and colonial self-reliance. Though imperialism was a factor, colonial forces continued to shape local societies. Louis XIV's obsession with Europe allowed local factors and personal ambitions to influence the outcome of colonial developments, revealing, in yet another way, the empire's elusiveness.

---

[1] Jean Meyer, *et al.*, *Histoire de la France coloniale*, Vol. 1, *des origines à 1914* (Paris: Armand Colin, 1991), 39–41.

The War of the League of Augsburg is a misnomer. The name fails to link the great maritime struggle between 1689 and 1697 to the European continental conflict. Known in American and English historiography as King William's War or the War of William III, these names do not capture its complexity either. Various Indian nations in North America were major participants rather than imperial pawns. Some historians have recently referred to it as the War of the English Succession, for it was the arrival of an heir to James II of England in the summer of 1688 and William of Orange's *coup d'état* in early November that rapidly transformed Louis XIV's attack in the Rhineland into a larger war involving the United Provinces, the Emperor, Spain, and England, and reached across the Atlantic to the Americas, but this new designation ignores the fact that Louis XIV initiated the war. Though not entirely satisfactory, the neutral appellation, the Nine Years' War, is used hereafter.

Initially unprepared for a war at sea and subsequently preoccupied with plans for landing troops in the British Isles and restoring James II to his throne, France had neither the will nor the strength to oppose the English or the Spanish overseas. Aside from locally mounted operations in several colonies, the French sent very little assistance to the colonies during the first four years of the war. Any help that arrived was grudgingly dispatched. In the meantime, the English sent several strong expeditions to the colonies and encouraged local ones as well, all with the intention of conquering French territory and driving the French out of the Americas. The result was paradoxical. Despite sending four metropolitan expeditions to the West Indies and mounting two colonial ones against Acadia and New France, the English were weaker in 1694 than they had been in 1689, while the French, vastly outnumbered and left largely to their own devices, appeared to be strengthened. During the final three years of war, the French moved from the defensive to the offensive. They changed their focus from the English to the Spanish and pursued naval policies in both the north and south that proved effective in the short term. However, the result was ambiguous, for while it contributed coincidentally to knocking Spain out of the war, the war also demonstrated the limited ability of naval power to increase French colonial security. The remainder of this chapter deals with the various campaigns in the Caribbean and off the east coast of New France in order to assess their significance while illustrating the disproportion, ambiguity, and complexity of the Nine Years' War in America.

7.2 THE WINDWARD ISLANDS

War began quickly in the West Indies. Tensions between the French and English over the behaviour of Island Caribs and the question of access to the island of Dominica were nearing a flash point before hostilities commenced.

A memoir from Martinique in 1688 called for 20 warships and 2,000 troops supported by colonial detachments to destroy Barbados.[2] In October, the marquis de Seignelay informed the governor-general and the governors of each island, independently, that Louis XIV's resolve to declare war on the Dutch Republic would undoubtedly cause a rupture with Spain and advised them to take defensive measures: inspecting fortifications and militia units, readying artillery batteries, and issuing orders to assemble local defence forces.[3] The only aid they could expect from France was two privateers from Saint-Malo destined to attack Dutch shipping. Highlighting the ambiguity of French policy, these ships were also to establish direct trade with the Spanish on *Terre firme*.[4] A month later, Seignelay instructed the comte de Blénac to attack St. Eustatius, raze the small fort there, and deport all the inhabitants. Only local forces were to be employed, and the costs were to be met from the sale of captured slaves. In a second, secret communication Seignelay ordered that all Huguenot exiles found on the island be transported to France as prisoners.[5] News that three or four large Dutch privateers were departing for the West Indies led the minister to reconsider. Also, several of the smaller French islands were indefensible, and news that privateers were pillaging them reached him before the year's end.[6] Seignelay dispatched *La Perle*, 52 guns, to Martinique in March of 1689, and the following month, after Louis XIV declared war on Spain, he ordered *Le Mignon* and *La Friponne*, frigates, to the islands with instructions to safeguard the colonies, assure French trade, and wage war against the Zealand privateers.[7] Seignelay, who was a great advocate of privateering war, had granted four warships to naval captains, but in May, after learning that England had declared war on France, he ordered them placed at Governor-General Blénac's disposition.[8]

French colonial leaders took advantage of the English refusal to cooperate with their Dutch allies in the West Indies. In April, acting in complete secrecy, Governor-General Blénac seized St. Eustatius and in July he took advantage of recently arrived warships and news that a quasi-civil war between Irish Jacobites and King William's supporters existed on St. Christopher to attack

[2] Philip P. Boucher, *Cannibal Encounters: Europeans and Island Caribs, 1492–1763* (Baltimore and London: The Johns Hopkins University Press, 1992), 90–3; and Col., C⁸ᴮ 1, no. 9.
[3] Col., B 14, f. 52 Seignelay to Blénac and nine others, 7 October 1688.
[4] Ibid., ff. 55–5v same to same, 8 November 1688.
[5] Ibid., ff. 59, 60 same to same, 29 November 1688; also Col., C⁸ᴬ 5, ff. 204–6 Blénac to Seignelay, 27 April 1689; and ibid., f. 398 "Compte de recettes et dépenses faites à l'occasion de la prise de St. Eustache", 16 December 1689.
[6] Col., B 14, f. 62 Seignelay to Blénac 21 December 1688; and Col., C⁷ᴬ 3 Hinselin to Seignelay, 27 December 1688.
[7] Marine, B⁴ 12, f. 12 Orders to Sieur de la Motte–Genouillés, 9 April 1689; Col., B 14, f. 88 Seignelay to Blénac, 30 April 1689.
[8] Col., B 14, ff. 90–1v King to Blénac, 18 May 1689; ibid., ff. 91–2 same to Guillotin and Du Casse, same date.

the English section of the island. Placing himself at the head of six men of war and 16 smaller ships, Blénac landed on the island on 27 July. The English surrendered Fort Charles on 15 August, and were quickly deported to Nevis.[9] A French attack on Dutch Surinam led by Captain Du Casse commanding four naval vessels was a failure. He encountered vastly superior Dutch forces at the mouth of the Surinam River and was forced to withdraw. Fierce resistance at Fort Barbiche, 60 leagues farther west, again forced him to withdraw. The accidental sinking of a warship at Barbiche and the loss of most of the locally recruited men left Cayenne virtually defenceless.[10]

The seizure of St. Christopher spread consternation throughout the English Leeward Islands, but the French success was short-lived. At the end of December, the English captured St. Bartholomew. They sent the governor, 60 prisoners, and slaves to Nevis while transporting cattle and other plunder and burning all the houses. The French repulsed a similar attack on St. Martin after Captain Du Casse landed a party to aid the colonists in driving the English off.[11] Early in January, the English attacked Marie Galante with greater success, withdrawing only after burning 50 sugar works, great quantities of sugar in cask, all the houses, and the cane fields. They also seized 80 slaves and killed most of the livestock.[12] The French learned that the English planned to attack Martinique and were only awaiting ships to transport a landing force estimated to number 2,300; eight warships were being fitted out in England for the task.[13] The English governor Sir Christopher Codrington estimated there were only about 5,000 Frenchmen in the Windward Islands and that 2,000 soldiers from England would give the English mastery over all French possessions in the Caribbean.[14]

Governor-General Blénac at Martinique had received upwards of 30 merchantmen escorted by four warships early in 1690, but he chose to do nothing. Moreover, the deportation of his English prisoners from St. Christopher to nearby Nevis instead of to Jamaica, and the withdrawal of his army to Martinique leaving insufficient men and munitions to defend his recent

9   Nellis M. Crouse, *The French Struggle for the West Indies, 1665–1713* (New York: Octagon Books, [1943] 1966). 149–52, 153–4, 155–6; Christian Buchet, *La Lutte pour l'espace caraïbe et la façade atlantique de l'Amérique centrale et du sud (1672–1763)*, 2 vols. (Paris: Librairie d'Inde, 1991), 1: 162–3 citing BN, Clairambault, 876, ff. 272–3; also Col., C⁸ᴮ 1, nos. 106 and 107.

10 Col., C¹⁴ 2, f. 65 Du Casse's agreement with La Barre, 26 April 1689; also Marine, B⁴ 12, ff. 120–3v Journal de navigation de l'escadre de Ducasse jusqu'à Cayenne et Suriname [sic]; ibid., 484–6 Du Casse to Seignelay, 1 March 1690. Also Philippe Hrodej, *L'Amiral Du Casse: l'Évolution d'un Gascon sous Louis XIV*, 2 vols. (Paris: Librairie de l'Inde, 1999), 1: 86–90.

11 Crouse, *The French Struggle*, 157–60; CSP, CS, 1689–92, no. 789.

12 Ibid; BN, Clairambault, 879, ff. 56–7 Guitaud and Dumaitz to the King, 4 October 1691.

13 Col., B 14, ff. 110–10v Seignelay to Blénac, 18 December 1689.

14 CSP, CS, 1689–92, no. 789. Governor Codrington to Lords of Trade and Plantations, 1 March [o.s.] 1690.

conquest, left the island vulnerable to a counterattack, which was not long in coming. In May, Commodore Lawrence Wright with 10 vessels and two fireships reached Barbados with a regiment of troops. Strongly reinforced by local militia, the English swiftly recaptured St. Christopher in June and St. Eustatius the following month. After leaving a strong garrison on St. Christopher, Wright withdrew to Barbados for the hurricane season. Mortality among his crews was very high, and news that a French squadron had reached the islands combined with a falling out among senior army and colonial leaders led him to abandon plans to attack Guadeloupe.[15]

Seignelay had spared no thought or extra resources for the Americas. Preoccupied with naval preparations leading to the Battle of Béveziers or Beachy Head (July 10) between the French and a combined Anglo-Dutch fleet, he concluded that no resources could be spared for the colonies. Indeed, while granting Governor-General Blénac's request to return to France, he only appointed his successor in May and made no effort to hasten his departure to the islands. Seignelay continued to leave the colonies to their own resources, advising the new governor-general designate, François d'Alesso, marquis d'Eragny, that he would assign naval escorts for merchantmen bound for the West Indies only at the end of the European campaign.[16] The war in Europe did not allow dispatch of a naval force, and he left d'Eragny largely on his own with just one 36-gun frigate, a naval transport or *flûte*, and 300 troops.[17] Even these meagre resources failed to get away as scheduled. The ship carrying the governor was forced back to France and he departed, escorting 8 merchantmen, only in mid-December.

The marquis de Seignelay's death in early November may actually have led to a slight improvement in the colonial situation. For the new minister, Louis Phélypeaux, comte de Pontchartrain, received a detailed briefing on conditions in the West Indies and the need for defensive reinforcements from Jean-Baptiste de Lagny, director of commerce in the naval ministry. At the year's end, a small squadron commanded by Captain Du Casse left Le Havre for Saint-Domingue.[18] During the entire year of 1690, however, the French Windward Islands had been open to attack. Fortunately for the French, the English leaders fell out among themselves and, despite the end of the rainy season, a five-month delay occurred before Commodore Wright's squadron headed for Marie Galante and Guadeloupe late in March of 1691.

[15] W. T. Morgan "The British West Indies during King William's War (1689–1697)", *The Journal of Modern History*, 2, no. 3 (September, 1930): 386–8; Buchet, *La Lutte pour l'espace caraïbe*, 1: 163–4.

[16] Col., B 14, ff. 121–1v Seignelay to Eragny, 6 August 1690.

[17] Ibid., ff. 122–8v Instructions to Eragny, September 1690.

[18] Col., C^8A 6, ff. 261–4v Memorial by de Lagny, endorsed, "written for Mgr de Pontchartrain, Nov. 1690"; Col., B 14, f. 184v, 209 Pontchartrain to Bégon, 17 December, 1690 and 5 January 1691; Marine, B^4 13, ff. 529–33 Chevalier d'Arbouville to Pontchartrain, 21 April, 1691.

The English quickly seized the former at the beginning of April and left it totally destroyed and depopulated,[19] but they were much less successful at Guadeloupe.

Learning that the English had landed, the marquis d'Eragny, who reached Martinique on 25 January, took the four warships at Fort Royal and three armed merchantmen and rushed two companies of naval infantry and 600 militia and freebooters to Guadeloupe, where they landed at Gosier, intending to march overland and catch the English from behind. The English naval commander immediately prepared to meet the French squadron. The English forces besieging Fort St. Charles near Basseterre had already lost nearly 400 of the 1,500 men who had landed. General Codrington had no choice but to break off land operations, re-embark his army, even abandoning some of his guns and wounded, and sail with Commodore Wright who failed to meet the French squadron at Cul-de-Sac despite possessing naval superiority.[20] Wright sailed to Barbados, where he left half his forces and returned to England. There he was court-martialed for cowardice and dismissed from the service. Meanwhile, the French colonies received unexpected reinforcements in June when a squadron of six vessels arrived from the East Indies.[21] Regrettably, they were heavily laden with rich cargoes and could not remain long in the islands, but their presence gave the French local superiority and proved reassuring.[22] So, too, did the capture in July of two English frigates of 42 and 48 guns, respectively.[23] This was just as well because disease ran rampant in the French colonies that summer; Governor-General d'Eragny was one of those who died after contracting yellow fever.[24]

During the summer the comte de Pontchartrain decided to send a squadron to the West Indies, the first significant naval force to be destined for the Americas since the beginning of the war. It was initially to be composed of half a dozen third rates and a frigate, but its composition was gradually whittled away. The commanding officer was renamed four times before Sieur de Vaudricourt was designated to sail with three men of war, *Le Vermandois*,

[19]   Crouse, *The French Struggle*, 172; Buchet, *La Lutte pour l'espace*, 1: 165; *CSP, CS*, 1689–92, no. 1557, pp. 461–2.
[20]   Morgan, "The British West Indies", 390; Crouse, *The French Struggle*, 172–5.
[21]   See Robert Challe, *Journal d'un voyage aux Indes orientales (1690–1691)*, 2 vols. (Paris: Mercure de France, 1979), 2: 236–63 for an account of the ships' stay at Martinique.
[22]   Col., C^{8A} 6, ff. 312–13v Eragny to Pontchartrain, 4 July 1691; ibid., f. 428, 429, Dumaitz to Pontchartrain, 16 and 30 August 1691.
[23]   These were HMS *Constant Warwick*, and HMS *Mary Rose*; see William Laird Clowes, *The Royal Navy, a History from the Earliest Times to the Present*, 7 vols. (London: Sampson, Low, Marston and Co., 1897–1903), 2: 465n2.
[24]   Pierre-Regis Dessalles, fils, *Annales du conseil souverain de la Martinique, ou tableau historique du gouvernement de cette colonies depuis son premier établissement jusqu'à nos jours*, 2 vols. (Bergerac: Chez J.B. Puynesge, 1786), 1: 313.

58 guns, *Le François*, 46 guns, and *Le Neptune*, 46 guns, escorting four large armed naval transports carrying provisions, munitions, and stores to supply the colonial garrisons and to extend the warships' stay in the islands. Two of the flutes were actually men of war, *L'Éole*, 50 guns, and *Le Bizarre*, fitted out "en flûte", carrying all but their lightest ordnance as ballast. Once in the islands they were to mount them for war,[25] but in the face of the enemy's growing strength this arrangement proved inadequate. After learning of the marquis d'Eragny's death, Pontchartrain added two more warships, including *Le Vaillant*, 48 guns, and sent the comte de Blénac back to the islands as governor-general. With 10 warships, a frigate, and two fireships under his command Blénac would enjoy naval superiority in the Windward Islands. Blénac's instructions were to attack Barbados and afterward pass through the English Leeward Islands, destroying everything belonging to the English colonists rather than land at Martinique.[26]

At the end of December of 1691, Captain Duparc, commanding *Le Cheval Marin*, captured HMS *Jersey*, 48 guns, but this good news was offset by the loss soon afterwards of one of the naval transports.[27] Nevertheless, Blénac's arrival at Martinique in early February proved timely, for ships of the second English squadron sent to conquer the French West Indies had just arrived. Under command of Commodore Ralph Wrenn, the squadron of five warships to which he joined four smaller vessels after reaching Barbados arrived at the end of January.[28] When Blénac reached Martinique on 4 February he outnumbered the English, but his local superiority came to nought. Though the two squadrons met on 1 March, the English commander protected his convoy of merchantmen and broke off the action. Through maladroitness the larger French force missed the opportunity to become master of the Lesser Antilles.[29] Despite their instructions, neither squadron could afterwards mount an offensive. To do so would weaken the defences of the respective islands as long as the other continued to exist; and, as the English had learned to their chagrin during the previous year's attack on Guadeloupe, landing troops on enemy islands put them and their warships at great risk. Each squadron needed to seek out the other and destroy it as a preliminary to any land operations.[30] Yet, it is not at all clear that contemporary naval officers saw the situation with such clarity. The presence of an enemy squadron in the Caribbean effectively removed any aggressive opportunity for one's own naval force.

[25] Col., B 14, ff. 265–72 Instructions for Nesmond, 17 September 1691; ibid., ff. 296–9v King to Nesmond and Vaudricourt, 24 September 1691.

[26] Col., F³ 67, ff. 171–2 Instructions for the comte de Blénac, 15 November 1691.

[27] Col., C⁸ᴬ 7, ff. 94–7 Dumaitz to Pontchartrain, 12 January 1692.

[28] Morgan, "The British West Indies", 390–2; Buchet, *La Lutte pour l'espace caraïbe*, 1: 166.

[29] CSP, CS, 1689–1692, no. 2, 110; Crouse, *The French Struggle*, 180–1.

[30] Buchet, *La Lutte pour l'espace caraïbe*, 1: 167–8.

Yellow fever destroyed the English squadron, causing the death of Commodore Wrenn himself in 1692. French naval crews also suffered. An unknown epidemic reigned in the French islands. By early June, disease was causing the comte de Blénac more worry than the enemy. By the beginning of July, there were insufficient sailors to man the warships on station; after laying up two ships only three remained fit for service. One was taken out of service.[31] Despite Blénac's failure to initiate any offensive operations in the Antilles, Pontchartrain appeared pleased with his conduct, dispatching additional provisions with instructions to undertake only defensive operations for the remainder of the summer.[32]

During 1692, the English decided to fit out yet a third expedition to attack French possessions in the Windward Islands and thence to proceed to further operations against Canada.[33] This largest naval expedition to date, commanded by Sir Francis Wheler, comprised a squadron of seven warships from 40 to 60 guns, four frigates, three fireships, a bomb ketch and three lesser vessels, and more than a score of transports and merchantmen. Despite intelligence that Martinique was the expedition's target, Pontchartrain sent nothing in response; *Le Jersé* (formerly HMS *Jersey*) and *L'Émerillon* sailed as escorts for the usual autumn convoy.[34] Circumstances forced the King to keep all his troops in the kingdom. Only 100 recruits were sent to reinforce those in the colonies. Much like his predecessor, Pontchartrain advised Blénac that colonists and their leaders must look to their own resources. An engineer, Sieur de Caylus had sailed to Martinique with Blénac, and during 1692 he directed extensive defensive preparations to receive an attack while the governor organised the island's militia, who numbered nearly 1,400. Reflecting a growing awareness of the limitations on naval power imposed by tropical conditions, Pontchartrain also ordered the five navy vessels currently in the islands, including those sent during the fall, to be gone by 1 March 1693.[35] The colonists were truly on their own under the redoubtable leadership of their tough, irascible, septuagenarian governor-general.

Admiral Wheler appeared off Martinique in mid-April, but military operations only commenced a week later after all elements of surprise had been lost. After sailing around the island and making several landings south of Fort Royal in the Cul-de-Sac Marin, the English put back to sea and sailed

---

[31]   Col., C⁸ᴬ 7, ff. 36, 135. Blénac to Pontchartrain, 9 June 1692 and Blénac and Dumaitz to same, 2 July; ibid., 59v–60 Blénac to Pontchartrain, 18 August 1692; and ibid., 83–6 procès verbal, 19 and 20 December 1692.

[32]   Col., B 14, ff. 367–8v Pontchartrain to Blénac, 7 May 1692; and ibid., f. 370v The King to chevalier de Lanion, same date.

[33]   See Stephen Saunders Webb, "William Blathwayt, Imperial Fixer: Muddling Through to Empire, 1689–1717", *William and Mary Quarterly*, 3rd Series, 26 (1969), 381–92.

[34]   Col., B 14, ff. 393v–6 Pontchartrain to Captain Buisson de la Varenne, 20 August 1692.

[35]   Ibid., ff. 416–18v Memoir of the King to Blénac and Dumaitz, 10 September 1692.

to St. Pierre, where they landed nearly 3,000 men at Fond Canauville.[36] There they were met by Captain Louis Collet's infantry company and some militia who delayed their landing and disputed their march. Led by the island's governor, Jean de Gabaret, the French conducted a vigorous defence of St. Pierre, but their small force of 1,000 men slowly gave way before the superior numbers of English soldiers. After Governor-General Blénac arrived with reinforcements from Fort Royal, a company of *troupes de la marine* and 500 to 600 militia, the English abandoned their siege on 4 May and their troops reembarked.[37]

The English failure has been chiefly attributed to lack of cooperation between colonial and naval leaders, but a more detailed explanation can be found in the minutes of an English council of war. News that the French had been reinforced led to general discouragement and a belief among the English that they were fewer in number. The fact that a third of the invading troops were Irish also led senior English officers to question their loyalty. The French defence had been very aggressive; colonial marksmen took a deadly toll. The deep ravines running down the slopes of Mount Pelée to the sea made the terrain very difficult to march over and impossible to haul the heavy guns needed to take the fort. In the wake of the Guadeloupe fiasco, fear that the army would be unable to regain their ships in the event of defeat was also a factor. Finally, high mortality among the troops influenced the withdrawal. After just three days ashore 800 were reported killed, wounded, or sick, and Wheler's squadron, not including the colonial militia, claimed 668 additional casualties.[38]

French losses were surprisingly modest in view of the enormity of the attack. Fewer than 50 were killed or wounded, and property damage was no greater than might be expected: 46 houses, 26 mills, and 27 boiling houses destroyed along with drums and boiling pans, boats and livestock, chiefly sheep and pigs, but only 68 slaves and 324 casks of sugar were reported carried off.[39] Indeed, a violent storm which smashed into Martinique six months later, destroying the entire cane harvest, caused far greater

---

[36]   Col., F³ 26, ff. 263–5, "Journal du Sr. Auger, gouverneur de Marie Galante, commandant au cul de Sac Marin". For an English account of the attack on Martinique see University of Minnesota Libraries, James Ford Bell Collection, No. L 398 "A Journal of the Transactions of Their Majesties Forces sent to the West Indies under command of the Honorable Sir Francis Wheeler (*sic*) and Col. Foulke, Anno 1693", by Captain Christian Lilly, R. E. See also Jean-Baptiste Labat, *Nouveau voyage aux Isles de l'Amérique* (La Haye: P. Husson, T. Johnson, P. Gosse, Jvan Duren, R. Atberts, and C. Le Vier, [1724] 1722), 1²: 56–7 and Crouse, *The French Struggle*, 181–9.

[37]   Col., C⁸ᴬ 7, ff. 247–51v Blénac to Pontchartrain, 3 May 1693; ibid., ff. 471–4 Gabaret to Pontchartrain, 4 May 1693; and ibid., ff. 320–4 Dumaitz to Pontchartrain, 4 May 1693 for three accounts of the French repulse of the English attack.

[38]   *CSP, CS*, 1693–1696, no. 281; ibid., no. 339; Buchet, *La Lutte pour l'espace caraïbe*, 1: 170–1; also Morgan, "The British West Indies", 395–6.

[39]   Col., F³ 26, "Estat de degast fait par les anglois", 20 May 1693.

devastation, including the destruction of 200 houses in one district alone.[40] Hurricanes were far more destructive than the cross-ravaging of the colonies during the war. One that struck Martinique, Guadeloupe, and Marie Galante on 5 October 1694 destroyed 253 buildings at St. Pierre alone and sank so many ships in the region that navy crews were easily reinforced from the numerous sailors who found themselves ashore without a ship.[41]

Louis XIV learned of Blénac's successful repulse of the English attack at Mézières on 17 June while returning from visiting the army at Namur, and although he acknowledged the need for naval reinforcements, the worsening economic and social crisis caused by the widespread failure of the previous harvest and the growing financial exhaustion of the kingdom forced a delay until the following year.[42] As usual, a fourth rate, *Le Faucon*, 44 guns, and two transports laden with munitions were sent off early in the fall and a frigate and a flute departed at the year's end, but that was all.[43] So isolated did the French colonies become through 1694 that the comte de Blénac proposed to the minister that he reactivate the treaty of neutrality negotiated and signed during the mid-1680s while attempting, himself, to encourage English desires for peace with the colonists on Antigua.[44]

The repulse of the strong English expeditionary force from Martinique gave the outnumbered French colonists renewed confidence in their leaders and in themselves. It may also have demonstrated to the minister that sea power was unnecessary to ensure colonial security. Strong fortifications and well-organised, disciplined militias led by good officers and supported by regular infantry seemed the best way to defend the colonies. Naval power appeared ineffective. Warships were often laid up soon after reaching the Caribbean as their crews fell prey to disease and malnutrition. The scantness of their provisions, which could only be obtained in France, exacerbated their poor living conditions. In addition, complaints about the commercially motivated behaviour of naval officers, who often ignored the needs of colonial defence to pursue their own interests, had appeared continuously since the beginning of the war.[45] Nothing, neither confiscation of their cargoes

---

[40]   Labat, *Nouveau voyage aux Isles*, 2: 224.

[41]   AN, SOM, G¹ 470bis no. 54 "Estat des maisons et cazes qui ont este emportees par la mauvais temps au quartier du fort St. Pierre", 10 November 1694; and Col., C⁸ᴬ 8, ff. 216–35, 273–83 Dumaitz and Gabaret to Pontchartrain, 6 and 10 November 1696.

[42]   Louis Charpentier, *D'Amblimont, chef d'escadre de Louis XIV*, (Paris: Société d'éditions de géographiques maritimes et coloniales, 1928), 77–8.

[43]   Col., B 14, ff. 562–4 Instruction for Sr. Roland, 29 July 1693; ibid., ff. 576–7v Instructions for Sr. de Ste. Marie, 20 October 1693.

[44]   Col., C⁸ᴬ 8, ff. 78, 94v Blénac to Pontchartrain, 30 March and 31 May 1694.

[45]   E. g. Col., B 14, ff. 445v, 446, 455v–6 Pontchartrain to Germain and same to Desgrassières, 17 and 20 September 1692; ibid., 456 ordinance forbidding naval officers to trade in the colonies, 22 October 1692; and Col., C⁸ᴬ 8, f. 197 Dumaitz to Pontchartrain, 26 August 1694.

nor even imprisonment on their return to France, deterred naval officers, who often prolonged their sojourn in the islands unduly.

The dispatch of Admiral Wheler's force to the Windward Islands and the sailing of Anglo-Dutch fleets in 1693 and 1694 to aid the allied war effort in Italy and Spain marked a major shift in the balance of the war away from the Low Countries to the south and to a lesser extent overseas. Indeed, with the check to French naval power in the western Mediterranean, the two wars, continental and maritime, that had been waged simultaneously but independently of each other in Europe now became one.[46] After 1693, French and English roles in the Americas became reversed. English aggression declined and French aggression took on new life, but with a very significant difference.

The first proposals to send privately armed warships to the Americas appeared at the end of 1693 and developed momentum during the following year.[47] Intended to make war for the private accounts of their investors, the object of these proposals was neither to defend French colonies and their trade nor to attack the English. Their chief aim was to plunder the ports of Spanish America and the treasure fleets that sailed to Cadiz. This activity was not simply privateering. *La course* had broken out as soon as the war commenced. At least 400 men left Martinique in 1693 to go privateering at the same time as the English landed on the island.[48] Nor was it a precursor of commerce raiding as conducted by modern states during the nineteenth and the twentieth centuries. The new form of warfare introduced into the West Indies with the active participation of the state was privately financed and conducted warfare, which, for want of a better phase, can be given its French appellation, *la course royale* or royal privateering, in which the king's ships were employed for the pursuit of profit by private investors.

The navy's reduced role became evident in the instructions issued in October of 1694 to Captain chevalier Camille de Digoine du Palais commanding the frigates *La Badine* and *Le Wesp*. His principal object was the security of the merchantmen under his escort. He was also ordered to preserve his crews from contagion and to remain in the islands for only one month, cruising wherever the comte de Blénac might dictate. Afterward, he was to return to Martinique and assemble the merchantmen gathered there under his escort and return to France.[49] The navy's role had been reduced

[46] A. T. Mahan, *The Influence of Sea Power upon History, 1660–1783* (Boston: Little, Brown and Co., 1890), 188.

[47] E. g. Col., C^{8A} 7, ff. 503–7 "Mémoire concernant l'employ des fregattes de roy *l'Aigle* et *le Favory* et de deux autres vaisseau de cinquante à cinquant–cinquante–quatre canons qu'il conviendroit de leur joindre pendant l'année 1694 ..." by La Boulaye, Commre. de la marine, 7 December 1693; also Marine B^4 15, f.68 "Projet d'armement pour Vera Cruz et Panama", January 1694.

[48] Col., C^{8A} 7, ff. 338–40 Dumaitz to Pontchartrain, 16 June 1693.

[49] Col., B 18, ff. 86v–8 The King to Digoine, 23 October 1694. On Digoine's activities see Marine B^4 15, ff. 394–439 Journal du voyage que Monsieur le chevalier de Digoine, capne. de vau. . . . , May 1695.

to that of a workhorse, transporting vital stores, provisions, and munitions to colonial garrisons and escorting merchantmen on their perilous voyage beyond the European capes, across the Atlantic, and safely through tropical waters infested by Dutch, English, and Spanish cruisers, privateers, and pirates. Once safely arrived at their destinations, the escorts had but little time to make ready for the return voyage to France.

The English never again attacked Martinique or Guadeloupe. The French government reduced naval expenditures by between one-quarter and one-third in 1694 and by nearly one-quarter again the next year.[50] Ineffectiveness in the West Indies and lack of finances at home reduced the navy's mission in the Caribbean. The war in the Windward Islands became increasingly local as privateers roamed unimpeded. Between 1690 and 1695, French privateers inflicted losses on Dutch vessels and cargoes amounting to 258,000 guilders.[51] In July of 1695, an English planter on Antigua complained that "the French have 14 small craft with 600 men in them, which are daily watching these islands".[52] During the first 4 months of 1696, privateers carried 25 prizes into Fort Royal.[53] Colonists became well-armed and remained on guard. Fort Louis de la Grande Terre, Guadeloupe, may have been no more than "un méchant parallelogram", good for nothing, but Sieur de La Pompe's militia company at Goyave was at full strength, having 80 men including mulattos and free Africans. Few possessed swords, but all were armed with the weapon of choice in the West Indies, the heavy buccaneer flintlock (*fusil boucanier*), bayonets, and cartridge pouches; most also carried a pistol.[54] Meanwhile, the struggle shifted northward to Saint-Domingue, where Spain had emerged as France's chief enemy in the Americas.

7.3 SAINT-DOMINGUE

Most of Saint-Domingue's colonists were destitute and facing increasing poverty at the beginning of the war. Yet, the war ultimately benefited the colony. It brought new capital in the form of the king's bounty, refugees, and additional slaves who opened new plantations, and incited buccaneers to become planters. The loss due to disease, departure, and capture of about

---

[50] Henri Legohérel, *Les Trésoriers généraux de la Marine, 1517–1788* (Paris: Éditions Cujas, 1965), fp. 180.

[51] Wim Klooster, *Illicit Riches: The Dutch Trade in the Caribbean, 1648–1795* (Leiden: KITLV Press, 1995), 101.

[52] *CSP, CS*, 1693–1696, nos. 183 and 530, quoted in Donald H. Alkenson, *If the Irish Ran the World, Montserrat, 1630–1730* (Montreal and Kingston: McGill-Queen's University Press, 1997), 120–2.

[53] Jacques Petitjean-Roget, *La Gaoulé: la révolte de la Martinique en 1717* (Fort-de-France: Société d'histoire de la Martinique, 1966), 46.

[54] Col., C7A 4 (nonfoliated) "Etat du gouvernement de la Guadeloupe", by Governor Auger, 17 July 1696.

1,400 freebooters during the late 1680s had substantially weakened the colony; Governor de Cussy could scarcely count on 1,000 good men.[55] In the wake of the collapse of the tobacco market, the economy was stagnant. Opening hostilities heightened the precariousness of trade. Indigo production and sugar cultivation was just beginning.[56] Destitution was the major cause of unrest. A revolt at Cap Français led to the arrest and execution of two leaders.[57] Saint-Domingue's defences left little to the imagination.[58]

Perhaps all these considerations led Governor de Cussy to delay opening hostilities until 1690. Even then it remains unclear why he initiated them. He may have wished to destroy Spanish land forces or to plunder Spanish cattle herds, but the need to assert some control over the independent, fickle buccaneers and settlers may have been a consideration. Many had sought the governor's commission to go privateering since the previous June. Understanding that they were Saint-Domingue's chief if unreliable defenders, de Cussy persuaded them to support him by proposing an attack on Santiago de los Cavelleros deep inside Santo Domingo on the Monte Christi River.

The buccaneers agreed, and setting out by sea from Port de Paix on 19 June, their little army of 400 mounted men, 150 foot, and 150 blacks landed at Cap Français two days later. After reassembling and provisioning themselves, the buccaneers set off overland for Santiago.[59] Following a hard skirmish outside the town a few days later, the French overran the Spanish positions and entered a deserted town. After finding nothing to plunder, they burnt the town in frustration and withdrew to Saint-Domingue. The long march had sorely fatigued the whole army and nothing had been accomplished except perhaps that royal authority was more firmly acknowledged in the colony. Nevertheless, any future success, the governor informed the minister, would have to be made from the sea.[60]

French authorities ignored the effect of this inconsequential engagement. Indeed, Seignelay continued to view hostilities in the Americas as local in origin and best left to colonial leaders to deal with as they saw fit. His chief interest lay in commercial penetration of Spanish America rather than military conquest. Beyond asking some Saint-Malo merchants, fitting out privateers for trade in the Gulf of Mexico to cruise off the north coast of Hispaniola while sailing to and from their destinations, he advised de Cussy to expect nothing.[61]

55 Col., C^{8A} 5, ff. 32v–36 Extrait des lettres de Sr. de Cussy, 1688.
56 Charles Frostin, *Les Révoltes blanches à Saint-Domingue aux XVIIe et XVIIIe siècles (Haiti avant 1789)*, (Paris: École, 1975), 123–6.
57 Col., C^{8A} 5, ff. 272–3 Extrait des lettres de Cussy [1689].
58 Col., C^{9A} 1 (nonfoliated) certificate, 29 April 1688.
59 Based on Pierre-François-Xavier Charlevoix, *Histoire de l'isle espagnole ou de S. Domingue*, 2 vols. (Paris: Jacques Guerin, 1730–1731), 2: 215–20.
60 Ibid., 2: 220.
61 Col., B 14, f. 170 Seignelay to de Cussy, 4 October 1690.

The Spanish were not so perfunctory. They quickly moved to counterattack the French colony. In January of 1691, a small Spanish naval force, the Armada de Barlovento or Windward Squadron, arrived off Cap Français with 2,600 men who were joined by an army of 700 that had marched overland. At Limonade, east of Le Cap, the Spanish invaders met the French and killed Governor de Cussy, his two senior military officers, Major de Gramont and king's lieutenant François de Pardieu de Franquenay, along with 30 officers and 400 to 500 men. Afterward they burned the town, carrying off women, children, and slaves and massacring the men. It was the worst French military debacle experienced in the colonies during the war. The buccaneers were noticeable by their absence.[62]

News of the disaster caused dismay in France, where the comte de Pontchartrain had just assumed the direction of the ministry of marine. In the wake of de Lagny's strong recommendation in favour of Jean-Baptiste Du Casse – "of all officers in the navy, the one who knows best the strength and weakness of America" – Pontchartrain lost no time in appointing him governor to replace de Cussy.[63] Though he had never exercised command ashore, the new governor had been active in the slave trade for nearly 15 years and a naval officer since 1686. A man with strong connections to merchant communities in the Channel seaports, Du Casse was committed to the development of Saint-Domingue. His attack on Dutch Surinam in 1689 had not succeeded, but with the ships under his command he took part in Blénac's recent attack on St. Christopher, and he had saved the French position on St. Martin during the summer. He was in France when news of de Cussy's death arrived, and he promptly offered to lead an expedition to retake Cap Français.[64] Pontchartrain accepted and sent him off with *Le Solide*, 48-guns, *Le Cheval Marin*, 40 guns, and *L'Émerillon*, 36-guns. The marquis d'Eragny was ordered to render him all the assistance necessary for the enterprise. Captain d'Arbouville, already at Martinique in *Le Mignon*, was ordered to remain there and sail with Du Casse to Saint-Domingue.[65]

Du Casse reached Martinique in May of 1691 just in time to render aid to Governor-General d'Eragny. It was his ships that forced the English to withdraw from Guadeloupe. Consultations with d'Eragny kept him in the Windward Islands, but an outbreak of yellow fever during the summer hastened his departure. When he finally reached Léogane, his letters of state as governor of Saint-Domingue awaited him.[66] As new governor, he immediately

62 Charlevoix, *Histoire de l'isle espagnole ou de S. Domingue*, 2: 222–5; Crouse, *The French Struggle*, 177–8.
63 Col., C⁸ᴬ 6, 262v Memorial of M. de Lagny, November 1690.
64 See Hrodej, *L'Amiral Du Casse*, 1: 15–121 for his career before 1691.
65 Col., B 14, ff. 226–7v Pontchartrain to Herbouville, 25 March 1691.
66 Ibid., f. 230 Provisions de gouverneur de Saint-Domingue pour le Sr. Du Casse, 1 June 1691; ibid., f. 231v lettres d'état, 10 June 1691; also ibid., f. 242 Pontchartrain to Du Casse, 18 June 1691.

plunged into his duties and responsibilities, organising the colony's defences and sending clear reports to the minister concerning its needs.[67]

Saint-Domingue's defenceless state was undoubtedly why the French did not attack Jamaica in 1692 in the wake of a devastating earthquake that killed a reported 2,000 people in June. Additional losses, estimated to have reached 3,000, followed a subsequent epidemic.[68] The French had lost their best opportunity to capture the island. The presence of Admiral Wheler's expeditionary force and his attempt on Martinique in the spring of 1693 deterred the French from attacking Jamaica the following year. By the same token, Wheler's failure at Martinique prevented any joint Anglo-Spanish attack on Saint-Domingue if any was contemplated.[69]

The chief danger to Saint-Domingue, however, remained the Spanish, who had occupied Hispaniola for two centuries and refused to acknowledge French sovereignty over any portion of the island. Despite the rodomontade and bellicosity emanating from Jamaica, only the Spanish, who had no more desire to see the English occupy the western portion of the island than the French, could retake Saint-Domingue. French-Spanish animus remained as harsh as ever. In Spanish eyes, all Frenchmen were murderous pirates to be dealt with as brutally as possible. Concern for French prisoners sent to Cadiz as galley slaves and 130 others known to be imprisoned at Santo Domingo in 1694 led Louis XIV to order a similar number of Spanish prisoners be put in irons; any held in Saint-Domingue were to be sent to France to be used in exchanges.[70]

Intelligence that a reinforced Windward Squadron was to attack Saint-Domingue led Pontchartrain in January of 1694 to order *Le Téméraire*, 60 guns, *L'Envieux*, 50 guns, and *Le Hazardeux*, *en flûte*, carrying provisions for soldiers in the colony and victuals for *Le Solide*, to sail to Saint-Domingue under command of Captain du Rollon. His first priority was the defence of the colony, but if Du Casse agreed, he might cruise against either Jamaica or the Spanish coast of Hispaniola.[71]

French buccaneers of course continually cruised off Jamaica, picking off a small vessel here and there or landing in order to seize slaves and other plunder. In December of 1693, they carried off 370 slaves and much plunder.[72] Du Casse was well-informed about enemy movements, but the challenge

[67]   BN, Clairambault, 878, ff. 20–2v, 35–40 Du Casse to Pontchartrain, 23 October 1691, and 24 November 1692.

[68]   Sir Alan Burns, *History of the British West Indies*, rev. 2nd ed. (London: Allen & Unwin, 1965), 381.

[69]   According to *CSP, CS*, 1689–1692, no. 2504, Wheler's instructions initially called for him to proceed to Jamaica and afterward to attack French settlements on Hispaniola.

[70]   Col., B 18, f. 17 Pontchartrain to Du Casse, 27 January 1694.

[71]   Ibid., f. 15v Pontchartrain to Du Casse 27 January 1694; ibid., f. 23 Instructions for du Rollon, same date.

[72]   Burns, *History of the British West Indies*, 382.

facing him, as de Cussy before him, was to subordinate these fair weather fighters to his authority by showing them opportunities for plunder and directing their petty attacks in ways that might contribute to the defence of Saint-Domingue rather than simply fueling Jamaican animosity. He sent off 400 or 500 men in six ships under the command of Major Jean Legoff de Beauregard to plunder the east end of Jamaica in March of 1694, but the appearance of an English frigate of 40 guns quickly put them to flight and led to the loss of one of the French vessels. Captain du Rollon reached Saint-Domingue on 6 April, and three days later Du Casse ordered him to cruise off Jamaica. Losing no time, du Rollon sent a local privateer inshore as a decoy to draw out the coast guard ship that had recently taken the buccaneers' vessel and captured HMS *Falcon*, 40 guns.[73] In France, intercepted intelligence revealed that the Anglo-Spanish plan for a joint attack on the French colony had been postponed to the end of the year, and the comte de Pontchartrain railed at the cost of fitting out the warships for Saint-Domingue. In the minister's eyes, the warships intended to provide local superiority over the Windward Squadron in the spring of 1694 had become a useless expense.[74]

No such considerations stopped Governor Du Casse. The French warships, reinforced by their recent prize, gave him local superiority, and he intended to take full advantage of it. Quickly assembling a small fleet of colonial brigantines and sloops, some 16 in all, he embarked 1,500 men and set sail for Jamaica.[75] Eight ships entered Port Morant at the island's east end and the remainder anchored in Cow Bay some 15 miles east of Port Royal on 27 June. The English had been forewarned, and the vigorous English governor had defence preparations well in hand by the time the French arrived. The French spent the next six or seven weeks plundering the eastern portion of Jamaica and sections of the north coast, but appeared to have no strategic or even tactical end in view.

Believing Port Royal and Kingston to be too well-defended, Du Casse put a large force of 1,500 men ashore at Carlisle Bay, 35 miles to the west, at the end of July, and though they routed the defenders, the chief end was again rounding up cattle and slaves and plundering plantations. Some English planters proved much more effective at defending their own property than the colony. Many French raiding parties were beaten off and failed to raze the countryside or collect much booty. The French reembarked at Carlisle Bay on 3 August and sailed for Port Morant, where they landed their prisoners, gathered the rest of the ships, and presently sailed to Petit Goâve. The expedition's richest prize was undoubtedly the 1,300 to 3,000 captured

73 Charlevoix, *Histoire de l'isle espagnole ou de S. Domingue*, 2: 255.
74 Col., B 18, f. 27v Pontchartrain to Bégon, 7 April 1694; ibid., same to Du Casse, 28 April 1694.
75 Paragraph based on Marine, B⁴ 15, ff. 445–9 "Relation de ce qui s'est passé à l'expedition de la Jamaique par M. du Rollon" (not signed).

slaves, who proved crucial to the immediate, future prosperity of the French colony.[76]

If Du Casse could declare the attack on Jamaica a success, the same conclusion could not be made by the navy. By August, sickness was swiftly reducing crew numbers. *Le Solide*, which had been long in the Islands, was immediately sent back to France, her crew being too diminished for further use. *Le Téméraire* had lost 50 of her best sailors and the captain of the English prize now called *Le Faucon* had died. By September, *L'Envieux* had lost 100 men including her captain, and disease claimed Captain du Rollon of *Le Téméraire*. The four warships, including *Le Hazardeux*, departed Cap Français in early October, but further disaster awaited them in the Atlantic. *L'Envieux* lost her foremast in a storm, became separated from the others, and reached La Rochelle only in mid-December.[77] *Le Téméraire* did not reach France at all. In terrible condition with eight feet of water in her hold, she, too, became separated, driving on alone until on 8 December she was discovered by an English fourth rate off Ireland. The next day HMS *Montague*, 58 guns, joined the attack. After being wounded three times, Acting Captain Descoyeux was taken below and command devolved on his first lieutenant, Captain du Rollon's son. He was killed 2 hours later. Command passed to the ship's second lieutenant, M. de Beaumont, by which time the ship had been reduced to a floating hulk. Determined to resist to the last, Descoyeux had himself carried up to his quarterdeck, but mercifully the captain of the *Montague* sent his first lieutenant on board to demand he surrender to avoid boarding. Learning that no quarter would be granted and all crew members would be thrown into the sea if the English were forced to board, a quick council of war, aided it seems by the Englishman who had come on board, persuaded Descoyeux he could surrender his ship, now exhausted of all munitions, entirely dismasted and sinking. Indeed, *Le Téméraire* was so badly damaged that she never reached land. The English set her on fire soon afterward.[78] This brief account illustrates that French naval officers seemed to consider personal courage the chief if not the sole end of naval tactics.

The comte de Pontchartrain remained committed to reducing naval operations or else finding alternative means of financing them. Despite intelligence reports in October that the English were embarking two regiments for Jamaica, and cannons, mortars, and bombs, the minister refused to send a second naval squadron to protect Saint-Domingue. Instead, he advised

[76] *CSP, CS*, 1693–1696, no. 1236 Lt. Gov. Beeston to the Duke of Shewsbury, 18/28 August 1694 for a detailed English account of the French attack; also Crouse, *The French Struggle*, 191–6 and Burns, *History of the British West Indies*, 383.

[77] Marine, B[4] 15, ff. 452–4 Acting Captain de Brouste to Pontchartrain, 14 December 1694.

[78] Marine, B[4] 15, ff. 456–9v Descoyeux to Pontchartrain, Kinsal (*sic*), Ireland, 8/18 January 1695.

Governor Du Casse to remain on guard, take all precautions, and complete the fortifications under construction.[79]

The new English expedition under Commodore Robert Wilmot's command was composed of five warships, two fireships, and 12 transports carrying 1,800 troops and departed England in January of 1695. It was joined by three warships in the Americas and 1,700 soldiers from the Spanish garrison of Santo Domingo. The object of the expedition was to destroy all French forces on Hispaniola and the town of Petit Goâve, the governor's seat. This fourth English naval force sent to the West Indies was the first to sail to Jamaica where instructions directed Wilmot to withhold some of his objective from his Spanish allies, namely, the English intent to occupy the lands taken from the French. Commodore Wilmot and the commander of the 1,800 British troops, General Luke Lillingston, who had served in Wheler's expedition, soon fell out and their quarrels were compounded by the Spanish general's refusal to cooperate with either officer. Indeed, Saint-Domingue's chief defence in 1695 was the complete confusion among the allies, for as usual the buccaneers had fled from any opportunity for serious fighting.

Governor Du Casse had few resources. The former notorious buccaneer leader, Laurens-Corneille Baldran, sieur de Graff, recently appointed king's lieutenant at Le Cap, displayed no military ability at all, and at the end of May the allies quickly overran the town and burnt it. Later, in July, they undertook separate attacks on Port de Paix, where the situation was no better. The populace mutinied against the weak king's lieutenant, Thomas Le Clerc de La Boulaye, and fled the town without a fight.[80] Though the entire Northern District was in Anglo-Spanish hands by the end of July, the allies failed to consolidate their control. The uneven distribution of booty exacerbated army and navy rivalry and English and Spanish susceptibilities. The English and Spanish generals refused outright Commodore Wilmot's orders to attack Petit Goâve and the other French settlements in the Western District where Du Casse had been organising the defence in his usual vigorous fashion. Wilmot sailed for Jamaica.[81]

Lives, livestock, and property had been lost on Saint-Domingue as at Jamaica the year before, but the numbers added up to a relatively small portion of the colony's wealth, and cross-ravaging could be quickly repaired. Something else was required to achieve a larger end. With no funds to fit out new squadrons for America, Pontchartrain's solution was to encourage the development of private naval warfare. He arranged for the king to lend

79 Col., B 18, ff. 89–9v Pontchartrain to Du Casse, 23 October 1694.
80 Frostin, *Les Révoltes blanches*, 134; also Crouse, *The French Struggle*, 196–211, and Buchet, *La Lutte pour l'espace*, 1: 172–6.
81 *CSP, CS*, 1693–1696, no. 1980 Commodore Wilmot to Wm. Blathwayt, 26 [o.s.] July 1695 for his official account; see also ibid., no. 1983 "Commissary Murrey's Journal of the expedition to Hispaniola" [31 July [o.s.] 1695].

warships to naval officers, who found private investors to pay for crews' wages and victuals in return for a portion of any booty acquired during subsequent voyages.

The practice had existed before the war. It can be traced as far back as 1677, when Vice-Admiral d'Estrées fitted out ships to retake Cayenne and Tobago. However, during the current war in America, the practice began in Newfoundland in 1693 and reached its apogee during 1696 and 1697 in the West Indies when the French sent no fewer than three expeditions all directed at Spanish America rather than the English colonies. Although these armed raiders had no other aim than plunder, their impact had unforeseen consequences that were crucial to bringing the Nine Years' War to a successful conclusion and influenced later French attitudes toward imperial defence.

7.4 SPANISH AMERICA

The dream of penetrating Spanish America runs continuously through the history of France overseas. Foreigners engrossed more than 90 percent of imports from Spanish America with the French taking about one-quarter.[82] The three expeditions directed toward Spanish America in 1696 and 1697 reflected the dream, but were also a response to worsening conditions in France. The previous year's expedition to Africa and the South Sea under the command of Captain Jean de Gennes was too. It arose from conditions in France, was directed against Spanish America, and conducted in the same form of royal privateering or *la course royale*. Private investors had fitted out their own expeditions to the Gulf of Mexico since 1693, and naval officers submitted proposals to plunder Spanish colonies in 1694. None of the latter received royal support before the spring of 1696.

A combined squadron of navy and private vessels commanded by Captain de Gennes departed La Rochelle early in June of 1695, bound for the South Sea via the Gambia River in Africa, Rio de Janeiro, and the Strait of Magellan.[83] The expedition involved an attempt to establish a monopoly over the Senegambian slave trade, a bizarre scheme to found a French colony on Magellan Strait, and a trading venture to the Pacific coast of South America. Six months after departing France and trying for six weeks to get through the Strait of Magellan, the ships turned back and made for Cayenne.

---

[82] Lyle N. McAlister, *Spain and Portugal in the New World, 1492–1700* (Minneapolis: University of Minnesota Press, 1984), 375.

[83] See [François] Froger, *Relation d'un voyage fait en 1695, 1696, 1697 aux côtes de l'Afrique par Monsieur de Gennes,* (Paris: Chez Nicolas Le Gras, [1700]). See also Marine, B⁴ 16, ff. 391–9v "Extrait du journal de navigation du Sr. de la Roque"; and Marine, 4JJ, 44, Journal de l'escadre de M. de Gennes de La Rochelle aux côtes d'Afrique, détroit de Magellan, Cayenne et Rochefort par M. de Torcy, ensigne de vaisseau sur *Le Faucon Anglais.*

Though it failed to challenge Spain in the Pacific, de Gennes' expedition was the precursor of two decades of commercial penetration of the South Sea previously the haunt of freebooters and buccaneers.[84]

The loss of Namur in the autumn of 1695 rather than de Gennes' risky venture was the true instigator of the three expeditions to the West Indies. Namur's loss was retrieved in part by the diplomatic detachment of Savoy from the Grand Alliance the following June, but Louis XIV lacked sufficient funds to employ the 30,000 troops released by diplomacy's success and became highly receptive to proposals to seize the Spanish treasure fleet. In August, the king advised Admiral Châteaurenault, sent to intercept the fleet off the Spanish coast, that "these ships carry immense riches and their capture would cause the collapse of Spain by diverting into other hands the succor on which the Spaniards base all their hopes for continuing the war".[85] Thus, while lack of funds led Pontchartrain to refuse any support to Governor Du Casse in the face of the largest allied expedition directed against Saint-Domingue during the war, the minister loaned four large warships under command of Captain Renau d'Eliçagaray for a combined naval and private expedition with the avowed aim of intercepting the Spanish treasure fleet in the West Indies.

Bernard Renau d'Eliçagaray (1652–1719) was perhaps the most intelligent naval officer in Louis XIV's navy. A geometer, mathematician, surveyor, and author, a Basque without personal wealth, and a naval engineer before such a profession existed, he became a protege of Colbert de Terron, who nicknamed him Petit-Renau on account of his youth and size and recommended him to Seignelay, who employed him in a variety of tasks during the 1680s. He served in Flanders under Vauban at the opening of the war, but returned to the navy and was present at the Battle of Béveziers or Beachy Head. In 1691, before returning to Flanders and the sieges of Mons and Namur, where he was wounded, Petit-Renau was commissioned a *capitaine de vaisseau*, although he possessed no prior naval grade. He designed *Le Bon*, 52 guns, which was completed at Brest in 1694, and commanded the vessel when she took a rich English East Indiaman.[86] A man of great intelligence and industry, already familiar with the growing importance of royal privateering and a devoted servant of the king, Renau was ideally suited for his mission to the Americas.

---

[84] Jean-Michel Deveau, "La rivalité franco-anglaise sur les côtes d'Afrique: la prise du fort Saint-James par Monsieur de Gennes en 1695" dans *Journées franco-anglaises d'histoire de la marine; Guerres et Paix, 1660–1815* (Vincennes: Service historique de la marine, 1987), 179–208; and Peter T. Bradley, *The Lure of Peru: Maritime Intrusion into the South Sea, 1598–1701* (Houndsmills: Macmillan, 1989), 181.

[85] Quoted in Geoffrey Symcox, *The Crisis of French Sea Power, 1688–1697: from the guerre d'escadre to the guerre de course*, (The Hague: Martinus Nijoff, 1974), 213; also William T. Morgan, "The Expedition of Baron de Pointis Against Cartagena", *American Historical Review*, 37, no. 2 (September, 1932), 240.

[86] Verge-Franceschi, "Dictionnaire des personnages et des batailles", 394–6.

On 7 February 1696, he obtained a lease on four warships from the crown.[87] His flagship, *L'Intrépide*, a second-rate ship of the line usually mounting 80 guns, carried only 60 in order to reduce the crew's size, increase the space for victuals, and lengthen the duration of her stay in the West Indies. The other large ships were similarly manned and provisioned: *Le Gaillard*, 48 guns, *Le Phoenix*, 50 guns, and *L'Esperance*, formerly HMS *Hope* of 70 guns, carrying 58 guns. Three privately armed vessels with the revealing names of *Le Pontchartrain*, 36 guns, *Le Renau*, 16 guns, and *L'Incognue* (*L'Inconnue?*), 12 guns, made up the remainder of the squadron.

Renau departed from La Rochelle early in April of 1696. The ships sighted Martinique a month later and continued through the Windward Islands to Léogane, which they reached on 24 May. There, they met *L'Esperance*, which had left France three weeks before them, lying at anchor alongside HMS *Dunkirk*, 44 guns, which she had captured a fortnight earlier. Also at Léogane were two small navy frigates that a later age would call sloops of war, *La Gracieuse* and *La Serpente*, each mounting 16 guns.[88]

The ships watered and the crews were refreshed. Du Casse laid up *La Serpente* in order to put her crew into *La Pontchartrain*, and on 3 June the reinforced squadron weighed anchor and set a course for the Bahama Channel off Cuba's north coast. Renau's objective was to capture the *flota*, the annual treasure fleet that sailed from Vera Cruz to Cadiz.[89] Renau detained two small French privateers en route and added them to his force. After reaching the waters off Havana, he established his ships along a northeast-southwest line and patrolled between Havana and the Dry Tortugas about 70 miles west of the Florida Keys. *Le Gaillard* captured a 38-gun Spanish man of war on 29 June. Several small English and Spanish prizes laden with sugar, cotton, hides, indigo, and dye wood were also taken during July, but the *flota* eluded the squadron.

By August, time was running out. Men were rapidly dying; disease carried off 300 in less than six weeks.[90] Moreover, Renau had known since late July that the governor of Havana had successfully warned the *flota* commander at Vera Cruz of the French presence. This intelligence, the impact of disease and mortality on crews, the wind's shift to the north, and the advancing hurricane season made it increasingly clear that the treasure fleet would not depart from Vera Cruz, and forced a return to France. The Spanish prize was burnt, the prisoners gathered over the summer were put ashore on the

---

[87]   Symcox, *Crisis of French Sea Power*, 211.

[88]   Marine, B⁴ 17, ff. 322–35, Extrait du journal de la route qu'a tenu l'escadre commandé par Mr. Renau, Capne de Vau. par M. de Mons, 10 October 1696.

[89]   Symcox, *The Crisis of French Sea Power*, 211 gives the expedition short shrift. Crouse, *The French Struggle*, 213–14 displays no grasp at all of what occurred for he relies entirely on hysterical but erroneous reports from Jamaica that the squadron was destined to attack the English colony.

[90]   Marine, B⁴ 17, ff. 332–4 Extrait du journal de Nos, 21 July 1696.

Cuban coast, and *Le Renau* departed for Placentia to escort the fishing fleet to France. Renau's buccaneer allies, including the ships privately armed in France, gradually departed with various shares of the spoils, and the four warships set a course for Aix Roads.[91] The pickings had been slim, and though the *flota* did not reach Spain in 1696, which severely constrained Spanish finances, that must have been small consolation to Louis XIV and none at all to Renau's private backers. The odds against capturing the *flota* had been enormous. The French had gambled and lost, but Pontchartrain's attention remained focused on the need to refill the king's coffers.

While Renau was still patrolling waters north of Havana, naval authorities were organising two more expeditions to the West Indies. The first one remains virtually unknown, while the second, normally considered an isolated phenomenon, is so famous as to leave a distorted understanding of French aims and intentions toward Spanish America.[92] The first expedition to sail after Renau, fitted out at Brest and Rochefort under command of Captain chevalier Desaugiers, a veteran of more than a score of years in the navy, was wholly naval in organisation and financing.[93]

While a junior officer, Desaugiers had been shot in the jaw during the retaking of Tobago in 1677. Ten year later he was promoted *capitaine de vaisseau* and commanded ships of the line at both Béveziers (Beachy Head) in 1690 and at Barfleur (La Hougue) in 1692. In the autumn of 1695, he commanded *Le Cheval Marin*, 44 guns, *Le Favori*, 36 guns, and *L'Aigle*, 36 guns, which carried the new intendant of the islands, François-Roger Robert, to Martinique, convoyed merchantmen there and to Saint-Domingue, and evacuated French colonists from Sainte-Croix.[94] Desaugiers' conduct, especially his diligence at keeping his crews healthy, drew strong praise from Robert, who strongly contrasted his conduct with other, more self-interested officers who found reasons to remain in harbour carrying on private trade and giving themselves over to pleasure.[95] Governor Du Casse also praised his conduct at Sainte-Croix. The intendant and governor's letters reached the minister soon after Desaugiers returned to France and probably influenced

[91] Ibid., ff. 336–41v Extrait du journal of Capt. Jacques Esnoul of *Le Renau*, 7 September 1696.

[92] E. H. Jenkins, *A History of the French Navy from its Beginnings to the Present Day* (London: Macdonald and Jane's, 1973), 90 thought the first expedition was intended to attack the English in the Caribbean.

[93] Buchet, *La Lutte pour l'espace caraïbe*, 603, 620, and 630 who is normally quite reliable ignores the presence of Desaugiers' two major units, which is why he dimisses the expedition too quickly.

[94] Col., B 18, f. 187v Instruction for Desaugiers, 12 October 1695; ibid., f. 192–3v Pontchartrain to Desaugiers, same date; ibid., ff. 222–3 same to same, 2 November 1695; and ibid., f. 224 Pontchartrain to Captain de Romegou-Blénac, same date; also Charlevoix, *Histoire de l'isle espagnol ou de S. Domingue*, 2: 288.

[95] Col., C⁸ᴬ 9, ff. 330–1 Robert to Pontchartrain, 12 May 1696.

his appointment to command the new squadron being readied in July. It was composed of *Le Bourbon*, 62 guns, *Le Bon*, 52 guns, the Bayonne-built frigates *L'Aigle* and *Le Favori*, each mounting 36 guns, *La Badine*, 32 guns, and *La Loire*, flute. His complicated instructions may reflect the minister's close interest in the expedition.

After assembling in La Rochelle's roadstead he was to sail to Sainte-Croix southeast of Puerto Rico and detach a frigate to Léogane with important dispatches for Governor Du Casse. He was then to cruise off Puerto Rico to await the Spanish Windward Squadron (*Armada de Barlovento*). If its ships were at Havana or not coming to Puerto Rico, Desaugiers was to make for Caracas and Spanish Main and seize all shipping available, but if they were at Puerto Rico he was to attack the *Armada* and thereby fulfill the expedition's twofold purpose: to damage Spanish commerce and to secure Saint-Domingue from attack. Afterward, whether on the Spanish Main or off Puerto Rico, he was to sail to Léogane and consult with Governor Du Casse concerning the advisability of ravaging Jamaica once again in revenge for the previous year's Anglo-Spanish attacks on the colony. Regardless of the decision, the frigates and the flûte from Rochefort were to unload their stores and munitions for Saint-Domingue at Léogane and prepare to escort the colony's merchant shipping to France. Afterward, Desaugiers could take his two largest warships into the Gulf of Mexico to attack the richly laden ships of the Honduran coastal trade. Desaugiers was given supplies for 10 months, and Pontchartrain advised him to cruise in the Bahama Channel if any time remained.[96]

Desaugiers got away during the second half of August and reached Grenada after a 40-day passage. There he took on wood and water, and on 5 October, he sailed for Puerto Rico. He had sent *L'Aigle* ahead in search of intelligence, and the frigate soon returned with news that he had missed the Windward Squadron by a month and the treasure fleet remained laid up in Havana. Renau's summer cruise had clearly shaken the Spanish. Desaugiers immediately detached *La Badine* and *La Loire* to Léogane and took his remaining ships to the Spanish Main. News of his coming may well have preceded him, for the French found few ships at sea. They did learn, however, that the galleon packet known as *La Marguerite* was at La Guaira, Caracas's seaport, completing her cargo before sailing to Cartagena, and Desaugiers resolved to seize her. Ordering *Le Bon* and the two frigates to engage the forts at the harbour entrance, his crew armed with muskets and grenades quickly overran the galleon and captured her. The principal cargo of the Spanish prize was approximately 9,000 quintals of cacao worth about

---

[96] Marine, B⁴ 17, ff. 362–7v Draft Instructions for Desaugiers, 12 July 1696; also Marine B² 113, ff. 12–22 Instructions for Desaugiers. The main part of these instructions are somewhat inaccurately printed in Charlevoix, *Histoire de l'isle espagnole*, 2: 292–5. See also Symcox, *Crisis of French Sea Power*, 273.

30 sols per livre weight or about 1,350,000 livres tournois and more than 91,000 piastres or pieces of eight, roughly 4 tonnes of silver. Learning that two merchantmen were at Portobelo, he sent off *Le Bon* and *L'Aigle*, but their mission proved fruitless. Desaugiers resolved to sail to Saint-Domingue. Off Jacmel he took an English merchantman from Cork and carried it and his prize into Léogane at the beginning of December.

Though mounting only 40 guns, the Spanish prize was pierced for 60. She was also brand new, colonial-built, and judged a good sailer. Desaugiers resolved to send her to France accompanied by *L'Aigle* escorting the merchant shipping at Léogane. Desaugiers drafted men from his own ships and pressed sailors from the merchantmen to man his prize. Lack of victuals at Saint-Domingue forced him to reduce his naval force and send his men and Spanish prisoners to France.

The galleon had been one of eight warships carrying silver from Portobelo. Captain Desaugiers resolved to sail to Cartagena in company with *La Badine*, where he hoped to meet up with the seven other Spanish ships. However, fresh intelligence from Havana and the worsening effect of fevers on his reduced crews forced a change in plans. On 8 December, Desaugiers sailed for the south coast of Hispaniola once more in search of the elusive Windward Squadron.[97] On 6 January, twelve leagues to windward of the city of Santo Domingo, the French sighted seven sail approaching from the east and gave chase under English colours. The Spanish ships fled. *Le Bourbon, Le Bon, Le Favori*, and *La Badine* chased all day and all night until at two the next morning the Spanish vice-admiral lost her foretopmast and maintopgallant sail. *Le Bon* overhauled her at dawn. Wind and high seas prevented boarding, but after a brief engagement she struck her colours.[98] The prize with less than 8,000 livres' worth of silver on board was a disappointment. She was *Le Christ de Marecaye* (*Santo Christo de Maracaibo?*), 46 guns, with a crew of 230, and was escorted into Léogane, where, owing to lack of victuals, she was immediately readied for the voyage to France, accompanied by yet a second frigate from the squadron to be reduced to a flute. Time in the tropics was exacting its toll. The once sprightly *Le Favori* sailed through the sea like a farm cart.[99] Making matters worse, the first prize, which sprang a leak at the Caicos Islands and returned to Petit Goâve for repairs, would not be ready to sail until mid-February.

Not only time, which rapidly wore out ships in the tropics, and disease and malnutrition that devoured their crews, but the inability to find fresh provisions, munitions, and stores in the French colonies seriously hampered navy effectiveness throughout the war. The need to transport everything

---

[97] Marine, B⁴ 17, ff. 377–81 Desaugiers to Pontchartrain, 6 December 1696; ibid., ff. 367–71v same to same, 3 February 1697.

[98] Marine, B⁴ 17, ff. 378–9v Captain Patoulet to Pontchartrain, 5 February 1697.

[99] Ibid., Desaugiers to Pontchartrain, 3 February 1697.

from France was proving to be the navy's greatest weakness in the Americas. Though less than six months out from France, the squadron was already substantially reduced. From his prisoners, Desaugiers learned that the treasure fleet remained in Havana and would not venture out before midsummer. Nothing remained for him but to continue his mission, and on 3 February he sailed for Honduras. Three months earlier, Pontchartrain had sent Desaugiers supplementary orders to support yet a third expedition about to depart France in 1696, but it is not clear whether he ever received them or ignored them in the light of his own reduced forces.[100] In any case, he took no prizes off Honduras and sailed for France without returning to Saint-Domingue, thereby missing the arrival of the largest French expedition of the war. Less than a month after Desaugiers left Léogane, a fleet of 12 warships and five smaller vessels sailed into Cap Français harbour in search of local reinforcements for a major assault on the Spanish Main.

The newest French expedition, under the command of Jean-Bernard-Louis Desjean, baron de Pointis (1645–1707), was long overdue when it finally reached Saint-Domingue on 3 March 1697. Pointis, who was a cousin of Marshal Jean d'Estrées and strongly connected at court, had proposed an attack on Spanish America as early as 1691. He also proposed to pillage Spanish American settlements early in 1694; Vera Cruz, Panama, Cartagena, and Portobelo were all considered as targets. The plan called for six ships of the line, eight lesser navy vessels, including four transports carrying 200 soldiers each, and 12 smaller tenders of various sorts and sizes, all requiring 4,000 men.[101] Pointis offered to fit out and careen the warships at his own expense and to purchase whatever was lacking to complete their armament. He estimated the total cost at 770,000 livres, which he claimed to be able to raise himself. He also thought that, after paying off the investors at 100 percent, he could give 200 to 300,000 livres to the admiral for his tenth of all booty and divide the remainder into five shares of which one-fifth would go to the Crown and the others to his backers. The proposal omitted sharing any booty among the officers and men of the expedition.[102]

Pointis was not alone in proposing attacks on Spanish America.[103] He had been anticipated by several wealthy ship owners who had the minister's ear. In June of 1694, *Le Comte de Toulouse*, owned by Joachim Descazeaux du Hallay of Nantes and Noël Danican, sieur de l'Espine of Saint-Malo, returned to France from a successful smuggling venture to Mexico loaded

100 Col., B 18, f. 402 Pontchartrain to Desaugiers, 6 November 1698.
101 Marine, B⁴ 15, ff. 62–7 Project d'armement pour les indes occidentales par M. de Pointis, 20 January 1694; also ibid., ff. 68–9v Projet d'armement pour la Vera Cruz et Panama, 1694.
102 Marine, B⁴ 15, ff. 70–6v halograph memorial by Pointis, 28 February 1694.
103 According to Dessert, *La Royale*, 251, Vice-Admiral d'Estrées was the true originator of the attack on Cartagena, but many others proposed similar assaults.

with gold and silver and towing an English prize. Both merchants were active investors in royal navy privateering with investments in *Le Furieux*, 60 guns, and *Le Vaillant*, 48 guns, and shared in other prizes brought in that summer.[104] At the end of November, Pointis submitted a proposal, his second of the war, to attack the Dutch at Curaçao.[105] The following January, the naval minister handed over 3 warships to the chevalier Damon to cruise in the Gulf of Mexico. Damon was later associated with the merchant investor Jean Saupin of Brest, himself closely connected in other privateering ventures to Descazeaux du Hallay, but nothing came of this Mexican expedition.[106] Pontchartrain was eager to penetrate Spanish America, but he only became receptive to Pointis' proposals early in 1696 in the larger context of Louis XIV's decision to knock Spain out of the war by capturing the annual treasure fleet and plundering Spanish American seaports.

In May, after Renau's squadron had left La Rochelle and three months before Desaugiers' ships got way, Louis XIV approved Pointis' expedition, granting him seven of the line between 56 and 70 guns, three frigates, and several smaller warships. The king was to share in the plunder. Louis XIV set the final, revised conditions in late July when Pointis also received his instructions.[107] The commander hoped to depart in September, but persistent peace rumours threatened his plans. Few investors were willing to subscribe and others repudiated their subscriptions. In October, Pontchartrain pointedly asked Pointis whether he had sent sufficient funds to Brest to provision his fleet, and the king suggested Pointis reduce the size of his force. Further delays occurred as lighters from Rochefort failed to arrive with provisions. It was only on 6 January 1697, after contrary winds abated, that the expedition's ships departed.[108] Pointis made for Saint-Domingue, where Governor Du Casse had been instructed to recruit 1,000 to 1,200 buccaneers to reinforce the expedition.[109]

Governor Du Casse was not happy about the expedition. Deeply committed to transforming Saint-Domingue into the chief French colony in the Americas, he favoured the conquest of Hispaniola or Jamaica, whereas the minister was preoccupied with penetration of Spanish America and sought to

[104] Jean Meyer, *La Noblesse bretonne au XVIIIe siècle*, 2 vols. (Paris: SEVPEN, 1966), 1: 339–41; Lionel Rothkrug, *Opposition to Louis XIV: The Political and Social Origins of the French Enlightenment*, (Princeton: Princeton University Press, 1965), 406.

[105] Col., C^{8A} 8, ff. 311–14 Memoire de Pointis sur un projet d'attaque contre Curaçao, 28 November 1694.

[106] Symcox, *Crisis of French Sea Power*, 207.

[107] Marine, B^4 17, ff. 404–5 Conditions accordées par le Roy au Sr. de Pointis … pour un armement en course, 25 July 1696.

[108] On the expedition's preparations, see Morgan, "The Expedition of Baron de Pointis Against Cartagena", 237–41; also Symcox, *The Crisis of French Sea Power*, 218–19.

[109] Col., B 18, f. 317v Pontchartrain to Du Casse, 26 September 1696, ibid., f. 319 same to Pointis, same date.

check Anglo-Dutch competition by seizing their wealth and creating a French colony similar to Curaçao somewhere close to the American mainland.[110] Du Casse viewed naval squadrons as possessing limited value to further his ambitions. The Spanish empire was dying, and, as he advised Pontchartrain, from the time of Queen Elizabeth I the English had the right idea of reducing Spain by undermining its American foundations, but Oliver Cromwell rather than John Hawkins was Du Casse's model. An expeditionary force was necessary. Naval squadrons alone accomplished little. The results of Renau d'Eliçagary's and Desaugiers' expeditions supported him. In Du Casse's opinion, ships served only to transport men to their destinations. Sailors only handled ships, according to the governor, and were useless to conquer territory. Men from Saint-Domingue were the key to success and would be much better employed led on a mission of conquest rather than plunder.[111] Baron de Pointis and Governor Du Casse were at odds from the beginning of their association. Pointis, the punctilious naval officer with a quarter of a century of service, hid his search for personal wealth beneath condescension, patronizing the aggressive, self-made, bourgeois governor, who boldly asserted that Saint-Domingue was worth a thousand Canadas.[112]

At Le Cap, Pointis found 400 freebooters and only a few more at Petit Goâve. He berated Du Casse for not having 1,500 men on hand. Seeking to intimidate and subordinate the governor and knowing nothing about buccaneers, their military customs, or the manner in which they waged war, Pointis' contempt for Saint-Domingue's obstreperous colonists only caused much useless delay. Executing rebellious buccaneers and threatening to burn their ships were empty gestures. Without Du Casse, he could recruit no one. The colonial reinforcements were on hand as ordered, but Du Casse wanted to change Pointis' destination in favour of Portobelo or Vera Cruz, and sought written assurances that captured booty would be divided according to the customs of the colony. Pointis, the naval commander-cum-entrepreneur, held fast to Cartagena as his objective. He readily signed an agreement to distribute booty in the same manner as was applied to the crews of his own ships, and the unsuspecting Du Casse was satisfied. On 19 March, Pointis' ships left Petit Goâve with about 1,600 buccaneers and colonists, including 2 companies of free blacks, in 10 ships, including Desaugiers' former prize, the *Santo Christo*.[113] Governor Du Casse sailed in *Le Pontchartrain*, 36 guns.

110   Charlevoix, *Histoire de l'isle espagnol ou de S. Domingue*, 2: 292; see Charles Frostin, "Les Pontchartrain et la pénétration commerciale française en Amérique espagnole", *Revue historique*, no. 245 (1971), 307–36 for a full discussion.

111   Col., C⁹ᴮ 1 Du Casse to Pontchartrain, 15 December 1696.

112   Marine, B⁴ 17, ff. 400v–1 Du Casse to Pontchartrain, 28 July 1697.

113   Patrick Villiers, *Marine royale, corsaires et trafic dans l'Atlantique de Louis XIV à Louis XVI*, 2 vols. (Dunkerque: Société dunkerquoise d'histoire et d'archaeologie, 1991), 1: 190; Buchet, *La Lutte pour l'espace caraïbe*, 1: 508; and Crouse, *The French Struggle*, 218.

The French reached Cartagena on 13 April and immediately began siege operations against the outer forts guarding the port. For more than two weeks the French slowly drove in the Spanish defences until the final assault began at the end of the month. Four days later, on 4 May, the Spanish signed articles of capitulation and the French began to take possession of Cartagena.[114]

Pointis turned his attention to collecting his booty while simultaneously duping Du Casse until he got it aboard his own virtually impregnable warships. He succeeded in remarkably easy fashion because the governor thought the sharing arrangements were beyond dispute. Du Casse was easily sent off with the bulk of the colonial forces on a wild goose chase in search of a Spanish army reportedly approaching the port. Pointis gathered up booty worth about 10 million livres into his ships before the buccaneers returned and found the gates of the city closed against them.[115] Aware that he had been duped, Du Casse withdrew from the city chiefly to organise provisions for the colonial forces in the face of Pointis' refusal to issue them victuals and attempt to dismiss them from the expedition. Du Casse faced a dilemma. Each day his men became more unruly as they saw the heavily guarded booty being loaded on board ships of the line, and he ran the risk of losing control over them, a control that relied less on royal authority than on his own domineering character and the freebooters' trust in him. As a king's commissioned officer and royal governor, however, he could not countenance rebellion. He had to be satisfied with Pointis' assurances that a fair distribution of booty would be made as soon as it was completely collected and inventoried while struggling to maintain discipline, which he did by promising to appeal to the king personally for justice.

By late May, with sickness taking a heavier toll than military casualties, and all the booty, including the guns from the forts and the bells from the churches, on board the warships, and after blowing up several outer forts, the freebooters, who numbered nearly one-quarter of the initial force, learned that far from receiving a quarter of the booty, they were to share in only one-tenth of the first million livres and one-thirtieth part of any additional millions. This paltry amount included no more than 40,000 écus (120,000 livres) to be divided among Du Casse's men, perhaps 25 *écus*, certainly no

---

[114] For an account of the siege of Cartagena see Sieur Pointis, *A Genuine and Particular Account of the Taking of Cartagena* (London, 1740), which is a translation of Pointis' own account that appeared as *Relation de l'expédition de Cathagène, faite par les françois en 1697* (Amsterdam: chez les héritiers de A. Schelte, 1698). Briefer accounts appear in Charlevoix, *Histoire de l'isle espagnole ou de S. Domingue*, 2: 297–353; and Crouse, *The French Struggle*, 219–32.

[115] Estimates of the booty range from eight to forty million livres; Charles de La Roncière, *Histoire de la Marine française*, 6 vols. (Paris: Plon, 1909–1932), 6: 290 gives 6,646,948 livres, which may be the value of gold and silver; Morgan, "The Expedition of Baron de Pointis", 247 estimated it at about ten million.

more than 40 *écus*, per man. If the governor was enraged, he could do nothing beyond promising to appeal to the king. His officers, who were less restrained, decided to sack what was left of Cartagena. Du Casse may have colluded with them. Pointis suddenly fell ill and could not see the governor or any officers who sought his support to maintain the king's authority. Instead, he ordered his ships to depart immediately.

The buccaneers lost no time. Locking all the male inhabitants in Cartagena's principal church and threatening them with horrible penalties that left nothing to the imagination, they demanded 5 million livres. The terrified inhabitants protested that Pointis had carried off everything; nothing remained. It was useless. The buccaneers were not to be denied, and after four days they obtained about 1,000,000 écus. Believing they had secured all that remained, they divided the gold and silver amongst themselves and set sail for Isle à Vache on the south coast of Saint-Domingue, where they intended to share the slaves and merchandise they had taken.[116]

The Cartagena expedition was not Louis XIV's greatest stroke at sea, nor can it have influenced greatly the Treaty of Ryswick, which was signed only three weeks after Pointis reached France. Though it may have contributed something to the king's revenues, it certainly did not fill his treasury or increase his interest in the West Indies.[117] For all its success, the differences between Du Casse and Pointis reduced the expedition's impact, as did the absence of a strategic plan. Besides, the greatest consequence of Pointis' expedition had nothing to do with its success. Its major consequence was unforeseen and due to the conduct of the Allies. It was the allied pursuit of Pointis to the Caribbean that enabled the French to knock Spain out of the war and Louis XIV to reach peace with William III.

The English learned of French preparations to attack Spanish possessions and were concerned about the French effort to take Spain out of the war by seizing the treasure fleet. During the previous two years, the Allies had been sending combined fleets to the western Mediterranean in support of the besieged city of Barcelona in order to keep Spain in the war. On learning of French preparations to attack Spanish America, including the assignment of Admiral Châteaurenault's fleet to cruise off Cadiz in wait for the treasure fleet, the English sent a messenger to overtake Vice-Admiral John Nevill who had sailed for the Mediterranean with 15 Allied men of war and a convoy bound for the Levant at Cadiz with orders to sail at once to Madeira and await reinforcements before sailing to the Caribbean.[118] These arrived under the command of Rear-Admiral George Mees only two months later,

116 Crouse, *The French Struggle*, 238–9.
117 These claims are to be found in Morgan, "The Expedition of Baron de Pointis", 254; also Villiers, *Marine royale, corsaires*, 1: 81.
118 John Ehrman, *The Navy in the War of William III, 1689–1697* (Cambridge: Cambridge University Press, 1953), 611.

at about the same time as Pointis' ships were appearing at Saint-Domingue. The English viewed the French expedition so seriously that for the only time during the war they overcame mistrust of their allies in the West Indies to assign a joint Anglo-Dutch force to seek and destroy Pointis.

Admiral Nevill reached Barbados on 27 April [N.S.] and spent a month before learning Pointis' whereabouts. Nevill first sailed to Antigua believing the French objective to be Santo Domingo, the *flota*, or both. He only learned they were at Cartagena on 26 May [N.S.], the same day that Pointis was making ready to depart. Nevill prepared to sail from Jamaica, where he had gone, but remained wind bound for more than a week before getting away. With his fleet now numbering 24 men of war he sighted Pointis on 7 June with 10 men of war and two transports, but Nevill failed to catch the short-handed, outnumbered French except for one of the flutes. During the next two days the weather blew "very fresh, with a great sea" and the English suffered much damage to masts and sails. They were unable to catch Pointis. Nevill finally made for Cartagena whence he sailed to catch the colonial force under Du Casse.[119] The true significance of these actions lay in Europe, where Admiral Nevill's diversion to the West Indies led to allied abandonment of naval support for the Spanish at Barcelona, which fell to a combined French land and sea attack on 22 June. Indirectly, then, the English response to the Pointis' expedition rather than the latter's successful capture of Cartagena contributed mightily to taking Spain out of the war.

In the West Indies, Du Casse was as good as his word, sending his second in command, king's lieutenant Joseph d'Honon de Galiffet, to carry his appeal directly to the king and to report to Pontchartrain.[120] Wisely ignoring events at Cartagena, Du Casse stressed Pointis' failure to capture the *flota* or to protect Saint-Domingue from the Anglo-Dutch naval forces currently besieging it. He also sent copies of his orders to captains and freebooters to remain obedient to the king's authority while acknowledging that Pointis had cheated them: "on nous fait une perfidie sans example".[121] The governor requested that each colonist who went to Cartagena be granted 100 *écus* from the king's bounty. Du Casse's accusation that Pointis was guilty of "une fraude scandaleuse" and of deceit (*la tromperie*) and his request for protection for himself and the colony was heard. In December, the Royal Council fixed the amount to be paid to the colonists and freebooters of Saint-Domingue at 1,400,000 livres.[122]

---

[119] R. D. Merriman, ed., *The Sergison Papers* (London: The Navy Records Society, 1950), 299 "Abstract of Vice-Admiral Nevill's journal of his voyage to the West Indies after M. Pointis".

[120] Hrodej, *L'Amiral Du Casse*, 2: 447–62 prints Gallifet's report.

[121] Marine, B⁴ 17, ff. 394–6v Du Casse to Pontchartrain, the younger, 30 June 1697.

[122] Ibid., ff. 398–411, same to same, 28 July 1697; Col., B 18, f. 591 arrêt du conseil, 2 December 1697.

After sailing away from Admiral Nevill in a gale, baron de Pointis touched at Cape Tibouron before sailing through the strait of Florida. Reduced manpower led him to sink three of his ships and lack of water forced him to make for Newfoundland. He anchored in Conception Bay, north of St. John's, which was occupied by Commodore Sir John Norris and ten ships of the English navy. After taking on water, the pugnacious French commander tested St. John's harbour despite Norris's superior numbers. The defences proved too strong, and the English refused to come out and contest the issue. On 8 August, Pointis set a course for France. About 250 miles off the Scilly Islands he encountered yet another English squadron. Though reduced to six ships after more than eight months at sea, he chose to contest the passage. After a three-hour battle the English broke off the engagement and the French sailed away, reaching Brest on 29 August.[123] A month later at Fontainbleau, Pointis presented Louis XIV with an emerald the size of a fist, and while the duc de Saint-Simon concluded that the account had all the appearance of a saga, it also had consequences for the French in the Americas.

Du Casse's charge that the recruitment of freebooters for Pointis' expedition had stripped Saint-Domingue of its defenders was accurate though less than forthright, for they had never been vigorous defenders of the colony. However, he was supported by the new governor-general of the West Indies, the marquis d'Amblimont, who claimed that Pointis could have been more usefully employed against the English at Barbados, which lacked a military commander.[124] The weakness of Saint-Domingue was demonstrated one last time, and the fact that the colony was no more secure in the final months of the war than before supports Du Casse's charge that Pointis' expedition failed to increase French security in the West Indies, but that may be beside the point. Pointis' great raid was never intended to advance the interest of the colonies or ensure their security.

Half an hour before dawn on 8 July about one mile east of Petit Goâve, the English, under the command of Admiral Mees landed a detachment of nearly 400 men who marched directly on the town. The raiders entered and overran the town so quickly that Du Casse escaped after leaping from a window wearing only his nightshirt. Reaching a previously assigned place, he rallied 55 to 60 men while Major Beauregard gathered about 100 men at the other end of town. They counterattacked simultaneously from both ends of the settlement. The raiders' discovery of a supply of liquor in the meantime greatly assisted French efforts, though the English were still able to blow up two storehouses containing gunpowder that set other fires, which destroyed about a quarter of the town. In addition to 42 houses burnt, 49

123   Morgan, "The Expedition of Baron de Pointis", 249–51.
124   Col., C⁸ᴬ 10, ff. 50–1, 72–3v Amblimont to Pontchartrain, 30 July 1697.

were killed, 17 or 18 taken prisoner, 5 were ships lost, and 140 to 150 slaves taken, all of which Du Casse blamed on Pointis.[125]

By the summer of 1697, all of this was little more than sound and fury. Peace negotiations had been seriously underway for a full year, ever since Savoy had withdrawn from the Grand Alliance. All parties needed peace and a means to reach it.[126] By 1697, William III was willing to negotiate a political settlement with France, and with the separation of Spain from the maritime powers, Louis XIV found means to achieve general peace. The fall of Barcelona in June forced the Spanish out of the war and compelled the Emperor to acknowledge that he could no longer fight France alone on the Rhine and the Ottoman army too.[127] It was merely a coincidence that news that Cartagena had been plundered was followed within three weeks by the signing of the Treaty of Ryswick.

7.5 NEW FRANCE

The French situation in North America differed markedly from what prevailed in the West Indies, though there too colonists were left largely on their own. The Crown sanctioned strategic gifts to the Indians but made no special provision to finance wartime alliances, leaving New France to defend itself with current levels of money and troops.[128] Nevertheless, the Nine Years' War marked a significant change in the status of natives in the growing French-English struggle in the Americas. In the West Indies, the Island Caribs ceased to play an important role in the conflict, but in North America the Abenaki in northern New England joined the Iroquois in New York in becoming independent parties in the war. Indeed, in 1689, the chief threat to New France was from Indians rather than the English. The threat was serious and remained so until the war's end.

Canada was blessed with formidable natural defences from both colonial and European enemies. Its still sparsely settled population lay hundreds of miles up the St. Lawrence River which was normally ice-bound for half the year and filled with a multitude of natural hazards to navigation during the other half. The only invasion route from the south, due north from the

[125] See Marine, B⁴ 17, ff. 398–401 Du Casse to Pontchartrain, 28 July 1697; ibid., ff. 402–4v Beauregard to Pontchartrain, 9 August 1697; and Merriman, ed., *The Sergison Papers*, 311–14 "An account of the burning of Petit Guaves the 28th June [o.s.] 1694 (*sic*) by the English under the command of Rear Admiral Mees".

[126] See Mark A. Thomson, "Louis XIV and William III, 1689–1697", *English Historical Review*, 76 (January 1961): 48–55 on 1696 peace initiatives.

[127] Wolf, *Louis XIV*, 485–88.

[128] Catherine Desbarats, "The Cost of Early Canada's Native Alliances: Reality and Scarcity's Rhetoric", *William and Mary Quarterly*, 3rd Ser., 52, 4 (October, 1995), 613.

Hudson River via Lake Champlain and the Richelieu River, was controlled by the strongest group of Indian nations in northeastern North America, the Five Nations Iroquois Confederacy. The western region, whence a threat might have come, remained a human desert still being laid waste by inter-tribal warfare in which the French actively participated. However, if the Iroquois were the only threat to New France, whose chief defence was a system of alliances with other nations, half a century of war against these formidable enemies had provided the colonists with harsh experience and valuable training. They had also been reinforced by regular infantry, once in the 1660s and permanently after 1683. By 1689, Canadians possessed skills acquired during the previous decades, and during the next nine years they would carry the warfare known as *la petite guerre* into New York and New England, creating a terror-myth whose impact remains fresh three centuries later.

New France and the Iroquois had long been at war when news arrived that France was at war with England. Previous efforts to intimidate the Iroquois had failed and brought home to senior French military officers in the colony the hardships and harshness of campaigns against such an elu-sive enemy. In 1688, Governor-General Jacques-René de Brisay, marquis de Denonville, sent Louis-Hector de Callière, Governor of Montreal and second-in-command in the colony, to France with a proposal to secure New France from the Iroquois by conquering New York. The plan was both origi-nal and bold; its chief recommendation lay in Denonville's assertion that less than half the forces needed against the Iroquois would be required. It called for two expeditions, one of 800 men from Canada to capture Albany, destroy it and nearby settlements and drive down the Hudson River to New York; a second expedition of six naval frigates and 1,200 men from La Rochelle would attack Manhattan by sea and ravage the coast northward as far as Boston. In addition to cutting off the Iroquois' source of arms and muni-tions, success would secure the French cod fishery, give France possession of an ice-free harbour and a fertile province, contain New England, and punish Huguenots who had fled New France and the West Indies and recently taken refuge in New York.[129] Callière presented the plan to Louis XIV early in 1689 and Seignelay rejected it. On 7 June, three weeks after England's dec-laration of war, Seignelay and the king revived the plan. They also modified it, reducing the forces involved. Instead of a two-pronged attack by land and by sea, a single overland force of 900 men was to attack Albany, and after taking it, move south to New York. The naval portion of the attack was reduced to a two-ship diversion off Manhattan. Something entirely new was

129   W. J. Eccles, *Canada Under Louis XIV, 1663–1701* (Toronto: McClelland and Stewart, 1964), 161; Zoltvany, "Callière, Louis–Hector de" *DCB*, 2: 113; also J. F. Bosher, "Huguenot Merchants and the Protestant International in the Seventeenth Century", *The William and Mary Quarterly*, 3rd ser. 52, 1 (January, 1995), 77–102.

also added. Former governor Louis de Baude, comte de Frontenac, was put in command and recalled as Governor-General of New France.[130]

Initially scheduled to sail on 14 June, the Canada convoy did not depart until five and a half weeks later, far too late to accomplish anything that year. Indeed, after continually battling fierce westerly winds, the ships reached Chedabouctou (present-day Guysborough, Nova Scotia), only late in September. There, Governor Frontenac issued his orders to Captain de La Caffinière commanding *L'Union* and *Le Fourgon* before boarding a merchantman for the long voyage to Quebec.[131] The warships carrying arms, munitions, and stores departed for Port Royal, but they never sailed beyond the Bay of Fundy. The late season and bad weather left Captain de La Caffinière with no choice but to return directly to France.[132]

Meanwhile, Canada's security had nearly collapsed. In early August, 1,500 Iroquois warriors attacked the settlement of Lachine on Montreal Island. Twenty-four colonists were killed, 70 to 90 were taken prisoner, and nearly three-quarters of the homes in the settlement were destroyed. More serious than the attack itself was the destruction of security, which spread fear and terror throughout the colony.[133] With the arrival of Governor Frontenac to replace Denonville came the news that France and England were formally at war. A second Iroquois attack, supported by a formal alliance with the English of New York, was a very real possibility. There could be no talk of attacking Manhattan; New France's defences needed serious reinforcement.

Governor Frontenac's solution to initiate peace negotiations with the Iroquois and launch a series of attacks on English frontier settlements in New York and New England was shortsighted and ineffective. He apparently hoped these spoiling attacks would dissuade the English from fully supporting the Iroquois, which they may have done, but they also undermined the colony's alliance system with western Indians and united the English colonies, especially through the adherence of Massachusetts, against New France.[134] In January, a war party of 114 Canadians and 96 allied Indians led by Nicolas d'Ailleboust de Manthet left Montreal and on 18 February attacked Schenectady, New York. English losses amounted to 60 killed and 27 men and boys taken prisoner together with many pack horses loaded with plunder. Failure to strike at Albany left the Iroquois' main source of arms and munitions intact and delivered only a message of

[130] Guy Frégault, *Iberville, le conquérant* (Montréal: Guérin, [1944] 1996), 366–7; Eccles, *Canada Under Louis XIV*, 163–4.

[131] Marine, B⁴ 12, ff. 107–9v Memoire pour servir d'instructions au Sieur de la Caffinière, 20 September 1689.

[132] Ibid., ff. 115–18 La Caffinière to Seignelay, 27 December 1689.

[133] Eccles, *Canada Under Louis XIV*, 164–5.

[134] Ibid., 169–70.

horror and hatred with no strategic content.[135] A second war party of 25 Canadians and 25 Indians led by François Hertel, sieur de La Fresnière, left Trois Rivières also in January. Though much smaller than the Montreal force, its exploits were equally devastating and also strategically empty. On 27 March, after a two-month march on snowshoes, hunting as they moved south, the raiders struck in the neighbourhood of Fort Rollinsford (near present-day Salmon Falls, New Hampshire). Within two hours they had wiped out everything. Losses were 34 killed and about 50 women and children taken prisoner. As Hertel's war party hustled their captives through the snowy woods they learned that an enemy force was moving to intercept them, and ambushed it at Wooster River, killing twenty. Sending some of his men to lead the captives to Quebec, Hertel led the remainder to intercept a third war party led by René Robineau de Portneuf, and after two months living off the land joined it. Composed of 50 Canadians and 60 Indians, this force had departed Quebec in late winter. It was reinforced by a strong force of Abenaki Indians allied to Jean-Vincent d'Abbadie de Saint-Castin, son-in-law of their paramount chief Madokawando at Pentagouet on the east side of the Penobscot River. In May, the enlarged war party struck Casco and Fort Loyal (present-day Falmouth and Portland, Maine, respectively). The result was similar to the earlier raids. The garrison was massacred and frontier settlements deserted as hundreds fled to larger colonial towns to the south, but of lasting effect there was little.[136]

Portneuf returned to Quebec late in June, having left most of his prisoners with the Abenaki, but New France's security had not been advanced. Instead, the bloody raids had so terrorized Massachusetts colonists that they achieved temporary unity, at least sufficient to plan a joint attack with New York, and to assemble a strong colonial force under command of Sir William Phips to strike at Quebec. The attack was to be half of a two-pronged assault intended to conquer New France: one composed of an 850-man army from New York to strike Montreal, and the other by sea from Boston to attack Quebec. Fortunately for the French, the overland force from New York broke up before it reached New France, and beyond a single damaging raid south of Montreal in early September, accomplished nothing. Phips's ships reached Quebec, but he too failed to gain his object. His arrival in mid-October was too late in the season and his force lacked either trained troops or sufficient munitions. After a week of demonstrations and rodomontade, calling on the French to surrender, the English colonial troops reembarked and Phips's ships stole downstream. In the absence of pilots and in the presence of worsening weather, the withdrawal turned into a rout. In January, one-third of the

[135]   Ibid., 172; Jean Blain, "Ailleboust de Manthet, Nicolas", *DCB*, 2: 13–14.
[136]   Eccles, *Canada Under Louis XIV*, 175–6; E. Taillemite, "Robineau de Portneuf, René" *DCB*, 2: 579–80; G. C. Salagnac, "Abbadie de Saint Castin, Jean Vincent d", *DCB*, 2: 4–7.

expedition's ships remained unaccounted for. In the words of the late Gerald Graham, "the wonder is that the expedition returned at all".[137]

Neither side displayed much military talent. A more enterprising general than Governor Frontenac, who enjoyed the advantages of defence and superior numbers including trained, regular infantry, might well have destroyed the 1,200-to 1,300-man English landing force had he chosen to; while Sir William Phips, completely without military experience and a protege of the Puritan divines who had transformed the expedition into a religious crusade, displayed no military talents at all.[138] Capturing New France was more difficult than the Protestant preachers had imagined, and they soon turned to conducting witch trials back home in Salem. At Quebec, the colonists offered solemn thanks to God, attributing their deliverance to the intercession of the Blessed Mother, naming their recently completed church in lower town Notre Dame de Victoire in her honour. Louis XIV struck yet another medal among the hundreds celebrating his glory, to mark the first French victory of the war in the Americas.

Astonishing though it may seem, New France suffered only one more English attack during the remainder of the war. In August of 1691, a combined force of New York militia and Iroquois numbering more than 400 fought a pitched battle against superior numbers of Canadians south of Montreal. Losses on both sides during the bloody struggle were high, and the English could claim a tactical victory over careless Canadian militia,[139] but the colony's greatest enemy remained the Iroquois, whose large war parties struck the western end of the colony, destroying farms and crops from the western end of Montreal Island to the mouth of the Richelieu River. From 1692, after the Mohawks ceased to function as a fighting force, however, senior military officers of the colony began to carry "the little war" to the Iroquois, sending out raiding parties to ambush the enemy while the government paid scalp bounties of 30 livres a piece.[140]

This policy also proved ineffective. It often conflicted with the goals of the fur trade. Rather than cementing alliances with the western Indians by combining with them to attack the Iroquois, Canadian traders were cutting their allies out of the trade as they voyaged ever farther west to trade with their allies' own clients.[141] Second, this kind of warfare proved very costly in both men and supplies, whereas the ministry's funds were being substantially reduced. Finally, Governor Frontenac's tactics were being increasingly

---

[137]   Gerald S. Graham, *Empire of the North Atlantic; The Maritime Struggle for North America*, 2nd. ed. (Toronto: University of Toronto Press, 1958), 71–5.

[138]   C. P. Steacy, "Phips, Sir William", *DCB*, 1: 545.

[139]   Eccles, *Canada under Louis XIV*, 186–7.

[140]   Francis Jennings, *Ambiguous Iroquois Empire: The Covenant Chain Confederation of Indian Tribes with English Colonies from its Beginnings to the Lancaster Treaty of 1744* (New York: W.W. Norton, 1984), 206.

[141]   Eccles, *Canada under Louis XIV*, 189.

criticized. In 1693, following a botched raid on a Mohawk village that resulted in heavy losses, Louis-Hector de Callière advocated a full-scale attack on the Iroquois homeland as the only means to halt the Iroquois capacity to wage war. The failure to destroy Albany in 1690 had been a grievous mistake. The colony's intendant Jean Bochart de Champigny supported Callière because the proposed attack would be undertaken by regular colonial infantry and enable the colonial militia to withdraw as New France's major offensive fighters and support their families,[142] but Governor Frontenac persisted in his attempt to conciliate the Iroquois. He successfully resisted all efforts to persuade him to change his tactics until July of 1696, and even then, the full-scale attack so long advocated in the colony was launched against the central Iroquois living south of Lake Ontario rather than the eastern Iroquois in the lower Mohawk Valley. An army of more than 2,000 regular infantry, colonial militia, and Indian allies destroyed many Oneida and Onondaga villages together with more than 1,000,000 bushels of corn, and even reasserted French authority in the West, but peace when it came owed little to the French and much to external circumstances.

The New York English refused to aid their erstwhile Indian allies who had borne the brunt of the war against Canada, while the French success brought wavering western Indian nations back to the Canadian alliance system, but demographics proved to be the major factor. The war had reduced the number of Iroquois warriors by one-half and by 1695 threatened their survival.[143] Peace negotiations only began at the end of the war in Europe and dragged on for four more years before they were concluded in 1701.[144]

While Canada suffered no serious English assaults after 1691, the war unleashed a bevy of American colonial privateers that found easy pickings in the Gulf of St. Lawrence. Only 3 of 11 merchant ships reached New France in 1690 in the wake of Phips's invasion. As a result, the new minister, Pontchartrain, ordered an escort for the next year's convoy. Even so, early in September of 1692, 200 raiders from two ships landed on the north shore and burnt Louis Jolliet's trading post at Mingan and later destroyed his establishment on Anticosti Island.[145] Declining shipping and rising freight rates also forced the minister to assume greater direction and control of the war in the colonies. Metropolitan merchants squeezed colonists between themselves and the financially embarrassed government. Freight rates rose from 50 to 75 livres per ton in 1691, payable in advance, in response to the government's requisitioning one-quarter to one-third of the cargo space on board ships bound for New France to send munitions, foodstuffs, and stores for

---

[142] Ibid., 190–2.
[143] Jennings, *Ambiguous Iroquois Empire*, 206–7.
[144] See Gilles Havard, *La grande paix de Montréal de 1701: Les voies de diplomatie franco-amérindienne* (Montréal: Recherches amérindiennes au Québec, 1992).
[145] Marine, B⁴ 14, ff. 213v–14, Journal du voyage d'Iberville.

the garrison.[146] By 1694, La Rochelle merchants were getting 80 livres per ton for freighting royal stores.[147] In August the same year, a Jamaican privateer in the Gulf of St. Lawrence captured a large merchantman belonging to a wealthy Montreal fur trader; colonial merchants lost cargoes worth an estimated 300,000 livres.[148] Without naval escorts, French merchants might well have abandoned the colony.

However reluctant the government might be, the navy had to participate in colonial defence. In 1691 and thereafter during each of the next 6 years, well-armed warships annually escorted convoys of merchantmen to New France.[149] Each year the number of men of war increased, and the naval commander's mission became more complex as ministry officials sought to attach seaborne assaults to convoy duties. On 12 July 1691, *Le Hazardeux*, 44 guns, commanded by Sieur du Tast and *L'Envieux, en flûte*, armed with only 20 guns, arrived at Quebec escorting 10 or 12 merchantmen. *Le Soleil d'Afrique*, 30 guns, Simon-Pierre Denys de Bonaventure commanding, had reached the port 12 days earlier.[150] On 3 September, all three warships, with the colony's entire supply of beaver pelts on board the largest, departed to cruise in the Gulf of Saint Lawrence against the growing menace from New England privateers. *Le Soleil d'Afrique* had the additional task of transporting Joseph Robineau de Villebon, brother of the Sieur de Portneuf and a protege of Governor Frontenac, to take up his appointment as commandant of Acadia.[151] The following year two more warships under the command of Pierre Le Moyne d'Iberville in *Le Poli*, 38 guns, and *L'Envieux*, now armed with 34 guns, with Denys de Bonaventure in command, sailed for Canada escorting 6 merchantmen. Once again the men of war sailed downstream to guard the seaward approaches to New France, patrol the waters of the Gulf, and carry supplies to Acadia.[152] In 1693, naval transports *Le Corossol* and *L'Impertinent* also sailed to Quebec in the company of Iberville and Bonaventure in *Le Poli* and *L'Indiscret*, respectively. The latter were to leave for a raid on English trading posts in Hudson Bay, but Governor Frontenac, who was no supporter of Iberville or his ambitions in the Bay, sent him and Bonaventure downstream to cruise in the Gulf and along the coast of Acadia.

[146] Marine, B², 78, ff. 637–8, 980 Pontchartrain to Bégon, 25 April and 16 June 1691; and Col., C¹¹A 11, f. 288 Champigny to Pontchartrain, 12 October 1691.

[147] E.g. Col., F¹A 9, f. 79 pay order, 31 January 1695.

[148] *RAPQ, 1927–28*, 186 Frontenac to Pontchartrain, 25 October 1694.

[149] Marine, B² 77, f. 415 Pontchartrain to Bégon, 21 March 1691; and ibid., 78, f. 666v same to same, 30 April 1691.

[150] Col., C¹¹A 11, ff. 58v–9 Relation … de novembre 1690 jusqu'au départ de 91.

[151] Ibid., f. 284v Champigny to Pontchartrain, 12 October 1691.

[152] Marine, B⁴ 14, ff. 203–30v Journal du voyage de Canada, 14 January 1693. Another account of the voyage is located in [Louis-Armand de Lom d'Arce] baron de La Hontan, *New Voyages to North America*, reprinted from the 1703 English edition, R. G. Thwaites, ed., 2 vols. (Chicago: A. G. McClung, 1905), 1: 274.

Privateers were still active in the lower St. Lawrence, and Governor Frontenac could not ignore the possibility of another seaborne invasion of the colony. Though he did not know it, that year Admiral Wheler was ordered to attack Canada after reaching Boston.

The growing financial crisis in France and the loss of Canadian trading posts in Hudson Bay led to a change in policy in 1693. Iberville and his brother, Joseph Le Moyne de Serigny, in *Le Poli*, 36 guns, and *La Salamandre*, 18 guns, escorted fishing vessels to the Grand Banks, then sailed ahead to Quebec, and with the minister's instructions in hand, they quickly recruited 110 Canadians before departing for Hudson Bay in mid-August. Meanwhile, navy transports *La Charente* and *La Bretonne*, carrying royal stores and munitions, escorted merchantmen to Quebec and Acadia, respectively. The following year, *La Bouffonne*, 26 guns, accompanied *La Charente* to Quebec. In an interesting experiment in colonial defence, the small frigate wintered at Quebec with a core of 30 sailors. The plan was to recruit a new crew the following spring and cruise for a second season in the Gulf of St. Lawrence. Intendant Champigny condemned the proposal, fearing the added costs would not realize any benefits, but he had been overruled by Frontenac.[153]

In June of 1696, Governor Frontenac put another of his proteges, Michel Le Neuf de Beaubassin, sieur de La Vallière, in command and sent him downstream to cruise in the lower St. Lawrence River, in the Gulf, and off the coast of Acadia. *La Bouffonne* was accompanied by a brigantine, *Le Frontenac*, which had been purchased the previous year and fitted out, armed, and manned by the governor and intendant for privateering. The ships once chased two small Rhode Island privateers but failed to catch them.[154] On 3 September, after three months spent cruising in the approaches to Canada, *La Bouffonne* met the merchant fleet from France in the St. Lawrence River and accompanied the ships back up to Quebec, but even before the cruise was finished questions were being raised. Champigny complained that the frigate had been of no value, adding that by mid-August none of the ships reaching Quebec had even sighted her.[155] The cost of keeping the vessel in the colony was prohibitively high, and the ship's presence in the Gulf in late spring could be achieved just as easily from France. Whether the whole affair was merely a ploy by Frontenac to increase his patronage and protect his investment in a local privateer is moot, but the experiment does indicate a degree of flexibility not normally attributed to the naval ministry.

[153]   Col., C^{11}A 15, f. 125 Champigny to Pontchartrain, 13 October 1695.
[154]   Marine, B⁴ 18, ff. 308–16v Journal de navigation de *la Bouffonne*, commandée per Sr. de la Villiere (*sic*) en 1696; also BN, Clairambault, vol., 881, f. 141v Iberville to Pontchartrain, 24 September 1696.
[155]   Col., C^{11}A 14, ff. 185–6v Champigny to Pontchartrain, 18 August 1696.

During the final two years of the war, hostilities against the English shifted to the east coast. Despite three squadrons being fitted out for the West Indies, in 1696, two large naval transports, *La Gironde*, 50 guns, and *La Charente*, 34 guns, carried royal provisions and stores to New France and escorted merchantmen to the colony. As in previous years, they were sent to Baie Saint-Paul following their arrival to load masts for the naval arsenal at Rochefort before departing late in the year.[156] *La Gironde* returned to Quebec during the next year with recruits for the garrison, accompanied by *L'Amphitrite*, 44 guns, transporting silver to pay the troops. As the French well knew, service to the monarch went only so far: as the saying went, "pas d'argent, pas de Suisse".[157]

The Nine Years' War is a misnomer, especially when applied to New France. Canada fought its own war against the Iroquois. The struggle nearly drove the colony to the wall owing to misplaced tactics and competing private interests. The growing European conflict touched it only occasionally and peripherally compared to other French colonies in the Americas. Massachusetts's seaborne assault and New York's attacks were colonial in both origin and resources employed. The regular dispatch of naval escorts to Quebec every year between 1691 and 1697 though was strong evidence that the colony was being drawn into the larger international Atlantic world. With the greater naval presence along New France's east coast, the war in North America contained a larger naval component than is normally acknowledged as a brief examination of local conflicts in Acadia, Newfoundland, and Hudson Bay clearly shows.

7.6 ACADIA, NEWFOUNDLAND, AND HUDSON BAY

An unofficial war between the French and English had been in progress in Acadia for at least two years before European hostilities began. The local conflict involving the Indians known as Abenaki was over sovereignty and influence along 150 miles of coast between the Kennebec and Sainte-Croix Rivers in present-day Maine and the access of New England fishermen to inshore waters off Acadia. Neither issue directly concerned Acadian colonists, whose relations with neighbouring New England were friendly and subordinate. In 1687, Governor Denonville at Quebec ordered Father Jacques Bigot, s.j., to journey to the East Coast to recruit Abenaki for the mission that he had just founded south of Quebec on the Chaudière River. The governor sought to build stronger ties with these natives whose lands were being pressured by New England speculators and settlers. At

---

[156] Ibid., ff. 194v–5, 199v; also Paul W. Bamford, *Forests and French Sea Power, 1660–1789* (Toronto: University of Toronto Press, 1956), 119.

[157] Col., F^{1A} 10, f. 67.

the same time, Abbé Louis-Pierre Thury, a secular priest of the Society of Foreign Missions from the Quebec seminary, was instructed to move from Miramichi and establish a new mission among the Abenaki at Pentagouet (present-day Castine, Maine) near Jean-Vincent d'Abbadie de Saint-Castin.[158] Denonville's aim to forge stronger ties with the Abenaki was intended to strengthen the colony's defences. Enthusiastic reports of Abenaki military virtues from the missionaries helped cement the French alliance against the English.[159] In the summer of 1688, the French government sent a small 16-gun corvette to defend the local fishery. In July, *La Friponne* arrested a New England fishing ketch off Cape Sable, but the vessel's presence was insufficient to halt a predatory New England attack on Chedabouctou in August, which left the Acadian Sedentary Fishing Company's establishment in ruins.[160] Indeed, New Englanders became more aggressive after receiving news of William of Orange's successful Protestant *coup d'état*. A Massachusetts force attacked the Abenaki and baron de Saint-Castin in their homes on the Penobscot River, and the following August, the Abenaki retaliated by attacking the English at Pemaquid.[161] Acadians, who did not live along the disputed coast or fish along Nova Scotia's southeast coast or at Chedabouctou, were largely isolated from the growing conflict, becoming caught in its entanglements only twice, in 1690 and again in 1696.

In the late summer and fall of 1689, the French frigates *L'Union* and *Le Fourgon*, part of Seignelay's reduced scheme to attack and take New York, captured six small New England fishing ketches and a large brigantine while en route from Chedabouctou to Port Royal, but despite the blow to the Massachusetts fishery, French policy continued to focus on exploiting the Abenaki land dispute.[162] French supplies and Canadian troops sent to support the Abenaki alliance were intended to secure New France. While this was a partial acknowledgement that Acadian settlements were indefensible, it chiefly reflected the greater influence and security needs of the St. Lawrence Valley colony.

[158]   See Kenneth M. Morrison, *The Embattled Northeast: The Elusive Ideal of Alliance in Abenaki-European Relations* (Berkeley: University of California Press, 1984), 114, 123–4; also T. Charland, "Bigot, Jacques", *DCB*, 2: 63–4; and R. Baudry, "Thury, Louis–Pierre", *DCB*, 1: 649.

[159]   John G. Reid, "Imperial Intrusions" in *The Atlantic Region to Confederation: A History*, eds., P. A. Buckner and J. G. Reid (Toronto: University of Toronto Press, 1994), 80.

[160]   Richard J. Johnson, *John Nelson, Merchant Adventurer: A Life Between Empires* (New York: Oxford University Press, 1991), 47.

[161]   See G. A. Rawlyk, *Nova Scotia's Massachusetts: A Study of Massachusetts-Nova Scotia Relations, 1630–1784* (Montreal and London: McGill-Queen's University Press, 1973), for a good account of the last years of peace and events leading up to the war.

[162]   Marine, B⁴ 12, ff. 115–18 La Caffinière to Seignelay, 27 December 1689; also Rawlyk, *Nova Scotia's Massachusetts*, 59.

Massachusetts' attack on Port Royal at the end of May in 1690 was in response to the attacks of combined French and Indian war parties sent out from Canada. The officially sanctioned private war begun in Massachusetts by land speculators, fishing interests, and Boston merchants was going nowhere until news of the Canadian attacks on Schenectady and Salmon Falls reached New England and reinvigorated the plan by allowing Puritan divines to portray the proposed attack on Port Royal as a religious crusade, disguising its true nature as an affair of pillage with no strategic or military objective.[163]

Sir William Phips in a frigate of 44 guns and six small sloops and ketches sailed from New England with about 700 men at the end of April. He anchored off Port Royal on 19 May [N.S.] and called on Governor Louis-Alexandre des Friches de Meneval to surrender, which he did. During the next three days the New Englanders broke the terms of the capitulation, plundered and sacked the settlement, including its church, leveled the fort, and removed the guns. Phips departed for Boston on 31 May after first directing two of his officers to plunder the remaining Acadian settlements in the Bay of Fundy and along the southwest coast of Nova Scotia.[164] The destruction of Port Royal served as a great tonic for the suffering New England frontiersmen, but it failed to yield sufficient booty to pay for the expedition. Nor did the English colony's annexation of Acadia in 1692 change anything. The French returned, and little was heard from New England until 1696 when Benjamin Church led a force of Christian Indians from southern Massachusetts and militiamen on a revenge attack against the Acadian settlement of Chignecto. Raised to scalp Abenaki for bounties of 100 pounds per adult male and 50 pounds for each woman and child, it had no strategic purpose. Moreover, no Indians lived at Chignecto. Murder and plunder were its *raison d'etre*.

After Port Royal's fall, French strategy focused more obviously on support for the Indians. Captain Joseph Robineau de Villebon arrived from France barely two weeks after Phips had carried off his prisoners to Boston. Finding the settlement in ruins, the official representative of the Crown immediately transferred himself and his 45 soldiers away from any settlements across the Bay of Fundy to the St. John River where they landed their munitions and stores upriver at Jemseg. Two English privateers entered the river and seized his ship; Villebon fled precipitously, making his way overland to Quebec. He then returned to France in search of aid.[165]

---

[163] Johnson, *John Nelson*, 60–5; also Rawlyk, *Nova Scotia's Massachusetts*, 61.

[164] Ibid., 67–70; Eccles, *Canada under Louis XIV*, 164–5.

[165] See J. C. Webster, ed. and trans., *Acadia at the End of the Seventeenth Century: Letters, Journals, and Memoirs of Joseph Robineau de Villebon, Commandant in Acadia, 1690–1700, and other Contemporary Documents* (Saint John: The New Brunswick Museum, 1934), 22–29 for more details.

Appointed commandant of Acadia on 1 April 1691, his instructions clearly spelled out French policy.[166] Stating that conditions in Europe did not permit reestablishing Port Royal, the king sent Villebon back to the Saint John River in *Le Soleil d'Afrique* with presents, munitions, and trade goods for the Abenaki. Villebon touched at Port Royal, but later during the summer he established a new fort about 90 miles upstream on the St. John River at the mouth of the Nashwaak River (opposite present-day Fredericton, N.B.). From Canada, two officers, Lieutenant Claude-Sébastien de Villieu and Ensign Jacques Testard de Montigny, were sent to command the garrison at the new fort called Naxouat. Early in October, the French captured the Boston merchant, John Nelson, and the newly appointed English military commander of Port Royal, Colonel Edward Tyng, at the mouth of the St. John River and sent them to Quebec.[167]

During the next three or four years Commandant de Villebon devoted himself to fur trading, going so far as to appropriate supplies for his own use and failing to furnish aid to regular troops and war parties from Naxouat.[168] If Villebon's reputation among Acadians that he was a thug who terrorised the countryside with the aid of family members in pursuit of his own interests, was accurate, it reinforced the Indian-centeredness of French policy.[169] Despite Villebon's conduct, Lieutenant de Villieu and his officers, strongly supported by Abbé Thury and baron de Saint-Castin on the Penobscot, carried *la petite guerre* to the frontier settlements of New England. In February of 1692, led by Madokawando, 150 warriors struck York in a bloody raid, killing 48 colonists and taking 92 more captive. Local privateering also revived. Pierre Maisonnat, known as Captain Baptiste, operated successfully against New England fishing and coastal craft. He fitted out two small ships in the St. John River in May, and the following month, captured a 45-ton brigantine within sight of Boston, bringing his total take during the first six months of the year to nine prizes. Late the next year, he sailed to France, where he obtained the loan of a small corvette, *La Bonne*, which he commanded off New England in 1694, taking five prizes. He apparently wintered in the Bay of Fundy, for in May of 1695 he lost his ship to two English vessels at Migascor (present-day Musquash, N.B.).[170]

Le Moyne d'Iberville's ships had reinforced the Abenaki in November of 1692, but the land war was going poorly.[171] The combination of Villebon's trading, including his inability to supply sufficient trade goods to meet Abenaki demand, Iberville's failure to carry out an assault from the sea in

---

[166] Col., B 16, ff. 46–7v Mémoire pour servir d'instructions au Sr. de Villebon, Comdt. en Acadie, 7 April 1691.

[167] Johnson, *John Nelson*, 69.

[168] Eccles, *Canada under Louis XIV*, 194–5.

[169] [In collaboration], "Robineau de Villebon", *DCB*, 1: 577.

[170] W. A. Squires, "Maisonnat, Pierre", *DCB*, 2: 449–50.

[171] Marine, B⁴ 14, f. 220v Journal du voyage d'Iberville.

conjunction with the Abenaki, and renewed Massachusetts diplomacy weakened French influence among the natives, who agreed to make peace with Massachusetts in August of 1693. Governor Frontenac's instructions to all concerned were to break up the negotiated peace as quickly as possible. The next year, Father Vincent Bigot, s.j., brother of the missionary at the St. Francis mission, journeyed to Pentagouet to establish a new mission there.[172] Abbé Thury's renewed efforts to bring the Abenaki back into the French camp were rewarded on 18 July 1694, when Villieu and his *troupes de la marine* accompanied the Abenaki on the bloodiest raid of the war. A large war party struck Oyster River (present-day Durham, New Hampshire), killing about 100 people and taking 60 captives.[173] Just as the French appeared to regain the upper hand, an epidemic swept through the Indian tribes, which together with the loss of Captain Baptiste's privateer, reduced French effectiveness on both land and sea. Though Denys de Bonaventure spent the entire season cruising off the east coast of New France, in the Gulf of Saint Lawrence, and along the south coast of Newfoundland in *L'Envieux*, 40 guns, his lack of a precise objective also contributed to French ineffectiveness.[174] Commandant de Villebon, ever in pursuit of his own commercial interests, proposed licensing enemy fishermen. Local privateers refused to attack fishing vessels with their smelly cargoes that quickly spoiled for want of a market, and by allowing fishermen access to Acadian waters, the number of New Englanders available for militia service against the Indians would be reduced.[175] However, the solution to the French position in Acadia was taken out of Villebon's, and for that matter Governor Frontenac's, hands; the final attack in the area came from France. In such ways local conflicts were slowly integrated into the larger one.

The question of Abenaki loyalty to the French cause remained foremost among Pontchartrain's concerns for New France and Acadia, and in 1696, he accepted Villebon's recommendation that the capture and destruction of Fort William Henry at Pemaquid at the mouth of the Penobscot River would ensure their security.[176] The Abenaki had long advocated such a move, and the French understood the need to support native objectives to gain their own. The 1696 campaign against New England was a complete success. In August, Le Moyne d'Iberville, commanding *L'Envieux* mounting her full complement of 50 guns, and *La Profonde*, 20 guns, commanded by Captain Denys de Bonaventure, sailed for Jemseg on the St. John River where he relieved Villebon, who was being blockaded by the English.[177] He captured

172   Charland, "Bigot, Vincent", *DCB*, 2: 64–5.
173   Rawlyk, *Nova Scotia's Massachusetts*, 78.
174   On the ship's movements see Marine, B⁴ 16, ff. 371–88 Journal de Denys de Bonaventure.
175   Rawlyk, *Nova Scotia's Massachusetts,* 79–80.
176   Morrison, *The Embattled Northeast*, 138–9.
177   BN, Claiambault, 881, ff. 135–43v Iberville to Pontchartrain, 24 September 1696 covers the events of the Acadia campaign from 27 June to his arrival at Placentia on 12 September.

a colonial frigate, the *Newport*, 24 guns, refitted his prize, put a crew commanded by Captain Baptiste on board, and sailed to Pentagouet, where he and his Mi'kmaq allies were joined by 240 Abenaki led by Saint-Castin and Sieurs de Villieu and de Montigny with troops from Fort Naxouat. Upon their arrival off Fort William Henry, the English garrison quickly surrendered, and the fort was razed. After the besiegers removed the guns, its munitions and stores were distributed to the Indians.

French prestige rose immeasurably among the Abenaki, who renewed their attacks on English settlements to within 25 miles of Boston. New England frontier settlements were virtually deserted. The destruction of the base on the Penobscot River also deprived local privateers of a safe refuge. More important than these concerns though, William Henry's destruction ensured French dominance over this vast contested area and gave strong support for advancing traditional claims that the border between Acadia and New England was as far west as the St. George River.[178] A month after Iberville's attack on Pemaquid, the English attacked the Acadian settlement of Chignecto. While en route home the raiders met and joined another New England war party intending to capture Fort Naxouat, but after a 36-hour siege the New England forces withdrew. This last gasp of New England aggression had proved futile.

Far from seeing the capture of Port Royal in 1690 as one more conquest of Acadia, it may be argued that during the Nine Years' War fewer than 1,000 Indians and a handful of Frenchmen strongly supported from seaward defeated Massachusetts. Entering the war on a wave of self-confident aggression, the commonwealth ended it with its economy in disarray, with hundreds killed or taken captive, frontier settlements pushed back, and pleading with King William for support from the metropolis.[179] Indeed, Joseph de Villebon, who had just finished resisting a New England attempt to take Fort Naxouat, was so confident that he offered the comte de Pontchartrain a plan to capture Boston. Dated 24 September 1696, it called for a squadron of six warships from France and a force of 600 men from Canada to join 400 Indians from Acadia at the mouth of the Kennebec River at the end of May or early June the next year and Boston, he vowed, would fall. The booty, he claimed, would pay the entire cost of the expedition.[180] While a combination of naval power and Indian allies had assured French success, the French government never grasped this important point, even after Iberville demonstrated its effectiveness once again in Newfoundland.

The French position in Newfoundland was extremely precarious when war broke out. Less than two weeks after England's declaration of war on

[178]   Eccles, *Canada under Louis XIV*, 194–5.
[179]   Rawlyk, *Nova Scotia's Massachusetts*, 84.
[180]   BN, Clairambault, 890, ff. 308–9 [Anonymous], but see ibid., ff. 353–5 Villebon to Pontchartrain, 24 September 1696.

France, the king appointed a new governor, Jacques-François de Monbeton de Brouillon and recalled the incumbent, Antoine Parat, but Newfoundland was far down on the list of navy and colonial priorities.[181] Seignelay assigned a warship to protect the fishery in August of 1689, but it is not clear if the vessel ever sailed.[182] The new governor's departure from France was delayed for nearly two years. He only arrived with a small contingent of soldiers and fishing apprentices in June of 1691.[183] In the meantime, Governor Parat had abandoned his post the previous September after having been tortured by members of a large party of English freebooters from Ferryland who pillaged Placentia in the late winter and early spring and following an outbreak of sedition and quarrels between the inhabitants and the commander of the military detachment.[184]

Defence of the French inshore fishery except at sea was all but impossible in the absence of a large body of resident fishermen and because of the migratory nature of the cod fish. In addition to the delayed departure of the new governor, the French deferred the dispatch of any warships. The first naval squadron to sail to Newfoundland reached Placentia only in 1692. In August, a strong squadron composed of *L'Aimable*, 70 guns, *Le Téméraire*, 52 guns, *Le Bon*, 52 guns, and three fireships under the command of Captain chevalier de Digoine departed from Brest. If he found no enemies in the St. Lawrence River, Digoine was to proceed to Placentia and put himself under Governor de Brouillon's command in order to "ruyner les habitations angloises de Terre-Neuve".[185] However, a departure so late in the season meant a long struggle against strong westerly winds, and the squadron reached St. Mary's Bay only on 19 September. Digoine immediately set a course for the Gulf. Three days later, the ships arrived at Cape Breton Island, where they landed more than sixty men suffering from scurvy. On 14 October, they sailed to meet *Le Poli* and *L'Envieux*, whose captains reported no enemy in the river or the gulf. While Iberville and Bonaventure sailed for Pentagouet and Mount Desert Island to attack English shipping, Digoine led his ships to Placentia, anchoring there on the 18th.[186] A hurricane struck the squadron the next day. *Le Bon's* anchor broke, and the ship drove ashore. Miraculously, only a few men drowned. Two fireships forced into Little Placentia broke their cables and went ashore in Ship Harbour and Long Harbour, four

---

[181]   See James Pritchard, "'Le Profit et La Gloire': The French Navy's Alliance with Private Enterprise in the Defence of Newfoundland, 1691–1697", *Newfoundland Studies*, 15, 2 (Fall 1999): 161–76 for more extended treatment.

[182]   Marine, B⁴ 12, f. 15 Plan de campagne de 1689.

[183]   R. Baudry, "Mombeton de Brouillon," *DCB*, 2: 478.

[184]   La Morandière, *Histoire de la pêche français de la morue*, 1: 441, 443–4.

[185]   Col., B 16, ff. 121v–3 Instructions pour M. d'Amblimont, 23 July 1692; also La Morandière, *Histoire de la pêche français*, 1: 453.

[186]   Marine, B⁴ 14, ff. 187–94 Abrège du journal de navigation de l'escadre du chevalier de Digoine ...", 1692.

to six leagues northeast of the port. Le Téméraire rode out the storm and got into Placentia with the two remaining ships three days later. There, they remained before departing on 20 November, having accomplished nothing of note. On their arrival in France, L'Aimable had 42 dead and 140 men unable to rise, and Le Téméraire had as many dead and half the remaining crew unfit to serve.[187] The costly expedition had been a complete write-off.

The chief lesson from these experiences was that the best defence of Placentia and similar French colonies was achieved by reinforcing local for-tifications and launching local attacks against the enemy. Expensive, sickly naval squadrons seemed least effective of all. In the first place, the enemy had come and gone before Digoine's ships arrived. In mid-September Com-modore Williams's squadron of five warships had anchored before Placentia and begun a sharp cannonade. After pillaging fishing shacks at Pointe Verte and on Saint-Pierre Island, however, the English suddenly sailed away.[188] Baron Lahontan later claimed credit for repulsing the English attack, but Governor de Brouillon gave chief credit to a young, recently arrived cap-tain, Philippe de Pastour de Costebelle, who was beginning a quarter of a century of service on New France's eastern coast.[189] Costebelle's arrival at Placentia earlier that year emphasized the fragility and unreliability of naval defence. Le Joli, carrying him and 25 recruits, was wrecked 20 leagues from Placentia and the survivors took shelter on an island until Governor de Brouillon sent a shallop to take them off.[190] Secondly, a small French war party led by Captain de Costebelle had succeeded in driving the English from Trinity Bay early in September.

Placentia faced its greatest challenge in 1693. The outcome may have reinforced a growing propensity to encourage local garrisons and support aggressive military action rather than rely on warships for defence. On 28 August, Admiral Wheler, on his way home from the West Indies via Boston after failing to capture Martinique or to attack Canada as instructed and seeking something to offer his political masters, anchored his squadron of 24 sail before Placentia. Although his nine warships appeared formidable, yellow fever and scurvy had seriously reduced their manpower. Only 700 to 800 men, including seamen, were available as a landing force. Moreover, Brouillon had successfully stretched a chain across the mouth of the harbour and placed a small but effective three-gun battery on the hill overlooking it, where he had also built a redoubt. For two days both sides exchanged cannon fire, but on 3 September the English suddenly departed after sacking

[187] Ibid., ff. 191–4.
[188] La Morandière, Histoire de la pêche française, 1: 450–2.
[189] Lahontan, New Voyages to North America, 1: 275–9; also Col., C[11C] 1, ff. 209–10v Brouillion to Pontchartrain, 1 October 1692.
[190] G. C. Salagnac, "Pastour de Costebelle, Philippe", DCB, 2: 510.

Saint-Pierre Island and burning 200 to 300 fishing boats and all the houses and fish.[191]

A French seaborne raid on Ferryland the following year contributed nothing to the defence of Placentia. Its only significance lies in it being an early example of *la course royale* in America. The French squadron owed its origins to the remarkably destructive, profitable attack on the Dutch whaling fleet at Spitz Bergen in 1693, which was chiefly sponsored by the duc de Gramont, governor of Bayonne. A former buccaneer, Jacques Gouin de Beauchesne, who was associated with other privateers at Bayonne and St. Jean de Luz, proposed the plan to de Gramont, who convinced Louis XIV and Pontchartrain to grant them *Le Pelican*, 50 guns, and two new Bayonne-built 36-gun frigates, *L'Aigle* and *Le Favori*, to be joined to three strong, privately owned privateers. The raiders destroyed about one-third of the Dutch whaling fleet in early August of 1693, and de Gramont, who prided himself as the "director" of the Basque "corsariat", had no difficulty obtaining several of the same warships, all to be fitted out at Bayonne to attack the English codfish trade at Newfoundland.[192]

The squadron, composed of *Le Gaillard*, 54 guns, *Le Pelican*, 50 guns, *L'Aigle*, 36 guns, and a Malouin privateer, a fireship, and a smaller ship rigged as a bomb ketch, was under the command of Captain Pierre de Saint-Clair, who invested 1,000 *écus* in the venture.[193] Most of the other captains also invested in the expedition, but despite great expectations it met with no success. After crossing the Atlantic, the ships attacked a well-fortified Ferryland (*Forillon*) on 10 September. There *L'Aigle* ran aground at the entrance to the harbour, and part of the crew mutinied and fled in the ship's boats to Placentia.[194] After refloating the frigate, Captain Saint-Clair set a course for St. John's, but like Admiral Wheler the previous year at Placentia, he found a chain or cables stretched across the harbour entrance. He declined

---

[191] Lahontan, *New Voyages to North America*, 1: 275. Two first-hand accounts by the expedition's commissary and engineer, respectively, are in Merriman, ed., *The Sergison Papers*, 296–8; and University of Minnesota, James Ford Bell Library, No. L 398, "A Journal ..." by Captain Christian Lilly.

[192] Philipe Henrat, "Une victoire française au Spitzberg, le combat de la baie aux Ours, (6 août, 1693)", *Cols bleus*, no. 1623, (26 juillet 1980). John Bromley, *Corsairs and Navies*, 189; also, Col., C⁸ᴬ 7, ff. 503–7. This memoir by Commissaire de la marine Louis-Hyacinthe Plomier de La Boulaye, 7 December 1693, which proposed joining these ships to attack the codfish trade at Newfoundland rather than in the Irish Sea is mistakenly bound in the general correspondence of Martinique.

[193] La Morandière, *Histoire de la pêche française*, 1: 454–5 incorrectly identifies Saint-Clair as a privateering captain from Saint-Malo. See E. Taillemite, "Saint-Clair, Pierre de", *DCB*, 2: 590–1.

[194] Marine, B⁴ 15, ff. 374–82 Information fait contre Sieurs Detcheverry et Daspiouette, 15 September 1694; *CSP, CS*, 1696–1697, no. 417 gives the date of the attack as 1 August [o.s.] 1694, but this is clearly an error for 31 August [o.s.], i.e. 10 September [N.S.].

to attempt an attack from seaward and sailed to Placentia.[195] Saint-Clair sailed for France on 13 October, escorting 34 fishing vessels and merchantmen. The expedition's obvious failure infuriated Governor Brouillon.

In the wake of the major social and economic crisis that had stricken France during 1693 and 1694, Pontchartrain could do little more to support Placentia than continue to contract with private merchants to supply the settlement in return for granting them a monopoly on its trade. As in the West Indies, *la course royale* provided opportunities only to mount destructive raids on English property. In 1696, Noël Danican, sieur de l'Espine, Saint-Malo's leading merchant-privateer, contracted to conquer all of the English settlements in Newfoundland. Danican de l'Espine, who sent ships to the Gulf of Mexico in 1693 and fitted out two ships for the Spitz Bergen raid, may have been involved in Saint-Clair's 1694 attempt.[196] In 1696, he agreed to supply six frigates including one of 50 guns to which the king added *Le Pelican*, 50 guns.[197] The land army was to be partially recruited in New France and commanded by Le Moyne d'Iberville.

The six privateering ships reached Placentia in July. Governor Brouillon immediately set off with over 400 soldiers and sailors commanded by his town major and engineer, Jacques L'Hermite, and his nephew, Lieutenant Joseph de Monbeton de Brouillon *dit* Saint-Ovide. The force struck Bay Bulls, but was back in Placentia in late October having failed, like its predecessor, to attack St. John's from the sea. The attack on the Avalon peninsula had been as disappointing as Saint-Clair's raid two years before. What followed only reinforced the idea of the ineffectiveness of sea power if unsupported by land.

During the next five months, Iberville and his Canadians laid waste to almost all the English settlements in Newfoundland. Between the time of Iberville's arrival in *Le Profond* and *L'Envieux* and Brouillon's return with the squadron of Malouin privateers, Jean Leger de la Grange, commanding *Le Wesp*, 32 guns, arrived with *Le Postillon* from Quebec. He transported a war party of 30 Canadians, 50 regular troops, and 3 officers, and provisions and munitions for the forthcoming expedition. During the summer, Denys de Bonaventure had easily recruited men anxious to fight under Iberville's leadership.[198] After Iberville arrived, fresh from his success at Pemaquid,

---

[195] Ibid., 379–81v several documents including a chart of St. John's and its defences. For the attack on St. John's see Olaf Uwe Janzen, "New Light on the Origins of Fort William at St. John's, Newfoundland, 1693–1696", *Newfoundland Quarterly*, 83, no. 2 (Fall, 1987): 24–31.

[196] On Danican see Rothkrug, *Opposition to Louis XIV*, 405 n72, 406 n76, and 407; Symcox, *The Crisis of French Sea Power*, 211–12.

[197] AN, G5 [NAC transcripts], Carton 5 ², pp. 13–19 Articles et conditions accordés par le roi à Noel de Lespine-Danican pour l'entreprise de Plaisance, 20 February 1696; also La Roncière, *Histoire de la marine française*, 6: 271.

[198] Col., C11A 14, ff. 125v, 195, 243v, 250–3.

Placentia became a base from which to conduct a number of raids against the English during the winter. St. John's was burnt before Christmas; by 1 May 1697, the French had destroyed all but two settlements on the eastern coast of Newfoundland.[199] English losses amounted to 200 killed, 700 prisoners, and 200,000 quintals of cod.[200] Like the Anglo-Spanish attacks on Saint-Domingue's north coast in 1695 though, Iberville's winter campaign had little lasting effect beyond inspiring the English to begin seriously fortifying St. John's. Despite the failure of Danican's venture to Newfoundland, Pontchartrain turned to another successful privateer-entrpreneur, Jean-Baptiste Levesque, sieur de Beaubriand, from Saint-Malo to provision Placentia in 1697. A former sea captain and member of a family of ship owners and outfitters that had recently moved from Granville to Saint-Malo, Pontchartrain loaned him *Le François*, 48 guns, for the Placentia venture.[201]

The French successes in Acadia and Newfoundland in 1696, reinforced by the losses and angry protests of English West Country fish merchants, led the English to fit out a large naval squadron and send it to recapture St. John's early in the spring. Preparations began in January, departure occurred in mid-April, and the first English warships arrived at the southern extremity of Conception Bay on 7 June [N.S.]. Ten days later, Commodore Sir John Norris entered St. John's harbour with 10 men of war and three smaller warships and 1,500 troops. They found not a house standing and immediately began to rebuild the port's defences.[202]

In France, the minister of marine learned of a rumored attack on Canada and that the English had recaptured their posts in Hudson Bay. Commerce raiding had failed to provide a defence for the colonies, and independent of the Levesque-Beaubriand contract, Pontchartrain decided to assemble a large naval force and to give its commander several tasks. The expedition was intended to conserve French Placentia, protect Iberville's recent conquests in Newfoundland, and secure the mouth of the St. Lawrence River. Finally, reviving the marquis de Denonville's prewar proposal to conquer

---

199 Alan F. Williams, *Father Baudouin's War: D'Iberville's Campaigns in Acadia and New Foundland 1696, 1697*, ed., Alan G. Macpherson (St. John's: Memorial University of Newfoundland, 1987) is the most recent account of the war. It is chiefly interesting for a unique interpretation of the route that Iberville followed to capture St. John's. The discussion of the larger aspects of the war is based on very old, unreliable secondary sources, and aside from publishing the original French text of Abbé Baudouin's journal (pp. 173–91), is of little interest.

200 Frégault, *Iberville, le conquérant*, 230.

201 Col., B 19, f. 129 Pontchartrain to Bégon, 26 January 1697; ibid., f. 134 same to Sr. de Bonnaire, 30 January 1697; and ibid., f. 136 same to Beaubriand, 6 February 1697. Also Bromley, *Corsairs and Navies*, 201, 304–5.

202 See John J. Murray, "Anglo-French Naval Skirmishing off Newfoundland, 1697" in *Essays in Modern European History*, ed., J. J. Murray (Bloomington: Indiana University Press, 1951), 74–5; *CSP, CS, 1696–7*, 15, 320, 377, 433–5, 440, 452, 522; also Graham, *Empire of the North Atlantic*, 77–8; and Janzen, "New Light", 27.

New York and ruin New England, 1,500 Canadians were to be assembled to attack the former.[203] Pontchartrain advised Governor Frontenac of the rumored English invasion and ordered him to be ready to prepare the troops for transport to New York.[204] Thirteen warships and four fireships, the largest force yet destined for the Americas, were assembled under the command of André, marquis de Nesmond. The minister also assembled a second, smaller force consisting of *Le Pelican* and four smaller ships under contract to Iberville and his backers commanded by his brother, Le Moyne de Serigny, at Rochefort. He ordered Serigny to sail to Placentia with instructions for Iberville to take command and sail into Hudson Bay to retake the fur trading posts recently lost to the English.[205]

Lieutenant général des armées navales the marquis de Nesmond (1641–1702) was a logical choice to command the large expeditionary force fitting out at Brest and Rochefort. He had a quarter of a century of naval service. He had commanded ships in both the North Sea and the West Indies during the Dutch War and transported troops to Ireland early in the present war. He also commanded ships at Bévéziers, Barfleur, and Lagos, and in 1695 he commanded *L'Excellent*, 56 guns, and four Malouin privateers on the richest single commercial raid of the war.[206] He also captured HMS *Hope*, 70 guns, the largest naval prize to fall into French hands during the war. Later, these royal privateers took two East Indiamen after sinking their escort. The booty was enormous, selling for 3,150,000 livres, excluding the diamonds and other precious stones found on board.[207] In 1696, Nesmond fitted out ships to cruise in the English Channel, where they seized all eight ships of the Ostende fleet sailing to Cadiz, which yielded him yet another rich prize.[208]

Despite his previous experiences and good fortune, Nesmond's cruise to Newfoundland and North America was a complete failure. He got away from France only at an unconscionably late date and spent a month at Placentia before sailing to St. John's, where he arrived on 28 August. He never encountered baron de Pointis, who had set his course from St. John's to France three weeks earlier. Though Nesmond's force of ten warships mounting 50 to 70 guns was the most formidable by far to reach Newfoundland

---

[203]   Marine, B⁴ 18, ff. 237–41v Projet d'instructions à Mr. le Marquis de Nesmond, 1 April 1697.
[204]   *RAPQ*, 1928–29, 327 Louis XIV to Frontenac, 21 April 1697.
[205]   Col., B 19, f. 191v, 197 Instructions pour le Sr. de Sérigny, 9 March 1697; and Pontchartrain to Sérigny, 19 March 1697.
[206]   E. E. Albert de Rochas l'Aiglun, *Vauban, sa famille, et ses écrits, ses oisivrtés et sa correspondances, analyse et extraits*, 2 vols., reprinted (Genève: Slatkine, [1910] 1972), 1: 438 Vauban to Pontchartrain, 18 September 1695 acknowledged investing 1,000 *écus*.
[207]   Vergé-Franceschi, "Dictionnaire des personages et des battailles", 376–7.
[208]   Symcox, *Crisis in French Sea Power*, 209–11; also ibid., 245–8 for the full text of Nesmond's contract with the government, dated 13 June 1695.

during the war, it was powerless before Commodore Norris's refusal to come out of St. John's and his excellent defensive arrangements. Nesmond sent a 50-gun third rate and a bomb ketch to test the defences, but after a brief exchange of gun fire they hauled off and the following day, 3 September, after a council of war, Nesmond withdrew his entire fleet.[209] His long crossing and arrival so late in the season allowed no time to carry out the remainder of his instructions.

Peace negotiations may have influenced his conduct, though one cannot help but wonder whether commerce raiding had undermined discipline and the military dimensions of naval warfare. The French navy's overwhelming presence in American waters in 1697 in the shape of three squadrons commanded by the baron de Pointis, the marquis de Nesmond, and Pierre Le Moyne d'Iberville suggests that neither coordination between the forces nor a strategic objective existed. Moreover, after failing to provide an adequate naval defence of Placentia at the beginning of the war, the French chose to fortify the port, contracted with private merchants to supply it, and used it as a base from which to launch overland attacks against the English settlements to the east. While this tactic appeared to deliver Newfoundland into French hands, in the long run it may have guaranteed its loss.

The French situation in Hudson Bay was not much different. The wartime campaigns are interesting chiefly because they illustrate even better than events in Newfoundland the intersection between private and state interests: how commercial competition and conflict in the colonies forced themselves on nation-states despite the best efforts of statesmen to ignore them. In the summer of 1688, well before any declaration of war in Europe, the marquis de Seignelay loaned Iberville a small navy frigate, *Le Soleil d'Afrique*, to enable colonial fur traders to pursue their private interests against English rivals in Hudson Bay. After sailing to Quebec, where the colonial *Compagnie du nord* fitted out and armed two small merchantmen to accompany him, Iberville departed for James Bay at the bottom of Hudson Bay. During the winter he left the English in peace, but in the spring he accepted the surrender of the starving Englishmen at Fort Albany and captured two ships sent from York Fort to James Bay before returning triumphant to Quebec at the end of 1689. The Nine Years' War began with the French in possession of the fur trading posts in James Bay.

The next year, Iberville returned to Canada with three ships to capture the one remaining English post, York Fort at the mouth of the Nelson River where it empties into the southwest corner of Hudson Bay. On his arrival in August he found three English ships already there and one drove him out of the river. After destroying a smaller Hudson's Bay Company post at

---

[209]   Marine, B⁴ 18, ff. 270–1 "Relation de la campagne ..." signed by all the officers and Nesmond contains a narrative of events from 16 August to 2 September 1697; La Roncière, *Histoire de la marine française*, 6: 292.

Severn River and seizing its furs, he departed for France.[210] Though Iberville commanded navy vessels during the next three years, he never succeeded in getting back into Hudson Bay. In the interim, the English Hudson's Bay Company sent four ships into the Bay, recaptured the post from the French, reinforced York Fort, and shipped furs to England, leaving the abandoned French and Canadian fur traders to make their way overland to Canada. In 1693, the English seized Fort Sainte-Anne at the Severn River, thereby regaining control of the entire Hudson Bay.

Private, commercial war had taken on a harder edge. Though the English company was unable or unwilling to fortify and garrison its posts adequately, it had secured acceptance of its case as a matter of state and a royal commission for its governor at York Fort.[211] Like the French, the English company also received support from the nation's navy, but it remained vulnerable to the new French policy of *la course royale*. In 1694, Iberville received an independent command and a mission to sail to Hudson Bay to retake the posts seized by the English. This was to be done at minimal cost to the government. In return for a three-year monopoly on the northern fur trade, Iberville and his backers received *Le Poli*, 36 guns, and *La Salamandre*, 18 guns, from the navy in return for agreeing to fit them out at their own expense.[212] Iberville's new associates were La Rochelle merchants because neither capital nor credit was available in sufficient quantities in the colony.[213]

Control of Hudson Bay centered on York Fort at the outlets of the Hayes and Nelson Rivers. These drained the best beaver region in the northern part of the continent, and as long as the French held this post they controlled a strategic point from which they could keep pressure on the posts in James Bay and ultimately drive the English from them.[214] In October of 1694, Iberville captured York Fort. Following news of his success, the Hudson's Bay Company obtained the loan of two ships from the English navy, and in 1696 reentered the Bay and recaptured York Fort. The English reached the mouth of the river only two hours before the French ships, which were then forced to depart. The French garrison surrendered. By then, both French and English private merchants had become surrogates of their respective states. Neither side could allow its surrogate to lose the contest. Peace negotiations were under way during the second half of 1696, but both sides intended to stake national claims even though, in the French case, the market for beaver was glutted. While Pontchartrain ordered closure of western fur trading posts, he

210   E. E. Rich, *The Fur Trade and the Northwest to 1857* (Toronto: McClelland and Stewart, 1967), 62.

211   Ibid., 56–7.

212   Marine, B⁴ 15, ff. 385–7 Articles et conditions que le Roy a accordé au Sr d'Iberville, ... pour l'entreprise de la baye d'Hudson, 17 March 1694.

213   Frégault, *Iberville, le conquérant*, 180 n. 11.

214   Rich, *The Fur Trade and the Northwest*, 80.

loaned five ships to Iberville and his merchant associates for the reconquest of York Fort. In England the navy loaned HMS *Hampshire*, a large 52-gun fourth rate, to reinforce the Company's two armed merchantmen.

On 25 August, while the marquis de Nesmond was still off St. John's and the baron de Pointis was nearing France, French and English forces met at the entrance to Hudson Bay. Ice brought both squadrons to a standstill before they were within range of each other. The next day the English ships got free first and attacked *La Profonde* and, leaving it for lost, made for Port Nelson. After breaking free of the ice, *La Profonde*, accompanied by *Le Wesp* and *La Violente,* made for the Churchill River to avoid the English and to make necessary repairs. Iberville, in *Le Pelican*, assumed they had gone after the enemy and when his ship got free made for York Fort. Arriving there, he discovered that he was alone. On 5 September, sighting three sails, Iberville weighed anchor to meet them. Believing them to be French, he discovered they were English. What followed was the only naval engagement ever fought in Hudson Bay. It lasted two hours until, passing each other on opposite tacks, *Le Pelican* fired her broadside and the *Hampshire* immediately sank, probably after striking a shoal, which ripped her bottom out. One of the remaining English ships surrendered, and the other fled leaving the French in possession once again of York Fort. Iberville received the post's surrender on 13 September one week before the signing of the Treaty of Ryswick, but the treaty mattered not a wit in Hudson Bay. The terms called for the restoration of the *status quo ante*, in other words, for the French to hold the posts in James Bay and the English to occupy York Fort, but the opposite situation prevailed. For the next 16 years the French held the post at Port Nelson, calling it Fort Bourbon. However, the example of merchant enterprises as surrogates of the state illustrates in yet another way how, during the Nine Years' War, the European struggle gradually integrated separate colonial conflicts, transforming them into a single rivalry of imperial dimensions.

7.7 CONCLUSION

Historians have long viewed the Nine Years' War as the first stage of imperial conflict between France and England for the domination of the Americas, but insofar as this view prevails it remains limited. It does not account for the independent roles of Amerindian nations in the conflicts in North America, and it is too Anglocentric when applied to the West Indies. There, France struggled against three European powers rather than one. Moreover, French ambition focused increasingly on penetration of Spanish America rather than conquest of English islands. It is significant that all French attacks on English West Indian possessions originated in the colonies, though they sometimes received support from France, while attacks on Spanish possessions originated largely with the metropolitan government. In North America, the conflicts remained primarily colonial. The major enemy of New France was the Iroquois rather than the English and the major enemy of Massachusetts was the Abenaki rather than the French. It would appear that English antipopery blinded New Englanders to the reality of their situation. The Indians were not simply pawns in an imperial struggle, and the degree to which that is acknowledged is recognition of the nonimperial nature of the Nine Years' War in the Americas. The French sought to harness Abenaki grievances and energies to their own cause, but as the hiatus during 1693 and 1694 indicates, they were not entirely successful. During the Nine Years' War, the conflicts in both North America and the West Indies also became increasingly entangled in the greater struggle between the European powers. The war in the Americas illustrates how well the integrative function of war transformed local conflicts into parts of a much larger, fiercer conflict.

The war also clearly revealed the grudging reluctance of the French minister of marine to defend the colonies. Whether expressed by Seignelay in 1689 or Pontchartrain in 1696, the ministers and the king believed strongly that colonies should defend as well as pay for themselves. The war showed, too, especially in the case of Canada, that the scarce numbers and low proportion of adults among youthful colonial populations placed a major burden on the colonists not only to feed but defend themselves at the same time. In the case of Saint-Domingue, the burden proved too great. In 1695, the colonists of the northern district refused to defend the settlements. Placentia could only be maintained by turning the inhabitants over to metropolitan merchants, who agreed to supply them in return for a monopoly on their trade. Demographic and economic weaknesses like these forced the French government to come to the aid of the colonies. French overseas defence was chiefly a matter of necessity. In Hudson Bay, however, the affairs of merchants became matters of state, as surrogates could not be permitted to lose the contest, but this only contributed to the ambiguity and general incoherence of an elusive empire.

Royal privateering, *la course royale*, was not an effective means to support French colonies. It deeply undermined the entire, if unacknowledged, question of overseas naval defence. It ran directly counter to the commercial need for convoys and escorts for merchant shipping, which carried the life blood of the colonies. Naval forces were instructed to escort merchant shipping to the colonies, but under royal privateering such tasks remained secondary to earning returns for investors. The privately outfitted warships that left France for the Americas from 1694 onward, whether for Newfoundland, Hudson Bay, or the Spanish Main, had serious consequences for the future of France in the Americas and for the French navy itself. The plundering of Cartagena is best known, but the process had been in effect since Saint-Clair had sailed to Newfoundland three years earlier. Considering the totality of privateering operations in the Americas involving the king's warships, little or no coordinated effort existed. Their miscellaneous character, confused objectives, and wide dispersal left naval operations during the war unusually incoherent. Moreover, privateering encouraged conduct prejudicial to good order and naval discipline. In a society of hard-to-discipline nobles, privateering seems about the worst activity they could engage in. At the same time, warships fitted out by the ministry do not appear to have accomplished anything more. The exception may be the escorts that sailed annually to the Windward Islands, New France, and Acadia without incident between 1691 and 1697. The squadrons sent to the West Indies early in the war failed to exploit naval superiority when they had it, and those dispatched to Newfoundland in 1692 and 1697 proved to be costly failures. One sent to the West Indies in 1696 may have paid for itself, but was not a success. The Nine Years' War in America contributed significantly to the creation of the early French empire and policy, yet, paradoxically, events undermined the establishment of a system of naval defence that was necessary for its survival.

8

The War of the Spanish Succession in America, 1702–1713

8.1 INTRODUCTION

Louis XIV's acceptance of the succession to the Spanish throne on behalf of his grandson, Philippe d'Anjou, late in 1700 might have received assent from other European states but for three subsequent actions. They were the king's sudden occupation of the southern Netherlands on his grandson's behalf; his securing privileged access to Spanish America for French merchants by acquiring the *asiento* or royal monopoly to sell African slaves in Spanish America; and finally, Louis XIV's recognition of James II's son as the King of England, thereby violating the terms of the Treaty of Ryswick. The War of the Spanish Succession was about whether or not France would gain hegemony in Europe, but more than ever before it was also about colonies and trade in America. The last Spanish Hapsburg died on 1 November 1700, and the French king's grandson ascended the Spanish throne as Philip V. In September of 1701, England, the United Provinces, and the Emperor renewed the Grand Alliance and sought to impose their collective will on both Spain and France.[1] During the next 11 years, well-trained, well-led armies engaged in some of the bloodiest campaigns in European history prior to the twentieth century. Though allied might could deeply wound, it could not destroy Louis XIV's France. Changing political circumstances in England in 1710 and Austria in 1711 could no longer keep the Allies together, and under the impetus of mutual betrayal, peace occurred in 1713. French and Spanish kingdoms were to remain forever separate; Spanish territories in Europe and French overseas colonies were ceded to the Emperor and to Great Britain,

---

[1] Gerald S. Graham, *Empire of the North Atlantic: The Maritime Struggle for North America*, 2nd ed. (Toronto: University of Toronto Press, 1958), 83–4 indicates that Article VIII of the Grand Alliance agreement signed secretly on 7 September 1701 denied France exclusive trade of Spanish America.

which also gained direct commercial access to Spanish America. In Europe, the territories previously assembled by Louis XIV remained French, but in the Americas some were lost.

The War of the Spanish Succession differed from all previous French wars in the New World chiefly because Spain was an ally rather than an enemy. Moreover, the chief aim of French policy was to protect and exploit Spanish America rather than to defend French colonies or ruin those of France's enemies, which included Portugal after 1703. The Spanish navy reached its nadir around 1700 and its renewal was delayed until after the war.[2] This weakness threw the entire burden of defence of the Spanish Indies on the French, whom Spanish Americans were loath to trust, though they acknowledged that only Louis XIV's grandson sought to keep the Spanish empire whole. This burden was doubly onerous because the French navy was also declining in size and relative importance. Between 1695 and 1715, the number of its ships declined by more than half, and displacement tonnage fell by almost the same proportion.[3]

The French West Indies emerged much stronger at the end of the War of the Spanish Succession than at the beginning despite the savage little wars fought between the colonists of the Windward Islands. The rapid expansion of the plantation complex, there and on Saint-Domingue, more than offset the effect of the loss of St. Christopher in 1702 and the collapse of Louisiana. The war had an immediate impact on the carrying trade. Many metropolitan merchants withdrew until its end or reinvested in privateering or explored commercial opportunities in Spanish America. These developments forced colonial officials to ignore restraints on foreign trade and turn a blind eye toward contraband. The *asiento* failed to produce the contracted number of slaves, but it established government collusion in the already large smuggling trade. The collapse of the French navy and the decline in the number of prizes in European waters after 1708 led to the reappearance of *la course royale* in the West Indies during the last five years of the war. Well-armed, privately fitted-out squadrons of warships from France increasingly attacked Dutch, English, and Portuguese possessions in American waters.

Canada survived the war in better condition than might be expected chiefly because of the vigour of the colonists, the resilience of their new society, the neutrality of Canada's chief native enemy, the nonaggressive stance of the colony of New York, and the policies pursued by political leaders, particularly Governor-General Philippe de Rigaud, marquis de Vaudreuil. The greatest handicap facing Canadian colonists was certain policy decisions made by the secretary of state for the marine.

---

[2] Jan Glete, *Navies and Nations: Warships, Navies, and State Building in Europe and America, 1500–1860*, 2 vols. (Stockholm: Almqvist & Wiksell International, 1993), 1: 229.

[3] Ibid., 2: 576–7.

Considerable debate surrounds the impact of the War of the Spanish Succession on the French colonies in the Americas because of clauses in the Treaty of Utrecht and the claims of some historians.[4] Although Great Britain gained Hudson Bay, Newfoundland, Acadia, Saint Christopher, and the *asiento* at the peace table, these prizes arose from France's general exhaustion and military defeat in Europe rather than the execution of a successful British strategy in the Americas.[5] The war in the West Indies was not a side issue on a small scale that led to no results, as Admiral Mahan once claimed.[6] The British failed to defend both their trade in the West Indies and their fishery in Newfoundland. They also failed to capture Guadeloupe or Canada or Hudson Bay. Moreover, French success in exploiting the trade of Spanish America was unequaled by any other European power. The transporting and escorting of Spanish treasure to Europe also aided immeasurably in allowing the exhausted nation to continue the war for eleven long, hard years. It is important, then, to disentangle events in the Americas from the general account of the War of the Spanish Succession. The challenge is not to lose sight of their relation to the whole.

The comte de Pontchartrain's chief aim in the Americas following the Nine Years' War was to increase France's already dominant position in the transatlantic trade of the Spanish Indies, which was worth far more than the trade of its own colonies.[7] His project had four parts: first, to create a company to develop trade with the Pacific coast of South America; second, to establish a privileged company with rights to trade with Mexico and the Spanish Main and to settle the southern region of Saint-Domingue; third, to rediscover the mouth of the Mississippi River and found a French settlement on the north coast of the Gulf of Mexico to block English traders from

---

4 See, for example E. H. Jenkins, *A History of the French Navy from Its Beginnings to the Present Day*, (London: Macdonald & Jane's, 1973), 105 for the claim that almost all French ships were taken in the West Indies and that "every French overseas possession lay at England's mercy"; also Patrick Crowhurst, *The Defence of British Trade, 1689–1815* (Folkstone: Dawson, 1977), 17 for a similar inaccurate statement that French fishing expeditions to Newfoundland were halted during the war.

5 For a critical view of British strategy in America see Admiral Sir Herbert Richmond, *The Navy as an Instrument of Policy, 1588–1727* (Cambridge: Cambridge University Press, 1953).

6 A. T. Mahan, *The Influence of Sea Power upon History, 1660–1783* (Boston: Little, Brown & Co., 1890), 208; and Paul Kennedy, *The Rise and Fall of British Naval Mastery*, (London and Basingstoke: The Macmillan Press, 1976), 84.

7 Michel Morineau, *Incroyables gazettes et fabuleux métaux: Les retours des trésors américains d'après les gazettes hollandaises (XVIe-XVIIIe siècles)*, (Cambridge: Cambridge University Press, 1985), 286 shows that in 1686 French manufactures were worth 39.4% of the value of all European goods on board the Spanish fleets. See also Stanley J. Stein and Barbara H. Stein, *Silver, Trade, and War: Spain and America in the Making of Modern Europe* (Baltimore and London: The Johns Hopkins University Press, 2000), 109–16 for a brief account of French penetration of Spanish America during the last half of the seventeenth century.

Carolina from doing the same; and fourth, to acquire the monopoly to trade African slaves in the Spanish empire.[8] Though all four projects were quickly implemented, war intervened before they could take effect. Moreover, the need to secure the transatlantic passage of Spanish *galeones* and the *flota* placed unforeseen burdens on the French navy, adding a fifth dimension to Pontchartrain's Spanish American plan.

During the twelve years between 1702 and 1713, the ambiguous French aim of protecting Spanish America while exploiting its commercial opportunities proved too much. Though usually portrayed as strong evidence of a French or royal imperial design, Pontchartrain's American policies were driven by European dynastic considerations and remained at the mercy of domestic political demands, requirements, and fiscal expediency. They represented the dreams and ambitions of a few men at court and elsewhere, including the colonies, but they were designed for the short term and subject to alteration or abandonment at any time. Spanish America survived not only French, but allied attempts at dismemberment, and French foreign policy remained continentalist.

New political arrangements in the French government also undermined the plans of Pontchartrain and his supporters. In 1699, the comte de Pontchartrain relinquished his office of secretary of state for the marine to his son, Jérôme, marquis de Pontchartrain, who had collaborated with him to seize control of Spanish American trade, but the younger Pontchartrain never entered the Council of State. He never became a minister of the Crown, and his influence was further reduced when the office of controller general of finances passed from his father to the new Secretary of State and Minister for War Michel Chamillart. Between 1701 and 1710, French naval expenses fell substantially from previous levels to vary with one exception, to between 11 and 14 percent of France's total military expenditures.[9] Chamillart no longer furnished previously agreed-upon funds. He began deducting previously assigned, unspent funds from those assigned for the current fiscal year. In 1701, for the first time, the treasurers-general of the marine began to pay naval creditors with their own notes issued by their clerks in the arsenals, ports, and colonies. With no controls in place, however, they soon began to protest (i.e., refuse to pay) them.[10] As early as 1703, they were unable to

---

8   Frostin, "Les Pontchartrain et la pénétration commerciale française en Amérique espagnole", *Revue historique*, no. 245 (1971), 307–36. John C. Rule, "Jérôme Phélypeaux and the Establishment of Louisiana" in *Frenchmen and French Ways in the Mississippi Valley*, ed., John F. McDermott (Urbana: University of Illinois Press, 1969), 179–97 does not deal with the larger context.

9   Henri Legohérel, *Les Trésoriers-généraux de la marine, 1517–1788* (Paris: Cujas, 1965), 179.

10   Didier Neuville, *Etat sommaire des archives de la marine antérieurs à la révolution* (Paris: Librairie Militaire de L. Baudoin, 1898 [Krause Reprint 1977]), 611–12; and Legohérel, *Les Tresoriers-général de la marine*, 203, 212.

meet their financial obligations. Thus, on the eve of the succession war the permanent insufficiency of funds supplied to the treasurers-general of the marine marked a new characteristic of the French naval, including colonial, finances.[11]

Anything called a naval policy melted away soon after the war began. Secretary of State Pontchartrain was increasingly reduced to encouraging and coordinating the overseas commercial operations of merchant-entrepreneurs and financiers rather than drafting policy to be executed by naval forces. Privateering or *guerre de course* that came to characterise the French war at sea was part of the larger phenomena of declining financial resources and eroding central authority. The navy sent small divisions, sometimes single ships, often privately fitted out, to escort merchantmen out to the colonies and home again, but colonists were pretty much left to defend themselves. Private capital increasingly substituted for declining royal authority overseas, superseding any imperial ambitions that the Pontchartrains may have had.[12] Indeed, by the end of the war, the neglected French colonies served chiefly as pawns to be sacrificed or exchanged to maintain French territory and influence in Europe rather than as jewels in a nonexistent imperial crown.[13]

8.2 THE TRADE AND TREASURE OF SPANISH AMERICA

On the eve of the succession war, the commercial connection with Peru, Spain's richest American possession, was all but severed. No supplies had been received from Spain since 1696, and for the next decade the vice-royalty remained cut off from Cadiz.[14] At the same time French merchants trading to Spain desperately sought to outflank the legal trade bonds at Seville by shipping textiles and hardware directly to South America's Pacific coast. Uninterested in defending the monopoly of the nearly defunct East India Company or allowing its assets to be liquidated, Pontchartrain had the Company lease its privileges to Saint-Malo merchants who created the variously styled *Compagnie royale de la mer pacifique* or *Compagnie de la mer du sud* in August of 1698.[15] Noël Danican de L'Epine of Saint-Malo and Jean Jourdan de Groué of Paris were the prime investors.

[11] Ibid., 187–90.
[12] See Geoffry Symcox, "The Navy of Louis XIV", *The Reign of Louis XIV*, ed., Paul Sonnino (New Jersey and London: Humanities Press International, 1990), 139.
[13] See Dale Miquelon, "Envisioning the French Empire: Utrecht, 1711–1713", *French Historical Studies*, 24, 4 (Fall 2001), [653]–77 presents a different perspective.
[14] Geoffrey Walker, *Spanish Politics and Imperial Trade, 1700–1789* (Bloomington and London: Indiana University Press, 1979), 21–2.
[15] Holden Furber, *Rival Empires of Trade in the Orient, 1600–1800* (Minneapolis: University of Minnesota Press, 1979), 118–19.

The new South Sea Company received a 30-year monopoly to trade along South America's Pacific coast. In December 1698, four ships under the command of another Malouin privateer-entrepreneur, Jacques Gouin de Beauchesne, left La Rochelle bound for the South Sea. Only two of them reached America. They spent six months struggling through the Strait of Magellan before reaching the Pacific coast of South America. There they traded for a year before departing in January of 1701. After rounding Cape Horn, they reached France in August. The venture resulted in a financial loss, but offered sufficient hope to inspire a second attempt. Legal trade through Cadiz was so bound up by taxes and draconian regulations that incentives to engage in direct, though illegal, trade were overwhelming.[16] Political anarchy in the Spanish colonies, the corruption of officials, and the very great demand made a second venture exceedingly attractive. The returns from two ships that arrived back in 1703 were said to be worth 1,270,000 livres. Perhaps more importantly, the French traders had obtained the adherence of the *corregidor* and the local bishop at Concepción, Chile, to the Bourbon claimant, Philip V.[17] From 1703 to 1713, 100 very large ships with a total capacity of well over 30,000 tons left Saint-Malo for the South Sea.[18] Additional ships, some that attracted a wide circle of investors from as far a way as Germany and Switzerland, departed from Marseilles.[19] The South Sea trade became the basis for mobilizing large capital amounts in France.[20] Annual investments grew from 500,000 livres in 1701 to 3.5 and 4 million in 1705, 1706, and 1707. After declining during the next three years, investment never fell below 4 million from 1710 until 1716.[21]

Though 97 to 98 percent of the returns from this seaborne trade were in silver, estimates of its total value are difficult to establish.[22] Jourdan de

---

[16] Anne Morel, "Les Armateurs malouins et le commerce interlope" in *Les Sources de l'Histoire Maritime en Europe: Actes du Quatrième Colloque Internationale d'Histoire Marime*, éds. M. Mollat et al. (Paris: SEVPEN, 1962), 311–15.

[17] Charles de La Roncière, *Histoire de la marine française*, 6 vols. (Paris: Plon, 1909–1932), 6: 564–5.

[18] Jean Delumeau, *Le Mouvement du port de Saint-Malo; 1681–1720, bilan statistique* (Paris: Librairie C. Klincksieck, [1966]), 288 gives 90 ships with known tonnage totaling 29,800 tons.

[19] Eric W. Dalgren, "Voyages français à destination de la Mer du Sud avant Bougainville (1695–1749)", *Nouvelles archives des missions scientifiques et littéraires*, 14, pt. 4 (1907): 423–568 indicates that 116 of 175 vessels sailing from French ports to the South Sea left before the end of 1713 though he also acknowledged that his list is incomplete.

[20] Charles Carrière. *Negociants marseillais au XVIIIe siècle: contribution à l'étude des économies maritimes*, 2 vols. (Marseille: Institut historique de Provence, 1973), 1: 87.

[21] André Lespangol, *Les Messieurs de Saint-Malo: une élite négociante au temps de Louis XIV* (Saint-Malo: Editions l'Ancre de Marine, 1991), 554.

[22] Jean Meyer, *La Noblesse bretonne au XVIII siècle*, 2 vols. (Paris: SEVPEN, 1966), 1: 345 estimated the total value of goods brought into Breton ports between 1688 and 1713 at between 400 and 500 million livres. Louis Dermigny, *La Chine et l'occident, le commerce à Canton au XVIIIe siècle, 1719–1823*, 3 vols + album (Paris: SEVPEN, 1964), 1: 426

Groué, cofounder of the South Sea Company, claimed that imports of precious metal had passed 300 million livres by 1711. Saint-Malo's deputy of commerce estimated that ships from that port alone imported 400 million livres between 1703 and 1720. This amount, suggests Anne Morel, represented two-thirds of Peru's entire silver production during the first 20 years of the century, which is close to a more recent estimate based on Spanish sources.[23] It gives French returns from Spanish Pacific trade between 1698 and 1724 as 47 million pesos or 65 percent of Peru's foreign trade.[24]

The cargoes of three Malouin ships that returned from the South Sea in 1703 yielded more than 7 million livres.[25] A single Marseilles ship reportedly landed a staggering 650,000 piastres or silver pesos, worth more than 3 million livres at Port Louis in 1704.[26] Three ships returning the next year were estimated to be worth 9 million livres; the returns from one ship in 1706 came to 4.5 million.[27] A ship fitted out the same year by Joachim Descazeaux du Hallay, who began his close association with Pontchartrain in 1691 at Placentia, returned with 724,529 piastres worth about 2.9 million livres on board.[28] Two ships fitted out by Lepine-Danican in 1707 brought back 784,159 pieces of eight. The net sum distributed to investors eight years later was more than 1.5 million livres.[29]

The only real failure among these astonishing voyages belonged to the East India Company, which was on the verge of bankruptcy in 1706. Pontchartrain persuaded its directors to ready three ships for South America, but due to the Company's indebtedness and lack of close management by its directors, the vessels were poorly fitted out. The directors' aims were also confused, and later the ships' officers refused to cross the Pacific. One ship sailed through the Strait of Magellan and on to Pondicherry, but the other two returned to France, where the venture was judged a failure.[30]

supposed that between 979,000 and 1,223,000 kilograms of silver entered France between 1700 and 1730.

[23]　Morel, "Les Armateurs malouins", 313; Frostin, "Les Pontchartrain", 310–11 cites the marquis d'Argenson for a later claim that the South Sea trade brought back 100 million livres annually!

[24]　Wim Klooster, *Illicit Riches: Dutch Trade in the Caribbean, 1648–1795* (Leiden: KITLV Press, 1995), 200 n. 1 citing Carlos D. Malamud, "El comercio directo de Europa con America en el siglo XVIII", *Quinto Centenario*, 1: 25–52. More recently, this author estimated that during the war years, 1702–12, French silver returns amounted to 24,146,764 pesos; see table in Carlos Daniel Malamud y Rikles, *Cadiz y Saint Malo en el comercio colonial peruano, 1698–1725* ([Cadiz]: Diputacion Provincial de Cadiz, [1986]), 67.

[25]　La Roncière, *Histoire de la marine française*, 6: 565–6.

[26]　Carrière, *Négociants marseillais*, 1: 86.

[27]　Morel, "Les Armateurs malouins et le commerce interlope", 313.

[28]　J. S. Bromley, "The French Traders in the South Sea: The Journal of Lieutenant Pitouays 1706–8" in *Corsaires and Navies, 1660–1760* (London and Ronceverte: The Hambleton Press, 1987), 329 n. 19.

[29]　Ibid., 328–9.

[30]　Anne Kroell, "The Search of the French East India Company for New Markets in South America, 1706–1709" in *Global Crossroads and the American Seas.* ed., Clark

The French defeat at Ramillies in 1706 and Allied occupation of Madrid had an electric effect in the Americas, where most colonists and officials had remained hostile to the Bourbon monarchy. In August of 1707, Pontchartrain dispatched two warships to the South Sea to assist Bourbon loyalists should other Spanish creoles revolt in support of the Hapsburg claimant to the throne. One turned back before reaching Cape Horn, but *L'Aimable*, 70 guns, continued to the west coast of South America. Despite strong Spanish American hostility to the ship's presence, no revolt occurred, and in November of 1708, *Chef d'escadre* de Chabert sailed from Concepción, escorting eight other ships carrying 10 million piastres.[31] By this time, Malouin merchants had become the king's bankers. Returns were delivered directly to the nearest royal mint. The Controller-General did not hesitate to match and even exceed commercial exchange rates to ensure the merchants' cooperation.[32] The value of the eight ships that arrived at Port Louis was estimated at 27 or 28 million livres.[33]

Attempting to appease the Spanish, Pontchartrain forced the Malouins to pay an indult or tax of 6 percent, ostensibly to the Spanish treasury, but this duty levied on the value of all goods returning to France from the South Sea, while nominally paid to the King of Spain for indulging in illegal trade, was levied on French merchants to pay for their naval protection.[34] The Malouins objected. Their heavily armed vessels did not need naval protection. The indult broke faith with their willingness to deliver silver to the mints. They abandoned Pontchartrain and turned for support to the new Controller-General of Finances Nicolas Desmaretz, who had replaced Chamillart in February of 1708. Pontchartrain opposed any further South Sea trade, but Desmaretz would not hear of it. Peruvian silver was too important to the exhausted state, and until the end of the war French ships continued to sail in ever growing numbers despite a total prohibition of the trade.[35]

G. Reynolds (Missoula, MA: Pictorial Histories Publishing Co., 1988), 1–7. Also Paul Kaepplin, *La Compagnie des Indes Orientales et François Martin: étude sur l'histoire du commerce et des établissements français dans l'Inde sous Louis XIV (1664–1719)*. reprinted (New York: Burt Franklin [1908] 1967), 571–2, 578–9.

[31] La Roncière, *Histoire de la marine française*, 6: 569–70. Bromley, "French Traders in the South Sea", 331.

[32] Lespangol, *Les Messieurs de Saint-Malo*, 624, 626–7 gives 98 to 100 percent.

[33] Morel, "Les armateurs malouins", 313. The ninth ship returned to Coruna with over 300,000 pieces of eight remitted by Lima to Spain.

[34] Dahlgren, *Les Relations commerciales*, 432–4.

[35] Lespagnol, *Les Messieurs de Saint-Malo*, 556. To obtain some idea of the enormity of these silver cargoes consider that, when Commodore George Anson's men from HMS *Centurion* boarded *Nuestra Senora de Covadonga* off Manilla in June of 1743 and seized 1,373,843 pieces of eight, the prize was one of the richest treasures ever taken by an English ship. Glyndwr Williams, "English Projects and Ventures in the South Seas, 1670–1750", in *Perspectives of Empire: Essays Presented to Gerald S. Graham*, eds. J. E. Flint and G. Williams (London: Longman, 1973), 49.

Pontchartrain's reversal of policy was part of the perpetual struggle between political, financial, banking, and commercial interests that characterised French politics during this period.[36] The political case for halting the trade was to appease the Spanish, who daily grew angrier at the French presence off Chile and Peru and to remove a major cause for enemy complaint while peace feelers developed at the Hague. In 1711, however, the major reason to ban commercial sailing was to obtain an official commercial concession to trade in Spanish America in return for an enforced prohibition of expeditions to the South Sea. This was not to be. The Spanish sought an unconditional return to the prewar monopoly that confined all transatlantic traffic to America to Cadiz.

Pontchartrain's ban proved ineffectual in any case. After declining in 1708 and 1709, annual investment in the trade did not fall below the previous high of 4 million until after 1716.[37] There was no decrease in the number of sailings. Twenty-seven ships left Saint-Malo for the South Sea between 1711 and 1713. Sixteen more sailed the following year.[38] During the ban on trade to the Pacific, French merchants also employed associates from Genoa to cover their activity. This probably accounts for a report that, in November of 1713, seven ships at Concepción had been fitted out at Marseilles for Genoese accounts.[39]

French commercial penetration of the South Sea was remarkably successful and deserves to be better known. One indication of its success lies in the complaints of the governor of Jamaica in 1710 and 1711 that the English contraband trade had almost disappeared owing to competition from French goods finding their way inland from the Pacific coast and via Buenos Aires.[40] In addition to mobilizing large capital amounts, realising enormous profits, yielding up vast quantities of silver, and driving the English out of the contraband trade, the South Sea trade was responsible for several significant feats of navigation, including the first French circumnavigation of the globe.[41] Shortly after the war, one of the Malouin ships also became the first European vessel to voyage around the world by sailing eastward.[42]

French commercial penetration of Spanish America via the ports of South America's Atlantic littoral, *Terre firme*, the West Indies and the Gulf of Mexico was equally important. At least 229 French ships have been identified

36 Lespagnol, *Les Messieurs de Saint-Malo*, 586. See also Herbert Lüthy, *La Banque protestante en France*, vol. 1, *Dispersion et regroupment (1685–1730)*, (Paris: SEVPEN, 1959) for a lucid history of this struggle.
37 Lespagnol, *Les Messieurs de Saint-Malo*, 554.
38 Delumeau, *Le mouvement de port de Saint-Malo*, 286.
39 Carrière, *Négociants marseillais*, 1: 87–88.
40 *CSP, CS*, 1710–1711, 109, 111, 428 cited in Williams, "English Projects and Ventures", 35.
41 John Dunmore, *French Explorers in the Pacific*, Vol. 1, *The Eighteenth Century* (Oxford: Clarendon Press, 1965), 19.
42 Ibid., 19–20, 25.

at Puerto Rico, Caracas, Cartagena, and Buenos Aires in Spanish America.[43] In 1707, authorities estimated 20 to 30 French ships were calling annually at Havana. Between 1701 and 1710, 23 ships arrived at Saint-Malo from eastern Spanish American ports.[44] The account books of a single commercial partnership at Marseilles reveal the company sent two ships annually to Spanish America between 1705 and 1709.[45] Ships from other ports, including Bordeaux, were also involved.[46]

Spain never relaxed its claim to a monopoly on all transatlantic trade with its American possessions. Royal decrees of 1701, 1702, 1703, and 1705 prohibited trade with French vessels entering Spanish American ports to purchase provisions and other necessaries, but these enactments were fictions designed to maintain honour. In August of 1701, French ships calling at Cartagena unloaded linens, hats, tools, wax, guns, wine, pepper, and liquor. The next year, the Council of the Indies complained that Malouin ships had introduced French textiles directly into New Spain and *Terre firme*. One vessel carried away 108,000 silver pesos and an unassessed quantity of gold, while another sailed with 100,000 pesos on board. Spanish merchants in Seville estimated in May of 1707 that, since the beginning of the war, 116 French ships had called at Campeche, Vera Cruz, and ports along the Spanish Main in comparison to 15 that had reached the South Seas.[47]

Under cover of war, a preexisting system of illegal trade in the Caribbean world expanded throughout the West Indies and the American mainland. The war encouraged market forces to flourish as never before. The French, English, Dutch, Danish, and others traded shamelessly in Spain's New World possessions. It may be that more trading than fighting occurred during the middle years of the war in the Americas. Entrepôts like Curaçao and St. Thomas flourished. The French, no less than others, gave themselves over to profitable illegal trade with the Spanish colonies. St. Pierre boomed. Between 1705 and 1709, at least 65 French merchantmen called at Vera Cruz and Campeche.[48] In 1710, the governor of Havana was accused of allowing 56 French ships to land illegal merchandise during the previous two and a half years.[49]

---

43 Pablo Emilio Perez and Mallaina Bueno, *Politica Naval Espanola en el Atlántico, 1700–1715* (Sevilla: Escuela des Estudos Hispano-Americano de Sevilla, 1982), 142–69.

44 Delumeau, *Le Mouvement du port de Saint-Malo*, 281 notes that no malouin ships sailed for these ports during the previous score of years. cf. 282–5.

45 Carrière, *Négociants marseillais*, 1: 81–2.

46 Huetz de Lemps, *Géographie du commerce de Bordeaux à la fin du règne de Louis XIV* (Paris-La Haye: Mouton, 1975), 362–3.

47 Based on Henry Kamen, *The War of Succession in Spain, 1700–1715* (London: Weidenfeld & Nicolson, 1969), 143–6; Stein and Stein, *Silver, Trade, and War*, 127.

48 Kamen, *The War of Succession*, 147 gives 42 ships for the years 1705 and 1707, but see Perez and Bueno, *Politica Naval Espanola en el Atlántico*, 144–50.

49 Lilian Crété, *La Traite des nègres* (Paris: Perrin, 1989), 225, citing C. A. Arauz Monfante, *El contrabando holandés en el Caribe durante la primera mitad del siglo XVIII*, 2 vols. (Caracas 1984), 1: 141, 163.

Despite complaints from colonial authorities about the voyages to Spanish colonies, trade to the West Indies grew. Though Bordeaux's trade suffered serious losses from English and Dutch privateers, recent revisions indicate these disguise the entry of new local merchants into colonial trade. Elsewhere, the total picture of West Indies trade was even more positive.[50] After 1704, Nantes's West Indian traffic surpassed the 1700 level. At La Rochelle, in 1705 and 1708, the only years for which evidence exists, the volume of West Indian shipping not only passed the best known figure for the seventeenth century but also the average for the eighteenth.[51] The *asiento* itself seems to have been chiefly a cover for widespread traffic in contraband.

One of Philip V's first acts was to transfer the *asiento* to French interests. In order to obtain the monopoly, Pontchartrain helped adjust disputes between the Spanish government and Portuguese holders of the contract and sent Jean Du Casse to Madrid to negotiate the concession to the French Guinea Company. The Company, founded in 1685, was reorganised in July of 1701 under the direction of seven powerful financiers close to the French government in anticipation of this development. Samuel Bernard, who became court banker the same year, was the most important international banker in France.[52] Other financiers included Antoine Crozat, Receiver-General of Finances at Bordeaux and the greatest financier of Louis XIV's reign; Joseph Legendre d'Arminy, Crozat's brother-in-law and a tax-farmer; Pierre Thomé, one-time Parisian merchant banker and current Treasurer-General of the Galley Corps; Jacques de Vanolles, Treasurer-General of the Marine; Etienne Landais, Treasurer-General of Artillery; and Vincent Mayon de Chambon, a former tax-farmer and current contractor to the army.[53] All seven men together with the kings of France and Spain, and Governor Du Casse and eight others became shareholders in the new company. On 15 November 1701, two weeks after the associates ratified the *asiento* contract, they established the *Asiento* Company to carry out its terms.[54] Three years earlier Bernard, Crozat, Mayon, and Thomé had created the highly successful

50 Huetz de Lemps, *Géographie du commerce de Bordeaux*, 159.
51 J. S. Bromley, "Le commerce de la France de l'ouest et la guerre maritime (1702–12)", reprinted in *Corsairs and Navies*, 404–5.
52 See Jacob M. Price, *France and the Chesapeake: A History of the French Tobacco Monopoly, 1674–1791 and its Relationship to the British and American Tobacco Trades*, 2 vols. (Ann Arbor: University of Michigan Press, 1973), 1; 55–60; and Lüthy, *La Banque protestante*, 1: 121–5; Frostin, "Les Pontchartrain et la pénétration", 317 mistakenly dismisses Bernard's role.
53 Frostin, "Les Pontchartrain et la pénétration", 317–19; Daniel Dessert, *Argent, pouvoir et société au Grand Siècle* (Paris: Fayard, 1985), 514–16, 535, 565–6, 576, 618, 628, 645, and 697.
54 Col., F²ᴬ 7 acte de société, 15 November 1701. See Frances G. Davenport, *European Treaties Bearing on the History of the United States and its Dependencies*, 4 vols. (Washington: Carnegie Institutions, 1917–37). 3: 51–3, and 65–74 for an English translation of this document.

company that leased the tobacco monopoly from the government.[55] These same financiers and Du Casse also founded the Saint-Domingue Company. Three others, Legendre, Landais and Vanolles, were also shareholders in the South Sea Company along with naval administrator and businessman, Michel Bégon de Montfermeuil, *premier commis* of the navy's funds office (*bureau des fonds*) and younger brother and namesake of the naval intendant at Rochefort.[56] Two of Pontchartrain's personal secretaries, Charles de Salaberry and Joseph de La Touche, along with naval commissary Hyacinthe Plomier de La Boulaye and Governor Du Casse, also held shares in the Saint-Domingue Company. "For all practical purposes", concluded Jacob Price, the tobacco lease, the South Sea Company, the Saint-Domingue Company, and the Asiento Company, "were one and the same interest".[57] This tightly knit group of financiers and naval administrators strongly supported Pontchartrain, but their dreams of profit should not be labeled French imperialism.

By the terms of the *asiento* contract, which was to last 10 years, or 12 if the terms remained unfulfilled, the new Company undertook to provide 38,000 slaves in wartime (48,000 in peacetime) to Spanish America. The King of Spain's duty was fixed at 33 1/3 piastres or 100 livres per head, the better part of which the Company agreed to pay in advance. Between 1702 and 1713, the Company delivered only about half the slaves called for in the contract.[58] Under its cover, though, a great deal of contraband trade along the coasts of the Spanish Main and the Gulf of Mexico took place, reinforced by the close relations between its major investors and the shareholders in the Saint-Domingue Company. Ostensibly established to settle the uninhabited southern district of Saint-Domingue, the Company possessed rights to trade with Spanish America and Jamaica.

The Spanish colonies never recognised the *Asiento* Company's monopoly. Spanish creoles continued to trade with the Dutch at Curaçao, which remained the chief conduit for slave imports throughout the war. The Dutch West India Company continued to ship slaves from Africa and to participate in illicit trade between Curaçao and Caracas. Between 1700 and 1712 it delivered more than 16,000 slaves to the mainland colonies.[59] The French did

55 Price, *France and the Chesapeake*. 1: 52–7.
56 See Yvonne Bezard, *Fonctionnnaires maritimes et coloniaux sous Louis XIV: les Bégon* (Paris: Albin Michel, [1932]), 230–44 for more about Bégon's varied investments in maritime trade and privateering during the war. Additional information is located in the Bégon Papers at the Université de Montréal.
57 Price, *France and the Chesapeake*, 1:55.
58 Philippe Hrodej, *L'Amiral Du Casse: l'Évolution d'un Gascon sous Louis XIV*, 2 vols. (Paris: Librairie de l'Inde, 1999), 1: 292–7; Michel Devèze, *Antilles, Guyanes, La mer des Caraïbes de 1492 à 1789* (Paris: SEDES, 1977), 219.
59 Joannes Menne Postma, *The Dutch in the Atlantic Slave Trade, 1600–1815* (Cambridge: Cambridge University Press, 1990), 41–52.

not seem to mind. Indeed, they appear to have encouraged it. In 1707, two Curaçao merchants contracted with the Saint-Domingue Company for three or four consignments of slaves. Soon afterwards, Jean (Juan?) Chouria, the son of the Spanish consul at Amsterdam and agent of the *Asiento* Company at Cartagena, sought to establish an office at Curaçao. Chouria experienced business difficulties, and the French appointed Phelipe Henriquez, one of the island's most successful merchants, as their agent.[60] Initial proposals that the Dutch company renew its participation in the slave trade also came to naught, but in 1711, Chouria successfully negotiated a slave contract for 400 adult male slaves from the West India Company over the objections of local private traders. He continued to frequent the Dutch colony in subsequent years, purchasing slaves for the *Asiento* Company. Chouria may have purchased 50 percent or more of approximately 4,000 slaves landed at Curaçao during the 1711–15 period.[61]

In view of the bullionist concerns of European statesmen, it is no surprise to learn that both French and English governments sent naval forces to the West Indies in anticipation of the coming war. The first to arrive was a small French squadron commanded by *Lieutenant-general des armées navales* Alain-Emmanuel, marquis de Coëtlogon, intended to strengthen the defenses of several Spanish American ports and to escort the Spanish *flota* containing two years' production of bullion to Europe. In October of 1701, William III sent his own naval expedition commanded by Vice-Admiral John Benbow to seize Cartagena. The English government had decided to seize the Spanish treasure fleet and provoke war in the Caribbean in order to export it to Europe.[62] Toward the end of the year, with war threatening, France sent a much larger force of 30 hastily fitted out warships under command of the marquis de Châteaurenault, newly appointed *vice-amiral* by Louis XIV and captain-general of the seas by Philip V, to reinforce Coëtlogon, but the Spanish kept the *flota* at Havana. In January of 1702, having exhausted his provisions and unable to obtain more, Coëtlogon had no option but to abandon the second part of his mission and depart empty-handed for France.[63]

After reaching the Caribbean, Châteaurenault found some of his ships in such poor condition and his crews so sickly that he reduced their number to fifteen and sent the rest home. The newly enlarged French escort, Spain's growing needs, and the presence of two years' accumulation of treasure

60 See Cornelis Goslinga, *The Dutch in the Caribbean and the Guianas, 1680–1791* (Dover, NH: Van Goram, 1985), 77–82 for more on Chouria; also Klooster, *Illicit Riches*, 67.

61 Postma, *The Dutch in the Atlantic Slave Trade*, 51.

62 Ian K. Steele, *The English Atlantic, 1675–1740: An Exploration of Communications and Community* (New York: Oxford University Press, 1986), 168, 364 n. 1.

63 Christian Buchet, *La Lutte pour l'espace Caraïbe et la façade atlantique de l'Amérique centrale et du sud, (1672–1763)*,2 vols. (Paris: Librairie de l'Inde, 1991), 1: 208–9.

finally led the Spanish to agree to depart with the French. The fleet of 32 French ships and 24 Spanish, including 12 *galeones* carrying an estimated treasure of 60 chests of gold and 200 chests of silver, as well as silver pigs, sows, and plate, sailed from Havana in July of 1702.[64] On reaching the Azores and learning that war had been declared and an English fleet was awaiting them off Cadiz, Châteaurenault opted to sail to France, but the Spanish commander refused, believing that the treasure would never reach Spain. The two men agreed to make for Vigo Bay on the northwest coast of Spain. Upon their arrival, Châteaurenault reinforced the defences at the entrance to the deep bay and the Spanish began unloading the treasure, which is how the English fleet found them nearly a month later while returning from Cadiz. After forcing the defences and reaching the bottom of the bay, the Anglo-Dutch fleet created havoc among the French and Spanish ships.[65]

The French lost everything: five vessels and two frigates destroyed, four of the line run aground, and six ships captured. Dishonour was the inevitable accompaniment of such a disaster. Chateaurenault's unpreparedness because his ships of the line were laden with merchandise and unable to fight was inexcusable. He never went to sea again, though he continued to receive the king's bounty.[66] Meanwhile, the Spanish lost very little. Silver totaling more than 13.5 million pesos had been removed well before the Allied fleet arrived and nearly half of it entered directly into the royal treasury. It was the largest sum ever obtained in a single year by a Spanish king. Anglo-Dutch merchants trading to Spanish America through Seville, who owned nearly one-third of the treasure in the fleet, lost everything because Philip V confiscated 4 million pesos in reprisal for the attack.[67] During the remaining years of the war, the French navy protected the treasure of the Indies with much greater success.

Shortly before the disaster at Vigo, a small French squadron achieved success in the West Indies. In April of 1702, hoping to present Spanish Americans with a French officer they might find more sympathetic, Governor Du Casse, who had been promoted to *chef d'escadre* to negotiate the *asiento* contract the year before, was given command of six warships and the tasks of escorting a convoy of Spanish troops to Cartagena and carrying the new viceroy of Mexico, the Duke of Albuquerque, to his destination.[68] After reaching Puerto Rico from Coruna, Du Casse sent two ships with the

64 Ruth Bourne, *Queen Anne's Navy in the West Indies* (New Haven: Yale University Press, 1939), 152. Estimates of its value vary from 11 to 12 million to 18 to 20 million pesos, see Morineau, *Incroyables gazettes et fabuleux métaux*, 311.

65 Henry Kamen, "The Destruction of the Spanish Fleet at Vigo in 1702", *Bulletin of Historical Research*, 39 (1966): 165–70.

66 Daniel Dessert, *La Royale, vaisseaux et marins du Roi–Soleil* (Paris: Fayard, 1996), 258–60.

67 Kamen, "The Destruction of the Spanish Fleet", 171–3.

68 See Hrodej, *L'Amiral Du Casse*, 1: 302–11 for details; also J. H. Owen, *War at Sea under Queen Anne*, 1702–1708 (Cambridge: Cambridge University Press, 1938), 76–7.

vice-regal entourage to Vera Cruz while he continued escorting the troops to Cartagena with the remaining four. Late in August, while running along the Spanish Main off Santa Marta, the Franco-Spanish force of 10 ships met the English expedition, which had been sent to seize the very port to which they were carrying reinforcements. Action continued for five days, and although superior in number, the English failed to prevail, owing to the desertion of Admiral Benbow by several of his captains. So disgraceful was their conduct that shortly afterward four English captains were court-martialed. Two were shot, a third died during his trial, and a fourth was dismissed from the service and imprisoned. Du Casse delivered his charges safely to Cartagena. The following spring, in 1703, he sailed for France with the extraordinary cargo of 6 million pieces of eight. He personally profited immensely from the voyage. A short time later, his daughter, with a dowry of 300,000 livres, married the chevalier de Roucy, Pontchartrain's brother-in-law – a remarkable illustration of a former Protestant slave trader's social advancement.[69] In November, Du Casse submitted a proposal to shore up the defences of four Spanish America port cities, Havana, Vera Cruz, Cartagena, and Panama, in order to reassure the Spanish and discourage the English. He also called for four or five French warships to be fitted out to support the Spanish in America,[70] but Du Casse's proposal called for the expenditure of scarce naval funds, and it came to naught.

In the wake of the Vigo disaster, Du Casse appeared to influence Philip V, who ordered that henceforth ships of the *galeones* and the *flota* were to sail in small numbers at unscheduled times to be less likely to be captured. No fleets sailed from Cadiz in 1703, 1704, or 1705. The Spanish remained very reluctant to risk their treasure.[71] In conjunction with the Spanish king's orders and reflecting ever decreasing French naval resources, a special force of six frigates left France for Vera Cruz in December of 1707 under the command of baron d'Oroigne. During the next two years it remained undisturbed in the Gulf of Mexico. Only endemic sickness forced the ships home. They arrived at Cadiz with a cargo of 10 million piastres on board in March of 1710.[72]

Twice more the king entrusted Du Casse with command of French squadrons to protect Spanish treasure, and twice more he escorted it safely to Europe. The problem remained of getting the Spanish to agree to the French escort. A shortage of silver forced the Spaniards to send the *galeones*, the first fleet in a decade, to Cartagena in 1706. The following year, Du Casse sailed to the Caribbean in command of eight capital ships to escort the treasure

69 La Roncière, *Histoire de la marine française*, 6: 475.
70 Marine, B4 17, ff. 24-5v Mémoire par M. du Casse, November 1703.
71 Morineau, *Incroyables gazettes et fabuleux métaux*, 311; Bourne, *Queen Anne's Navy in the West Indies*, 162.
72 Morineau, *Incroyables gazettes et fabuleux métaux*, 312; Buchet, *La Lutte pour l'espace caraïbe*, 1: 231-2.

ships that were ready to return to Cadiz.[73] He was expected home in March of 1708, but on reaching Portobelo, Du Casse learned the *galeones* were not ready. The last ships of the *flota* were also just beginning to be careened at Vera Cruz and would not be ready for four or five months. Failing to persuade any *galeones* to accompany him to Havana, he sailed without them to await the *flota*. At Havana, weeks turned into months. French crews sickened and died, provisions grew scarce, and quarrels with Spanish officials increased. A British fleet captured several *galeones* as they exited Cartagena to join Du Casse at Havana. Only in mid-July did Du Casse finally sail with part of the *flota* and a few *galeones*.[74] Nevertheless, it was the largest treasure fleet of the war. Du Casse returned to Spain with treasure estimated to be worth 20 million pesos, but the lack of cooperation between the French and Spanish was obvious for all to see.[75]

Two years later, desperate conditions and news that many laden *galeones* were laid up at Cartagena and Portobelo and the *flota* was at Havana encouraged the French to fit out yet a third expedition to bring America's treasure to Europe.[76] Du Casse's squadron, numbering just three capital ships and two frigates, reached Cartagena in July of 1711. There, in a ruse reminiscent of an earlier stratagem, he ordered the treasure ships to sail to Havana without him. The British squadron waiting outside the port pursued and took two of the ships, but were later lured away to Jamaica by false rumours of a French attack. Du Casse, with 8 to 10 million piastres on board his own ships, slipped away unnoticed. A hurricane later scattered his ships off Newfoundland and forced all but one back to Martinique to repair and refit.[77] It was only in mid-March of 1712 that he reached France.[78] By then the Congress of Utrecht was in progress, and in June, French and English ministers agreed to a temporary cessation of hostilities in Flanders, which was then extended worldwide in August.[79]

Often thought to be absent from the Americas, the French navy was present, but its role was limited to protecting the treasure ships of a mistrustful ally that deeply resented having to rely on it. Nevertheless, French warships escorted treasure worth nearly 45 million pesos to Spain, probably more than the wealth carried from the South Sea. At no time during the war

73   Geoffrey J. Walker, *Spanish Politics and Imperial Trade, 1700–1789*, (Bloomington: Indiana University Press, 1979), 23–4; Hrodej, *L'Amiral Du Casse*, 2: 368–74, 593.

74   Bourne, *Queen Anne's Navy*, 169–70.

75   Morineau, *Incroyables gazettes et fabuleux métaux*, 312.

76   Hrodej, *L'Amiral Du Casse*, 2: 397–402, 600; Bourne, *Queen Anne's Navy*, 174.

77   Morineau, *Incroyables gazettes et fabuleux métaux*, 312 reports one French warship arrived at Cadiz in November 1711.

78   Ibid., 175–7; Buchet, *La Lutte pour l'espace caraïbe*, 1: 233–5.

79   Col., B 34, ff. 85v, 478v Pontchartrain to Phélypeaux and others, 9 August 1712. See Max Savelle, *The Origins of American Diplomacy: The International History of Anglo-America, 1492–1763* (New York: Macmillan, 1967).

did the navy fit out capital ships to defend French colonies from attack or lead assaults against the possessions of the king's enemies. That became the ever-increasing task of a growing alliance between the secretary of state for the marine and a group of private merchant entrepreneurs and naval officers who often had their own agendas.

8.3 TRADE AND WAR IN THE CIRCUM-CARIBBEAN

The French government left the colonies on their own well before the outbreak of hostilities. Even before Louis XIV accepted the heavy burden of protecting his grandson's Spanish inheritance, Sébastien Le Prestre de Vauban had counseled Pontchartrain to trust the defence of the colonies to permanent masonry fortifications, which French engineers excelled in building, garrisoned by regular troops and colonial militia.[80] In 1699, Pontchartrain dispatched the distinguished naval engineer, Captain Bernard Renau d'Eliçagaray and naval commissary Hyacinthe Plomier de La Boulaye on a joint mission to inspect the defences and fortifications of the West Indies.[81] These two men made a thorough review of the French defences and as a result, new works were being constructed in several colonies on the eve of the war. All along the colonial littoral and in the West Indies, local conditions and circumstances rather than government policies played crucial roles in affecting the war's outcome. In general, the amount of fighting during the twelve years of warfare in the Caribbean has been exaggerated. Except during the first two years, the French islands remained relatively untouched, and with one exception, in 1706, metropolitan attacks on English, Dutch, and Portuguese colonies were confined to the final three years of the war owing to changing conditions in Europe.

The French West Indies had been without a governor-general since the marquis d'Amblimont's death at Martinique on 17 August 1700. Neither of his successors left their mark. The comte d'Enos succumbed three months after arriving at Martinique, and the marquis de Rosmadec died eight months

---

80 Three of Vauban's essays on colonies and privateering can be found in Albert Rochas d'Aiglun, *Vauban: sa famille et ses écrits, ses oisivetés et sa correspondance, analyse et extraits*, 2 vols., reprinted (Genève: Slatkine, [1910] 1972), 1: 413–61. See also two letters from Vauban to Maurepas (that is, Jérôme Phélypeaux), dated 1699 in Louise Dechêne éd., *La Correspondance de Vauban relative au Canada* (Québec: Ministère des Affaires Culturelles, 1968), 23–30, 37–44. Also Frederick J. Thorpe, "Fish, Forts, and Finances: French Construction at Placentia, 1699–1710", The Canadian Historical Association, *Historical Papers, 1971* (Ottawa, 1971), 53; and Dale Miquelon, *New France, 1701–1744: A Supplement to Europe* (Toronto: McClelland and Stewart, 1987), 10–14.

81 Col., B 21, f. 382 Pontchartrain to Robert, 2 August 1699. In 1699, Renau was made a member of the Royal Academy of Sciences. La Boulaye was already a director of the Saint Domingue Company; soon afterward he became a director of the *Asiento* Company.

later at Havana without ever reaching the islands.[82] When hostilities broke out in July of 1702, the French colonies had been under the interim command of the governor of Martinique for the past 15 years. He was Knight Commander of the Order of Malta Charles de Guitaud, who expired on 7 September.[83] The only senior authority remaining was François Robert, intendant since 1695.[84] Robert had no military influence, although he had much responsibility for ensuring that the local defence forces were clothed, armed, and fed.

With no senior military authority in the islands, defence became a wholly local affair, uncoordinated and idiosyncratic. Fortunately, the colonial militias had grown and become well-dispersed over Martinique and Guadeloupe, though the same was not true of St. Christopher, where the French were still struggling to assume control of the north and south portions of the island. Elsewhere, the militias had been reconstituted into regiments under the command of colonels and lieutenant-colonels drawn from the ranks of the large planters.[85] Little wonder that the French were in some confusion at the beginning of the war, hastily evacuating their smaller islands while preparing to receive enemy attacks. They sent to France for naval assistance, which was not forthcoming.[86]

The loss of St. Christopher immediately following the commencement of hostilities could have been predicted. On 14 July the English appeared with 21 sail and 2,500 troops commanded by Major General Walter Hamilton, who immediately called on the comte de Gennes to surrender after informing him that their two nations were at war. The 400 Frenchmen able to bear arms were divided between the north and south sections of the island, and a council of war advised de Gennes to surrender on the best terms available. The garrison received the honours of war; the Irish were allowed to depart unmolested with the French, and all were to be repatriated to Martinique. Unfortunately for de Gennes, he and his men had not fired a shot

---

[82] Col., B 24, ff. 34–46 "Memoire pour servir d'instructions au comte d'Esnos … ", 9 February 1701; Col., C⁸ᴬ 13, ff. 138–43 Robert to Pontchartrain, 11 July 1701 reports his arrival and ibid., ff. 190–3 same to same, 8 October 1701 reports his death. The marquis de Rosmadec was appointed to succeed D'Esnos on 4 January 1702 (see Col., B 24, f. 321). Ibid., f. 432 Pontchartrain to Machault, 28 June for his death.

[83] See Col., C⁸ᴬ 12, ff. 319–20. Guitaud's petition for appointment as governor-general 22 August 1700. Also ibid., 14, f. 52 Gabaret to Pontchartrain, 14 September 1702 announcing Guitaud's death.

[84] Col., B 24, f. 482 Pontchartrain to Robert, 25 October 1702.

[85] Jacques Petitjean-Roget, *La Gaoulé: la révolte de la Martinique en 1717* (Fort-de-France: Société d'histoire de la Martinique, 1966), 65.

[86] See Col., C⁸ᴬ, 13 f. 267–70 Commandeur de Guitaud to Pontchartrain, 29 March 1701; ibid., 14, ff. 4–6 Machault to Pontchartrain, 14 October 1702 asking for warships to be placed on station at Martinique; ibid., f. 99 Robert to Pontchartrain, 21 April 1702; ibid., ff. 165–88 same to same, announcing evacuations of Marie Galant, St. Martin, and St. Barthélémy.

in their own defence, and later he was court-martialed, attainted for trea-
son, found guilty of cowardice, and degraded of his nobility and honours.
De Gennes appealed to the king but was captured en route to France and
died soon afterward in Plymouth, England.[87] The French had their revenge
in 1706, but St. Christopher was permanently lost from France's American
possessions.

English strategy was to immediately prepare a second larger expedition
to conquer Martinique. A fleet of six warships and 10 transports carrying
4,000 men under the command of Commodore Hovenden Walker reached
Barbados in January of 1703. There, a quarter of his manpower died of
infectious disease, scurvy, or drink, and the English authorities abandoned
Martinique for Guadeloupe. On 6 March, the English fleet numbering 45
men of war, merchantmen, and other craft, and carrying 4,000 soldiers,
including colonists from Barbados, who had replaced the men lost during
the ocean crossing, arrived off Guadeloupe. Governor Charles Auger, aided
by the fiery preaching friar Jean-Baptiste Labat, did their best to organize
the island's defences, but numbers had their effect. During the next two and
a half weeks the English steadily drove in the French defences, finally taking
the fort at Basseterre.[88]

On 3 April, Nicolas de Gabaret arrived from Martinique with reinforcements and assumed command. Late in March, the new Governor-General
Charles de Machault de Bellemont reached Martinique, where he found
Intendant Robert preparing to send reinforcements under Gabaret's
command to the beleaguered islanders. He had brought with him Gabaret's
promotion to king's lieutenant of the general government of the Islands,
which meant that he was second-in-command to the governor-general.[89]

After reaching Guadeloupe, Gabaret implemented new defensive tactics,
falling back from the enemy, systematically destroying areas beforehand,
and drawing the English deeper into the island where they could be more
easily harassed while waiting for the inevitable effects of disease, drink, and
diminishing resources to do their work.[90] Planters strongly objected in view

[87] See Nellis M. Crouse, *The French Struggle for the West Indies, 1665–1713* (New York: Octagon Books, [1943] 1966), 252–5 for a brief account of the loss of St. Christopher. Louis XIV later restored de Gennes' former honours and emoluments to his widow and children.

[88] Ibid., 268–90 presents a brief account of the siege of Guadeloupe based entirely on English accounts and Jean-Baptiste Labat *Nouveau voyage aux Isles de l'Amerique* (La Haye: P. Husson, T. Johnson, P. Gosse, Jvan Duren, R. Alberts, and C. Le Vier [1724], 2: 387–443, which stresses his own primary role in the struggle.

[89] Crouse, *The French Struggle*, 286 n6 incorrectly identifies him as Jean Gabaret who died in 1697 despite the assertion to the contrary. In 1711, Nicolas de Gabaret was named Governor of Saint-Domingue.

[90] Col., C8A 15, ff. 146–7 Gabaret to Pontchartrain 24 May 1703. L. Guet, *Origines de la Martinique – Le colonel Français de Collart et la Martinique de son temps – Colonisation, sièges, révoltes et combats de 1625 à 1720,*(Vannes: Lafoyle, 1893), 234–46 contains a

of the property destruction as did the bellicose Père Labat, but in the absence of naval forces Gabaret's was a prudent strategy.[91] There is no doubt that it worked. On 15 May, the English commanders admitted defeat, withdrew their troops, and three days later sailed away.

The French surrendered their half of Saint Martin to the Dutch in July, but for nearly three years little military activity occurred in the Lesser Antilles.[92] The quality of recruits from France was terrible and the colonists were basically left on their own.[93] Privateering and illicit trade appeared to be the order of the day. Between September and December of 1702, nearly 600 slaves taken from English prizes entered Martinique.[94] Nearly a score of vessels from Martinique, Guadeloupe, and Saint-Domingue attacked enemy shipping in 1703; 30 privateers reportedly took 163 prizes the next year.[95] French privateers were trading captured goods in Spanish American ports and underselling the English.[96] Between May of 1703 and July of 1704, prizes sold at Martinique alone were worth 2.1 million livres.[97] The *Boston News Letter* of 8 May [O.S.] 1704 reported 130 odd vessels taken by the French since the beginning of the war and that 17 privateers were out,[98] but privateering is only one part of the story and perhaps has been given too much emphasis in comparison with trade.

Lack of evidence of illegal trade has seriously distorted accounts of the war. According to one historian, if data were available, illegal trade between the English mainland colonies and the French West Indies, which had become a permanent feature of colonial commerce, would probably show a marked ascent during the war.[99] The failure of French merchants to provision the colonies adequately was apparent everywhere. In the West Indies, soldiers were fed cassava or manioc flour, while in Louisiana corn mush became

detailed account of the defence of Guadeloupe based on more than Labat's somewhat self-serving one.

[91] Cf. Patrick Villiers, *Marine royale, corsaires et trafic dans l'Atlantique de Louis XIV à Louis XVI*, 2 vols. (Dunkerque: Société dunkerquois d'histoire et d'archaeologie, 1991), 1: 191.

[92] Col., C⁸ᴬ 15, ff. 30–2 Machault to Pontchartrain, 19 July 1703.

[93] Col., C⁸ᴮ 2, no. 69 Extract from Mithon to Pontchartrain, 22 December 1703.

[94] Col., C⁸ᴬ 14, ff. 247–51, 285–9, and 290–5 Robert to Pontchartrain, 25 September, 3 December and 25 December, 1702.

[95] Sir Alan Burns, *History of the British West Indies*, rev. 2nd ed. (London: Allen and Unwin, 1965), 414; also Owen, *War at Sea under Queen Anne*, 63.

[96] Ian K. Steele, *The Politics of Colonial Policy: The Board of Trade in Colonial Administration, 1696–1720*, (Oxford: Oxford University Press, 1968), 104.

[97] Petitjean-Roget, *La Gaoulé*, 46; also try Col., C⁸ᴬ 15, 425–52 Mithon to Pontchartrain, 24 October 1705.

[98] J. Franklin Jameson, ed., *Privateering and Piracy in the Colonial Period: Illustrative Documents*, reprinted (Augustus M. Kelly, [1923] 1970), 276–7.

[99] Frank Wesley Pitman, *The Development of the British West Indies, 1700–1763*, (New Haven: Yale University Press, 1917), 190.

their staple diet.[100] Only one small bark laden with bad wine reached Cayenne during the 15 months ending in February of 1709.[101] Governor Machault and Intendant Vaucresson received special authority to trade Martinique's sugar for provisions, especially salt beef, at St. Thomas.[102] Foreigners also introduced mules and slaves. The number of slaves on Martinique increased by 28.8 percent between 1702 and 1709.[103] In 1707, the governors of Martinique and Barbados agreed upon a cartel to exchange prisoners, but all acknowledged that it served chiefly to promote trade and intelligence between the two colonies.[104]

The attacks on Saint-Christopher and Nevis in 1706 had nothing to do with local privateering. They were organised from France. Late in August of 1705, Pierre Le Moyne d'Iberville, who had been recovering his health and pursuing his private interests in France since returning from Louisiana three years earlier, received 10 ships in accord with his proposal to drive the English from Carolina.[105] Pontchartrain had called regularly upon Iberville, who was still the senior commanding officer in Louisiana, for advice concerning the colony. Iberville had sought to return to Louisiana, but his deteriorating health, military duties in France, and declining naval funds dictated several postponements until the summer of 1705, when success in attracting private investors to his venture finally led Pontchartrain to support his plans.[106] The expedition appeared initially to be a response to growing English threats to Spanish Florida and to the French settlement on Mobile Bay, but by the time the ships reached the Americas, the venture had become devoid of any strategic intent.

Iberville's plan called for the force to be divided into two squadrons. The first, fitted out by the navy at Brest, was commanded by Captain Louis-Henri, comte de Chavagnac, who departed from Brest in December and reached Martinique in January of 1706. Governor-General Machault had no interest in assisting him to recruit colonists, and condemned the plan as badly arranged and predicted it would have no beneficial effect.[107] Chavagnac obtained recruits easily with the help of two senior militia officers and local notables, Jean du Buc, militia commander, and François de Collart, who had become a leading privateer. Within a week they gathered some 700

[100]   Marcel Giraud, "France and Louisiana in the Early Eighteenth Century", *Mississippi Valley Historical Review*, 36 (1950), 663–4.

[101]   Col., C^{14} 5, ff. 127–32 D'Albon to Pontchartrain, 23 February 1709.

[102]   Guy Josa, *Les Industries du sucre et du rhum* (Paris: Les Presses modernes, 1931), 87.

[103]   See Col., G^1, 470bis nos. 3 and 11.

[104]   Pitman, *The Development of the British West Indies*, 196.

[105]   Buchet, *La Lutte pour l'espace caraïbe*, 1: 222–4; Guy Frégault, *Iberville, le conquérant* (Montréal: Guérin, [1944] 1996), 371–86 discusses these plans in detail.

[106]   Giraud, *Histoire de la Louisiane*, 1: 99–100.

[107]   Col., B 25, f. 159 Pontchartrain to Machault, 2 September 1705; Col., C^{8A} 15, ff. 396–400 Machault to Pontchartrain, 14 December 1705.

colonists and buccaneers to which Machault reluctantly added four companies of regular troops. Wasting no time, Chavagnac departed for Guadaloupe where he recruited 300 more militiamen before sailing, nine days later, with his five warships, two merchantmen, and 24 brigantines manned by freebooters and 1,200 men for the landing parties. Failing to effect a landing on Nevis because of the weather, he made for St. Christopher, which he reached on 21 February.[108] The landing parties quickly went ashore. Pillage was their only aim. Chavagnac had no artillery for a siege, and the English repulsed the French attack on the fort. The French systematically burnt and pillaged the plantations to within cannon range, but upon receiving a false report that an English fleet was expected, they reembarked precipitously, taking only 600 of the best slaves, but leaving piles of boiling-house coppers and mill machinery on the beach, and returned to Martinique. One estimate placed the damage at more than 3 million livres, but the raid was not a success.[109]

The second squadron, commanded by Iberville, appeared at Martinique a few days after Chavagnac's return. Iberville had experienced many delays getting away from France and only reached the colony on 9 March.[110] Later that month, he sailed to Guadeloupe and there, with a force of 12 men of war, eight merchantmen, and 28 brigantines, and smaller craft transporting several hundred soldiers, colonists, and 1,100 freebooters, he made his plans and disposed his forces. The grandiose project of the previous summer had shrunk to an attack on Antigua and Nevis. Finding a 44-gun frigate sheltering under the former island's guns, Iberville redirected his forces toward Nevis. On 1 April, after separating his forces into three divisions, Iberville attacked in buccaneer fashion employing ruses and feints and defeated the island's militia with little difficulty. So small was the English population and so sudden and ruthless was the assault that all resistance on the island ceased on Easter Day, 4 April. During the next fortnight the French gave themselves over to pillage.[111] Slave resistance and reports of enemy ships approaching led Iberville to hasten his ransom demands. On 19 April, the English agreed

[108] Col., F³26, ff. 355–8 Mithon to Pontchartrain, 15 February 1706; Crouse, *The French Struggle for the West Indies*, 293–5.

[109] Ibid., 296–9; For another account see Marine, B⁴31, ff. 111–32 "Journal de ce qui s'est passé depuis le départ de l'escadre de la Martinique jusques à son retour de la dite isle" by comte de Chavagnac. Richard S. Dunn, *Sugar and Slaves: The Rise of the Planter Class in the English West Indies, 1624–1713* (New York: W.W. Norton, 1972), 136–9, 317 reports that English planters who claimed over 600 slaves were taken – 61 percent of them males – set damage claims at £145,000.

[110] Crouse, *The French Struggle for the West Indies*, 299–305, and Buchet, *La Lutte pour l'espace caraïbe*, 1: 223.

[111] For Iberville's own account of his actions and the terms of capitulation see Marine, B⁴, 31, ff. 138–43 "Relation depuis mon départ de la Martinique" by Iberville, dated 8 April 1706. For another copy see University of Minnesota Libraries, James Ford Bell Collection, "Relation de la Prise et Capitulation de l'isle de Nieue appartenant aux Anglois par M. d'Iberville en 1706".

to deliver 1,400 slaves to Martinique within six months and a week later Iberville returned to Martinique with nearly 3,200 slaves and other booty, including 22 merchant ships.[112] Despite conquering the entire island and blowing up the English fort, the raid was a travesty of military operations, and its repercussions were far more damaging to the French than the English. Pillage appeared to be the least of Iberville's activities. Fraud was his major aim and its consequences were serious and wholly unforeseen.

The fraud involved Iberville, his brothers, Joseph, sieur de Serigny, and Antoine, sieur de Châteauguay, their investors and outfitters, and nearly every officer in the squadron. Even before the ships reached the West Indies, Pontchartrain ordered a commission to inquire into allegations by some investors of fraudulent practices in the initial provisioning of the vessels and the embarkation of merchandise for purposes of illicit trade.[113] Deliberate obfuscation and poor recordkeeping concerning the prizes and other booty compounded the confusion. Le Moyne de Serigny commanded *Le Coventry,* which was loaded with cargo destined for Louisiana. Immediately following the French withdrawal from Nevis though, he sailed to Vera Cruz, where he exchanged a cargo of captured slaves for a staggering 400,000 pesos worth of indigo and silver.[114] Iberville dispatched the much smaller *L'Aigle* to Louisiana carrying only part of the provisions and stores destined for the isolated colony while he sailed with the main force to Saint-Domingue where he owned two plantations. There, more than 1,900 slaves were disposed of to his own profit rather than those who invested in the expedition.[115]

Iberville remained at Saint-Domingue for some time attending to his affairs. According to Charlevoix, he sailed to Le Cap, where he fitted out a 14-gun brigantine and manned it with 120 men for an attack on Jamaica. He sent Chavagnac's force back to France and dispatched his four remaining ships to Léogane to await him before sailing to Havana.[116] Perhaps he hoped to encourage the Spaniards to join in his planned attack, or perhaps he was pursuing commercial interests. We shall never know, at least not until further evidence comes to light. On 9 July, on board his flagship at Havana, Iberville died, reportedly of yellow fever. Thus ended, as abruptly as it began, the French policy of reprisals directed at the English in the Lesser Antilles. The entire enterprise had been Iberville's brain child. As a result of

---

[112] Col., C⁸ᴬ 16, ff. 153-4v Traité fait entre d'Iberville et les habitants de Nièves … ", 19 April 1706.

[113] See NAC [transcripts] MG 3I/, V⁷ , 214 for the records of the extraordinary commission.

[114] Hrodej, *L'Amiral Du Casse*, 2: 372. For a good discussion of the frauds perpetrated during the expedition see Giraud, *Histoire de la Louisiane*, 1: 104–16. *Le Coventry* was a large, 54-gun English warship of 670 tons captured in July of 1704, see Winfield, *The 50-Gun Ship*, 29–30. *L'Aigle* had less than half this capacity.

[115] NAC [transcripts], MG 3I/V7 214 p. 191.

[116] Pierre-François Xavier Charlevoix, *Histoire de l"isle espagnol ou de S. Domingue*, 2 vols. (Paris: Jacques Guerin, 1730–1), 2: 386-7.

his betrayal, Pontchartrain no longer trusted any member of the Le Moyne family. Bienville's days in Louisiana were numbered, the colony's security was ignored, and it was plunged deeper into isolation. With Iberville and his brothers no longer pursuing their private interests trading with the Spanish, other merchants became uninterested in sending ships to the colony.

Illicit trade and privateering continued in the Windward Islands, but these were simply opposite sides of the same coin of local initiatives. By 1706, privateers at Saint-Pierre made up about one-half of the adult white population. The number of cabarets and houses of ill repute and the presence of merchants who fitted out privateersmen made Saint-Pierre the best location for them to gather.[117] It possessed an open roadstead; it had no harbour. Saint-Pierre's location on the leeward side of the island allowed ships to arrive quietly at any time of the day or night and just as silently slip away pursuing their business. According to Commissary Mithon, a small number of freebooters came from the island's first families seeking to prove their valour and gain a good opinion of themselves. Others were *petit blancs* and artisans, the dissolute and indentured servants who sought escape from their harsh toil and were prepared to risk their lives at sea. The largest group of privateersmen were merchant seamen who deserted their ships, disguised themselves, changed their names, and deceived authorities despite all efforts to discourage these practices and to punish them. Seamen's registers were not maintained in the colony, which made desertion virtually impossible to halt, and the crews of merchantmen continued to provide a large pool of ready recruits for the privateers that sailed until the end of the war.

The impact of these colonial privateersmen cannot be determined with any accuracy because many prizes were carried into colonial ports by metropolitan vessels en route from France. One global estimate gives 408 prizes and ransoms carried into West Indian ports between 1695 and 1713. We can be certain that most of these occurred after 1702.[118] Though most English colonial commerce fell to privateers in the English Channel, colonial privateersmen also contributed to the sharp decline of English sugar imports between 1702 and 1707.[119] English West Indian planters and merchants computed their losses for one year at £380,000 sterling. In 1704, 27 out of a fleet of 33 ships were taken.[120] The average annual value of English sugar imports declined by 43.5 percent from the peacetime average for 1700

---

[117]   Col., C⁸ᴬ 16, ff. 109–16 Mithon to Vaucresson, 10 May 1706 quoted in Petitjean-Roget, *La Gaoulé*, 45–6. Labat, *Nouveaux voyages aux Isles*, 1: 26 gives the population of two parishes and three districts constituting Saint-Pierre as about 2,400 communicants and as many slaves and children; included in the first number are soldiers and freebooters.

[118]   Jean Delumeau, "La guerre de course française sous l'ancien régime", *Actes du colloque internationale d'histoire maritime*, typescript (San Francisco: 1975), 284.

[119]   Steele, *Politics of Colonial Policy*, 103.

[120]   Richard B. Sheridan, *Sugar and Slavery: An Economic History of the British West Indies, 1623–1775* (Baltimore: The Johns Hopkins University Press, 1974), 410.

and 1701. Wartime annual valuations fluctuated widely and surpassed the peacetime annual average only in 1710.[121] Privateers also struck hard at the vital provisions trade. In mid-July [N.S.] of 1707, the English islands were reported "almost starving for want of provisions from the continent of America, the French taking all or most of the ships that come from thence so that few or none will venture".[122]

Colonial privateers also mounted small raids on Dutch and English colonies. Spanish and French freebooters raided the outskirts of Charleston, South Carolina, in 1704 and 1706.[123] In 1708, eighteen French ships bombarded Willemstad, Curaçao, whose citizens paid a heavy ransom to avoid capture. Meanwhile, French and Spanish from Petit Goâve landed on New Providence in the Bahamas, surprised the fort, took the governor prisoner, burnt the town of Nassau, and carried off half the slaves. In October, the French returned alone and caught most of those who had fled to the woods during the first visit, so the English abandoned the island.[124] The same month, three heavily armed Martinican privateers attacked the Dutch settlement of Essequibo (in present-day Guyana). Though the fort did not surrender, the French departed only after receiving a ransom worth 50,000 guilders consisting principally of 163 slaves. The following year, two more privateers again attacked and damaged the remaining plantations, carrying off more slaves and boiling coppers, nearly wiping out the settlement. As a result 480 more slaves were introduced into Martinique.[125] Other privateers struck St. Eustatius, destroying all the buildings on the island and carrying off 264 slaves.[126] The French attacked Montserrat four times: in 1707, December 1708, June 1710, and June 1711. Individual planters suffered serious losses, but overall damage was minor.[127] Costs were sometimes heavy, as in 1711 when a colonial privateer lost 70 to 80 men and gained only 50 to 60 slaves in booty.[128] Early the following year at least 11 vessels, including a slaver and the King's ship *La Loire*, were lost to English frigates stationed at Antigua and Barbados.[129] Nevertheless, by the war's end French privateers and

---

[121]   Crowhurst, *The Defense of British Trade*, 177–8.

[122]   Great Britain, Board of Trade, *Journal of the Commissioners for Trade and Plantations*, Vol. 1, *from April, 1704 to February, 1708/09* (London: HMSO, 1920), 398.

[123]   Ian K. Steele, *Warpaths: Invasions of North America*, (New York: Oxford University Press, 1994), 155.

[124]   Postma, *The Dutch in the Atlantic Slave Trade*, 50; and Captain Thomas Southey, *Chronological History of the West Indies*, 3 vols., reprint (London: Frank Cass, [1827] 1968), 2: 202.

[125]   Col., C⁸ᴬ 17, f. 89v Vaucresson to Pontchartrain, 18 April 1709.

[126]   Postma, *The Dutch in the Atlantic Slave Trade*, 190–1, 198.

[127]   Donald H. Akenson, *If the Irish Ruled the World: Montserrat, 1630–1730* (Kingston and Montreal: McGill-Queen's University Press, 1997), 121, 139–40.

[128]   Lucien-René Abénon, *La Guadeloupe de 1671 à 1759, Étude politique, économique et sociale*, 2 vols., (Paris: L'Harmattan, 1987), 1: 163n113.

[129]   Col., C⁸ᴬ 18, ff. 405–6 Vaucresson to Pontchartrain, 9 March 1712.

freebooters had become major suppliers of foodstuffs. Without them, wrote Lieutenant Colonel de Buc of Martinique, "we would die of hunger".[130] Sometimes they brought in more than food. In 1709, the privately fitted out frigate, *La Valeur*, 36 guns, met and captured HMS *Adventure*, 44 guns, off Martinique.[131] Three years later, a local privateer took a Portuguese East Indiaman laden with silks and other rich textiles, which along with packets of diamonds and gold dust were estimated to be worth 1,000,000 livres.[132]

Little in the way of hostilities occurred at either Saint-Domingue or Louisiana. The war opened with a successful attack on several ships at Léogane in August of 1702, during which Admiral Benbow's ships ran the king's flûte *La Gironde* aground and burnt it, but little beyond the usual interisland privateering followed.[133] In 1707, the new governor, the comte de Choiseul-Beaupré, tried to revive buccaneering and direct it against the English in order to increase the colony's security, but his offer of amnesty to buccaneers who returned from Spanish America proved ineffective.[134] Intermittent hostilities continued. In May of 1711, *La Thétis*, frigate, 42 guns, fell victim to two English warships while transporting the governor of Saint-Domingue to Havana. Governor de Choiseul-Beaupréand several others were killed during the action. The following month, corsairs carried several prizes laden with flour, salt beef, and 700 to 800 slaves into Petit Goâve,[135] but most colonists appeared more interested in trade and economic development. Piracy and freebooting were more closely related to the poverty of the participants than to economic conditions, which improved during the war.

Isolation kept Louisiana out of the war. Scarcity of provisions was the most pressing problem. As the colony's leaders developed trade connections with Spanish officials at Vera Cruz, Havana, and Pensacola, uncertainty rapidly increased. Pontchartrain had little choice but to turn to private enterprise to support the colony. In the wake of Iberville's betrayal, Pontchartrain considered confiding the colony to a private company and asked his officials at Saint-Malo and La Rochelle to explore merchants' willingness to invest in colonies if they were conceded to companies of their own making. He also investigated giving free passports to merchants willing to transport provisions and stores to Louisiana or to fit out a warship to the colony,[136] but several proposals lacked sufficient capital. The vision of quick and certain

---

130 Quoted in Petitjean-Roget, *La Gaoulé*, 47.
131 Bourne, *Queen Anne's Navy in the West Indies*, 100.
132 Petitjean-Roget, *La Gaoulé*, 47.
133 Col., C⁸ᴬ 14, f. 296 Procès verbal établi par Jean Marie, 12 August 1702.
134 Charlevoix, *Histoire de l'isle espagnole ou de S. Domingue*, 2: 387.
135 Col., C⁹ᴮ 2 "Extrait de M. de Charite", 23 June 1711.
136 Giraud, *Histoire de la Louisiane*, 1: 101, 121, 130–54; Gwendolyn Midlow Hall, *Africans in Colonial Louisiana: The Development of Afro-Creole Culture in the Eighteenth Century* (Baton Rouge and London: Louisiana State University Press, 1992), 12–13 presents a brief, accurate, unflattering portrait of the Le Moyne brothers' activities.

profits was so absent as to discourage all but the richest investors or those who saw support as a means to another goal. Offers were too self-interested or their authors too discredited. At La Rochelle the navy's growing inability to pay its bills discouraged more knowledgeable investors.[137] Louisiana survived largely owing to the continuing support from Spanish authorities at Vera Cruz, Havana, and Pensacola. Eventually, Pontchartrain turned to one of the Crown's chief financiers with overseas interests, but nearly five years passed before Louisiana was ceded to Antoine Crozat in 1712.

After reviewing the evidence, it seems quite wrong to say the islands suffered more than usual from attacks by the English navy or by English colonial privateers. Trade was the crucially overlooked factor. Economic development continued apace. Crossravaging by enemy raiders did not seriously damage the French, English, or Dutch colonies. During the decade between 1701 and 1711, the number of sugar works on Martinique grew by 30 percent (to 1709) and increased by more than 50 percent on Guadeloupe.[138] The 50 sugar works on Saint-Domingue in 1702 had grown more than one and a half times to 138 by 1713.[139] As Richard S. Dunn points out, despite all the raids and plundering, English and French planters in the eastern Caribbean prospered during the war.[140] By 1713, Saint-Domingue's population surpassed Martinique's. The War of the Spanish Succession, by breaking the stifling forces of regulation and control and introducing freer trade than ever before witnessed, may have been the most important stimulus to economic growth in France's colonial history.

8.4 *LA COURSE ROYALE* REAPPEARS IN THE AMERICAS

By 1707 it was clear to all in the government that the navy was approaching bankruptcy. The government was increasingly living hand to mouth. Samuel Bernard, the Protestant court banker whose international credit alone continued to support it, was encountering difficulties. Two years later, not even he, backed by the resources of other leading financiers in the kingdom, could continue. His declaration of bankruptcy had serious repercussions throughout France and abroad.[141] The financial resources of the state for the years 1710–13 were so encumbered that the entire floating debt was transformed into annuities on the Hotel de Ville of Paris.[142] In the middle of 1710,

---

[137]   Giraud, *Histoire de la Louisiane*, 1: 122, 124–5.

[138]   Based on Col., G¹, 470bis, no.11; 497, no. 6; and 498, nos. 59 and 63bis.

[139]   Frostin, "Les Pontchartrain et la pénétration", 309 n. 5; and Col., G¹, 509, no. 12.

[140]   Dunn, *Sugar and Slaves*, 147.

[141]   Dessert, *Argent, pouvoir et société*, 165–7, 192–7, and 522; also Bromley, "Duguay-Trouin: The Financial Background", in *Corsairs and Navies*, 305.

[142]   Paul Harsin, "La finance et l'Etat jusqu'au système de Law", in Braudel and Labrousse, dirs. *Histoire économique et sociale de la France*, Tome 2, *Des derniers temps de l'âge*

Pontchartrain swore that the treasurers-general of the marine had no funds and were unable to acquit the navy's most pressing expenses. He advised creditors to invest the sums owed them into some of the navy's newly created venal offices![143] Controller-General Nicolas Desmaretz did nothing to aid Pontchartrain.[144] The huge, growing mass of uncontrollable naval debt reached a critical threshold early in 1711, and in February a royal edict transformed the debt into perpetual annuities on the General Receipts paying 5 percent.[145]

Pontchartrain, who had begun granting warships to entrepreneurs in return for carrying recruits, arms, munitions, and provisions in support of colonial garrisons now began lending the king's ships in greater numbers than ever before. The subsequent expeditions harken back to Iberville's raid of 1706, but they differ from those of the previous war, when court aristocrats and naval officials ventured a few thousand livres on a patriotic flutter, in being financed by practical businessmen in the seaports. Nevertheless, the new expeditions represented a reversion to royal privateering (*la course royale*) when the primary target had been the weakest enemy overseas. While Spain had been the target during the 1690s, the new enemy was Portugal, whose possessions in the Americas were attracting French notice by shipping large quantities of gold to Europe.[146]

Between 1703 and 1709, French privateers attacked Portuguese shipping wherever they found it. They burnt the town of Benguela in West Africa in 1705, sacked the island of Principé in the Gulf of Guinea the following year, and visited the same destruction on Sao Tomé in 1709,[147] but the principal French assaults were launched against the source of the gold, Brazil. Pontchartrain advised the chevalier Desaugiers to attack Rio de Janeiro if his 1706 ambush of Dutch East Indiamen off Cape of Good Hope failed.[148]

The first of these Brazilian expeditions, which occurred in 1710, involved only a few ships and a commander of low rank and minor reputation. Jean-Baptiste Duclerc was a colonist, the son of a former major at Guadeloupe. He held a captaincy in the colonial infantry on that island before being appointed

seigneurial aux préludes de l'âge industriel (Paris: Presses universitaires de France, 1970), 2: 272.

[143] Henri Legohérel, *Les Tresoriers-généraux de la marine, 1517–1788* (Paris: Éditions Cujas, 1965), 189; also Dessert, *Argent, pouvoir et société*, 187.

[144] On Desmaretz's relations with Pontchartrain see Meyer, *Colbert*, 346; also Thomas Schaeper, *The French Council of Commerce, 1700–1715: A Study in Mercantilism After Colbert* (Columbus: Ohio State University Press, 1983), 226.

[145] Legohérel, *Les Trésoriers-généraux de la marine*, 257.

[146] See Morineau, *Incroyables gazettes et fabuleux métaux*, 128, 135 for a record of wartime gold shipments from Rio, Bahia, Pernambuco, and estimated values.

[147] C. R. Boxer, *The Golden Age of Brazil 1695–1750: Growing Pains of a Colonial Society* (Berkeley: University of California Press, 1969), 85–7; Alain Roman, *Saint-Malo au temps des négriers*, (Paris: Karthala, 2001), 275.

[148] Bromley, "Duguay-Trouin: The Financial Backgound", 313.

major at Petit Goâve in 1701. During the war, he became a privateer-outfitter, obtaining command of the naval transport *La Gaillarde* in 1705 and receiving *La Valeur*, frigate, and 36-guns three years later. The next year, during a successful cruise in the West Indies, he captured HMS *Adventure*, which led to his promotion to junior naval grade and command of a squadron destined to attack Rio de Janeiro.[149]

Duclerc was promoted *capitaine de frégate* shortly before his departure from France with a force of six ships of the line, several smaller craft, and 800 soldiers, all privately fitted out and paid for by the Chastelain-de Neuville Company of Brest and La Rochelle.[150] He appeared off Rio on 16 August 1709, but failed to force the harbour entrance. A month-long delay allowed the Portuguese plenty of time to prepare their defences, and the French landing and assault failed. Hundreds of French sailors and soldiers, including Captain Duclerc, were taken prisoner. Later Duclerc was murdered. It was, concluded La Roncière, "a mad escapade".[151]

A far more ambitious attack had been incubating, at least since 1708, when the great Malouin privateer leader René Duguay-Trouin failed at the Azores by just a few days to intercept the Brazil fleet carrying gold to Lisbon.[152] In 1710, he proposed to intercept the fleet at its point of departure in Rio. Captain Duclerc's murder provided the pretext, if not the motive, for the expedition.[153] Duguay-Trouin persuaded a consortium to create a company with a capital of 700,000 livres, Shares each worth 50,000 livres were subscribed largely by Malouin shippers, including Duguay-Trouin and four of his relatives. Two other investors were the comte de Toulouse, Admiral of France, who put up 75,000 livres, and Jean Nicolas, a Parisian banker and former associate of Samuel Bernard.[154] Despite some reluctance, Pontchartrain fell in with the plan, supporting it even though Duguay-Trouin selected the officers commanding the ships. Pontchartrain finally provided seven sail

---

[149] Neuville, *Etat sommaire*, 167 n. 4; Taillemite, *Inventaire analytique . . . Série B*, 284; also Col., B 18, ff. 134, 309; B 21, ff. 194, 713; B 26, f. 58; B 28, ff. 680, 695; B 31, ff. 8–9, 11, 474.

[150] J. F. Bosher, "Partners of the French Navy in Supplying Canada, 1701–1713", in *Business and Religion in the Age of New France, 1600–1760, Twenty-Two Studies* (Toronto: Canadian Scholar's Press, 1994), 25–6. mistakenly thought the squadron was bound for Canada, but correctly identified the chief outfitter, Pierre Mirleau de Neuville, *receveur des tailles et octrois* of La Rochelle.

[151] La Roncière, *Histoire de la marine française*, 6: 527–30; and Boxer, *The Golden Age of Brazil*, 87–91.

[152] René Duguay-Trouin, *Mémoires de Duguay-Trouin*, éd. Philippe Clouet (Paris: France-Empire, 1991), 120.

[153] Though frequently seen as a revenge raid, Duguay-Trouin himself explained the raid as such (see *Mémoires*, 128), Duclerc's murder occurred in March of 1711, long after the expedition had been decided upon; see François Bluche, *Louis XIV*, trans. by Mark Greenglass (Oxford: Basil Blackwell, 1990), 560–1.

[154] Bromley, "Duguay-Trouin; Financial Background", 310–15.

of the line, from 58 to 74 guns, seven frigates, three lesser warships, and 5,400 men, including more than 2,200 soldiers, while surrendering any share in the prizes owing to the consortium's need to supply the funds to fit out the king's ships in the arsenals.[155]

Although the Portuguese were forewarned, the French attack on Rio in mid-September of 1711 went off without a hitch, and though resolution, bravery, and luck were with the attackers, the Portuguese leaders, who failed to defend the heavily fortified city, were chiefly responsible for Duguay-Trouin's victory.[156] The destruction was terrible, and the booty enormous. Seven Portuguese warships and about 60 merchantmen were destroyed and Rio was thoroughly plundered. The French obtained a ransom of 610,000 cruzados in gold dust, bar, and coin, 1,484 chests of sugar, and 200 head of cattle. In addition, Duguay-Trouin "permitted" merchants and colonists to buy back from the French such of their own ships and property as they could afford.[157] Duguay-Trouin loaded the European manufactures, chiefly textiles, seized at Rio into two ships and dispatched them around Cape Horn to Peru, where they were sold for close to three million livres.[158] Finally, in mid-November, after taking on board about 360 survivors from Duclerc's expedition, Duguay-Trouin's ships departed. They reached Brest about 12 weeks later.

Though the damage to Rio was great – Duguay-Trouin claimed it amount-ed to 20 million livres – the loss of treasure-laden ships, including the 74-gun *Le Magnamine* and 60-gun *La Fidèle*, during the return voyage struck a serious blow against the financial success of the raid.[159] Nevertheless, returns from the two ships sent to the South Sea, along with the remaining gold, sugar, and other booty paid for the expenses of the armament and gave a 92-percent return to the shareholders.[160] It is doubtful whether the attack influenced Portugal to sign a suspension of arms. England and France signed one in late July of 1712, and the Franco-Portuguese armistice was signed

---

[155] Duguay-Trouin, *Mémoires*, 130–3, 217–26; Bromley, "Duguay-Trouin: The financial background", 316; La Roncière, *Histoire de la marine française*, 6: 530–40; Bluche, *Louis XIV*, 564; and Etienne Taillemite, *Histoire ignorée de la marine française* (Paris: Perrin, 1988), 126–8.

[156] See Duguay-Trouin, *Mémoires*, 134–64 for his own account of the campaign; also La Roncière, *Histoire de la marine française*, 6: 530–40 for a brief account; and Boxer, *The Golden Age of Brazil*, 96–100 for a view from the Portuguese side of the hill.

[157] Duguay-Trouin, *Mémoires*, 152–5; see also Michel Vergé-Franceschi, "Duguay-Trouin (1673–1736); un corsaire, un officier général, un myth", *Revue historique*, no. 598, (avril-juin 1996), 347–8.

[158] See Marine, B⁴ 36, ff. 76–81 for lading lists of booty taken into the French ships.

[159] Ibid., ff. 45–8 for a copy of the printed *Relation de la prise de Rio de Janeiro* (7 pages) for the damage claim.

[160] Duguay-Truin, *Mémoires*, 162–3; and Bromley, "Duguay-Trouin: The Financial Background," 317–20 gives a fuller evaluation.

four months later.[161] Not even another French assault on Portugal's overseas possessions appeared to have much effect, though during the greatest French raid of the war the French seized the island of Santiago in the Cape Verde archipelago and destroyed the island's fortress, houses, and other property evaluated at 4.5 million livres just for starters.

Like Duguay-Trouin, Jacques Cassard had never before left European waters. His appearance overseas may have reflected the improving security of Allied maritime trade, but the growing presence of Portuguese gold also drew him westward. An experienced Nantes sea captain when war broke out, Cassard spent the first six years capturing prizes in the English Channel, where he earned a reputation as an audacious leader. A royal commission in the king's navy and Pontchartrain's protection quickly followed. In 1709, famine stalked the land, and in the south grain imports from abroad were required to relieve the distress. Pontchartrain sent Cassard to the Mediterranean with a special mission, and during the next two years he attacked English privateers and escorted grain ships from North Africa to Toulon. His success earned him further promotion, and he continued sailing on similar missions, escorting two large convoys from Turkey and fighting a large provisions convoy into Pensacola, Spain, to relieve the French army.[162]

Where the idea for his overseas expedition originated is unclear, but Pontchartrain cannot be ruled out. Marseilles merchants closely connected to Saint-Malo were probably behind the contract that Cassard signed with naval authorities in December 1711 for six warships, including three, from 56 to 66 guns, to which he joined two armed merchantmen to make war for eight months. The arrangement was similar to those signed between Pontchartrain and Iberville, Duclerc, and Duguay-Trouin. Cassard and five Marseilles merchants assumed all the fitting out costs for the eight ships. Cassard himself reportedly invested more than 300,000 livres in the expedition.[163]

In February, unknown to the merchant investors, Pontchartrain issued secret instructions to Cassard, directing him to exact reprisals on the overseas colonies of the king's enemies. French diplomats were already negotiating with the Allies at Utrecht. French colonies were clearly identified as pawns to be sacrificed to strengthen France's position in Europe.[164] However, in what appeared to be a reversion to Louis XIV's violence and terror in the Spanish Netherlands 30 years before, Cassard was "to blow up with mines, works and fortifications, houses, magazines, and all other buildings without exception; he was to burn all sugar cane and other field crops; and carry out

[161] Both Bluche, *Louis XIV*, 568; and Taillemite, *Histoire ignorée*, 129.
[162] Taillemite, *L'Histoire ignorée de la marine française*, 129–31.
[163] La Roncière, *Histoire de la marine française*, 6: 546.
[164] Savelle, *Origins of American Diplomacy*, 136–8.

generally all practicable damages *in the lands we seek to devastate*".[165] Cassard sailed first to the Cape Verde Islands in May, where he and his men burst onto the island of Santiago like a thunder clap. After following his instructions by blowing up Fort La Praya, burning the town, and destroying all that he could, he sailed away to the West Indies.[166] Upon reaching Martinique in July, Cassard approached three senior officers of the colonial militia, all of them influential men: Colonel François de Collart and lieutenant-colonels Jean du Buc and Louis du Prey, with a request that they each furnish 600 men, promising in return a share of the booty. They were also included in the council of war that settled on attacking Antigua. Within three days the colonial leaders recruited 1,500 men.[167]

Cassard's ships along with local vessels arrived off Antigua on 16 July, but strong winds prevented the French from landing, and their forces anchored instead off the coast of Montserrat, where the sudden attack by some 3,500 men quickly put him in possession of the island. Thereafter, the French gave themselves over to 12 days of looting. According to one report, they carried off between 1,200 and 1,400 slaves, boiling coppers, and stills.[168] The raid represented a major disaster for the islanders. The loss of slaves alone represented roughly one-third of the island's black population.[169] An English estimate placed the total value of these losses at £180,000. The appearance of English ships off Montserrat's chief town led the French to withdraw to Guadeloupe where Cassard shared the booty with the colonial privateers.[170] Afterward, he refitted his ships in preparation to attack Dutch colonies.

Two of Cassard's ships, which had earlier appeared at the mouth of the Surinam River, were repulsed in July, but when he arrived within sight of Paramaribo in October with eight warships, a large number of smaller craft, and 1,100 men, there was no stopping him.[171] Cassard sailed up river, passed the settlement, and created havoc among the undefended plantations before returning to negotiate with the Dutch governor. After some stalling, the Dutch paid an enormous ransom worth nearly three-quarters of a million florins or guilders, including cash, bills of exchange, sugar, and slaves,

---

[165] Italics added; quoted in Guet, *Origines de la Martinique*, 277; also Taillemite, *L'Histoire ignorée*, 131.

[166] La Roncière, *Histoire de la marine française*, 6: 541–2; Carrière, *Negociants marseilleais*, 1: 93.

[167] Guet, *Origines de la Martinique*, 274–97 gives a full account; Crouse, *The French Struggle for the West Indies*, 307.

[168] CSP. CS, 1712–1714, nos. 8, 23, 33 and ibid., 1714–1715, 2; also La Roncière, *Histoire de la marine française*, 6: 542–3.

[169] Akenson, *If the Irish Ran the World*, 140.

[170] Crouse, *The French Struggle for the West Indies*, 306–8.

[171] Based on La Roncière, *Histoire de la marine française*, 6: 543; and Cornelius Ch. Goslinga, *A Short History of the Netherlands Antilles* (The Hague: Martinus Nijoff, 1979), 98.

coppers, and provisions. The 750 slaves were valued at 262,500 guilders.[172] Cassard also besieged the settlement of Berbice and ransomed it for a sum of 300,000 guilders in sugar and slaves; Essequibo, attacked twice before in 1708 and 1709, paid 50,000 guilders to keep the French from again occupying the port and ruining the plantations.[173] Cassard appeared to pursue his own and his investors' interests rather than Pontchartrain's profitless, bloody-minded reprisals.

Cassard returned to Martinique in January of 1713 and recruited six boats manned by volunteers. Three more boats similarly manned by colonists joined from Guadeloupe, and before the month's end, Cassard sailed for St. Eustatius. After quickly obtaining the island's surrender, however, he discovered that it had not recovered from an earlier French raid and he was forced to accept a miserable 3,400 pieces of eight worth about 13,500 livres.[174] The ransom, including 67 chickens and 23 turkeys, was so small that the raid might better be characterised as petty larceny.[175] Neither discouraged nor deterred and joined by men from Martinique and Guadeloupe, Cassard sailed for Curaçao. There his luck ran out.[176] He failed to take his objective. His flagship was lost on a shoal offshore, Cassard was wounded, and his squadron and men were further reduced in numbers. The Dutch refused his demands for a large ransom. After a series of meetings, chiefly given over to haggling, both parties agreed that 115,000 pesos sufficiently massaged Cassard's dignity to permit him to depart.[177]

Cassard carried out perhaps the single most destructive raid against the king's enemies in the entire history of the French navy, striking hard at the colonial possessions of Portuguese, English, and Dutch enemies and inflicting losses estimated at more than 30 million livres, but the sale of booty, amounting to less than 2.3 million livres, failed to cover the expedition's

---

172   Marine, B⁴ 36, f. 194 Compte general, December 1712; and ibid., f. 195 convention, 27 October 1712. La Roncière, *Histoire de la marine française*, 6: 543 gives half a million *écus*. According to Postma, *Dutch in the Atlantic*, 182, 193, 40 percent of the ransom was paid immediately in sugar and slaves and the remainder, 181,000 guilders, in bills of exchange drawn on the Dutch absentee landlords, were protested. The family offered instead to turn the whole settlement over to the French. After two years of negotiations, four Amsterdam merchants agreed to pay 108,000 guilders in return for control of the settlement.

173   Berbice and Essequibo are in present-day Guyana, not Surinam.

174   Guet, *Origines de la Martinique*,281–3; La Roncière, *Histoire de la marine française*, 6: 544; and Goslinga, *A Short History of the Netherlands Antilles*, 82.

175   Marine, B⁴ 36, Articles of capitulation, 25 January 1713.

176   Marine, B⁴ 36, f. 294 "Liste des bastimens commandez par les habitants de la Martinique et Guadeloupe qui sont joints à l'Escadre du Roy pour l'expedition de Corossol", 26 January 1713.

177   Ibid., ff. 239–43 "Relation de la desente à l'isle de Curassol", 5 March 1713; La Roncière, *Histoire de la marine française*, 6: 544; and Goslinga, *A Short History of the Netherlands Antilles*, 61–2.

expenses. Cassard's Marseilles backers, who had viewed the enterprise in commercial terms, turned on him. Cassard lost his entire investment. Shortly afterward, he also lost his protector, Pontchartrain. Rejected by the navy's officer corps, stung by the idea that he was responsible for the losses of others, and proud of his word, the fighting bourgeois sea captain gradually lost his sanity, spending his days in a lunatic's padded cell and later shut up in the Chateau of Ham.[178]

The importance of these three privateering raids from Europe does not lie in the damage they caused, but in what they reveal about the navy's collapse and its growing irrelevance to the defence of French colonies. Well before the war but increasingly after 1705, when Iberville's expedition was being planned, the navy fell under the influence of wealthy entrepreneurs and dashing privateering captains who used the king's ships and sailors to pursue their private interests. Well before 1712, the navy was unable to fit out a single warship to sail to the Americas, and the colony of Louisiana had to be handed over to a financier in order that it might survive. It remains to be seen how these same conditions worked themselves out in North America.

8.5 NORTHERN COLONIES ABANDONED

Conditions in Canada changed considerably during the decade before the outbreak of hostilities. With the decline of the navy already apparent, Governor-General Vaudreuil sought to preserve Iroquois neutrality when he acceded to office in the spring of 1703. Later, he acknowledged that the Five Nations rather than New York were the major threat to New France's security.[179] For Vaudreuil, Iroquois neutrality effectively cancelled the superior demographic weight of New York and, by threatening to throw the full force of Canadian strength against the Five Nations should they ally themselves with Albany, he effectively preserved the peace in the crucial central theatre of operations. Fortunately, the Iroquois also actively pursued the same policy of remaining neutral in the face of a war between whites.[180]

The ruinous state of the Canadian fur trade also aided peace in the central region of New France. Canadians increasingly smuggled beaver pelts

[178] La Roncière, *Histoire de la marine française*, 6: 546 n. 3; Carrière, *Négociants marseillais*, 1: 93; and Taillemite, *L'Histoire ignorée de la marine francaise*, 132–3.

[179] Wm. J. Eccles, *The Canadian Frontier, 1534–1760*, rev. ed. (Albuquerque: University of New Mexico Press, [1969] 1983), 133. Much that follows is indebted to Dale Miquelon, *New France, 1701–1744: "A Supplement to Europe"* (Toronto: McClelland & Stewart, 1987), 33–48; see also Yves Zoltvany, *Philippe de Rigaud de Vaudreuil, Governor of New France, 1703–1725* (Toronto: McClelland & Stewart, 1974), 33–8, 46.

[180] Francis Jennings, *Ambiguous Iroquois Empire: The Covenant Chain Confederation of Indian Tribes with English Colonies from its beginnings to the Lancaster Treaty of 1744*, (New York: W.W. Norton, 1984), 208–13.

to English merchants at Albany via the domiciled Iroquois at Montreal and naturally sought to preserve conditions that encouraged the flow of furs from the western Indians.[181] This behaviour admittedly weakened French influence among the Indians in the far west, and the major challenge during the war was its reestablishment.

In 1700, Pontchartrain's solution, after listening to one of his proteges, Antoine Laumet, better known as Lamothe Cadillac, was to authorise the establishment of a new French settlement at Detroit about 1,000 kilometres west of Montreal and situated between the upper and lower Great Lakes. The plan was for the new settlement to attract all the allied Indian nations to settle nearby. This, Cadillac persuaded Pontchartrain, would intimidate the Iroquois and forestall Anglo-American westward expansion. Pontchartrain's views concerning the establishment of Louisiana, which was intended to forestall Carolina traders from gaining access to the North American interior, may have influenced his decision.[182]

Over the objections of the governor and intendant, the project went ahead during the war, but the new settlement accomplished neither of Pontchartrain's objectives. It undermined the French position among the western Indians in the interior, and the Iroquois began to question the need to maintain their neutrality with the French. Pontchartrain refused to acknowledge that Detroit was a mistake or to order that it be abandoned and the post at Michilimackinac, 400 kilometres northwest, be restored. Vaudreuil allowed traders to operate there and supported renegade *coureurs de bois* who asserted a French presence elsewhere in the west.[183] The success of this local policy, however, owed as much to New York's nonaggression as to Governor Vaudreuil's adroit political maneuvering among the tribes.

The war had an immediate impact on the precarious maritime carrying trade to Canada. Many French merchants withdrew owing to the hostilities or to reinvest in privateering or to explore opportunities in the newly opened regions of Spanish America and in the growing economy of Saint-Domingue. Trade to Canada and other northern colonies virtually ceased. The capture of the flûte *La Seine* bound for New France in August of 1704 resulted in losses of munitions and provisions worth an estimated 1.3 million livres as well as military officers and priests, including the bishop of Quebec, who were captured.[184] As early as 1705, the treasurer at Rochefort, acting on the orders of the treasurer-general of the marine, refused to accept bills of

---

181   Thomas E. Norton, *The Fur Trade in Colonial New York, 1686–1776* (Madison: University of Wisconsin Press, 1974), 128–35; Zoltvany, *Philippe de Rigaud de Vaudreuil*, 37.

182   Zoltvany, "Laumet, Antoine", *DCB*, 2: 353.

183   Zoltvany, *Philippe de Rigaud de Vaudreuil*, 38, 56, 60.

184   *RAPQ*, 1938–39, 43 Pontchartrain to Vaudreuil, 3 September 1704. The naval storeship, *La Seine*, 36 guns, was a substantial vessel, for she was surveyed, taken into the English navy, and rated and manned as a 54-gun ship, see Winfield, *The 50-Gun Ship*, 32–3.

exchange drawn on Quebec. Few ships at all sailed to Canada.[185] In 1707 and 1708, the king's ship that sailed annually to the colony was the only vessel that returned directly to France, making it terribly difficult for hard-pressed merchants to acquire sufficient trade goods for subsequent years.[186] Economic conditions in New France brought about by the collapse of the fur trade, the government's financial difficulties, and new commercial opportunities in the West Indies and elsewhere relegated Canada to a stagnant backwater in which few were interested. Indeed, before the war was over colonial merchants at Quebec had initiated commercial ventures to Acadia, Newfoundland, Martinique, and even Europe in a remarkable display of local initiative in response to virtual abandonment by France.

The situation at Newfoundland was equally bad. Lack of naval protection immediately impacted the fishery. The number and tonnage of Malouin ships departing for Newfoundland immediately declined to less than 30 percent of the average for the five years between 1698 and 1702 and remained below that level during the remainder of the war.[187] More than 150 French fishing ships, compared with 88 merchantmen in the West Indies trade, were carried as prizes into England during the war to which must be added those taken into English colonial prize courts, captured by the Dutch, or both. Such declines and losses coincide loosely with the claim of the Council of Commerce in 1709 that 250 fishing vessels sailed annually in peacetime, but only 120 in wartime.[188] Nevertheless, the claims of some historians that French fishing expeditions halted during the war are wrong.[189] Indeed, the war may have damaged the English fishery more than the French.[190]

The English attacked the French residential fishery in 1701 before war was declared, destroying fishing vessels in Trepassey Bay and seizing a small fort on Saint-Pierre Island. In April of 1703, Rear Admiral John Graydon, on his way home from the West Indies, attacked Placentia with 16 ships but to no effect. During the summer, munitions arrived from Bayonne, and the French attacked Ferryland.[191] In August, two French warships, *Le Juste*,

[185] John S. Bromley, "Le commerce de la France de l'ouest et la guerre maritime, (1702–1713)" in *Corsaires and Navies*, 404.

[186] *RAPQ*, 1939–40, 402, 463 Vaudreuil and Raudot to Pontchartrain, 15 November 1707 and 14 November 1708.

[187] Delumeau, *Le Mouvement de port de Saint-Malo*, 273.

[188] Bromley, "Le commerce de la France de l'ouest", 403.

[189] E.g., Crowhurst, *The Defence of British Trade*, 17; La Morandière, *Histoire de la pêche français de la morue*, 1: 498–501 shows annual catches of 71,200 and 123,000 quintals in 1703 and 1704, respectively, and that 52 and 45 ships visited Placentia in 1706 and 1707. Cf. Steele, *The English Atlantic*, Table 5.1, 302.

[190] In 1704 the French captured the entire English fishing fleet with 68,000 quintals, see BL, Egerton. Mss. 921, 4v.

[191] BN, Clairambault, 869, f. 479 Estat des munitions chargées ... pour Plaisance, 16 May 1703; ibid., ff. 481–4 and Col., C11C 4, ff. 6–9 "Journal fait par moi, Amarition, lieutenant d'un detachement de Fort Louis de Plaisance [n.d.]".

66 guns, and *Le Hazardeux,* 50 guns, privately fitted out by Beaubriand-Levesque, arrived to aid the French defence during English preparations for a second attack. Their appearance forced the enemy to withdraw to St. John's. Governor Subercase did not think the time was ripe for an attack on English settlements.[192] Beaubriand had provisioned Placentia during the final year of the previous war, but this appeared to be his last involvement with Newfoundland.[193] Thereafter, colonists from Canada took an increasing part in defending the fishing port and attacking the English. Colonial ships sailed regularly from Quebec with detachments of soldiers, militia, and Indians as well as materials for use in attack as well as defence.[194] At Placentia, these local vessels found transocean cargoes off-loaded by ship captains from France seeking to avoid the long treacherous voyage up the St. Lawrence River. Like other northern colonies, Newfoundland was left on its own, and also like them its defence was exceptionally vigorous.

Canada's security on the eastern seaboard was seriously at risk. Acadia remained as defenceless as during the previous war and, like Newfoundland, soon found itself abandoned by France. Governor-General Vaudreuil incorporated both colonies into his concerns for Canada's defence.[195] He really had no option but to renew earlier policies of exploiting Abenaki grievances against the incursions of New England settlers, disrupting their negotiations with Massachusetts's representatives, and promoting border raids by distributing gifts and appealing to the natives to join Canadian war parties to attack new, expanding settlements. All of the horrors of "the little war" were once again visited on near helpless settlers. In August of 1703, Lieutenant Alexandre Leneuf de Beaubassin led a small detachment of French, Mission Indians, and 500 Abenaki into New England, laying waste along a 50-mile line from Wells to Casco, killing and capturing more than 160 persons.[196] Sporadic attacks continued during the autumn, and in March of 1704, Jean-Baptiste Hertel de Rouville and 50 Canadians, Iroquois from Kanawake, and 200 Abenaki attacked Deerfield, Massachusetts. The raid was in response to requests for support from both the governor of Acadia and the Abenaki who had been recently attacked. Fifty-four settlers were killed and 120 taken prisoner. Later the same year, Rouville led another

192 La Morandière, *Histoire de la pêche française de la morue,* 1: 491–3.

193 Col., B 24, ff. 332, 345 Pontchartrain to Beaubriand-Levesque, 11 and 25 January 1702.

194 *RAPQ,* 1938–39, 20, 24, 57, 96–7 Vaudreuil and Beauharnois to Pontchartrain, 15 November 1703, 17 November 1704, and Vaudreuil to Pontchartrain 3 April 1704 and 19 October 1705.

195 See also James Pritchard, "Canada and the Defense of Newfoundland During the War of the Spanish Succession, 1702–1713" in *Canadian Military History Since the 17th Century.* ed., Yves Tremblay (Ottawa: Department of National Defense, 2001), 49–57.

196 K. M. Morrison, *The Embattled Northeast: The Elusive Ideal of Alliance in Abenaki-Euroamerican Relations* (Berkeley: University of California Press, 1984), 158; Zoltvany, *Philippe de Rigaud de Vaudreuil*; Eccles, *The Canadian Frontier,* 139, gives 160 persons.

group of Abenaki to Placentia, where they visited the same horrors on English fishermen.[197] During the remainder of the war, smaller parties continually attacked New England settlements and French Newfoundland continued to be incorporated into Canada's defence. In 1708, Vaudreuil sent Rouville and Jean-Baptiste de Saint-Ours Deschaillons with 100 Frenchmen and 60 Abenaki to attack Portsmouth, New Hampshire. At the last minute the objective was switched to the harmless village of Haverhill, which they laid waste. The next year, Rouville returned to Deerfield once more in support of the colony's native allies. Vaudreuil reported that two-thirds of all the fields north of Boston were untended.[198]

Even before the beginning of hostilities, colonial ships from Quebec carried building materials and foodstuffs to Placentia. There they picked up cargoes of dried cod for transport to France. Colonial merchants were developing trade downstream along the north shore of the St. Lawrence as far as Labrador. After the war began, it was a simple extension of an already existing pattern to sail to Placentia, especially after 1703 when scarcity drove Governor Subercase to dispatch a ship to Quebec in search of supplies.[199] In May of that year, Joseph Riverin and Louis Aubert Duforillon formed a partnership to acquire the ketch *La Prospérité* and send it with provisions to Placentia.[200] Antoine Pascaud sent *La Marguerite* to Placentia. Jacques Cochu sailed *La Marie* to Port Royal with 10,000 livres worth of supplies and munitions.[201] Similar ventures continued, attracting additional colonial merchants such as Antoine de La Garde, Louis Landrin, and Nicolas Martin. They also expanded to include privateering and voyages to Martinique.

Hopes of booty inspired some Canadian activity. In June of 1704, several Quebec merchants, including Nicolas Dupont de Neuville, Louis Prat and Antoine Pascaud, invested in two locally built vessels, *Le Joybert* and *Le Phélipeau*, commanded by Jean Léger de La Grange and Claude Pauperet, respectively, for a raid on English settlements in Newfoundland. La Grange found at least 26 men willing to sign on as crew with their own weapons and no wages, but for a share of the booty.[202] On 29 August, the Canadians descended on Bonavista, where they burned one small ship, ran another aground, and captured the *Pembroke Galley*, 250 tons, which they sailed to

[197] Raymond Douville, "Hertel de Rouville, Jean-Baptiste", *DCB*, 2: 285.

[198] Zoltvany, *Philipe de Rigaud de Vaudreuil*, 79–80; Douville, "Hertel de Rouville", *DCB*, 2: 285; and C. J. Russ, "Saint-Ours Deschaillons, Jean-Baptiste de", *DCB*, 3: 579; and Eccles, *The Canadian Frontier*, 139.

[199] Col., C¹¹ᴬ 22, f. 32.

[200] C. J. Russ, "Aubert de la Chesnaye, Louis", *DCB*, 3: 22.

[201] Chamballon 2: 15, 16, 23, 63; and Col., F1A, 13, f. 21.

[202] Pierre G. Roy, "Un corsaire canadien, Jean Léger de La Grange" *BRH*, 24, (1918), 41–3 reprints the acte de société, dated 4 January 1704.

Quebec where she and her cargo were sold for 61,700 livres.[203] Later, the ship, laden with 2,500 quintals of cod, departed for Bilbao, Spain, and each man received about 40 *écus* from the sale of the cargo. In general though, privateering without a base in commerce proved unprofitable.[204]

Lieutenant Jacques Testard de Montigny, like Léger de La Grange, was a colonial-born veteran of Iberville's raids on New England and Newfoundland during the previous war. His family of Montreal merchants was connected to the Le Moynes. Based at Fort Nashwaak during the 1690s whence he led his men on joint raids with the Abenaki in New England and against St. John's, he was experienced in all the tactics of forest warfare. He was an ideal choice to revisit the "little war" on the English fishermen of Newfoundland when Governor Subercase decided the time was ripe. In January of 1705, a French force of 450 under command of the governor besieged St. John's but was repulsed with heavy losses.[205] Between March and June, however, de Montigny led about 100 Canadians and Indians on a destructive raid against the English settlements on the Avalon peninsula, capturing shallops, a brigantine, and boats and using them to move along the coast from Ferryland through Trinity and Conception Bays to Bonavista. The raid caused enormous destruction estimated at 4 million livres, but it had no strategic impact. Governor Subercase later complained that it yielded a miserable 2,600 livres. This may not be true, as Montigny shipped most of his booty directly to Quebec from the bottom of Trinity Bay.[206] It was several years before a similar raid occurred again, but these raids and privateering took their toll on the English fishery. During the first five years of the war, the highest annual volume of the English catch was less than half the lowest volume harvested during the previous four years of peaceful enterprise. The number of English fishing vessels dropped to 46 from more than 200 that were annually employed in peacetime.[207]

Governor Subercase reaped the chief benefits from Montigny's success, for Louis XIV made him a knight of St. Louis and in the spring of 1706 appointed him to the governorship of Acadia. Philippe Pastour de Costebelle, king's lieutenant since 1695, succeeded Subercase as governor of Placentia. Like his predecessor, he concerned himself with strengthening fortifications and defences. Lacking any resources of his own to launch another attack on the English, Costebelle reached an unspoken agreement with them, exchanging

---

203 AN, G⁵, 213 [NAC transcript], pp. 72–81 procès verbal, Quebec, 18–27 October 1704.

204 David Lee, "Léger de La Grange, Jean", *DCB*, 2: 387–8.

205 Jean-Pierre Proulx, *The Military History of Placentia: A Study of French Fortifications, Placentia, 1713–1811* (Ottawa: National Historic Sites and Parks Branch, 1979), 146; Col., F3, 54, ff. 409–14 Costebelle to Pontchartrain, 22 October, 1705; and Baudry, "Auger de Subercase", *DCB*, 2: 36.

206 Louise Dechêne, "Testard de Montigny, Jacques", *DCB*, 2: 625; *RAPQ*, 1922–23, 293–8 "Journal de Sr de Montigny".

207 Steele, *The English Atlantic*, Table 5.1, 302.

prisoners for nearly two years. By late 1708, however, he had assembled a force of 170 men under the command of the new king's lieutenant, the veteran Joseph Monbeton de Brouillan *dit* Saint Ovide, to attack St. John's once again.[208] Even the frigate *La Vénus*, loaned to Quebec merchants for a privateering venture, was appropriated. At the end of December, the French force moved overland from Placentia and at dawn on New Year's Day struck the town. All resistance ceased after a few hours, but Saint-Ovide was at a loss as to what to do with 800 prisoners. He certainly could not feed them, and in March, with the onset of the fishing season, Governor Costebelle resolved to abandon the English settlement. Guns, shot, and powder were shipped to Placentia, the forts were blown up, and the French withdrew. The French success was a mixed blessing at best, for it brought fears of a counterattack. It was all Pontchartrain could do to rush 200 regular troops and two warships, which reached Placentia in June. However, the feared counterattack never arrived, and during the final years of the war Costebelle fell back on his earlier policy of reaching an unspoken accord with the English authorities at St. John's.

Acadia suffered from a lack of sailors. In 1707, a group of Quebec merchants financed the cruise of *La Biche*, newly built at Port Royal, with a crew of 60 Canadians under command of Louis-Denis, Sieur de La Ronde, who earlier had also served under Iberville. They arrived just in time to assist in the defense of Port Royal in May. After sailing to France with news of the successful defence, *La Biche* proved unfit to return, and La Ronde contracted with the secretary of state for *La Vénus*, a small frigate, which he intended to employ off Massachusetts the next year.[209] Also in 1707, the accomplished war leader, Leneuf de Beaubassin, formed a partnership with two Quebec merchants, Joseph Riverin and Guillaume Gaillard. Riverin furnished his new brigantine, *La Notre Dame de Victoire*, in return for one-quarter of the gross sales of any prizes, and Gaillard, who victualed and fitted out the ship for sea, was to receive half the remaining prize money. Captain de Beaubassin, who had led the terror raid to Wells and Falmouth four years earlier and was to recruit the crew and command the expedition, was to obtain his share from the remaining half allotted to the officers and crew. Intendant Raudot, who invested in the venture, later claimed that few ships were at sea and little booty was to be had, but another report claimed success off Newfoundland where several prizes were taken.[210]

[208] Georges Cerbelaud de Salagnac, "Pastour de Costebelle, Philippe", *DCB*, 2: 511.

[209] *RAPQ, 1939–40*, 385 Pontchartrain to Vaudreuil, 19 October 1707; Noel Belanger, "Amiot de Vincelotte, Charles-Joseph", *DCB*, 2: 17–18; and Bernard Pothier and Donald J. Horton, "Denys de La Ronde, Louis", *DCB*, 3: 176–9.

[210] Col., C^{IIA} 26, f. 240 Raudot to Pontchartrain, 13 November 1707; and Dièreville, *Relation of the Voyage to Port Royal in Canada or New France*. trans. by J. C. Webster (Toronto: Champlain Society, 1933), 215.

New England's response to Indian attacks and the privateers' depredations was to attack Acadia. Massachusetts possessed no group of men nor any Indian allies to course through the wilderness to attack far distant Canadian settlements, and, surprisingly, in view of the colony's strong maritime activities, seemed equally ineffective in defending its fishery and local trade. In July of 1704, a maritime expedition led by Colonel Benjamin Church destroyed the Acadian settlements of Grand Pré, Pigiquit, and Cobequid in the Minas Basin but failed to attack Port Royal though it was poorly fortified. The new governor of Acadia, Auger de Subercase, and a small force of Acadians, Abenaki, and Canadians routed two New England assaults in June and August of 1707. However, bravery and gallant service could not hide the fact that the northern colonies had been abandoned in their hour of need. Port Royal had been rescued in June by Canadians and in August by buccaneers from Saint-Domingue. One week before the second New England attack, Pierre Morpain, captain of *L'Intrépide*, sailed into Port Royal with several prizes and carrying more than 600 barrels of flour, which he delivered to Governor Subercase.[211]

Military defeats in Europe – Blenheim (1704), Ramillies (1706), and Oudenarde (1708) – shattered the prestige of French arms, and the collapse of the navy increasingly left the northern colonies on their own. Pontchartrain had never considered them very valuable and had no resources to succor them even had he thought otherwise. In 1708, the thoroughly beaten New Englanders, on the other hand, appealed to England for aid. It finally arrived off Port Royal two years later in the form of a fleet of 34 vessels including seven warships and a landing force of 1,500 troops.[212] Governor Subercase mustered less than 300, including 150 men of the garrison, to oppose them. A week later, after the British went through the formalities of a siege, setting up batteries and opening trenches, Subercase signed a capitulation and with his garrison marched out of the fort with all the honours of war. A court-martial in France rapidly acquitted him of negligence.[213] Pontchartrain toyed with the idea of retaking Acadia, but with the first negotiations having already been made, it was far too late in the war to give credence to the idea.[214]

[211] Robert Le Blant, "Un corsaire de Saint-Domingue en Acadie", *Nova Francia*, 6 (1931), 195–6; Bernard Pothier, "Morpain, Pierre", *DCB*, 3: 374–6.

[212] J. D. Alsop, "Samuel Vetch's 'Canada Survey'd': The Formation of a Colonial Strategy, 1706–1710", *Acadiensis*, 12, 1 (Autumn, 1982), 39–58 provides a thorough discussion of the development of British policy and draws some revisionist conclusions. G. A. Rawlyk, *Nova Scotia's Massachusetts: A Study of Massachusetts-Nova Scotia Relations 1630–1784*, (Montreal and London: McGill-Queen's University Press, 1973), 108–19 discusses the lengthy plans and preparations for this attack.

[213] René Baudry, "Auger de Subercase, Daniel", *DCB*, 2: 38–9.

[214] Col., C^{11D}, 7, ff. 126–7 "Projet d'un armement pour reprendre l'Acadie … " joined to Beauharnois to Pontchartrain 11 January 1711; and Col., B 33, ff. 262–5v Pontchartrain to Beauharnois, 30 March 1711. See also A.D. MacLachlan, "The Road to Peace,

A similar fate almost befell Canada. A maritime expedition from New England failed to reach the French colony in 1709, and as with Acadia, appeals to Great Britain gave rise to a major invasion force bound for Quebec. An expeditionary force of 15 warships and 31 transports carrying 5,300 troops under the command of Admiral Sir Hovenden Walker, who had been repulsed from Guadeloupe in 1703, sailed into Boston harbour in June of 1711. It departed for Quebec reinforced by 1,200 colonial soldiers at the end of July. It was supported by an army of 2,300 colonial militia under command of the conqueror of Port Royal, Colonel Francis Nicholson, but the campaign was a repeat of Phips's 1690 expedition in more ways than one. The army never reached New France, and nature intervened to emphasize the defects of inadequate preparations and lack of intelligence. Gales and fog made navigation increasingly difficult as the expeditionary force moved into the Gulf and St. Lawrence River. On the night of 23 August, the ships found themselves amongst the surf, rocks, and islands of the north shore near Île aux Oeufs, where eight transports, a sloop, and 884 soldiers and sailors were lost.[215] Admiral Walker sailed to Cape Breton Island, but after intercepting a letter from Governor Costebelle to Pontchartrain containing news that his garrison numbered 2,000, Walker erected a cross on the shore of his anchorage claiming the surrounding territory for Queen Anne and sailed for England.

The people of Quebec, having some experience in these matters and knowing they owed precious little to Louis XIV, understood whom to thank for their deliverance. Even "the least devout were closely affected by the enormity of the miracle", recorded Mother Juchereau de Saint-Ignace, superior of the Religious Hospitallers of Quebec's Hotel Dieu. Quebec merchants subscribed 6,000 livres for a public devotion of seven masses dedicated to the Virgin, and, thanking the Blessed Mother once again for their preservation, the colonists rededicated their parish church to Our Lady of Victories.[216] This time Louis XIV did not order a medal struck in celebration.

Between 1702 and 1712, colonists successfully defended the northern colonies and carried the war to their enemies with the resources they had on hand with very little support from France. Despite prewar ambitions emanating from Versailles, the colonists were left on their own. They pursued no campaign of imperial aggression. Indeed, by the end of the war French

1710–1713" in ed., Geoffry Holmes, *Britain After the Glorious Revolution, 1698–1714*, (London: Macmillan, 1969), 206; and Miquelon, "Envisioning the French Empire", 663.

[215]   Graham, *Empire of the North Atlantic*, 92–102, and his collection of documents, *The Walker Expedition to Quebec, 1711* (Toronto: The Champlain Society, 1953) provide details of the expedition.

[216]   Jeanne-Françoise de Juchereau de Saint-Ignace and Marie Andrée Duplessis de Sainte-Hélène, *Les Annales de l' Hotel Dieu de Québec, 1636–1716*, éd., Dom Albert Jamet (Quebec: à L'Hôtel Dieu, 1939), 365, 369–70. I thank Dr. Kenneth Banks, who provided this reference.

imperial ambitions lay in ruins. Colonists employed the few resources at hand and they succeeded. They preserved peace with the Indians in the western interior and also with their greatest enemies, the Iroquois. Canada had been defended. Though Port Royal was lost, Acadia was not, and Placentia had yet to be successfully attacked. Once again the English settlements of Newfoundland had been laid waste. By 1712, New Englanders dared not venture beyond their fortified strong points. All of this was a credit to colonial resources, leadership, and diplomacy. From a colonial viewpoint nothing accounted for the huge surrenders of French territory in the Americas that arose from the Treaty of Utrecht that France signed with her European enemies on 12 April 1713. French colonists would learn that the Americas were to be won or lost on the battlefields of Europe rather than at sea or in the New World.

8.6 CONCLUSION

Well before 1713, Pontchartrain's correspondence to French diplomats at Utrecht revealed that French colonies were to be sacrificed in order to make up for French military defeat and financial exhaustion at home and to preserve the unity of the French state and the territories gained through conquests earlier in the reign.[217] In June of 1712, the minister advised Vaudreuil and Bégon of the possibility that Placentia and Acadia might be ceded to the English and of the boundaries between French and English in the Americas.[218] If French hegemony in Europe was denied in 1713, French territorial integrity was preserved but at the expense of France's American colonies. The terms of the Treaty of Utrecht ceded to Great Britain: Hudson Bay (Article 10), Acadia "with the ancient boundaries" (Article 12), and Newfoundland (Article 13). France also acknowledged British suzerainty over the Iroquois and access to trade with the Indians in the West (Article 15). In the tropics, France ceded its claim to Saint Christopher (Article 12).[219] The *asiento* was a matter for a separate agreement already achieved.[220]

A strong case may be made that, by the treaty's terms, France shed liabilities overseas rather than assets. The French had failed to meet the terms of the *asiento* and could well do without it. French trade with Spanish America did not contract but grew after 1713. Though St. Christopher was the mother colony of the French West Indies, the two French sections at

[217] Marine, B³, 194, f. 160 Champigny to Pontchartrain, 3 November, 1711 printed in La Morandière, *Histoire de la pêche française de la morue*, 1: 505; Miquelon, "Envisoning the French Empire", 656–60 examines Pontchartrain's memorandum for the negotiators.

[218] *RAPQ 1947–48*, 149–50, Pontchartrain to Vaudreuil and Bégon, 26 June 1712. For a fuller discussion see Miquelon, "Envisioning the French Empire", [653]-77.

[219] Davenport, *European Treaties Bearing on the History of the United States*, 3: 211–13.

[220] Ibid., 167–85.

each end of the island had long been a liability, and their economic significance had been replaced elsewhere. Expanding sugar output in Martinique
and Guadeloupe more than compensated for the loss of St. Christopher. The
claim of British suzerainty over the Iroquois ignored the latter's nonacquies-
cence. In Newfoundland, the French preserved their fishing rights along the
north coast from Bonavista to Point Riche on the west coast, and though
they lost their right to fish along the island's south coast, they moved across
Cabot Strait and installed themselves on Cape Breton Island, regaining what
they had surrendered.[221] France relinquished Fort Bourbon on Hudson Bay
where no action occurred during the war, but this mattered little until the
British moved inland. This occurred only 40 years later. Acadia's "ancient
boundaries" were never agreed upon. British claims extended the new territory to the St. Lawrence River, while French claims successfully confined
British sovereignty to peninsular Nova Scotia and conserved all the islands
in the Gulf of St. Lawrence, including Cape Breton Island, and the mainland
from the Chignecto isthmus as far south as the Kennebec River. This territory
continued to be occupied by the people of the Abenaki Confederacy.

Although the French appeared to shed liabilities, such an interpretation
ignores the way eighteenth-century states perceived power and the fact that
the British made no strong attempts to implement the sweeping terms they
had obtained until more than a generation afterwards. The Treaty of Utrecht
dealt any French dream of empire a serious blow from which it never recovered. The plans of a few men at the end of the seventeenth century lay in ruins.
Louisiana was in private hands. French possessions in the New World remained as before, separate colonies in an uncertain empire. French colonists
ignored these considerations and, during the next two decades, gave themselves over to constructing their societies as never before. As they had done
in the past, so they continued to do in the future.

---

[221]   See the interesting essay by Jean-François Brière, "Pêche et politique à Terre-Neuve au
XVIIIe siècle: la France véritable gagnante du traité d'Utrecht", *Canadian Historical
Review*, 64, 2 (June 1983): 168–87.

9

Elusive Empire

9.1 INTRODUCTION

The year 1713 ushered in three decades of peaceful growth and unusual development in the French colonies. Their economies, especially in the West Indies, leapt forward in size and value, but development occurred independent of growing foreign trade and of naval power, usually considered vital prerequisites. Moreover, colonial development evolved separate from French foreign policy, which remained focused on the continent of Europe. The increasing transformation of colonial societies into slave societies was irrelevant as to whether France was a "reluctant imperialist" or its empire was elusive.[1] Local developments posed much greater threats to the continuity and security of French possessions in the Americas than foreign commercial rivalry or imperial ambition. The conduct of Indian relations remained the primary responsibility of Canadian colonial officials. Colonists looked after themselves, shaping their society in their own image. In the West Indies, local unrest and the depredations of pirates following the peace were far greater problems than illicit commerce with British North American colonies or threats of attack from British colonies in the Caribbean.

By the end of hostilities, virtually all navy vessels proceeded to sea only after being fitted out and provisioned by private merchants. In 1713, private investors readied *L'Affriquain* for Quebec, *Le Semslack* for Plaisance, *Le Ludlow* for Cayenne, *L' Heros* for Martinique, and *Le Baron de la Fouche* for Louisiana, and the practice continued for many more years. After Louis XIV's death, the beleaguered French government and its creation, the Navy Council (*conseil de marine*) concluded that the navy played a negligible role

[1] The phrase is in Glen R. Conrad, "Reluctant Imperialist: France in North America" in *LaSalle and his Legacy: Frenchmen and French Ways in the Lower Mississippi Valley*, ed., Patricia Galloway (Jackson: University Press of Mississippi, 1982), 93–105.

in colonial security and could be safely neglected in the interests of economy and the pursuit of a continental foreign policy. At the same time as the army was reduced by 50 percent of its effective strength, the navy budget that included colonies was slashed by as much as 70 percent, declining from 15,166,000 livres in 1715 to 6 million the following year to 4.5 million in 1718, the lowest level during the century preceding 1789.[2] During the late 1720s and 1730s, even after French finances recovered and monetary stability was reestablished, navy funding never amounted to more than 5 percent of total annual military expenses in contrast to the 13- to 23-percent range obtained during the 1670s or even the 11 to 14 percent during the worst years of the War of the Spanish Succession. Under the Regency and the comte de Maurepas, when the navy's ordinary expenses were established at 8 million livres and extraordinary expenses disappeared, navy funding remained below the levels of expenditure first made available to Colbert sixty years before.[3] The colonies were not a drain on the Crown.

Warships returned to the colonies during the 1720s, but during subsequent years the navy failed to find a role in the development and defence of empire, which became very elusive indeed. Colonies increasingly assumed their own direction and development. Several areas in this elusive empire – French- and British-Indian relations in the interior of North America, the outbreak of French-Spanish hostilities in America, Anglo-French relations in the West Indies, and the upsurge of piracy in both the West Indies and North Atlantic fishery – reveal the continuing ambiguity, disproportion, and uncertainty across a broad spectrum.

9.2 RIVALS FOR A CONTINENT

Article 15 of the Treaty of Utrecht granting the British access to trade with the Indian nations in the North American interior seriously threatened the future of New France. Though the state had few resources with which to respond or to assist, colonial leaders had no intention of allowing this threat to develop. Pontchartrain pulled the unsavory Lamothe Cadillac from Detroit, intending the post should die, and sent him off to Louisiana. Under the leadership of Governor-General Rigaud de Vaudreuil, Michilimackinac was reopened in 1712–13 and re-garrisoned. Trade was restored to the Illinois-Michigan area by 1715. Aided by a recovery in the price of beaver in 1714, fur traders departed westward in numbers not seen in years. The Navy Council approved returning to the interior. Between 1716 and 1726, Vaudreuil established eight

2 Henri Legohérel, *Les Trésoriers-généraux de la marine, 1517–1788* (Paris: Éditions Cujas, 1965), table, facing page 180; and Claude Sturgill, "Philip d'Orlean's [*sic*] "No Colonies" Policy, 1715–22" in *Proceedings of the Tenth Meeting of the French Colonial Historical Society*, ed., Philip Boucher (Lanham: University Press of America, 1985), 133.

3 Legohérel, *Les Trésorier-généraux de la marine*, 182–3.

new trading posts. Three built on Lake Superior and two more erected farther north began successfully intercepting furs traveling to Hudson Bay (see Map 9.1).[4] Three new posts built southwest of Lakes Erie and Michigan directly challenged Anglo-American traders venturing from Pennsylvania. West of Lake Michigan, a new post reopened trade with the Sioux.[5] In 1727, under Vaudreuil's successor, soldiers and traders constructed Fort Beauharnois near the site of an earlier post on Lake Pepin (in present-day western Wisconsin) among the Dakota. On the lower Great Lakes, where the threat was most direct and aggressive, Vaudreuil arranged to erect a post on Seneca territory at the mouth of the Niagara River in 1720. During the next eight years of intense diplomacy, the French built two barks on Lake Ontario to reinforce the new post's connection to Fort Frontenac at the lake's eastern end and replaced the palisaded post at Niagara with a stone fort. Employing scarce resources where they were most needed, Forts Frontenac, Niagara, and a revived establishment at Detroit became King's posts where trade goods were subsidised in order to keep prices as low as possible to meet the competition. Nevertheless, British competition seriously eroded French trade in the area. Finally, in 1731, the French moved to the southern end of Lake Champlain and constructed another stone fort, Fort St. Frédéric, at Point à la Chevalure (today Crown Point, New York) in order to block the invasion route to the heart of New France itself.[6]

All of this activity occurred within a context of "aggressive instability" that characterised relations between the peoples in the interior of the continent for thirty years after the peace.[7] Declining native demography altered relations between nations, and increasing economic pressure from competing European traders caught French, English, and Indian nations up in a vast, seething cauldron of conflict. War between the Fox Indians and New France, which absorbed colonial energies and limited metropolitan resources, was the most intractable, transforming the nature of French power in the West.

Like their predecessors in the seventeenth century, the Algonquian-speaking Fox, originally from the Wisconsin River area west of Lake Michigan, aimed to become middlemen between French traders and the Indian nations south and west of the Great Lakes. The Fox attacked French allies in the Illinois country, and the conflict persisted for more than a score of years after 1713.[8]

---

4   These were Kaministiquia, 1717; Nipigon, 1717; La Pointe (Chagamigon), 1718; Témiscamingue, 1720; and Michipicoten, 1726.

5   These were La Baie, 1717; Pimitoui, 1718; Miamis, 1719; and Oiatenon, 1720.

6   Wm. J. Eccles, *The Canadian Frontier, 1534–1760*, rev. ed. (Albuquerque: University of New Mexico Press, [1969] 1983), 141–5; Dale Miquelon, *New France, 1701–1744, "A Supplement to Europe"* (Toronto: McClelland & Stewart, 1987), 166–76.

7   The phrase is in Ian K. Steele, *Warpaths: Invasions of North America* (New York: Oxford University Press, 1994), 165.

8   See R. David Edmunds and Joseph L. Peyser, *Fox Wars: the Mesquakie Challenge to New France* (Norman: Oklahoma Press, 1993) for the most complete treatment.

Map 9.1. The French North American interior, *circa* 1730.

Previous history, the character of the Fox, the French policy of vigorous westward expansion manifested in the erection of so many trading posts, armament of native allies, and division amongst the French themselves are only some of the reasons the bloody conflict continued for so long.[9] In 1717, at John Law's behest and over Governor-General Vaudreuil's objections, the Navy Council placed the Illinois territory, including the newly established Canadian posts, under the authority of the governor of Louisiana, who was quite unable to oppose the Fox so far away from the Gulf colony.

In 1715, Governor Lemoyne de Bienville had supported native allies resisting English penetration of the lower Mississippi Valley much further south in what became known known as the Yamasee War.[10] Afterwards, vigorous expansion also occurred in Louisiana under the aegis of the India Company. During the five years following construction of Fort Rosalie in 1716, some 400 kilometers above the mouth of the Mississippi, a network of French trading posts appeared on the Tallapoosa, Yazoo, Red, and Arkansas Rivers that, by 1726, annually funneled 50,000 deerskins to New Orleans,[11] but this was as far as the small colony could venture. The distant Illinois demanded nonexistent resources. Officers sent there proved inexperienced and inept, and were no match for Fox leaders, who increasingly directed their attacks on upper Louisiana. Canadian fur traders, with the support of the governor-general, struggled desultorily against the Fox, hesitating to resolve a favourable situation that prevented furs from moving down the Mississippi. Vaudreuil's support of the traders had become so complicit by 1725 that only his death at age 78 may have prevented Maurepas from ordering his recall to France.[12] By then, the Fox barrier to further western expansion had grown intolerable, and in 1727, Vaudreuil's successor, the marquis de Beauharnois, launched the first of five bloody expeditions to exterminate the nation. The mission was finally accomplished eight years later, but at a terrible cost from which the French obtained little benefit. Though they went on to explore the continent east of the Rocky Mountains, the French were weaker than before. The result of the Fox wars made clear that fear rather than Christianity or trade goods had become the basis of French-Indian relations in the West.

Canada's southeastern defences were very much weaker than in the west and south. Though the British claimed Acadia's "ancient boundaries" extended to the St. Lawrence River and included Cape Breton Island, the French successfully confined their rivals' claims to peninsular Nova Scotia for half

9   Miquelon, *New France, 1701–1744*, 178–9.
10 Marcel Giraud, *Histoire de la Louisiane*, 4 vols. (Paris: Presses universitaires de France, 1953–1974), 1: 302–3.
11 Daniel H. Usner, Jr., *Indians, Settlers, and Slaves in a Frontier Exchange Economy: The Lower Mississippi before 1783* (Chapel Hill and London: University of North Carolina Press, 1992), 28–31.
12 Yves Zoltvany, *Philippe de Rigaud de Vaudreuil, Governor of New France, 1703–1725* (Toronto: McClelland & Stewart, 1974), 205–6.

a century, retaining occupation of the mainland from the Musquash River on the Chignecto Isthmus to the Kennebec River. Governor-General Vaudreuil employed his predecessor's old defensive measures, offering material and moral support to the Abenaki to resist New England traders and settlers while maintaining the existence of Anglo-French entente. Significantly, neither Pontchartrain nor the Navy Council instructed Vaudreuil to invite Acadians to settle in the St. John Valley. Present-day New Brunswick and northeastern Maine were to remain a native buffer zone between French and English. Such weak measures met with limited, short-term success, and when Massachusetts declared war on the Abenaki in 1723, the Canadian governor did nothing to halt it. Indeed, by abandoning the natives to their fate, he prolonged their agony.[13]

By 1730, Canadians had learned that their problems brought little support from France. They were largely responsible for their own defence, and during the previous 15 years the major strengths and weaknesses of their place in North America were well-defined. Threats of violence had given way to employing force, a sign of growing weakness in the colony's pattern of expansion. Taken together, the New England-imposed peace on natives in the East, the growing tension on Lake Ontario, and the unfinished Fox wars in the west left Canada much less secure in 1730 after 17 years of peace and Anglo-French détente than before. Canada was far from Versailles, scarcely known to any but a few merchants. The wilderness was no longer a buffer between English and French traders in the west nor between native allies and the press of settlers in the east. No imperial policy for Canada's defence existed beyond the constant pleas of its governors for support.[14]

Despite the tensions on all the colony's frontiers, the St. Lawrence Valley colony grew and prospered. The physical threat to its survival disappeared. Indian wars were far away, increasingly fought by colonial infantry and fur traders, including Métis, who lived in the west. Between 1715 and 1730, the population of the St. Lawrence heartland increased by more than two-thirds from 20,000 to over 34,000 people. The number of arpents under cultivation grew from 55,201 to 130,791, an increase of 137.3 percent.[15] The per capita number of arpents under cultivation increased rather steeply from 2.7 to 3.8 during the same period. Land was being cleared at a much faster rate than population growth, though immigration had virtually ceased. The wheat crop increased by nearly 88 percent from 244,177 to 458,722 minots, but per capita production of wheat increased only slightly from

[13] Zoltvany, *Philippe de Rigaud de Vaudreuil*, 196–8; Eccles, *The Canadian Frontier*, 142; Miquelon, *New France, 1701–1744*, 108.

[14] Ibid., 165.

[15] J. E. A. Lunn, "Economic Development in New France, 1713–1760" (unpublished Ph.D. thesis, McGill University, 1942), 443–4. The above data for 1715 is the median of Lunn's data for 1714 and 1716. For more on population, land, livestock, and crops see Miquelon, *New France, 1701–1744*, 202, 205.

12.1 to 13.4 minots. Yields remained about the same. Livestock per capita also increased, but only slightly. By 1730, the most significant development in Canadian history had begun. The transformation of a small, disparate group of French immigrants into a homogeneous Canadian peasant society had been underway for a generation, and its continuing ruralisation would not cease for another century.

9.3 FRANCO-SPANISH HOSTILITIES

Despite the renunciation of his right to succeed to the French throne in 1713, Philip V of Spain believed this was a matter for God to decide rather than man, and that he possessed the strongest claim of any man should Louis XV die. The duc d'Orléans, the Regent, saw in Great Britain a strong supporter of his own claim to the French throne in the event of the boy-king's death. The new German-speaking George I similarly sought support for his claim to the British throne in the face of challenges from James III. Worsening events in northern Europe and the harsh military reality of demobilised armies and navies and exhausted treasuries led to the Anglo-French alliance in January of 1717, which preserved peace between France and Great Britain for nearly three decades.[16]

By the beginning of 1717, the Spanish government was preparing for war in the Mediterranean, and for the next 18 months, until the signing of the Quadruple Alliance, French foreign policy aimed to preserve the peace while checking Spanish ambitions in Italy. This failed, and with great reluctance, early in 1719 a French army invaded Spain.[17] In the Americas, the war that broke out between France and Spain was the outcome of years of tension between the two powers in the Gulf of Mexico.[18] The handing over of Louisiana to the India Company (*Compagnie des Indes*) in August of 1717 gave rise to renewed fears among Spanish colonial authorities concerned for the security of Mexico that war could not be far off. In Louisiana, French officials pursued aggressive anti-Spanish activities, and at Havana, Spanish hostility led Company agents to forbid their captains to call at the port.[19] This hostility may have been local because in 1718 the Regent ordered authorities at Saint-Domingue to live in harmony with the Spanish coinhabitants of Hispaniola.[20] In Louisiana, however, authorities quickly determined on war.

---

[16] Jeremy Black, *Natural and Necessary Enemies: Anglo-French Relations in the Eighteenth Century* (London: Duckworth, 1986), 8–11.

[17] Claude Sturgill, "From Utrecht to the Little War with Spain: Peace at Almost Any Price Had to be the Case" in *The Origins of War in Early Modern Europe*, ed., Jeremy Black (Edinburgh: John Donald, 1987), 176–84.

[18] Robert S. Weddle, *The French Thorn: Rival Explorers in the Spanish Sea, 1682–1762* (College Station: Texas A&M University Press, 1991), 212 virtually ignores the war.

[19] Giraud, *Histoire de la Louisiane*, 3: 297, 299–300.

[20] Ibid., 298–9.

In view of the navy's weakness, the decision was surprising. It reveals the Regent's narrow focus on the new colony and his reliance upon John Law to bring stability to French finances.

On 12 May 1719, three ships commanded by another of the ubiquitous Lemoyne brothers, Joseph, sieur de Serigny, left Île Dauphine for Pensacola. Their arrival from France during the previous three weeks bearing the declaration of war against Spain and orders from the India Company to seize the Spanish outpost on the Florida panhandle amounted to the largest naval force dispatched to the colonies since the previous war. Two of the vessels had been fitted out by the India Company. Ships' companies sighted Pensacola the next day, and following a brief cannonading, received its surrender on the 14th. Twenty-four hours later another Lemoyne brother, Antoine, sieur de Chateauguay, arrived overland with an Indian war party.[21] Two ships immediately sailed off with the Spanish garrison as agreed in the terms of surrender, but were seized at Havana by Spanish authorities who immediately employed them together with ten of their own ships in a successful counterattack. Following the mass desertion of 50 French soldiers and the refusal of the remainder to fight, Chateauguay had no alternative but to surrender. After imprisoning the French, the Spanish sailed to Île Dauphine prior to seizing Mobile, but Serigny successfully repulsed the landings, and the Spanish departed toward the end of August.

The next month, three more warships, commanded by the comte Desnos de Champmelin, and two more fitted out by the India Company, sailed from Île Dauphine to Pensacola and, in cooperation with yet another war party of 150 Canadians and volunteers and about 400 Indians commanded by Governor Bienville, retook the fort along with more than 1,200 prisoners and several ships, including the two belonging to the India Company. More than half the prisoners were sent to Havana in exchange for the French already in Spanish hands, but again the governor refused to cooperate. French forces were too weak to defend Pensacola against an expected Spanish attack from combined Vera Cruz and Havana squadrons, but the plague kept Spanish warships at Vera Cruz, and the French remained in possession of Pensacola at the suspension of hostilities in January of 1720.

In July, the Navy Council had ordered three more warships fitted out under command of the chevalier de Saujon to support the three ships already sent to defend Louisiana, but lack of funds and resources in the arsenal led to endless delays, and the small division got away from Brest only in late November.[22] The navy also contracted with the India Company to arm two

[21] Pierre Heinrich, *La Louisiane sous la compagnie des Indies, 1717–1731*, reprinted [New York: Burt Franklin, 1970], 53–8 for a detailed account. Also Giraud, *Histoire de la Louisiane*, 3: 297–315.

[22] Marine, B² 254, f. 16 Navy Council to Buisson, 5 July 1719; ibid., f. 523, Council to Robert, 6 December 1719; Col., B 41, ff. 129–9v Instructions to Saujon; Marine, B¹ 43, ff. 20v–5v project de mémoire, 24 September 1719.

frigates to support Saujon's squadron in attacking Spanish warships, but this proved to be a waste of scarce resources. Disease and bad weather disposed of the Spanish vessels, and on 26 January, the King of Spain announced his adherence to the Quadruple Alliance. This was just as well. The weak, poorly equipped French ships were likely to have been insufficient to resist the Spanish squadron from Cadiz sent with the express purpose of retaking Pensacola and destroying the French settlements at Île Dauphine and Mobile, but which made instead for Havana on news of the truce.

There was no doubt that France wanted to keep Pensacola, first, to prevent any other European power from becoming established there and second, to enjoy untroubled access to Mobile and New Orleans. However, French diplomats failed utterly to convince the Spanish that Louisiana posed no threat to their position in the Gulf of Mexico. Though France had no understanding, let alone sympathy, for the Spanish view of the Gulf of Mexico, both nations had a mutual interest in keeping the English out. France quickly agreed to return Pensacola in the face of Spanish insistence, and the post was grudgingly handed over in June of 1722 after both powers agreed to guarantee each other's possessions everywhere in the world.[23]

Hostile mistrust persisted while clandestine trade was renewed. Spanish governors seized French vessels trading along their coasts and French authorities feared their colonists would exact reprisals. The little war with Spain brought no benefits to Louisiana. Great effort amounted to pure loss. The ephemeral victories at Pensacola demonstrated the dreadful state of French colonial troops. Following the second capture of the post, nearly 140 renegades were seized, 12 were hanged and 35 others sentenced to a lifetime of servitude to the India Company.[24] The dispatch of three separate naval forces in penny packets in defence of Louisiana chiefly demonstrated the weakness of the service.

9.4 PIRACY'S RESURGENCE

Under Article 2 of the Treaty of Utrecht, France and Great Britain agreed jointly to struggle against piracy, but the French government proved unable or unwilling to act for nearly a decade.[25] Colonial authorities tried to check the pirate menace, but received no support from home. Between April of 1715 and June of 1717, Spanish pirates captured or pillaged 20 French

[23] Frances G. Davenport, *European Treaties Bearing on the History of the United States and its Dependencies*, 4 vols. (Washington: Carnegie Institution, 1917–1937) 4: 23.

[24] Jack D. L. Holmes, "Dauphin Island in the Franco-Spanish War, 1719–22" in *Frenchmen and French Ways in the Mississippi Valley*, ed., John F. McDermott (Urbana: University of Illinois Press, 1969), 123 n. 114.

[25] Col., A 24, f. 210 extract from Article 25 of the Treaty of Utrecht; also Davenport, *European Treaties*, 3: 210.

ships along the coast of Saint-Domingue.[26] In 1716, the Navy Council denied Jean Cassard's request for a frigate to be joined to two privately armed vessels to cruise against pirates, and Governor-General Blénac and Intendant Mithon issued an ordinance forbidding colonists on Saint-Domingue to furnish provisions to pirates.[27] Governor Blénac ordered a navy ship, *L'Indien*, to cruise around Saint-Domingue over the strong protests of the private investors who had fitted her out for the voyage to the colonies; the Navy Council later rejected their request for compensation.[28] In the fall of 1717, pirates seized seven French ships, including four merchantmen from Nantes and La Rochelle. The navy commissary at Nantes, M. de Lusançay, complained that Nantes' outfitters were threatening to withdraw from the trade. The directors of Bordeaux's Chamber of Commerce claimed insurers were refusing to cover vessels bound for the colonies.[29] Governor-General Chateaumorant and Intendant Mithon complained that the "colony's commerce was ruined". They asked that two frigates and row galleys be sent to cruise in defence of trade, but the Council's only response to appeals from both merchants and colonial authorities was to request more information about piracy.[30] Nothing like the executions of 600 Anglo-American pirates between 1716 and 1726 occurred in the French colonies.[31] Instead, the government issued a royal amnesty to all pirates who abandoned their criminal ways. In 1718, after extending it to all naval deserters and pirates, French officials extended it for six months, and then abandoned even this weak effort.[32] In the Council's opinion the amnesty attracted new recruits and persuaded pirates they could continue pillaging, but in a revealing afterthought, members concluded that, as the British navy had recently been so successful against pirates, no further action was required.[33] The governor-general and intendant at Martinique extended the pirate amnesty until 1720 but again with no visible results.[34] Yet, still nothing was done.

---

[26] Col., C⁹ᴬ 14, (nonfoliated) Etat des batiments françois pris en mer par les gardes côtes et forbans espagnols.

[27] Col., A 28, f. 54 ordinance, 8 October 1716.

[28] Marine, B² 254, ff. 122–3 Navy Council to Beauharnois, 14 August 1719.

[29] Marine, B³ 243, ff. 439–40 Lusançay to Navy Council, 24 December, 1717; ibid., 251, f. 203 same to same, 6 January 1718; ADG, C4261, Chamber of Commerce to M. de Machault [Intendant of Commerce] and the comte de Toulouse, 8 January 1718.

[30] Marine, B³ 252, ff. 105–6 Clairambault to Council, 10 January 1718; Col., C⁹ᴮ 5 décisions du conseil, 18 March 1718 re: letter from Chateaumorant and Mithon, 15 November 1717.

[31] Clinton V. Black, *Pirates of the West Indies* (Cambridge: Cambridge University Press, 1989), 24–5.

[32] Col., A 28, f. 88 ordinance, 5 September 1718; also Charles Frostin, *Les Révoltes blanches à Saint-Domingue aux XVIIe et XVIIIe siècles (Haiti avant 1789)*, (Paris: L'École, 1975), 211.

[33] Marine, B¹ 43, ff. 88–93v décisions fait.

[34] Col., C⁸ᴬ 27, f. 18 Feuquières and Bénard to Navy Council, 10 January 1720.

The upsurge in piracy in the West Indies and elsewhere as privateersmen, including crews of privately armed French warships, fell out of employment and the British navy demobilised is well-known. The growing prosperity of American and the West Indian colonies and increased shipping made the Caribbean a more profitable cruising ground than before. Pirates expanded their field of plunder, first to the Bahamas and then northward to the Carolinas and Virginia, along the American mainland to the Grand Banks of Newfoundland, across the Atlantic to the coasts of Sierra Leone, Guinea, and Angola, and shortly thereafter to the Madagascar Channel, the Red Sea, and Persian Gulf.[35]

The common view of the pirate resurgence as a local, Anglo-American phenomenon and of pirates as unemployed privateersmen and sailors ignores piracy's multicultural and social origins.[36] Some pirates may have gained sailing experience in the Caribbean, but perhaps the majority had not. Fernand Braudel long ago pointed to the connection between piracy and social unrest, which should not be ignored in the Caribbean case. Like banditry on land, piracy often followed the suspension of major hostilities, subsuming as it were the energies of a social war that never surfaced.[37] Louis Dermigny related the increase and ubiquity of piracy at the time to the breakup of great empires: Turkish, Spanish, Mughal, and Chinese.[38] Others have drawn political and economic connections between piracy and trade monopoly, seeing both as responses to territorially based merchant empires.[39]

In the West Indies, the social origins of piracy are worth considering. In the late seventeenth century, next to cattle killing, piracy attracted the least stable elements in colonial societies. The largest portion of white colonists in the islands were not planters, merchants, or other representatives of colonial elites, but those less favoured and much poorer. They included not only subjects of modest means, well-integrated into the "plantation complex", but a large

---

35 Jennifer Marx, *Pirates and Privateers of the Caribbean* (Malabar, FA: Krieger Publishing Co., 1992), 191; Edward Lucie-Smith, *Outcasts of the Sea: Pirates and Piracy* (New York and London: Paddington Press, 1978), 214; Marcus Rediker, *Between the Devil and the Deep Blue Sea: Merchant Seamen, Pirates, and the Anglo-American Maritime World, 1700–1750* (Cambridge: Cambridge University Press, 1987), 254–55; Ian K. Steele, *The English Atlantic, 1675–1740: An Exploration of Community and Communications* (New York: Oxford University Press, 1986), 225; Richard Pares, *War and Trade in the West Indies, 1739–1763*, reprint (London: Franck Cass & Co., [1936] 1963). 17.

36 Rediker, *Between the Devil and the Deep Blue Sea*, 214, 281–2 stresses declining wages and oppressive working conditions in the English merchant navy in the face of surplus labour as the chief cause of piracy, which he views solely as an Anglo-American phenomenon.

37 Fernand Braudel, *The Mediterranean World in the Age of Philip II*, 2 vols. trans., Siân Reynolds (New York: Harper and Row, [1949] 1966), 2: 865–71, 890.

38 Louis Dermigny, *La Chine et l'Occident, le commerce à Canton aux XVIIIe siècle, 1719–1833*, 4 vols. (Paris: SEVPEN, 1964), 1: 92–4.

39 See Anne Pérotin-Dumon, "The Pirate and the Emperor: Power and the Law of the Seas, 1450–1850" in *Political Economy of Merchant Empires*, ed., James D. Tracy (New York: Cambridge University Press, 1991), 196–227.

floating population, both temporary and constantly renewed, of masterless men (*gens sans aveu*), leading aimless lives in an atmosphere of vagrancy, idleness, beggary, and petty crime; growing numbers also came from military deserters and indentured prisoners. It was from this social environment that most pirates were recruited.[40] The resurgence of piracy, Anglo-American, French, and the rest, may have owed its appearance partly to the sudden de-mobilisation of national fleets, but it no less resulted from growing postwar poverty and social upheaval among *petit blancs* that marked the rapid expansion of the French West Indian sugar economy, especially at Martinique and Saint-Domingue between 1716 and 1725.

Why the French government failed to move against pirates is significant. The explanation that the government stayed its hand against them owing to its desire to reintegrate the malefactors into colonial society is not convincing and needs further demonstration.[41] This view hides the navy's inability to secure trade and even the colonies themselves from the pirates' savage assaults. Following the outbreak of war with Spain in January of 1719, it is significant that the government did not issue letters of marque to French pirates, thereby transforming them into privateers. On 1 January 1720, Governor-General Feuquières and Intendant Bénard sent the strongest protest yet over the government's inaction against pirates: "These rovers (*vagabonds*) daily cover our seas pillaging our ships sailing to Quebec and Saint-Domingue".[42] As late as 1722, the government only timidly tried to limit recruitment. Pirate ships could still be found openly recruiting men on Saint-Domingue's south coast.[43]

The French navy was in no position to act before 1720. The history of fitting out, arming, and dispatching the half-dozen men of war and frigates to the Gulf of Mexico during the war with Spain bears telling only to affirm that the navy had reached its nadir. During the decade after 1710, the French fleet declined by as much as 120,000 tons. By 1720, the navy was reduced to only 50,000 tons of mainly wornout ships, a quarter of the strength of three decades earlier. A force that once contained more than 30 percent of the entire European battle fleet had fallen to less than 8 percent.[44] The number of frigates able to proceed to sea between 1715 and 1719 fell drastically from 94 to 59. These "effectives" often included hulks unfit to leave port.[45]

40   Frostin, *Les Révoltes blanches*, 168–9, 205.
41   Paul Butel, *Les Caraïbes aux temps des flibustiers, XVIe–XVIIe siècles* (Paris: Aubier Montaigne, 1982), 158.
42   Col., C⁸ᴬ 27, ff. 1–1v Feuquières and Bénard to Navy Council, 1 January 1720.
43   Frostin, *Les Révoltes blanches*, 209–10.
44   Jan Glete, *Nations and Navies: Warships, Navies, and State Building in Europe and America, 1500–1860*, 2 vols. (Sockholm: Almquist & Wiskell International, 1993), 1: 241–2, 227.
45   Patrick Villiers, *Marine royale, corsaires et trafic dans l'Atlantique de Louis XIV à Louis XVI*, 2 vols. (Dunkerque: Société dunkerquoise d'histoire et d'archaeologie, 1991), 1: 204.

In March of 1720, the Regent finally ordered two frigates to the West Indies, but his response was a case of too little, too late.[46] No sooner had *L'Atalante* reached Martinique in July than she went alongside the careening wharf for more than two months, after which the governor-general and intendant employed her to carry them to Grenada and Guadeloupe.[47] Earlier that year, *Le Triton*, 54 guns, with the new intendant, Charles Bénard, on board, reached Martinique in such dangerous condition that she was stripped of her masts, spars, and rigging, her hull sold within the month and her guns installed ashore on Guadeloupe and Grenada.[48] *La Fortune*, ordered to Martinique in 1721 to cruise against pirates and smugglers, proved too small, old, and weak to undertake the voyage and was withdrawn.[49] Little wonder that piracy and illicit trade flourished thoughout the French colonies. Imperial defence lacked a maritime component.

The navy's decline after the peace and only partial recovery during the following period to 1748 reinforced the defence policy that had appeared at the turn of the century, emphasizing local forces supported by regular infantry and new fixed fortifications. The navy was excluded from defence and reduced to a workhorse transporting military supplies, even to the extent of carrying stone for colonial fortifications from France to the colonies. Despite increased colonial production and maritime trade, the government's financial exhaustion denied the navy any role in imperial defence. By 1721, the Navy Council, which included Marshal d'Asfelt, chief of the Royal Corps of Engineers, was already committed to building large fortifications at Louisbourg on Île Royale and was planning new installations at Saint-Domingue, Cayenne, Guadeloupe, and Martinique.[50] In the postwar world of economic growth and prosperity, fitting out and arming warships for the defence of colonial trade received no priority at all.

The first signs of change affected the fishery rather than transatlantic trade. Reports of pirates plundering fishing vessels on the Grand Banks reached France during the summer of 1717.[51] By December, pirates had pillaged

---

[46] Marine, B² 257, ff. 172-2v Navy Council to Beauharnois, 19 March 1720; ibid., ff. 175-5v Council to Champmeslin, 19 March 1720; ibid., same to Purveyor-General, 19 March 1720.

[47] Col., C⁸ᴬ 27, ff. 57–8 Feuquières and Bénard to Navy Council, 19 July 1720; and ibid., 119–22 Journal.

[48] Col., C⁸ᴬ 27, ff. 24–7 minutes of inspection of *Le Triton*, 19 April 1720; ibid., ff. 247–53, 262–9 Bénard to Navy Council, 12, 13, 24 April, and 4 May 1720.

[49] Col., F²ᶜ 2, ff. 249–50 décisions du conseil, 21 July 1721.

[50] Fred. J. Thorpe, *Remparts lointains: La politique française des travaux publics à Terre-Neuve et à île royale, 1695–1758* (Ottawa: Éditions de l'Université d'Ottawa, 1980), 44–5 and the same author's "In Defence of Sugar", in *Proceedings of the Nineteenth Meeting of the French Colonial Historical Society*, at Providence, R.I. May 1993, ed., James Pritchard (Cleveland: FCHS, 1994), 68–86.

[51] Marine B³ [NAC transcripts, MG/2] 241, ff. 241–3, 328v-9 Champigny to Navy Council, 3 and 28 September 1717; ibid., 242, ff. 219-9v Marin to same, 17 September 1717; ibid., 244, ff. 433v-5 Clairambault to same, 13 December 1717.

42 French fishing ships and seized 25 fishermen to augment their crews.[52] Not seen for nearly a century, such attacks reflected the expansion of piracy after 1713. Fish were the least of the reasons for the attacks. From first to last during the next eight years, reports of pillage recorded losses of masts, spars, sails, rigging, other gear including navigational instruments, and surgeons' chests – sometimes the surgeons, too – and provisions.[53] Above all, pirates preyed on fishing ships for men. In 1720, 25 English and as many French fishing ships were plundered and sunk off the Grand Banks and their crews marooned at Bay Bulls near St. John's, and 50 young sailors were pressed into pirate crews.[54] Three French pirates who seized several ships on the Banks in 1721 stripped them of clothing, provisions, fishing gear, and young men.[55] Fitted out to remain on the Banks for months at a time, fishing vessels were well-stocked with everything pirates needed to remain at sea. They were also numerous and unarmed, and their small crews were not aggressive. High-sided fishing ships with deep holds not designed for speed and manned by honest working men rarely escaped their ruthless predators. Yet, despite serious losses to the fishing industry, four years passed before the French navy offered any assistance and only after repeated appeals for help. In 1721, following advice from naval officials in the ports that continued neglect threatened the fishery's future, the Navy Council ordered two warships fitted out to patrol the Grand Banks.[56] The focus on defence of the fishery rather than colonial trade may reveal the relative importance of the former to members of the Navy Council, but on the other hand, it may not. The chief reason to fit out and arm the warships was likely the temporary failure of the Franco-British entente in 1721 after George I appointed a new, anti-French secretary of state for foreign affairs.[57] The Regent acknowledged at the time that French-British disputes in the Americas could not be resolved as easily as those in Europe.[58]

Surprisingly, in light of the previous half decade of inadequate responses, no effort was spared. In mid-June a 56-gun third rate and a new 40-gun

---

52 Ibid., f. 436–7 captains' declarations, 11 December 1717.

53 Col., C⁸ᴬ 27, ff. 92-2v Surgeon Rousell's declaration, 21 October 1720; Marine, B³ 269, ff. 188-91v, 208v-9 Tilly to Navy Council, 5 and 27 September 1721.

54 Marine B³ 264, ff. 174–5 Champmort to Navy Council, 14 October 1720.

55 Marine, B³ 269, ff. 24, 188v-91, 230–31, 304-4v and 524–5 Benneville to Navy Council, 31 August 1721, Tilly to same, 5 and 27 September 1721, Berigny to same, 13 September 1721; see also Charles de La Morandière, *Histoire de la pêche française de la morue dans l'Amérique septentrionale*, 3 vols. (Paris: Maissonneuve & La Rose, 1962–1966), 2: 620.

56 Marine, B² 261, f. 364v Council to Rancé, 17 September 1721; Marine, B³ 269, f. 226 Tilly to Navy Council, 7 November 1721; also La Morandière, *Histoire de la pêche française*, 2: 620.

57 Derek McKay and Hamish Scott, *The Rise of the Great Powers, 1648–1815* (London and New York: Longman, 1983), 119.

58 Col., F²ᶜ 3, ff. 45–8 Chammorel to Navy Council, 29 December 1721 with minutes of the Council's decisions of 18 January 1722; and ibid., ff. 105–7 same to same, 1 February 1722, with the Regent's acknowledgment in the marginalia.

frigate departed Brest on a five-month cruise ostensibly to act against pirates on the Grand Banks. The cruise was judged a success, but reports that British naval officers were ordering French fishermen off the Banks disturbed the Council.[59] Subsequent investigation revealed little substance to the claim, and no warships were sent the following year despite continuing losses to pirates.[60]

Major changes in naval administration in 1723 may also explain why no warships were sent. On 25 February, the Regency Council disappeared when Louis XV declared his majority.[61] On 10 May, Cardinal Dubois informed the Navy Council of its own demise; the comte de Morville assumed the duties of secretary of the state for the marine.[62] Finally, on 2 December, the duc d'Orléans died, and the king named the duc de Bourbon as his prime minister. Fisheries' protection and colonies, ignored for the past eight years, may simply have become lost amidst all the changes at the most senior levels of government. Reports of British attempts to drive the French from the Grand Banks and pirates sinking and pillaging fishing vessels continued to reach France.[63] Pirates also captured sieur de La Boularderie's ship *La Dauphine* that year, ruining his attempt to found a colonial fishing settlement at Ingonish on Île Royale.[64]

Maurepas turned to the new foreign secretary for assistance after receiving more reports that English naval officers were threatening fishermen on the Banks.[65] Morville lodged a strong protest with the English minister at Paris and instructed the French representative in London to do the same, but diplomacy had its limits. Fish merchants at Saint-Malo, Nantes, and elsewhere were threatening to cease sending ships.[66] British aggressiveness rather than pirate depredations probably accounted for the decision to send two strong ships to cruise on the Grand Banks in 1724 and again in 1725.[67]

59 Marine, B⁴ 38, ff. 235–9 Extrait de journal de la campagne des Vˣ du roy, *L'Eclatant* et *l'Amazonne*, frigate destinez pour allez croiser sur le grand bank contre les forbans en 1722.

60 Marine, B³ 278, ff. 302-2v, 340-40v Hocquart to Navy Council, 20 November and 6 December 1722; ibid., 286, (n.f.) same to same, 24 January 1723.

61 Michel Antoine, *Le Conseil du roi sous le règne de Louis XV*, (Paris: Droz, 1970), 118.

62 Sydney Daney, *Histoire de la Martinique depuis la colonisation jusqu'en 1815*, 3 vols., facsimile (Fort-de-France: Société d'histoire de la Martinique, [1846] 1963), 2: 52 for copy of Dubois to Superior Council of Martinique, 10 May 1723.

63 Marine, B³ 286, ff. 420–1 Le Brun to Maruepas, 22 October 1723; ibid., 288, ff. 101-1v, Bigot de la Mothe to Morville, 22 June 1723; ibid., 124-6v, 181-1v, 287 captains' declaration 29 and 31 July, 6 and 11 August, and 9 October 1723.

64 Marine, B³ 286, f. 342-2v declaration, 26 October 1823; ibid., f. 225v Bigot de la Mothe to Maurepas 24 August 1723; for more on this attempt see Dale Miquelon, "Poupet de La Boularderie", *DCB*, 2: 417–18.

65 Marine, B³ 290, ff. 81-1v Morville to Maurepas, 10 November 1723.

66 Ibid., 288, f. 170 Bigot de la Mothe to Morville, 30 July 1723; ibid., 293, f. 36 Tilly and de Villiers to Maurepas 6 January 1724; ibid., 294, f. 43 Marin to Maurpas, 23 April 1724.

67 Marine, B² 269, f. 5 Roquefeuil's instructions, 12 March 1724; Marine, B⁴ 38, ff. 367-75 King's Memoir to Capt. de Benneville, 25 March 1725.

Pirates did not disturb investors or the government's image of itself in quite the same way as did the British navy.

The first cruise proved uneventful. Naval officers counted 110 French fishing vessels in 1724 compared to the 40 sighted two years earlier. Life appeared to have returned to normal. Chasing down a report of a pirate and two prizes in the area revealed only one French and two English fishing ships gathered "to drink a lot of wine together".[68] No further attempts to chase French fishermen from the Banks occurred. Though four British frigates patrolled the fishery that year, on meeting them French officers exchanged no more than pleasantries with their once and future enemies.[69] Both French and British warships encountered pirates, and although weather frequently made their task difficult, they effectively brought an end to piracy of the Grand Banks. The following year, a similar cruise was deemed unnecessary. The only warship to sail across the Banks was bound for Louisbourg with troops and munitions.[70] With a single exception, 1732, no further fishery protection cruises occurred for nearly 20 years.[71]

9.5 COLONIES IN SEARCH OF A NAVY

While the Anglo-French entente did not reduce tensions between the two powers in America, it undoubtedly prevented war from breaking out on at least two occasions and permitted the limited naval response that France mounted against Spain in the Gulf of Mexico. As was the case in Canada, relations with English colonies were left largely in the hands of colonial authorities, who relied chiefly on their own wits and limited local military resources. What sometimes passes for imperialist ideology among some historians was little more than pleas to the Navy Council for greater support. The Canso Affair occurred in September of 1718 when a British navy captain acting on the orders of the governor of Massachusetts seized French fishermen at their base on Canso Island off the southwest shore of Île Royale and transported them and their boats, gear, and provisions to Boston. The incident gave rise to the establishment of commissioners to consider all the larger issues of the Acadian boundary the next year.[72] The issue was resolved in September of 1720. French diplomats, with the Regent's full support, insisted that Canso Island was a part of Île Royale, and the British accepted that any islands lying north of the mainland (i.e., peninsular Nova Scotia) and in the Gulf of St. Lawrence were French possessions. After another two

68 Marine, B⁴ 38, f. 229 Extrait du journal de la campagne de V^aux du Roy *L'Hercule* [54 guns] et *Le Prothée* [44 guns], (n.d.).
69 La Morandière, *Histoire de la pêche française*, 2: 622.
70 Marine, B⁴ 39, ff. 29-30v Chaon to Maurepas, 6 November 1726.
71 BN, n.a.f., 2550; La Morandière, *Histoire de la pêche française*, 2: 622-3.
72 Ian K. Steele, *Politics of Colonial Policy: The Board of Trade in Colonial Administration, 1696-1720* (Oxford: Oxford University Press, 1968), 165-9.

years, the British government compensated the chief victim of the seizure for his losses.[73] The result spoke to the success of French diplomacy in the absence of the navy in protecting French interests overseas, but its effectiveness was strictly limited.

An equally serious incident arose at the same time in the Windward Islands over possession of Dominica, St. Lucia, and St. Vincent, later called the Neutral Islands, that constrained French diplomacy in the face of increasing British hostility. During the post-Utrecht era, Frenchmen who planted crops, logged timber, and traded gradually settled on these islands amidst the Carib occupants. Though the natives, metropolitan authorities, and the English disapproved of this development, local colonial officials encouraged the practice over objections from the English islands. All three islands were adjacent to the French on Guadeloupe, Martinique, and Grenada and possessed strategic value. Occupation relieved demographic pressure on *petit blancs*, and produced scarce timber and ground provisions for which there were inexhaustible demands on the sugar islands. On St. Vincent, Island Caribs desperately sought French allies in their losing struggle with Black Caribs for control of the island.[74] Naturally, the English objected in the strongest terms. In February of 1715, a British warship evicted French loggers from St. Lucia and seized their timber.[75] Pontchartrain advised Governor-General Duquesne that, although the island was certainly a French possession, he was not to provoke the English.[76]

Until the duc d'Orléans was confirmed as the sole regent, the Navy Council was established, and John Law's schemes were adopted, nothing was attempted. The reduction of the navy and refocusing and militarisation of colonial policy on Louisiana and Île Royale led Marshal comte d'Estrées, president of the Council, to ask for and obtain royal letters dated August 1718, giving him ownership of Saint Lucia. The following year, his agents took formal possession of the island in the name of the king.[77] D'Estrées had a detachment of troops and settlers sent there.[78]

About the same time, December of 1718, colonial officials on Martinique moved to reinforce the French position on St. Vincent by concluding a treaty

[73] Miquelon, *New France, 1701–1744*, 98–9.

[74] Philip P. Boucher, *Cannibal Encounters: Europeans and Island Caribs, 1492–1763* (Baltimore and London: The Johns Hopkins University Press, 1992), 95, 104–5.

[75] Col., C^{8A} 20, ff. 241–9, 250–7 Duquesne to Pontchartrain 17 February and 24 March 1715. Also *CSP, CS*, 1714–1715, no. 244i Duquesne to Governor Lawthor of Barbados, 24 February, 1715.

[76] Col., B37, f. 278 Pontchartrain to Duquesne, 25 August 1715.

[77] Col., A 25, f. 93v King's letter, August 1718; Col., C^{8A} 26, ff. 98–9 Feuquières and Bénard to Navy Council, 12 July 1719; and ibid., ff. 297-7v Bénard to Navy Council, 2 August 1719.

[78] Ibid., ff. 102-3v Feuquières and Bénard to Navy Council, 17 August 1719; and Marine, B^1 43, ff. 81-1v same to same, 30 October 1719.

with the Island Caribs, but their actions backfired. Island Caribs ceded their rights to the island to the King of France in return for protection against the Black Caribs, identified as "les nègres, nos Ennemis", and assurances not to settle on the island.[79] Behind this attempt to increase French sovereignty, however, lay a baser motive: to sell Black Caribs into slavery on Saint-Domingue. A joint Island Carib-French expedition turned into a debacle as Black Caribs reminded them what fierce fighters they were, damaging both French prestige and pretensions.[80]

Meanwhile, in April strong British protest and the absence of any naval support forced the Navy Council to order local authorities to withdraw the expedition from St. Lucia.[81] Evacuation occurred during the summer, but not before the island commander died of wounds inflicted during an English assault on his family and servants by men from a ship he had earlier arrested for trading.[82] As British attacks on ships increased, French policy reverted to the traditional one of no settlements and island neutrality.[83] Settlement clashed with local interests that favoured contraband trade, which grew rapidly on both St. Lucia and Dominica.

In 1722, the English reinforced the humiliation of having to withdraw in the face of murder when George I appointed Lord Carteret as British foreign secretary of state, and granted St. Lucia and St. Vincent to his protégé, John Duke of Montagu.[84] French weakness was not as great as four years before, however, and the duc d'Orléans ordered the forcible eviction of the British. After sending presents to the Black Caribs, the avowed enemies of English settlers on St. Vincent, Governor-General de Feuquières dispatched the marquis de Champigny to St. Lucia with 100 troops and about 1,000 militia from Martinique to evict the English, who withdrew immediately.[85]

During the mid-1720s, the Franco–British entente became easier to maintain. The growing dynastic stability in both kingdoms did not undermine the relationship. In Britain, the weakness of Hanover in the face of Prussian hostility, and in France, the alarming prospect of an Anglo-Austrian alliance kept British and French diplomats on the same side for several more years.[86]

St. Lucia, St. Vincent, and Dominica remained bones of contention between them for the next 36 years. By the late 1720s, over 300 French

79 Col., F²ᴬ 11, (Copy) Traité entre le Roy et les Caraybes ..., 3 December 1719.
80 Boucher, *Cannibal Encounters*, 104.
81 Col., C⁸ᴬ 27, ff. 161–3 Feuquières to Navy Council, 9 June 1720.
82 Ibid., ff. 252-3v, 284–5 and 314–17 Bénard to Navy Council, 13 April, 6 June and 8 August 1720.
83 Col., C⁸ᴬ 26, f. 239 Feuquières to Navy Council, 30 December 1719.
84 Miquelon, *New France, 1701–1744*, 99 ignores events on St. Lucia prior to 1722 and incorrectly identifies Lord Carteret as Prime Minister. John, 1st Viscount Carteret (later 1st Earl Granville), was appointed one of two foreign secretaries under Robert Walpole in 1721.
85 Marine B⁴ 38, ff. 291–2 Bénard to Navy Council, 21 January 1723.
86 Black, *Natural and Necessary Enemies*, 15–17.

settlers resided on Dominica, a sign of waning Carib resistance; the governor-general appointed a commandant for the island. Other attempts to settle the islands remained unfulfilled, probably owing to the benefits enjoyed by French and English merchants and planters from keeping the islands free for clandestine trade.[87] The English could be counted on to purchase French sugar for 10 percent more and to sell their salt beef for 10 percent less than French merchants offered.[88] English traders in concert with Saint-Pierre merchants took all the French sugar and cacao offered at St. Lucia "with unbelievable ease".[89] A French report of December 1730 claimed that 15 or 20 English ships could be found anytime at Le Carénage (today Castries) on Saint Lucia trading chiefly salt beef, flour, and dry goods for sugar and other commodities from Martinique.[90]

9.6 ELUSIVE EMPIRE

There is a long tradition in French colonial historiography that colonial and maritime themes occupy a prominent place in French national history and in defining French national interests. Those who ignored this, ran the argument, did so to the detriment of France. Historians like the late Pierre Pluchon assumed that a national interest existed and was obvious to the participants, who were morally bound to strive to achieve it despite any factors that obscured its perception.[91] Indeed, some earlier historians appeared unable to conceive of colonies existing prior to policy.[92] I have argued that theory is hard to find and expediency was always the chief factor shaping the organizational policies of the Bourbon empire. From the moment Louis XIV assumed direct control of his American possessions, the European recession that was especially severe in France shaped royal initiatives toward the Americas, in particular abbreviating them and leaving in their wake ill-conceived, often contradictory, and incomplete policies. French colonial ambitions, in short, quickly succumbed to the exigencies of local ambitions and circumstance.

Imperial communications between France and its colonies that accompanied the growth of trade after 1713 occurred too late and proved insufficient

---

[87] Boucher, *Cannibal Encounters*, 105.

[88] Marine, B⁴ 38, f. 292 Bénard to Navy Council, 21 January 1723.

[89] Col., C⁸ᴬ 36, f. 39v Blondel to Maurepas, 8 April 1726; ibid., ff. 77 Feuquières and Blondel to Maurepas, 16 June 1726.

[90] ADLA, C 735, f. 6 memoir of Sieur Rossel, December 1730; also ADG., C 4269, f. 129 memoir of the Chamber of Commerce of Bordeaux, 22 August 1730.

[91] See Pierre Pluchon, *Histoire de la colonisation française*, Tome 1, *Le Premier empire coloniale des origines à la Restauration* (Paris: Fayard, 1991), is a passionate, magisterial survey that provides a recent example of this nationalist tradition.

[92] E.g. Pierre Bonnassieux, *Les Grandes compagnies* (Paris: Plon, 1892); Gabriel Hanoteaux et Alfred Martineau, *Histoire des colonies et de l'expansion de la France dans le monde*, 6 vols. (Paris: Plon, 1929–33).

when combined with the state's financial exhaustion and the severe decline of the navy during the Regent's reordering of priorities. It undermined reliability, rendered the formation of lasting links impossible and too often left colonial authorities on their own.[93] Together with local environments, limited economic development, and demographic weakness, the failure in communications prevented colonial integration and centralisation of French political institutions. Economic growth and social interaction remained decentralised. Continentalist ambitions also ran more strongly through French history than among other European colonial powers. Strong politicians opposed Colbert's and his successors' efforts to endow France with a navy and overseas possessions. Influential royal advisors like Vauban, whose entire life's work was to develop the policy of "the dueling ground (*la politique du pré carré*)", pursued a continentalist policy for France.[94] Though colonial possessions were closely tied to the monarch after they were reunited to the Crown during the 1660s, European and colonial policies were not different aspects of a single ambition of national expansion. Louis XIV's sacrifice of colonies in 1713 and the Regent's subsequent abandonment of the navy, though damaging the monarch's prestige, illustrates the royal family's commitment to continentalism's political programme, which viewed colonialism as a form of adventurism leading to a weaker France. Colonial possessions were not so tied to the Crown as ever to place colonialism above continentalism. Not even growing colonial trade was sufficient to divert the state from its continental ambitions. Colonists increasingly traded with neutral and enemy shipping in peace as well as in war. In France, profit and power, trade and dominion, it seems, were separable.[95] By 1730, despite growing profits, colonial possessions were political and military rather than economic in character.

The elusive empire existed and continued to exist, even as its economic significance grew, but its demographic disproportion increased and was never resolved. By 1730, fewer than 42,000 French colonists, widely settled in North America from Île Royale, the St. Lawrence Valley, and upper and lower Louisiana, confronted 400,000 British-Americans established between the Appalachians and the Atlantic. The disparities were less in the West Indies though the 18,000 French men and women of 1685 scarcely numbered 32,000 45 years later. The growing pressures of war and royal

93 Kenneth Banks, "'Lente et assez fâcheuse traversée': Navigation and the Transatlantic French Empire, 1713–1763", *Proceedings of the Twentieth Meeting of the French Colonial Historical Society* ed., A. J. B. Johnston (Cleveland: FCHS, 1994), 80–94.

94 André Corvisier, *La France de Louis XIV, 1643–1715: Ordre intérieur et place en Europe*, (Paris: SEDES, 1979); Luc-Normand Tellier, *Face aux Colbert: Les Le Tellier, Vauban, Turgot ... et l'avenement du liberalisme* (Sillery: Presses de l'université du Québec, 1987), 145–6, 607.

95 Cf. Paul Kennedy, *The Rise and Fall of the Great Powers: Economic Change and Military Conflict from 1500 to 2000* (London and Sydney: Unwin Hyman, 1988), 83.

ambition rather than the integrative function of expanding markets allowed the scattered settlements in North America to shape themselves. Colonists and their leaders were shaped by circumstances far more than might be expected in light of absolutism's image of itself and attempts to regulate and control development. During the decades between 1670 and 1730, France was always too preoccupied with dynastic (i.e., continental) interests and conflict to expend time, manpower, and wealth on colonies.

Appendixes

Appendix 1. *Estimated Population of French America by Race and Region, 1670–1730.*

Region	1670	1685	1700	1715	1730
1. Canada:					
Red	c.1,000	2,100	2,200	2,300	2,600
White	6,631	10,904	14,656	20,701	34,753
Black	—	—	—	—	—
Total	7,631	13,004	16,856	23,001	37,353
2. Acadia:					
Red	<1,000	c.850	c.700	1,300	1,500
White	c.500	c.900	c.1,450	2,500	5,000
Black	—	—	—	—	—
Total	1,500	1,750	2,150	not included	not included
3. Placentia-Île Royale:					
Red	—	—	—	156	?
White	73	c.175	c.200	1,450	4,645
Black	—	—	—	—	—
Total	73	c.175	c.200	1,606	4,645
4. Louisiana-Illinois:					
Red	c.200,000	160,500	104,000	77,000	59,000
White	—	200	100	300	c.2,000
Black	—	—	—	100	c.4,000
Total	c.200,000	160,700	104,100	77,400	65,000

Appendix 1. *(cont.)*

Region	1670	1685	1700	1715	1730
5. St. Christopher and the French "Leeward" Islands:					
Coloured	21	144	30	—	—
White	4,450	4,598	1,061	230	325
Black	4,901	5,294	722	132	220
Total	9,372	10,036	1,813	362	545
6. Guadeloupe and Marie Galante:					
Coloured	98	229	403	814	1,262
White	3,444	3,670	4,466	6,022	8,147
Black	4,482	5,257	6,855	14,200	28,811
Total	8,024	9,156	11,724	21,036	38,220
7. Martinique and Grenada:					
Coloured	—	358	533	1,120	1,424
White	4,177	5,183	6,774	9,391	12,558
Black	6,393	10,611	15,266	29,247	47,866
Total	10,570	16,152	22,573	39,758	61,848
8. Cayenne (Guiana):					
Coloured	—	—	17	20	76
White	100	175	327	332	554
Black	50	1,507	1,418	2,563	3,836
Total	150	1,682	1,762	2,915	4,466
9. Saint-Domingue:					
Coloured	—	219	?	1,404	?
White	3,100	4,386	4,560	6,668	10,449
Black	—	2,939	9,082	35,451	79,545
Total	3,100	7,544	13,642	43,523	89,994
10. Total North America:					
Red	c.202,000	163,450	106,900	79,456	61,600
White	c.7,204	12,179	16,406	22,451	41,398
Black	—	—	—	100	4,000
Total	c.209,204	175,629	123,306	102,007	106,998
11. Total West Indies and Guiana:					
Coloured	119	950	983	3,358	2,762
White	15,271	18,012	17,188	22,643	32,033
Black	15,826	25,608	33,343	81,593	160,278
Total	31,216	44,570	51,514	107,594	195,073

Appendix 1. *(cont.)*

Region	1670	1685	1700	1715	1730
12. Total French America:					
Red/Coloured	202,119	164,400	107,883	82,814	64,362
White	22,475	30,191	33,594	45,094	73,431
Black	15,826	25,608	33,343	81,693	164,278
Total	240,420	220,199	174,820	209,601	302,071

Sources: 1. *Canada.* The estimate of Canadian population in 1670 was obtained crudely by dividing the difference between the two closest estimates straddling that year by the appropriate number of years between them and multiplying the result to obtain an estimate to be added to the known estimate of the first of the years. See Hubert Charbonneau, *Vie et mort de nos ancêtres, Étude démographique* (Montréal: Presses de l'université de Montréal, 1975), 30. The other Canadian estimates are taken from Richard Lalou and Mario Boléda, "Une source en friche: les denombrements sous le régime française", *RHAF*, 42, 1 (été, 1988): 55. Amerindian population figures are taken from J. A. Dickinson et J. Grabowski, "Les populations amerindienes de la vallée laurentienne, 1608–1765" *Annales de démographie historique,* (1993): 51–66.
2. *Acadia.* See Andrew Hill Clark, *Acadia: The Geography of Early Nova Scotia to 1760* (Madison: University of Wisconsin Press, 1968), 121, 123, 128, 201. Amerindian demographics for Acadia are no more than guesswork based on a view that aboriginal populations continued to decline until the first quarter of the eighteenth century. See footnote 5.
3. *Placentia-Île Royale.* The 1670 population estimate is based on the 1671 census, which is printed in Charles de la Morandière, *Histoire de la pêche française de la morue dans l'Amérique septentrionale,* 3 vols. (Paris: G.-P. Maisonneuve et La Rose, 1962–1966), 2: 1009–10. See Canada, Dominion Bureau of Statistics, *Censuses of Canada, 1931,* vol. 1 (Ottawa: King's Printer, 1936), 135–6 for population figures for Placentia from 1678 and 1698 that were used as estimates for 1685 and 1700. See ibid., 137–8 for Île Royale, both aboriginal and white, for 1714 and 1716. The mean of these two censuses was used to obtain the 1715 estimated population. The 1730 estimate is taken from B. A. Balcolm, *The Cod Fishery of Isle Royale, 1713–58,* (Ottawa: Parks Canada, Environment Canada, 1984), 4.
4. *Louisiana-Illinois.* Amerindian population estimates are adjusted from Peter H. Wood, "The Changing Population of the Colonial South: An Overview by Race and Region, 1685–1790" in *Powhatan's Mantle: Indians in the Colonial Southeast,* eds., P. H. Wood, G. A. Waselkov, and M. T. Hatley (Lincoln: University of Nebraska Press, 1989), 38–9. The white and black estimates for 1730 are from Daniel H. Usner Jr., *Indians, Settlers, and Slaves in a Frontier Exchange Economy: The Lower Mississippi Valley Before 1783* (Chapel Hill and London: University of North Carolina Press, 1992), 41; also Gwendolyn Midlo Hall, *Africans in Colonial Louisiana: The Development of Afro-Creole Culture in the Eighteenth Century* (Baton Rouge and London: Louisiana State University Press 1992), 10.

Sources to Appendix 1.(*cont.*)

5. *St. Christopher and the French "Leeward" Islands* includes St. Martin, St. Barthélémy, and Sainte-Croix. The 1670 population estimate is taken from C. W. Cole, *Colbert and a Century of French Mercantilism*, 2 vols. (New York: Columbia University Press, 1943), 2: 43–4. The 1685 estimate was obtained by drawing a linear interpolation, as described earlier in Section 1 between the estimates of 1682 and 1687 for St. Christopher, St. Martin, and Saint-Barthélémy, which are found in AN, SOM, G1 472, f. 317 and 498, no. 101, and adding the 1685 census for Sainte-Croix, in ibid., no. 75. For the 1700 estimate see ibid., vol. 472, f. 348 for the St. Christopher census and vol. 498, nos. 6a & b for the same for St. Martin. The population of Saint-Barthélémy was estimated to be only 108, including 87 whites, by assuming that its decline paralleled St. Martin's since the mid-1680s. Sainte-Croix was not included, having been evacuated in 1696. The 1715 and 1730 estimates are for St. Martin; see Col., C^{8B} 3, no. 73 and G^I 498, no. 7, respectively, to which the number 100 has been arbitrarily added for Saint-Barthélémy's population.

6. *Guadeloupe and Marie Galante.* The 1671 enumeration AN, SOM, G^I 468, "Denombrement de terres ..." was used for the 1670 population estimate. The 1685 estimate was obtained by establishing a linear interpolation between the censuses for 1682 and 1686 located in G^I 469, ff. 120 and 122. The mean of the 1699 and 1701 census, vols., 469, f. 138 and 498, no. 63bis, was the basis of the 1700 population estimate. For the 1715 estimate see the census for the same year in vol. 497, no. 8. The final estimate is taken from the 1730 census printed in Maurice Satineau, *Histoire de la Guadeloupe sous l'ancien régime, 1635–1789*, (Paris: Payot, 1928), 382–3.

The settler's roll (*rolle des habitants*) for Marie Galante, see G^I 498, no. 16, was substituted for 1670 as the only one available. For the 1685 estimate see ibid., no. 18. The 1700 population estimate is taken from C. Schnakenbourg, "Recherches sur l'histoire de l'industrie sucrière à Marie Galante", Extrait du *Bulletin la la Société d'Histoire de la Guadeloupe*, nos., 48–50 (1981): 19–20. A linear interpolation between the censuses of 1712 and 1719, see Col., C^{8B} 3, no. 42 and AN, SOM, G^I 498, no. 21, provided the 1715 estimate, while the 1726 census, in ibid., no. 22, enabled a linear projection from 1719 through 1726 to provide the 1730 estimate.

7. *Martinique and Grenada.* The appropriate Martinique censuses are located as follows: AN, SOM, G^I 499, no. 3 (1670); ibid., no. 4 (1685); vol. 470bis no. 1 (1700); Col., C^{8A} 21, f. 250 (1715). The 1730 estimate was determined by a linear interpolation between the censuses for 1716 and 1731, see Col., C^{8A} 37, f. 14 and L. Guet, *Origines de la Martinique-Le colonel François de Colbert et la Martinique de son temps-colonisation, sièges, révoltes et combats de 1625 à 1720* (Vannes: Lafolye, 1893), 380.

The 1670 and 1685 population estimates for Grenada are based on the 1669 and 1686 censuses, respectively, see AN, SOM, G^I 498, nos. 28 and 35. The 1700 estimate is taken from George Brizan, *Grenada, Island of Conflict, From Amerindians to Peoples' Revolution, 1498–1979*, (London: Zed Books Ltd., 1984), 25. The 1715 estimate is based on a linear interpolation between 1704 and 1718, see G^I 498, nos. 40 and 41, respectively. The 1730 estimate has yet to be made and is not included.

8. *Cayenne-Guiana*. The 1670 population estimate is no more than a guess about the number of survivors from the La Barre expedition of 1664, when some 350 whites and 50 blacks arrived. For 1685 see Col., C^{14} 2, f. 166. The 1700 estimate was based on a linear interpolation between the census of 1698 and 1704, see Col., C^{14} 3, f. 227 and ibid., 4, f. 253, respectively. The 1715 population estimate is the mean of the 1714 and 1716 censuses, see Col., C^{14} 8, f. 171 and ibid., 9, ff. 281-1v, respectively. The 1730 estimate was made from a linear interpolation between the census for 1722, see Col., C^{14} 13, ff. 277–96 and data for 1735 taken from Bernard Chérubini, *Cayenne – ville créole et polyethniqu, essai d'anthropologie urbain* (Paris: Karthala-Cenaddom, 1988), 31.

9. *Saint-Domingue*. The 1670 population estimate is based on Col., C^{9A} 1 [nonfoliated], which contains both Bertrand Ogeron's 1669 estimate of 1,500 fighters, hunters, and settlers and *engagés* on Tortuga and the north coast of Saint-Domingue and "Mémoire sur l'état de la colonie de St. Domingue" joined to Captain Louis Gabaret's letter to Colbert dated June 1671. The 1685 estimate is based on a linear interpolation between the two closest censuses, "Denombrement générale de l'isle de la Tortue et coste de St. Domingue, en mai 1681", in ibid. and the 1687 census in AN, SOM, G^1 498, no. 59. The 1700 and 1715 estimates are based on censuses in ibid., 509, no. 8 (1700) and nos. 13, 17 and 18 and Col., C^{9B} 2, extract for St. Louis (1715). The 1730 estimate is taken from Charles Frostin, *Les Révoltes blanches à Saint Domingue aux XVIIe et XVIIIe siècles (Haiti avant 1789)*, (Paris: L'École, 1975), 28–9, 144–5.

Appendix 2. *Slave Populations of the French West Indies, 1670–1730.*

Year	Martinique	St. Christopher	Guadeloupe	Grenada	S. Domingue	Guiana	Total
1671	6,582	4,468	4,267				
1672							
1673							
1674							
1675							
1676							
1677						1,422	
1678							
1679							
1680							
1681					2,102		
1682	9,372	4,301	4,109				
1683	9,364	4,301	4,109	220			
1684							
1685	10,343					1,507	
1686		4,348	4,625	292			
1687	10,801	4,470	4,602	297	3,358	1,157	24,685
1688				279			
1689		4,017					
1690				398			
1691						1,220	
1692	12,857					1,133	
1693							
1694	12,887						
1695						1,190	
1696	13,126		6,431	474			
1697	13,458						
1698	13,596		5,719			1,520	
1699	13,292	465	6,185				
1700	14,566	659			9,082		
1701	16,688	901	7,143				
1702	17,382						
1703	18,898						
1704	19,466			925		1,215	
1705	19,509						
1706	20,063						
1707	20,333		8,626			1,532	
1708	20,082		8,626				
1709	22,384					1,877	
1710			9,706				
1711			11,000			2,114	
1712			10,697				
1713					28,632	2,488	

Appendix 2. (*cont.*)

Year	Martinique	St. Christopher	Guadeloupe	Grenada	S. Domingue	Guiana	Total
1714			12,562		28,632	2,488	
1715	26,865		13,271		30,651		
1716			14,481		36,096	2,637	
1717			14,910		37,474	2,637	
1718			16,042	2,779	41,876		
1719	35,472		16,654				
1720			17,184		47,077	2,774	
1721			17,581	2,656			
1722				3,045		2,907	
1723			21,094	3,106			
1724			22,965				
1725			31,359	3,580			
1726	40,403			3,476			
1727							
1728							
1729							
1730			26,801		79,545		

Sources: Slave Populations of the French West Indies and Guiana, 1670–1730.

Martinique:

1671	Colonies, G^I 499, no. 5.
1682	" " " 12.
1683	" C^{8B} 17, no. 9.
1685	" G^I 499, no. 14.
1687	" " 498, no. 59.
1692	" " 499, néant
1694	" " " no. 27.
1696	" " " no. 28.
1697	" " " no. 29.
1698	" " " no. 31.
1699	" " " nos. 32a and b.
1700	" " 470bis no. 1.
1701	" " " no. 2.
1702	" " " no. 3.
1704	" " " no. 4.
1705	" " " no. 5.
1706	" " " nos. 7 and 8.
1707	" C^{8B} 2, no. 89.
1708	" G^I 470bis nos. 9 and 10.
1709	" " " no. 11
1715	" C^{8A} 21, f. 250; also C^{8B} 2, no. 73.
1719	" G^I 470bis no. 33.
1726	" C^{8A} 37, ff. 14–38.

Sources to Appendix 2. (*cont.*)

Saint Christopher:

1671	Colonies,	G^I 471, a register of 147 pages.
1682	"	" 498, no. 100; also G^I 472, f. 317.
1883	"	C^{8B} 17, no. 9.
1686	"	G^I 472, f. 321.
1687	"	" 498, no. 101.
1689	"	" 472, ff. 330–1.
1699	Colonies,	G^I 472, f. 340.
1701	"	" 498, no. 63G^{bis}.

Guadeloupe:

1671	Colonies,	G^I 468 register.
1682	"	" 469, f. 120.
1683	"	C^{8B} 17, no. 9.
1686	"	G^I 469, f. 122.
1687	"	" " f. 131.
1696	"	" " f. 13.
1697	"	" " f. 134.
1698	"	" " f. 137.
1699	"	Satineau, *Histoire de la Guadeloupe*, 380–1.
1701	"	" 498, no. 63bis.
1707	"	" 497. no. 3.
1708	"	C^{8B} 2, no. 89.
1710	"	G^I 497, no. 5.
1711	"	" " , no. 6.
1712	"	C^{8A} 19, ff. 1–74; and C^{8B} 3, no. 42.
1714	"	G^I 497, no. 7.
1715	"	" " , no. 8.
1716	"	C^{7B} 1, no. 20.
1717	"	G^I, 497, nos. 9 and 10.
1718	"	" " , no. 11; and C^{7A} 8, ff. 100–1v.
1719	"	" " , no. 12; and C^{7B} 1, no, 92.
1720	"	" 469, f. 140.
1721	"	" " , f. 142.
1722	"	" " , f. 144.
1723	"	" " , f. 146.
1724	"	" " , f. 148.
1730	"	Satineau, *Histoire de la Guadeloupe*, 382–3.

Grenada:

1683	Colonies	C^{8B} 17, no. 9.
1686	"	G^I 498, no. 35.
1687	"	" " no. 36 and 59.
1688	"	" " no. 37.
1690	"	" " no. 38.

1696	"	"	" no. 39.
1704	"	"	" no. 40.
1718	"	"	" no. 41.
1721	"	C^{8B} 7, no. 34.	
1722	"	G^{I} 498, no. 42.	
1723	"	"	" no. 43.
1725	"	"	" no. 44.
1726	"	"	" no. 45.

Saint-Domingue:

1681	Colonies,	G^{I} 509, no. 2.
1687	"	" 498, no. 59.
1700	"	" 509, no.8.
1713	"	" " no. 12
1714	"	C^{9B} 2, summary of letters, 24 November 1715.
1715	"	G^{I} 509, no. 13.
1716	"	C^{9B} 3, summary of letters, 15 July 1716.
1717	"	G^{I} 509, no. 14; and C^{9B}4, summary of letters 18 November 1717.
1718	"	C^{9B} 5, summary of letters 26 July 1719; and Marine, (Paris), B^{I}43, ff. 95v–6v.
1720	"	G^{I} 509, nos. 17 and 18.
1730	"	Frostin, *Les Révoltes blanches à Saint-Domingue*, 144–5.

Guiana:

1677	Colonies,	C^{14A} 1, f. 220.
1685	"	" 2, f. 166
1687	"	" 2, f. 185.
1691	"	" 2, f. 201–1v.
1695	"	" 3, f. 215.
1698	"	" 3, f. 227.
1704	"	" 4, f. 253.
1707	"	" 5, ff. 263–71.
1709	"	" 6, ff. 183–9.
1711	"	" 7, ff. 229–41.
1713	"	" 7, ff. 242–50.
1714	"	" 8, f. 171.
1716	"	" 9, ff. 281–1v.
1717	"	" 10, ff. 232–41.
1720	"	" 12, ff. 351–2v.
1722	"	" 13, ff. 295–6.

Appendix 3. *Provisional List of Colonial Administrators, 1670–1730.*[1]

1. Governors-General
2. Intendants
3. Governors and Commandants
4. *Commissaires-ordonnateurs*

1. Governors-General

New France

1665–1672	Daniel de Rémy de Courcelle (1626–1698).
1672–1682	Louis de Buade, comte de Frontenac (1622–1698).
1682–1685	Joseph-Antoine Le Febvre de La Barre (1622–1688).[2]
1685–1689	Jacques-René de Brisay, marquis de Denonville (1637–1710)
1689–1698	Louis de Buade, comte de Frontenac (1622–1698) died in office.
1699–1703	Louis-Hector de Callière (1648–1703) died in office.
1703–1725	Philippe de Rigaud, marquis de Vaudreuil (*c.* 1643–1725) died in office.
1725–1747	Charles de Beauharnois de la Boische, marquis de Beauharnois (1671–1749).

The West Indies (*les Îles de l'Amérique*)

1667–1677	Jean-Charles de Baas, died at Martinique.
1677–1690	Charles de Courbon, comte de Blénac (1622–1696).
1691	Francois-Alexandre d'Alesso, marquis d'Eragny (*c.* 1650–1691) died at Martinique six months after his arrival.
1691	Charles de Peychepeyrou-Comminge de Guitaud, interim commandant.
1691–1696	Charles de Courbon, comte de Blénac (1622–1696) died at Martinique.
1696–1700	Thomas-Claude Renard de Fuschamburg, marquis d'Amblimont (1642–1700) died of yellow fever at Martinique.
1700	*Commandeur* de Guitaud, interim commandant.[3]
1701	Charles, comte Des Nos (or D'Esnots) (*c.* 1645–1701) died of yellow fever at Martinique.
1701	*Commandeur* de Guitaud, interim commandant (d. 1702).
1702	Marc-Hyacinthe, marquis de Rosmadec, died at Havana in 1702 en route to his post.
1702–1709	Charles-François de Machault de Bellemont (1641–1709) died of yellow fever at Martinique.
1711	Nicolas de Gabaret, interim commandant (d. 1712).
1709–1713	Raymond-Balthazar de Phélypeaux du Verger (*c.* 1650–1713) died at Martinique.[4]

The Windward Islands (*les Îles du Vent*)[5]

1714–1717	Abraham de Belleprat, marquis Duquesne-Guitton (*c.* 1650–1724).
1717	Antoine, marquis d'Arcy de La Varenne (*c.* 1656–1732).
1717–1727	François de Pas de Mazencourt, marquis de Feuquières (*c.* 1660–1731).[6]
1728–1748	Jacques-Charles de Bochart, marquis de Champigny (*c.* 1673–1754).[7]

Saint-Domingue (*Les Îsles sous le Vent*)

1714–1716	Louis de Courbon, comte de Blénac (d. 1724), named first governor-general of the Leeward Islands in 1714.[8]
1717–1719	Jean-François Joubert de La Bastide, marquis de Chateaumorant.
1719–1723	Léon, marquis de Sorel (d. 1743).
1723	Gilles, comte de Nos de Champmeslin (*c.* 1653–1726), named *commandant-général* of all seas, islands, and the mainland of South America.[9]
1723–1724	Etienne Cochard du Pernot de Chastenoys, governor of Le Cap Français, named interim governor-general.
1723–1731	Charles-Gaspard de Goussé, chevalier de La Rochallart (1670–1748).

2. Intendants

New France

1665–1668	Jean Talon (1626–1694).
1668–1670	Claude de Boutroue d'Aubigny (1620–1680).
1670–1672	Jean Talon (1626–1694).
1675–1682	Jacques Duchesneau (d. 1696).
1682–1686	Jacques de Meulles (d. 1703).[10]
1686–1702	Jean Bochart de Champigny (*c.* 1645–1720).
1702–1705	François de Beauharnois de La Chaussaye (1665–1746).[11]
1705–1710	Jacques (1638–1728) and Antoine-Denis Raudot (1679–1737), father and son, respectively.
1710–1726	Michel Bégon de la Picardière (1667–1747).[12]
1724	Edmé-Nicolas Robert, died at sea en route to New France.[13]
1725	Henry de Chazel, died in shipwreck en route to New France.
1725–1728	Claudy-Thomas Dupuy (1678–1738).
1728–1749	Gilles Hocquart (1694–1783).[14]

The Windward Islands

1679–1683	Jean-Baptiste Patoulet (d. 1695).[15]
1684	Michel Bégon de la Picardière (1638–1710).[16]
1684–1695	Gabriel Dumaitz de Goimpy.[17]
1695–1702	François-Roger Robert (d. 1736).[18]
1702	Louis Bigot de Gastines, named but never took up his post.[19]
1704–1715	Nicolas-François Arnoul de Vaucresson (d. 1726).[20]
1716–1717	Louis-Balthazar de Ricouart, comte de Herouville.
1718	Constant de Silvecane, died of yellow fever less than eight weeks after reaching Martinique.
1719–1722	Charles Besnard (or Bénard).[21]
1723–1728	Charles-François Blondel de Jouvancourt.[22]
1728–1738	Jacques Panier d'Orgeville, died 1739 at Saint-Domingue en route home.[23]

Saint-Domingue (*Isles sous le Vent*)

1718–1720	Jean-Jacques Mithon de Senneville (d. 1737), named first intendant of the Leeward Islands, 19 August 1718, after 21 years of service in the islands.[24]

Appendix 3. *(cont.)*

1722–1725 François de Montholon, died 1725 at Saint-Domingue.
1729–1735 Jean-Baptiste Dubois Duclos, named intendant late in 1729; died at Léogane in 1737.[25]

3. Governors and Commandants[26]

Acadia
1670–1673 Hector d'Andigné de Grandefontaine (1627–1696).
1673–1678 Jacques de Chambly (d. 1687).[27]
1676–1678 Pierre de Joybert de Soulanges (c. 1644–1678) interim administrator.
1678–1684 Michel Le Neuf de La Vallière de Beaubassin (1640–1705) commandant.
1684–1687 François-Marie Perrot (1644–1691).[28]
1687–1690 Louis-Alexandre Des Friches de Meneval (*fl.* 1687–1703).
1691–1700 Joseph Robinau de Villebon (1655–1700) commandant, died in Acadia.
1700–1701 Claude-Sébastien de Villieu (*fl.* 1674–1704) acting commandant.[29]
1701–1705 Jacques-François de Mombeton de Brouillon (1651–1705) died in Acadia.
1705–1706 Simon-Pierre Denys de Bonaventure (1659–1711) interim commandant.
1706–1710 Daniel d'Auger de Subercase (1661–1732).[30]

Cap Français (Saint-Domingue)
1695–1698 M. de Boissiramé (d. 1698).
1706–1710 Jean-Pierre de Charrite (1658–1723), king's lieutenant since 1698.[31]
1711 Paul de La Grange, comte d'Arquian (d. 1745).
1713 Jean-Joseph de Paty (1664–1723)
1723–1737 Etienne Cochard du Pernot de Chastenoys, interim governor-general in 1724.

Cayenne (Guiana)
1673 M. d'Estienne, major of the colony, interim commandant.
1675–1679 Cyprien Lefebvre de Lézy.[32]
1679–1684 Pierre-Eléonore de La Ville, marquis de Férolles, commandant.[33]
1684–1687 Pierre Sainte-Marthe de Lalande (d. 1692).[34]
1687–1691 François Lefebvre de La Barre.
1691–1705 Pierre-Eléonore de La Ville, marquis de Férolles (d. 1705).[35]
1706–1713 Rémy Guillouet d'Orvilliers (1633–1713) died at Cayenne.[36]
1713 Chevalier de Béthune.[37]
1713–1715 Pierre de Morthon de Grandaval, interim commandant.[38]
1715–1728 Claude Guillouet d'Orvilliers (1668–1728).[39]

Grenada
1669–1670 M. Vincent.
1671–1674 Louis de Canchy de Lerole.[40]
1675–1679 Pierre Sainte-Marthe de Lalande.[41]
1679–1680 Jacques de Chambly (d. 1687).[42]
1680–1689 Nicolas de Gabaret (d. 1712).[43]
1690–1695 Louis Ancelin de Gemostat (d. 1695).[44]

Appendix 3. (*cont.*)

1696–1700   M. de Bellair de Saint-Aignan, naval captain; returned to the navy in 1700.
1701–1708   M. de Bouloc (d. 1708).[45]
1709–1710   Laurent de Valernod (d. 1711).
1711–1715   Chevalier de Maupeou-Ribaudon (d. 1725) naval officer.[46]
1716–1717   François, marquis de Pas de Feuquières.[47]
1717   Chevalier de Lespinay (*c.* 1667–1721).
17??–1722   M. de Hou (d. 1722).
1722   Bonaventure-François de Boisfermé (1661–1722).[48]
1723–1727   Robert Giraut du Poyet (1665–1740).[49]
1727–1734   Charles Brunier, marquis de Larnage, died 1746 at Petit Goâve.[50]

Guadeloupe[51]
1669–1677   Charles-François du Lion (d. 1677).
1677   M. de Baas de l'Herpinière, (may not have served).[52]
1677–1694   M. Hinselin (d. 1694).[53]
1695–1703   Chevalier Charles Auger (*c.* 1634–1705).[54]
1702–1705   Bonavanture-François de Boisfermé (1661–1722), interim.
1703–1705   Joseph d'Honon de Galiffet (d. 1706), absent appointee.
1705–1717   Robert Cloche de La Malmaison (d. 1717).[55]
1717   François, marquis de Pas de Feuquières.[56]
1719–1727   Charles Vaultier de Moyencourt.
1727–1735   Robert Giraut du Poyet (1665–1740).[57]

Île Royale (Cape Breton Island)
1714–1717   Philippe de Pastour de Costebelle (1661–1717), died at Île Royale.[58]
1717–1739   Joseph de Mombeton de Brouillon *dit* Saint Ovide (1676–1755).[59]

Louisiana
1707   Nicolas Daneaux du Muy, died at Havana en route to his post.
1710–1716   Antoine Laumet *dit* de Lamothe Cadillac (1658–1730).
1717–1726   Jean-Baptiste Le Moyne de Bienville (1680–1767).
1727–1731   Etienne Perier, the elder.

Marie Galante
1670–1677   Marquis de Témericourt (d. 1677).
1679–1686   Charles-François d'Angennes, marquis de Maintenon.
1686–1695   Charles Auger.[60]
1695–1696   M. de Laurière (d. 1696).
1696–1702   Bonaventure-François de Boisfermé (1661–1722).
1725–1729   Pierre Le Bègue (d. 1729).[61]

Martinique
1663–1672   Robert Le Fricot-Desfriches, chevalier de Clodoré.
1672–1679   Antoine-André de Sainte-Marthe de Lalande (*c.* 1610–1679).
1680–1687   Jacques de Chambly, died 1687 at Martinique.[62]
1687–1689   Charles de Peychpeyrou-Commigne de Guitaud (d. 1702).
1689   Chevalier de Saint Laurent, died one month after being named.[63]
1698–1703   Nicolas de Gabaret (d. 1712).[64]
1711   Jean-Pierre de Charrite (*c.* 1658–1723), never occupied the post.
1720–1727   Jacques-Charles de Bochart de Noray de Champigny (d. 1754).[65]

Montreal (Canada)

1669–1684   François-Marie Perrot (1644–1691).[66]
1685–1699   Louis-Hector de Callière (1648–1703).[67]
1699–1703   Philippe de Rigaud, marquis de Vaudreuil (*c.* 1643–1725).[68]
1704–1724   Claude de Ramezay (1659–1724).
1724–1729   Charles Le Moyne de Longueuil, first baron de Longueuil (1656–1729).[69]
1730–1733   Jean Bouillet de La Chassaigne (1654–1733).

Petit Goâve (Saint-Domingue)

1713   Jean-Joseph de Paty (1664–1723).

Placentia (Newfoundland)

1670–1684   M. La Pioppe, *lieutenant de vaisseau*, died 1684, probably at Placentia.
1685–1690   Antoine Parat, *capitaine de brulot* (d. 1696).
1691–1702   Jacques-François de Mombeton de Brouillon (1651–1705) died in Acadia.
1697–1702   Joseph de Monic (d. 1707) acting governor while Brouillon was on leave in France.
1702–1705   Daniel d'Auger de Subercase (1661–1732).[70]
1708–1714   Philippe de Pastour de Costebelle (1661–1717).

Saint Bartholomew

1713–17??   Charles Gabriel Vaultier de Moyencourt

Saint Christopher

1670–1689   Chevalier de Saint-Laurent (d. 1689).[71]
1689–1702   Charles de Peychpeyrou-Comminge de Guitaud (d. 1702) interim commandant.
1699–1702   Jean de Gennes (d. 1705) naval officer, died at Plymouth.[72]

Sainte-Croix[73]

1669–1674   Chevalier Dubois (d. 1674) received his royal commission in 1672.
1679–1694   M. de La Saulaye (d. 1694).
1695–1696   Joseph d'Honon de Galiffet.

Saint-Domingue
(Île de la Tortue et coste de Saint-Domingue)

1665–1676   Bertrand d'Ogeron (1613–1676).
1675–1676   Pierre-Paul Tarin de Cussy (d. 1691).
1676–1683   Jacques de Nepveu de Pouançay.[74]
1684–1690   Pierre-Paul Tarin de Cussy, killed in action during Spanish attack at Limonade in 1691.
1690   Jean-Jacques Dumas, interim governor, died at Léogane 1695.[75]
1691–1700   Jean [*dit* Jean-Baptiste] Du Casse (1646–1715).
1700–1703   Joseph d'Honon de Galiffet, interim governor.[76]
1703–1705   Charles Auger (1634–1705) interim governor.
1706   Jean-Pierre de Charrite (1658–1723) named governor of Cap François and interim governor.
1706–1710   Francois-Joseph, comte de Choiseul-Beaupré, *capitaine de vaisseau*; recalled September 1710; died of wounds on board *La Thétis*, 18 May 1711.

Appendix 3. *(cont.)*

1711–1712   Nicolas de Gabaret (d. 1712), interim governor.
1712–1714   Louis de Courbon, comte de Blénac, named first governor-general in
            1714.

Saint Louis (Saint-Domingue)
1720–1723   Jean-Joseph de Paty (1664–1723).
1724–1738   Jean-Joseph de Brach d'Elbos (1660–1755).

Saint Martin
1676   M. de Magne, killed in action in 1676.

Trois Rivières (Canada)
1672–1689   René Gaultier de Varennes (*c.* 1635–1689).[77]
1690–1699   Claude de Ramezay.[78]
1699–1702   François Provost (1638–1702).
1703–1709   Antoine, marquis de Crisafy-Grimaldi (d. 1709).
1709–1720   François de Galiffet (1666–1746).[79]
1720–1724   Charles Le Moyne de Longueuil (1656–1729).
1726–1730   Jean-Bouillet de La Cassaigne (1654–1733).[80]
1730–1733   Jean-Marie-Josué Dubois Berthelot de Beaucours (*c.* 1662–1750).[81]

4. Commissaires-Ordonnateurs

Cayenne
1712–1746   Paul Lefebvre d'Albon, died at Cayenne 1746.[82]

Guadeloupe
1723–1729   Charles Mesnier (d. 1729).[83]

Île Royale
1714–1718   Pierre-August de Soubras (d. 1725).
1718–1731   Jacques-Sébastien Le Normant de Mézy (d. 1741).

Louisiana
1712–1718   Jean-Baptiste Dubois Duclos.[84]
1716–17??   Marc-Antoine Hubert.
1720–1722   Michel Léon Duvergier, *directeur-ordonnateur.*
1722–1724   Du Saunoy and Jacques de La Chaise, *commissaires-extraordinaires.*
1724   Perrault.
1725–1731   Jacques de La Chaise, commissary-general.

Saint-Domingue
1703–1707   André Boureau Deslandes, named first *commissaire-ordonnateur.*[85]
1708–1718   Jean-Jacques Mithon de Senneville, named first intendant of the
            Leeward Islands, 19 August 1718.[86]

Endnotes:
[1] I welcome corrections and additions to this list. The chief sources are Etienne
Taillemite, "Index alphabetiques des noms propres", dans *Inventaire analytique de
la correspondance générale avec les colonies, Départ, Série B,* [Tome] I, *Registres
1 à 37 (1654–1715),* (Paris: Ministère de la France d'outre-mer, 1959), 271–312,
several volumes of the *DCB,* and Annexe I in Michel Vergé-Franceschi, "Fortune
et Plantations des Administrateurs coloniaux aux îsles d'Amérique aux XVIIIe et

XVIIIe siècles", dans *Commerce et Plantations dans la Caraïbe, XVIIIe et XIXe siècles*, éd., Paul Butel (Bordeaux: Maison des Pays Ibériques, 1992), 127–42.

2 See also Cayenne.

3 *Commandeur* indicates a senior grade in the ranks of the Knights of Malta.

4 Cousin of Jérôme de Pontchartrain.

5 In 1714, the West Indies was divided into two separate jurisdictions, each headed by a governor-general; the first encompassed the Lesser Antilles known to the French as the Windward Islands *(Îsles du vent)*, and the second, called the Leeward Islands *(Îsles sous le Vent)* comprised the western half of Hispaniola better known as Saint-Domingue.

6 Former governor of Grenada.

7 Governor of Martinique since 1720.

8 Son of the former governor-general of the West Indies.

9 Younger brother of the comte Des Nos, who died at Martinique in 1701.

10 Like his brother-in-law, Michel Bégon, appointed intendant of the West Indies, De Meulles was related by marriage to Colbert.

11 Related to the Phélypeaux de Pontchartrain family and brother-in-law of Michel Bégon who succeeded him in New France.

12 Son of the intendant of the Windward Islands between 1682 and 1685.

13 Father-in-law of Dummaitz de Goimpy, intendant of the islands.

14 Served as *ordonnateur* until 1731 when he was named intendant.

15 Served as Jean Talon's secretary in New France and in Cayenne in 1677 before being appointed the first intendant of the West Indies.

16 Related to Colbert by marriage; he left Martinique to become, successively, intendant of the galleys at Marseille, naval intendant at Rochefort, and provincial intendant of La Rochelle. His son and namesake later became intendant of Canada between 1710 and 1726.

17 Former commissary-general in the galley corps.

18 Former commissary-general at Toulon; later promoted to naval intendant at Dunkirk and Brest.

19 Appointed naval intendant of Dunkirk in 1703.

20 Former commissary-general in the galley corps; later, in 1719, promoted intendant of the galley corps.

21 Former naval comptroller at Rochefort.

22 Former commissary-general in the galley corps.

23 A *maître des requètes* rather than a naval officer of the pen, related by marriage to Maurepas.

24 Promoted intendant of Toulon in 1720; left a great fortune in plantations on Saint-Domingue.

25 Formerly *commissaire-ordonnateur* in Louisiana since 1712; named acting intendant before being appointed intendant.

26 I have translated *gouverneur particulier* as deputy-governor, though each of these men ruled as governor in their respective jurisdictions.

27 Promoted governor of Grenada (1679) and later became governor of Martinique.

28 Formerly governor of Montreal from 1669.

29 Le Neuf de La Vallière's son-in-law.

30 Former governor of Placentia.

[31] Several times appointed interim governor of Saint-Domingue; in 1711 named governor of Martinique, but did not take up the appointment.

[32] A former director of West India Company and brother of Antoine Le Febvre de La Barre who founded the colony after seizing the territory from the Dutch in 1664.

[33] Cayenne had no governor for five years following Lézy's departure.

[34] Son of the governor of Martinique and former governor of Grenada.

[35] Named governor-general of the islands and *Terre firme* in 1701, but the title did not stick.

[36] Son-in-law of colony's first governor, Antoine Le Febvre de La Barre. Married Anne-Marie Le Febvre, legitimised daughter of Antoine. He accompanied La Barre to Canada as captain of his guards. Also served as interim commandant during Férolles' absence in 1700 and 1701.

[37] Though named governor, this naval officer did not take up his post. In 1716 he also refused appointment to Martinique.

[38] A former lieutenant colonel of the Guienne Regimant and king's lieutenant at Cayenne since 1709, he appeared to be the senior military officer in the colony.

[39] Son of a former governor; born at St. Christopher; served in New France between 1684 and 1694 and afterwards in the navy at Rochefort. Promoted *capitaine de frégate* in 1712. Died at sea while sailing to France.

[40] He may have been a cousin of Lieutenant-General Alexandre de Prouville de Tracy.

[41] See note 33.

[42] Former governor of Acadia and future governor of Martinique.

[43] Appointed governor of Martinique in 1689 and interim governor of Saint-Domingue in 1711.

[44] Engineer since 1672 and king's lieutenant at Martinique since 1675.

[45] Half-pay lieutenant colonel of the D'Artagnan Regiment and later king's lieutenant at Port de Paix, 1699, and at Ile à Vache, Saint-Domingue.

[46] Lieutenant in Canada, 1691; returned to France and entered the navy in 1695; capitaine de vaisseau 1707.

[47] Later governor of Guadeloupe, 1717, and governor-general of the Windward Islands, 1717–1727.

[48] Former governor of Marie Galante, 1696.

[49] Later governor of Guadeloupe, 1727.

[50] Aide de camp to Governor-General Phélypeaux, king's lieutenant at Marie Galante, 1714, Guadeloupe, 1721, and Martinique, 1722, governor of Guadeloupe, 1734, and governor-general of Saint-Domingue from 1737 to 1746.

[51] Between 1669 and 1677 the administration of Guadeloupe was joined to Martinique.

[52] Governor-General de Baas' nephew, named following du Lion's death.

[53] Son-in-law of the island's lord-proprietor, Charles Houel.

[54] Born on St. Christopher. A knight of Malta, named king's lieutenant at Marie Galante, 1683, and governor in 1692; appointed governor of Saint-Domingue in 1703; died at Léogane 1705.

[55] King's lieutenant of Guadeloupe since 1694.

[56] See footnote 46.

[57] Former governor of Grenada and king's lieutenant on Guadeloupe since 1721.

[58] Formerly governor of Placentia.

[59] A nephew of Jacques-Francois Monbeton de Brouillan under whom he served at Placentia during the 1690s; also served there under Costebelle during the 1700s.

[60] Brother-in-law of the preceding governor. Was named governor only in 1692.

[61] Served as king's lieutenant on Martinique since 1690.

[62] Served previously in Acadia.

[63] Former governor of St. Christopher, 1666–1689; named commandant in the absence of the governor-general, 1682.

[64] Former governor of Grenada.

[65] Brother of the intendant of New France; appointed governor-general of the Windward Islands in 1727.

[66] Became governor of Acadia.

[67] Younger brother of François de Callières, one of Louis XIV's private secretaries "who held the pen". He succeeded Frontenac as governor-general of New France.

[68] Succeeded Callière as governor-general of New France.

[69] Older brother of Pierre Le Moyne d'Iberville and Jean-Baptiste Le Moyne de Bienville, founder and governor of Louisiana, respectively.

[70] Former governor of Placentia.

[71] Governor since 1666, received the king's commission in 1670.

[72] Cashiered for having surrendered St. Christopher in July of 1702 to the English without firing a shot.

[73] After the evacuation of the island's population to the northern district of Saint-Domingue in 1695 these appointees became known as governors of Sainte-Croix and Cap Français.

[74] Governor Ogeron's nephew.

[75] Officer in the colonial infantry; named king's lieutenant at Léogane in 1685; assumed temporary charge of the government until Du Casse's arrival.

[76] Named to governorship of Guadeloupe but did not leave Saint-Domingue.

[77] Son-in-law of the previous governor of Trois Rivières.

[78] Left to become commandant of troops in Canada; later appointed governor of Montreal.

[79] Brother of Joseph d'Honon de Galiffet, governor of Saint-Domingue.

[80] Named governor of Montreal in 1730.

[81] A naval officer and engineer, he had earlier been refused the governorships of Trois Rivières and Montreal.

[82] After becoming a naval commissary in 1703, he was named *inspecteur de marine* at Cayenne in 1706. He was appointed *ordonnateur* and first councillor of the Superior Council six years later. The next year he was named deputy (*sub-delégué*) to the intendant of the Windward Islands.

[83] Arrived in the West Indies in 1695 as Intendant Robert's private secretary; named *contrôleur* at Martinique in 1701 and councillor of the Superior Council in 1713; he may have been the first *ordonnateur* appointed to Guadeloupe.

[84] Prior to this appointment, government accounting had been carried on by the storekeeper Poirier and before him by Nicolas de La Salle, naval scrivener.

[85] Prior to this appointment the intendant of the islands had appointed several naval scriveners to the colony as his deputies or *subdelégués*.

[86] Became a naval scrivener in 1690, sent to Martinique in 1697 as acting commissary and promoted the following year; appointed to the Superior Council in 1703 and named first councillor a year before going to Saint-Domingue.

Bibliography

Manuscript Sources

Canada

National Archives of Canada (NAC)

Manuscript Group 1, Archives des Colonies (Paris), microfilms of:

Série B	Minister's Correspondence, letters sent, Volumes 1 to 55.
Série C^{8A}	General Correspondence, Martinique, 1660–1730, Volumes 1 to 41.
Série C^{11A}	General Correspondence, Canada, 1660–1730. Volumes, various.
Serié C^{11C}	North America, Newfoundland (Placentia), 1662–1717, Volumes 1 to 7.
Série C^{11D}	General Correspondence, Acadia, Volumes 1 to 4, 7.
Série F^{1A}	Fonds des colonies, Volumes 1, 9, 10.
Série F^{2C}	Décisions du Conseil de Marine, 1715–1723, Volumes 1 to 3.
Série F^{3}	Collection Moreau de Saint-Méry, Vol. 54, Terre-Neuve et Saint-Pierre et Miquelon, 1640–1803.
Série G^{1}	Vol. 467, Census, 1687, and Recensement générale des habitants de Plaisance en l'Isle de Terreneuve en 1698 (transcripts).

Dépôt des fortifications, Amérique septentrionale, Selected reports on Acadia and Newfoundland (microfilm reel no. F-5).

Manuscript Group 2, Archives de la Marine (Paris), microfilms of selected volumes of:

Série B^{2}	Letters sent.
Série B^{4}	Campaigns, Volumes 7 to 39 (1678–1729).
Série B^{3}	Letters Received, *transcripts* of selected volumes concerning piracy on the Grand Banks, 1717–1727.

Manuscript Group 3, Archives Nationales (Paris) *transcripts*

Série G⁵   Admiralty and Prize Council, of selected cartons (microfilm no. 12,540).
Série V⁷   Extraordinary Commissions of the Council of State, Carton 214
             re: Iberville's 1705–06 expedition.

Manuscript Group 7, Bibliothèque Nationale, (Paris) *transcript*

Fonds français, vol. 11,332, ff. 661–700 "Situation du Commerce
Exterieur du roïaume exposée à Sa Majesté par M. Le Comte De
Maurepas Secretaire d' Etat aïant le departemt. de la Marine dans le
Conseil roïal de Commerce tenu à Versailles le 3 Octobre 1730".

Université De Montréal

Fonds Bégon

France

Archives Nationales (AN)

Serié F¹²   Carton 1834A "Tableau générale contenant la progression annuelle de
              la valeur intrinsique des marchandises étrangères de toutes especes, entrées
              en France comparée avec la valeur intrinsique des marchandises de France
              de toutes especes sorties pour l'étranger formant la Balance du Commerce
              de la France avec L'Étranger depuis et compris l'année 1716 epoque du
              travail ordonné par l'arrêt du Conseil du 29 février 1716".
Série G⁷   Carton No. 1,312, Western Domain, 1673 à 1707.
Série K   No. 1360, Marine, nos. 1 and 45 to 51.

Archives des colonies (Colonies)

Serié A   Acts of Sovereign Power, Volumes 1, 24, 25, 27, and 28.
Serié B   General Correspondence, Départ, Volumes 1 to 54.
Serié C⁷ᴬ   General Correspondence, Guadeloupe, Volumes 1 to 11.
Serié C⁷ᴮ   General Correspondence, Guadeloupe, Volume 1.
Serié C⁸ᴬ   General Correspondence, Martinique, Volumes 1 to 41.
Serié C⁸ᴮ   General Correspondence, Martinique, Volumes 1 to 9, 17, 19, and 23.
Série C⁹ᴬ   General Correspondence, Saint-Domingue, Volumes 1, 12, 13, 14, and 16.
Série C⁹ᴮ   General Correspondence, Saint-Domingue, Volumes 1 to 9. Though
              supplementary to the main series, this series contains a wealth of detail on
              population, production, and trade with France.
Série C¹⁰ᴬ   General Correspondence, Petites Antilles, Volume 1.
Série C¹³ᴬ   General Correspondence, Louisiane, Volumes 1 to 4.
Série C¹⁴   General Correspondence, Guiana, Volumes 1 to 13.
Série D²ᴬ   Colonial Recruits, Registers 1 to 5.
Série F²ᴬ   Compagnies de Commerce, *Asiento* Company, Volumes 7 to 11.

Série F³   Moreau de Saint-Méry Collection, Vol. 23 Miscellaneous; Vol. 26
            Martinique; Vol. 53 St. Christopher; Vol. 68 Instructions aux
            Administrateurs, 1702–1719.

Archives de la Marine (Marine)

Série B⁷   Commerce with America, Vol. 493, 1685–1788.
Série 3JJ   Vol. 278, bundle 1, Cahier des routes dans le golphe du Mexique et de
            divers journaux de navigation, 1665–1732.
Série 4JJ   Vol. 44, Journal de l'escadre de M de Gennes de La Rochelle aux côtes
            d'Afrique, détroit de Magellan, Cayenne et Rochefort par M. de Torcy,
            enseigne de vaisseau sur Le Faucon Anglais.

Archives Nationales, Section d'Outre mer (Aix-en-Provence)

Archives des colonies

Série G¹   Civil State, Cartons 468 to 472, 497 to 499, and 509.

Bibliothèque Nationale (Paris)

Salle des Manuscrits

Collection Clairambault, Vols. 869, 873 to 890, Mélanges sur la marine.
Mélanges de Colbert, Vols. 173 to 176ᵇⁱˢ, documents concerning the d'Estrées
expeditions to the West Indies, 1676 and 1677.
n.a.f. 9,323 to 9,336, part of the Margry Collection concerning the West Indies.

Archives Départementales de la Gironde (Bordeaux)

Série C   Fonds de la Chambre de Commerce de Guienne.
                Nos. 4251, 4252, 4261, 4267, and 4269.
Sous-Série 7B Fonds des Négociants,
                Nos. 1755–1962 Papiers de Jean Pellet
                Nos. 1968–1973 Papiers de Jacques Pradie, fils
                Nos. 2310–2314 Papiers d'Odet Brand et Pierre Borain
                Nos. 2549–2553 Papiers de Pierre Forestan
                Nos. 2630–2633 Papiers de Paul Hugon
                Nos. 2772–2773 Papiers de Jean Marchais
                Nos. 2811–2816 Papiers de Jean-Baptiste Montuy
                Nos. 3100 Documents isolées

Bibliothèque de Bordeaux

Ms. No. 734   "Extrait du mémoire de M. de Courson [Intendant] sur la généralité
              de Guienne (sans date)".

Ms. No. 736   "Mémoires concernnant la Généralité de Bordeaux et la Province de
Béarn contenant la description et le denombrement de la Guyenne du
Périgord, de l'Agenois, Condomois & c: du Béarn, et de la Basse
Navarre. Le premier composé par Mr de Bezons. Le second par
Mr. Guyet, Intendants, année 1698".

Great Britain

British Library (London)

Egerton Manuscripts, vol. 921
Stowe Manuscripts, vol. 201

United States of America

Newberry Library (Chicago)

Ayer Collection: Census of Acadia, 1708

University of Minnesota Library, (Minneapolis)

James Ford Bell Collection:

- Relation de la prise et capitulation de l'isle de Nieuve
appartenant aux anglois par M. d'Iberville en 1706.
- A Journal of the Transactions of Their Majesties Forces
sent to the West Indies under the Command of the
Honorable Sir Francis Wheeler and Col. Foulke, Anno
1693 by Captain Christian Lilly, R.E.

Guides to Research

Bondois, Paul-M. *Catalogue des manuscrits de la collection des Mélanges de Colbert*, 2 vols.,
(Paris: Éditions Ernest LeRoux, 1920–22).
Boucher, Philip P. *The Shaping of the French Colonial Empire: A Bio-bibliography of the Careers
of Richelieu, Fouquet, and Colbert.* (New York and London: Garland Publishing, 1985).
Favier, Jean. dir., *Les Archives nationales, État général des fonds*, Tome III, *Marine et Outre
Mer.* (Paris: Archives nationales, 1980).
Giteau, Françoise. *Répertoire numérique du fonds des négociants (7B 1001 à 3154)*, (Bordeaux:
Archives départementales de la Gironde, 1960).
Gras, M. et M. A. Gouget. *Inventaire-sommaire des Archives départementales anterieur à 1790,
Gironde, archives civiles-Série C (no. 1 à 3132).* (Paris, 1877; Reprinted 1983).
Krakovitch, Odile. *Arrêts, déclarations, édits et ordonnances concernant les colonies, 1660–
1779: Inventaire analytique de la série Colonies A.* (Paris: Archives nationales, 1993).
Lauer, Philippe. *Catalogue des manuscrits de la collection Clairambault*, Bibliothèque nationale,
3 vols., (Paris: Éditions Ernest Leroux, 1923–32).
Menier, Marie-Antoniette. "Images des Iles et documents d'histoire", *Revue historique de
l'armée*, (1963), 39–49. See for an idea of the material in the collection "Dépôt des cartes et
plans des colonies".
Menier, Marie-Antoinette, Étienne Taillemite, et Gilberte des Forges. comps., *Inventaire des
Archives Coloniales, Correspondance à l'arrivée en provenance de la Louisiane*, tome I,
(articles C¹³ᴬ 1 à 37). (Paris: Imprimerie natinale, 1976).

Neuville, Didier. *Etat sommaire des Archives de la Marine antérieurs à la Révolution.* (Paris: 1898; Reprinted Krause, 1977).

Parker, John. "Materials on French Overseas Expansion Before 1800 in the James Ford Bell Library, University of Minnesota", *French Historical Studies*, no. 2 (1978): 113–21.

Ragatz, Lowell Joseph. *Early French West Indian Records in the Archives Nationales*, 2nd ed., (Washington: Educational Research Bureau, [1941] 1949).

Taillemite, Étienne, *Inventaire analytique de la correspondance générale avec les colonies, Départ, Série B,* [Tome]I, *Registres 1 à 37 (1654–1715).* (Paris: Ministère de la France d'Outremer, 1959).

Taillemite, Étienne. *Inventaire de la série Colonies C^{8A}, Martinique (correspondance à l'arrivée),* Tome 1, *(Articles 1 à 55).* (Paris: Imprimerie nationale, 1967). Also Tome 3, (C^{8B} *articles 1 à 27 et index*). Paris: 1984.

Védère, Xavier. *Archives municipales de Bordeaux – Catalogue des Manuscrits.* (Bordeaux: Imprimerie E. Castera, 1938).

Wroth, Lawrence. *Acts of French Royal Administration concerning Canada, Guiana, The West Indies, and Louisiana prior to 1791.* (New York: The New York Public Library, 1930).

Primary Printed Sources

[Anonymous]. *Collection de manuscrits contenant lettres, mémoires, et autres documents historiques relatifs à la Nouvelle-France,* 4 vols., (Quebéc; 1883–85).

[Anonymous]. *Code de la Martinique,* 2 vols., (St. Pierre: Imprimerie P. Richard, 1767).

Baudouin, Abbé Jean. *Journal de l'expédition de D'Iberville en Acadie et Terreneuve, par l'abbé Beaudouin (sic), lettres de D'Iberville, éditée* par Auguste Gosselin. (Evreux: l'Eure, 1900).

[Baudeau, Abbé Nicolas]. *Commerce.* 3 vols. Encyclopédie méthodique, vols. 78–80. (Paris: Chez Panckoucke, 1783–84).

Camus, Michel. éd., "Correspondance de Bertrand Ogeron, gouverneur de l'île de la Tortue et coste de Sainte-Domingue au XVIIe siècle", *Revue de la Société Haitienne d'histoire et de géographie*, 43, no, 146 (mars 1985): [1]-188.

Canada, Assemblée Legislative du. *Edits, ordonnances royaux, declarations, et arrêts du conseil d'état du roi concernant le Canada,* 3 vols., (Québec: E.-R. Fréchette, 1854–56).

Canada, Dominion Bureau of Statistics. *Seventh Census of Canada, 1931,* Volume 1, *Summary.* (Ottawa: King's Printer, 1936).

Canada, Government of, *Censuses of Canada, 1665–1871: Statistics of Canada,* Vol. 4. (Ottawa: Queen's Printer, 1876).

Challe, Robert. *Mémoires, correspondance complète; Rapports sur l'Acadie et autres pièces.* éd., Frédéric Deloffre. (Genève: Libraire Droz, 1996).

Challe, Robert. *Journal d'un voyage aux Indes orientales (1690–1691),* éds., Frédéric Deloffre et Melâhat Menemencioglu. (Paris: Mercure de France, 1979).

Charlevoix, Pierre-François-Xavier, SJ, *Histoire de l'Isle espagnol ou de S. Domingue ecrit particulièrement sur les mémoires manuscrits du P. Jean-Baptiste Le Pers.* 2 vols. (Paris: Jacques Guerin, 1730–31).

Charlevoix, Pierre-François-Xavier, SJ, *Histoire et description générale de la Nouvelle-France, avec le journal historique d'un voyage fait par ordre du roi dans l'Amérique septentrionale,* 6 vols. (Paris: Chez P.-F. Giffart, 1744).

Colbert, Jean-Baptiste. *Lettres instructions et mémoires de Colbert.* Pierre Clément, éd., 7 vols., bound as 9 and one vol. of errata and index. (Paris: Imprimerie impériale, 1859–82).

Conrad, Glenn R., trans. and ed. *Immigration and War, Louisiana: 1718–1721 from the Memoir of Charles Le Gac.* (Lafayette: University of Southwestern Louisiana Press, 1970).

Davenport, Frances Gardiner. *European Treaties bearing on the History of the United States and its Dependencies.* 4 vols. (Washington: Carnegie Institution, 1917–37).

Dechêne, Louise. éd. *La Correspondance de Vauban relative au Canada.* (Québec: Ministère des affaires culturelles 1968).

Denys, Nicolas. *The Description and Natural History of the Coasts of North America (Acadia).* Translated by Wm. F. Ganong. (Toronto: The Champlain Society, [1672] 1908).

[Dessalles fils, Pierre-Regis]. *Annales du Conseil Souverain de la Martinique, ou Tableau Historique du Gouvernement de cette colonie depuis son premier établissement jusqu'a nos jours,* 2 vols. (Bergerac: Chez J. B. Puynesge, 1786. Reprinted Fort-de-France, Martinique, Société des Amis des Archives, 1995; and Paris: L'Harmattan, 1995).

Dièreville, Sieur de. *Relation of the Voyage to Port Royal in Acadia or New France,* ed. J. C. Webster. (Toronto: The Champlain Society, 1933).

Duguay-Trouin, *René. Mémoires de Duguay-Trouin, lieutenant-général des armées navales, commandeur de l'ordre royale et militaire de S.-Louis,* éd. Philippe Clouet. (Paris: France-Empire, 1991).

Duhamel du Monceau, Henri. *Traité générale des pesches et histoire des poissons,* 3 vols. (Paris: Sailant & Nyon et Désant, 1769–77).

Du Tertre, Jean-Baptiste. *Histoire générale des Antilles, habitées par les François,* 4 vols. (Paris: T. Jolly, 1667–71).

Exquemelin, Alexandre Olivier. *Histoire des avanturiers flibustiers qui se sont signalez sans les Indes,* nouvelle éd. 4 vols. ([Paris?] A. Trevoux, Par la compagnie, 1744).

Exquemelin, Alexander Olivier. *The Buccaneers of America,* trans. Alexis Brown, intro. by Jack Beeching. (Harmondsworth: Penguin Books, 1969). First translation from the Dutch original published in 1678.

[France]. *Le Code noir, ou receuil des reglements rendus jusqu'à present.* (Basse-Terre: Société d'histoire de la Guadeloupe, [1767] 1980).

[France]. *Mémoires des commissaires du roi et de ceux de Sa Majesté britannique, sur les possessions et les droits respectifs des deux Couronnes en Amérique: avec les actes publiques et pièces justificatives.* 4 vols. (Paris: De l'Imprimerie royale, 1755–57).

Froger, François. *Relation d'un voyage fait en 1695, 1696, et 1697 aux côtes d'Afrique, Detroit de Magellan, Brézil, Cayenne, et Isles Antilles, par un escadre des vaisseaux du roi, commandé pas M de Gennes.* (Paris: Chez Nicolas Le Gras, 1700).

Great Britain, Board of Trade. *Journal of the Commissioners for Trade and Plantations,* 14 vols. (London: H[is] M[ajesty's] S[tationary] O[ffice], 1920–38).

Great Britain. *Calendar of State Papers, Colonial Series, America, and West Indies,* ed. W. Noel Sainsbury. 45 vols. (London: Longman & Co., 1880–1938).

Labat, Jean-Baptiste. *Nouveau voyage aux Isles de l'Amérique.* 2 vols. La Haye: P. Husson, T. Johnson, P. Gosse, Ivan Duren, R. Atberts, and C. Le Vier [1722] 1724.

Lahontan, [Louis-Armand de Lom d'Arce] Baron de. *New Voyages to North America.* 2 vols. ed. Reuben Gold Thwaites. (Chicago: A.C. McClung & Co., [1703] 1905).

[Le Moyne d'Iberville, Pierre], *Iberville's Gulf Journals.* ed. and trans. Richebourg Gaillard McWilliams. (Tuscaloosa: University of Alabama Press, 1991).

Le Page du Pratz, Antoine. *Histoire de la Louisiana, contenant la decouverte de ce vaste pays; sa description géographique.* 3 vols. (Paris: De Bure l'ainé, 1758).

Lower Canada, Legislative Assembly. *Edits, ordonnances royaux, déclarations et arrêts du Conseil d'État du Roi, concernant le Canada,* 2 vols. (Québec: P.-E. Desbarats, 1803–06).

Margat [de Tilly], Jean-Baptiste. [4 letters, dated 1725, 1729, 1730 and 1743] in *Lettres édifiantes et curieuses écrites des missions étrangères.* nouvelle édition, Tome 7. *Mémoires d'Amérique.* (Paris: Chez J. G. Merigot, le jeune 1781), 107–255.

Margry, Pierre. éd. *Rélations et mémoires inédits pour servir à l'histoire de la France dans les pays d'outre-mer.* (Paris: Challamel, 1867).

Merriman, Cdr. R. D. ed. *The Sergison Papers.* (London: The Navy Records Society, 1950).

Moreau de Saint-Méry, [Médéric-Louis-Elie]. *Description topographique physique, civile, politique, et historique de la partie française de l'isle de Saint-Domingue,* éds. B. Maurel et E. Taillemite, 3 vols. (Paris: Société française d'histoire d'autre-mer, [1784–1790] 1984).

Plumier, Charles. "Saint-Domingue en 1690; Les observations du père Plumier, botaniste provençal", éd. Philippe Hrodej, *RFHOM*, 84 no. 317 (1997): 93–117.

Québec, Province de. *Collection de manuscrits contenant lettres, mémoires, et autres documents historiques relatifs à la Nouvelle-France*, 4 vols. (Québec: A. Côté et cie., 1883).

Quebec, Archives de la province de. "Correspondance échangé entre la cour de France et le gouverneur de Frontenac pendant sa première administration (1672–1682)". éd. Pierre-Georges Roy. *RAPQ pour 1926–27*, (Québec: Rédempti Paradis, 1927), 3–144.

Québec, Archives de la province de. "Correspondance échangé entre la cour de France et le gouverneur de Frontenac pendant sa second administration, 1689–1699". *RAPQ pour 1927–28*, (Québec: Rédempti Paradis, 1928), 1–211; and *RAPQ pour 1928–29*. (Québec: Rédempti Paradis, 1929), 247–384.

Quebec, Archives de la province de, "Correspondence échangée entre la cour de France et l'intendant Talon pendant ses deux administrations dans la Nouvelle-France". éd. Pierre-Georges Roy. *RAPQ pour 1930–31*, (Québec: Rédempti Paradis, 1931), [3]-182.

Québec, Archives de la province de. "Correspondance entre M de Vaudreuil et la cour". éds. Pierre-Georges Roy et Antoine Roy. *RAPQ pour 1938–39, 1939–40, 1942–43, 1946–47, et 1947–48*. (Québec: Rédempti Paradis, 1939–48).

Québec, Archives de la province de. "La Prévoté de Québec: ses officiers – ses registres", *RAPQ pour 1943–44*. éd. Gareau, Jean-Baptiste. (Québec: Rédempti Paradis, 1944), 51–125.

Raveneau de Lussan, sieur de. *Raveneau de Lussan: Buccaneer of the Spanish Main and early French filibuster of the Pacific*. trans. Margurite Eyer Wilbur. (Cleveland: Arthur C. Clark, 1930). Translation of *Journal du voyage fait à la Mer du Sud avec les flibustiers de l'Amérique en 1684 et années suivantes*, published in Paris in 1689.

Rochas d'Aiglun, E. Albert de. *Vauban, sa famille et ses écrits, ses oisivetés et sa correspondence, analyse et extraits*, 2 vols. (Paris, 1910; reprinted Genève: Slatkine, 1972).

Roussier, Paul, "Instructions données à l'Intendant des Iles françaises du Vent, le 25 août 1716", *RHC*, 45, (1924), 67–106.

Savary, Jacques. *Le Parfait négociant ou instruction générale pour ce qui regarde le commerce des marchandises de France, et des pays estrangers*, 7eme éd., par Jacques Savary des Bruslons, 2 vols. (Paris: Michel Guignard et Claude Robustel, [1675] 1713).

Symcox, Geoffrey. ed. *War, Diplomacy and Imperialism, 1618–1763*. New York: Harper Torchbooks 1973.

Webster, John Clarence. ed. *Acadia at the End of the Seventeenth Century: Letters, Journals and memoirs of Joseph Robineau de Villebon, Commandant in Acadia, 1690–1700, and Other Contemporary Documents*. Saint John: The New Brunswick Museum 1934.

Wickham-Legg, L. G. "Torcy's Account of Matthew Prior's negotiations at Fontainbleau in July 1711", *English Historical Review*, 21 (1914), 525–32.

Secondary Sources

Abénon, Lucien-René. "Blancs et libres de couleur dans deux paroisses de la Guadeloupe, Capesterre et Trois-Rivières, 1699–1779", *RFHOM*, 3e trim. (1973), 297–329.

Abénon, Lucien-René. *Guadeloupe de 1671 à 1759, étude politique, économique et sociale*. 2 vols. (Paris: L'Harmattan, 1987).

Abernethy, David B. *The Dynamics of Global Dominance: European Overseas Empires, 1415–1980*. (New Haven: Yale University Press, 2001).

Allain, Mathé, "L'Immigration française en Louisiaine, 1718–1721", *RHAF*, 28, 4 (mars 1975), 555–64.

Allain, Mathé, *'Not Worth a Straw': French Colonial Policy and the Early Years of Louisiana*. (Lafayette: Center for Louisiana Studies, University of Southwestern Louisiana, 1988).

Allaire, Gratien. "Fur Trade Engagés, 1701–1745", in *Rendezvous: Selected Papers of the Fourth North American Fur Trade Conference, 1981*, ed. Thomas C. Buckley, [n.p., n.d.], 17–26.

Allaire, Gratien. "Le commerce des fourrures à Montréal: documentation et méthode d'analyse", in *Le Castor Fait Tout: Selected Papers of the Fifth North American Fur Trade Conference.* eds. B. Trigger, T. Morantz and L. Dechêne. (Montreal: [n.p.] 1987), 93–121.

Allaire, Gratien. "Officiers et marchands: les sociétés de commerce des fourrures, 1715–1760", *RHAF*, 40, 3 (hiver 1987), 409–28.

Alsop, J. D. "Samuel Vetch's 'Canada Survey'd': The Formation of a Colonial Strategy, 1706–1710", *Acadiensis*, 12, 1 (Autumn 1982), 39–58.

Alsop, J. D. "The Age of the Projectors: British Imperial Strategy in the North Atlantic in the War of the Spanish Succession", *Acadiensis*, 21, 1 (Autumn 1991), 30–53.

Alsop, J. D. "British Intelligence for the North Atlantic Theatre of the War of the Spanish Succession", *The Mariner's Mirror*, 77 (1991), 113–18.

Altman, Ida and James P. P. Horn. eds. *"To Make America", European Emigration in the Early Modern Period.* (Berkeley: University of California Press, 1981).

Altman, Morris. "Seigniorial Tenure in New France, 1688–1739: An Essay on Income Distribution and Retarded Economic Development", *Historical Reflections/Réflexions Historiques*, 10, 3 (Fall 1983), 335–75.

Altman, Morris. "Economic Growth in Canada, 1695–1739, Estimates and Analysis", *The William and Mary Quarterly*, 3rd. Series, 45, 4 (October 1988): 684–711.

Akenson, Donald Harman. *If the Irish Ran the World: Montserrat, 1630–1730.* (Kingston and Montreal: McGill Queen's University Press, 1997).

Antoine, Michel, *Le Conseil du Roi sous le règne de Louis XV.* (Paris: Droz, 1970).

Arseneault, Samuel P. "Geography and the Acadiens", in *The Acadiens of the Maritimes*, ed. Jean Daigle. (Moncton: Centre d'études acadiennes, 1982), 87–124.

Balcom, B. A. *The Cod Fishery of Isle Royale, 1713–58*, Studies in Archaeology, Architecture, and History. (Ottawa: Park Canada, Environment Canada, 1984).

Banbuck, C. A. *Histoire politique, économique et sociale de la Martinique sous l'ancien régime (1635–1789).* (Paris: Marcel Rivière, 1935).

Banks, Kenneth. *Chasing Empire across the Sea: Communications and the State in the French Atlantic, 1713–1763.* (McGill-Queen's University Press, 2002).

Banks, Kenneth. "'Lente et assez fâcheuse Traversé': Navigation and the Transatlantic French Empire, 1713–1763" in *Proceedings of the Twentieth Meeting of the French Colonial Historical Society*, Cleveland, May 1994, ed. A.J.B. Johnston. (Cleveland: French Colonial Historical Society, 1996), 80–94.

Barreau, Jean. "Les Guerres en Guadeloupe au XVIIIe siècle, (1703, 1759, et 1794)". Extrait du *Bulletin de la Societé d'Histoire de la Guadeloupe*, nos. 25, 27, 28 (1975–76).

Barrett, Ward. "Caribbean Sugar Production Standards in the Seventeenth and Eighteenth Centuries" in *Merchants and Scholars: Essays in the History of Exploration and Trade*, ed., John Parker. (Minneapolis: University of Minnesota Press, 1965), 147–70.

Bardet, J.-P. et H. Charbonneau. "Cultures et milieux en France et en Nouvelle-France: la différentiation des comportements démographiques". dans J. Goy et J.-P. Wallot. éds. *Evolution et éclatement du monde rural: structures, fonctionnement, et évolution différentielle des sociétés françaises et québecoises XVIIe–XIXe siècles.* (Paris and Montréal: École des hautes études en sciences sociales et Presses Université de Montréal, 1986).

Bates, Réal. "Les conceptions prénuptiales dans la vallée du Saint Laurent avant 1725", *RHAF*, 40, 2 (automne 1986), 253–72.

Baudrillart, Alfred [Cardinal]. *Philippe V et la cour de France, 1700–1715.* 5 vols. (Paris: Firmin-Didot, 1890–1901).

Baudrit, André. "Charles de Courbon, comte de Blénac, (1622–1696), gouverneur-général des Antilles françaises (1677–1696)", *Mémoires de la Société d'historie de la Martinique*, 2 (1967), 1–205.

Baugh, Daniel A. "Maritime Strength and Atlantic Commerce, The uses of 'a grand marine empire'" in *An Imperial State at War: Britain from 1689 to 1815*, ed., Lawrence Stone. (London and New York: Routledge, 1994), 185–223.

Beckles, Hilary McD. *White Servitude and Black Slavery in Barbados, 1627–1715.* (Knoxville: University of Tennessee Press, 1989).

Beik, William. *Absolutism and Society in Seventeenth-Century France: State Power and Provincial Aristocracy in Languedoc.* (Cambridge: Cambridge University Press, 1985).

Betts, Raymond F. *Europe Overseas, Phases of Imperialism.* (New York: Basic Books, 1968).

Bezard, Yvonne. *Fonctionnaires maritimes et coloniaux sous Louis XIV, les Bégon.* (Paris: Albin Michel, [1932]).

Black, Jeremy. *Natural and Necessary Enemies: Anglo-French relations in the eighteenth century.* (London: Duckworth, 1986).

Black, Jeremy. *The Rise of the European Powers, 1679–1793.* (London: Edward Arnold, 1990).

Black, Jeremy. "British Naval Power and International Commitments: Political and Strategic Problems, 1688–1770" in *Parameters of British Naval Power, 1650–1850.* ed. Michael Duffy. (Exeter: University of Exeter Press, 1992), 39–59.

Blackburn, Robin. *The Making of New World Slavery: From the Baroque to the Modern, 1492–1800.* (London and New York: Verso, 1997).

Blérald, Philippe-Alain. *Histoire économique de la Guadeloupe et de la Martinique, du XVIIe siècle à nos jours.* (Paris: Karthala, 1986).

Blet, Henri. *Histoire de la colonisation française*, Vol. 1. *Des origines à 1789.* (Grenoble-Paris: B. Arthaud, 1946).

Bliss, Michael, *Northern Enterprise; Five Centuries of Canadian Business*, (Toronto: McClelland & Stewart, 1987).

Bluche, François. *Louis XIV.* trans. Mark Greenglass. (Oxford: Basil Blackwell, 1990).

Blussé, Leonard and Femme Gaastra, *Companies and Trade: Essays on Overseas Trading Companies during the Ancien Règime.* (The Hague: Martinus Nijhoff, 1981).

Boleda, Mario. "Trente mille Français à la conquête du Saint-Laurent", *Histoire sociale/Social history*, 23/45 (May 1990), 153–77.

Bondois, Paul M. "Colbert et la question du sucre, la rivalité franco-hollandaise", *Revue d'histoire économique et sociale*, 11 (1923), 12–61.

Bondois, Paul M. "Les Centres sucriers français au XVIIIe siècle", *Revue d'histoire économique et sociale*, 19, 1 (1931), 27–76.

Bondois, Paul M. "L'Industrie sucrière française au XVIIIe siècle: la fabrication et le rivalités entre les raffineries", *Revue d'Histoire économique et sociale*, 19, 3 (1931), 316–46.

Bonnassieux, Pierre. *Les Grandes compagnies de commerce: étude pour servir à l'histoire de la colonisation.* (Paris: Plon, 1892).

Bosher, J. F. *The Canada Merchants, 1713–63.* (Oxford: Clarendon Press, 1987).

Bosher, J. F. *Men and Ships in the Canada Trade, 1660–1760: A Biographical Dictionary.* (Ottawa: Environment Canada, Parks Service, 1992).

Bosher, J. F. *Business and Religion in the Age of New France, 1600–1760: Twenty-two Studies.* (Toronto: The Canadian Scholars' Press, 1994).

Bosher, J. F. "Huguenot Merchants and the Protestant International in the Seventeenth Century", *William and Mary Quarterly*, 3rd. Series, 52, 1 (January 1995), 77–102.

Bouchard, Gérard et Joseph Goy. éds. *Famille, économie et société rurale en context d'urbanisation (17e–20e siècles).* (Chicoutimi et Paris: Centre interuniversitaire SUREP/École des hautes études en sciences sociales, 1990).

Boucher, Philip P. "Comment se forme un ministre coloniale: l'initiation de Colbert, 1651–1664", *RHAF*, 37, 3 (décembre 1983), 431–52.

Boucher, Philip P. "A Colonial Company at the Time of the Fronde: The Compagnie de la Terre ferme de l'Amérique ou France équinoxiale", *Terrae Incognita*, 11 (1979), 43–58.

Boucher, Philip P. *Les Nouvelles Frances: France in America, 1500–1815, An Imperial Perspective.* (Providence: The John Carter Brown Library, 1989).

Boucher, Philip P. *Cannibal Encounters: Europeans and Island Caribs, 1492–1763.* (Baltimore: The Johns Hopkins University Press, 1992).

Boudriot, Jean. *Le Navire marchand, ancien régime, étude historique et monographie [Le Mercure, 1730].* (Paris: Jean Boudriot, 1991).

Boulle, Pierre, H. "French Mercantilism, Commercial Companies, and Colonial Profitability" in *Companies and Trade: Essays on Overseas Trading Companies during the Ancien Régime*, eds. Leonard Blussé and Femme Gaastra. (The Hague: Martinus Nijhoff, 1981), 97–117.

Bourne, Ruth. *Queen Anne's Navy in the West Indies.* (New Haven: Yale University Press, 1939).

Boxer, Charles R. *The Golden Age of Brazil, 1695–1750: Growing Pains of a Colonial Society.* (Berkeley and Los Angeles: University of California Press, 1969).

Boxer, Charles R. "Some Second Thoughts on the Third Dutch War, 1672–1674", *Transactions of the Royal Historical Society*, 5th Series, 19 (1969), 67–94.

Bradley, Peter T. *The Lure of Peru: Maritime Intrusion into the South Sea, 1598–1701.* (Houndsmills: Macmillan, 1989).

Braudel, Fernand. *Civilization and Capitalism, 15th–18th Century*, 3 vols. trans. Siân Reynolds. (London: Collins, 1982–4).

Braudel, Fernand. *The Identity of France*, Vol. 2, *People and Production*, trans. Siân Reynolds. (London: Collins, 1990).

Brière, Jean-François. "Pêche et politique à Terre-Neuve au XVIIIe siècle: la France véritable gagnant du traité d'Utrecht?", *Canadian Historical Review*, 64, 2 (1983), 168–7.

Brière, Jean-François, *La Pêche française en Amérique du Nord au XVIIIe siècle.* ([Saint-Laurent] Fides, 1990).

Brière, Jean-François. "The French Fishery in North America in the 18th Century" in *How Deep is the Ocean? Historical Essays on Canada's Atlantic Fishery.* ed. James E. Candow et al. (Sydney: University College of Cape Breton Press, 1997), 45–64.

Brizan, George *Grenada, Island of Conflict, from Amerindians to People's Revolution, 1498–1979.* (London: Zed Books, 1984).

Bromley, John S. *Corsairs and Navies, 1660–1760* [a collection of 22 essays]. (London and Ronceverte: The Hambleton Press, 1987).

Brujin, Jaap. *The Dutch Navy of the Seventeenth and Eighteenth Centuries.* (Columbus: University of South Carolina Press, 1993).

Buchet, Christian. *La Lutte pour l'espace Caraïbe et la facade Atlantique de l'Amérique Centrale et du Sud (1672–1763).* 2 vols. (Paris: Librairie de l'Inde Editeur, 1991).

Buchet, Christian. "The Royal Navy and the Caribbean, 1689–1763", *The Mariner's Mirror*, 80, 1 (February 1994), 30–44.

Buffon, Alain. *Monnaie et crédit en économie coloniale; contribution à l'histoire économique de la Guadeloupe (1635–1919).* (Basse-Terre: Société d'histoire de la Guadeloupe, 1979).

Burke, Peter. *The Fabrication of Louis XIV.* (New Haven: Yale University Press, 1992).

Burns, Sir Alan. *History of the British West Indies.* rev. 2nd ed. (London: Allen and Unwin, 1965).

Butel, Paul. *Les Négociants bordelais, L'Europe et les îsles au XVIIIe siècle*, (Paris: Aubier-Montaigne, 1974).

Butel, Paul. *Les Caraïbes au temps des flibustiers, XVIe–XVIIe siècles.* (Paris: Aubier-Montaigne, 1982).

Butel, Paul. "Un Nouvel âge coloniale: Les Antilles sous Louis XIV" in *Histoire des Antilles et de la Guyane.* éd. Pierre Pluchon. (Toulouse: Edouard Privat, 1982), 79–118.

Butel, Paul. "France, the Antilles, and Europe in the seventeenth and eighteenth centuries: renewal of foreign trade", in *The Rise of Merchant Empires, Long Distance Trade in the Early Modern World, 1350–1750.* ed. James D. Tracy. (New York: Cambridge University Press, 1990), 153–73.

Butel, Paul. *L'Économie française au XVIIIe siècle*, (Paris: SEDES, 1993).

Cahall, Raymond Du Bois. *The Sovereign Council of New France: A Study in Canadian Constitutional History.* (New York: Columbia University, 1915).

Camus, Michel. "Aux origines de la colonisation française de St. Domingue", *Revue de la Société Haitienne d'histoire et de géographie*, 45, 154 (mars 1987), 55–67.

Carnes, Marc C., *Mapping America's Past: A Historical Atlas*. (New York: Henry Holt, 1996).

Carrière, Charles. *Négociants marseillais au XVIIIe siècle: contribution à l'étude des économies maritimes*. 2 vols. (Marseille: Institut historique de Provence, 1973).

Cassel, Jay. "Les troupes de la marine en Canada, 1683–1760: Men and Materiel", Unpublished history Ph.D. thesis, University of Toronto, 1987.

Cassilly, Thomas Alex. "The Anticolonial Tradition in France: The Eighteenth Century to the Fifth Republic". 2 vols. Unpublished history Ph.D. thesis, Columbia University, 1975.

Cauna, Jacques. *Au temps des isles à sucre; histoire d'une plantation de Saint-Domingue au XVIIIe siècles*. (Paris: Karthala et A.C.C.T., 1987).

Cauna, Jacques de. "Aux origines du peuplement des "Iles de l'Amérique": les ports de l'Aquitaine et Saint-Domingue, (XVIIe–XVIIIe siècles)", dans *Négoce, ports et océans, XVIe–XIXe siècles*. dirs. Silvia Marzagalli et Hubert Bonin. (Bordeaux: Presse universitaires de Bordeaux, 2000), 195–213.

Cavignac, Jean. *Jean Pellet, commerçant en gros, 1694–1772: contribution à l'étude du négoce bordelais du XVIIIe siècle*. (Paris: SEVPEN, 1967).

Charbonneau, Hubert *et al.* "Le recensement nomiatif du Canada en 1681", *Histoire Sociale/Social History*, 7 (avril 1971), 77–98.

Charbonneau, Hubert. *Vie et mort de nos ancêtres: étude démographique*. (Montréal: Presses de l'Université de Montréal, 1975).

Charbonneau, Hubert et Yves Landry. "La politique démographique en Nouvelle France", *Annales de démographie historique*, (1979), 29–57.

Charbonneau, Hubert. "Trois siècles de dépopulation amérindienne" dans *Les populations amérindiennes et inuit du Canada, aperçu démographique*, dirs., Louise Normandeau et Victor Piché. (Montréal: Presses de l'Université de Montréal, 1984), 28–48.

Charbonneau, Hubert and Normand Robert, "The French Origins of the Canadian Population, 1608–1759" in *The Historical Atlas of Canada*, Vol. 1, *From the Beginning to 1800*. ed. R. C. Harris. (Toronto: University of Toronto Press, 1987), Plate 45.

Charbonneau, Hubert, André Guillemette *et al. Naissance d'une population; les Français établis au Canada au XVIIe siècle*. (Paris et Montréal: Institut National d'Études Démographiques/Presses de l'Université de Montréal, 1987). trans. by Paola Colozzoa as *The First French Canadians, Pioneers in the St. Lawrence Valley*. (Newark: University of Delaware Press, 1993).

Chard, Donald F. "The Price and Profits of Accommodation: Massachusetts Louisbourg Trade, 1713–1744" in *Seafaring in Colonial Massachusetts, a conference held by the Colonial Society of Massachusetts*, November 21–22, 1975. (Boston: [n.p.] 1980), 131–52.

Chard, Donald F. "Canso, 1710–1721: Focal Point of New England-Cape Breton Rivalry", *Collections of the Nova Scotia Historical Society*, 39 (1977), [49]-77.

Charpentier, Louis. *D'Amblimont, chef d'escadre de Louis XIV*. (Paris: Société d'éditions géographiques maritimes et coloniales, 1928).

Chaudenson, Robert. *Creolization of Language and Culture*. Revised in collaboration with Solikoko S. Mufwene. translated by Sheri Pargman, Solikoko Mufwene, Sabrina Billings and Michelle AuCoin. (London and New York: Routledge, [1992] 2001).

Chauleau, Liliane. *Case-Pilote, Le Prêcheur, Basse Pointe: Étude démographique sur le nord de la Martinique, XVIIe siècle*. (Paris: L'Harmattan, 1990).

Chauleau, Liliane. *Dans les îles du vent: La Martinique XVIIe–XIXe siècles*, (Paris: L'Harmattan, 1993).

Chénier, Rémi. *Quebec: A French Colonial Town in America, 1660 to 1690*, Studies in Archaeology, Architecture, and History. (Ottawa: Parks Services, Environment Canada, 1991).

Chérubini, Bernard. *Cayenne: ville créole et polyethnique, essai d'anthropologie urbain*. (Paris: Karthala-Cenaddom, 1988).

Chiappeli, Fredi. ed. *First Images: The Impact of the New World on the Old.* 2 vols. (Berkeley: University of California Press, 1976).

Choquette, Leslie. *Frenchmen into Peasants, Modernity and Tradition in the Peopling of French Canada.* (Cambridge: Harvard University Press, 1997).

Clark, Andrew Hill. *Acadia: The Geography of Early Nova Scotia to 1760.* (Madison: University of Wisconsin Press, 1968).

Clark, John G. *La Rochelle and the Atlantic Economy during the Eighteenth Century.* (Baltimore and London: The Johns Hopkins University Press, 1981).

Clowes, William Laird. *The Royal Navy: A History from the Earliest Times to the Present.* 7 vols. (London: Sampson Low Marsten and Co., 1897–1903).

Coates, Colin. *The Metamorphoses of Landscape and Community in Early Quebec.* (Montreal and Kingston: McGill-Queen's University Press, 1999).

Cohen, William B. *The French Encounter with Africans: White Response to Blacks, 1530–1880.* (Bloomington: Indiana University Press, 1980).

Cole, Charles Woolsey. *Colbert and a Century of French Mercantilism.* 2 vols. (New York: Columbia University Press, 1939).

Cole, Charles Woolsey. *French Mercantilism, 1683–1700.* (New York: Columbia University Press, 1943).

Coleman, D. C. ed. *Revisions in Mercantilism: Debates in Economic History.* (London: Methuen, 1969).

Collins, James B. *Fiscal Limits of Absolutism: Direct Taxation in Early Seventeenth-Century France.* (Berkeley: University of California Press, 1988).

Cook, S. F. and Woodrow Borah. "The Aboriginal Population of Hispaniola" in *Essays in Population History: Mexico and the Caribbean.* 3 vols. (Berkeley: University of California Press, 1971), 1: 376–410.

Cooke, Jacob Ernest. ed. *Encyclopedia of the North American Colonies.* 3 vols. (New York: Charles Scribners Sons, 1993).

Corvisier, André, *La France de Louis XIV, 1643–1715: Ordre intérieur et place en Europe.* 2ème éd. (Paris: SEDES, 1979).

Crété, Liliane. *La Traite des nègres sous l'ancien régime, le nègre, le sucre et la toile.* (Paris: Perrin, 1989).

Crosby, Alfred W. *Ecological Imperialism: The Biological Expansion of Europe, 900–1900.* (New York: Cambridge University Press, 1986).

Crouse, Nellis M. *The French Struggle for the West Indies, 1665–1713.* (New York: Octagon Books, [1943] 1966).

Crouzet, François. "Économie et société (1715–1789)" dans *Bordeaux au XVIIIe siècle.* dir. Fr.-Geo. Pariset. (Bordeaux: Fédération historique du Sud-Ouest, 1968), 155–369.

Crowhurst, Patrick. *The Defence of British Trade, 1689–1815.* (Folkstone: Dawson, 1977).

Curtin, Philip D. *The Atlantic Slave Trade: A Census.* (Madison: University of Wisconsin Press, 1969).

Curtin, Philip D. ed. *Imperialism.* (New York: Walker and Co., 1971).

Curtin, Philip D. *The Rise and Fall of the Plantation Complex: Essays in Atlantic History.* (New York: Cambridge University Press, 1990).

Dahlgren Eric. W. "Voyages français à destination de la Mer du Sud avant Bougainville (1695–1749)", *Nouvelles archives des missions scientifiques et littéraires,* 14, pt. 4 (1907), 423–568.

Dahlgren, Eric W. *Les Relations commerciales et maritimes entre la France et les côtes de l'Ocean Pacifique,* Tome 1, *Le commerce de la Mer du Sud jusqu'à la paix d'Utrecht.* (Paris: Librairie Ancienne Honoré Champion, 1909).

Dahlgren, Eric W. "L'expédition de Martinet et la fin du commerce interlope français à la mer du sud espagnole", *RHC,* 1 (1913), 257–332.

Daigle, Jean. "'Nos amis les ennemis': relations commerciales de l'Acadie avec le Massachusetts, 1670–1711". Unpublished history Ph.D. thesis University of Maine, Orono, 1975.

Daney, Sydney. *Histoire de la Martinique depuis la colonisation jusqu'en 1815.* 3 vols. [facsimile]. (Fort-de-France: Société d'histoire de la Martinique, [1846] 1963).

Daniels, John D. "The Indian Populations of North America in 1492", *The William and Mary Quarterly*, 3rd Series, 49, 2 (April 1992), 298–320.

Davies, J. D. "The Navy, Parliament, and Political Crisis in the Reign of Charles II", *Historical Journal*, 36 (1993), 271–88.

Davies, David, "The Birth of the Imperial Navy: Aspects of English Naval Strategy c. 1650–90", *Parameters of British Naval Power, 1650–1850*, ed., Michael Duffy. (Exeter: University of Exeter Press, 1992, 14–38.

Davies, K. G. *The North Atlantic World in the Seventeenth Century*, (Minneapolis: University of Minnesota Press, 1974).

Davis, Ralph. *The Rise of the English Shipping Industry in the Seventeenth and Eighteenth Centuries.* (Newton Abbot: David and Charles, [1962] 1972). Reprinted National Maritime Museum [n.d.].

Davis, Ralph. *The Rise of the Atlantic Economies.* (London: Weidenfeld and Nicolson [1973] 1975).

Debien, Gabriel. "Les Engagés pour les Antilles, 1634–1715", *RHC*, 37 (1951), 2–277.

Debien, Gabriel. *Une Plantation de Saint-Domingue: La Sucrerie Galbaud du Fort 1690–1802.* (Cairo: Les Presses de l'Institut français d'archéologie orientale du Caire, 1941).

Debien, Gabriel. "Engagés pour le Canada au XVIIe siècle vus de La Rochelle", *RHAF*, 6 (1952–53), 177–233; 374–407; 456; 536–9.

Debien, Gabriel. "L'Emigration poitevin vers l'Amérique au XVIIe siècle", *Bulletin de la société des antiquaires de l'ouest*, 2e série, 2 (1952), 277–306.

Debien, G., M. Delafosse, et M. Gaucher. "Les engagés pour le Canada au XVIIIe siècle", *RHAF*, 13 (1959–60), 247–61; 402–21; 550–61; et 14 (1960–61): 87–108; 246–58; 430–40; 583–602.

Debien, Gabriel. *Les Esclaves aux Antilles (XVIIe–XVIIIe siècles).* (Fort-de-France/Basse-Terre: Société d'histoire de la Martinique/Société d'histoire de la Guadeloupe, 1974).

Dechêne, Louise. *Habitants and Merchants in Seventeenth-Century Montreal*, trans. Liana Vardi. (Montreal and Kingston: McGill-Queen's University Press, [1974] 1992).

Deerr, Noel. *The History of Sugar.* 2 vols. (London: Chapman and Hall, 1949–50).

Delafosse, Marcel. "La Rochelle et les Iles au XVIIe siècle", *RHC*, 36 (1949), 238–81.

Delalande, J. *Le conseil souveraine de la Nouvelle France.* (Québec: Imprimeur du roi, 1927).

Deloffre, Frédéric. "Chronique de Chedabouctou: La colonie rocheloise de Chedabouctou racontée par un témoin" in *France in the New World: Proceedings of the 22nd Annual Meeting of the French Colonial Historical Society.* ed. David Buisseret. (East Lansing: Michigan State University Press, 1998), 91–106.

Delumeau, Jean. "Les Terres-neuviers malouins à la fin du XVIIe siècle", *Annales (Économies-Sociétés-Civilisations)*, 164 (1961), 665–85.

Delumeau, Jean. dir. *Le mouvement du port de Saint Malo, 1681–1720: bilan statistique.* (Paris: Librairie C. Klincksieck, [1966]).

Delumeau, Jean. "La Guerre de course française sous l'ancien régime", dans *Course et piraterie, études présentées à la Commission Internationale d'Histoire Maritime à l'occassion de son XVe colloque internationale pendant le XIVe Congrès Internationale des Sciences Historiques*, typescript, (San Francisco, Centre Nationale de la Recherche Scientifigue, 1975), 271–95.

Denis, Serge. *Trois siècles de vie française, Nos Antilles.* (Paris et Orléans: Maison du Livre Français, 1935).

Desbarats, Catherine. "Agriculture within the Seigneurial Régime of Eighteenth-Century Canada: Some Thoughts on the Recent Literature", *Canadian Historical Review*, 73, 1 (March 1992), 1–29.

Desbarats, Catherine. "The Cost of Early Canada's Native Alliances: Reality and Scarcity's Rhetoric, *The William and Mary Quarterly*, 3rd Series, 52, 4 (October 1995), 609–30.

Desbarats, Catherine. "France in North America: The Net Burden of Empire During the First Half of the Eighteenth Century", *French History*, 11, 1 (1997), 1–28.

Deschamps, Hubert. *Les Methodes et les doctrines coloniales de la France (du XVIe siècle à nos jours)*. (Paris: Armand Colin, 1953).

Dessert, Daniel et J.-L. Journet. "Le Lobby Colbert: un royaume ou une affaire de famille", *Annales, (Économies-Sociétés-Civilisations)*, 30 (1975), 1303–36.

Dessert, Daniel. *Argent, pouvoir et société au Grand Siècle*. (Paris: Fayard, 1984).

Dessert, Daniel. *La Royale: vaisseaux et marins du Roi-Soleil*. (Paris: Fayard, 1996).

Deveau, Jean-Michel. "La Rivalité franco-anglaise sur les côtes d'Afrique: la prise du fort Saint-James par Monsieur de Gennes en 1695" dans *Guerres et Paix, 1660–1815: journée franco-anglaises d'historie de la marine*. (Vincennes: Société historique de la Marine, 1987), 197–208.

Devèze, Michel. *Antilles, Guyanes, la Mer des Caraïbes de 1492 à 1789*, (Paris: SEDES, 1977).

De Vries, Jan. *The Economy of Europe in an Age of Crisis, 1600–1750*, (London and New York: Cambridge University Press, 1976).

Dichason, John A. *Justice et justiciables, la procédure civile à la prévoté de Québec, 1667–1759*. (Québec: Les Presses de l'université Laval, 1982).

Dickason, Olive P. *Canada's First Nations: A History of Founding Peoples from Earliest times*. (Toronto: McClelland and Stewart, 1992).

Dickinson, John A. "The Pre-contact Huron Population: A Reappraisal", *Ontario History*, 72, 1 (March 1980), 173–9.

Dickinson, John A. *Law in New France*. Canadian Legal History Project, Working Paper Series. (Winnepeg: University of Manitoba, 1992).

Dickinson, John A. and Jan Grabowski. "Les populations amérindiennes de la vallée laurentienne, 1608–1765", *Annales de démographie historique*, (1993), 53–66.

Dingli, Laurent. *Colbert, marquis de Seignelay: le fils flamboyant*. (Paris: Libairie Academique Perrin, 1997).

Donovan, Kenneth. "Slaves and Their Owners in Île Royale, 1713–1760", *Acadiensis*, 25, 1 (Autumn 1995), 3–32.

Donovan, Kenneth. "A Nominal List of Slaves and Their Owners in Île Royale, 1713–1760", *Nova Scotia Historical Review*, 16, 1 (1996), 151–62.

Doyle, Michael W. *Empires*. (Ithaca: Cornell University Press, 1986).

Doyle, William. *The Old European Order, 1660–1800*. (Oxford and New York: Oxford University Press, 1978).

Dubé, Jean-Claude. "Clients des Colbert et des Pontchartrain à l'intendance de Québec" dans *Hommage à Roland Mousnier, Clienteles et fidelitiés en Europe à l'époque moderne*. éd. Yves Durand. (Paris: PUF, 1981), 199–212.

Duffy, Michael. ed. *Parameters of British Naval Power, 1650–1850*. (Exeter: University of Exeter Press, 1992).

Dunn, Richard, S. *Sugar and Slaves: the Rise of the Planter Class in the English West Indies, 1624–1713*. (New York: W.W. Norton, 1972).

Dupâquier, Jacques. *La Population française aux XVIIe–XVIIIe siècles*. (Paris: Presses universitaires de France, 1979).

Easterbrook, W.T. and Hugh G.J. Aitken. *Canadian Economic History*. (Toronto: Macmillan [1956], 1970).

Eccles, William John. *Frontenac, The Courtier Governor*. (Toronto: McClelland & Stewart, [1959] 1979).

Eccles, William John. *Canada Under Louis XIV, 1663–1701*. (Toronto: McClelland & Stewart, 1964).

Eccles, William John. *The Canadian Frontier, 1534–1760.* revised ed. (Albuquerque: University of New Mexico Press, [1969] 1983).

Eccles, William John. *France in America.* revised ed. (Toronto: Fitzhenry & Whiteside, [1972] 1990).

Eccles, William John. *Essays on New France.* (Toronto: Oxford University Press, 1987).

Edmunds, R. David and Joseph Peyser. *Fox Wars: the Mesquakie Challenge to New France.* (Norman: University of Oklahoma Press, 1993).

Ehrman, John. *The Navy in the War of William III, 1689–1697.* (Cambridge: Cambridge University Press, 1953).

Eid, Leroy. "The Ojibwa-Iroquois War: The War the Five Nations did not Win", *Ethnohistory,* 26, 4 (Fall 1779), 297–324.

Ekberg, Carl J. *The Failure of Louis XIV's Dutch War.* (Chapel Hill: University of North Carolina Press, 1979).

Ekberg, Carl J. *French Roots in the Illinois Country: The Mississippi Frontier in Colonial Times.* (Urbana and Chicago: University of Illinois Press, 1998).

Ekelund, Robert and Robert D. Tollison. *Mercantilism as a Rent-seeking Society: Economic Regulation in Historical Perspective.* (College Station: Texas A&M University Press, 1981).

Elisabeth, Leo. "The French Antilles", in *Neither Slave Nor Free: The Freedmen of African Descent in the Slave Societies of the New World,* David W. Cohen and Jack P. Greene eds. (Baltimore and London: The Johns Hopkins University Press, 1972), 134–71.

Elliott, John H. *Spain and its World,1500–1700.* (New Haven and London: Yale University Press, 1989).

Eltis, David "The Slave Economies of the Caribbean: Structure, Performance, Evolution, and Significance" in *General History of the Caribbean.* Vol. 3. *The slave societies of the Caribbean.* ed. Franklin W. Knight. (London: UNESCO Publishing, 1997), 105–37.

Eltis, David, Stephen D. Behrendt, David Richardson, and Herbert S. Klein. eds. *The Trans-Atlantic Slave Trade: A Database on CD-ROM.* (Cambridge: Cambridge University Press, 1999).

Eltis, David. *The Rise of African Slavery in the Americas.* (Cambridge: Cambridge University Press, 2000).

Eltis, David. "The Volume and Structure of the Transatlantic Slave Trade: A Reassessment", *The William and Mary Quarterly,* 3rd Series, 58, no. 1 (January 2001), 17–46.

Emmer, P. C. "European Expansion and Migration: The European Colonial Past and Intercontinental Migration; An Overview" in *European Expansion and Migration from Africa, Asia, and Europe.* eds. P. C. Emmer and M. Möner. (New York and Oxford: Berg, 1992), 1–12.

Engerman, Stanley L. and B. W. Higman. "The Demographic structure of the Caribbean slave societies in the eighteenth and nineteenth centuries" in *General History of the Caribbean,* Vol. 3. *The slave societies of the Caribbean,* (London: UNESCO Publishing, 1997), 45–104.

Faribault-Beauregard, Marthe. *La Population des forts français d'Amérique, (XVIIIe siècle).* 2 vols. (Montréal: Editions Bergeron, 1982–4).

Faure, Edgar. *Le Banqueroute de Law.* (Paris: Gallimard, 1977).

Fauteux, Joseph-Noël. *Essai sur l'Industrie au Canada sous le régime français.* 2 vols. (Québec: Ls.-A. Proulx, 1927).

Feiling, Keith G. *British Foreign Policy, 1660–1672.* (London: Macmillan and Co., 1930).

Filion, Conrad. "Essai sur l'évolution du mot habitant (XVIIe-XVIIIe) siècles", *RHAF* 24, 3 (décembre 1970), 375–401.

Fischer, David Hackett. *The Great Wave, Price Revolutions, and the Rhythm of History.* (New York: Oxford University Press, 1996).

Flandrin, Jean-Louis. *Families in Former Times: Kinship, Household, and Sexuality in Early Modern France.* (Cambridge: Cambridge University Press, 1977).

Flinn, M. W. *The European Demographic System, 1500–1820.* (Brighton: The Johns Hopkins University Press, 1981).

Forster, Robert. "Slavery in Virginia and Saint-Domingue in the Late Eighteenth Century" in *Proceedings of the Thirteenth and Fourteenth Meetings of the French Colonial Historical Society*, ed. Philip P Boucher. (Lanham: The University Press of America, 1989), 1–13.

Francis, Daniel and Toby Morantz. *Partners in Furs: A History of the Fur Trade in Eastern James Bay, 1600–1870.* (Kingston and Montreal: McGill-Queen's University Press, 1983).

Frégault, Guy. *Iberville, le conquérant.* (Montréal: Guérin, [1944] 1996).

Frégault, Guy. *Le XVIIIe siècle canadien: études.* (Montréal: HMH, 1968).

Frostin, Charles. "Les Pontchartrain et la pénétration commerciale française en Amérique espagnole", *Revue historique*, no. 245 (1971), 307–336.

Frostin, Charles. *Les Révoltes blanches à Saint-Domingue aux XVIIe et XVIIIe siècles (Haiti avant 1789).* (Paris: L'École, 1975).

Frostin, Charles. "Du peuplement pénal de l'Amérique française aux XVIIe et XVIIIe siècles: hésitations et contradictions du pouvoir royal en matière de déportation", *Annales de Bretagne*, 85 (1978), 67–94.

Frostin, Charles. "L'Organisation ministérielle sous Louis XIV: cumul d'attributions et situations conflictuelles (1690–1715)", *Revue historique de droit française et étranger*, 4ème série (1980), 201–26.

Galloway, J. H. *The Sugar Cane Industry: An historical geography from its origins to 1914.* (Cambridge: Cambridge University Press, 1989).

Galloway, Patricia, ed. *La Salle and His Legacy: Frenchmen and Indians in the Lower Mississippi Valley.* (Jackson: University Press of Mississippi, 1982).

Garnault, Emile. *Les Rochelais et le Canada.* [La Rochelle: [n.p.] 1893].

Gaudet, Placide. "Les seigeuries de l'ancienne Acadie", *Bulletin des Recherches Historiques*, 33 (1927), 343–7.

Garrigus, John D. "Blue and Brown: Contraband Indigo and the Rise of a Free Coloured Planter Class in French Saint-Domingue, *The Americas*, 50 (1993), 233–63.

Gaultier, Arlette. "Les esclaves femmes aux Antilles françaises 1635–1848", *Historical Reflections/Réflexions historiques*, 10, 3 (Fall 1983), 409–33.

Gaultier, Arlette. *Les Soeurs de Solitude – la condition féminine aux Antilles du XVIIe au XIXe siècle.* (Paris: Éditions Caribbéenes, 1985).

Gaultier, Arlette. "Traité et politique démographiques esclavagistes", *Population*, 41, 6 (1986), 1005–24.

Geggus, David. "Sex Ratio, Age, and Ethnicity in the Atlantic Slave Trade: Data from French Shipping and Plantation Records", *Journal of African History*, 30 (1989), 23–44.

Geggus, David. "Sex ratio and ethnicity: A reply to Paul Lovejoy", *Journal of African History*, 30 (1989), 395–7.

Geggus, David. "The Demographic Composition of the French Caribbean Slave Trade" in *Proceedings of the Thirteenth and Fourteenth Meetings of the French Colonial Historical Society.* ed. Philip P. Boucher. (Lanham: University Press of America, 1989), 14–30.

Geggus, David. "The Major Port Towns of Saint-Domingue in the Later Eighteenth Century" in *Atlantic Port Cities: Economy, Culture, and Society in the Atlantic World, 1650–1850.* eds. Franklin W. Knight and Peggy K. Liss. (Knoxville: University of Tennessee Press, 1991), 87–116.

Girard, Albert. *Le Commerce français à Seville et Cadix au temps des Habsbourg.* (Paris: 1932). (Reprinted New York: Burt Franklin, 1967).

Giraud, Marcel. *Histoire de la Louisiane française*, 4 vols (Paris: Presses universitaires de France, 1953–74).

Giraud, Marcel. *A History of French Louisiana.* vol. 5. *The Company of the Indies, 1723–1731.* (Baton Rouge: Louisiana State University Press, 1974).

Gisler, Antoine, CSSP . *L'Esclavage aux antilles françaises (XVIIe–XIXe siècle): Contribution au problem de l'esclavage.* (Fribourg Suisse: Éditions universitaires Fribourg Suisse, 1965).

Glete, Jan. *Navies and Nations, Warships, Navies, and State Building in Europe and America, 1500–1860.* 2 vols. (Stockholm: Almquist & Wiksell International, 1993).

Goslinga, Cornelis Ch. *The Dutch in the Caribbean and the Wild Coast, 1580–1680.* (Gainesville: University of Florida Press, 1971).

Goslinga, Cornelis Ch. *A Short History of the Netherlands Antilles and Surinam.* (The Hague: Martinus Nijhoff, 1979).

Goslinga, Cornelis Ch. *The Dutch in the Caribbean and in the Guianas, 1680–1791.* (Dover: Van Gorarm, 1985).

Goubert, Pierre. *Louis XIV and Twenty Million Frenchmen.* translated by Anne Carter. (New York: Vintage Books, [1966] 1970).

Goubert, Pierre. "Le tragique dix-septième siècle" dans F. Braudel et E. Labrousse, éds., *Histoire économique et sociale de la France.* Vol. 2. *Des derniers temps de l'âge seigneurial aux préludes de l'âge industriel,* (1660–1789). (Paris: Presses universitaires de France, 1979), 329–65.

Goubert, Pierre. *Mazarin.* (Paris: Fayard, 1990).

Gouger, Lina. "Montréal et le peuplement de Détroit, 1701–1765" in *Proceedings of the Eighteenth Meeting of the French Colonial Historical Society.* ed. James Pritchard. (Cleveland: French Colonial Historical Society, 1993), 46–58.

Gould, Clarence P. "Trade Between the Windward Islands and the Continental Colonies of the French Empire, 1683–1763", *The Mississippi Valley Historical Review,* 25, (1939), 473–90.

Goy, J. et J.-P. Wallot. éds. *Evolution et éclatement du monde rurale: structures, fonctionnement, et évolution differentielle des sociétés françaises et québecoises XVIIe–XIXe siècles.* (Paris et Montréal: École des hautes études en sciences sociales/Presses de l'Université de Montréal, 1986).

Grabowski, Jan. "Searching for the Common Ground: Natives and French in Montreal, 1700–1730" in *Proceedings of the Eighteenth Meeting of the French Colonial Historical Society.* ed. James Pritchard. (Cleveland: French Colonial Historical Society, 1992), 59–73.

Grabowski, Jan. "French Criminal Justice and Indians in Montreal, 1670–1760", *Ethnohistory,* 43, 3 (Summer 1996), 405–29.

Graham, Gerald S. *Empire of the North Atlantic: The Maritime Struggle for North America.* 2nd ed. (Toronto: University of Toronto Press, 1958).

Greene, Jack P. *Colonial British America: Essays on the New History of the Early Modern Era.* (Baltimore: Johns Hopkins University Press, 1984).

Greene, Jack P. *Negotiated Authorities: Essays in Colonial Political and Constitutional History.* (Charlottesville and London: University Press of Virginia, 1994).

Greer, Allan. *Peasant, Lord, and Merchant: Rural Society in Three Quebec Parishes, 1740–1840.* (Toronto: University of Toronto Press, 1985).

Greer, Allan. *The People of New France.* (Toronto: University of Toronto Press, 1997).

Griffiths, Naomi E. S. *The Context of Acadian History, 1686–1784.* (Montreal and Kingston: McGill-Queen's University Press, 1992).

Guet, L. *Origines de la Martinique – Le colonel François de Collart et la Martinique de son temps – Colonisation, sièges, révoltes, et combats de 1625 à 1720.* (Vannes: Lafolye, 1893).

Hall, Gwendolyn Midlo. *Social Control in Slave Plantation Societies: A Comparison of St. Domingue and Cuba.* (Baltimore and London: The Johns Hopkins University Press, 1971).

Hall, Gwendolyn Midlo. "Saint Domingue" in *Neither Slave Nor Free: The Freedman of African Descent in the Slave Societies of the New World.* eds. David W. Cohen and Jack P. Greene. (Baltimore and London: The Johns Hopkins University Press, 1972), 172–92.

Hall, Gwendolyn Midlo. *Africans in Colonial Louisiana: The Development of Afro-Creole Culture in the Eighteenth Century.* (Baton Rouge and London: Louisiana State University Press, 1992).

Hamelin, Jean. *Économie et société en Nouvelle France.* (Québec: Les Presses Universitaises Laval, 1960).

Hamscher, A. N. "The Conseil Privé and the Parlements in the Age of Louis XIV: A Study in French Absolutism", *Transactions of the American Philosophical Society,* 72, 2 (1987), i–v, 1–162.

Hanoteaux, Gabriel et Alfred Martineau. *Histoire des colonies et de l'expansion de la France dans le monde.* 6 vols. (Paris: Plon, 1929–33).

Hardy, Jr., James D. "The Superior Council in Colonial Louisiana" in *Frenchmen and French Ways in the Mississippi Valley.* ed. John F. McDermott. (Urbana: University of Illinois Press, 1969), 87–101.

Haring, Clarence Henry. *The Buccaneers in the West Indies in the XVII Century.* (London: Methuen & Co., 1910).

Harms, Robert. *The Diligent: A Voyage Through the Worlds of the Slave Trade.* (New York: Basic Books, 2002).

Harris, Richard Cole. *The Seigneurial System in Early Canada: A geographical study.* 2nd ed. (Montreal and Kingston: McGill-Queen's University Press, [1966] 1984).

Harsin, Paul. "La finance et l'État jusqu'au système de Law (1660–1726)", dans *Histoire économique et sociale de la France.* Tome 2. *Des derniers temps de l'âge seigneurial aux préludes de l'âge industriel (1660–1789).* éds. E. Labrousse et F. Braudel. (Paris: Presses universitaires de France, 1970), 267–399.

Harvey, Daniel Cobb. *The French Regime in Prince Edward Island.* (New Haven: Yale University Press, 1926).

Hatton, Ragnhild and J. S. Bromley. eds. *William III and Louis XIV: Essays, 1680–1720, by and for Mark A. Thomson.* (Toronto: University of Toronto Press, 1968).

Hatton, R[agnhild] M. "Louis XIV and his Fellow Monarchs" in *Louis XIV and the Craft of Kingship.* ed. J. Rule. (Columbia: Ohio University Press, 1969), 155–95.

Hatton, Ragnhild. *War and Peace, 1680–1720: An Inaugural Lecture.* (London: Weidenfeld and Nicholson, 1969).

Haudrère, Philippe. "Les Premiers colons de Léogane, 1666–1735" dans *Commerce et plantations dans la Caraïbe.* (Bordeaux: Maison des Pays Ibériques, 1992), 71–80.

Havard, Gilles. *La Grande paix de Montréal de 1701: Les voies de diplomatie franco-amérindienne.* (Montréal: Recherches amérindienne au Québec, 1992).

Hayot, Émile. "Les Gens de couleur libres du Fort Royal, 1679–1823", *RFHOM*, 56, (1969), 5–163.

Heinrich, Pierre. *La Louisiane sous la compagnie des Indes, 1717–1731.* (New York: Burt Franklin, [1908] 1970).

Henripen, Jacques. *La Population canadienne au début du XVIIIe siècle; nuptialité – fécondité – mortalité infantile,* Institut national d'études démographiques, Travaux et documents, cahier no. 22. (Paris: Presses universitaires de France, 1954).

Holmes, Jack D. L. "Dauphin Island in the Franco-Spanish War, 1719–22" in *Frenchmen and French Ways in the Mississippi Valley.* ed. John F. McDermott. (Urbana: University of Illinois Press, 1969), 103–25.

Hornstein, Sari. *The Restoration Navy and English Foreign Trade: A Study in the Peacetime Use of Sea Power.* (Aldershot: Scolar Press, 1991).

Hôtel de la Monnaie. *La Medaille au temps de Louis XIV.* (Paris: Imprimerie nationale, 1970).

Hrodej, Philippe. *L'Amiral Du Casse: l'Évolution d'un Gascon sous Louis XIV.* 2 vols. (Paris: Librarie de l'Inde, 1999).

Huetz de Lemps, Christian. *Géographie du commerce de Bordeaux à la fin du règne de Louis XIV.* (Paris-La Haye: Mouton, 1975).

Huetz de Lemps, Christian. "Indentured Servants Bound for the French Antilles in the Seventeenth and Eighteenth Centuries" in *"To Make America": European Emigration in the Early Modern Period.* eds. Ida Altman and James Horn. (Berkeley: University of California Press, 1991), 172–203.

Huguet, Edmond. *Dictionnaire de la langue française du seizième siècle,* 7 vols. (Paris: E. Champion, 1925–1966).

Hurault, Jean. *Français et Indiens en Guyane, 1604–1972.* (Paris: Union générale d'éditions, 1972).

Hynes, Gisa. "Some Aspect of the Demography of Port Royal, 1650–1755", *Acadiensis*, 3, 1 (1973), 3–17.

Ingersoll, Thomas N. *Mammon and Manon in Early New Orleans: The First Slave Society in the Deep South, 1718–1819.* (Knoxville: University of Tennessee Press, 1999).

Innis, Harold Adams. *The Fur Trade in Canada: An Introduction to Canadian Economic History.* rev. ed. (Toronto: University of Toronto Press, [1930] 1970).

Innis, Hanold Adams. "Cape Breton and the French Regime", *Transactions of the Royal Society of Canada*, 3rd ser., 29, sec. 2 (1935), 51–87.

Innis, Harold Adams. *The Cod Fisheries: The History of an International Economy.* rev. ed. (Toronto: University of Toronto Press, [1940] 1954).

Jaenen, Cornelius J. *The Role of the Church in New France.* (Toronto: McGraw-Hill Ryerson, 1976).

Janzen, Olaf Uwe. "New Light on the Origin of Fort William at St. John's, Newfoundland, 1693–1696", *Newfoundland Quarterly*, 83, 2 (Fall 1987), 24–31.

Jenkins, E. H. *A History of the French Navy From its Beginnings to the Present Day.* (London: Macdonald and Jane's, 1973).

Jennings, Francis. *Ambiguous Iroquois Empire: The Covenant Chain Confederation of Indian Tribes with English Colonies from its beginnings to the Lancaster Treaty of 1744.* (New York: W.W. Norton, 1984).

Johnson, Richard R. *John Nelson, Merchant Adventurer: A Life Between Empires.* (New York: Oxford University Press, 1991).

Johnston, A. J. B. *Religion in Life at Louisbourg, 1713–1758.* (Kingston and Montreal: McGill-Queen's University Press, 1984); reprinted 1996 as *Life and Religion at Louisbourg, 1713–1758.*

Johnston, A. J. B. "The People of Eighteenth-Century Louisbourg", *Nova Scotia Historical Review*, 11, 2 (December 1991), 75–83.

Johnston, A. J. B. "The Fishermen of Eighteenth-Century Cape Breton: Numbers and Origins", in *Aspects of Louisbourg*, ed., E. Krause *et al.* (Sydney: University College of Cape Breton, 1995), 198–208.

Johnston, A. J. B. *Control and Order in French Colonial Louisbourg, 1713–1758.* (East Lansing: Michigan State University Press, 2001).

Jones, J. R. "Limitations of British Sea Power in the French Wars, 1689–1815" in *The British Navy and the Use of Naval Power in the Eighteenth Century* eds. Jeremy Black and Philip Woodfine. ([n.p.]: Leicester University Press, 1988), 33–50.

Jones, J. R. *The Anglo-Dutch Wars of the Seventeenth Century.* (London and New York: Longman, 1996).

Josa, Guy. *Les Industries du sucre et du rhum à la Martinique (1639–1931).* Thèse de droit. (Paris: Les Presses modernes, 1931).

Julien, Charles A. *Les Français en Amérique de 1713 à 1784.* 2 vols. (Paris: SEDES, 1977).

Kaeppelin, Paul. *La compagnie des Indes orientales et François Martin: étude sur l'histoire du commerce et des établissements français dans l'Inde sous Louis XIV (1664–1719).* (Reprinted New York: Burt Franklin, [1908] 1967).

Kamen, Henry. "The Destruction of the Spanish Fleet at Vigo in 1702", *Bulletin of the Institute of Historical Research*, 39 (1966), 165–73.

Kamen, Henry. *The War of the Spanish Succession in Spain, 1700–1715.* (London: Weidenfeld & Nicolson, 1969).

Kay, Jeanne. "The Fur Trade and Native American Population Growth", *Ethnohistory*, 31 (1984), 265–87.

Kennedy, Paul M. *The Rise and Fall of British Naval Mastery.* (London: Macmillan, [1976] 1983).

Kennedy, Paul M. *The Rise and Fall of the Great Powers: Economic Change and Military Conflict from 1500 to 2000.* (London and New York: Unwin Hymen, 1988).

Kettering, Sharon. *Patrons, Brokers, and Clients in Seventeenth-Century France.* (Oxford: Oxford University Press, 1986).

Kettering, Sharon. *Judicial Politics and Urban Revolt in Seventeenth-Century France: The Parlement of Aix, 1629–1659.* (Princeton: Princeton University Press, 1987).

Keyes, John. "Un commis des trésoriers généraux de la marine à Québec, Nicolas Lanouillier de Boisclerc", *RHAF.* 32, 2 (1978), 181–202.

Kilby, Kenneth. *The Cooper and his Trade.* (London: John Baker, 1971).

Kiple, Kenneth F. and Kriemhild C. Ornelas. "After the Encounter: Disease and Demographics in the Lesser Antilles" in *The Lesser Antilles in the Age of European Expansion.* eds. Robert L. Paquette and Stanley L. Engerman. (Gainsville: University Press of Florida, 1996), 50–67.

Klein, Herbert S. *The Middle Passage: Comparative Studies in the Atlantic Slave Trade.* (Princeton: Princeton University Press, 1978).

Klein, Herbert S. *African Slavery in Latin America and the Caribbean.* (New York and Oxford: Oxford University Press, 1986).

Klooster, Wim. *Illicit Riches: The Dutch Trade in the Caribbean, 1648–1795.* (Leiden: KITLV Press, 1995).

Knight, Franklin W. and Peggy K. Liss. eds. *Atlantic Port Cities: Economy, Culture, and Society in the Atlantic World, 1650–1850.* (Knoxville: University of Tennessee Press, 1991).

Knight, Franklin W. ed. *General History of the Caribbean.* Vol. 3. *The slave societies of the Caribbean.* (London: UNESCO Pubishing, 1997).

Knight-Baylac, Marie-Hélène. "La vie à Gorée de 1677 à 1789", *RFHOM,* 57, (1970), 377–420.

Kondert, Reinhart. "Les Allemands en Louisiane de 1721 à 1732", *RHAF,* 33, 1 (juin 1979), 51–66.

Kroell, Anne. "The Search of the French East India Company for New Markets in South America, 1706–1709", in *Global Crossroads and The American Seas.* ed. Clark G. Reynolds. (Missoula: Pictorial Histories Publishing Co., 1988), 1–7.

Laberge, Alain. "État, entrepreneurs, habitants, et monopole: le privilège de la pêche au marsouin dans la Bas Saint-Laurent, 1700–1730", *RHAF,* 37, 4 (mars 1984), 543–56.

Labrousse, Elisabeth. *La révocation de l'Édit de Nantes: une foi, une loi, un roi?* ([n.p.]: Éditions Payot, [1985] 1990).

Lachance, André, *Crimes et criminels en Nouvelle-France.* (Montréal: Boréal Express, 1984).

Lachance, André. *La Vie urbaine en Nouvelle-France.* (Montréal: Éditions du Boréal Express, 1987).

Lachance, André. *Vivre, aimer et mourir en Nouvelle-France, la vie quotidienne au XVIIe et XVIIIe siècles.* (Montréal: Édition Libre Expression, 2000).

Lachance, Paul. "L'Effet de déséquilibre des sexes sur le comportement matrimonial: comparaison entre la Nouvelle France, Saint Domingue, et la Nouvelle Orléans", *RHAF,* 39, 2 (autumne 1985), 211–31.

Lachance, Paul. "The Demography of French Slave Colonies, Part I (1700–1760)", Unpublished paper delivered to Social Science History Association at Chicago, November 1998.

Lafleur, Gérard, *Les Protestants aux Antilles françaises du vent sous l'ancien régime,* (Basse-Terre: Société d'histoire de la Guadeloupe, 1988).

Lafleur, Gérard. *Les Caraïbes des Petites Antilles.* (Paris: Karthala, 1992).

Lalou, Richard et Mario Boléda. "Une source en friche: les denombrements sous le régime français", *RHAF,* 42, 1 (été 1988), 47–72.

La Morandière, Charles de. *Histoire de la pêche française de la morue dans l'Amérique septentrionale.* 3 vols. (Paris: Maissoneuve & La Rose, 1962–6).

Landry, Yves et Rénald Lessard. "Les causes de décès aux XVIIe et XVIIIe siècles d'après les registres paroissiaux québecois", *RHAF,* 48, 4 (printemps 1995), 509–26.

Landry, Yves. *Orphelines en France, pionnières au Canada: les Filles du roi au XVIIe siècle.* (Montréal: Leméac, 1992).

La Roncière, Charles de. *Histoire de la marine francaise.* 6 vols. (Paris: Plon, Nourrit et Cie, 1909–1932).

Lasserre, Guy. *La Guadeloupe, étude géogrpahique.* 2 vols. (Bordeaux: Union française d'impression, 1961).

Lavallée, Louis. *La Prairie en Nouvelle France, 1647–1760, étude d'histoire sociale.* (Montréal et Kingston: McGill-Queen's University Press, 1992).

LeBlant, Robert. *Un Colonial sous Louis XIV, Philippe de Pastour de Costebelle, gouverneur de Terre-Neuve, puis de l'Île Royale (1661–1717).* n. p. 1935.

LeBlant, Robert. "Un corsair de Saint-Domingue en Acadie: Pierre Morpain, 1707–1711", *Nova Francia*, 6 (1931), 193–208.

LeBlant, Robert. "Une sédition basque à Terre-Neuve en 1690", *Revue historique et archéologique de Béarn et du pays Basque,* (janvier 1932), 46–64.

Leclerc, Jean. *Le Marquis de Denonville, gouverneur de la nouvelle-france, 1685–1689.* (Montréal: Fides, 1976).

Leclant, Jean. "Coffee and Cafés in Paris, 1644–1693" in *Food and Drink in History: Selections from the Annales, Economies, Sociétés Civilisations.* Vol. 5. eds. Robert Forster and Orest Ranum, trans. Patricia M. Ranum. (Baltimore: The Johns Hopkins University Press, 1970), 86–97.

Le Goff, T. J. A. "The Labour Market for Sailors in France" in *"Those Emblems of Hell"? European Sailors and the Maritime Labour Market, 1570–1870,* eds. Paul C. van Royen, Jaap Bruijn, and Jan Lucassen, (St. John's: International Maritime Economic History Association, 1997), 287–327.

Legohérel, Henri. *Les Trésoriers généraux de la marine (1517–1788).* (Paris: Éditions Cujas, 1965).

Lemieux, Denise. "La famille en Nouvelle France: des cadres de la vie matérielle aux signes de l'affectivité" dans *De France en Nouvelle-France: société fondatrice et société nouvelle.* dir. Hubert Watelet. (Ottawa: Les Presses de l'université d' Ottawa, 1994), 45–70.

Léon, Pierre et Charles Carrière. "L'Appel des marchés" dans *Histoire économique et sociale de la France.* Vol. 2. *Des derniers temps de l'âge seigneurial aux préludes de l'âge industriel (1660–1789).* (Paris: Presses universitaires de France, 1970), 161–215.

Le Roy Ladurie, Emmanuel. *The French Peasantry, 1450–1660.* trans. A. Sheridan. (Aldershot: Scolar Press, 1987).

Le Roy Ladurie, Emmanuel. *L'Ancien régime de Louis XIII à Louis XV, 1610–1770.* (Paris: Hachette, 1991).

Lespagnol, André. *Messieurs de Saint-Malo: une élite négociante au temps de Louis XIV.* (Saint-Malo: Éditions l'Ancre de Marine, 1991).

Lossky, Andrew. "The Nature of Political Power according to Louis XIV" in *The Responsibility of Power; Historical Essays in Honor of Hajo Holborn.* eds. L. Krieger and F. Stern. (Garden City: Doubleday Anchor Books, 1969), 115–32.

Lossky, Andrew. "The General European Crisis of the 1680s" *European Studies Review,* 10 (1980), 177–98.

Lossky, Andrew. *Louis XIV and the French Monarchy.* (New Brunswick: Rutgers University Press, 1994).

Lowenthal, David. "Colonial experiments in French Guyane, 1760–1800", *Hispanic American Historical Review,* 32 (February 1952), 22–43.

Lunn, Jean. "Economic Development in New France, 1713–1760". Unpublished history Ph.D. thesis, McGill University, 1942; published as *Développement économique de la Nouvelle France, 1713–1760,* trans. Brigitte Monel-Nish. (Montréal: Les Presses de l'universitéde Montréal, 1986).

Lunn, E. J. "The Illegal Fur Trade Out of New France, *1713–1716*", *Canadian Historical Association Report, 1939*, 61–76.

Lüthy, Herbert. *La banque protestante en France.* Vol. 1. *Dispersion et regroupement, (1685–1730).* (Paris: SEVPEN, 1959).

Ly, Abdoulaye. *La compagnie du Sénégal.* (Paris: Présence Africaine, 1958).

Lynch, John. *Spain under the Hapsburgs.* 2 vols. 2nd ed. (New York: New York University Press, 1984).

Lynch, John. *Bourbon Spain, 1700–1808.* (Oxford: Basil Blackwell, 1989).

Lynn, John A. *Giant of the Grand Siècle, The French Army, 1610–1715.* (Cambridge: Cambridge University Press, 1997).

Maclachlan, A. D. "The Road to Peace, 1710–13" in *Britain after the Glorious Revolution, 1689–1714.* ed. Geoffry Holmes. (London: Macmillan, 1969), 197–215.

Maduell, Jr., Charles R. *The Census Tables for the French Colony of Louisiana from 1699 through 1732.* (Baltimore: Genealogical Publishing, 1972).

Mahan, Alfred Thayer. *The Influence of Sea Power Upon History, 1660–1783.* (Boston: Little, Brown and Co., 1890).

Malamud-Rikles, Carlos Daniel. *Cadiz y Sainto Malo en el comercio colonial peruano, 1698–1725.* (Cadiz: Diputacion Provincial de Cadiz, 1986).

Mannion, John and Gordon Hancock. "The 17th Century Fishery" in *The Historical Atlas of Canada.* Vol. 1. *From the Beginning to 1800.* ed. R. C. Harris. (Toronto: University of Toronto Press, 1987), Plate 23.

Marchand-Thébault, Mme. M.-L. "L'esclavage en Guyane française sous l'ancien régime", *RFHOM,* 47 (1960): 5–75.

Martin, Gaston. *Nantes au XVIIIe siècle: L'ère des négriers (1714–1774).* (Paris: F. Alcan, 1931).

Martin, Gaston. *Histoire de l'esclavage dans les colonies françaises.* (Paris: Presses Universitaires de France, 1948).

Martineau, Alfred et Louis-Philippe May. *Trois siècles d'histoire antillaise, Martinique et Guadeloupe de 1635 à nos jours.* (Paris: Leroux, 1935).

Marx, Jenifer. *Pirates and Privateers of the Caribbean.* (Malabar: Krieger Publishing, 1992).

Mathieu, Jacques. "Province de France (1663–1700)"; "Un Pays a statu colonial, (1701–1755)" dans *Histoire du Québec.* dir. Jean Hamelin. (Montréal: France-Amérique, 1976), 127–230.

Mathieu, Jacques. *Le commerce entre la Nouvelle France et les Antilles au XVIIIe siècle.* (Montréal: Fides, 1981).

Mathieu, Jacques et Réal Brisson. "La Vallée Laurentienne au XVIIIe siècle: Un paysage à connaitre", *Cahiers de Géographie du Québec,* 28 (avril-septembre 1984), 107–24.

Matthews, George T. *The Royal General Farms in Eighteenth-Century France.* (New York: Columbia University Press, 1958).

May, Louis-Philippe. *Histoire économique de la Martinique (1635–1763).* (Fort-de-France: Sociétéde distribution et de culture, [1930] 1972).

Maze-Sencier, Geneviève. co-ord. *Dictionnaire des maréchaux de France du Moyen Âge à nos jours.* (Paris: Perrin, 1988).

McAlister, Lyle N. *Spain and Portugal in the New World, 1492–1700.* (Minnesota: University of Minnesota Press, 1984).

McClelland, III, James E. *Colonialism and Science: Saint-Domingue in the Old Regime.* (Baltimore and London: The Johns Hopkins University Press, 1992).

McCusker, John J. "Weights and Measures in the Colonial Sugar Trade: The Gallon and the Pound and their International Equivalents", *The William and Mary Quarterly,* 3rd. Ser., 30 (October 1973), 599–624.

McCusker, John J. *Money and Exchange in Europe and America, 1600–1775: A Handbook.* (Chapel Hill: University of North Carolina Press, 1978).

McCusker, John J. *Rum and the American Revolution: The Rum Trade and the Balance of*

Payments of the Thirteenth Continental Colonies. 2 vols. (New York and London: Garland Publishing, 1989).

McCusker, John J. and Russel R. Menard. *The Economy of British America, 1607–1789.* (Chapel Hill and London: University of North Carolina Press, 1985).

McDermott, John Francis, ed. *Frenchmen and French Ways in the Mississippi Valley.* (Urbana: University of Illinois Press, 1969).

McKay, Derek and H. M. Scott. *The Rise of the Great Powers, 1648–1815.* (London and New York: Longman, 1983).

McLennan, J. S. *Louisbourg from its Foundation to its Fall, 1713–1758.* (London: Macmillan, 1918).

Meinig, D. W. *The Shaping of America: A Geographical Perspective on 500 Years of History.* Vol. 1. *Atlantic America, 1492–1800.* (New Haven and London: Yale University Press, 1986).

Merrick, Jeffrey. "Politics and Pedestals: Royal Monuments in Eighteenth-Century France", *French History*, 5 (1991), 234–64.

Mettas, Jean. *Répertoire des expéditions négrières françaises au XVIIIe siècle.* 2 vols. éd. Serge Daget. (Paris: Société française d'histoire d'outre-mer et Librairie orientaliste Paul Geuthner, 1978–84).

Meyer, Jean. *La Nobless bretonne au XVIIIe siècle.* 2 vols. (Paris: SEVPEN, 1966).

Meyer, Jean. *Colbert.* (Paris: Hachette, 1981).

Meyer, Jean. *Histoire du sucre.* (Paris: Éditions Desjonquères, 1989).

Meyer, Jean, Jean Tarrade, Annie Rey-Goldzeiguer, et Jacques Thobie. *Histoire de la France coloniale.* Vol. 1. *des origines à 1914.* (Paris: Armand Colin, 1991).

Michell, A. R. "The European Fisheries in Early Modern History", *The Cambridge Economic History of Europe.* Vol. 5. eds. E. E. Rich and C. H. Wilson. (London: Cambridge University Press, 1977), 133–84.

Miller, Virginia P. "Aboriginal Micmac Population: A Review of the Evidence", *Ethnohistory*, 23, 2 (Spring 1976), 117–27.

Miller, Virginia P. "The Decline of Nova Scotia Micmac Population, A.D. 1600–1850", *Culture*, 2, 3 (1982), 107–20.

Mims, Stewart L. *Colbert's West India Policy.* (New Haven: Yale University Press, 1912).

Minchington, Walter. ed. *Mercantilism: System or Expediency?* (Lexington: D.C. Heath, 1969).

Mintz, Sidney W. *Sweetness and Power; The Place of Sugar in Modern History.* (New York: Viking, 1985).

Mintz, Sidney W. "Pleasure, Profit, and Satiation" in *Seeds of Change: A Quincentennial Commemoration.* eds. H. J. Viola and C. Margolis. (Washington and London: Smithsonian Institution Press, 1991), 112–29.

Miquelon, Dale. *New France, 1701–1744: "A Supplement to Europe".* (Toronto: McClelland & Stewart, 1987).

Miquelon, Dale. "Canadas Place in the French Imperial Economy: An Eighteenth-Century Overview", *French Historical Studies*, 15, 3 (Spring 1988), 432–43.

Miquelon, Dale. "Jean-Baptiste Colbert's 'Compact Colony Policy' Revisited: The Tenacity of an Idea" in *Proceedings of the Seventeenth Meeting of the French Colonial Historical Society.* (Lanham: University Press of America, 1991), 12–23.

Miquelon, Dale. "Envisioning the French Empire: Utrecht, 1711–1713", *French Historical Studies*, 24, 4 (Fall 2001), 653–77.

Moitt, Bernard. "Women, Work, and Resistance in the French Caribbean" in *Engendering History: Caribbean Women in Historical Perspective.* eds. Verene Sheperd, Briget Bereton, and Barbara Bailey. (New York: St. Martin's Press, 1995), 155–75.

Moitt, Bernard. *Women and Slavery in the French Antilles, 1635–1848,* (Bloomington: Indiana University Press, 2001).

Moogk, Peter N. "'Thieving Buggers' and 'Stupid Sluts': Insults and Popular Culture in New France", *William and Mary Quarterly*, 3rd ser., 36, 4 (October 1979), 524–47.

Moogk, Peter N. "'Les Petites Sauvages': The Children of Eighteenth-Century New France" in *Childhood and Family in Canadian History*. ed. Joy Parr. (Toronto: McClelland & Stewart, 1982), 17–43.

Moogk, Peter N. "Reluctant Exiles: Emigrants from France in Canada before 1760", *William and Mary Quarterly*, 3rd ser., 46, 3 (July 1989), 463–505.

Moogk, Peter N. *La Nouvelle France: The Making of French Canada – A Cultural History*. (East Lansing: Michigan State University Press, 2000).

Moore, Christopher. "The Other Louisbourg: Trade and Merchant Enterprise in Ile Royale, 1713–1758", *Histoire Sociale/Social History*, 12, 23 (1979), 70–96. Reprinted in *Aspects of Louisbourg*. ed. Eric Krause et al. (Sydney: University College of Cape Breton Press, 1995), 228–49.

Moore, Christopher. "Cape Breton and the North Atlantic World in the Eighteenth Century" in *The Island: New Perspectives on Cape Breton History, 1713–1990*. ed. Kenneth Donovan. (Fredericton: Acadiensis Press, 1990), 31–48.

Morel, Anne. "Les Armateurs malouins et le commerce interlope", dans *Les sources de l'histoire maritime en Europe: Actes du quatrième colloque international d'histoire maritime*. éd. M. Mollat *et al.* (Paris: SEVPEN, 1962), 311–15.

Morgan, William Thomas. "The British West Indies during King William's War (1689–1697)", *The Journal of Modern History*, 2, 3 (September 1930), 378–409.

Morgan, William Thomas. "The Expedition of Baron de Pointis Against Cartagena", *The American Historical Review*, 37, 2 (January 1932), 237–54.

Morineau, Michel. "Quelques recherches relatives à la balance du commerce exterieur français au XVIIIe siècle: ou cette fois un egale deux" dans *Aires et structures de commerce française au XVIIIe siècle*. dir. Pierre Leon. (Paris: Centre d'histoire économique et sociale de la région lyonnaise, 1975), 1–45.

Morineau, Michel. "Les hésitations de la croissance (1580–1730)", dans *Histoire économique et sociale du monde*. 3 vols. (Paris: Presses universitaires de France, 1977–82), Vol. 2.

Morineau Michel. *Incroyables gazettes et fabuleux métaux; les retours des trésors américains d'après les gazettes hollondaise (XVIIe–XVIIIe)*. (Cambridge/Paris: Cambridge University Press/Editions de la Maison des Sciences de l'Homme, 1985).

Morineau, Michel. "La vraie nature des chose et leur enchaînement entre la France et l'Europe (XVIIe–XIXe siècle)", *RFHOM*, 84 (1997), 3–24.

Morrison, Kenneth M. *The Embattled Northeast: The Elusive Ideal of Alliance in Abenaki-Euroamerican Relations*. (Berkeley: University of California Press, 1984).

Morrissey, Marietta. *Slave Women in the New World: Gender Stratification in the Caribbean*. (Lawrence: University Press of Kansas, 1989).

Mousnier, Roland E. *The Institutions of France under the Absolute Monarchy, 1598–1789*. trans. Brian Pearce. 2 vols. (Chicago: University of Chicago Press, 1979–84).

Mousnier, Roland E. dir. *Un Nouveau Colbert: Actes du Colloque pour le tricentenaire de la mort de Colbert*. (Paris: SEDES, 1985).

Munford, Clarence. *The Black Ordeal of Slavery and Slave Trading in the French West Indies, 1625–1715*. 3 vols. (Lewiston: Edwin Mellen Press, 1991).

Murat, Inès. *Colbert*. trans. by R. F. Cook and J. Van Asselt. (Charlottesville: University Press of Virginia, [1980] 1984).

Murray, J. J. "Anglo-French Naval Skirmishing off Newfoundland, 1697" in *Essays in Modern History Written in Memory of William Thomas Morgan*. ed. J. J. Murray. (Bloomington: Indiana University Press, 1951), 71–85.

Musgrave, Peter. *The Early Modern European Economy*. (London: Macmillan, 1999).

Nardin, Jean-Claude. "Encore des chiffres: La traite négrière française pendant la première moitié du XVIII siècle", *RFHOM*, 58, (1970), 421–46.

Neal, Larry D. "The Integration and Efficiency of the London and Amsterdam Stock Markets in the Eighteenth Century", *Journal of Economic History*, 47 (March 1987), 97–115.

Neal, Larry. *The Rise of Financial Capitalism: International Capital Markets in the Age of Reason.* (New York: Cambridge University Press, 1990).

Newson, L. A. "The Demographic Collapse of Native Peoples of the Americas, 1492–1650" in *The Meeting of Two Worlds, Europe and the Americas, 1492–1650.* ed. W. Bray. (London: The British Academy, 1993).

Newton, Arthur Percival. *The European Nations in the West Indies, 1493–1688.* (London: A. & C. Black, 1933).

Norton, Thomas E. *The Fur Trade in Colonial New York, 1686–1776.* (Madison: University of Wisconsin Press, 1974).

Olivier-LaCamp, Gael et Jacques Legaré. "Quelques caracteristiques des ménages de la ville de Québec entre 1666 et 1716", *Histoire sociale/Social History,* 12, no. 23 (1979), 66–78.

Olivier-Martin, François. *L'Absolutisme française.* (Paris: Éditions Loysel, [1951] 1988).

O'Neill, Charles Edward. *Church and State in French Colonial Louisiana.* (New Haven: Yale University Press, 1966).

Ormrod, David. "The Atlantic Economy and the 'Protestant capitalist international', 1651–1775", *Historical Research,* 66 (1993), 197–208.

Ouellet, Fernand. "Seigneurial Property and Social Structure 1663–1840" in *Economy, Class, & Nation in Quebec: Interpretive Essays.* ed. and trans. Jacques A. Bernier. (Toronto: Copp Clark Pitman, 1991).

Owen, J. H. *War at Sea Under Queen Anne, 1702–1708.* (Cambridge: Cambridge University Press, 1938).

Pagden, Anthony. *Lords of All the World: Ideologies of Empire in Spain, Britain, and France, c.1500–c.1800.* (New Haven and London: Yale University Press, 1995).

Palmer, Colin. *Human Cargoes: The British Slave Trade to Spanish America, 1700–1739.* (Urbana: University of Illinois Press, 1981).

Paquette, Lyne et Réal Bates. "Les naissances illégitimes sur les rives du Saint-Laurent avant 1730", *RHAF,* 40, 2 (automne 1986), 239–52.

Parker, David. *The Making of French Absolutism.* (London: Edward Arnold, 1983).

Parker, David. *Class and State in Ancien Regime France: The road to modernity?* (London and New York: Routledge, 1996).

Parry, J. H., Philip Sherlock, and Anthony Maingot. *A Short History of the West Indies.* 4th ed. (London and Basingstoke: Macmillan, 1987).

Peabody, Sue *"There Are No Slaves in France": The Political Culture of Race and Slavery in the Ancien Regime.* (New York: Oxford University Press, 1996).

Peabody, Sue. "A Dangerous Zeal": Catholic Missions to Slaves in the French Antilles, 1635–1800", *French Historical Studies,* 25, 1 (2002), 53–90.

Perez, Pablo Emilio and Mallaina Bueno. *Politica Naval Espanola en el Atlántico, 1700–1715.* (Sevilla: Escuela des Estudios Hispano-Americanos de Sevilla, 1982).

Pérotin-Dumont, Anne. "French America", *The International History Review,* 6, 4 (November 1984), 551–69.

Pérotin-Dumont, Anne. "Cabotage, Contraband, and Corsairs: The Port Cities of Guadeloupe and Their Inhabitants, 1650–1850" in *Atlantic Port Cities: Economy, Culture, and Society in the Atlantic World, 1650–1850.* eds. Franklin W. Knight and Peggy K. Liss. (Knoxville: University of Tennessee Press, 1991), 58–86.

Pérotin-Dumon, Anne. "The Pirate and the Emperor: Power and the Law on the Seas, 1450–1850" in *The Political Economy of Merchant Empires.* ed. James D. Tracy. (Cambridge: Cambridge University Press, 1991), 196–227.

Pérotin-Dumon, Anne, *La Ville aux Iles, la ville dans l'île; Basse-Terre et Point-à-Pitre, Guadeloupe, 1650–1820.* (Paris: Karthala, 2000).

Perrot, Jean-Claude. "Les dictionnaires de commerce du XVIIIe siècles", *Revue d'histoire moderne et contemporaine,* 28 (1981), 36–67.

Petitjean-Roget, Jacques. *Le Gaoulé, la révolte de la Martinique en 1717.* (Fort-de-France: Société d'histoire de la Martinique, 1966).

Petitjean-Roget, Jacques. *La société d'habitation à la Martinique: Un demi siècle de formation, 1635–1685.* 2 vols. (Lille-Paris: Université de Lille III-Librairie Honoré Champion, 1980).

Pétré-Grenouilleau, Olivier. *Les Négoces maritimes français XVIIe–XXe siècle.* (Paris: Belin, 1997).

Petyraud, Lucien. *L'Esclavage aux Antilles francaises avant 1789, d'après des documents inédits des Archives coloniales.* (Paris: Hachette et Cie., 1897).

Phillips, Carla Rahn. "The Galleon *San José*, Treasure Ship of the Spanish Indies" *The Mariner's Mirror,* 77 (1991), 355–63.

Pitman, Frank Wesley. *The Development of the British West Indies, 1700–1763.* (New Haven: Yale University Press, 1917).

Pluchon, Pierre. ed. *Histoire des Antilles et de la Guyane.* (Toulouse: Privat, 1982).

Pluchon, Pierre. *Nègres et juifs au XVIIIe siècles: le racisme au siècle des lumières.* (Paris: Tallandier, 1984).

Pluchon, Pierre. *Histoire de la colonisation française.* Tome 1. *Le Premier Empire coloniale des origines à la Restauration.* (Paris: Fayard, 1991).

Postma, Johannes Menne. *The Dutch in the Atlantic Slave Trade, 1600–1815.* (Cambridge: Cambridge University Press, 1990).

Pothier, Bernard. "Acadian Emigration to Ile Royale after the Conquest of Acadia", *Histoire Sociale/Social History,* 6, (1970), 116–31.

Price, Jacob M. *France and the Chesapeake: A History of the French Tobacco Monopoly, 1674–1791 and its Relationship to the British and American Tobacco Trades.* 2 vols. (Ann Arbor: University of Michigan Press, 1973).

Pritchard, James. "Ships, Men, and Commerce: A Study of Maritime Activity in New France". Unpublished history Ph.D. thesis, University of Toronto, 1971.

Pritchard, James. "The Pattern of French Colonial Shipping to Canada before 1760", *RFHOM,* 63, no. 231 (1976), 189–210.

Pritchard, James. "The Franco-Dutch War in the West Indies, 1672–1678: An Early 'Lesson' in Imperial Defence", in *New Interpretations in Naval History: Selected Papers from the Thirteenth Naval History Symposium.* ed. William M. McBride. (Annapolis: Naval Institute Press, 1998), 3–22.

Pritchard, James. "'Le Profit et La Gloire': The French Navy's Alliance with Private Enterprise in the Defence of Newfoundland, 1691–1697", *Newfoundland Studies,* 15, 2 (Fall 1999), 161–75.

Pritchard, James. "Canada and the Defence of Newfoundland during the War of the Spanish Succession, 1702–1713", *Canadian Military History Since the 17th Century.* ed. Yves Tremblay. (Ottawa: Department of National Defence, 2001), 49–57.

Pritchard, James. "The French West Indies during the Nine Years' War, 1688–1697: A Review and Reappraisal", *French Colonial History* (2002), 2, 45–60.

Proulx, Gills. *The Military History of Placentia: A study of French fortifications: Placentia 1713–1811.* (Ottawa: National Historic Sites and Parks Branch, 1979).

Rambert, Gaston. "Marseille et le commerce "interlope" en Mer du sud (1700–1723)", *Provence historique,* 17, (1967), 32–60.

Rambert, Gaston. *Histoire du commerce de Marseille.* vol. 6. *De 1660 à 1789, les colonies.* (Paris: Plon, 1959).

Rawley, James A. *The Transatlantic Slave Trade: A history.* (New York and London: W.W. Norton, 1981).

Rawlyk, George A. *Nova Scotia's Massachussetts: A Study of Massachussetts-Nova Scotia Relations, 1630–1784.* (Montreal and London: McGill-Queen's University Press, 1973).

Reddy, William. *The Rise of Market Culture: The Textile Trade and French Society, 1750–1900.* (Cambridge: Cambridge University Press, 1984).

Rediker, Marcus. *Between the Devil and the Deep Blue Sea: Merchant Seamen, Pirates, and the Anglo-American Maritime World, 1700-1750.* (New York: Cambridge University Press, 1987).

Reese, Armin. *Europäische Hegemonie und France d'outre-mer: Kolonial Fragen in de französichen Aussen politik, 1700-1763.* (Stuttgart: Steiner, 1988).

Reible, Marcel. "L'Emigration coloniale en Angoumois sous Louis XIV et la question protestante", *Mémoires de la société archeologique et historique de la Charente,* 1958, (Angouleme, 1959), 97-[178].

Reid, John G. "1686-1720: Imperial Intrusions" in *The Atlantic Region to Confederation: A History.* eds. Philip A. Buckner and John G. Reid. (Fredericton: Acadiensis Press, 1994), 78-103.

Rennard, Jean. "Organisation des paroisses" dans *Nos Antilles.* éd. Serge Denis. (Paris: Maison du Livre Français, 1935), 131-59.

Rennard, Jean. *Histoire religieuse des Antilles françaises des origines à 1914 d'après des documents inédits.* (Paris: Société de l'histoire des colonies française et Librairie Larose, 1954).

Revert, Eugène. *La Martinique, étude géographique et humaine.* (Paris: Nouvelles Editions Latines, 1949).

Rich, E. E. "Russia and the Colonial Fur Trade", *Economic Historical Review,* 2nd Series, 7 (1954-55), 307-28.

Rich, E. E. *The Fur Trade and the Northwest to 1857.* (Toronto: McClelland and Stewart, 1967).

Richard, Robert. "A Propos de Saint-Domingue: La monnaie dans l'économie coloniale (1674-1803), *RHC,* 41 (1954), 22-46.

Richet, Denis. *La France moderne: l'esprit des institutions.* (Paris: Flammarion, 1973).

Richmond, Admiral Sir Herbert. *The Navy as an Instrument of Policy, 1588-1723.* ed. E. A. Hughes [published posthumously]. (Cambridge: Cambridge University Press, 1953).

Roberts, W. A. *The French in the West Indies.* (Indianapolis: The Bobbs Merril Co., 1942).

Rogozinski, Jan. *A Brief History of the Caribbean from the Arawak and the Carib to the Present.* (New York: Meridian Books, 1994).

Roman, Alain. *Saint-Malo au temps des négriers.* (Paris: Karthala, 2001).

Roosen, William. "The Origins of the War of the Spanish Succession" in *The Origins of War in Early Modern Europe.* ed. Jeremy Black. (Edinburgh: John Donald, 1987), 151-75.

Rothkrug, Lionel. *Opposition to Louis XIV: The Political and Social Origins of the French Enlightenment.* (Princeton: Princeton University Press, 1965).

Rowen, Herbert F. *The Ambassador Prepares for War: The Dutch Embassy of Arnauld de Pomponne, 1669-1671.* (The Hague: Martinus Nijhoff, 1957).

Rowen, Herbert F. *The King's, State.* (New Brunswick: Rutgers University Press, 1980).

Roy, Muriel K. "Settlement and Population Growth" in *The Acadians of the Maritimes, Thematic Studies.* ed. Jean Daigle. (Moncton: Centre d'études acadiennes, 1982), 125-96.

Rule, John C. "Jérôme Phélypeaux and the Establishment of Louisiana, 1696-1715" in *Frenchmen and French Ways in the Mississippi Valley.* ed. John Francis McDermott. (Urbana: University of Illinois Press, 1969), 179-97.

Rule, John C. "Colbert de Torcy, an emergent bureaucracy and the formulation of French foreign policy, 1698-1715" in *Louis XIV and Europe.* ed. Ragnhild Hatton. (London: Macmillan, 1976), 261-88.

Saintoyant, Jules F. *La Colonisation française sous l'ancien régime (du XVe siècle à 1789).* 2 vols. (Paris: La Renaissance du Livre, 1929).

Sala-Molins, Louis. *Le Code noir ou le calvaire de Cannan,* 3 éd. (Paris: Presses universitaires de France, [1987] 1993).

Satineau, Maurice. *Histoire de la Guadeloupe sous l'ancien régime, 1635-1789.* (Paris: Payot, 1928).

Saugera, Eric. *Bordeaux, port négrier: chronologie, économie, idéologie XVIIe–XIXe siècles.* (Paris: Karthala, 1995).

Savelle, Max. *The Origins of American Diplomacy: The International History of Anglo-America, 1491–1763.* (New York: Macmillan, 1967).

Scammell, G. V. *The First Imperial Age, European Overseas Expansion, c. 1400–1715.* (London: Unwin Hyman, 1989).

Scelle, Georges. *La Traite négrière aux Indes de Castille, contrats et traités d'assiento.* Paris 1906; translated by Edna K. Hoyt as "The Slave Trade in the Spanish Colonies of America: the Assiento", *American Journal of International Law*, 4 (1910), 612–661.

Schaeper, Thomas J. *The French Council of Commerce, 1700–1715: A Study of Mercantilism after Colbert.* (Columbus: Ohio State University Press, 1983).

Schmitt, Eberhard. "The Brandenburg Overseas Trading Companies in the 17th Century" in *Companies and Trade: Essays on Overseas Trading Companies during the Ancien Régime.* L. Blussé and F. Gaastra eds. (Leiden: University Press, 1981), 159–76.

Schnakenbourg, Christian. "Note sur les origines de l'industrie sucrière en Guadeloupe au XVIIe siècle (1640–1670)", *RFHOM*, 55 (1968), 267–315.

Schnakenbourg, Christian. "Statistiques pour l'histoire de l'économie de plantation en Guadeloupe et en Martinique (1635–1835)", *Bulletin de la Société d'histoire de la Guadeloupe*, 31 (1977).

Schnakenbourg, Christian. "Le 'terrier' de 1671 et le partage de la terre en Guadeloupe au XVIIe siècle", *RFHOM*, 67 (1980), 37–54.

Schnakenbourg, Christian. *Histoire de l'industrie sucrière en Guadeloupe XIX–XXe siècles.* Vol. 1. *La Crise du system esclavagiste, 1835–1847,* (Paris: L'Harmattan, 1980).

Schnakenbourg, Christian. "Recherches sur l'histoire de l'industrie sucrière à Marie Galante", Extrait du *Bulletin de la société d'histoire de la Guadeloupe*, nos. 48–50, (1981), 18–19.

Schubert, Eric S. "Innovations, debts, and bubbles: International integration of financial markets in Western Europe, 1688–1720", *Journal of Economic History*, 48 (1988), 299–306.

Scoville, Warren C. *The Persecution of Huguenots and French Economic Developments, 1680–1720.* (Berkeley: University of California Press, 1960).

Shennan, J. H. *Philippe, Duke of Orléans, Regent of France, 1715–1723.* (London: Thames and Hudson, 1979).

Sheridan, Richard B. *Sugar and Slavery: An Economic History of the British West Indies, 1623–1775.* (Baltimore: The Johns Hopkins University Press, 1974).

Shomette, Donald G. and Robert D. Haslach. *Raid of America, The Dutch Naval Campaign of 1672–1674.* (Columbia: University of South Carolina Press, 1988).

Snow, Dean R. and Kim M. Lanphear. "European Contact and Indian Depopulation in the Northeast; The Timing of the First Epidemics", *Ethnohistory*, 35 (1988): 15–33.

Solow, Barbara L. ed. *Slavery and the Rise of the Atlantic System.* (New York: Cambridge University Press, 1991).

Sonnino, Paul. *Louis XIV and the Origins of the Dutch War.* (Cambridge: Cambridge University Press, 1988).

Southey, Captain Thomas. *Chronological History of the West Indies*, 3 vols. (London: Frank Cass & Co., [1827] 1968).

Speck, W. A. "The International and Imperial Context" in *Colonial British America: Essays on the New History of the Early Modern Era.* ed. Jack P. Greene. (Baltimore: The Johns Hopkins University Press, 1984), 384–407.

Steele, Ian K. *Politics of Colonial Policy, The Board of Trade in Colonial Administration, 1696–1720.* (Oxford: Oxford University Press, 1968).

Steele, Ian K. *Warpaths: Invasions of North America.* (New York: Oxford University Press, 1994).

Stein, Robert Louis. *The French Slave Trade in the Eighteenth Century: An Old Regime Business.* (Madison: University of Wisconsin Press, 1979).

Stein, Robert Louis. *The French Sugar Business in the Eighteenth Century*. (Baton Rouge: Louisiana State University Press, 1988).

Stein, Stanley J. and Barbara H. Stein. *Silver, Trade and War: Spain and America in the Making of Early Modern Europe*. (Baltimore: Johns Hopkins University Press, 2000).

Stone, Lawrence. *An Imperial State at War: Britain from 1689 to 1815*. (London: Routledge, 1994).

Sturgill, Claude, "Philippe of Orlean's [sic] "No Colonies" Policy, 1715-22", *Proceedings of the Tenth Meeting of the French Colonial Historical Society*, April, 1984, ed., Philip Boucher. (Lanham: University Press of America, 1985), 129-37.

Sturgill, Claude, "From Utrecht to the Little War with Spain: Peace at Almost Any Price Had to be the Case" in *The Origins of War in Early-Modern Europe*. ed. Jeremy Black. (Edinburgh: John Donald, 1987), 176-84.

Symcox, Geoffrey. *The Crisis of French Sea Power, 1688-1697: From guerre d'escadre to the guerre de course*. (The Hague: Martinus Nijhoff, 1974).

Taillemite, Etienne. *Dictionnaire des marins français*. (Paris: Editions Maritimes et d'Outre-mer, 1982).

Taillemite, Etienne. "Colbert et la marine" dans *Un Nouveau Colbert*. dir. Roland Mousnier. (Paris: SEDES, 1985), 216-28.

Taillemite, Etienne. *L'Histoire ignorée de la marine française*. (Paris: Perrin, 1988).

Thomson, Mark A. "Louis XIV and William III, 1689-97", *English Historical Review*, 76 (January 1961), 37-58.

Thomson, Mark A. "Louis XIV and the Origins of the War of the Spanish Succession", in *William III and Louis XIV: Essays, 1680-1720, by and for Mark A. Thomson*, eds. Ragnhild Hatton and J. S. Bromley. (Toronto: Liverpool University Press and University of Toronto Press, 1968), 111-33.

Thomson, Mark A. "Louis XIV and the Grand Alliance, 1705-10", *Bulletin of the Institute of Historical Research*, 34 (1961), 16-35.

Thomson, Mark A. "Self-determination and collective security as factors in English and French foreign policy" in *William III and Louis XIV: Essays, 1680-1720, by and for Mark A. Thomson*. eds. Ragnhild Hatton and J. S. Bromley. (Toronto: Liverpool University Press and University of Toronto Press, 1968).

Thornton, John. *Africa and Africans in the Making of the Atlantic World, 1400-1680*. (Cambridge: Cambridge University Press, 1992).

Thorpe, Frederick J. "Fish, Forts, and Finance: The Politics of French Construction at Placentia, 1699-1710", *The Canadian Historical Association Historical Papers, 1971*. (Ottawa: 1971), 52-64).

Thorpe, Frederick J. *Remparts lointains: La politique française des travaux publics à Terre-Neuve et à l'île royale, 1695-1758*. (Ottawa: Éditions de l'université d'Ottawa, 1980).

Thorpe, Frederick J. "In Defense of Sugar: The Logistics of Fortifying the French Antilles under the Regency, 1715-1723" in *Proceedings of the Nineteenth Meeting of the French Colonial Historical Society*, Providence, RI, May, 1993, ed., James Pritchard. (Cleveland, 1994), 68-86.

Tracy, James D. ed. *The Rise of Merchant Empires: Long Distance Trade in the Early Modern World, 1350-1750*. (Cambridge: Cambridge University Press, 1990).

Tracy, James D. ed. *The Political Economy of Merchant Empires: State Power and World Trade, 1350-1750*. (Cambridge: Cambridge University Press, 1991).

Tramond, Joannès. "Les troubles de Saint-Domingue en 1722-1724", *RHC*, 22 (1929), 487-512; 549-98.

Trudel, Marcel. "Louis XIV et son projet de déportation, 1689", *RHAF*, 3 (1950-51), 157-71.

Trudel, Marcel. *L'Esclavage au Canada français; histoire et conditions de l'esclavage*. (Québec: Presses de l'université de Laval, 1960).

Trudel, Marcel. *Dictionnaire des esclaves et de leurs propriétaires au Canada français*. (La Salle: Hurtubise HMH, 1990).

Trudel, Marcel, *Histoire de la Nouvelle France*, Tome 4. *La seigneurie de la Compagnie des Indes occidentales, 1663–1674*. (Montréal: Fidès, 1997).

Tulloch, Judith. "The New England Fishery and Trade at Canso, 1720–1744" in *How Deep is the Ocean? Historical Essays on Canada's Atlantic Fishery*. ed. James E. Candow *et al.* (Sydney: University College of Cape Breton Press, 1997), 65–73.

Turgeon, Laurier. "Le temps des pêches lointains: permanences et transformations, vers 1500–vers 1850" dans *Histoire des pêches maritimes en France*. éd. Michel Mollat. (Toulouse: Privat, 1987).

Turgeon, Laurier. "Colbert et la pêche française à Terre-Neuve" dans *Un Nouveau Colbert*. dir. Roland Mousnier. (Paris: SEDES, 1985), 255–68.

Unger, Richard W. "The Tonnage of Europe's Merchant Fleets, 1300–1800", *The American Neptune*, 52, 4 (Fall 1992), 247–61.

Usner, Jr., Daniel H. *Indians, Settlers, and Slaves in a Frontier Exchange Economy: The Lower Mississippi Valley before 1783*. (Chapel Hill: University of North Carolina Press, 1992).

Vachon, André. "The Administration of New France" in *DCB*, 2, xv–xxv.

Vaissière, Pierre de. *Saint-Domingue: la société et la vie créole sous l'ancien régime (1629–1789)*. (Paris: Perrin et Cie, 1909).

Valdman, Albert. "Creole, the Language of Slavery" *Slavery in the Caribbean Francophone World: Distant Voices, Forgotten Acts, Forged Identities*. ed. Doris Y. Kadish. (Athens and London: University of Georgia Press, 2000), [143]-63.

Vergé-Franceschi, Michel. "Fortune et plantations des administrateurs coloniaux aux îles d'Amérique aux XVIIe et XVIIIe siècles" dans *Commerce et Plantation dans la Caraïbe XVIIIe et XIXe siècles*. (Bordeaux: Maison des Pays Ibériques, 1992), 115–42.

Vergé-Franceschi, Michel. "Duguay-Trouin (1673–1736), un corsaire, un officier général, un mythe", *Revue historique*, 598 (avril-juin, 1996), 333–52.

Vignols, Léon. "L'Asiento français (1701–1713) et anglais (1713–1750) et le commerce franco-espagnol vers 1700 à 1730, avec deux mémoires français de 1728 sur ces sujets", *Revue d'histoire économique et sociale*, 17 (1929), 403–36.

Villiers, Patrick. *Marine royale, corsaires et trafic dans l'Atlantique de Louis XIV à Louis XVI*. 2 vols. (Dunkerque: Société Dunkerquoise d'histoire et d'archéologie, 1991).

Viola, Herman J. and Carolyn Margolis. eds. *Seeds of Change: A Quincentennial Commemoration*. (Washington and London: Smithsonian Institution Press, 1991).

Walker, Geoffrey J. *Spanish Politics and Imperial Trade, 1700–1789*. (Bloomington and London: Indiana University Press, 1979).

Wallerstein, Emmanuel. *The Modern World System*. Vol. 2, *Mercantilism and the Consolidation of the European World-Economy, 1600–1752*. (New York: Academic Press, 1980).

Ware, Christopher J. "The Royal Navy and the Plantations, 1720–1730" in *Global Crossroads and The American Seas*. ed. Clark G. Reynolds (Missoula: Pictorial Histories Publishing Co., 1988), 121–7.

Watts, David. *The West Indies: patterns of development, culture, and environmental changes since 1492*. (Cambridge: Cambridge University Press, 1987).

Webb, Stephen Saunders. "William Blaythwayt, Imperial fixer: Muddling through to empire, 1689–1717", *William and Mary Quarterly*, 3rd series, 26 (1969), 373–415.

Webster, Jonathan Howes. "The Merchants of Bordeaux in Trade to the French West Indies, 1664–1717". Unpublished history Ph.D. thesis, University of Minnesota, 1972.

Weddle, Robert S. *The French Thorn: Rival Explorers in the Spanish Sea, 1682–1762*. (College Station: Texas A&M University Press, 1991).

Wells, Robert V. *The Population of the British Colonies in America before 1776: a survey of census data*. (Princeton: Princeton University Press, 1975).

Wein, Thomas. "Selling Beaver Skins in North America and Europe, 1720–1760: The Use of Fur

Trade Imperialism", *Journal of the Canadian Historical Association*, New Series, 1, (1990), 293–317.

Wein, Thomas. "Castor, peaux et pelleteries dans le commerce canadien des fourrures, 1720–1790" in *Le Castor Fait Tout: Selected Papers of the Fifth North American Fur Trade Conference*. eds. B. Trigger, T. Morantz, and L. Dechêne. (Montreal: [n.p.] 1987), 72–92.

Williams, Alan F. *Father Baudoin's War: D'Iberville's Campaigns in Acadia and Newfoundland 1696, 1697*. ed. Alan G. Macpherson. (St. John's: Memorial University of Newfoundland, 1987).

Williams, Eric. *From Columbus to Castro: The History of the Caribbean, 1492–1969*. (London: André Deutsch, 1970).

Williams, Glyndwr. "The Inexhaustable Fountain of Gold: English Projects and Ventures in the South Seas, 1670–1750" in *Perspectives of Empire: Essays presented to Gerald S. Graham*. eds. John E. Flint and Glyndwr Williams. (London: Longman, 1973), 27–53.

Wolf, John B. *Louis XIV*. (New York: W.W. Norton, 1968).

Young, Kathryn. *Kin, Commerce, and Community: Merchants in the Port of Quebec from 1717 to 1745*. (New York: Peter Lang, 1995).

Zahedieh, N. "Trade, plunder, and economic development in early English Jamaica, 1655–89", *Economic History Review*, 39 (1986), 205–22.

Zahedieh, N. "The Merchants of Port Royal, Jamaica and the Spanish Contraband Trade, 1655–1692", *William and Mary Quarterly*, 3rd series, 43, 4 (October, 1986), 570–93.

Zahedieh, N. "A Frugal, Prudential, and Hopeful Trade: Privateering in Jamaica, 1655–89", *Journal of Imperial and Commonwealth History*, 18, 2 (1990), 145–68.

Zoltvany, Yves F. ed. *The Government of New France: royal, clerical or class rule?* (Scarborough: Prentice-Hall of Canada, 1971).

Zoltvany, Yves F. "Esquisse de la Coutume de Paris", *RHAF*, 25, 3 (1971), 365–84.

Zoltvany, Yves F. *Philippe de Rigaud de Vaudreuil, Governor of New France, 1703–1725*. (Toronto: McClelland and Stewart, 1974).

Index